# ELIZABETHAN LIFE:

## *HOME, WORK & LAND*

© ESSEX COUNTY COUNCIL, 1976

ISBN 0 900360 47 X

*To*
MARC FITCH,
D.Litt., F.S.A., F.R.Hist.S.,
without whose generosity many Essex and other
historical works would never have been published

# ELIZABETHAN LIFE:
## *HOME, WORK & LAND*

From Essex Wills and Sessions and Manorial Records

### F. G. EMMISON
Author of *Elizabethan Life: Disorder*
and *Elizabethan Life: Morals & the Church Courts*

ESSEX RECORD OFFICE
in collaboration with
THE FRIENDS OF HISTORIC ESSEX
1991

*Published by the*
ESSEX RECORD OFFICE
County Hall, Chelmsford, Essex CM1 1LX

© Essex County Council 1991

All rights reserved — This book may not be reproduced, in whole or in part, in any form, without written permission from the publishers.

*British Library Cataloguing in Publication Data*
Emmison, F. G. (Frederick George)
Elizabethan life.
Home work & land: from Essex wills and sessions and manorial records.
I. Essex. Social life, 1558-1603
I. Title
942.67022

ISBN 0-900360-78-X
Essex Record Office Publication No. 69

*Cover illustration:*
Detail from the late 16th-century Bradford Table Carpet
by courtesy of the Board of Trustees of the Victoria and Albert Museum, London.

Printed in Great Britain by the Essex County Council Supplies Department

# Contents

INTRODUCTION     vii

### PART 1—HOME (from Essex Wills)

*1* THE HOUSE
- Rooms     1
- Fixtures     8

*2* FURNITURE AND FURNISHINGS
- Beds and Bedding     12
- Other Furniture     16
- Musical Instruments     23
- Tableware and Household Implements     24
- Food and Drink     29
- 'Second best bed'     31

*3* AGRICULTURE
- Crops     33
- Livestock and Farm Implements     44
- Timber     55

*4* SHIPPING AND FISHERIES     59

*5* CRAFTS AND TRADES     74
- Markets and Fairs     90
- Debts and Loans     91

*6* FAMILY AND HOUSEHOLD
- Wives     95
- Children and Other Relations     102
- Disputes     115
- Education and Books     118
- Apprentices and Servants     125

*7* WEAPONS AND ARMOUR     132

*8* DEATHBED AND PROBATE
- Sickness     138
- Preambles, Witnesses, Executors and Overseers     140

### PART 2—WORK (from Essex Petty & Quarter Sessions Records)

*9* EMPLOYMENT
- The Statute of Artificers     146
- High Constables' Petty or Hiring Sessions     147
- Wages     164
- Apprentices     168

CONTENTS

## 10 DEALERS IN FOOD SUPPLIES
*Licensing*   175
*Illegal Dealing and Food Shortage*   177

## 11 CONTROL OF TRADE (see also chapter 19)
*Weights and Measures and the Clerk of the Market*   190
*Fairs and Miscellaneous*   193

### PART 3—LAND (from Essex Manorial Records)

## 12 MANOR COURTS: THE SOCIAL BACKGROUND   197

## 13 THE LORD AND THE TENANTS   204

## 14 ORIGINAL PRESENTMENTS   220

## 15 THE MANORIAL OFFICERS   223

## 16 PUNISHMENTS   229

## 17 OFFENCES
*Felonies*   232
*Assault, Barratry and Rescue*   233
*Poaching and Unlawful Games*   237
*Archery Practice*   240
*Highway Duty*   242
*The Commons*   243
*The Tenants' Buildings*   259
*Cottages and Inmates*   268
*Clothes and Caps*   274

## 18 NUISANCES
*Rivers, Bridges and Ditches*   278
*Highway Obstructions*   286
*Public Health*   290

## 19 CONTROL OF TRADE (see also chapter 11)
*Prices, Markets and Assizes of Commodities*   299
*Unwholesome Food*   304
*Bad Workmanship*   306
*The Flemings at Halstead*   306

## 20 CONTEMPT OF COURT   309

## 21 CUSTUMALS, BYE-LAWS AND SURVEYS   311

## INDEX OF SUBJECTS   334

## INDEX OF PERSONS AND PLACES   345

# Introduction

The project for publishing much of the information in the extremely rich Elizabethan archives in the Essex Record Office, commissioned by the County Council in 1968, envisaged a trilogy. The previous volumes are *Elizabethan Life: Disorder, mainly from Essex Quarter Sessions and Assize Records* (1970) and *Elizabethan Life: Morals and the Church Courts, from Essex Archidiaconal Records* (1973). The three parts of the present, third volume are based on the following sources :—

*Part 1.* The 10,000 Wills proved in the two local Probate Courts (Archdeacons of Essex and Colchester).

*Part 2.* The Quarter Sessions Rolls, relating to Employment and Trade (the other subjects having been dealt with in Volume I).

*Part 3.* The Court Rolls, etc., of 74 manors, selected as being representative of urban, rural, coastal, forestal, enclosed and open-field Manors.

The County Council having stipulated that each book should be restricted to about 360 pages, it was clear, when the entire series of Wills had been read and extracts made of all noteworthy clauses or items, that some of the material could not be included because of the length of the volume. As the series so far relates largely to the lower classes, the County Archivist (the General Editor of the E.R.O. Publications) and I felt that the best course was to leave out of Volume III the information taken from the Wills of esquires, gentlemen, and the affluent yeomen, clothiers and other merchants, and the clergy.[1] In the meantime the Council had authorized a fourth volume (to be published about 1977-8), to comprise the Wills of the upper classes proved in the Prerogative Court of Canterbury (formerly kept at Somerset House and now in the Public Record Office).[2] The material for Volume IV, however, is being prepared (and is nearly completed) on a different basis. Instead of narrative chapters on the various *subjects* (e.g. Sedition, Highway Robbery, Religious Offences), the text will be in the form of *detailed abstracts* giving every personal and place name and omitting only legal verbiage and repetitive phrases. The corresponding locally-proved Wills of the richer testators, not dealt with in Volume III, will, if authorized by the Council, form a fifth and final book.[3]

Although emphasized in the two previous Introductions, it is unfortunately necessary to repeat that the publication of the Quarter Sessions Rolls, let alone even part of the vast bulk of Archidiaconal Court Books and Manor Court Rolls, in calendar form is *absolutely out of question*.

INTRODUCTION viii

Twenty years ago my recommendation for printing the typescript calendar of the Sessions Rolls for 1556-1603 at an estimated cost of £20,000 was not unreasonably rejected. By 1976 the comparable figure would be not far short of £100,000 : no local authority in the near future could contemplate such a publishing venture. Yet, despite my firm remarks in Volumes I and II about impracticability of printing calendars of such records, the present method, fully approved by the County Archivist and omitting little of value, was recently dismissed as a 'dangerous compromise'.[4] A realistic attitude appears an impossibility for a few scholars who still cry for the moon in a period of economic stress. All I need add is that, as already explained, the Essex County Council, despite the crisis, is continuing to publish material from its records at a reasonably steady rate.

Below is indicated the kind of information that has been extracted or omitted. Following the formula used in Volumes I and II, the *Note on Editorial Method* (p. x) gives particulars under the relevant subjects :—

> *Part 1—Wills.* Excluding those of the richer testators as stated, four out of five average testaments yield little or nothing of interest except to the parish and the family historian and the genealogist. From the remainder have been used as many passages as possible.
>
> *Part 2—Employment and Trade.* Of the unique records of the High Constables' Petty (or Hiring of Servants) Sessions a lengthy account has been compiled, with several analyses. Apprenticeship, Wages, Dealers, and Food Shortages have been treated almost as fully. The chapter on Trade Control quotes all the relevant Quarter Sessions documents, also the shrievalty account-book in the Petre family archives—a very rare type of record. The Essex Q.S. rolls have already been used for Purveyance,[5] which I have not studied afresh.
>
> *Part 3—Manors.* From the multitudinous membranes of Court Rolls which were read hundreds of representative entries have been extracted about the heterogeneous aspects of social and economic life controlled by the courts. The countless cases of assault, unscoured drains, and sale of bread and beer without licence or at excessive prices call only for a few typical entries, but the less common offences and nuisances have been treated fairly fully. Virtually nothing is said about the innumerable entries of changes of tenancy by inheritance or sale.

The present volume, as before, is based on classes of records of which surprisingly little has been published for any county for the Elizabethan period. The object remains the same : to present to the economic and social historian, as well as the local historian, a substantial corpus of new evidence. The series is therefore largely source material for specialists on their own subjects. There is one qualification to the statement that the Essex sources are immensely rich. Inventories are very deficient, only a small number having been preserved in the E.R.O. probate court records and almost none in the P.C.C. series for our period. Many testators, however, refer to articles of furniture and household and farming implements, and some testators are so detailed in this respect as to suggest that they specified all their possessions in allocating them to the legatees. Such documents are often more descriptive than inventories. Shakespeare's (and others') 'second best bed' would normally appear as 'one bed', and 'one great chair and one hooped chair in the hall' merely as '2 chairs', in the relevant inventory.

---

[1] The Introduction to Volume II (p. xiii) stated that chapters on 'Work and Play on Sundays' and 'Tithes and Perambulations' would appear in the present volume. The County Archivist and I now feel that they would be alien in subject for Volume III, and indeed there would be no space. They will, however, be included in a volume of studies to be published September 1976 in honour of a distinguished antiquary, in a chapter entitled 'Tithe, Perambulation and Sabbath-Breaking in Elizabethan Essex' (ed. F. G. Emmison).
[2] Negative photostats of *all* the P.C.C. Essex Wills, 1558-1603. had been purchased by the Friends of Historic Essex several years ago (not yet available in the E.R.O.).
[3] The Friends of Historic Essex Committee has already promised a substantial contribution towards the cost.
[4] See review of *Elizabethan Life: Morals and the Church Courts* in *Archives* (the journal of the Brit. Rec. Assoc.), no. 53, pp. 36-37, and my rejoinder in no. 54, p. 82.
[5] Allegra Woodward, 'Purveyance for the royal household in . . . Elizabeth' (*Trans. Amer. Philos. Soc.*, n.s., xxxv, pt. 1, Philadelphia, 1945).

## NOTE BY THE GENERAL EDITOR, 1990

Two further volumes in the Elizabethan Life series were printed subsequently. **Wills of Essex Gentry and Merchants proved in the Prerogative Court of Canterbury**, a volume of abstracts, appeared in 1978 (ISBN 0 900360 50X) and was followed in 1980 by the complementary volume, **Wills of Essex Gentry and Yeomen, preserved in the Essex Record Office** (ISBN 0 900360 47X). The latter is now out of print.

Dr Emmison's work on abstracting Elizabethan wills of Essex people has since expanded into the **Essex Wills** series, of which eight volumes, covering all the Archdeaconry Court wills, from 1538 to 1603, will have been published by the end of 1992. A further four volumes covering the Essex and Hertfordshire Division of the Bishop of London's Commissary Court, will follow.

Details of all these books are available on request from the Essex Record Office.

V W GRAY

## ACKNOWLEDGEMENTS

Again I have to thank the Library, Museums and Records Committee of the Essex County Council for their continuing support, and, on behalf of the Council, the Executive Committee of the Friends of Historic Essex for their very substantial grant towards the cost of production. Mr K. C. Newton, M.A., F.R.Hist.S., the County Archivist—author of *The Royal Manor of Writtle* and an acknowledged expert on manorial records—has read Part 3 and assisted me in this and other directions, for which I am deeply obliged. Assistance with other chapters is therein acknowledged. I am grateful again to my part-time secretary, Miss Olwen Hall, for typing my much-corrected draft chapters and for drafting the Index of Persons and Places.

The Trustees of the Pilgrim Society and of the Plimoth Plantation, Plymouth, Massachusetts, having regard to the amount of material bearing on the social background of the immediate forefathers of the early immigrants to New England, agreed to make a joint contribution of $1.000 to the County Council towards the cost of production of the book. This is greatly appreciated by the Council, especially at the present time, and the County Archivist and I wish to record our thanks to Mr L. D. Geller, M.A., F.R.S.A., the Director of the Pilgrim Society, for his practical interest in the matter.

*Ingatestone Hall, December 1975* F.G.E.


## NOTE ON EDITORIAL METHOD

All dates between 1 January and 24 March are expressed in modern style, which has also been adopted for the quotations and the names of parishes. Enlarging on statements made on p. viii, the following indicates for each chapter whether all or only select cases have been extracted from the documents, apart from purely repetitive items, e.g. looms in chapter 5.

> *Nearly all cases quoted*: ch. 4 (Shipping and Fisheries), ch. 5 (Crafts and Trades), ch. 6 (section on Education and Books), ch. 7 (Weapons and Armour), ch. 9 (Employment), ch. 10 (Dealers in Food Supplies), ch. 11 (Control of Trade).
>
> *Selection only*: ch. 1 (The House), ch. 2 (Furniture and Furnishings), ch. 3 (Agriculture), ch. 6 (Family and Household), ch. 8 (Deathbed and Probate), chapters 12-21 (i.e. all Part 3, Manor Courts).

*Abbreviations*: *Trans. E.A.S.*, *Transactions of the Essex Archaeological Society*; *Ess. Rev.*, *Essex Review*; *E.L.*: *Disorder*: *Elizabethan Life*: *Disorder* (1970); likewise *E.L.*: *Morals and the Church Courts* (1973).

# PART 1—HOME
(*from Essex Wills*)

## 1
## The House

### Its Rooms

The majority of the buildings referred to in our wills are undoubtedly of late medieval date. The remainder, with few exceptions, probably fall within the first part of the 'Great Rebuilding' period of about 1570-1640, during which so many old houses—not only farmhouses but also cottages—were being enlarged or improved. Scattered over Essex may also be seen a remarkably large number of farmhouses newly built about this time. Many, however, when their interiors are examined, reveal alterations, especially the addition of an upper floor or a cross-wing, to an earlier structure. But very few of the smallest Elizabethan cottages, except those mainly rebuilt towards the end of the period, are still existing. In the view of a distinguished local historian, none 'seems to survive before the late seventeenth century. If it is genuine, it is almost invariably in origin a husbandman's house and not a labourer's cottage at all'.[1] Apart from a few of these rude, one-room dwellings, it seems probable that the majority of our Elizabethan Essex testators live in a single-storey cottage with two rooms. These are the hall, used for cooking and eating, while the second, known as the parlour or chamber, is the bedroom of the husband and wife, other members of the household sleeping in the hall. The latter is open to the roof, the smoke escaping as best it can through a hole in the roof. Against the side or backwall of the hall, there may be a lean-to used as a buttery, pantry or larder for storing beer, food or household utensils.

Slightly larger cottages have what some social historians call a service-room, in which food, etc. is prepared. It is often separated from the hall by a narrow cross-passage called the 'screens', the origin of which was probably to keep out draughts. Fig. 1 shows the fairly general arrangement of the rooms in both types of dwelling, the screens passage and the room beyond being absent in the case of the smallest cottages; the fireplace may be ignored for the moment.

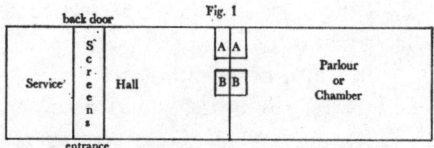

A and B show alternative positions of a double fireplace, if inserted.

It will be noticed that the plan does not use the word kitchen, because some Elizabethan kitchens are little buildings, detached from the dwelling so as to reduce fire-risk. An additional bay may of course have been added to a medieval house, and this is perhaps implied in some wills that mention 'the parlour and the chamber adjoining'; what appears to be a third room—a 'buttery' or the like—may be little more than a division in the hall.

Still larger houses have one or two cross-wings. Fig. 2 shows a fairly common plan of a late medieval house after upper rooms have been inserted or added during partial rebuilding, or of a new house erected in the Elizabethan period; H indicates the hearths or fireplaces.

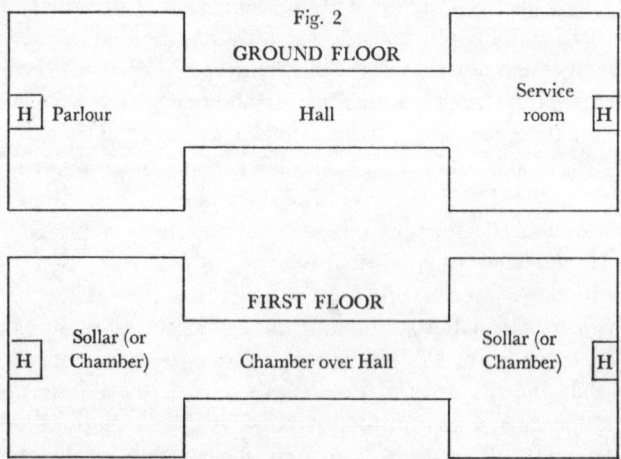

As relatively few Essex probate inventories are extant, analyses showing the sizes of houses with the number and names of the rooms and outhouses, which some Tudor social historians have compiled from them, cannot be done in any large way for this county. The fortunate survival, however, of 248 inventories for Writtle and Roxwell, 1635-1749, left behind in Writtle church chest in 1858 when the wills were taken to Somerset House, led to their being published in full, with a helpful introduction including some useful tables.[2] To attempt to analyse such details in the 11,000 Elizabethan wills is outside the writer's terms of reference. In any case the naming of rooms is a purely arbitrary act on the part of each individual testator and the amount of time involved in dealing with incomplete facts would be out of all proportion to its very limited value. We shall therefore use the imperfect material in our wills only to illustrate the structure of houses, though some wills throw light on certain aspects not illustrated in inventories.

Reverting to the humblest dwellings, remarkable confirmation of the belief that most medieval and many Tudor cottagers as well as some husbandmen lived in single-storeyed dwellings of two rooms or even one room is evidenced by the fact that at least 6 of the 24 houses on one side of Ingatestone High Street were depicted as late as 1601 in John Walker's very accurate map as having only one storey.[3]

'My chamber wherein I lie called the parlour' occurs occasionally; 'the chamber next the hall' commonly; 'my bed in the parlour' very frequently. With the gradual introduction of brick by about the 1570s, but slightly later in the smallest cottages, the central hearth is replaced by a single or double (back-to-back) fireplace, which accordingly heats one or both rooms (Fig. 1), or by hearths at one or both ends (Fig. 2), and one or two chimneys are built.

'A new chimney to be set up' is referred to in a number of wills, thus bearing out Harrison's well-known comment about 'the multitude of chimneys lately erected'.[4] A postscript to the will of Jeremy Debenham of Belchamp Walter reads: 'I have sold unto John Froste the quantity of 5 foot of my free ground to build thereon a chimney' (1592). The effect of introducing a chimney into a late medieval building is well expressed in a recent Essex parish history: 'The building of chimney stacks had more important results than the elimination of smoke. It facilitated the construction of upper chambers under the rafters. The parlour then provided some privacy for the head of the household'.[5] The managing curator of many early New England houses, who has carefully studied their contemporary counterparts in Essex and other counties, has equally helpful comments on the parlour in the larger cottages: 'The 17th century parlour' (and this applies also in our period) 'has no exact parallel in the 20th century house. It had multiple uses, all related to the character of the best room. Here was the best furniture; here company was entertained; and wills and inventories show that it was the room in which the parents slept'.[6]

Installation of brick hearths and chimneys thus allowed the roof space to be utilized by the addition of one or two upper 'sollars', which may be reached by new but probably unguarded stairs or by ladders with or without trapdoors and are either bedrooms or store-lofts. Some of the cottages shown on the same Ingatestone map of 1601, which were single-storeyed 'at the beginning of the reign, had recently been entirely rebuilt.'[7] At the manor court in 1601 Thomas Hinde, tenant of a house backing onto the churchyard, is presented for lighting a fire in a room that has no 'chimney' (i.e. fireplace) and is ordered to build one or pay a fine of 10s. Conversion of roof-space is indicated by Gilbert Isaac of Rayleigh: 'My wife shall lay with boards the lofts or garrets and nail down or lay with planks in the hall and both the shops of my said house' (1597). Adaptation of the central one-storeyed hall with parlour and kitchen on either side, or rebuilding with an extra storey to provide one or more bedrooms, is occasionally implied. Among early wills, William Archer of Theydon Garnon mentions 'a new chamber over the parlour that Harry my son did build' (1559); and William Payne of Elmstead, yeoman, refers to 'two new chambers over the hall' and 'a little new soller' (1568). But 'new' as applied to a room (or soller or loft) is rare before about 1585, and a total of 38 other wills using the adjective with no detail has been noted, in nearly all of which an upper floor seems to be suggested.

Instead of 'sollar' or 'soller', some, especially modern, writers give it as 'solar', a spelling that commonly leads to a false pronunciation and indeed rarely appears in Essex wills though it is a contemporary alternative elsewhere. Stow (*Survey of London*, 1598) has 'two shops, with solars and sellars', perhaps using this form to distinguish them, but Tusser, an Essex man, adopts 'soller'. The numerous uses to which the sollar is put are shown thus : 'my bed that I lie in in the sollar'; 'one bed in the soller'; 'the sollar where my servants lie'; 'the north and south sollers'; 'the chamber going up into the sollar'; 'the corn soller'; 'the corn in my sollars'; 'the rye in the sollar'; 'the malt in the sollar' (where it is drying); 'the apple sollar'; 'the store soller'; 'the cheese sollar'; 'my wool in the sollar'. 'Loft' is in less common use, but occurs in such phrases as 'the loft over (or in) the hall'; 'the loft wherein I lie'; 'the bedstead in the loft over the parlour'; 'the loft soller'; 'the blind loft'; or, in one tanner's will, 'the bark loft'.

We also find fairly often 'the chamber over the hall' ('over the parlour' or 'over the buttery'), 'upper (bed) chamber' and 'nether (bed) chamber'; though it would be wrong to assume that a 'chamber', as opposed to a 'soller', is reached by a staircase rather than a ladder. 'The chamber' (or 'loft') 'at the stair's head' or 'the stair chamber', which are self-explanatory, occur somewhat infrequently. In houses with a separate 'entry' there may also be a small 'chamber over the entry'. 'Study' is a very rare term in the wills of ordinary people. A Wrabness yeoman gives his son 'all my books which are in my study', but in our period the word may also mean a private room or office, which is possibly implied in the will of Joan Vygerous, a Langham widow (1567). In three houses, those of Joan Alline of Little Burstead (1591), Agnes Meade of Berden (1601), and Alice Eve of Great Dunmow (1593), there is mention of 'the guest's chamber' or 'the gessing chamber'.

The nomenclature of the other rooms in Elizabethan houses is amply exemplified in later sections. Use of the hall as sleeping as well as living accommodation is illustrated by such phrases as 'in my chamber within the hall' (1583). In our period 'cellar' apparently denotes a small store-room or closet, normally on the ground floor, underground cellars being mostly confined to inns or other substantial buildings. Seldom used, it is found in fact only twice in the wills, viz. 'cellars and sollars' and 'the chamber over the cellar'. The occasional occurrence of 'the great chamber' and 'the little chamber' does not necessarily denote a somewhat larger house; it may mean that the original open-to-roof hall was fairly long, thus enabling two rooms to be inserted above.

As already explained, the kitchen is often a separate little structure, and phrases such as 'with the barn and kitchen in the backside of my house' are quite common. 'After my decease', John Turner of Great Waltham determines, 'my wife shall build up at her cost one kitchen house as followeth, in length 30 foot, in width 18 foot, one storey, a purloined roof and cut roof ends, with one partition in the same, and thatch and daub the same' (1592).

In addition to the kitchen, there is a very wide range of 'service rooms'. Such a room may be under the same roof as the dwelling, a lean-to, or an outbuilding. The 'backhouse', commonly found and usually implying a service-room or store-room, may be part of the dwelling or may be in the yard. Caution is needed in reading an illiterate will that uses 'bakehouse' or 'backehouse' for backhouse or bakehouse, though the context is often a guide to the right interpretation. Apart from Harris's will, to be quoted, 'long house' (in which is the quern) occurs only once. Many wills refer to the buttery (for brewing), bakehouse, milkhouse or cheesehouse (for making cheese and butter), millhouse or quernhouse (for grinding corn), malthouse, 'yealding house' (where the beer wort is left to ferment), or hayhouse (though the hay may be drying in the loft). A carpenter assigns to his wife 'the garner and the one end of the sheepen' (1587), properly a shippon meaning a cattle-shed or cow-house and not a sheeppen; the word has also been found, 'half the shippen, barn and garner', in a yeoman's will.

Among the most pleasant features of our Essex heritage is the survival of so many late-16th and early-17th century mansions, farmhouses and cottages often with their picturesque gables, shadowing eaves and broad chimney-stacks.[8] The vast amount of new construction, rebuilding and extensive modernisation that took place in this period is explained as being due not so much to the increased population, which was relatively small, as to the improved economic status of the yeomen and to a lesser extent of the husbandmen. A sharp look-out for evidence was kept by the writer. While this is sporadic and scanty, a few items are significant, but surviving buildings usually provide better evidence.

Belonging to earlier years, the remarkably informative will of Solomon Whiskerd, a Fryerning glover, noted also under leather craftsmen, has this clause (1561):

> My executors shall see my frame set up honestly and finished in all points and to leave remaining about the house two hundred of board beside that which shall be spent about the same new house, and after my frame is finished they shall sell all my timber and wood to the use of my will.

We are indebted to Thomas Hayward of Wrabness, husbandman, for the fullest details. He describes his plan to his executors (1569):

to build a dwelling house of 44 foot long and 18 foot broad between the sills, with two pike walls in the said house, that is to say, he is to make three shifts in the house with ceiling all over, and the house to be double storey, which I will the nether storey to be seven foot and the upper storey 5½ foot between the joints with the wideness also of 16 inches between stud and stud of each storey, and finished with thatching, daubing, pinning and flowering'.

Such a specification leaves a few problems. 'Ceiling' in our period may stand for the lining with woodwork or plaster of either the floor or the walls. A 'pike-wall' is one converging to a point at the top, i.e. a gable wall: a rare term and its sole occurrence in the wills. Much as one would like to think that 'flowering', in its obsolete sense of decoration, is an Essex or local term for pargeting (plastering), it probably means flooring. 'Shifts' is not easy to explain. Tudor buildings, as here, are often distinguished from those of later date by the narrow distances between the studs (wooden timbers, with infilling of clay-daub or bricks). Regrettably, this is the only will setting out such particulars, but there are several giving similar facts about new outbuildings.

The charitable intentions of William Benoll of Hockley (1589) for providing an almshouse for two poor men or women are expressed in an instruction to his son William:

> to lay out of my free ground by the streetside 4 rods of length and 2 rods of breadth and therein to set and build one house of 34 foot of length and 12 foot of breadth, and in the middle of the house to set up a double chimney of brick to serve to put in two dwellers (so) that they may have in either of the ends one hall and a chamber for their bed to stand in.

Timber for intended construction is occasionally mentioned. Richard Smyth *alias* Baylye of Great Sampford, yeoman, bequeaths to his son Thomas 'so much of my timber as well hewen and sawen as rough, which do lie in my yards and which is already felled and lying yet in the groves or woods, as shall serve to make one barn of 5 or 6 and 30 foot long and 17 foot broad, if there be so much' (1585); and George Badcocke of London, grocer, 'now dwelling at Rayleigh', leaves to his son 'all my timber to build up a new frame adjoining to my house I now dwell in' (1588).

The cost of a new house is mentioned only once. Elizabeth Hammon of Danbury, widow, leaves to her eldest son 'the building and cost I bestowed upon my tenement called Rallins in Danbury which cost me £40' (1585), which may be compared with £18 for a three-bay new house at £6 a bay,[9] and with figures drawn from a recent study by Dr Petchey:[10]

HOUSE PRICES AT MALDON
(average no. of transactions per decade, 24)

| Average value 1561-70 | 1571-80 | 1581-90 | 1591-1600 |
|---|---|---|---|
| £26.76 | £26.19 | £34.90 | £41.90 |

The 'old' as well as the 'new' house may appear. Two sons of William Foockes of West Mersea are to get 'my new builded house which I myself builded called Sowthes alias Perrells' and 'my old builded house, with free ingress into the pond for water' (1582); and Thomas Beane of St. Peter, Maldon, husbandman, orders that 'my old house be divided into three parts to my two daughters and one son, and my new house after my wife's decease likewise into four parts to my four other children' (1592). In general, however, the evidence from wills seems mainly to incline towards rebuilding and conversion rather than completely new construction.[11]

Fitting out what seems to be a new room, perhaps after the building of a chimney, is described by Anthony Bret of Langford, yeoman (1588):

> A true note of the charges which he did lay out in trimming of a chamber, in anno domini 1584.
> Paid to the joiner of Maldon for the half pace and making of the hearth in the same chamber, 5s. 4d.
> To John Steven for three score ells of a canvas which doth hang the said chamber, 37s. 2d.
> To the goodman Laye the painter for painting the cloths, 51s. 8d.
> Paid to his wife for sewing the cloths, 2s. 6d.
> To the joiner for making of the little door and for hinges which hang the door, 2s. 6d.

'Pace' denotes either a step or part of a floor raised by it.

Thomas Harris of Great Waltham, 'pailemaker' (fence pales, not pails), gives some elaborate instructions (1600):

> To John my son one parcel of a long house belonging to my tenement that standeth against the street, that is to say, the great gates and the garret over the gates. And also all the residue of the house as it standeth along from the gates and garret eastward.
> And further my mind is that my son John shall within two years next after the decease of me and my wife take down remove and carry away the said parcel of the long house with the gates and garret and put it in some other place to such use as he shall think meet, and the ground whereon they now stand to remain to Thomas my son and his heirs for ever.
> I will that Agnes and Margery my two daughters shall have their dwelling and use of my kitchen that joineth to my hall at the west end of my house and the buttery there and the chamber over it, rent free during the time they live unmarried, with ingress, egress and regress into and from the same.
> I will that my son John shall not take down the parcel of the long house until he hath obtained a licence from the lord of the manor of Much Waltham.[12]

The maintenance of the dwelling-house (whether freehold, copyhold, or leasehold) in good repair is often requested, directed, or in some wills stipulated, as a condition of the gift or life-term. This may even apply in the case of a cottage occupied by a casual tenancy at will. More frequent, however, is a prohibition against 'strip or waste', the lawyer's terms for a tenant's offence in cutting down trees or hedges or allowing buildings to fall into disrepair. Common phrases are : 'to be kept in good and sufficient reparations', 'well maintained against wind and rain', 'windtight and watertight', or the like; occasionally the devisee is to have 'all in timber that I have towards the reparations of my tenement'. The wife, as tenant for life, may be told 'to find reparation of clay and straw'; 'to keep good reparation with timber, tiling, thatch, clay, hedging and ditching'; 'not to fell any oak or ash or any other wood, saving alder wood for reparations'; 'to make no strip or waste but to take so much wood yearly as shall serve for eithers (i.e. edders, or flexible wood such as osiers for interlacing hedge stakes) and stakes and one load of firewood'; 'to make no strip or waste, neither shall fell but for mere need of the house, and shall keep the house in good reparation with thatch, clay and other necessaries'; or 'not to take, spoil or cut any timber trees than shall be needful in the necessary repairing of the houses and fences'.

Robert Weeles of St. Mary, Colchester, cutler, imposes a severe penalty for any dilapidations (1582). His wife is to have his two houses, provided that she 'bestow at the end of 10 years after my decease 40s. yearly in reparations during the term of her life, and if she neglect and default then the next heir of my blood shall enter into both messuages and quit and clean expel, amove and put out' his wife. (His debts are given on p. 86). An unusual maintenance clause is embodied in the will of Thomas Wast of Tolleshunt Major, weaver : 'to find the fourth penny towards repairing the house' (1595).

Normally, of course, a tenant has the right to take a reasonable amount of fire-wood for fuel and necessary repairs from his land. This is set out in various archaic prefixes to the Old English word '-boot' or '-bote', meaning use, e.g. 'no strip or waste except for firebote', or 'for hedgebote and fencebote'; but other testators, or more likely their attorneys, choose to roll off an even longer list.

To obviate any boundary disputes John Pecke of Great Wakering, using a pair of almost unknown words, charges his wife 'to maintain all my outmarks and inmarks of all the hedges and fences' (1589).

Although some Elizabethan deeds refer to covenants for repairing local sea-walls, they have been noticed only once in our wills. Edward Duke of Brightlingsea senior, yeoman, reminds his son 'to repair the houses and maintain the sea walls belonging to the manor' (1572).

## *Fixtures*

An interesting provision by a surprisingly large number of testators is the stipulation that various fixtures, such as window-glass, 'shall remain' in the house, though nowadays considered an integral part of it. We use 'fixtures', although 'heirloom' in its original sense would be a better word, to include also some of the principal articles of furniture or large or essential household implements that could readily, but must not, be taken away. A contemporary but much rarer term is 'standards' or 'standers'. In imposing a veto, some testators think fit to specify them in detail.

In its simplest forms such directions occur as: 'I will that my table and frame in the hall with the benchboard and form shall remain in my house for ever to them that have the house'; 'the table board and the bench with the form and the great chair which standeth in the hall shall be standards and remain in the house for ever'; similarly with 'my long tables and ceilings and benches', in which ceilings are undoubtedly wall-linings of woodwork; 'the bench-board and back settles in the hall'; or 'a portal door in the parlour'.

Glass, being still relatively novel and too readily removable, is quite commonly listed in conjunction with locks and so forth. But most dwellings merely have 'lattices', that is, the window-openings are filled with narrow laths, interlaced and sometimes nailed together, with some spaces between the laths; or thin horn is used. They let in draughts but little light, and they seldom find mention in wills. Glazed windows are now gradually coming into fashion because the increased production of cheap glass has made its use possible in ordinary houses.[13] It is obtained in small diamond-shaped 'quarrels' mounted between lead strips.

John Manninge of Maldon, shoemaker, leaves 'to my wife Elizabeth my tenement in the parish of All Saints called by the sign of the Spread Eagle during her life, provided she shall not remove any of the wainscot (i.e. panelling) nor the glass' (1581). Gilbert Isaac of Rayleigh stipulates that 'all the glass in the windows of my house, the windows, doors, locks, bolts, benches, shelves, all the boards and planks in the garrets and upper chambers and floors beneath, nailed and unnailed, the gates and pales of my yard and iron work, as they now stand, to remain to the house' (1597). Occasionally painted cloths—the cheap substitute for tapestries—are included in the ban: 'not to take away any of the glass, wainscot, benches, shelves, doors, windows, painted cloths, portals or settles, locks or keys' (1597); or 'all the stained cloths hanging anywhere upon the walls of my house do there still remain' (1596). John Jenkyn of St. Runwald, Colchester, adds an implement to his sanctions: 'all the wainscot, glass, locks, keys, harps, hingles (i.e. the part of the hinge attached to the door), doors, windows, shelves, ceilings, pavements and lattices belonging to the house, and all the joined benches and forms fastened to the house, with all the leads, gutters, also a brewing lead in the backhouse, I will shall remain where they now be during the natural life of Katherine my wife' (1563). William Danyell of St. Giles, Colchester forbids the removal of 'all manner of ceilings, with the glass, the horse-mill, a lead (i.e. cauldron) and a brass, and the great vats belonging to the brewing' (1567); and John

Trott of Little Hallingbury husbandman directs that 'the cistern of lead belonging to my malthouse shall remain and belong to my heirs' (1588).

Removal of important household or 'shop' utensils is prohibited in a few other cases. Henry Harkewood of Crondon Hall in Stock (probably a tenant farmer of Sir John Petre) determines that 'the quern, the kneading trough and the moulding board', as well as the table, bench and form in the hall, must stay (1589). The same instruction is given by Katherine widow of John Grene of Shelley: 'the cauldron hanging in the brewhouse and my great andirons and my great spit' (1593); by Thomas Bruce, rector of Little Burstead—'a quern in the kitchen with the house as pertaining to the same'; by John Ponde of Fryerning yeoman—'my great powdering (i.e. salting) trough for powdering of hogs' (1573); by William Foster, a Romford smith—'all the implements in my shop, as boards, shelves, the great chest, and the spice mortar' (1573). John Brooman of South Weald wills that 'a bar of iron, 2 pothooks, a quern standing, a powdering trough, a boulting trough, a cauldron that is a furnace, a table and a form in the hall, all these to be standers to the house' (1574).

Kitchen 'fixtures' are dealt with by William Glascocke of Fyfield, yeoman: 'My son nor nobody shall remove the cauldron that hangeth in the kitchen chimney, nor the bar of iron with the pothooks, nor shall take out the iron hooks out of any of the chimneys' (1579); and Robert Keble of Great Oakley dictates: 'I will that my wife shall have and occupy my copper pan during her life, and after her decease I will that it shall remain unto the house I dwell in as a standard of the same' (1564). 'All my 3 ladders which serve to go into 3 lofts shall serve still to the use of my son' is willed by one man; and another insists on 'leaving the ladder to my house', perhaps as a fire precaution for a thatched dwelling. Perhaps the most unusual item is 'two pease hooks to remain in the house'. In a different sense, John Moyse of Thorpe debars disturbance by his executors: 'To my wife Margaret all my household where I now dwell even whole as it standeth, with corn, fish, cheese, butter and bacon, and all other hostilments (i.e. furniture, etc.) whatsoever' (1558).[14]

It is disappointing to find only rare mention of gardens. Humphrey Garralde of Downham devises 'to my wife Ellen the house that she now dwelleth in, with the yard extending to the cloth hedge, the great pear tree growing at the south end of the hedge, also the paled garden in the other yard' (1601). Another will refers to cherry and walnut trees. Only once de we read of a 'herb garden'. Not unnaturally, wills say nothing of vegetables or flowers.[15]

---

[1] W. G. Hoskins, *Local History in England* (2nd edn., 1972), 'The Rebuilding of Rural England, 1570-1640' (*Past and Present,* 1953, 44-59), reprinted in his *Provincial England* (1963).

# FOOTNOTES

² F. W. Steer, *Farm and Cottage Inventories of Mid-Essex, 1635-1749*. For other counties, see 'Jacobean Household Inventories', ed. F. G. Emmison (*Beds. Histl. Rec. Soc. Publns.*, xx, 1938; 'Notts. Household Inventories' (1516-62), ed. P. A. Kennedy (*Thoroton Soc. Rec. Series*, xxii, 1962); *Household and Farm Inventories in Oxfordshire, 1550-90*, ed. M. A. Havinden (*Oxfordshire Rec. Soc. Publns.* no. 44, 1965).

³ E.R.O., D/DP P8 (see centre-spread re-drawing in colour of High Street in *Elizabethan Essex* (E.R.O. Pubns., several edns.), also smaller plate in Emmison (ed.) *Catalogue of Maps in E.R.O.* (1st. edn. only, 1947).

⁴ William Harrison (rector of Radwinter, 1559-93), *The Description of England* (1st. edn., 1577, 2nd. edn., 1587, ed. G. Edelen, Cornell Univ. Press, 1968), cf. *Elizabethan Life: Morals and the Church Courts*, index.

⁵ G. C. S. Curtis, *The Story of the Sampfords* (1974), 90-1.

⁶ A. L. Cummings, *Rural Household Inventories* (Society for Preservation of New England Antiquities, 1964), xv; I am grateful to him and to Bertram Little, his predecessor, for showing me these historic buildings in Massachusetts; cf. Nina F. Little, *Country Arts in Early American Homes* (New York, 1975), pl. 1.

⁷ *Elizabethan Essex*, caption to centre-spread map.

⁸ *Royal Comm. on Hist. Monuments, Essex*, vols. i-iv (1916-23); the pioneer work of Mr A. C. Edwards of Essex has shown that many '17th century' dwellings belong in fact to the late 16th century or even much earlier.

⁹ M. W. Barley, *The English Farmhouse and Cottage* (1961), 53.

¹⁰ W. M. Petchey, 'The Borough of Maldon, 1500-1688' (unpubld. Leicester Univ. Ph.D. thesis, copy in E.R.O.).

¹¹ Cf. Petchey, *op. cit.*, app. 3, 'Domestic Building Operations in Maldon, c. 1508-1682'. New; enlarged; rebuilt; and subdivided houses—1558-85 and 1586-1603 respectively: 5, 3; 2, 1; 1, 1; 4, 6.

¹² For licences for tenants' new buildings, see that section under Manors *infra*.

¹³ Barley, *op. cit.*, 70.

¹⁴ The *O.E.D.* derives 'hostlement' from Old French '(h)ostil', utensils. Spelt here as 'ostyllment', the only other occurrences noted are 'hostelments of household' (1560) and 'huslement' (p. ).

¹⁵ For these, see Harrison, *op. cit.*, 264-5, 270.

# 2
# Furniture and Furnishings

Except for the homes of the wealthy, with which we do not deal in this volume,[1] most Elizabethan furniture is fairly rude and essentially utilitarian, judged by the standards of the next century. It is mainly the product of the carpenter. But the craft of the joiner, who uses joints and may turn out superior or more ornamental pieces, is coming to the fore in our period. Significantly, some testators distinguish 'joined' or 'joint' beds, chairs, chests and so on, while naturally those 'of carpenter's work' are rarely specified as such. Indeed, a choice article of furniture may occasionally be identified in the testaments of grandfather, father and son. Although some yeomen's and a few husbandmen's and craftsmen's dwellings seem to be adequately equipped, the fact remains that most homes are sparsely furnished. The slightly lighter and more ornamental 'Jacobean' furniture will in due course largely replace the heavy 'Tudor Gothic' style in the less humble homes, but the periods indicated by the modern terms are only approximate.

## Beds and Bedding

There is an extraordinary wealth of evidence about bedrooms and their furnishings in Elizabethan wills. 'Bed' is often used to include, besides the bedstead, the mattress, bolster, sheets, and coverlet. Otherwise all the equipment is merely referred to as the 'furniture', as in 'my second best bed with the furniture' bequeathed by Shakespeare to his wife or 'a good featherbed furnished with all the things necessary to it'. 'Bedsteadle', a word less commonly used than 'bedstead', is apparently a somewhat infrequent term outside Essex. Only once do we find 'bedstock' (1581), which may, however, denote the front and back parts of the bedstead; once also, 'a boarded bedsteadle'; and one testator leaves only 'the timberwork of bed', i.e. the framework.

As the most valuable domestic asset in many houses, the bedstead is often the first bequest, though the table sometimes has priority. While the bed is generally not qualified with an adjective, the 'joined bed' and the 'posted bed' are fairly common: or it may be a 'wainscot bed', or once 'my joined bed, the head being of asp' (a kind of poplar, the timber of which is very seldom mentioned). Very frequent is the legacy of the 'best bed', varied occasionally with 'great bed' or 'chief bed', which often implies a posted bed. Four-posters (a much later term) are generally described as 'the bed with a ceiling and tester' (once 'without a ceiling'), 'the joined bedstead with a joined ceiling' (or 'wainscot ceiling'), 'the posted bed with the ceiling and cording', or 'the great joined bedsteadle with a joined ceiling': phrases that often signify the owner's pride of possession. Seven wills mention 'a half-headed bed'; one, 'a demi-ceiling tester', meaning presumably that it has only a head-cover; another refers to 'my half-headed bedstead with the ceiling and curtain rods'. We can all visualize what a dealer's catalogue calls a four-poster or a tester bed; but the Elizabethan 'ceiling' and 'tester', as the extracts show, are not identical terms. At this period tester may still denote the vertical headboard and not necessarily the canopy, while the latter may be called the ceiling.[2]

Many Elizabethan 'standing beds' have a low 'trundle bed' on wheels, pushed underneath in daytime. The word has two variants, as in 'my trindle bed under my posted bed' and 'my standing bed with a trindle bed', or 'a truckle bedstead'. Such beds serve for maidservants or children: menservants probably sleep in the hall. A 'trussing bed in the nether chamber', found only once (1588), implies one that can be packed up for storing or travelling. Handed down to the next generation are 'one cradle of wainscot' and 'a child's cradle', but only a few others are mentioned.

Rarely is a value attached to articles of furniture in wills, though a normal feature of inventories. John Gilden, vicar of Ridgewell, however, gives his son Thomas his 'joined post bedstead which should cost me 20s.' (1585), which may be compared with 'two standing beds each valued at 40s.' occurring in an early Quarter Sessions document (1563).

The better-class bedsteads have colourful curtains, or curtains, rods and valances about them, mostly of Essex 'say', 'green and red say', 'yellow and red say', or 'blue and yellow say', or once 'three curtains of yellow buckram and red'. We read of 'the bedstead with a painted tester' or 'a painted testorn'; 'three joined bedsteadles with painted ceilings'; 'stained' (or 'painted') 'cloths hanging about the bed' (very common); 'bedstead with a tester and hangings of a painted cloth'; 'bedstead and a tester of painted cloth'; 'posted bed and a stained cloth for the heading of the bed'; 'the five painted cloths about the bed'; 'my carved bedsteadle in the parlour'; or 'one posted bed carved, with the tester and curtains of dornix paned'. Only in the last two wills is there any suggestion of decorated work. More ornate beds with caryatids or other embellishments are not found in the ordinary homes; 'the bedstead with plain posts' is one testator's clear description.

A remarkably high proportion of wills also describe in some detail what is now termed the bed-linen. It is about the improvement in bedding comfort that Harrison, while rector of Radwinter, wrote that vivid paragraph, often cited, though rarely with any confirming or challenging comment from contemporary documents. It will be followed by evidence from the wills of his own county. According to the greybeards of Radwinter—[3]

> Our fathers, yea, and we ourselves have lien full oft upon straw pallets, on rough mats covered only with a sheet, under coverlets made of dagswain or hap-harlots, and a good round log under their heads instead of a bolster or pillow. If it were so that our fathers or the goodman of the house had within seven years after his marriage purchased a mattress or flock-bed, and thereto a sack of chaff to rest his head upon, he thought himself to be as well lodged as the lord of the town, that peradventure lay seldom in a bed of down or whole feathers, so well were they contented and with such base kind of furniture. Pillows (said they) were thought meet only for women in childbed. As for servants, if they had any sheet above them it was well, for seldom had they any under their bodies to keep them from the pricking straw that ran oft through the canvas of the pallet and rased their hardened hides.

The worthy cleric felt it necessary to interpolate after 'dagswain and hap-harlots', both meaning coarse coverlets, '(I use their own terms)', seemingly because he had never seen them, despite his rural environment and certainly not for prudish reasons as he uses plenty of crude vernacular elsewhere. But, although familiar to scholars because of Harrison (and earlier use of the words is known to lexicographers), they are both very rare. We find the elusive hap-harlot in a solitary will: Richard Faukoner *alias* Stockmer of Castle Street, Walden, leaves to Agnes Rabbett 'my old covering called an happharlett' (1579). We also note, for example, 'one mat and one mattress'; 'a bed stuffed with straw'; 'the canvas for the straw bed'; 'a chaff bed'; 'the trundle bed with the mats and lines'; 'a girted (corded round?) bedstead with a mat or strawbed' (1571, the other extracts being from later wills). Some of these are the sole bedding of poor testators, while others are probably for the use of menial servants, many of whom virtually sleep on the floor, as we know from other sources.

Luxury is represented by the mattresses (usually termed 'beds') and pillows being filled with feathers, down or flock. Here we have ample confirmation of Harrison (whose first edition came out in 1577) from the gradually increasing recurrence of featherbeds and the like. Except in the earlier decades, flock-beds, down-beds and feather-beds are common. When Stephen Virgin of Barnston, a bricklayer, determines that Clemence his daughter shall have 'one featherbed with all that belongeth thereunto' at 21, and in the meantime Agnes his wife 'shall have the occupying of the same featherbed', we are left in no doubt about this important asset (1566). Of the less common items we note: 'a bed of down priced the bed at £3' (1582); 'a bed half of feathers and half of flocks'; 'the bed stopped with flocks being a mattress'; 'a wool bed'; and 'one flock bed of Coggeshall combs' (1573). The last, belonging to a testator living twenty miles from this clothing village, must refer to combed-out refuse wool.

Of sheets there are, for example: '8 pair of sheets whereof 4 pair flaxen and 4 pair towen' (tow is the shorter, or inferior, flax fibres); 'two pair of towen sheets being of her own spinning'; 'one pair of sheets of canvas of 9 ells in the pair and my best sheets wrought with the herring bone'; 'a pair of flaxen sheets with open seams'; 'two pair of best canvas sheets and one canvas pillow'; 'a fine holland sheet with a bone lace set on' (1597); 'my flax sheet wrought with a herring bone lace'; 'one pair of holland sheets marked with these letters T.J. and A.'

The quality of coverlets (often called 'coverlid', 'kiverlet' or 'kivering') also shows a wide range: 'a coverlet made of broadcloth and lined with canvas'; 'my best northern coverlet'; 'a covering of my wife's own spinning of red and blue'; 'one white coverlet striped with yarn'; 'a red wadmole covering' (a coarse woollen material); 'a black and yellow homemade coverlet'; 'a coverlet and the bolster and the underbed of flax'; 'a covering with a canopy'; 'a thrum coverlet' (i.e. with a fringe of threads or tassels); 'four grounds for coverlets'. 'A covering of dornix' (heavy, coarse linen) appears in many variants—darnick, darnacle, dernacle, e.g. 'a darnack covering and another country housewife's covering of blue and red' and 'a coverlet of Flanders dornix'. Woven and embroidered coverlets in imitation of tapestry appear as 'a tapestry covering which lieth on my bed'; 'my best coverlet of tapestry work'; 'a coverlet of tapestry work lined with canvas'; 'ten coverlets of tapestry with images'; 'a covering of carpet work' (on a bed, not a table); 'a coverlet of arras work'; and 'a coverled wrought with birds'.

We have considered each article of bedroom furniture and linen separately, but of course the more detailed wills list them together. Among the less usual descriptions we quote only two: 'a Spanish new bedstead, one new canvas bed stopped with feathers, one tick bolster, a new fustian pillow, a linsey woolsey pillow' (Alice Eve of Great Dunmow, widow, 1593); and '1 featherbed, 2 wool beds made mattress fashion, 3 fustian pillows, 1 bolster of feathers, 4 blankets, 1 coverlet, 8 pair of sheets, 1 bearing sheet' (Nicholas Holman of Hornchurch, tanner, 1580). Listed very occasionally among bed-linen, as in the last extract, a bearing sheet is used for carrying a child to church for baptism. It may be of fine quality and embroidered. John Joyce of Rettendon records after the bed-linen 'my best bearing sheet and my best casting sheet' (1583). Two other casting sheets have been found, but the meaning is not known to the writer. Blankets with descriptive additions are: 'a white kersey blanket', 'a great russet blanket', ' a pair of linsey woolsey blankets of the best', and 'a Spanish blanket'. Of the other articles of bed-linen, there is an abundance from which to select, and some of the linen is embroidered: 'one new pillow stuffed with feathers'; 'a pillow of feathers with a bere' (pillowcase); 'two pillows and the beres to them'; 'a pillow-bere with great black seams'; 'one bolster stopped (i.e. stuffed) with feathers'; 'two bolsters, the one of feathers, the other of flocks'; 'a bolster of tick stopped with feathers'; 'a pillow of down covered with a fustian tick'; 'a pair of pillow-beres, one wrought with black silk lace, the other with white work'.

The chamber vessel enclosed in a stool or box (the predecessor of the Victorian commode) always goes by the name of close-stool, except for one 'close-chair' and one 'close little chair of rods' (1588). Velvet-covered seats are a luxury found only in a few houses of the wealthy.[4] The humble chamber-pot rarely merits testamentary mention unless it happens to be one of pewter. Surprisingly, a 'warming pan', to contain live coals, occurs only once (1598). A privy, apparently a little moveable shelter, appears in the will of John Thorowgood, a Witham yeoman: 'Whereas Mr Archer hath in his possession goods of mine, viz. one house of easement which cost 40s. and one cupboard which did cost 18s., he is to pay my executors or leave them to God and his conscience'! (1602).

## Other Furniture

The evolution of the table in the Tudor and Stuart period is well known. Originally the ordinary type consisted only of a 'board' (or more commonly a 'plank', which was sometimes regarded as thicker than a board) that rested on trestles: the top is the 'table', which can be lifted off when the pegs holding the two stretchers to the trestles are pulled out, and the separated pieces can be stacked against the wall, giving more space in the room. Thus we have 'a table lying on two trestles', 'a table and trustles', or, just as frequently, 'a plank table'; also 'a small plank table and trestles, with a little form to it', 'a plank' (or 'two planks') 'to make a table'; 'a table or plank, to make a table on (i.e. of) and two other small planks to make forms on'; 'an elmen table or plank'; 'one slab or plank'; or 'an elm table planed of two planks and headed with oak'.

The rigid sort of table is supported by solid ends joined by a long, single fixed stretcher or rail underneath the table proper: 'table', or 'board', as before, denotes the top; the legs and stretcher are the 'frame'. Thus, '3 planks and as many quarters which shall make a frame with 6 feet', and the utterly common 'table with the frame', 'joined table lying on a frame', or perhaps the 'table made of elm with the frame of oak' or 'table of fir with a frame of elm'. Such permanent tables are occasionally called 'dormant tables', a term used by Chaucer but not in our wills, though we find 'a table with a pair of dormans' (1592) and 'in the hall an old plank table standing upon dormans' (1603).

About the beginning of the Elizabethan period a new kind appears. It stands on four or more legs of the bulbous type. The legs are joined by stretchers near the floor level. These tables are sometimes very cumbersome as compared with the trestle type, and some are of great size, especially those in the larger houses or in farmhouses, for by ancient usage the labourers ate there. (Some surviving examples are the so-called 'refectory tables'.) They may well be represented by the not uncommon 'long joined table' in the hall or kitchen or 'my long table in the hall to remain still in my house', i.e. in the nature of a 'fixture'. But the 'long table' is not necessarily a single piece of furniture, as the occasional 'long table, with a frame of joiner's work, in the hall' shows. Space is also saved where needed, by a table that can be drawn out at one or both ends, and such is called a 'leaf table' (1559). Thus we find, now and again, 'a table shot with leaves' (1582); 'a table in the parlour with a leaf'; 'a short two-leaved table' (1565); 'a little table with two leaves' (1591); 'one table folded, three-leaved'; 'a table with half a leaf'; and 'a drawing table in the kitchen' (1567); 'my shut table' (1570); and 'my leaf table of peartree'. An alternative term, 'draw table', does not seem to occur in the Essex wills. What is later known as the gate-legged table is called a 'falling table' (1587, 1594), but these are fairly rare. 'A little table with four stacks' occurs once (1589).

Other wills refer to 'a little square table on a frame' (1584); 'one joined round table of elm standing in the chamber where I lie' (1591); 'a round table with a chest in the frame of it'; and 'a little round table having a chest in it'. The exact meaning of counter-table is not clear. It is found in eight wills, from 1559 onwards, e.g. 'a counter table in the hall and a counter table in the parlour', and 'my long counter table standing in the hall'. A useful adjunct to the dining-table is the 'side table in the hall' or, once, 'a side table with turned feet'. The livery table, on which the 'liveries' or servants' rations are put, occurs only rarely in households of lesser size than that of the yeoman, e.g. 'one livery table in the hall' (1598).

Floor carpets or floor mats have been noticed by one or two writers in and indeed before the Elizabethan period (rushes or straw being the usual coverings), but none has been seen in the Essex wills, which refer solely to carpets laid on tables—the normal meaning at this time for a thick covering, generally made of wool. 'A table and the carpet for the same', 'a carpet for a table', 'a carpet on table', 'the table with the carpet that belongeth to it', and 'my green carpet to make her a covering' exemplify its use. There is a solitary mention of 'my side table and carpet to it in the parlour'. 'My greatest Turkey carpet lying on the table in the hall', left by Elizabeth Harwoode of St. Nicholas, Colchester (1594), evidently a tradesman's widow, is the only appearance of the superior and much-prized type, either imported from Turkey or made in the style of such richly-coloured wool carpets.

As would be expected, cushions are an uncommon feature. They are mostly embroidered or of similar workmanship: 'my great cushion'; 'a wrought cushion'; '3 cushions of thromes' (perhaps in this context meaning tasselled); 'a cushion marked with a blue thread'; '3 cushions of green say with the griffins in them'; 'a cushion of carpet work'; and 'half a dozen cushions of tapestry work'.

Furniture to sit upon is of the rudest sort in most dwellings. Even by 1603 nearly everyone sat on stools. The single chair is the prerogative of the head of the family—the origin of 'chairman', or 'to take the chair'— though there may be a second chair for the chief guest. Seating for the rest of the family is admirably described as 'all the benchboards or seats placed to the sides and walls of the hall and kitchen to sit on or for other uses or services' (1594). The Elizabethan heavy chair with panelled base had passed through various stages from its origin in the chest. 'My great chair', 'my great joined chair', 'the best turned chair' (1570), 'a joined chair which her own mother did commonly sit in' (1573), or the like, is a treasured possession of the husband or widow. We also find: 'the best chair with a high back' (1570); 'one great chair and one hooped chair in the hall' (1576), 'the chair with the hoop' (1594); 'one oaken table and one oaken chair that standeth at the table's end' (1559); 'a chair of turner's work'; 'my lowest turned chair' (1578); and 'three chairs with bottoms of bullrushes' (1594). Two wills mention a 'wicker chair' (1592). Some of the finest examples of contemporary and slightly later chairs may still be seen in the chancels of Essex churches, as elsewhere.[5] 'Two fair joined chairs which cost 13s. 4d.' is the only item thus valued.

The chair is usually followed by a form or stools, e.g. 'the long table in the hall with the form'; 'my long joined table with the stools thereunto belonging'; 'my frame table in the chamber with 6 stools'; 'the joined table and half a dozen joined stools belonging to it'; 'one high joined chair and two high joined stools' (1585); 'the table with the frame and 6 joined stools price 20s.' Occasionally, in the poorest homes, even a chair may be absent, e.g. 'the table in the hall with the form and three stools belonging to the same' (1598), or merely 'a little plank and form in the hall'. But Matthew Dale of Great Greenwoods in Stock, yeoman, is clearly proud of his 'great joined table, 6 joined stools, and one walnut-tree chair in my great parlour' (1586).

More comfortable chairs and stools are few and far-between in the ordinary houses, but we discover 'my embroidered chair and three embroidered stools' (1598), 'my red chair wrought with gold' (thread) (1591), and 'three cushion stools' (1591). Low stools occur now and again as 'three buffet stools' (1575), 'two buffet joined stools' (1588), and 'three round buffet stools' (1598). Among other unusual items are 'one twigged stool', apparently made of wicker (1576, earliest reference in *O.E.D.*, 1643); a box-stool, described as 'a little coffer stool' (1595), 'my oaken stool with a back and a walnut-tree stool' (1578); and 'two buckstools' (1586), not recorded by lexicographers but apparently meaning a washing-stool: it occurs in the will of a widow of Steeple Bumpstead, where there is still a ford.

Made to seat three or four persons, but of course not as common as stools, are forms, benches, and settles, the last having an arm at each end and a high back. 'Benchboards'—a frequent word in wills but strangely missing from the *Oxford Dictionary*—'are sometimes mentioned together with benches, and it would appear that the framing of the bench is often regarded as a separate item from the board that forms the seat.[5] Exemplifying the usual place of the settle or bench on one side of the fireplace in the hall or the kitchen are: 'a settle in the hall standing against the chimney' (1584); 'the great board now standing in the kitchen' (1569); 'two wainscot settles standing in and about the hall' (1585); 'a backbench and a form thereunto belonging' (1588); and 'one benchboard and the backboard joined together as they now stand in the hall' (1584).

Generally indicative of the furniture commonly used for eating, seating and preparing food are such common items as 'the great table with the form, bench and benchboards in the hall and all that belongeth thereto and three turned stools' (1584); 'one long table, one plain form, one bench and benchboard in the hall' (1590); 'the long table in the hall with the bench and backboard unto the same' (1584); 'one table, trestles, form and benchboard in the hall' (1574); 'the form with all benchboards now standing in the hall' (1575); 'a settle, a bench and a long form'; and similar phrases extracted in the section about Fixtures. A puzzling entry is 'a long joined table in the hall, a long wyned settle, and a little settle' (1597). Found only in one other will—'the lattice wyned to the wall'—'wyned' apparently means that the long settle is affixed to the floor.

The humbler kind of chest is made of boards nailed together; the better type, made to prevent splitting, is framed, the panels being free to shrink in their grooves.[7] Coffers and chests are sometimes regarded as synonymous, but 'the Oxfordshire inventories distinguish between them, coffers being mentioned more frequently' (168 coffers, 43 chests).[8] In the Essex wills, however, chests occur more often than coffers or hutches, and coffers are probably used for the more valuable articles. It is of course very usual to find one, or the only, chest standing at the foot of the bed, and its main use is either for storing linen or valuables or both. Indeed, scores of wills refer to 'my chest at the bed's feet'; once 'the oaken chest that standeth at the bed's head' (1560); once also, 'all such linen as is usually locked up in a chest'.

Many testators regard this important piece of furniture as meriting more than the bare word. Thus, for example, 'my great chest' (common), 'my chest and a little chest', 'two of the biggest chests', 'chest of joiner's work', 'boarded chest with ledges on it', 'little chest with a compartment lid with lock and key', 'broad great chest' (no doubt about its size), 'long chest', 'chest that standeth in the parlour betwixt the cupboard and the bedstead', 'chest standing under the window', 'chest under the stairs', 'great leathern chest', 'the two fairest chests'. A 'painted chest' stands in several houses; we also find 'a danske painted coffer' and once 'the hutch that is painted with a St. Catherine wheel' (1569).

The exact use of 'my great ware chest' belonging to Thomas Jenynges of Harlow, who does not give his occupation, is not apparent, though it presumably refers to some sort of goods kept in it (1558); nor is 'a little chest with a compass lid with lock and key', among the possessions of Bartholomew Church of Earls Colne, in which 'compass' seems to imply either a mariner's compass fixed to the lid or a dial-lock.

Occasionally, however, the chest is merely a 'box', e.g. 'two of my best boxes' (1595), 'my great box with three locks and keys', or 'all my chests and boxes'. 'Danske' chests often appear in English (especially mariners') wills from the middle of the century, e.g. 'a danske chest wherein my linen doth lie' (1587), and less often a 'Flemish chest' or 'Flanders chest', with which we may note 'the coffer that my woollen lieth in', and 'a little hutch with all the linen therein'. The solitary 'casket' (written above 'plain box' struck through) in the will of Sibyl White of Great Baddow (1598) is probably a small jewel-box. A few chests and hutches are specifically described as of oak or wainscot, of elm, cypress (a kind of cedar, often corrupted into Cyprus), fir or spruce, all coniferous trees; rarely, of walnut, e.g. 'my walnut tree chest' and 'my hutch of walnut tree'; and once of 'pear tree'. One testator leaves his son 'three boards to make him a chest' (1573).

Very common is the 'ship chest', so common in fact as to be slightly problematical. Although 'my ship chest in the chamber over the parlour', or the like, occurs in some sailors' or fishermen's wills, the term is apparently used in most cases merely for a strong chest. Thomas Hunwycke (or Honicke), a miller of Little Waltham, for example, has 'a great ship chest standing at the stair's head betwixt the doors' (1597).

Typical references to hutches are: 'my hutch standing at the bed's feet' (common); 'a hutch that was my father's and a little hutch standing by the chimney side in my chamber'; 'the great hutch that was my father's'; 'the long hutch'; 'a carved hutch'. Their uses are exemplified by 'the hutch in the parlour to lay clothes in'; 'my hutch that all my holy-day linen lieth in'; 'the little hutch wherein I use to put my writings'; 'the hutch that my evidences (i.e. title-deeds and leases) lie in'; and '6s. 8d. in the till of my hutch'. Only four wills mention a trunk, including 'the trunk standing over my bedchamber'; and one gives 'a trunk hutch' (1592).

In the first volume a good deal of evidence emphasized the prevalence of burglaries and housebreakings.[9] With virtually no facilities for insuring valuables or banking cash, the demand for strong chests is natural enough. The need is by no means confined to the rich. A few yeomen, having apparently no substantial assets, mention iron-bound chests or hutches. Thus: 'a round barred chest'; 'a chest covered with iron bars'; 'a great chest in the chamber to lock up'; 'my hutch or coffer with a spring lock'; 'a spring lock hutch', 'my hutch with a lock and key'; 'the great hutch with one broken hasp'; 'one great box with three locks and three keys' (1571), and '1 fair joined chest with a double lock which cost 6s.'

Joan Dale, a Stock widow, possesses as well as the usual bedroom chest a 'barred chest' and a third 'with a keep over the hole' (1586); 'keep' is apparently an unrecorded noun in this sense, though its meaning (a slide- or hinged-cover) is obvious.

Our typical modern cupboards, with a pair of doors and standing on the floor, have little similarity to the various kinds of Elizabethan cupboards. In its original form, as the name denotes, it was simply a 'board' (like the humble stretcherless table-top), on which to put or display cups and the like; and doubtless the unqualified 'cupboard' in some of our early wills is little more than this. Where the Elizabethan household includes a few servants, their liveries, or rations, of food may be placed in or on a 'livery cupboard', which is probably doorless or has columns or other openings for ventilation. 'My livery cupboard in the hall' is fairly common and occasionally seen in the parlour. A parallel and slightly later development produces the 'court cupboard', or open buffet or sideboard, often highly ornamental in the richer households. Only near the end of the period do we come across two examples, both in the homes of apparently unsubstantial yeomen: 'my court cupboard in the great parlour' (1597) and 'the court cupboard in the chamber' (1594). Exceptional items are 'a glass (i.e. glazed) cupboard' and 'a steel glass to look in (i.e. a mirror) and a coffer covered with leather' (1595).

In his valuable introduction to the Writtle inventories, Dr. Steer writes: 'Cupboards before the sixteenth century were not necessarily receptacles in which things were deposited, but rather side-tables on which they were placed; in other words, the original cupboard was simply a board supported by legs and covered with a cloth or carpet, on which household plate and vessels, especially drinking cups, were put. Hence the word "cup-board". But, by the early sixteenth century, the difference between cupboards, aumbries and presses had become definitely established', although, he adds, 'the terms soon became interchangeable, and the medieval plate cupboard was more generally quoted as, or superseded by, the court cupboard. This was either of two open tiers rather like a sideboard, or else with the lower tier enclosed by doors and the upper fitted with small recessed cupboards leaving a shelf for cups and other articles'.[10] Examples of the use of the three words and of the covering carpet follow, but none occurs frequently and only six aumbries have been noticed: 'my greatest cupboard which standeth in the parlour'

(1594); 'a great cupboard and a cupboard cloth' (1603); 'my cupboard standing on my table in the hall' (1595); 'a cupboard made in the hall window (recess)' (1573); 'a joined cupboard with a press'; 'one cupboard with a press'; 'a pear tree cupboard with a press in it' (1600); 'a cupboard fastened to the wainscot' (1588); 'a wainscot press' (1594); 'my press standing in the parlour where I lie'; 'a press to lay clothes in' (1581); 'a cupboard press in the parlour with the carpet thereto belonging' (1567); 'a little aumbry' (1590); and 'an aumbry in the kitchen' (1574).

To keep out draughts in timber-framed dwellings and to provide colour, wall-hangings are often found in the main living and sleeping rooms. In the smaller houses, the very common substitutes for tapestries are the large 'painted cloths', 'stained cloths' being the less frequent term. Much rarer is 'halling', signifying canvases hanging on the hall walls and once defined : 'the painted cloths in the hall being the halling' (1576). The cloths are painted with religious, classical, mythological, floral, arboreal or similar scenes or designs, with human or animal figures or merely biblical text. Three wills describe what they depict. 'One piece of stained cloth of forest work hanging about the south and north parts of the parlour' is in the house of John Wood of North End in Great Waltham, surgeon (1585); 'all the stained cloths that hang behind mine old cupboard and a little story of Tobias that hangeth over it' in that of his namesake, a mercer of Earls Colne (1584); and 'a painted cloth of Robin Hood that hangeth in the hall' in that of Thomas Shouncke of Pyrgo Street in Havering (1589). Another painted cloth is referred to as 'of antique work' (1569). '(All) the painted cloths hanging around the parlour' ('round the hall', or 'about the chamber'), or merely 'hangings', occur in hundreds of wills; there may be 'six painted cloths' or some such number. A few mention painted cloths in several rooms, including 'in the chimney', 'before my chimney in the hall', or 'all my stainings and hanging cloths in and about my chamber'. Other examples are : 'a painted cloth of half a dozen yards'; 'the uppermost painted cloth in the hall'; 'a halling cloth painted'; 'the halling in the hall'; and 'the halling against the wall'. Margery Graye, widow (the Grays of Coggeshall are engaged in the cloth industry), leaves 'the hanging of the hall at the high dais' (1568), the sole occurrence of the word. Less often we see 'the stained cloth over the bed'; occasionally, 'one painted cloth hanging over the bench in the hall', 'two pieces of painted cloths which hang over the table', or 'the piece of stained cloth that hangs over the door'. They are to disappear gradually in the Stuart period.

Apart from the homes of the gentry and the more affluent yeomen and merchants, tapestry is specifically mentioned by Ralph Lee, vicar of Gestingthorpe (1558), who leaves 'a covering of tapestry work which hath a leopard upon it', and only by three others, whose rank or occupation is not given.

## Musical Instruments

As we exclude from this volume the gentry, we did not expect to find many musical instruments among the possessions of the less affluent testators, but their wills have yielded a few illuminating items, mostly of course relating to stringed instruments.

Noticed by chance in Marian wills are 'two gitterns and a lute' which Richard Maryffe, priest of Stapleford Abbots, bestows on 'my master, Robert, the parson' (Robert Day *alias* Bury, rector, 1519-57), who we hope enjoyed them in the last two years of his old age. Roger Rede of Hornchurch, smith, bequeaths to his servant Stephen Prentice 'the viol that he brought to me and my treble' (1573), the latter probably being a treble viol and the former a tenor or bass viol. In the next generation an inventory of Sir John Petre's 'singing books and instruments' has 'the chest of viols, viz. 2 trebles, 2 tenors and the bass'.[11] John Truelove, also of Hornchurch, yeoman, whose books we mention in another section, leaves 'one lute and case thereto' (1574). Another yeoman, John Ayers of Brightlingsea, gives to 'Mary Sanden, my wife's daughter, £4 and my best virginals at the age of 18' (1585); other legacies show that he is related to the Beriffs, merchants of the same parish. Thomasine Baron of Layer Breton widow (of John, who had termed himself a yeoman in his will a year earlier [12]) directs that 'my son Richard Baron shall have my virginals' (1591). Remarkable interest attaches to the will of John Bentley, 'servant to the right honourable Sir John Petre of Ingatestone', whose belongings include 'all my sets of song books and songs in rolls and my books for the virginals, and one pair of virginals' (1597). His master, if not personally accomplished, encouraged music in the household. As far back as 1561-62 Sir William Petre had seen to this : 'A Cullen lute bought for Master John Petre, 13s.' and 'Mr Lychefeild's man for bringing certain songs for Master John Petre, 2s.' The lute came from Cologne or was of a Cologne type, and the songs were presumably sold by Henry Lichfild, who has been described as 'one of the smaller figures among the English madrigalists and composer of some pleasant songs'. Other evidence of Sir John's devotion to music and of the close friendship which developed later between him and William Byrd is related elsewhere.[13]

Of singular interest is the nuncupative will of Anthony Bret, a Langford yeoman (1588). He states that he has laid out money for a 'Mr Jerome', whose identity has not been traced :

> For taking of (off?) the belly of a lute and for gluing her, and for new pins and strings for the said lute, 4s.
> For cotton for to line the case 18d.
> For 2 calf skins to cover the case 3s.
> For workmanship of the case 2s.
> For lace to bind the case about 2s. 8d.

For a lock for the case 10d.
For carrying the lute to London and down again 8d.

While the nature of Bret's transactions with Jerome is unknown, it is clear that the belly of the lute had been removed for re-gluing.

## Tableware and Household Implements

On Elizabethan tableware Harrison has an invaluable passage, in which he cites the improvement in this—the last of the three things 'marvellously altered'; 'They (his elderly parishioners) tell of the exchange of vessel, as of treen platters into pewter, and wooden spoons into silver or tin. For so common were all sorts of treen stuff in old time that a man should hardly find four pieces of pewter (of which one was peradventure a salt) in a good farmer's house'.[14] To Harrison treen and wooden are synonymous, the latter being a relatively new word. Naturally, the cheaper ware is still in evidence, even in late Elizabethan wills, or appears in joint use with pewter. Mention of wooden tableware is infrequent because of its trifling value, and only a dozen bare references to 'all the treen dishes' and/or 'treen spoons' occur, with an occasional 'biggest wooden platter'. A yeoman mentions 'two white treen platters and two other treen platters', spelt 'tryen' (1594); a widow, 'an elm bowl'. Other yeomen may list both pewter and treen, e.g. '10 pewter dishes and platters, 3 wooden dishes, 3 trenchers, and 2 wooden platters' (1597); '6 pewter platters, 6 pewter spoons, 6 treen dishes', (1600). The assets of John Cripes senior of Foulness include 'a dozen of pewter and 3 pieces of my best pewter' (1586), and those of Elizabeth Pettican of Wormingford, a yeoman's widow, '30 pieces of pewter lying in the new chest' (1598). A tailor leaves 'all my brass and pewter whatsoever, with all manner of treen dishes and spoons' (1592). A few ordinary folks' tables are graced by a salt and candlesticks of pewter; especially treasured, if of silver. A contemporary fashion is the painted fruit platter or trencher,[15] to which two wills yield reference: 'a painted platter' (1592) and 'one painted platter and two trenchers' (1601). We read neither of knives (each brought his own to the table) nor forks (which do not appear until the next century). Much of the meat being torn from the bone, a towel or napkins or an ewer and basin may be used to cope with messy fingers. Thus we find 'a towel of blue work', 'a towel wrought with blue', and 'a napkin which hath a gold lace round about it'. Tablecloths, of holland, calico or 'home-made cloth', are occasionally mentioned, or the wider term 'napery' (table linen) is used.

Wills that specify articles of furniture often continue with culinary and ancillary utensils and finish with equipment in the service-rooms or outhouses, if any (see p. 5). Using its manifold resources and skills to the full, with nearly every implement specially fashioned to serve its purpose, the average Elizabethan household is largely self-supporting, amazing as it may be to our own generation, accustomed to push-button and other labour-saving gadgets and public utility facilities.

We will begin with the hearth and its fittings. From a swing-bar, fixed at one side of the chimney in many Elizabethan halls or kitchens, hang a chain and pothook on which is suspended the big cooking-pot. The chain bears a crook or rack, the joint device being known as a trammel, by which the height of the pot above the fire can be varied. Under the revolving spit, supported by a pair of large fire-dogs called andirons or cobirons (the difference perhaps being that cobirons are knobbed), lies the essential dripping-pan (once 'my great dripping pan'). The modern hotplate is perhaps represented by the chafing-dish (a small portable grate filled with burning charcoal or wood embers for warming meat and the like). The 'fire-pan' and the 'gridiron' are also portable iron grates, with short legs and a long handle, placed in the fire and used for broiling meat; both words are fairly rare, the latter appearing in such odd forms as 'gyrtyron' and even 'gregeone'. There is also the inevitable pair of bellows.

The hearth, often with a superabundance of pots and pans, is a familiar sight in any good museum having an Elizabethan 'reconstruction'. In fact, it assumes the appearance of 'a culinary obstacle course', as Dr. Cummings aptly describes the display in some New England historic house museums.[16] Later often bricked-up (perhaps to be re-opened in this century by proud owners of Elizabethan houses), the great size of the opening of the hearth, even in ordinary dwellings, testifies to the then abundance of wood. We quote only a few examples of what the testators look at in the long evenings when seated in the coziest place in the house— the chimney-corner, now belovedly but anachronistically termed the ingle-nook by estate agents : 'all ironwork, as trammels, spits, tongs, firepan, bearers, gridiron'; 'the trammel with the chain as it hangeth in the hall chimney'; 'the pair of trammels'; 'the trammels and bars of iron and other engines thereto belonging in the chimney in the hall'; 'a fire fork, a fire pan, two trammels, two pair of pothooks'; 'one of the great spits, the lesser of the twain'; 'a crooked handle spit'; 'a spit being the best, the trammels with the pothooks'; 'my jack in the chimney' (the sole reference, 1602), this automatic device for turning the spit having only recently been invented; '2 cobirons in the hall, my fire pan, my fire fork, my tongs, a spit with a foot; and 'a pair of Flanders cobirons and a pair of tongs suit like to them'.

We may visualize, except in the poorest homes, an astonishing array of pots and pans, mostly of brass, used for cooking and other purposes. Some are of big capacity, usually with one or two 'ears', 'bails', or handles for lifting. We see, for instance : 'a great brass pot with the long legs'; 'my biggest brass pot and my brass boiler'; 'my great cauldron with iron ears'; 'a great brass pot of 53 lb. in weight'; 'my middlemost pan with two ears'; 'a curbled pan' (i.e. with a raised rim); 'my frying pan and best dripping pan'; 'my frying pan with a bail'; '4 pewter pots, one a thirdendale, another half a thirdendale, the third a quarter pot, the fourth a flour pot' (a 'thirdendale' apparently holds three pints).[17] Incidentally, the word 'bronze' was not to appear until the eighteenth century and Elizabethan 'brass' generally denotes the former alloy.

That ubiquitous culinary couple that charms the ear with its metallic, if not musical, ring—posnet and skillet—both predecessors of the saucepan, or boiling-vessel, is self-defined in many wills: 'a posnet with three feet' or, 'a posnet with a handle', 'a posnet of brass', 'a potbrass posnet without a handle', and often 'a little posnet', varied occasionally with 'deep', 'broad' 'thick brass' posnets. Solitary examples are 'the lesser posnet basin of pewter', 'my posnet bound round with iron', 'a great posnet of pot brass'; and 'a little brass posnet with feet, having a patch in the bottom' is one of a poor widow's few kitchen utensils. The three legs or feet enable it to stand in the embers of the fire; its legs are short, its handle long. Similarly we find 'my three-footed skillet'. But, somewhat strangely, while the Writtle and Roxwell inventories of later date yield more references to skillets than posnets,[18] skillets are much less common than posnets in our Essex wills and 'a skillet pan with a band' is among the very few descriptive items.

There may also be one or more pottingers or porringers—those twin words derived from pottage, a thick vegetable soup (the present sense of porridge is not to appear until three centuries later): '1 broad pewter pottinger'; '4 round porringers without ears'; and 'a dozen of round footed porringers'.

The care with which so many of these utensils are described is a criterion of their importance. The multitude of kitchen vessels is further illustrated below in our little discourse on the theme of 'Second best'.

The indispensable kettle is spoutless and usually coverless; in other words, more like a pot or cauldron; and it is generally one of several, except in the humblest cottages. A range of 'greatest', 'middle' and 'least', or the like is therefore a common feature, e.g. 'my great kettle without a ringle', 'one great kettle bottomed with a basin', even 'the lesser of my two bigger kettles'. We also note the occasional copper or brass kettle, 'my copper kettle', 'a kettle of pot brass', 'my three-footed kettle of brass', 'a kettle with the brazen bottom', or 'a hanging kettle', even 'my kettle with a hole'! Some are 'bound with a band of iron' or 'banded', e.g. 'the brass kettle banded with iron, 4 gallons'; others are distinguished as 'without a band', 'unbound', 'bailless', or 'never branded'. The big ones are valuable, hence 'my great kettle with a patch' or 'my great kettle with the broken band' is by no means rare. A very frequent item is the 'tinker's kettle'; once, 'my kettle and a piece on the bottom with tinker's work'. William Sommers of Rayleigh, a tinker, bequeaths 'one great tinker's kettle and so many of other smaller sorts as are rated in my shop at 20s. and one of my biggest posnets' (1586). 'The tinker's kettle commonly used to wash vessels in' tells of other uses. As to kettles' capacity we note with some surprise: 'in the buttery the greatest kettle, an old tinker's kettle of a pottle' ($\frac{1}{2}$ gallon), and 'a tinker's kettle of 6 quarts'; 'my brass kettle of 6 gallons, the other of 3 gallons'; 'my kettles whereof one holdeth 6 gallons, the other 3 and the third 2'; 'the great kettle of 9 gallons'; 'the greatest kettle, the gallon kettle and the pottle kettle'; 'the kettle or cauldron with 2 rings'. Cauldrons, usually of brass, are probably used for boiling large joints and for heating water for washing.

Saucers, often mentioned, are unlike the modern article but shallow dishes for sauces and condiments. The Elizabethans have need for an ample supply to give zest to their monotonous diet, especially dried fish and meat far from fresh. 'Six saucers of pewter' is an early reference (1560).

From culinary vessels we pass to brewing equipment, often found in a separate little building usually referred to as the brewhouse. There may also be a malt-house and a buttery in which the barrels are stored. Brewing, generally the task of the housewife, entails the use of numerous big utensils, such as 'vats' (nearly always spelt 'fats'), some with names strange to modern ears. These include the yotting vat in which the barley is soaked; the mashing vat or tun in which hot water is added to the malt to soak and form the wort; the lead or large pot or cauldron for boiling the wort, originally of lead but often of copper, sometimes merely called a copper, but occasionally a furnace; the keeler (or cooler); and the yealding vat in which it is left to ferment. (An inventory of the brewhouse at Ingatestone Hall reveals even more equipment.[19]) Representative items of brewing equipment seen in the wills are: 'the great vat which we use to water barley in'; a 'yauthing vat'; 'the barley vat and mashing vats, the lead in the yotting vat'; 'my brewing kettle, my greatest brewing cauldron'; 'the two leads in the brewhouse and the two great tubs or vats'; 'the one the yealding tub and the other the mashing vat'; 'all my leads and coppers as they be placed in the furnace'; 'a cauldron in the entry hanging in a furnace'; 'the furnace in the brewing house'; 'my vessel called a lead for a furnace'; 'one great lead or furnace'; 'the great copper pan that I brew withal commonly called the lead'; 'one pair of malt querns as they stand, one brewing tub, and one little keeler;' 'my yotting vat in the yotting house and a malt quern there'; '2 keelers, a wort keeler, a mashing keeler, and the least brewing tub.' The brewing-tub may be called a kimnel, a word also denoting a tub used for kneading, salting meat, and other household purposes. Finally, there are the barrels holding the finished product, such as 'all my brewing vessels as 9 barrels and firkins and 6 tubs more or less', 'half the barrels in the yeilding house', or 'all the earthen ale pots'. Once we find 'my brewing pan with a curb'

(1574), meaning the frame around the top, which is 90 years earlier than the first example of this sense in the *Oxford Dictionary;* perhaps a 'broad-chined pan' (1567) has the same meaning, as with 'two porringers with broad verges' (1564). The undated will of Robert Leonard of Chelmsford, buried in 1576, has : 'all my brewing vessels, the copper, the mash tun, the yeal tun and the wort tun, the cooling vats, the flotts (a rare word also meaning a cooling-vat), and the underback, the tunnel, the barrels, kilderkins, firkins and pipkins.'

Bread-baking requires a 'boulting trough' ('tub', or 'tun'), in which the flour is sifted from the bran, a 'kneading trough', and a 'moulding board', or bench on which the loaves are shaped. All these are common terms, and a separate 'boulting house' is sometimes mentioned. Once we have 'a pair of baking irons', referring perhaps to the oven peel, or flat shovel with a long pole, for inserting and taking out the loaves; once also, 'a great bread bin'. The solitary 'pair of wafer irons' produces light thin cakes, baked between them.

Equally important are butter-making, with its churn, and cheese-making, demanding a little more equipment. The mould in which the curds are pressed is called the cheese press or cheese-mote and its cover the cheese-board, both terms being mentioned occasionally. A separate cheese chamber is found in more than one yeoman's house, but a dairy is a rare occurrence. In that of Joan Adeslie of Great Bardfield, a widow (1598), the buttery has both brewing and cheesemaking implements : 'the drink stalls in the buttery, the cheese press, the brewing tubs, a keeler, my great cheese board and a cheese mote, all my leaden weights, my greatest treen bowl, a cheese tub with two ears'.

The imperative need for salting pork and other meat to preserve it and make it more palatable during the long winter months calls for the common 'powdering trough' or 'salt trough'. In some wills a pepper box or a mustard quern (or mill) also occurs, and now and again a pestle and mortar for grinding, a cleaver (or cliver) for cutting meat into joints, and other knives. The will of Emme Maiston, a widow of Marks Tey (1593), contains two rare terms : 'a cliver, a brazen mortar with a pestle, a brazen ladle, a brazen strainer, a grate, a brazen chafing-dish, a pair of malt querns, a powdering trough with a cover, the battleden, and a rolling pin'. 'Grate' is presumably a grater for powdering ginger or nutmegs, and 'battleden' (unrecorded by lexicographers?) seems in the context of mortar and pestle to mean a beetle, or crusher.

There is probably no clearer aspect of the average household's independence of outside resources than in the preparation and storage of nearly all their food and drink. Among the few exceptions is the fact that most families have to pay the miller his toll for grinding their corn, although quern or handmill, or more rarely a horsemill, producing the flour is an adjunct of the husbandman's or yeoman's house.

## Food and Drink

Of the three staple foods—bread, dairy produce and meat (the last is too dear for the poorest folk), only cheese, salted butter and bacon can be kept in store for a fairly long time. The considerate Elizabethan testator, wishing to provide a supply of food or drink for his widow, generally bequeaths hard cheese or salt butter, or both; less commonly, bacon, fruit or honey; or corn or malt (for brewing). Being virtually without means of refrigeration, he knows that nearly all other food is perishable; nor can beer or ale be kept beyond a few weeks.

Cheese and butter are occasionally called whitemeat, a term noted only once—by Thomas Sterne of 'Much' Fordham, yeoman, who bequeaths to Dorothy his wife 'all the whitemeat in my house, 10 bushels of wheat, 10 bushels of maslin (mixed corn), and 18 bushels of malt towards bringing up my children' (1599). We find 'all my whitage, as butter and cheese' (1561) mentioned by James Harrys of Wickford, unaware that his definition could have proved helpful four centuries later to the compilers of the *O.E.D.* when apparently baffled by 'the whitage of the kine' left by a slightly earlier testator, meaning, as we now see, dairy produce.

First, however, a word about measures. Cheese is reckoned by the lead or wey; butter, by the dish, pot, firkin or barrel. The lexicographers do not define any of the small measures. Use of the wey is confined mainly to two counties. According to works published in 1596 and later (quoted in *O.E.D.*), the Essex and the Suffolk wey contain 336 lb. and 256 lb. respectively. The former is confirmed by St. Osyth's Priory accounts, 1512. Two contemporary Essex records prove that the lead is accounted as 56 lb. and is made up of a varying number of cheeses according to their size—from nine 'small cheeses' to three large ones.[20]

A dish has been given as 24 oz., but an Essex farmer was to be indicted in 1709 with selling 'a dish of butter, which ought to weigh $2\frac{1}{2}$ lbs.'[21] A pot, according to the Act of 14 Chas. II, c.26 (1662), 'ought to weigh 20 lb., viz. 14 lb. of good and merchantable butter neat and the pot 6 lb.'; and two of our wills equate it to a number of dishes. The firkin of butter was originally reckoned as a quarter of the barrel, or half a kilderkin; the latter varying according to the commodity between 8 and $10\frac{1}{2}$ gallons.

Four men bequeath $\frac{1}{2}$, $1\frac{1}{2}$, 2 and $2\frac{1}{2}$ weys of cheese. Some refer to both cheese and butter: John Haryson of the island of Foulness leaves '$2\frac{1}{2}$ wey of good cheese, 2 firkins of salt butter yearly, and 2 dishes of sweet butter weekly' (1577); William Wright of Canewdon, '2 lead of cheese and 5 dishes of salt butter' (1564); Anthony Graunthame, a yeoman of the same creekside parish, 'wey of cheese and barrels of salt butter', but forgets to fill in the numbers (1565); and Nicholas Warren, a Little Baddow miller,

'4 leads of cheese and 4 pots of good butter, every pot containing 8 dishes, viz. 2 leads and 2 pots before Christmas and the other on Lammas Day (1 August) ensuing' (1603). Richard Clarke of Mundon, husbandman, leaves '2 leads of hard cheese and 2 pots of butter containing 6 dishes apiece, to be put up betwixt this and Michaelmas when my wife shall think best' (1590). Several refer to hard cheese, one to 'half the cheese in my garret', and one to 'a dozen cheeses of the best'. Thomas Cole of Stansgate (in Steeple), yeoman, mentions 'a cheese press, the motes (i.e. moulds), and cheese boards' (1585). John Byrde senior of Ingatestone, yeoman, 'a churn for butter, two cheese motes, and the cheese layer (board?) (1574). Cheese presses occur in many wills; '4 keelers to put milk in' is among several referring to cooling vessels; and once we have 'a butter flasket' (basket). (A unique entry in a tithe suit recorded in an Archdeaconry deposition book gives 'one cheese to be made of the milk of 34 milk kine'.)

The useful product of industrious bees—frequently given in the old plural 'been'—is noted a score of times : 'a pot of honey, and a hive of been' and 'all my bees with their hives and honey'. Roger Huen of Springwell in Walden leaves to his son his 'stock of bees except 12 hives' to his wife (1593); John Dyer of Great Maplestead, husbandman, can also boast of eleven hives (1570); and William Styleman of Ulting, yeoman, has ten 'hives with been', six of which he leaves to his maidservant among other bequests, and one to Francis Sea the vicar (1584). Several men have as many as nine 'stocks of bees'; another, '4 skeps or hives of bees'. A Romford man named Empsall is able to leave 'to my dame a swarm of bees which I have at Noak Hill' (c. 1570); three other testators are lucky enough to have taken a swarm; and a widow bestows her four hives and a swarm among five friends.

Of beer, the Elizabethans' staple drink, we find an interesting and unique mention in the nuncupative will of Anthony Bret of Langford, yeoman (1588) : 'a lead to wheel wey in, one whole brewing of beer of three bushels of malt and one bushel of corn, three bushels of very good wheat meal and two bushels of good beer corn, two bushels of oats more for beer corn when they were threshed for his landlady, a firkin of good butter and two pots of good butter, with oat meal, bay salt and white, 14 bushels of good wheat, to the estimation of two wey of cheese being of them in number (blank)'. As would be expected, wine is not mentioned in any of our ordinary folks' wills.[22] William Cooke of Stebbing gives his wife '6 cheeses, one of the great pots of butter, and a flitch of bacon of the best' (1581). 'I will that my wife', writes John Stayworthe of Paglesham, clerk, 'shall have towards her living 2 bushels of wheat, a bushel of malt, a lead of cheese, and 10 dishes of butter' (1562). John Bridges had been instituted as rector of Paglesham in 1562; Stayworthe, rector of Foulness, evidently finds the rigours of the island too harsh or inconvenient for his abode.

Edward Radmoll, a tailor of Bradwell-juxta-Coggeshall, mentions '2 bacon flitches that hang in my house and one store pig and 2 hens' (1592). Appearing in other wills are '8 flitches of bacon and 2 firkins of salt butter'; 'the flitch of bacon hanging from the rafters'; and 'a flitch of bacon, if there be any of them left'.

Robert Coote of Radwinter, husbandman, leaves his wife 'every year 1 quarter of wheat, 1 quarter of malt, 1 quarter of my best hard cheese, and 1 of my best hogs, and every week 1 lb. of butter, and when God send them the fourth part of my fruit' (1585). Not many testators, however, bother to mention their fruit. John Battell of Eastwood, yeoman, arranges that Ellen his wife shall have 'during her widowhood yearly out of my orchard six bushels of the best apples, if they be growing there' (1597), and another bequeaths 'half the fruit growing upon the ground, viz. apples, pears, plums, peas and beans'. There is a solitary reference to a crab press, to make verjuice, a kind of very sharp cider; also to 'a verjuice barrel with verjuice'.

## 'Second best bed'

The Elizabethan testator usually shows clear ideas about the disposition of his house, but his goods and clothes may give rise to a big problem where two or more children have to be considered. It is not confined to the well-to-do. We sense that division among wife and children worry less affluent men even more, and some impecunious widows or spinsters go to much trouble in distributing their few chattels. We can watch many a woman trying to decide who is to have each of her treasured articles. The result may be almost as good as an inventory. We thus have in the wills a large number of partial substitutes for inventories, though the goods are not valued.

Despite the theme-title of this section now being a literary Aunt Sally, the extracts cited illustrate, quite apart from their intrinsic interest, the normality of Shakespeare's legacy to his wife of the 'second best bed' more fully than in any other work. While experts have derided, though in general terms, the earlier nonsense written about his supposed ill provision, we are able to add, after reading all the Essex wills of the period, that at least a hundred use the identical or a similar phrase in relation to the wife. It is the eldest son, not the widow, who usually gets the best bed, and the second is represented, to quote only one example, by 'a bed next the best' left by John Brewre of Hornchurch to his wife Margaret (1559).

From the great number of wills that refer to the order or quality of beds and other articles we select typical phrases. The best, second, third and fourth beds are left by William Crips of Foulness to his four sons

(1581); Rose Dennis of Weeley, a widow, allocates to different legatees her best, second, third, fourth and fifth beds (1585). 'One other bedstead and featherbed, the fourth best in goodness', may be compared with 'an indifferent feather bed', 'my least trundle bedstead', 'my best holyday linen and my seconds sort linen', and the ingenuous phrase, 'a pair of holland cloths a little worse than new.' In this context 'worst' is far from uncommon, and it is necessary to emphasize that the Elizabethan usage of the word is not necessarily derogatory and may merely mean the last or least valuable. Furthermore, *pace* modern grammarians, the lesser of *two* may be called 'the worst'; hence 'my worst bed', 'my worst diaper cloth', and so on. One imagines how dilettante historians would have interpreted Shakespeare had he used 'worst bed' instead of 'second best bed'.

The assortment of culinary and other kitchen utensils produces the widest range of terms. The legacy may be only the simple division of a pair, such as 'the best brass pan of twain and the best posnet of twain', or 'one brass pot, the worst of the twain'; or of three, as 'my great brass pot, my middlemost brass pot, and my little brass pot with the long feet'. Some phrases conjure up larger numbers of useful vessels: 'the third pot of my three biggest brass pots', 'the least kettle of the three biggest kettles', or 'two kettles one of the biggest and one of the meanest'.

That 'worst' is not disparaging is amply confirmed by our final quotations of fairly normal 'mixed' bequests: 'three of my best platters, two of my second, and two of my worst'; 'my worst salting trough of the two in the buttery and three pieces of pewter pots not of the best nor of the worst'; and 'the worst of my three feather beds, four of my mean pewter platters which are used every day, two handsome pewter platters, my worst flaxen towel save one, and four fair pewter platters'.

[1] See Introduction, p. vii.
[2] In reading the wills, the writer found no other survival of the medieval 'tester and ceiling' (i.e. back and top, cf. *O.E.D.* under 'tester', which however omits under 'ceiling' the sense of bed-canopy). [3] Harrison, *op. cit.*, 201.
[4] As many as five such covered close-stools at Ingatestone Hall, Essex (Emmison, *Tudor Secretary*, 38).
[5] *Royal Historical Monuments Commission, Essex,* index, 'Furniture (chairs)'.
[6] F. W. Steer, *Farm and Cottage Inventories of Mid-Essex*, 14.
[7] G. W. Hayward, *English Period Furniture* (14th edn., 1971), 14 (fig.).
[8] Havinden, *op. cit.*, 322. [9] *E.L.: Disorder,* 262-71. [10] Steer, *op. cit.*, 15.
[11] E.R.O., D/DP E25/1. [12] P.C.C., 19 Drury.
[13] Emmison, *Tudor Secretary*, 212-14. [14] Harrison, *op. cit.*, 201.
[15] Illustrated in Joyce I. Whalley, *English Handwriting, 1540-1853* (V. & A. Mus., 1969, plates 10b, 11b). [16] See p. 11, n. 6.
[17] *O.E.D.* and Halliwell, quoting North Country refs. [18] Steer, *op. cit.*, 25.
[19] Emmison, *Tudor Secretary*, 149, from *Inventory of Ingatestone Hall in 1600* (1954), 17. [20] *Ibid.,* 136n., quoting all three sources. [21] *Ibid.*
[22] Some exceptionally interesting details of wine occur in Sir William Petre's accounts (*ibid.,* 150-1).

# 3

# Agriculture

## *Crops*

In Elizabethan Essex the soil, relief and coastline and the proximity of the south-western part to the London food market all combined to produce an agricultural pattern of great diversity, and in consequence there was a wide range in profitability. In attempting to provide a picture of the main farming areas, we may begin by repeating what John Norden wrote in 1594, although it is only a very rough sketch and lamentably brief in its mention of crops.

Instead, however, of using the oft-quoted printed account,[1] we will quote from the recently-found manuscript, now in the Essex Record Office.[2] This is a slightly earlier version, differing somewhat in phraseology and a trifle in fact, and it has not yet appeared in print (here modernised).

> As touching the fertility of this Shire, thus I think that it may be called English Goshen, the fat of England, yielding infinite commodities exceeding (as I take it) any other Shire in regard of the variety of the good things it yieldeth. And it is to be observed how every particular commodity hath, as it were, its proper limit and peculiar quarter, allotted, as it were, by the natural disposition of the soil. As the Hundreds of Rochford and Dengie ... yield most deep feedings, which again do yield most great abundance of butter and cheese, so that it may be said of those parts that they flow with these commodities as Palestine or Canaan did with milk and honey. And in these hundreds especially are the great and huge cheeses of such admiration for weight and magnitude made, which are also in Tendring Hundred in small quantity. And there are also many wicks as they there term them, namely dairy houses, wherein they make their butter and cheese. But this Tendring hundred yieldeth many barren places also.
>
> A second commodity though newly found out seemeth to challenge the hundreds of Lexden, Hinckford, Dunmow and Froswell, which hundreds lie in the north part of the Shire, and they abound greatly with hops, a commodity of great and continual use, but draweth with it an apparent inconvenience, the destruction of young springs (i.e. saplings). This commodity increaseth daily, yielding large requital for the pains and charge they require.[3] In these hundreds are also good feedings, and corn in competent measure.
>
> About the north-west part of this Shire as about Walden, the Chesterfords and the borders of Cambridgeshire the soil differeth, both in nature and colour, from the rest of the Shire, it is more white and chalky and aptest for grain. About the town of Walden is great store of a commodity which

is not general in England, namely saffron, and the abundance of it about this place giveth unto this town the adjunct Saffron Walden.

To continue unto the hundreds placed in the west part of the Shire, as Waltham, Becontree and Harlow and their confines, they are for the most part disposed to woods. And in these is a great circuit of woody grounds which carrieth the name of Waltham Forest and thrusteth itself into many hundreds near adjoining . . .

The Forest of Waltham aboundeth with deer red and fallow, who seem no good neighbours to the forest inhabitants, but I suppose the kindness they receive of the forest may work their patience towards the game . . . There is also a chace called Hatfield Chace, a ground well replenished with fallow deer, which lieth in Harlow hundred.

Barstable hundred yieldeth good store of oats, so do also Rochford and Dengie in reasonable measure . . .

This Shire is not much inclined to sheep pastures, neither is it anywhere furnished with flocks of sheep, but here and there ewes for dairy. The most barren heathy grounds yield the most finest wool, viz. Kingswood Heath, Lexden Heath, Mistley Heath, about Ardleigh, Alresford, Frating, Thorrington, Elmstead, and Tiptree Heath, these places for the most part yield singular good wool.

The 'new' document refers to cheese production in Tendring hundred 'in small quantity', whereas the printed one credits it with 'many wicks or dairies'. The former would seem to be preferable, as we shall see later, judging by the solitary mention of milch ewes—at Great Clacton—in this hundred. Another curious difference lies in the third sentence of our quotation, where Rochford and Dengie hundreds are credited with flowing with milk and honey, whereas the other account bestows this richness on the whole county. The same sentence is not followed, as in the printed version, by Norden's personal complaint about 'the most cruel quartan fever' which the coastal marshes inflicted on him, which is expressed in a later passage. The chief dissimilarities, however, occur in the second paragraph about the north-west, for which the alternative reads: 'The hundreds of Uttlesford, Chelmsford, Clavering, and those parts are reasonable apt for corn, and especially Uttlesford hundred; the rest are here and there much interlaced with woods and rugged grounds'. And the newly-found document gives a longer account of saffron cultivation (quoted below). It also inserts the brief paragraph 'It (i.e. the county) is full of parks' between mention of Hatfield Chace and Barstable hundred.

Very little has been published about Tudor Essex agrarian history,[4] hence the value of Norden's short 'Description'. We have, however, a reasonably comprehensive account by Dr F. Hull, on which we shall draw heavily.[5] 'There is no easy course to adopt', he writes, 'for discovering the farming methods or the crops grown by the Essex farmer. Information is scattered and on the whole scanty'.[6] He emphasizes that his best evidence is in the Petre estate archives;[7] but we do not deal with substantial landholders in the present volume. To Norden's account Hull offers five modifications: maslin and bullimong, mixed crops to which we shall refer later, are also commonly sown; the greater part of central and north Essex is given over to mixed farming; in the south-west and south, cattle are extensively fattened for the London market; much barley is grown on the chalky soil of the north-west corner; oats are not a common crop, though found in the south, and rye a little-sown crop. Our wills generally confirm all five points. Perhaps the only aspect on which the wills—a source not used by him—provide evidence differing from his own is on saffron, for which his material yielded little information, leading him to believe that Norden's and Camden's comments on its intensive cultivation around Walden were exaggerated. The wills, as we shall see, amply bear out their remarks and illuminate other aspects of Essex agriculture.

In broad outline, therefore, the picture is as follows. The coastal marshes of the east, south-east and Thamesside in Elizabethan Essex are mainly devoted to pastoral farming, flocks of milch ewes being perhaps the dominant feature. Sheep are bred both for their wool and mutton chiefly on the sandy heaths of the north-east, and folded for their dung on the after-harvest stubble and fallow in the north-west. Wheat is the main crop elsewhere, especially in the south-east, except of course in the marshlands and Waltham Forest, then far more extensive than its present survivals of Epping and Hainault Forests.

As wills are very imperfect in comparison with those probate inventories that list grain, it would be a futile exercise to attempt any analysis of the areas and extent of the various cereals growing in Elizabethan Essex. We shall therefore only select those few wills that mention special features or methods of farming,[8] but we have to confess at the outset that they throw little light on contemporary improvements or innovations in agricultural techniques, especially arable farming.

Fertilizers appear only once. Henry Casse of Aythorpe Roothing, in devising his lands to his wife, stipulates that 'a hundred load of marl and dung be laid yearly upon my ground by mine executrix' (1591). Finding a similar but solitary covenant in a lease of 1588 of a farm in north-west Essex, Dr Hull remarks, 'This reference to marl is of the greatest significance, for it was the constant admixture of the chalk with the boulder clay in this part of Essex which made it so much better arable land than the London clay of southern Essex.'[9] Our will suggests that marling was also a husbandry practice in the heavy clay area in Elizabethan times, as we know would apply in a later period.

Apart from the occasional legacies of a few quarters of seed corn, we note a covenant made by Thomas Grenelefe of Copford with Nicholas Crammer 'to sow two acres of barley land, and he must find seed to sow the same, and so to part it at harvest following by the shock, and Nicholas to sow it again the next year after the same sort' (1558).

Of mixed crops, the seed having been sown together for simultaneous harvesting, meslin (usually rye and wheat), bullimong (often oats, pease and vetches), and dredge (generally oats and barley), occur fairly commonly, more or less in this order of frequency; but no testator bothers to define them. Typical phrases are 'a bushel of peasen and a bushel of meslin', '3 acres wheat, 3 acres barley and 4 acres bullimong', and 10 seams of barley and 3 seams of dredge'. Maslin produces a fairly high quality bread. Mention of rye as a single crop, whether growing or harvested, is scanty. 'To every poor household in Chadwell a peck of rye' (1562), an unusual bequest, will make them some coarse bread. 'So much rye as shall serve for seed, which seed rye did grow upon the hills', referring to the rising ground above the Mucking marshes, is an exceptional clause (1571). Another is a legacy of 'one coomb of rye and a coomb of acorns and all the rowen in the house' made by William Howe senior, a Langham carpenter, rowen being the grass aftermath (1599). In times of distress, such as the end of the 1590s, some of the poor supplement their bread, made from rye, meslin or barley, with acorn-bread.[10] This is the sole mention of acorns. A few wills use, in addition to quarters and bushels, two now unfamiliar terms. In one of his didactic chapters Harrison defines them: coomb, 4 bushels, and seam, 8 bushels or a quarter.[11] Tusser equates a coomb with 10 sacks. Thus we not uncommonly find such bequests as 'one coomb of barley', '3 coomb of rye and a coomb of oats', 'a coomb of wheat and a coomb of malt', 'a seam of bread corn', '4 seams of wheat at harvest'; and once a testator provides his own definition, 'one quarter otherwise one seam of pease'. Occasionally both harvested and unharvested grain is left, as 'all my corn on my ground and in my barn' or 'half the corn in barn and half the corn sown'. John Frith of Cranham, yeoman, gives 'a quarter of wheat of the foremost goff or mow' (1574), both words meaning a quantity of mown grain or hay.

Haymaking is best exemplified by Thomas Fuller the elder, a Great Burstead yeoman: 'William Bryckett oweth me for the first crop of my More Meadow to be taken off by midsummer 14s., and John Norrys butcher oweth me 23s. for the first crop of grass to be taken off one meadow lying on the backside of my house at Billericay by the Feast of St John the Baptist next' (1585). An otherwise unrecorded compound-word occurs in 'two loads of trussband (i.e. bundled) hay' (1596). Nothing like the following occurs in any other will: Thomas Damote of Coggeshall (1567) bequeaths

> to Agnes my wife my cow and two bullocks and also pasture for the same, putting away the old cow as shortly as she conveniently may, and she to have pasture for the other two bullocks in the ground that belongeth to my mill, reasonably sparing the meadow that belongeth to the same in due time for the best keeping of the two bullocks, or two other kine for them for want of the said two bullocks, with the hay of the meadow, so much

of the same hay as shall reasonably serve the two kine in the winter season as men commonly use to serve their kine, without check or let during the term of years in the lease of my mill yet to come called Pointell Mill.

Husbandry covenants about crop rotation and especially those prohibiting conversion of pasture into arable (common enough in leases of farms) are seldom mentioned. Of two Great Waltham yeomen, Henry Barnard insists that, 'during her six years, my wife shall take but two crops and a summer tilth, and not break up, plough or put in tillage any other lands than are now in tillage' (1586); and John Turner that 'my wife shall have but two crops without a summer fallow' (1592). An unusual covenant with a legatee, made by James Roe of Aveley, runs thus: 'in consideration of ploughing the 13 acres in the Marsh of Aveley, he is to have the grass of the doles and the feeding of the whole Marsh till Michaelmas and half the corn, paying half the rent' (1590). One of the few references to piecework is made by Robert Barthlett, curate of Little Thurrock: 'to Richard Austen to be performed by covenant (i.e. contract) four score shocks of barley straw and oat straw, paying 1d. a shock' (1587).

While we shall later draw deeply from the records of Manor Courts for information about commons and heaths, wills yield little about them. We may, however, interpolate here an exceptional item from the Quarter Sessions records which was overlooked in our first volume. In 1567 Matthew Stephen of Fordham, yeoman, was indicted for 'enclosing part of the common called le Shrebbey at Stanway, to wit, 30 acres of wood, which the tenants and inhabitants of Stanway from time immemorial have been accustomed to use for common of pasture', for which he was fined 20d. There is in fact very little enclosure for sheep-breeding in Tudor Essex. Hence the vociferous grievance of many Englishmen against such enclosure is not among the numerous complaints against the rich uttered by Harrison, though he does fulminate against enclosure for creating parks.

In contrast, scores of wills mention ownership of land in the common fields or common meadows. From these we shall quote a few to illustrate this aspect of Essex agriculture. We do so partly because of categorical statements, based perhaps on inaccurate remarks by some Tudor and Stuart writers, made by more than one recent agricultural historian about the absence of open fields in Essex. The truth is that, whilst most of the county had been enclosed direct from woodland or waste at an early date, the ancient common-field system with its intermixed arable strips covering the English Midlands and beyond extends deep into north-west Essex and right along its northern and western boundaries and was to remain so until the parliamentary enclosure period which in this county ranged from 1800 to 1860.[12] Traces of champion fields also occur in a few scattered parishes in central and south Essex.[13]

William Smythe of Hatfield Broad Oak, yeoman, for example, describes his four strips under crops :

> One piece of barley growing in Witche Field (perhaps named from a solitary wych elm), one end thereof butting upon Eadie Field gap. One other piece of barley in the same field, the middle piece at the gate coming in, to take and carry away at harvest time next. One acre of wheat growing upon a shott called Knowles next unto Perry Croft, to take and carry away at harvest time. One acre of pease called Skootye Piece in a field called Langlye on the further side next to Horse Croft.

These lands are left to his son William, who is also to get 'one quarter of seed barley at barley seed time next after my decease at Michael-tide' (1588). John Barber of Clavering, husbandman, devises 31 acres in the common fields there :

> 3 half-acres in Berden Mill Field between my Lady Ramsey's land and Father Day's. 3 roods in Bowsters Field between Robert Hunt's land and John Hagger's.

These are followed by a further twenty strips ranging from $\frac{1}{2}$ to $3\frac{1}{2}$ acres. Description of intermixed arable strips, and other agricultural and topographical details, are of course commonplace in deeds and manor court rolls. In a well-known passage, Tusser has no doubt about the advantages of several over common-field land.

Consolidation of strips is illustrated, for instance, by the will of Stephen Nyghtyngale of Newport, yeoman (1565) :

> 'To Stephen my son 9 acres of land in Shortgrove Field between the land of the Hospital of the one part and that of John Cocket of the other, the one head abutting upon the land of divers men towards the south and the north.

Before the Dissolution, Newport Hospital was under the jurisdiction of the Dean of St Martin-le-Grand, London. Or the description may be in the form used by John Hubbert of Walden, yeoman :

> To Roger Hubbert my brother 13 acres of arable land whereof 12 acres be copyhold land holden of the several manors of Walden and Pouncys and 1 acre thereof is free land lying in the fields of Little Walden in several shotts there, the one called Brockolde Shotte and the other Little Walden Shott (i.e. furlong).

Where no manor court rolls or deeds are extant, a will may thus perhaps provide evidence of a hamlet such as Little Walden, or, in another will, Little Wenden, having its own independent common-field system.[14]

Some wills may also refer to open meadows, as along the Stort, in that of Thomas Hayver of Harlow, husbandman (1562) :

> To William Haiver son of Henry Haiver one piece of free land lying in the common field called Port Lane by estimation 3 acres, the one head abutteth upon Loxhempstall upon the south and the other head on the

double ditch against Byrd Field; and one half acre of meadow lying in Sawbridgeworth Holme betwixt Harlow Marsh on the south part and the river on the north part.

Common meadows are also mentioned, e.g. along the Chelmer : 'an acre and a half of meading in Much Baddow Mead near the fulling mill' and 'the common mead called Kewton Mead in Springfield'; along the Lea in Nazeing Mead; along the Colne in Nunnery Common Meadow in Sible Hedingham; and common marshes along the Thames in Barking and Dagenham. A North-country term very rarely used in Essex is found in two separate 'carrs of meadow' at Wix on the Stour estuary (1586). The Dedham manor byelaws governing the common meadows are noted under Manors.

Robert Farrant of Hadstock, lying on the chalk hills, furnishes some interesting items. He decides to leave (1574) :

> All my land to my son George, paying out of such lands to my daughter Alice yearly 3 acres of corn, i.e. 1 acre of barley and another of wheat and another of bullimong, and she to choose the first three acres of all his corn as well winter corn as bullimong, and she also to choose the second 3 acres or else he give unto her for the wheat 33s. 4d., for the barley 33s. 4d., and for the bullimong 13s. 4d. And she shall have during her life the going and finding of 1 cow both winter and summer yearly and 1 hog of the age of 1 whole year, fair and clean, delivered unto her at the Feast of All Saints, fat and able to kill.

And he also gives several coombs of barley to various people.

Of the extensive sheep-walks in north-west Essex, Thomas Sawarde of the 'Bell' inn, Thaxted, refers to 'all such arable land' (in Langley) 'as at that season ought to be for fallow by reason of any usage or custom, and also upon the sheepwalk, sheeps' course or fold course belonging to the same' (1588); and Robert Aspland of Heydon (now in Cambridgeshire) mentions that 'goodman Cook must have my course during the year which began at Michaelmas last' (1564).

We shall now consider what the wills reveal about two specialized crops.

As a flavouring for beer, hops are generally believed to have been first intensively grown in England, and probably also in Essex, about 1525; but Dr Steer thinks that Norfolk could claim such cultivation from at least 1482.[15] So far our earliest Essex reference seems to be the 'hopgarden' at Ingatestone Hall in 1548.[16] Tusser has one of his encouraging comments :

> Get into thy hop-yard with plenty of poles,
> and those same hillocks, divide them by doles.
> Three poles to a hillock (I pass not how long),
> shall yield thee more profit, set deeply and strong.

And in one of his supplementary articles, 'The Hopyard—A Digression' :

> Meet plot for a hop-yard, once found as is told,
> Make there of account, as a jewel of gold.[17]

Harrison tells us a lot more in sober prose :

> Of late years, also, we have found and taken up a great trade in planting of hops, whereof our moory hitherto and unprofitable grounds do yield such plenty and increase that there are few farmers or occupiers in the country which have not gardens and hops growing of their own, and those far better than do come from Flanders unto us . . . And this I know by experience, that some one man, by conversion of his moory grounds into hopyards, whereof before he had no commodity, doth raise yearly by so little as twelve acres in compass two hundred marks (i.e. £133 6s. 8d.), all charges borne toward the maintenance of his family. Which industry God continue! though some secret friends of Flemings let not to exclaim against this commodity as a spoil of wood, by reason of the poles, which nevertheless after three years do also come to the fire and spare other fuel.[18]

Norden's briefer remarks, clearly based on Harrison, have already been noted.

Comparing literary with testamentary statements, our best will is that of Richard Bretten of Sible Hedingham, who, in dealing with 'my acre of hopground in Codham New Park', enjoins his wife that, 'when she hath taken of her crop of hops, she shall stake it with poles and dig up the hop ground and dress it at the seasonable time of the year, and when time is, to pole it and pare it and weed it at her cost' (1595). Hops do not occur earlier than the casual mention of 6 lb., which, with three load of wood are to be received yearly by the wife of William Cooke of Stebbing, not far from the recognized centre around Castle Hedingham (1581). There, at the same date, John Lyddye directs : 'If it shall please Almighty God of his goodness to send good increase of hops upon my ground this next year, then I will that my wife shall pay unto each of my sons £5 apiece more'. References in the next two decades have been noted in all parts of the county, mostly to hopgardens, hopyards, or profits from them, but they lack details; and 'hop-bagging' is mentioned once among goods. Quarter Sessions records have brief notes about a theft of hops worth 40s. at Great Maplestead (1571), drying hops at Shalford (1588), and obstructing the highway at Fordham with piles of hop-poles (1599).

The one crop—saffron—that is almost peculiar to East Anglia and especially to Essex figures frequently in wills, but rarely outside the north-west corner of Essex. Although an authoritative history of saffron-growing is still awaited, an excellent article written seventy years ago still serves as the best account, from which we draw generally in our introductory remarks.[19] Saffron had been grown for centuries in the Middle East for use in colouring and flavouring table dishes, as a yellow dye in other products, and as a perfume. It is as a tithable crop that saffron is first definitely recorded in Essex—in an agreement dated 1445 between the abbot and the vicar of Walden. (The town's distinctive prefix is first found in 1582.[20])

By far the fullest description of its culture and of the estimated costs, yields and profits is bequeathed to us by Harrison.[21] Living at Radwinter on the edge of the area in which the crocus-growing is concentrated, he is well qualified to do so; and we are for ever in his debt for writing at great length on a matter appealing to his inquisitive nature. In the second edition of his work (1587), he added other passages.[22] His chapter, 'Of our Saffron and the Dressing thereof', bears all the evidence of first-hand knowledge of the work of the 'crokers', or 'saffron men'. 'Saffron', he says, '(besides the manifold use that it hath in the kitchen and pastry, also in our cakes at bridals and thanksgivings of women), is very profitably mingled with those medicines which we take'. According to him, the 'heads' (i.e. bulbs) are taken out of the ground in July and then 'set' again in rows until September, about the end of which the flowers (purple, not yellow, as popularly supposed) are gathered before dawn (the chives being first removed) and dried in little kilns over a gentle fire, pressed into cakes, and finally bagged. In good years 100 lb. of wet saffron may be produced from an acre of ground, yielding, after being dried, 20 lb. or more. (Estimates of later writers indicate that 1 oz. of saffron takes about 4,000 flowers to produce.) Since the price is usually about 20s. a lb., 'it is easy to see what benefit is reaped by an acre of this commodity towards the changes of the setter'. (A Quarter Sessions indictment of 1587 refers to a theft of 3 oz. of saffron worth 5s.) He gives details of the cost of the dung and of the various operations, too long to quote here. The culture from first setting to final gathering is carried out in a three-year cycle; the first year's yield being small, the next crop greater, and the third the largest. Then, he remarks, 'the ground will serve well, and without compost, for barley for the space of 18 or 20 years together' (but this is surely an exaggeration); and 'after twenty years the same ground may be set with saffron again'. In a typically anecdotal passage, which occurs in both editions, he declares: 'Such was the plenty of saffron about 20 years past that some of our townsmen of Walden ... not thankful for the abundance of God's blessing bestowed upon them (as wishing rather more scarcity thereof, because of the keeping up of the price), in most contemptuous manner murmured against Him, saying that he did shit saffron, therewith to choke the market'. But, he adds, the Almighty claimed retribution and great scarcity followed, 'until now of late within these two years men began again to plant and renew the same, because of the great commodity'.[23] So, if his facts are accurate, the revival took place about 1575. Once again Harrison's statements are borne out. According to some depositions taken in 1571, 'the grounds about Walden have been oft set and much wearied of saffron and worn out of heart with too much and often setting of saffron, and therefore doth not bring forth such plenty of saffron as they have done in time past, and that doth discourage men to do cost; therefore the grounds be not apt to bear saffron that hath been set within twenty years before but will be fainty (i.e. sickly) and rot the heads'.[24] Indeed, no Walden wills of Elizabeth's first two decades mention saffron plots. But we follow shortly with evidence of its cultivation at this period in the surrounding parishes. In the second edition, Harrison, ever patriotic, concludes with a fulsome note. 'Would to God', he declaims, 'that my countrymen had been heretofore (or were now) more careful of this commodity! Then would it, no doubt, have proved more beneficial to our island than our cloth or wool'.

About the same time, Camden declares that Walden stands 'in the midst of fields smiling with the most beautiful crocus'.[25] It is probably this sentence that misled a leading social historian, although living near the area of its former cultivation, to refer to 'the great fields of saffron in Essex';[26] whereas in fact the crop is raised, as our quotations will show, in enclosed garden plots; in fact, only twenty or forty foot square, according to Tusser. Norden, in his 'Description of Essex' (1594), writes: 'About the town of Walden groweth great store of saffron whose nature, in yielding her fruit, is very strange, and bindeth the labourer to great travail and diligence: and yet at length yieldeth no small advantage to recomfort him again'. But, in the recently-discovered version, saffron cultivation merits a longer paragraph as well as a coloured drawing of the flower in the margin.[27] 'The colour of the leaves', he notes, 'is a kind of watchet or pale blue, the leaves are near 2 inches long, and in one night it will grow to a perfect flower, nothing appearing in the evening. The saffron blades are the strings like unto threads which issue out of the heart of the flower, forked at the end, which they call chives, being of a fiery colour. It hath a round root of the form of an onion'; ending much as above.

In reading through the 11,000 Elizabethan wills, we have taken notes of the 60 references to saffron-growing. Without exception, they all occur in the Walden area, which would seem to testify to its cultivation being confined to the light, chalky soils. But 'saffron' is found in field-names in seven Essex parishes outside this area.[28]

Initial planting of the bulbs is implied in the will of Henry Hager of Great Chishall (now in Cambridgeshire), who bequeaths to his sons Richard and George 'my saffron ground, on condition that they give to Thomas my son 5 quarters of heads, so that he shall raise them at his own charges, and they shall deliver to Agnes my daughter 4 quarters of saffron heads' (1569). Harrison explains that an acre of ground requires 20 quarters of heads,[29] set in rows 2 inches apart, in long beds 8-10 feet wide. First-year setting may also be referred to in 'one saffron bed called the butt, being this year set, in my garden at the town's end', by John Roulles of Little Chishall (1574). Agnes Rookes of Great Chesterford, widow, passes to her two daughters one rood, 'to be chosen where they think good amongst other of my saffron grounds' (1585). Jane Runham, another Great Chesterford widow, leaves to her son William one rood of saffron 'of twelve months set' and to her daughters Jane and Anne two roods 'of two years set, together with all my saffron heads commonly called raising ground' (1572). Several others distinguish between new and second-year growth. William Baker of Great Chishall, husbandman, leaves his wife 'one rood of my saffron ground of last year's set and one rood of two years set lying next to Barley' (the adjacent parish in Hertfordshire) 'and she to take all the crops of saffron and saffron heads which shall arise on the same' (1568). John Sell the elder, a Littlebury yeoman, gives to John and Judith his children one rood of 'twelve month set saffron' and one rood of 'two year set saffron' and to Marcy his daughter 'my raising ground' (1601). Matured plants are mentioned only once, by John Brende of Newport, glover, who leaves his daughter Joan 'one rood of saffron ground, lying in Wicken (Bonhunt) parish, of three years set' (1572).

William Fyllupp of Great Wenden directs his wife to 'set for every one of my daughters one rood of saffron ground apiece' (1559); and Cecily Haughton, a Little Chesterford widow, plans what she hopes will turn out to be a lucrative little investment for her nine (named) grandchildren, each of whom will get 40s., 'to be used in a stock of saffron' (1596). William Romaine of Walden bequeaths two separate half-roods 'old and new set, with the profits' (1577), a hope expressed by others, such as John Shelford, a yeoman of North End in the same parish, who gives his son 'all my parcel of saffron ground with the heads of saffron and all other commodities of the said heads and saffron growing, increasing and arising' (1595). But Robert Hilles, a miller of Great Chesterford, is more cautious: 'one rood of saffron ground, if any remains in stock' (1585). The other references are to similar roods or half-roods, with no fresh details, and relate to the same or neighbouring parishes. Curiously enough, there is only one mention, by the same Robert Aspland, of the finished product: 'I owe Mr Barley, my son-in-law, 3 quarters of barley and 1 pound of saffron' (1564).

Not a single legacy or listed debt discloses anything about the actual profit or even the price fetched by sale, but mention of gifts to distinguished visitors in 1546 and 1561 in the account-book of the Guild of the Holy Trinity in Walden bears out Harrison's figure:

> A pound of saffron, to give my Lady Pagett, 12s.
> A pound of saffron given to the Queen's Attorney, £1 5s.

From the preceding century the saffron crocus had thus provided industrious Walden townsmen with a money crop much in demand. They acknowledged their indebtedness when rebuilding the magnificent church about 1500 by 'a beautifully executed representation of eight saffron flowers', which can be seen in the spandrels of one of the south aisle arches, and by incorporating three saffron flowers in the arms that ornament the borough charter of 1549.[30]

Solitary references occur to osiers (used in basket-making) in Bildon Mead at Chrishall (now also in Cambridgeshire) and Earls Colne and to broom (a cheap fuel) at Great Bromley. Although flax wheels are not a rare feature in wills, they yield no mention of flax as a crop, despite the Act of 5 Eliz., c. 5 (1563), 'for the maintenance of the navy', which included a clause enjoining every farmer to plant one acre with flax for every 60 acres of arable, in order to provide for an adequate supply of ropes and sacks. Like another almost unknown statute requiring certain numbers of milch cows and calves in proportion to land or stock (see following section), it appears only indirectly in the Quarter Sessions records, which contain a letter of 1589 from the Privy Council to the Essex justices to arrest several unnamed men who had been levying penalties under the Act without any authority. The silence of our county records, apart from this, tallies with Harrison's own comment: 'I see no success of that good and wholesome law, since it is rather contemptuously rejected than otherwise dutifully kept in any place of England'.[31] The reluctance is due to flax and hemp being troublesome crops to grow and dry; but worthy Tusser urges it, so that the women may spin their much-needed towen, or coarse, sheets, and the men may make ropes and halters.

Vital fodder is referred to in 'all my stover within the house and without for to keep his cattle'; 'all my stubber', apparently a colloquial form of 'stover'; and 'all my stover or fodder for the cattle of straw, chaff and hay'. John Sandell of Basildon (1588) and Thomas Wilham of Little Burstead (1593), yeomen, provide for their wives to have 'sufficient winter stover and provision for her cattle' and 'all the cattle freely maintained upon my farm with grass and winter stover during her life, she being at the charge to make the stover and tend the cattle'.

## Livestock and Farm Implements[32]

Passing from crop to animal husbandry, we are able to reconstruct from the wills a somewhat incomplete picture of the livestock kept by the smaller landholders.[33] Apart from the essential usefulness of some animals for draught and of all for dung, livestock is kept for their meat, milk, wool and hides. Most testators have the bare minimum of beasts for their families' subsistence, while others with larger herds are aiming at profitable sales at the local or London markets. As for the last, an incidental reference comes from an unexpected source. In 1597 West Ham—the nearest parish to the City—petitioned Quarter Sessions to reduce the heavy charges in conveying its arrested felons over 30 miles to the county gaol at Colchester Castle; 'the parishioners', so they declare, 'having very little of the lands in their occupation because the most part thereof is in the occupation of foreign graziers, butchers and innholders dwelling out of the parish'.

We again remind readers that use of the wills of the gentry and the rich yeomen is deferred to the next volume. This is unfortunate in the present context, as the distinction between substantial and other yeomen is bound to be somewhat arbitrary. Nevertheless, affluent testators' wills do not differ much, except in the actual size of herds and flocks, as to the kind of livestock kept in certain localities. Even so, they reveal no very large flocks commensurate with those kept by some Midland farmers. The number of animals mentioned may of course form only part of the testator's livestock, the remainder, if any, being in the unknown 'residue'. We shall quote from wills giving the fullest and most representative details about livestock, beginning with sheep and ewes, which greatly outnumber all other animals.

The marshes in the south and east of the county are given over to the making of butter and cheese. The peculiar features, as already seen, are that the cheeses are abnormally big and that both butter and cheese are produced from ewes' milk. Incidentally, the practice is a long-established one: the earliest mention of the wicks, or dairy sheds—'a building for making cheese from sheep'—occurs in 1301.[34] In another paragraph (which is not included in the 'new' version), Norden also remarks:

> Near the Thames mouth, below Benfleet, are certain islands called Canvey Islands, low marsh grounds; and for that the passage over the creeks is unfit for cattle, it is only converted to the feeding of ewes, which men milk, and thereof make cheese (such as it is), and of the curds of the whey they make butter once in the year, which serveth the clothier.[35]

Turning to William Camden's account, published 13 years later, we read that Canvey

> is indeed so low-lying, that often it is all overflown, except for the higher hillocks, on which there is a safe retreat for the sheep. For it pastures about 4,000 sheep, of very delicate flavour, which we have seen youths, carrying out a womanly task, milk, with small stools fastened to their buttocks, and make ewes' cheeses in those cheese sheds which they call there 'Witches'.[36]

'Cheese (such as it is)' recalls the vivid verse of the early 16th-century poet, John Skelton:

> A cantle of Essex cheese
> Was well a foot thick
> Full of maggots quick

> It was hugh and great
> And mighty strong meat
> For the Devil to eat
> It was tart and punicate.

Continuing his journey, Camden relates that Dengie hundred is

> passing plentiful in grass, and rich in cattle, but sheep especially where all their doing is in making of cheese; and there shall ye have men take the women's office in hand and milk ewes, whence those hugh thick cheeses are made that are vented and sold not merely into all parts of England but into foreign nations also, for the rustical people, labourers and handicrafts men to fill their bellies and feed upon.[37]

Cheese is of course a valuable winter reserve food, especially for the poor. The unpalatable quality, according to Harrison, is improved by adding some cows' milk to the ewes' milk, but not too much, 'whereby their cheese doth the longer abide moist and eateth more brickle (crisp) and mellow than otherwise it would'.[38] That such Essex cheeses would keep even longer than most clearly accounts for the profitability of the industry in supplying ships leaving the estuary on long voyages. (Christopher Martin, who provisioned the 'Mayflower', doubtless took a big stock of it.) Ten milking sheep have been equated with one cow.[39]

Let us now see to what extent the topographers' statements about the sheep-and-cheese economy of Canvey and the other east Essex marshes is borne out by our wills. Two separate parts of Canvey island 'belonging' to South Benfleet are undoubtedly the marshes referred to by seven testators of this parish. (The island in fact consists of as many as sixteen detached parts of nine mainland parishes.) John Harte, husbandman, leaves '10 shear sheep and 40 sheep as they run out of the fold' and 'the rest of my stock in the marshes, both sheep and lambs, with the lease' (1559); and Thomas Letten passes on '20 hoggerels (second- or third-year sheep) and 3 sheep now, and 3 lambs at doffing day' (1562). Nicholas Howell gives his son 'half the marsh called Lymard Wick with half the stock of all such cattle' ('cattle', to the Elizabethans, may include sheep) 'as is now going and feeding at this present' (1581). Thomas Reynolde, yeoman, bequeaths to his son Roger '120 sheep in Canvey Marsh, which sheep and the wool of them I will in time be sold to the best advantage and the money employed to his use and paid when he accomplish the age of 18 years' (1593). A lessee yeoman, Humphrey Drywood of South Benfleet, bequeaths 'all my stock of cattle, my 4 score and 12 sheep and 9 score and 10 lambs (i.e. 282 in all), now going upon the salt marsh called Rencheward' (1595). Although a supply of ewes' milk is presumably their main aim, two other South Benfleet men refer to 'my old wool, viz. 9 lb.' (1568) and 'all my lambs' wool' (1575). The latter will is in fact quite a catalogue: George Letton, perhaps a bachelor, divides his 37 sheep and 15 lambs; apart from the chief legacy of '27 of the best sheep' to Parnell Roberts, he gives away the rest in small numbers to twelve persons including 'Mary my master's maid one lamb'.

There is, then, no doubt about Canvey marshes feeding some big flocks, but there is no mention of milch ewes as such, and the only wills with specific mention are those of John Wheler senior, a Tollesbury yeoman, who has '8 milch kine and 30 milch ewes', doubtless on the Blackwater estuary marshes in that parish (1576), and of a Great Clacton farmer, quoted later under Cattle, whose stock includes '68 milch sheep', probably feeding on Jay Wick marshes. In fact the sole evidence found elsewhere is in the accounts of Sir William Petre of Ingatestone Hall, well inland, which record the purchase in 1550 of '3 pails to milk ewes in' and twice allude to a sheep-milker in 1555.[40] It could well be that the ewes'-milk cheese production is so normal in south-east Essex that testators have no need to distinguish 'milch' ewes, whereas the practice is rarer 20 or 30 miles away, as confirmed by Norden's remark, already quoted, about the 'small quantity' in Tendring hundred.

Wallasea ('Walflete' on Norden's map of 1594) island is likewise claimed by five mainland parishes,[41] and the last of the next three wills, referring to 'dry sheep' in the marsh pastures, may perhaps distinguish them from milch ewes. Stephen Tedemer of 'Wallets' (Wallasea) has '44 ewes, 15 hoggerel lambs, 2 lambs and a cow' (1564). A legatee of Nicholas Gawderne of Canewdon (which includes two parts of the island) gets '20 sheep called wethers and all the sheep and yearling lambs, saving 30 ewes and a ram' (1588). Although living 15 miles from the island, Thomas Emery, a Danbury yeoman, leaves his son 'my marsh lying in Wallets and the stock and store of sheep and lambs there, reserving 10 of the best dry sheep, also to have those Welsh runts (small cattle) and other dry cattle and beasts in the same marsh, to be sold for beef' (1602). A study of Foulness wills by the present writer, in advance of the next volume, reveals that John Haryson, the biggest lessee in the island, reckons his ewe flock at 300 (1577).[42]

Many of the wicks of the kind described by the two topographers are in other coastal and creekside marshes, and some of their names, although perhaps modified, are preserved in present-day farms. Robert Browne of Hadleigh, yeoman, for example, leaves his son John 'the lease of my marsh in Vange called Vange Wick with the whole stock belonging' (1560); and Richard Justys of Mundon refers to 'my lease in Goldhanger called Vaughty Wick Marsh and East Marsh and my whole stock of cattle now going upon the wick and marsh and all the profits' (1561). 'My wick vessels', occurring in the will of an Althorne man, may possibly allude to a milking-hut.

In the eight extracts which follow we have no means of knowing whether the ewes imply cheese production or normal pastoral farming. Thomas Cole, a yeoman of Stansgate (in Steeple), refers to '40 of my best sheep' (1585); William Hodge of Bradwell-juxta-Mare refers to his 'lease of Dillimers with stock of 28 kine and 5 score ewes' (1588); Giles Polley of Great Wigborough, yeoman, leaves his wife his 'stock of 46 kine and six score ewes', and he also has cornland (1574); Margaret Bowen of Tolleshunt Major, widow, mentions her son's stock of '8 milch kine, 2 oxen, 30 ewes, 2 rams, 2 horses, 2 wennels and 4 hogs' (1588); Thomas Stammer of Rettendon leaves '40 of my best sheep', apparently pasturing on Woodham Ferrers marshes (1571); and Thomas Alexander of Goldhanger leaves Thomas his son '50 of my best sheep of any age, as wethers, shear sheep or hoggerels' (1584); all five parishes have coastal marshland. William Sayer, a carpenter of East Mersea, gives his wife Susan '2 beasts, 31 sheep and 1 ram going upon Blockhouse Marsh' (1603). On the Stour estuary are '40 ewes and 60 wethers, one couple of oxen, 3 of my best horses, and 6 milch beasts' of Christopher Allen of Dovercourt (1566) and '10 milch beasts and 40 ewes' of John Marvyne of Ramsey, yeoman (1571), both with similar marshes.[43]

Turning to the Thames estuary marshes, the wife of John Brewer of West Tilbury gets '10 beasts and 30 sheep' (1600) and Susan Bretten of East Tilbury refers to her late husband having given each of their two daughters 10 kine and 30 sheep (1590); but 30 sheep at Milton and 20 sheep at Chalkwell, both hamlets in Prittlewell, may be feeding on the higher ground. At the head of the Roach Creek lies the farm of Anthony Graunthamme of Canewdon, yeoman, whose illuminating will (1565) reveals :

> To my son Edmund 12 steers and 100 wether sheep, to be sold, and of the money to buy so many ewes and milch kine as shall store the farm called Coombes in the parishes of Rochford, Little Stambridge and Eastwood which I have on lease; and William Ellyot shall be herd there, if he will take it upon him, his covenant to be rated by the governor of my child. The governor shall sell the wool, butter and cheese with the advice of my executors and overseers and they shall leave upon the farm both young farmable kine and young ewes and the said money from the sale of the wool, butter and cheese.

Ten miles inland from the Thames on the east bank of the Mar Dyke is the rich marsh pasture known as Bulphan Fen. Here Robert Humphrey bestows on his wife '12 of the best kine, 4 of the best horse, 30 of the best ewes, 30 of the best wethers, and all the corn unthreshed in the barn, with 5 quarters of oats and 2 acres of wheat that is now growing, with 2 acres of oats of the best' (1569); another Bulphan will is quoted later; and William Hurt of Orsett, yeoman, leaves Bridget his daughter 'all the profit of sheepground', doubtless in Orsett Fen, also next Mar Dyke (1559). Higher up on the Thames estuary, the marshland flocks are more likely to be fattening for the London meat markets; for example, 20 ewes at Wennington, 20 sheep at Rainham, 20 sheep at Barking, and '84 sheep and 25 hogs and pigs' owned by William Fuller, also of Barking (1558).

It is significant that only three ewe flocks are definitely found outside the marshland areas. Richard Glascok of Sandon asks his executors 'to let my farm called Sowlandes (Southlands), with the stock of 30 milch kine and 90 ewes, to the best value till my son Edward come to 20 years' (1570); Thomas Gelbard senior of West Hanningfield gives his eldest son Thomas 'the occupying and use of a stock of 12 milch kine and 26 ewes or sheep' (1570); and William Walker of Cold Norton Hall leaves his son William '25 kine, 1 bull and 90 ewes which I have now going manured in my copyhold lands' (1593); 'manured' is used in the early sense of abiding.

We know from sources other than Norden that the heaths around Colchester provide some of the wool for the town clothiers, but only a single will exemplifies the point, 'half a score of ewes with the wool and half a score of lambs' being left by John Wilson of Great Bromley (1575); and at Elmstead, near Colchester, William Payne, yeoman, has 20 ewes and a ram (1568). Of the big commons elsewhere, some of which were to survive the parliamentary enclosure period (all are shown on Chapman and André's atlas of Essex, 1777), their usefulness as rough pasture is reflected in a few wills, e.g. William Waller of South Weald has 16 kine, 40 sheep and 6 horses (1562); Anthony Graunt of Danbury '17 sheep that go at Horne Row and 30 sheep that be at St Clere's' (1561); and Richard Barber of Romford leaves to 'Nicholas Simpson, gentleman, 20 wethers, if they be found, that goeth upon the Common' (1578). (Overcharging commons is discussed under Manors.) Apart from south and east Essex and the commons, no other large flocks have been noticed, except those of William Stileman of Ulting, yeoman, who has '37 sheep, 4 beasts and a bull' (1584) and John Fenzham of Chigwell, surprisingly a carpenter, 63 sheep and 3 lambs (1595). Here again Norden's remarks are endorsed.

Among little-known words we may note '7 theeves and 6 hoggerels' left by William Almon of West Hanningfield, husbandman (1582). The former are ewes of the first year (in Essex, but of the second or third year in some other counties) and the latter are sheep of the second or third year; '1 theave sheep a year old' confirms the belief of two lexicographers. 'A brockfaced sheep' and '2 twelvemoning lambs' are unique terms in the Essex wills.

There are thus many gaps in our sketch of the pastoral economy. But certain features are sufficiently detailed as to leave no doubt, for example, about the intensive and apparently prosperous marshland farming. Some light also comes from an unexpected quarter—the numerous indictments for sheep-stealing, described in our first volume.[44] They yield a little more evidence of the flocks feeding on the heaths in the north-east and the sheep-folds in the north-west. In both areas the heavy incidence of theft is noticeable; less so, from the marshes, perhaps because of their inaccessibility except to the flock owners with their intimate knowledge of the treacherous tracks over the countless drains that take the place of hedges.

Unlike the fairly rich evidence about sheep flocks, that about cattle is relatively poor. We now quote the few wills that throw any light on cattle farming or husbandry methods. A very large number of testators have a single cow or perhaps a couple. While many of these are among the lower-rank husbandmen or farm labourers, some are small tradesmen or craftsmen, such as Stephen Clarke, a Billericay woollendraper, who bequeaths to his son-in-law 'my brown cow with her calf by her side, if God prosper it' (1589). It probably would prosper without divine help if it could feed in a home close or on the common, but if there were neither it would have to graze on the roadside verges and so perhaps earn its owner a fine in the manor court for being left untended. Without knowing Tusser's advice to his readers :

> Keep two beasts and one sow, and live at thine ease :
> And no time for need, buy they meat but thou please

the draper and others have seen the benefit, if not necessity, of doing so. In contrast, the only large herd noticed is '108 kine', owned by William Blackmore of Buttsbury, yeoman (1581), whose otherwise uninformative will does not suggest our excluding him from the present volume on account of wealth. Within this range there is of course a good deal of variety both in number and kind of stock, but little indication whether it is for dairying or fattening. Harry Daynse of Great Stambridge, another yeoman, leaves his wife 'my herd of beasts on Hampton Barns (Farm), with all the stock and store there of great cattle and small within the house and without' (1560) : one of the few hints in Essex wills that shelter for livestock may be under the same roof as the dwelling, though common enough in more remote parts of the country. But shelter only in a general sense is implied in 'the hostring and keeping of all my cattle' (1585).

This is what three of the more informative testators have to say about their livestock. William Alden of Great Clacton declares (1584) : 'I sold to Bretton 5 wether bullocks, for 3 of them 50s. apiece and for the other 2 46s. 8d. apiece, I have 21 milch beasts and bullocks, 4 two years old, 1 beast runt and a bull, 4 yearlings, 6 wennels (calves newly weaned), 12 horses and colts that work, 1 yearling, 3 suckles (probably unweaned calves), 68 milch sheep, 24 dry sheep, 9 wethers, 3 barren ewes, 24 lambs'. Ralph Bowtell, a Rayleigh yeoman, assigns all his stock to Martha Hardinge widow, 'my well beloved mother', who must have already outlived two husbands (1602) : '14 milch kine, 12 yearling bullocks, 1 bull, 51 sheep, 5 horses, geldings and mares, 3 colts, and 3 hogs, all which cattle are now going and feeding on my farm called Sprats Green in Rayleigh; also 37 dry sheep and 2 colts going and feeding on Beeches Common in Hockley'. Referring to the plentiful pasture adjoining Mar Dyke, William Wade of Bulphan (1559) bestows on Joan his wife 'the profit of all my milch kine and sheep run upon the ground between this and Michaelmas, which shall be delivered to her by tally and to save the poll of the milch kine and ewes; and if it fortune that any of the kine or ewes do die or any of the ewes do decay or be lost, then she shall deliver so many kine or ewes that are decayed or lost or else four nobles for every cow and 3s. for every ewe, at the election and choice of my son'. The testator's accounting conditions are interesting; 'poll', referred to again shortly, denotes head or number.

Several yeoman insist on a stock lease, e.g. 'My overseers to let my farm with a sufficient stock of cattle for a yearly rent and not to let it without a stock or to put it out to herd' (1601). Many men, in fact, arrange for the farming-out of their livestock, with hopes of profit for their beneficiaries. This may be expressed only in general terms, as by Roger Underwood of Southminster: 'To John Bonde the son of Mr Richard Bonde, parson of South Fambridge, £5, with which he should buy 2 kine and then to employ to the best use and profit for the behoof of John' (1600). In contrast are specific clauses in the will of John Lewger of Purleigh (1573). On his death, '10 ewe sheep of the best and 2 bullocks of a year old to be in the keeping of my brother-in-law Edward Durrisse', who is 'to pay for the farming of the said sheep 6s. 8d. a year to Mr Baron Lorde for the every year one lamb'; and 'because the sheep be already fermable' (fit to be farmed or let out) Durrisse 'shall ferm them by the poll' and deliver the livestock to the testator's son at 21. Durrisse is to have with the bullocks '10s. for stover (fodder) this winter'; 'and if it please God to let the 2 bullocks to live and prosper until Michaelmas come twelvemonth' he is 'to pay for ferm of them' 6s. 8d. a year. If the bullocks live to three years, he is 'to answer for them by the poll, but if they die before, he shall be quit of them and answer nothing'. William Burchett of Langham enjoins his heirs to maintain the herd intact: 'To my wife Joan and my son Richard the use and profit of my cattle, so that they keep whole the stock without diminishing the same or selling or putting them away' (1584). Witness, too, not uncommon legacies such as 'a bullock of one year and the vantage' (i.e. profit) and '4 of my ewes and 1 of my best sheep, with all the vantage'; also 'to keep the 2 bullocks till they be farmable, that is at 3 years of age, and then Mary and Susan my daughters receive the profits'.

Plough oxen, one would think, would be among the livestock calling for mention, but we have noted only two specific references. Nicholas Brest of Great Birch gives 'to the right worshipful Thomas Tey esquire' (of that parish) 'one yoke of oxen that now feedeth on the ground which I have under him' (1583); and William Lake, a yeoman of Theydon Garnon, possesses 'one yoke of steers of the lesser of 11 that go in Marsh Field and one yoke of steers of the same company' (1591). Six other wills mention 'a couple of oxen', '2 couple of oxen' or 'plough oxen'. The evidence is too scanty to bear on the question of preference of oxen to horses for turning over the heavy clay lands of much of the county.

Of mixed farming, there is more evidence, especially where the testator refers to ploughs, harrows or the like as well as to cows or sheep. But there is less information, outside the open-field areas, about arable farming only : not knowing what is included in a testator's residuary legacy does not justify our assuming that he owns no pasture animals although he mentions his tillage implements.

We have already referred to the small man's possession of one or a few beasts. How precious is this ownership is exemplified in the countless descriptive terms used by individual testators. The ways in which they mention their bovine animals reflect the care bestowed on them, for their contribution to the family's livelihood is often a vital one. Kept in the shed or in the pightle, or little close next to the house, their quasi-domestic relationship is more than apparent. Among the many items are a few archaic words not easy to explain : '2 kye and a bulchin and the red cow bullock of a year old, a pied bullock of 2 years old, and 3 yearling bullocks'; '3 cow bullocks of 4 years old'; 'a brended bullock of 3 years age'; 'my great grindle-bellied cow and brand bullock'; 'my red grinlet bullock's calf'; 'my black grimble cow'; 'the white milk bullock and the black howed bullock'; 'my other white pied bullock with the bell about his neck'; 'a great garled cow'; 'a black garled bullock'; 'my greatest dun cow, a farrow pied bullock, a black bullock that goeth kneebanded'; 'a black northern heifer'; and '5 milch beasts, one of them a herscalf great with calf, of the age of 3 years'; 'a dodkin cow'. Remembering a vital factor when bequeathing such beasts, a few testators add a rider, such as 'with sufficient summer feed and winter meat' or 'he shall pay nothing for the wintering and summering of his bullocks'. Another intimate aspect is afforded by the names given by Elizabethan farmers, e.g., 'a black northern cow called Gentle'; 'a cow called Brown Snout'; 'my 2 kine called Garle and Gold'; 'my cow called the black cow with a star in the forehead'; 'one black cow called Tytt'; 'a cow called Button and a bullock called Lovely'; '3 beasts, called Chill, Petchey and the black bullock'; '4 beasts, that is to say, Nut, Nan, Old Whitelock, and Hart'; and '4 kine, Northern Welman, Brown Howe, Brown Harvie, and old Brown Weald'.

Owing to the 'great scarcity of cattle' resulting from sheep-farming, a little-known Act, 2 and 3 Philip and Mary, c. 3 (1555), which was extended by that of 13 Eliz., c. 25 (1571), enjoined the keeping of a milch cow for every 60 shear sheep and every 10 oxen and the breeding and rearing of a calf for every 120 sheep and for each couple of milch kine, under the penalty of 20s. a month for each cow not kept or calf not reared, one-half of which could be claimed by an informer at the Royal Courts or Quarter Sessions. While the records of the County Bench reveal no presentments or indictments for any such offence, indictments for extortion are noted in 1591 against two men for pretending to discharge non-existent informations exhibited at the Exchequer 'under the statute for not rearing calves'. The accused are Roger Cawderon, a Chelmsford yeoman, for taking 5s. from John Poole at Langdon Hills, and Robert Maye, an Ingatestone cobbler, for levying small sums or a cheese from Poole and two other men. The result is not recorded; was the Act by now almost a dead letter?

While many cottagers have customary pasture rights on the commons for such cattle, sheep and horses as they may own, with or without stints, the use of commons and wooded wastes by swine, if allowed at all, is usually prohibited, as we shall see later, by manorial bye-laws unless they are ringed and yoked. Pigs appear infrequently both in Elizabethan wills and in the writings of modern agricultural historians.[45] Less than a dozen testators refer to their boar or to one or two 'bacon hogs'; a few others to '3 good hogs or shots', 'my 3 sheats' (in each case young pigs), 'my best shots and one great hog', 'a sow hog', '2 bacon hogs and 2 store hogs', '6 hogs which he did sell, the worst of them for 12s. each, the other 5 were spent in the house' (1588), '1 pig to be pigged of his sow', 'my red sanded sow being great with pig', and 'my black spotted pig with a bob tail'. Nicholas Ruste of Debden, yeoman, gives his wife Joyce '2 beasts and 1 hog to be pastured, fed and kept in such grounds in Debden where my milch beasts and hogs were wont to be pastured' (1597). The sole mention of a large stock is the '25 hogs and pigs' already mentioned with William Fuller's sheep flock at Barking. John Ponde of Fryerning has a 'great powdering trough for powdering (salting) of hogs' (1573).

Bearing in mind the Elizabethans' need of horses for travel as well as for draught and tillage and cartage about the farm and to market, the wills have little to say about this aspect. We know from sporadic references in other Essex records that they are bred in various parts of the county; Cold Fair at Newport is an important market for horse-dealing; and horse-stealing accounts for many indictments.[46] Only a few testators mention 'my whole team of horses' or 'my thill horse'—the shaft-horse or wheeler in a team, next to the waggon or cart, as opposed to the leader. Unusual is the will of Valentine Wheler of Buttsbury, rippier (one who carries fish inland to sell). His servant is rewarded with 'a grey gelding called Dycke, with packsaddle, pedder, halter, wanty, and girth, and a brown mare called Joan Twopence with two motley saddles, girths, stirrups and a bridle' (1590); a wanty is the band fastening the pack to the horse's back and a pedder is a wicker pannier. Representative items include 'a young grey mare which was never backed' (broken in); 'my grey hobby' (small ambling horse); 'to my wife one nag or handsome horse for her own riding' (the adjective is used in the early sense of 'easy to handle', but wives are generally carried on a pillion seat behind their men); 'a sorrel mare with a pannel and girdle'; 'a sorrel horse colt with a blazing star in the forehead'; 'my brown mare with a white strike on the face'; 'four mares viz. Hobb, Crabb, Brown and Morle'.

Owing to their small value poultry is seldom mentioned, and then sometimes as 'pullen', 'fowls or pullen', and once as 'pullery'; one man has 'a capon's coop standing in the kitchen'.[47] Of other fowls there is scarcely any mention apart from 'a brood goose' and '3 ducks and a drake'. A unique legacy, made by John Tubbes of Walden, shoemaker, is 'my 4 tame coneys' —for lining some of his products? (1594); another, by William Jonssone, vicar of Southminster, is 'my best gown furred with polecat fur' (1559).

As explained under Manors, a heriot—the deceased's best beast—is a common-place feature of court rolls, but proves to be a rare item in wills. The sole examples found occur in the wills of Margaret Bonner of Canewdon, widow : 'To John Sumner of Canewdon my cow called Loyter, and if the lord take her for an heriot then I give him one of my other kine' (1587) and of Henry Saffolde of Bradwell-juxta-Mare, yeoman : 'To my wife Martha my bay gelding, and if it be taken for an heriot then the price thereof' (1590).

Yeomen's and husbandmen's wills abound in lists of ploughs, carts, and a miscellany of farm implements, yet the Elizabethan farmer's equipment is astonishingly simple by modern standards. Most of it is the work of the smith, the carpenter, or the farmer's own family; for a harrow even an old thorn-bush may serve. Little known, but deservedly ranking as classic, is the three-page catalogue entitled 'Husbandly (*sic*) Furniture', which Tusser printed as one of the appendices to his *Five Hundreth Pointes of Husbandrie* (1571) :[48] a veritable inventory of everything a farmer should possess. Even so, our Essex wills provide a few additional items. Of the more detailed references to the indispensable plough we find : 'my plough with the plough chains, share, coulter and plough timber' (the plough being made wholly of wood except for the iron share); 'my plough and two chains with a foot shackle (coupling), a coulter and a share'; and '5 iron wedges with plough irons and plough chains'. Mention of 'my plough with sufficient irons and chains for one plough to be drawn by four horses and four pair of plough harness with sufficient collars' occurs in the will of George Eve, a yeoman of Aythorpe Roothing (1575), in the heavy boulder-clay area.

Equally common are carts, mostly 'long carts' for general transport,[49] and two-wheeled tumbrels (tip-carts) for dung, sometimes called coops or coups, with closed sides and ends; some are unshod. Farm transport occurs, for example, as 'a long cart with a pair of shod wheels and a dung cart'; '2 long carts and 2 dung carts'; '1 tumbrel or dung cart with the collars, harness and other furniture'; 'a tumbrel and draught and coop to the same'; 'a dung cart with the wheels ironed'; and 'an iron-bound cart'. Unique in the Essex wills is 'a pair of draughts for a bullock to draw in a cart', owned by Katherine Gunby of Fingringhoe, widow (1574). We may also note 'my body harness and a thill harness with a cart saddle' and '4 score extrees and 3 pair of thill shafts', extree being a rare spelling of axeltree, itself an archaic form of axle. With realistic comment John Ayme of Hutton yeoman gives his son 'all such ploughs, carts, and cart harness, harrows and such like as are not worn to pieces at the hour of my death' (1588): a reminder of the farmer's constant burden of repairs.

The clutter of smaller agricultural implements in the farmer's yard is well illustrated by such phrases as 'all my shovels, spades, mattocks, axes, bills, and all other furniture belonging to husbandry'. Among less common implements we note 'my scythe newly headed and unstocked' (i.e. without a handle); 'a broom hook and 8 wedges' (for splitting wood); and 'a spade, a scavel, tryes, a pair of mittens, a flail, and a rake' (a scavel is a small spade, a try is a sieve, perhaps for separating chaff from wheat, and the mittens are for use in hedging or reaping).

## Timber

The terms commonly found are those used in the statute of 1553, known as the Assize of Fuel (7 Edw. VI, c. 7),[50] viz. talwood, billet, faggot, and coals. All have prescribed sizes, set out in some detail in the Act. As for coal, it mentions only 'a sack of coals', i.e. charcoal;[51] but, as we shall see, one or perhaps two of our wills apparently refer to seacoal. Others refer mostly to 'loads', which could denote either a cart-load (mentioned once) or horseload, or a recognised measure; a mid-century source states that a load of charcoal is equivalent to 30 sacks of 3 bushels.[52] Two wills employ the 'hundred', which normally implies a total length of wood equivalent to 100 feet; the cubit, which the lexicographers only explain as a vague measure of about 18-22 inches, apparently contains, according to one will, one-fortieth of a load. The small miscellany of extracts that follow has only a minor bearing on Forestry; and the scarcity of timber is illustrated rather in the excerpts from manorial records on other pages.

A few testators leave standing trees or hewn or sawn timber. Thomas Andrewes of Noak Hill (1594) gives his brother 'my fee wood with the starlings and windfall as also those stubs which are in my house'; the first term is explained in a quotation of 1602 in the *O.E.D.*, 'mortuos arbores, Anglice the starveling trees and windfalls'. 'One hundreth of oak board and one hundreth of wych board' (i.e. wych-elm) are among the assets of Stephen Collyn of Beauchamp Roothing (1575). William Eve of the same parish refers to 'all my boards, planks and clampole' (1559); and Thomas Nevell of Willingale Doe gives his son Thomas 'all my part of the timber, board and clampole now growing on my lands' (1560); for 'clampole' see p. 82 below. John Pavyet of Great Dunmow, yeoman, dictates: 'To Thomas my son all new board and timber in the Parsonage yard; to my executors all the sawen, hewen and cleft timber which I have in Iverie Wood in Terling and Fairstead' (1584). 'All the timber, rails, pales and eaveslath now being in the yards' is left by John Fanne of Thaxted, yeoman (1602). Two Ashdon husbandmen, Thomas Newman and John Noble senior, mention 'my timber, wood, compost and dung which I have in my garden and house' (1584) and 'the timber now ready sawn and hewen about my house' (1597). 'Three pieces of timber lying in the street and two rails' and 'all my logs that lie in the street' are other typical entries.

Agnes Garrat the elder, daughter of William Merchaunt (no abode given), gives her own daughter Anne Hall 'two loads of wood yearly during her life, 40 cubits in the load' (1566). William Shaw of West Hanningfield, yeoman, instructs his executors to give to 'Peter Davy dwelling in Gracious Street one hundreth and a half of short faggots to be delivered him at his house' (1576). Three legatees of William Sharpe of Great Wakering are to benefit by 'half a load of talwood and half a load of faggots that Hankyn made' (1575). Referring to debts owed to him, one man records, 'I made 51 faggots of furzen' (1581).

The New Hythe, or port, figures in the will of widow Anne Barrington of St. Giles, Colchester, who leaves her son Richard 'half my shells and coals lying at the New Hythe' (1571), referring probably to lime-shells and to sea-coals shipped from Newcastle. John Clarke of 'St. Leonard at the New Hythe', mariner, has '2,000 of Colchester billet', which is wood cut for fuel (1573). Thomas Catonne, a Thaxted blacksmith, leaves his son 'a chalder of coal' (1582); a chaldron being a measure varying between 32 and 64 bushels and normally used for sea-coal, as apparently here, in which case it has presumably been carried from King's Lynn up the Ouse and the Cam as far as Walden or possibly Newport.[53] Under Manors we refer to a collier employed in charcoal-making in the big woods in Writtle. John Master, a yeoman of Stapleford Abbots, on the edge of Waltham Forest, provides: 'I give leave to Edward Master to fell four trees and the storven (i.e. died of disease) trees. I give all my talwood ready felled and all my coalwood at the collier's, that is, in old Berry pit' (1575). Other testators give permission to 'fell every year for their fuel one rod of wood' or direct that 'the bodies of two oaks be cut as far as they bear timber when they are barked'. Under Crafts we refer to several woodworkers' stocks of timber.

# FOOTNOTES

[1] *Speculi Britanniæ Pars: An Historical and Chorographical Description of the County of Essex*, by John Norden, 1594, ed. Sir Henry Ellis (Camden Soc., o.s., 9, 1840).

[2] E.R.O., D/DMsP1. See F. G. Emmison and R. A. Skelton, 'The Description of Essex, by John Norden, 1594' (*Geographical Journal*, cxxiii (1957), 37-41).

[3] This sentence occurs only in the E.R.O. copy.

[4] See *V.C.H., Essex Bibliography* (1959), 8-11. For the 13th-15th centuries, J. L. Fisher, *A Medieval Farming Glossary of Latin and English Words, mainly from Essex Records* (1968) may prove useful, and for the 17th-18th centuries the long introduction to F. W. Steer, *Farm and Cottage Inventories of Mid-Essex* (1950) is invaluable. Tudor agriculture, apart from the long accounts of 'Saffron Culture' and 'Hop Growing', is only touched upon in *V.C.H., Essex*, ii. Harrison's references, often useful, are dispersed through his book.

[5] F. Hull, 'Agriculture and Rural Society in Essex, 1560-1640' (London Univ. Ph.D. unpublished thesis, 1950), a copy of which the author presented to the E.R.O. [6] Hull, *op. cit.*, 83.

[7] The nearest Essex parallel to the Robert Loder and Henry Best farming accounts are those of Sir John Petre for 1580-81, which are detailed but only cover the single year (E.R.O., D/DP A19, full copy in Dr. Hull's thesis, appendix 2).

[8] Good use of inventories has recently been made in two articles by J. A. Yelling on crop production and rotation in Worcs., 1540-1867 (*Agric. Hist. Rev.*, xviii and xxi). [9] Hull, *op. cit.*, 89.

[10] For the various kinds of bread, see Harrison, *op. cit.*, 133, 216, and Emmison, *Tudor Secretary*, 134-5. [11] Harrison, *op. cit.*, 459.

[12] The chief printed sources (all late medieval but mainly applicable also to our period) are K. C. Newton, *Thaxted in the Fourteenth Century* (1960); D. Cromarty, *The Fields of Saffron Walden in 1400* (1966) (both E.R.O. pubns.); and G. Eland, *At the Courts of Great Canfield* (1949).

[13] Emmison (ed.), *Catalogue of Maps in the E.R.O.*, 2nd edn., 1969, Index, s.v. 'Open fields', 'Open meadows'; Newton, *The Manor of Writtle* (1970).

[14] Cf. A. L. Rowse, *England of Elizabeth* (1950), 86-88.

[15] *V.C.H., Essex*, ii, 366-69; Steer, *op. cit.*, 36.

[16] Emmison, *Tudor Secretary*, 148.

[17] Dorothy Hartley, *Thomas Tusser* (1931), 61, 89. [18] Harrison, *op. cit.*, 434-5.

[19] Miller Christy, 'Saffron Culture' (*V.C.H., Essex*, ii, 359-66).

[20] *Place-Names of Essex* (1935), 537; the writer has found no earlier reference.

[21] Harrison, *op. cit.*, 348-56.

[22] Virtually the whole account, omitting the introductory paragraphs, is reprinted in *V.C.H., Essex*, ii, 361-63. [23] Harrison, *op. cit.*, 352-3.

[24] E.R.O., D/DBy T9/3. [25] Camden, *Britannia* (1586), 248.

[26] Trevelyan, *English Social History*, 145. [27] See n. 2.

[28] *V.C.H. Essex*, ii, 360. [29] 16 quarters to an acre in 1678 (*ibid.*, ii, 363).

[30] *Ibid.*, ii, 361. [31] Harrison, *op. cit.*, 437; *V.C.H., Essex*, ii, 242.

[32] I wish to thank Mr G. C. S. Curtis, O.B.E., M.A., for advice; see n. 45.

[33] For the farm stock enumerated in the 248 Writtle and Roxwell inventories, 1635-1749, preserved by chance, see Steer, *op. cit.*, table opposite p.54.

[34] *V.C.H., Essex*, i, 372. [35] Norden, *op. cit.*, 10.

[36] Camden, *Britannia* (only in last edn., 1607). [37] *Ibid.*

[38] Harrison, *op. cit.*, 311.

[39] J. T. Rogers, *Six Centuries of Work and Wages* (14th edn., 1919), 94-5.

[40] Emmison, *Tudor Secretary*, 135-6.

⁴¹ See map in *V.C.H., Essex,* i, opp. p. 369.   ⁴² *Essex Journal,* x, 18.

⁴³ A flock of 180 sheep belonging to Ralph Choppyn of Tillingham in 1565 seems to be the largest recorded in the Quarter Sessions rolls.

⁴⁴ *E.L.: Disorder,* 280-83.

⁴⁵ In a helpful note to the writer, Mr Curtis emphasizes that the cow, not the pig, should be regarded as the mainstay of the Elizabethan cottager's economy. The cow could maintain itself by grazing, with assistance from a little hay in winter. The pig fed itself at shacktime from grain spilled from sheaves in the harvest field and in autumn from beech-nuts, acorns, crab-apples or berries in woods and hedgerows; but for much of the year it required regular feeding if it was to thrive. This would entail the diversion of cereals or dairy produce from human to animal use and was beyond the poor man's resources. And the Elizabethan hog did not multiply like the modern pig. Tusser, Mr Curtis adds, does not suggest that sows farrowed more than once a year, and he recommends five as the optimum number of a litter intended for stores and three for breeding stock. Not until the potato was cultivated generally did the pig become the humble man's animal. (Cf. his *Story of the Sampfords* (1974), 99.)

⁴⁶ *E.L.: Disorder,* 286-92, 316; A. C. Edwards, *John Petre* (1975), 59-66.

⁴⁷ For an elaborate hen-coop at Ingatestone Hall, see Emmison, *Tudor Secretary,* 35.

⁴⁸ Reprinted in *Thomas Tusser: His Good Points of Husbandry,* ed. Dorothy Hartley (1931), 142-44, with many marginal notes by the editor. Apart from a three-line reference to Tusser's appendix, G. E. Fussell, *History of British Farm Implements, 1500-1900,* provides little on Elizabethan times, though so useful for later periods. See also the several published series of inventories for other counties.

⁴⁹ Dr. Steer thinks that 'long cart' may be equated with waggon (*op. cit.,* 59). A very detailed non-probate inventory of the 'implements of husbandry' left in the charge of William Petchey at Ingatestone, 1600 (E.R.O., D/DP E2/15), is too long to quote here.

⁵⁰ Incomplete copy in R. H. Tawney and Eileen Power, *Tudor Economic Documents,* i, 238-40 (but given under 'mining').

⁵¹ For charcoal-making in Essex, see Emmison, *Tudor Secretary,* 155-6.

⁵² W. Beveridge, *Prices and Wages in England* (1939), 120.

⁵³ I have to thank Mr K. C. Newton for this opinion.

# 4

# Shipping and Fisheries[1]

From Barking to Harwich at the mouth of the river Stour, the Essex coastline is characterized by its numerous estuaries and deeply-indented creeks. The last word, to the Elizabethan Board of Customs, also denoted very small ports—some being widely-separated individual quays or wharves where of course no officer was stationed, but they provided 'ladings', or berths, for the fishermen and mariners. The more sizeable ports were Colchester with Wivenhoe and Brightlingsea, Maldon, Leigh, and Barking; Harwich, with its fine harbour, was rather a naval base, with only a limited coastal trade.

England's small navy demanded from the port towns a supply of armed merchantmen and other ships as a second line of defence to the men-of-war. Returns of such privately-owned ships yield valuable statistics. In 1565 Essex is thus recorded as having 187 'harbours, ports and creeks', 349 ships, vessels and boats, and 1,196 mariners and fishermen. But these totals do not tally with the actual details in the same return, which add up to only 186 ships and 785 mariners and fishermen—perhaps those ashore at the time of actual registration.[2]

|  | Vessels | Masters & Owners | Mariners & Fishermen |  | Vessels | Masters & Owners | Mariners & Fishermen |  | Vessels | Masters & Owners | Mariners & Fishermen |
|---|---|---|---|---|---|---|---|---|---|---|---|
| Harwich | 17 | 23 | 82 | Colchester | 35 | 39 | 182 | N. & S. Shoebury | 1 | 1 | 4 |
| Brightlingsea | 13 | 21 | 59 | East Mersea | 1 | 1 | 18 | Prittlewell | 10 | 14 | 36 |
| Wivenhoe | 12 | 12 | 51 | West Mersea | 1 | 1 | 16 | Burnham | 21 | 18 | 17 |
| Maldon | 16 | 18 | 27 | Barling | 23 | 15 | 48 | S. Benfleet | 5 | 5 | 15 |
|  |  |  |  | Leigh | 31 | 32 | 230 |  |  |  |  |

Two years later a register of coasting traders (that is, excluding fishing boats) belonging to most of the ports gives these figures :[3]

|  | 140 tons | 100 tons | 50-100 tons | 20-50 tons | Under 20 tons |  | 50-100 tons | 20-50 tons | Under 20 tons |  | 50-100 tons | 20-50 tons | Under 20 tons |
|---|---|---|---|---|---|---|---|---|---|---|---|---|---|
| Colchester | 1 | — | 5 | 17 | 6 | Manningtree | — | 3 | — | Leigh | 27 | 9 | 4 |
| Harwich | — | 3 | 6 | 3 | 4 | Bradwell | — | — | 1 | Milton Shore | 3 | — | 5 |
| Maldon | — | — | 4 | 6 | 8 | Walton | — | — | 1 | Rowhedge | — | — | 4 |
| Brightlingsea | — | — | 1 | 10 | — | Hullbridge | — | — | 2 | St. Osyth | — | — | 1 |
| Wivenhoe | — | — | — | 3 | — | Barling | — | — | 2 | Canewdon | — | — | 2 |

The predominance of Leigh is very noticeable. It must be remembered that some of the numerous little wharves up the creeks, not listed in either table, were usable only by shallow-draught near-shore boats. The Elizabethan Port Books reveal few Essex boats of more than 40 tons burden, with an average of about 15 tons.[4]

We may now look at the information found in the wills. Sturdy sailors and fishermen, giving careful thought to the disposal of their treasured craft, furnish much that is valuable and some is of considerable interest. It may be read in conjunction with a long Essex 'Maritime History' article which, however, deals mainly with sea-defences and naval operations and is based almost wholly on the public records available seventy years ago.[5]

Among the various terms for Elizabethan sea-craft are a number that are obsolete, little known, or differ somewhat from their modern usage. Ketch, or catch, according to the *O.E.D.*, applies to 'a strongly-built two-masted coasting vessel' as well as a smaller boat for trawling for fish or dredging for oysters; both senses occur in the wills. The dictionary defines crayer as a 'small trading vessel'; two wills give 'ketch or crayer' as alternative terms. A quotation of 1561 in the *O.E.D.* refers to 'catches or mongers' but the latter is merely explained as 'a kind of fishing vessel'; our four references to mongers are equally vague, except that one is of 6 tons burden. Hoy is defined as 'a flat-bottomed bargelike vessel, usually rigged as a sloop'. Caravel is 'a fast little ship or a light merchant ship without decks and with lateen sails'.[6] Other fishing craft include bark, 'a small sailing vessel'; peter-boat, 'a decked boat'; and stall-boat, or staw-boat, 'anchored at the mouth of a river'. Dredger is generally a boat used in dredging for oysters. Skey, unexplained in *O.E.D.* beyond being 'a kind of boat', is equated with 'dredging cock' in one will. Cock, or cock-boat, is the Elizabethan equivalent of dinghy. But long-boat, defined as 'the largest belonging to a sailing vessel', is probably used in a will, quoted later, of 1564 merely to differentiate it from a shorter one, as in the 'great boat' and 'small boat' bequeathed in 1571.

William Beylde senior of Manningtree, sailor—evidently fairly substantial as he refers to his 'capital mansion house wherein I dwell'—leaves to William his son 'the moiety of my catch or crayer with the moiety of all sail tackling as well for North Sea gear as also for staw boat gear', and to his son William 'the moiety of my vessel called the monger with the moiety of all such tackling' (1592). William Goodyn of Horndon-on-the-Hill, wax chandler, gives 'to Lancelot Andrews and Agnes Andrews, son and daughter of Thomas Andrews of London, mariner, my part in the ship called the Trinity of Carytes (*sic*) and of the crayer now called the Hearne of London' (1561). Charles Graye of St. Osyth, seafaringman, bequeaths to his wife 'the half part of my ketch called the Ann Graye with the half of all the rigging that belongeth to her as she goeth to sea, and the half part of my skiff, and the one other half to my son Samuel' (1583).

SHIPPING AND FISHERIES 61

John Grene of St. Osyth, mariner, endows Alice his daughter with 'the quarter of a crayer called the Peter' (1562). Two mariners of St. Leonard at the New Hythe, Colchester, also pass on their shares in crayers. Adam Pollye assigns to Agnes his wife 'one quarter of my crayer called the Grace of God' (1573), and the wife of Steven Storye gets 'my half ketch or crayer called the Rose, with all her nets, ropes, tables, sails, anchors, furniture and apparel,[7] and my sixth part of the good ship or hoy called the Mary and John' (1598). The 'catch or hoy bark called the Anne of Manningtree and the cock boat' are inherited by Joan the wife and Jane the daughter of Robert Polter of Mistley and the 'dredging-boat' by Henry his son (1590).

Of the thirteen hoys, the first three belong in whole or part to Leigh men. Richard Johnson mariner refers to 'my hoy called the Fortune and the cock or boat of the hoy' (1586). Robert Grove leaves 'to my eldest son John and his eldest son Emmanuel the half of my hoy called the Toby, to William Clay my daughter's son the third quarter of my hoy, to Richard son of Thomas Grove the fourth quarter, John having the use of all the boat until my debts be paid' (1593). An old legend, repeated by county historians, tells how John Vassall, a member of the Virginia Company, of Eastwood close to Leigh, set out a ship called the *Little Toby* at his own cost a generation later.[8] John Lambe, sailor, gives 'to my wife Beatrice three quarters of my hoy or barge called the John of Leigh and to Richard my son the fourth quarter; if my wife marry, her three parts to my two sons Joseph and John Lambe in even portions' (1592).[9] Of three Burnham testators, Edward Ince of Burnham directs, 'My hoy called the Mary of Burnham to be sold by my executrix and from the money arising I bequeath to my two sons John and Edward to each £13 6s. 8d. apiece at 21 years' (1575); Nicholas Filbye, seafaringman, leaves his wife Grace 'my half hoy called the Hare and my boat called the Nicholas' (1593); and Thomas Graye gives his wife Winifred 'my half of my hoy called Repentance, and my cock called the Wenne' (1580), perhaps a late example of the then nearly obsolete 'win', meaning joy. 'My half quarter of the hoy called the Coronation' is willed by John Petchie of Harwich, mariner, to Elizabeth his wife. Thus also two other Harwich hoymen. Christopher Tucket passes 'my part of a good ship called the Florington and also part of one hoy called the William to my daughter when she shall expire to (i.e. reach) the age of 18 years, and in the meantime I do give the use and profits to John Tucket and William Tucket my brethren' (1588); and William Tucket (or Tuckyt) declares, presumably when suddenly taken ill, 'I give to Lucy Gardener, whom by God's help I do mean to a-married, my quarter of my hoy called the Christopher' (1589). Shares in other hoys are left by William Fuller of Rettendon to his son Hugh, 'my one quarter of my hoy called The Gift of God, and my other quarter and half quarter of my hoy to my wife Elizabeth' (1588); John

Crips of Fobbing gives 'to Eleazar my son a quarter of my hoy and to Joan my wife the other quarter' (1597); and John Haywarde of Colchester bequeaths to 'Peter Randall my late wife's kinsman my half quarter of a hoy called The Gift of God of Colchester' (1597), a not infrequent name that appealed to the superstitious concepts of some sailors. Fuller's wharf is evidently by Battlesbridge, at the head of the very long Crouch creek.

Elaborate instructions for keeping a craft in the family's ownership are dictated by John Bedill of Prittlewell (1559): 'I have a monger called the Mary Fortune, of which I give (half) unto Alice my wife, the other half unto Roger my son-in-law that if he will pay £4 within half a year for a quarter of the boat unto Alice for the behoof of Susan my daughter or else to deliver it into my wife's hands, and she for to pay £4, and you taking the half must stand to half the charges, and then your mother the other half if you keep the half or else to have the quarter'.

Four more Leigh boats are recorded. Stephen Breadcake, mariner, leaves part of the ship called Elizabeth (1602), and Blanche Bower, widow, can only give her son William 'my sixteenth part of a good ship called the Primrose' (1596), but perhaps she is of more than average tonnage. Could it be the 120-ton vessel of that name, which had been provided by Essex ports in the Armada year? As is well known, however, some names, such as *Primrose*, are by no means uncommon:[10] a fact which has tantalized several historians, anxious to identify one of a number of contemporary or slightly earlier *Mayflowers* with the Pilgrim Fathers' ship. Here is one more, found still earlier, which we are not bold enough to add to the list of claimants, the strongest probably being a Harwich ship sailed by a Harwich master, Christopher Jones. Be this as it may, Robert Cuttle, one of several seafaringmen of that name in the district, leaves 'to my wife Ellen my part of the ship called the Maryflower (*sic*) and the profit arising of the same, provided that, if she shall fortune to come to any mischance or decay during her widowhood, then the legacies given to be paid out of the sale of the same ship shall be void' (1563). We shall come across another *Mary Flower* shortly. William Rawlin, mariner, bequeaths 'to Mary my wife and Henry my son my parts of the shipping which I have and the stocks to them belonging, equally divided between them' (1593).

John Golston of East Mersea, mariner, gives Thomas his son 'my great boat and my part of my small boat', conditional, however, on his paying 'for the same unto my five children, that is, old John and young John, Rose, Mary and Naomi, each of them 20s.' at 21 (1571).

Possible ancestors of the few surviving 'Thames sailing barges', those sturdy craft which plied along the Essex and Kent coasts, appear in two wills. Richard Theward of Grays Thurrock, bargeman, directs that 'the half part of my barge be delivered into the hands of my brother-in-law William Rogers', and the debts owing to him include the unspecified charge for a 'freight of corn' by John Johnson (1563); and Thomas Edwards of Hadleigh gives an annuity of 20s. to Jane Steven, 'to be paid out of my barge called the Edward so long as it is occupied' (1558).

James Fuller senior of St. Leonard, Colchester, sailor, is one of only two testators who give the tonnage: 'My ship called the James of the burthen of six score tons shall be sold by my executors' (1602). A rare term is used by Thomas Sharpenton, also of Colchester, 'master and part owner of the good ship called the Lion of Colchester, being a carvel' (1603). Samuel Purchas, ten years later, wrote, 'Thus Columbus is set forth with three carvels'.[11] It is the earlier and vernacular form of caravel.

Both before and after Elizabeth's time most of the fish destined for the London market were landed at the Town Quay of Barking, and fishing with its ancillary crafts and trades were the town's chief means of livelihood. But although we can visualize the busy scenes at the Quay, the Fish Shambles and the Fish Row, Barking is not one of the principal ports and its industry is apparently still confined in our period to the Thames estuary. Despite the large number of Barking testators who term themselves fishermen, not many seem to own their craft. The nine extracts that follow are all taken from Barking wills. It is of interest to note that salmon-fishing is mentioned in two wills of the Armada year.[12] Stephen Commynges bequeaths to his brother William 'my house near to the waterside in the town of Barking adjoining to the house now called by the sign of the Blue Anchor and one drove of salmon nets' (1588); and Stephen Birde gives 'to my brother's son William Birde of Erith (Kent) my old tideboat or lighter, my new lighter, 3 salmon nets, and one net called a trawling ground net', and to 'little Brown the fisherman one upper part of a trawling net and one new drag net' (1588). Peter Debbet senior, fisherman, leaves his son John 'half of my great boat called the Blessing of God with the stawboat net, provided that he pay to my executor £24' (1602); but, the father adds darkly, 'If he shall absent himself from his labour in the said boat, it shall be lawful for my executor to set her forth to work to the maintenance of her (evidently the testator's wife Margaret) and her children'. Nicholas son of Anthony Holderness, shipwright, gets 'my boat, anchor and tools belonging thereto' (1599); and William Gyllett, fisherman, leaves 'my lighter boat' (1586). Thomas Clark leaves to William Miller, his son-in-law, 'a cock boat lying in the shipwright's yard' (1574); Thomas Nickelsoun bequeaths to Thomas son of Thomas Wood 'my two fishing cocks and boats and the small peter boat' (1592). Thomas Woodland refers to 'my hebbing boat' (1587), and Thomas Gooson, fisherman, to 'my hebbing cock' (1589). A hebbing (or ebbing) weir is a device for catching fish at ebb-tide, and these boats are evidently used to row the fishermen to their weirs, about which we shall say more when dealing with the Foulness wills. What are we to make of 'a hokkar boat with her cabin and her oars, paying to my wife 12s. in money', bequeathed by Edward Mighell of West Ham, fisherman, to William Passeslye (1560)?[13]

Of other cock-boats John Hyde of Paglesham, 'servant with William Miller of the same, mariner', leaves him 'my half cock I have with him', and Henry Almon of Burnham, mariner, mentions 'my boats or cocks called the Helen and the Bronning' (both 1581).

William Damyon of Great Wakering, fisherman, refers to 'my house called Wakering Hall and all fishing craft belonging thereto' (1575); and Stephen Tedemar of Wallets (Wallasea island) in the parish of Canewdon to his 'long boat' (1564). At Burnham, Thomas Fowle arranges that his son Peter has 'my half boat called the Dorothy and £5 in money, to be paid to her at the court day which shall be holden for the manor of Burnham next after my decease' (1584); and Richard Camber, mariner, before his premature death, assigns to Richard his father 'a moiety or one half of my boat called the Anne of Burnham', also 'my Flanders sea gown' (1573).

Four men living near the Blackwater estuary do not describe their boats. Clement Bond of Bradwell-next-the-sea, mariner, gives his wife Margaret 'all my craft which I have towards the sea' (1573); Gregory Jacob of the same, sailor, leaves 'half my boat and half my nets' (1600); and William Trott, of Mundon, husbandman, directs that my boats and all the nets be equally divided between my sons' (1590). Affectionate and rare words are used by George Osbonde of Goldhanger : 'To my dear mother my half boat, also a bream net, and a new vagnet; to my brother-in-law Heard all things else pertaining to sea craft for the 6s. which I owe him' (1575). Under 'fagnet', the *O.E.D.* can go no further than 'some kind of fishing net'.

Andrew Cutler, calling himself a carpenter and living at Salcott at the head of the creek, has very definite wishes : 'My boat called the Bess of Salcott to my son at his full age of 26 years or else immediately after the death of my wife, she to leave it (in the meantime) on condition she do buy a new tilt (i.e. awning) and a pair of new oars and make new oarlops and hatches, and also frame the boat one strake pitcher, and keep the boat in sufficient reparations until my son shall enjoy it; and my son shall pay my wife 16d. every week so long as she shall live' (1575). A strake is a continuous line of planking on the side of a vessel, and 'pitcher' apparently means higher. This man, it may be observed, has a third occupation, for his few beasts show he is also a husbandman. But some fisherfolk doubtless eke out their precarious livelihood with occasional smuggling at secret hide-outs, especially along the long, lonely inlets.

On the north-east coast, Henry Mott of Moze plans that his two sons get 'my two boats, to be parted between them in even portions, but two of my best nets to my wife' (1560); and John Tylnye of Dovercourt, mariner, that his sons and his wife have 'the occupying and profits of my boat with all my nets for three years after my burial, part and part alike, afterwards to my son' (1570).

Other men, having no son or for different reasons, arrange for their boats to be sold. Thomas Hawes of East Mersea enjoins : 'My half quarter of the ship called the John shall be praised (appraised) by four indifferent persons, and the money coming thereof I will unto my brother John Hawes, provided that Robert Burde shall have the first offer to buy the half quarter, and the money to rest in my executor's hand in the meantime' (1581); and Thomas Walden of the same : 'My part of the ship called the Mary Flower shall be sold by my wife' and four named men (1574). Likewise William Nycholle of Burnham, seafaringman, requests his cousin William Lyse 'to sell my half boat presently after my death to the uttermost value' (1572); and Nicholas Meatham of Manningtree, sailor, tells his wife 'to sell all my nets and boats, to be bestowed on my funeral and burial' (1601).

Three fishermen of Stanford-le-Hope give, as few others do, a faint glimpse of their shore work. Richard Hache wills that 'my fishing room, the nets and my boat be sold to pay my debts' (1569); John Wright bequeaths to Matthew his son 'half my boat and to my wife the other half, and to my wife my fishing room next the land and two nets' (1574); and Christopher Bartholomew gives his wife '22 sheep and the fishing room with the nets and boat, then to my son Thomas at 20 years, with £7 to buy him nets and a boat' (1576). The *O.E.D*'s quotation (1879) explains fishing-room as a small stretch of the shore set apart for the curing and storing of fish, which presumably also applies three centuries earlier.

Very brief references occur in the wills of Richard Chapman, a Rainham labourer, who has 'part of a boat' (1559); Richard Clarke of West Ham, fisherman, 'to my wife Ellen all my fishing craft' (1589); Edward Morrisse of Salcott, sailor, 'my best boat' (1567); Andrewe Genye of Dovercourt, husbandman, 'to my son my boat' (1570); John Gale of Peldon, mariner, 'my boat' (1596); and Richard Dorrell of Fingringhoe, sailor (one of many Dorrells or Durrells who plied their maritime business hereabouts), 'to Tobias my son and Prudence my wife my boat' (1597). Two cases of theft of small boats were recorded in our first volume.[14]

Among others engaged in coastal trades are three more shipwrights. John Moptayd of Harwich enjoins his wife 'to keep my houses in good repair with the quay next unto the waterside' (1570); Jacob Ashlye of St. Leonard, Colchester, leaves his wife Joan 'my third part of my ketch called the Andrew with all the third part of her furniture, tackling and stall nets' (1595); but Thomas Wraight of Great Stambridge tells us nothing about his business (1592).

Another testator of St. Leonard-at-the-New Hythe, Nathaniel Lambarte, merchant, mentions his 'shipping' but with no details (1600); and 'my tenement called the Salt House with the shop thereto belonging, with the dock and quay' are left by Alice widow of William Bonner of Leigh to her son Abraham (1571).

Many other small vessels are of course around the Essex shores. Some testators do not refer to them; some owners or part-owners make no will. Of the former, we note that one of the Elizabethan lists of lading-places and quays names the lading-places of Richard Cock, William Gyles and John Maior, all at Wivenhoe,[15] two of whom term themselves sailors but make no mention of boats.

An interesting aspect of Essex mariners' lives is the occasional reference to voyages beyond the limits of the near coastal business, but we shall find little or no mention of distant trading ports, exploration, or sea-dogs' expeditions, though the perils of a long voyage are often uppermost in the minds of those about to sail into the 'North Seas'.

We will take the wills in order of date. John Love of Brightlingsea, mariner, refers to a payment which will be due 'at his coming home from Boston at the end of his voyage', and he leaves 'to every one of his partners an old angel' (1561). Thomas Clarke of Leigh, mariner, bequeaths 'to my two children Ellen and Thomas all that my quarter of my crayer called the Anne Gallant, and at the coming home again of the crayer upon this present voyage I will that the said quarter shall be praised by honest men and sold by my executrix, and the money to remain in the hands of my executrix, to be paid to my children by equal portions at their sundry days of marriage or at the age of 21 years' (1565). Thomas Hawes of East Mersea, whose one-eighth of the 'John' has already been noticed, in a nice touch, bequeaths to four men 'my best cloak, my best jerkin, my best breeches, and my best doublet' respectively, in each case adding, 'if God send him home; if not, I will it to my brother John' (1581). Are they members of the crew? At any rate, the first two apparently returned, as wills of 'John Slye of East Mersea mariner' (1588) and 'Edmund Osborne innholder' (1590) are preserved.

Thomas Estwood of East Donyland, sailor, provides: 'To John my son my monger; to Margery my wife and Edward my son my ketch; and if it please God to send her from the North Seas safe and sound, then the one half to my wife and the other half to my son, they to sell the ketch' (1583); and divine protection is also sought by Robert Honor of Harwich, mariner, who leaves 'to Ellen Martin my cousin a quarter of my bark, to be sold at the next return of her voyage or when it shall please God to send her back again' (1587). Three other wills refer to the same dangers: Joan Banks of Dovercourt, widow, reflects, 'If it do chance that my son Thomas do not come home of his voyage' (1587); William Coke junior of West Mersea gives his sister Joan Coke 'half my great boat or the price she is showed for' (i.e. valued in the probate inventory) and his father

SHIPPING AND FISHERIES 67

William Coke the residue of his goods (including debts amounting to 95s. 10d. owing to him by 9 persons), 'if I come not again' (1590); and William Tynge of Chipping Ongar, well inland, 'minded to go over the seas into Portugal, declares his (nuncupative) will, if he should not return again' (1592). Is he William Tinge of Stanford Rivers, who had amorously pursued a Chipping Ongar widow thirty years earlier?[16]

It seems more than a mere coincidence that the next testament is that of another Chipping Ongar man—James Fynch, 'singleman', who

> purposing, God willing, to adventure a journey beyond the seas, do make this my will of such goods and money as I shall leave behind me, of the which I do make my brother-in-law Matthew Glascocke of Stanford Rivers executor or attorney to gather up all such goods and money as I shall leave behind me, i.e. £10 in the hands of Francis Awsop of Chipping Ongar and £22 in the custody of the said executor, which I do leave behind me to mine own use if it shall please God to give me safe return again, if not then it is my will to bestow it in manner and form following. First I will that Dennice my youngest sister of High Laver shall have thereof £12 and to my other three sisters Joan, Grace and Margaret I do give to them £6 13s. 4d. apiece when the death of the said James Fynch shall be truly certified, which money I will that Francis and Matthew shall truly employ and use either until my coming again or a true and evident report of my death brought in.

Probate was given in 1594, the will being undated.

The burials of neither Tynge nor Fynch occur in the registers of Chipping Ongar, Stanford Rivers, or several other neighbouring parishes, so possibly we may assume that both of them failed to return home. The will of John Firlye of Colchester, sailor, reads: 'To my wife two quarters of my ketch and the half of her tackle and furniture, with all the profit of this last voyage from the North Sea, and my other quarter to my two sons equally between them' (1597).

Just before embarking on a return voyage in 1565, John Mylles of Harwich, taken sick in a foreign port, writes a letter to his wife—a laudable blend of affection for her, piety, and concern for his quarter share of the trading profits which she will be able to claim, should he die.

> Wellbeloved wife after my hearty commendations etc. These may be to certify you that I am at this time visited with God's hand as the master and the company can inform, so that I am not able to come home as yet for fear of worse inconvenience. I hope I shall shortly by the grace of God. In the meantime I shall desire you to pray for me, as I will do for you. You shall understand that the ship is now laden and ready to depart, God send her well home. When God shall please to send her home in safety you shall receive the freight clearly for the quarter, deducting the part of the men's wages, for I have clearly discharged her here for my part and owe nothing here to any man for it. Say my commendations to the goodman Russell and pray him to be your friend as I trust he will. I have laid out for the ship before my coming from home 12s. 3d. which you shall receive

of the rest of the owners except my part. The bill of the particulars you shall receive here inclosed. More you shall receive of John Frenche 7s. and Peter Johnson 10s. All other things I refer to God and you and what so ever God hath sent me. What so ever God doth with me, I do freely give it to you and make you my full and sole executrix, as knoweth the Almighty who send us of his grace and a merry meeting at his pleasure, Amen. Written in haste in Danske [17] the 12th day of July 1565.
Your loving husband.                                             JOHN MYLLES
In the presence of Richard Skynner, Richard Frenche, John Frenche, Peter Johnson and Robert Pygot the writer hereof.

He did not recover, and the document, which is addressed 'To the wife of John Mylles, deliver this in Harwich', was accepted for probate and duly endorsed 'To be registered'. 'Goodman Russell' is probably William Russell, ship-owner and merchant of Harwich, whose interesting will we hope to publish in the next volume.

Because of their ephemeral nature, cargoes rarely find mention in wills apart from sea-food generally. We know, however, from the Public Records of our period that the main Essex exports are cloth, corn, cheeses, butter, bacon, timber and boards, with imports of coal from Newcastle, dried and salted ling, wine, sugar, unrefined salt (to supplement the local brine product), dried fruit and spices;[18] but export of grain was prohibited, as we shall see in Part 2, in periods of dearth.

Oyster fisheries, among the most ancient of our industries, have of course a special place in the history of Essex, the most favoured oysters being 'natives', a term which covers those bred between Harwich and Margate in Kent. In our period, before giving way to Colchester natives, 'Wallfleet oysters' claim first place, but the location of Wallfleet is disputed between Roach Creek and Crouch and Blackwater estuaries.[19] Colchester wills yield virtually nothing, probably because the important Colne oyster-fishery is the preserve of the Corporation by royal charter. Richard Gynis of 'Colchester Hythe' (the quay), mariner, leaves 'a monger called Bartholomew and my little dredging boat' (1589); that is all. While much is in print about the early oyster-culture of the Colne, the reverse applies to the rest of the county. Yet productive oyster-beds (called 'laynes') are found in other creeks and fleets around the Essex coast. These occur in at least a dozen wills, but some of the little dredging-boats, or cocks, mentioned below may refer, not to oysters, but to mussels and other molluscs. Space does not allow of any description of the various phases of oyster-culture, for which good accounts are available.[20] It will be seen that most of the fisheries lie in the fleets of the Roach and Crouch.[21]

The oyster industry between Paglesham and Wallasea Island is prominent in four inhabitants' wills. William Thornton refers to 'my oysters and broods as lieth upon the laynes of Clam Fleet Marsh, to be taken at all such reasonable times according to the custom of the country before

Easter next coming'; these go to his wife Alice, who also gets his 'best boat', his 'second boat' going to his son Thomas (1558). William Cocke junior, mariner, leaves 'to my brethren Robert and Thomas 40 wash of oysters to be divided betwixt them' (1583). A 'wash' seems to be equivalent to about ten bushels. He names his father as residuary legatee and executor, to whom he disposes 'also my half boat and my part of the lease of Cock's Hall lay' (layne). Thomas Bowne, yeoman, passes on 'my lease of Cocksolla, with the water ship, the skey and the laynes with oysters and mussels' (1584) : the sole mention of mussels. The alternative name of the leased farm is Grapnells on Wallasea Island and reckoned as a detached part of Paglesham parish.[22] Thomas Cock, seafaringman, devises to his wife 'my house with the oyster layne, and my ketch or boat called the James with two stall nets, a stall anchor, and my half part of my ketch called the Bess, my dredging cock, my skiff, and all the oysters now lying upon the laynes which I hold of Lady Riche' (1591).

Thomas Lees of Canewdon, mariner, bequeaths 'my monger with the cock and all manner of implements belonging, as two trawls, three dredges and a new warp' (1560); a 'warp' is a hawser. Joan Vyncente, a Great Stambridge widow, mentions 'my oyster layne and fishing place which I hold by copy of court roll of the manor of Great Stambridge' (1581). Thomas Sapster of Great Wakering leaves 'one oyster layne in the parish called Yonges Lane' (1595); Great Wakering extends to Potton Creek and the greater part of Potton Island is a detached part of the parish. John Seaborowe of Little Wakering, mariner, gives his wife 'half of my ketch called the John, half of a skeye called the Swallow, half of my skeye or dredging cock called the James, and my skeye or dredging cock called the Prudence; all my oysters which now are in all my laynes to be taken and carried by her before Easter day next to her own use' (1580). He also leaves 'certain fishing grounds in the liberty of the borough of Maldon', whose jurisdiction reaches well below the town. John Ladd, also of Little Wakering, seafaringman, has 'two laynes lying in the manor of Barling' (1591).

The next two testators' abodes lie on the other side of the Crouch. John Crompe of Althorne dictates clear instructions. John his eldest son is to have 'my dredging cock and half the oysters that be now upon my layne; half my oysters to my other children part and part to be divided, i.e. Henry, John the younger, Sarah and Agnes' (1584); and the elder John is to 'dredge all the oysters betwixt this and Easter next and deliver the money for his brothers' and sisters' parts to my executors'. James Anderkyn, a Creeksea yeoman, devises to his wife Margaret 'my mansion house at the east side of the fleet in Creeksea, together with all (oyster) shelves and the east layne of oysters there, also a little dredging cock called the Cybbe', and to Nicholas Bownde of Burnham and to Marion his wife, 'my daughter, my messuage and six acres of land and the layne of oysters to the same messuage belonging and adjoining in the parish of Canewdon and abutting on the salt fleet' (1585).

Thomas Haukin of Salcott, mariner, gives his wife 'my hoy called Richard and a dredger boat called the Fox' (1591). Passing to the Stour estuary, William Oliffe *alias* Lambert, a Harwich mercer, devises 'to my wife Joan my monger of the burthen of 6 tons, my cock or boat with the nets, also my weir and weir ground called Polechere being under Fishe Banne with all fishings and dredgings belonging, in fee simple' (1603).

None of the wills affords any indication of the value or sale-price of oysters. Ten years before Elizabeth ascended the throne Sir William Petre of Ingatestone Hall got an occasional bushel for 8d. or 9d., or as little as 12d. for three bushels if bought by his acater at Battlesbridge.[23] There is an incidental mention of 'a firkin of sprats' in the will of John Battell of Leigh (1558).

Another method of catching fish (but without the need for boats) that is closely associated with the lower reaches of the Thames and the Essex shores though not peculiar to it, introduces two strange words—keddles, or kiddles, and wares, or weirs. A description of a kiddle occurs in a long judgement given by Justice Heschell after a complicated case in 1891: 'A kiddle consists of a series of stakes forced into the ground occupying some 700 feet in length, with a similar row approaching them at an angle. The stakes are connected by network, and at the angle, where the two rows approach, a large net or bag is placed for the purpose of catching the fish'.[24] Expressed even better by a recent writer: 'Weirs were substantial and permanent structures between high and low water marks, triangular in shape, built of oak posts, six to eight feet high, set several feet apart and thatched with wattling (small pliable lengths of wood and twigs). As the tide fell, large numbers of fish, chiefly plaice, dabs, soles and flounders, were trapped in the enclosure and scooped out at low tide and transported back to the shore by horse and cart. Kiddles worked on the same principle but were large square or V-shaped netting enclosures'.[25] The practice in Elizabethan times is prominently featured in the wills of Foulness inhabitants, who are also much engaged in wildfowling. Not surprisingly, they relate mostly to the longest established and prolific family, the Crippses, other members of which we met in the previous volume.[26]

John Cryps senior gives his son Robert 'all my fishing and fowling grounds belonging to the lordships of Foulness and Great Wakering' (1572). William Crips bequeaths 'my quarter of the great skiff to my four sons, John, Robert, William and Richard; to my son William my half quarter of my boat called the Grype; to my three sons aforesaid my part which is half of the fowling craft of New Wick' (1580). He also mentions 'my quarter of fishing crafts lying in the lordship of Wakering'.

# SHIPPING AND FISHERIES

In the same year John Cryppes describes the boundaries and adjoining owners of his keddles: 'In Foulness, one summer keddle called Saturday and one hoke or parcel of land containing 4 acres with the ditches about them in East Wick. In Wakering the one half of the half of one fishing, the park of Southminster and New Wick House on the south side and Rayleigh church and New Marsh House on the north side, and so directly from the ebb to Temsedge. And the half of one half of one keddle called the Half Ebb lying in Barnes Fleet on the north side and Waters Fleet on the south side' (1580). Another John Cripes senior arranges for his son James to get 'a summer keddle which I bought of William Cripes my brother and all my nets' (1586); and James Cripes, husbandman, for his wife Mary to have 'my tenement in East End with a keddle called the Pleck being a summer kiddle' (1596).

The vital part which these fish-traps play in the islanders' lives and the need to describe them accurately are even more apparent in the will of John Staples 'the eldest' (1586).

> To my son Thomas two cottages called Blarescotes and one keddle lying between Barnfleet Keddle and Crouch Keddle, and the pasture of two horses in East Wick, and the fowling on the marsh called Rugward Head as well within the walls as without, and one summer keddle between that late of John Hancocke late of John Frend called South Keddle and Crouch Keddle, and one keddle called the Half Ebb.
> To my son John Staples the elder one keddle called Spedewell, one keddle place lying between the keddle called Keddleman's Keddle and that called le Tepe upon the west, and the fowling on Nass Wick Head and Munken Barn Head as well within the walls as without.
> To my wife Joan one cottage wherein I dwell called Rauf Pecke alias Raynould Hocke, and the pasture of one horse in New Wick, and the keddles to the same belonging lying between the lands of Great Wakering and the Regge; also a certain place for laying of hooks and taking of fishes; until my son John the younger do accomplish the age of 19.
> To Thomas my son all the sea ground lying within Wakering Court (manor).

In a codicil (1586), he leaves Richard Peeke of Foulness 'half of one boat called the Bess'. In due course (1604) his son, 'John Stapell the elder', deals with much the same inheritance.

> To my son William the house that I now dwell in, with the land thereto belonging, and ten keddles, eight keddles being partable between old Damen and John Stapell, lying by north, i.e. the Old Friday, the Pleke, Elbow Teep and Waters, Spedwell and his Reddey and Whetaker, and one half of the Rayghe nets berth.
> To my son William two horses grass and a half on New Wick which I hold by copy (of court roll) of my Lord Riche belonging to the manor of Foulness Hall, and all my fowling in the isle, i.e. the fourth part in New Wick and the fowling in Nass Wick and Mumpen Barns, both within the walls as without.
> My wife Elizabeth shall have the land, fishing and fowling till my son

accomplish the age of 21 in consideration of my three daughters' portions, Emme, Rachel and Mary Stapell.
To my wife all my household stuff and all fishing nets and other engelments belonging to fishing and all the fowling nets and lines, and the moiety of a boat called the Bess.

Coming to weirs, it is interesting to notice that several are named after the patron saint of fishermen. John Ellyot of St. Osyth devises to his wife Joan 'my ware called Peter in Westness there lying, for her life' (1560); Westness, the furthest limit of Colchester's oyster-fishing charter rights, is the headland now called Westmarsh Point, opposite St. Osyth Stone Point. Richard Lun of Burnham leaves 'my half of the two wares called the Peter and Mary to the use of Grace my wife during her life and after to Hugh my son' (1574); and Thomas Maddock of Harwich gives his wife 'my ware called Peter' (1586).

We saw in the previous volume how the duty of manning the Crouch ferries was put forward as an excuse by several church absentees.[27] Ownership of one of the ferries is recorded in the will of John Bastwick of Burnham, yeoman : 'My lands in North Fambridge called Aylewins and a tenement called the Ferry house with passage, lands and boats thereto belonging called Fambridge Ferry, together with a lease I have of a third of the said lands and ferry' (1596). Another will mentions incidentally a debt 'owed to Thomson that hath half the ferry at Gravesend 5s. 4d.' (1569); and Edward Lea of Harwich, sailor, leaves to his sons Edward and Robert 'my ferry boat equally between them' (1597).

---

[1] Dr A. P. McGowan, Head of Department of Ships, National Maritime Museum, kindly read through this section and gave me several helpful corrections; I also wish to thank Mr F. V. Hussey of Ipswich.

[2] The two tables for 1565 and 1572 are copied from *V.C.H., Essex*, ii, 276.

[3] For a list of over 100 Essex lading-places and quays, with the number of ships, if any, at each, 1565-77, see *Trans. E.A.S.*, xvii, 153-64; for Brightlingsea ships, see E. P. Dickin, *History of Brightlingsea* (1939), 142-3, 163-8; for Harwich, see B. Carlyon Hughes, *History of Harwich Harbour* (1939), 21-26.

[4] See p. 63.

[5] *V.C.H., Essex*, ii, 259-312. For details of the Essex coastal trade using selected Port Books in the P.R.O., see F. Hull, 'Agriculture and Rural Society in Essex, 1560-1640' (unpublished London Univ. Ph.D. thesis, copy in E.R.O.), 183-215, 573-83.

[6] Dr McGowan writes: 'Whether the caravel was without decking is, I think, problematical'.

[7] Hereafter phrases referring to such ancillary equipment—usually the briefer 'with all her furniture and tackling' or the like, are omitted from our extracts.

[8] *V.C.H., Essex*, ii, 277, n. 10.

[9] Assigned to '1590?', there is a brief report on hoymen's rates of pay and the state of the hoys and small craft belonging to the Thames and to Kent and Essex ports (*Cal. State Papers Dom., 1581-90*, 710).

FOOTNOTES

[10] For some names of Essex ships in our period, see *V.C.H., Essex,* ii, 274, and *Trans. E.A.S.,* xvii, 160-1.  [11] *Purchas His Pilgrims* (1625-26).

[12] Three 'good fresh salmons of the largest sort taken within the waters of the marsh at South Benfleet between Candlemas and Bartholomewtide' (2 Feb.-24 Aug.) formed part of the rent paid by Sir William Petre's tenant there about 1550, and Petre paid him 3s. 4d. each for three more salmon (Emmison, *Tudor Secretary,* 147).

[13] Dr McGowan wonders if there is a relationship between 'hokkar' and the idiomatic term 'hooker', said to be derived from the Dutch *hoeker,* a small two-masted Dutch fishing vessel, adding, 'In view of the relative position of the Dutch and Essex coasts, it might be thought remarkable if there is no trace of *hoeker* in the language of the Essex coast'.

[14] *E.L.: Disorder,* 301.  [15] *Trans. E.A.S.,* xvii, 156.

[16] *E.L.: Disorder,* 197-8; see also *E.L.: Morals,* 136.

[17] Several experts from whom I sought advice disagree in identifying 'Danske' with either Danzig or Denmark.

[18] For the best accounts, see Dickin, *op. cit.,* and the theses of Dr Hull (p. 34) and Dr Petchey (p. 6).  [19] *Ibid.,* xli, 17, 205.

[20] Especially *V.C.H., Essex,* ii, 425-39 ('Wallfleet oysters', 435, citing Norden).

[21] Surprisingly, 'the 137 wills of the 16th century (i.e. both Archdeaconry and P.C.C.) make no reference to oysters nor layings', although Brightlingsea Creek is known to have such laynes (Dickin, *op. cit.,* 180); cf. *V.C.H., Essex,* ii, 428.

[22] *Place-Names of Essex* (ed. P. H. Reaney), 206; Cock's Hall lay is evidently a corruption of Cocksey lay.  [23] Emmison, *Tudor Secretary,* 139.

[24] *Ess. Rev.,* i, 42-47.

[25] J. R. Smith, *Foulness: A History of an Essex Island Parish* (E.R.O. Publns., 1970), 14.

[26] *E.L.: Morals and the Church Courts,* 91-2. For transcripts or detailed abstracts of 48 wills, see Emmison and Olwen Hall, 'Life and Death in Foulness, 1503-1632' (*Ess. Journal,* 1975, 2-28).

[27] *E.L.: Morals,* 80-1.

# 5
# Crafts and Trades[1]

In visualizing the work of Elizabethan craftsmen, we have to remember that most of their products come directly or indirectly from the land. By their industry and skill they convert the raw material through various stages into the finished article. In doing so, some, dedicated to their own craft, doubtless get a personal satisfaction, whether it is made for their employer or for their own sale. In either case, most of them are members of a closely-knit local community in which they and their handiwork are intimately known by all. These aspects are sometimes reflected in their testaments. But the products of some craftsmen are subject to inspection in most manors, and, as we shall see in Part 3, defective workmanship is a not infrequent offence presented at some manor courts. We also have to bear in mind that many craftsmen are also engaged in husbandry—an aspect of rural economy often overlooked—as witness quotations given under Agriculture showing how some grow or breed part of the family's food as well as plying a trade.

A substantial proportion of the adult population being fairly small master craftsmen or tradesmen, many of their wills refer prominently to their means of livelihood. The majority are concerned with passing on their business, 'shop' (usually workshop), implements, or stock-in-trade intact to their heirs or successors. Some are worried. Which member of the family has the ability to carry on my craft? Is my son willing to follow it? If a minor, at what age can I entrust him with the implements? Must I describe my tools fully, to avoid any dishonest handling? How vital all this may be is strikingly illustrated by the amount of detail into which some go, even on their deathbed. Others, however, specify a few implements and finish with, or indeed only use, an omnibus phrase such as 'all the implements of my occupation', which we normally omit from the excerpts that follow. Similarly we do not refer to wills that fail to mention any equipment, even if the craft is an uncommon one.

Apart from agriculture, clothworking takes the largest share of the labour market in Elizabethan times, embracing both full-time and part-time occupation. In the initial steps, the sheep-farmer sells his fleeces, directly or through the woolman, to the clothier, husbandman or weaver. While 'clothier' in our period usually signifies an employer who distributes the wool to be processed by others or employs weavers under his own roof, the term is sometimes interchangeable with 'clothmaker' or 'weaver'. The later stages are regular. The tangles in the wool having been removed by means of a pair of 'cards' (wooden-backed brushes with wire bristles), the wool is smooth and ready for spinning. By now the hand-distaff has mainly been replaced by the spinning-wheel. The spun yarn, after being woven in the loom, goes to the fulling-mill with its wooden mallets actuated by the big water-wheel, where the last of the natural grease is removed and the cloth thickened. The wet cloths are fastened with hooks to wooden frames called tenters (or tainters) in order to dry them evenly, are passed to the dyeing-vat, and then teasled (raising the nap) and 'finished' by the shearman's large pair of shears, leaving the surface even, for return to the clothier.

In our first volume we lamented the fact that there is still no comprehensive history of the Essex cloth industry in print,[2] though it is to be hoped that detailed study of the borough records of Colchester, its chief centre, will be undertaken before long. The other main centres were Dedham, Coggeshall, Braintree and Bocking. Our wills include those of many of the 'Dutch' (i.e. Flemish) settlers,[3] and we shall later narrate a little new evidence on their short-lived sub-colony at Halstead. Lack of space forbids our repeating anything about the numerous kinds of cloth manufactured in Essex, sometimes termed the 'Old' and 'New Draperies'.[4] Perhaps the most outstanding memorial of the industry's pre-Elizabethan prosperity is the noble church of Coggeshall, a village ever to be associated with the wealthy Paycockes.

Despite the number of sheep farmers in the county, the raw material is only occasionally mentioned in wills, e.g. 4 lb. fleece wool, 20 lb. of my sheep wool to be delivered to my wife yearly, 8 lb. of old wool. Thomas Wackefeilde of Radwinter, husbandman, leaves 'all the wool in my house to be equally divided between my wife, Joan my daughter and Anne Coote my daughter-in-law' (1569); Thomas Prentys of Rettendon is owed £5 for wool by Edward Vere (1570); Anthony Graunthamme of Canewdon, yeoman, mentions his 'packs of wool' (1565); and John Downes of Eastwood, husbandman, refers to '3 yards of ash coloured cloth which I had of my wool man' (1587). Edmund Clerke of Earls Colne, clothier, gives to 'my daughter Alice 7 score lb. wool, and Margaret my wife is to have the occupying of the same, paying to my daughter half the gain and profit' (1576). It is disappointing that none of the testators who specify debts refers to wool sold by the farmers to the clothiers.[5]

Carding and spinning being the sole means of livelihood of many spinsters (hence their name) and widows—and wives, too, are often so engaged to supplement the family income—cards and wheels are almost ubiquitous items in the poorer homes as well as in others. The wheel may also be plied by children from a very low age and by men in times of inclement weather or of unemployment in their own occupations. Two widows, for example, bequeath 'my best spinning wheel with my reel and a pair of woollen cards' and 'a spinning wheel and two quills' (reeds on which yarn is wound). For the first steps in production of linen—

> Now pluck up the flax, for the maidens to spin,
> First see it dried, and timely got in

there is little to add to Tusser. Numerous wills refer both to a woollen and a flaxen wheel, though wheels for spinning flax for linen cloth are less common; one man mentions 'a Dutch wheel' (1603) and once we find 'a long wheel'. Yarn figures now and again, e.g. '7 lb. flax yarn and 11 lb. towen yarn (for the difference, see p. 15) in the hands of Gilbert Thackerwree, weaver' (1598). On the stages, including bleaching, between yarn and bed-linen and table-linen, the wills are silent.[6] Found in the Quarter Sessions rolls, a solitary reference (1590) illustrates the next stage in the manufacture of woollen cloth: a yeoman of St Lawrence gives a Maldon weaver 46 lb. woollen yarn worth 30s. 'to be made into three coverlets of weaver's craft for certain payment agreed on between them'.

Weavers' wills—hundreds of them—abound with looms of various types and their ancillary equipment and mention some relatively unknown terms.[7] Typical references are 'a loom and four kersey slays' and 'a loom in my shop and my slays, both linen and woollen'. Slays, sometimes termed reeds, which separate the threads of the warp and beat up the weft, are among the loom's chief accessories. Where a testator has more than one son, careful distribution of his implements is noticeable. Francis Caster, 'one of the Dutch congregation' at Colchester, bequeaths 'one of my looms furnished and a pair of combs with the furniture likewise belonging to it' (1596). Several Coggeshall weavers' wills, mostly in the 1590s, are illuminating. William Tyll senior leaves 'to my son William my broad loom that stands in my shop, with my warping and all that belongs to it; to my son Thomas my broad loom that is at Rands with the narrow slays, the shotting board and trestles' (1594). Peter Saunder *alias* Haywards allocates 'to my son John the best kersey slay and the short board; to my son in law Cleiveland the second slay; to my son Edward the third slay and a narrow loom with a narrow slay and a gauge of shafts' (1596). John Connye refers to 'my narrow loom in the kitchen' (1597); while Thomas Bradey senior leaves 'to my son Thomas the two narrow looms standing in the shop, the warping standing in the kitchen, two winding wheels, with the slays and reeds belonging' (1599); and Joan Aunsell, 'widow, being aged', bestows 'my narrow loom and my broad loom with the wheel and blades and all the warping' (1597). John Clerke of Great Dunmow leaves 'to Israel my boy the bastard loom standing next the great yard, with a latch shuttle, two slays of woollen and two of linen, and all other shop gear as looms, lathes, shuttles, warping vats and bars, weights and scales excepted' (1574). Ralph Robinson *alias* Luter of Stebbing gives 'to Edward my son my best loom called a bastard loom and to Edward and Miles my sons all my slays to be equally divided' (1576). 'Bastard', in Mr Pilgrim's view, is perhaps a vernacular term for a loom used for weaving the 'new draperies', which had a worsted warp and a fine woollen weft, i.e. a cloth of mixed parentage. Another weaver bestows on his apprentice 'my tilt loom' (1583). John Badcock senior of Halstead, one of the more substantial weavers, directs that 'all my looms, slays, reeds, shuttles, wheels and blades' be equally divided between his two sons, and 'my stock of wool, yarn and bays' between his wife and sons (1594). Unique is the mention of 'two slays, one of xxx, the other of xxxiiii', given to John his son by William Manton of Great Waltham (1581).

Unfortunately very few dyers' and fullers' wills illustrate their crafts. Thomas Adsley of Great Bardfield, dyer, leaves 'to my son Thomas my dyeing bed, two pair of shearman's shears, and my tainter posts and rails' (1576). Agnes Halles of Thaxted, a widow, refers to 'the house wherein I dwell called the Dyehouse, with the stables, barns and tanhouses' (1587). Robert Osborne of Halstead, fuller, mentions 'four of my best twitches' (1579), apparently referring to tweezers or pincers (1579), and John Wyles *alias* Wylde of Felsted, fuller, gives 'to my eldest son Henry half my shop gear, saving the press, and one tainter' (1577). William Stamage of Langham lists among the debts owing to him 'two firkins of grease that he had of me that come to 30s.' and also refers to his woad, for dyeing his cloth blue (1593). There are bare references to 'the lease of my tainter yards' by Richard Tomlynson of Colchester (1564) and to 'my tenter yard' by John Steeven, a clothier of Ardleigh, who lives at the 'Cock' (1586). Tainters set up in the fields are marked on several old engraved maps of Colchester.

The solitary mention of teasel, by John Trewe senior, a Coggeshall clothier, is perhaps due to his having a good stock of it: 'to the poor of Coggeshall £9 and all my teasel, reserving out of my teasel 10s. which I give to Richard Trewe towards the dressing of the said teasel' (1576). Of the two Colchester shearmen's wills mentioning their equipment, Robert Browne merely dictates, 'To my son John my whole shop stuff with all those implements pertaining to the art of a shearman' (1570); and William Northen leaves 'one cloth being a short white, one cloth being a long white, and all my instruments and working tools, with one chest, wherein my havats and twitches lie' (1576). Commenting on 'havats', which he has not met before, Mr Pilgrim suggests that it is a local word for a wire device (usually called a gig) to raise a long and even a curled nap. Edmund Watson of Dedham bequeaths 'to my son my whole shop stuff with the press and papers, the tainter, and all the implements which belongeth' (1585); and Thomas Morris, of the same, passes on 'to Nicholas

Rose son of Elizabeth my sister my seven pair of shearman's shears that are in my shop, five pair whereof are French shears (1580). He adds : 'If Nicholas do depart this life before he enjoyeth my gift, then the whole stuff to be sold by my executor and half the money to be given to such as fear God and love the Gospel of Jesus Christ which are known to have most need, to the glory and praise of God, and the other half to my sister Elizabeth if she live to enjoy it, or else to the poor that fear God as the other part.' The will reveals the impact of the preaching of Dr Edmund Chapman, the leading divine of the Dedham 'classis' or presbyterian group of puritan ministers.[8] Morris appoints as supervisor his 'neighbour' Henry Shearman, a member of the well-established clothier family, from whom the renowned American General William Sherman (1820-91) is descended.[9] John Sharman, whose will (*circa* 1575) includes a 20s. legacy to Chapman, is one of several parishioners who showed their gratitude to the preacher. Ralph Cocke, also of Dedham, leaves his son Samuel 'my shop stuff, viz. my shearman's shears and handles and all other implements, my tainter and my folding table' (1601). We quote from two more shearmen's descriptive testaments. John Reve of Harlow bequeaths 'all my shop stuff, that is, three pair of shears, one pair of tainters, ten dozen handles, two burling crows, two slays, a press, a prime, a lard box, a cottoning board, a perch, a rackhead, and a shear board' (1569). Mr Pilgrim cannot explain 'crow' and 'prime', but states that 'burling' means teasling and 'cottoning' refers to napping pieces of cotton first imported from India, which (unlike modern cottons) had a long fleecy nap. Thomas Allen of Coggeshall leaves 'my three pair of shearman's shears, a shear board, a pair of trestles, a scrawe (a frame upon which fleeces are hung to drain), 16 pair of handles, and a press' (1570).

Only three of the ubiquitous tailors mention their equipment. John Sallisbury of Witham leaves 'my shopboard, pressing pan, shears and tailor's yard' (1559), and 'two pressing irons' and 'wafer irons' occur in the others. The Elizabethan tailor stocks very little cloth, this being brought to him by his customers to be made up.

Indirectly connected with textile workers are those who produce 'painted cloths' or 'stained cloths'. One such craftsman can apparently be identified as the deceased husband of Alice Gammedge of Walden. The widow leaves 'all my frames with painted pictures or stories in them, together with all my stones, colours and frames, and all other things belonging to the art, mistery, science or occupation of a painter' (1591). It seems unlikely that she herself had served an apprenticeship. The will of Thomas Gammige of Walden (1578) does not mention his wife or occupation. Apart from this, there are a few 'painters' whose wills are uninformative, but no 'limners' or 'painter stainers' except goodman Laye (p. 7). All three terms 'had wide meanings, ranging from one who painted portraits to the house-painter and decorator',[10] including the man who executed interior plaster-wall paintings, of which so many fine examples still survive.[11]

The leather crafts embrace tanners, curriers and tawyers, who process the raw hides, skins, and bark, and glovers and shoemakers, who make up the leather into the finished goods.[12] Oak bark is the source of tannin, in which the hides and skins are steeped. Among the tanners who refer to their equipment, ten merely mention their tan-house and tan-vats, but five others describe their craft assets—though not deemed assets by the local communities, having to put up with the unsavoury smells. Joan Bowyar, widow, of Braintree : 'to Thomas Gooddaye, my daughter's son, a hoppet (yard or small close) where my limepits be, and all the implements and tools pertaining to tanner's craft, as fats, bark, my stock of leather and hides tanned and untanned, and all manner of skins already within the fats or without' (1560); Thomas Swallowe of Hare Street in the parish of Hornchurch : 'to Margery my daughter a dicker (a lot of ten hides or skins) of leather' (1564); Thomas Fletcher of Barking: 'all my bark, tan fats, hides and leather to be indifferently valued and praised by the joint advice of Agnes my now wife, Robert Commyns, Thomas Fisher and William Preble, to be sold forthwith, and Thomas Fisher to have the refusal before any other' (1583); William Sparrow of Halstead : 'my tanhouse and all its vats, pits, cisterns and other vessels, and my messuage called the Bull in Halstead' (1602); and William Wailett of Lambourne, a fairly substantial tanner : 'to my son William £10 with all my fats, limepits, bark-mill, and all other instruments, tools and gins belonging to the trade of tanning', and he also gives £50 to his second son Thomas and £35 each to his two daughters Mary and Elizabeth (1603). John Uphaveringe, a yeoman who does not give his abode but is to be buried at Hornchurch, leaves 'to my son Richard the bark loft, the gatehouse with the vats, the three limepits in the yard, and the tools and the bark to dress the leather in the yard withal' (1585).

Of tawers (or tawyers) who produce white leather by applying alum and salt to the raw hides, the unhelpful William Purle senior of Great Dunmow merely records the legacy to his son William of 'all my tools and instruments' (1575). None of the few curriers mentions his tools.

Many towns and villages have a glover (a few have several), whose wares protect labourers' hands in their rough tasks as well as money in their purses. Solomon Whiskerd of Fryerning gives elaborate instructions (1561) :

> I will that all my occupation shall be dressed out into journey work as shortly as may be, and as soon as it is dressed to be laid up under lock and key and to be sold.
> I will to John Clarcke, my servant, 20s. and to Collin 6s. 8d. to take pains to see that which belongeth to my occupation honestly done, and to have 3s.

a hundred for sheep's leather and 2s. for lamb and to have for other a 4d. above the task (i.e. rate).

My executors shall ride to all my butchers and gentlemen that I had ware of on Saturday next after my decease to fetch in all such wares as is in their hands and to have it pulled and dressed, and whereas I owe anything on the score or by tally or by bill, to see it discharged forthwith.

And whereas any butchers are in my debt which I have bought, Clarcke shall have that ware both of the gentlemen and butchers the week next after my decease, so that he shall answer for that ware that I have bought and paid for to my butchers, and after that is come out Robert Clarke shall have all my said butchers and the gentlemen that I had ware of to his use to do with as he shall think good.

All the money that shall rise or grow of my occupation shall be gathered up to the performance of my will and to the use of my children, portion and portion alike.

Other glovers elucidate their stock. John Harte of Ardleigh specifies his tools, 'as knives, tubs and leather tawed as untawed which is made to sell as that which is not' (1570). Lawrence White of Great Baddow says : 'To my brother a C (hundred) of sheep's leather and all my lambs' leather; to Nicholas Livesgate my servant 40s. and all my leather and skins that I have in the pits to work; to my landlord John Cooke a dozen of sheep's leather for doublets'; and he also gives 20s. to each of his two apprentices (1571). Richard Richardson of St. Osyth, leaving his son William 'all my shop tools', adds : 'My stock of leather dressed and undressed shall be sold to the most advantage by mine executor to the use of my legacies' (1581); while John Chamberlayne of Peny House in Pond Street in the same village refers to 'all my leather wrought and unwrought' (1591); and the stock of John Hall is to be augmented by 'five calves' skins' under the will of Richard Vyvens, a Manningtree butcher (1593). John Browne of Prittlewell, who does not give his occupation, is apparently a tanner rather than a tawer or a glover : 'to my son William half a hundred of sheep and lambs' leather of that which was last dried, as it falleth one with another' (1595).

Even more numerous are the shoemakers, or cordwainers, the latter name being from the leather first made at Cordova in Spain, originally of goat-skin but later often of split horse-hide. Any contemporary distinction between shoemakers and cordwainers seems to be hypothetical. Mark Coppin of Harwich, 'cordiener', asks his executors to sell 'my shop gear, leather and tallow to pay my debts and funeral charges' (1570); and Richard Cooke of St. Peter, Colchester, 'cordyner', arranges for his son Lawrence to have '6 dozen of shoes of every size, sortlike as well of the least as of the biggest, 3 hides and 2 backs at the day of his marriage or age' (1583); Peter Wright of Hornchurch, shoemaker, passes 'to my two eldest sons all my implements and the tallow pan and the cauldron with two rings' (1573); and John Tubbes of Walden, shoemaker, 'all my boots and shoes and leather, lasts, and shop knives' (1594).

CRAFTS AND TRADES 81

Two minor crafts also using leather are each represented by a solitary will. John Bird of Chelmsford, a collarmaker (for horses, not humans), refers to 'all my sackcloth and sacking, all my wares and leather in the shop' (1594); and Anthony Nicholson of Lexden, a pointmaker, to 'all the implements of my occupation, together with all my ware, leather, points (metal tags for laces) and latten' (1601).

Three tallow-chandlers, who make candles from hard animal fat and probably also sell them, hand on the equipment to their sons. 'My great cauldron, tallow pan and tallow trough, my tubs, and braches' (boring tool?) are inherited by Richard son of Andrew Broman of South Weald (1591); 'all my ware in my workhouse and my great cauldron in the warehouse', by John son of William Cooke *alias* Barker of Layer Breton (1584); and 'my great cauldron or pan hanged in my workhouse, with all other my pans, moulds and other tools', by John son of Thomas Parker senior of Walden (1593), who calls himself a shoemaker (leather is dressed with tallow). By our period only a few butchers also make candles.

The few saddlers tells us nothing of their implements.

In a curious little 15th-century poem, *The Debate of the Carpenter's Tools,* the tools voice their views and merits. For example,

> The crow, the pleyn, and the squyre,
> Says we have arnyd wele our hyre.

No less than 24 other implements take part.[13] They differ little throughout the ages. For our period, there is a detailed inventory of the tools of Cornelius Eversson in his 'joiner's workhouse' at (Old) Thorndon Hall (1592).[14] The array of tools in the carpenter's workshop may be best visualized from the wills of William Mason of Fingringhoe, whose three legatees have to divide among themselves 'a drawing stock, a joint, 2 adzes, a hand saw, a framing saw, a twybill (axe with two edges for cutting mortises), a mortise wimble, a draught wimble, a long wimble (gimlet), two chisels, a piercer (another boring tool), and an axe' (1569), and of Edward Nycholas of Chigwell, senior, who leaves 'to Edward my son 3 pair of scrazes (a tool for scratching?), 3 long jointers, 1½ dozen of chisels, 1 broad axe, 2 scoring axes, 6 augers of the best, 1 tenon saw, 1 hand saw, 1 hammer, 1 square, 2 piercers, and 1 twybill', to be delivered at 17 and to remain in his mother's hands in the meantime, and 'all the rest of my carpenter's tools to be divided equally betwixt my two prentices' (1589). Incidentally, Edward Nycholas senior of Chigwell (also 1589) leaves his carpenter's tools to Edward his son (grandson of Edward the first?); and are John Nycholls of Buttsbury (1600) and Edmund Nicholes of St Nicholas, Colchester (1600), both carpenters, also related? John Roper, a Barking carpenter, mentions 'a sowe to draw timber out of a ditch and 2 crows of iron'. (1575). A North Weald carpenter, William

Wilkinson, bequeaths '200 of lath towards the repairs of the Church House' (1585). Other carpenters add a few more details to the general picture : 'My bench and benchboard and grindstone' (William Smith senior of Great Sampford, 1598); '2 axes, a hand saw, 6 wimbles, a square, a piercer, and a hammer' (William Ravens senior of Great Bromley, 1603); 'my scoring axe and 2 of my best iron wedges' (Robert Bateman of Bardfield Saling, 1603); and 'my timber rough and wrought and made ware' (Giles Sorby of Walden, 1588). Although calling himself a carpenter, Robert Coote of Hempstead mentions 'my plank boards and joiner's stuff' (1592).

Of joiners' implements, William Smith of Great Bardfield leaves 'my pump tools, my joiner's tools, 3 planks and timber sufficient to make a frame and table' (1602), and Michael Manners of Boxted bequeaths to his unnamed father of Colne Engaine, also a joiner, 'my hatchet, holdfast (vice?), bench hook, and fore plane' (1602). While failing to list his tools, William Wyther of Chelmsford sets out his stock of timber, viz. '200 of quarters, 200 of ½-inch board, and 100 of mountains' (1595); the meaning of the last term has not been traced. Thomas Quilter of Great Dunmow, who combines the twin crafts of joiner and turner, divides his 'working tools' equally between his two sons, giving each 'a turning lathe and a grindstone unhanged'; the elder son is to have the larger grindstone if he will teach his brother 'joining and turning in the best manner he can'; and his 'wheeling timber with spindles' (for cartwheels) and the rest of his timber are also to be shared when it is 'wrought'. Thomas Wheatlye of Buttsbury, who does not name his occupation, refers to 'all my boards, quarters and timber' (1585). The small number of turners' and sawyers' wills do not disclose anything about their ancillary tools.

Coopers, who make barrels, afford a few particulars. Richard Dale of St Botolph, Colchester : 'all my timber that is wrought and unwrought and milled' (sawn?) (1569); William Gouldthayte of Coggeshall : 'to my son Thomas all my timber, oak, ash, seasoned and unseasoned, wrought and unwrought' (1587); and Hugh Bennett of Stratford Langthorne in West Ham : '20 hundred of hoops' (1593). Here is the stock-in-trade of two fletchers : Francis Cowling of Witham, 'all my tools and timber to Harry my son' (1583); and John Symond of Walden, 'to Toby my son all my bows, bowstaves, shafts, shaft timber, heads, feathers, and all my working tools and shop gear' (1591). Robert Wallys of Pattiswick, palemaker, gives his son Richard 'all my pales and bottoms of pales and clampole and all my tools' (1603). 'Clampole' is possibly unrecorded outside Essex and is a variant of 'clapholt', or split oak; the Colchester wages assessment of 1583 gives those of splitters of 'cloboard and clampell' (see pp. 56, 165), and 'a clampole to make a yielding tub'—evidently a job for the cooper—occurs in a will of 1592.

'Wright', a worker in wood, is now an almost obsolete word, recognized only with a prefix. A few specialist wrights mention their implements. Of wheelwrights—William Walter of St. Osyth: 'to my son William all my working blocks, upon condition that he shall perform the heaving of all the said timber' (1589); and Erasmus Bedle of Hatfield Broad Oak: 'my tools, working blocks, and my grinding stone, except my two-hand saw' (1596); also perhaps Richard Marten of Finchingfield, who does not name his craft: 'my wimble, adze, shave (spokeshave?), best piercer, little thoyer (meaning?), and bench' (1570). One ploughwright—William Shipman of Walden: 'my grindstone and the trough with the standards whereupon the same lieth' (1587). One millwright—Henry Rayner of White Notley: 'a chipping axe and a berse (meaning?), and all my tools and timber' (1603). Two fanwrights, who make a special kind of baskets for winnowing grain—William Glascocke of Little Bardfield: 'to my brother Cooke all my rods, timber and fans, and all other my tools' (1597); and Avery Lacye of Stansted Mountfitchet, referring three times to his baskets (1600). Two shipwrights—George Forest of Thorrington: 'all my tools except an axe to cut wood, a hammer, and a pair of pinsons' (pincers) (1573); and John Ellyott of St Osyth; 'my biggest hand saw, the residue of my tools to be equally divided between my two sons' (1574). Four other shipwrights appear in the section on Shipping. Of ancillary crafts, William Fawbott, a roper of Dagenham (1569), says nothing, and for anchor-making there is only John Moris, anchor smith of Harwich, just beyond our period (1610). Thomas Vincent of Great Tey, who fails to state his craft, leaves 'all my tools, my axe excepted, all my timber wrought and unwrought, with my hewing blocks, planks, shelves, trestles and other engines in the shop in which I work' (1573).

Passing to metal workers, we find that the most informative testators include many mighty blacksmiths, who leave such a wealth of detail as to conjure up the busy, noisy scenes at their forges. In Essex, it may perhaps be assumed that those who call themselves smiths are all blacksmiths. Essentially a rural craft, the only exceptions might be found at Thaxted, with its cutlery industry (though on the decline); there William Blyth, who refers merely to his 'vice and moulds' (1578), identifies himself as a blacksmith. The extracts do not seem to fall into any groups, so they will be taken in order of date. From the extraordinary variety of tools we may visualize the skilled manufacture and repair of the smaller agricultural implements and other iron wares such as hinges, locks and chains, as well as the shoeing of horses.

John Yngold of Roydon: 'all my working tools pertaining to my occupation of smithcraft' (1560); John Darbye senior of Brentwood: 'to John my son one anvil for a smith, a great tool to make a nail for a church door, and 2 hammers in Harman's keeping, a vice in Rychards' keeping, a nailing stock in the keeping of Richard Greene, and a rockstaff in the custody of Keche of Kelvedon, with all the rest of my smith's gear in my house' (1561) (a rockstaff is 'part of the apparatus for working a smith's bellows', first recorded in the *O.E.D.* in 1677); Robert Peatchie of 'Norton' (probably Norton Mandeville) : 'to my brother Richard all the iron in the shop and all the coal' (charcoal), to my mother all the money that is owing to me in the shop and all the working tools in the shop, 2 anvils, and 20 sheep, and to Joan Peatchie the younger 2 kine' (1562) : another instance of combined occupations; Richard Yonger of St. Mary, Colchester : 'to my son Robert a great bellows in my shop and the great hammer, my chaffer (vessel for heating water), and my best stythe' (stithy, or anvil) (1571); Robert Taylor of Felsted : 'my wife to let the shop to my partner John Petche blacksmith before all other if he will have it, as he and she can agree for it reasonably, and to my son John the anvil in the hands of John Taylor of Stebbing blacksmith, 2 pair of smith's tongs to nail tools, and a middle hammer' (1578); William Baylye of Finchingfield : 'to my son John all my shop tools and two hundreth of iron' (1578); Thomas Catonne of Thaxted, blacksmith : 'to my son Nicholas my messuage in Thaxted, except and always reserved to John my son the great shop which I do now work in, also to Nicholas one chalder of coals' (1579); John Pearson of Great Easton : 'all manner of debts and duties due unto me upon tally, score or otherwise, and my iron tools in my shop' (1584); John Rogers of Steeple Bumpstead : 'to my son John all my steethes, hammers, bellows and other working tools, with my scools (scales) and weights, and he shall have the use of my shop with the room for his coals during all the time that I have in the same (i.e. lease), yielding yearly 10s. towards the payment of my rent, and he shall have as much iron, coal and money of the tales (count, or tallies?) and marks as shall pay Mr Lambert so much money as I owe unto him' (1584); John Bendlowe of Great Bardfield : 'to Clement my brother a pair of smith's bellows, 1 stythe called a pole stythe, 2 pair of crotched tongs, and 1 pair plain tongs, 1 butteris (a farrier's tool for paring a horse's hoofs), 1 shoe hammer, 1 pair of pincers, 1 hand hammer, and 2 nail tools' (1584); Thomas Danwood *alias* Beane of Brentwood : 'all my working tools to my son, the second best anvil, a great hammer, a lesser smiting hammer, a shoeing hammer, a pair of pincers, and a butteris' (1587); Henry Wuddall of Chrishall : 'to my son the wrench (screwwrench or spanner) of my grindlestone (grindstone)' (1591); Robert Person of Great Ilford : 'to James Campe, my man, all my working tools in my shop, all my iron and coals, and all my made ware both old and new, to pay to my executors £5 10s.' (1592); Thomas Mills of Great Hallingbury : '1 bloom anvil, 1 bolt hammer weighing 14 lb., 1 upright hammer, 1 hand hammer, 1 pair of foregate tongs, 1 pair of cracked tongs, 1 shoeing hammer, 1 pair of pincers, and 1 paring iron' (1593); William

Ferrer of Wethersfield: 'the old bloomer, a peld hammer, a hand hammer, an upright hammer, 3 pair of tongs, i.e. 2 pair of forebits and a pair of crotchets (iron hooks) with a hobnail tool' (1593); and William Dowsett of Moreton: 'the high cobiron, a yarn (iron) peel (a long-handled shovel), a fire shovel, a pair of tongs' (1601). The penultimate blacksmith's surname is derived from the medieval 'ferrer', a smith. Is it possible that the craft had been handed down from father to son for two or three centuries?

John Page of Southminster, smith (1583), draws up lengthy provisions for carrying on his business:

> My shop and all such tools as I have set down in an inventory belonging to the shop praised at £10 I will that John Learke my servant shall have for the term of 10 years, paying yearly for the first 4 years to my executrix and owner of the shop 40s. and for the 6 years following 30s. and upon condition that he shall do his uttermost endeavour to certify my executrix of all such debts and reckonings as shall be due to me at the hour of my death as may appear by my shop book or by any other means that he knoweth and to help her as much as he conveniently can towards the gathering in of the same. And he shall have all the iron made and unmade remaining in the shop, the wrought at 2½d. the lb., nail rods, and all the unwrought being new iron at 11s. the hundred, the old iron at ¾d. the lb.; and if there remain any more tools than are expressed in the inventory then he to pay for them after 3d. the lb., whereof he shall pay unto my ironmonger so much money as I shall be indebted to him in part of payment of my said wares. The rest of the money which shall amount for the same wares he shall pay to my executrix within 4 years after my decease, provided that he shall put in sufficient security in an obligation of £30 before he shall enter and leave my shop and tools to keep the shop in good repair, as also for the yearly payment of £10 to my wife for all such tools as are expressed in the inventory, and further to pay for the rest of the wares and iron abovesaid and not contained in the inventory to my wife and to my ironmonger at such days as are expressed.

Not specifying his craft, but apparently a smith or farrier, is Robert Fellexe of Great Oakley: 'a pair of bellows, a beckhorn (bickern, an anvil with two projecting taper ends), with two bolt hammers, an upright hammer, a hand hammer, a nailing hammer, with all my shoeing tools and shop tools' (1598).

Forges are also needed by cutlers. Indirect testimony to the decay of the flourishing medieval industry at Thaxted is afforded by the existence of only three cutlers' wills in our period. John Skoot gives his sons, John and Nathan, to be equally shared, 'all my tools and things belonging to my occupation and all my armour, swords, daggers, knives and such other like' (1583), which may perhaps suggest that certain weapons are as much a local product as knives. John Button merely divides his 'working tools' between his sons John and Thomas (1592); later we find that Thomas Browne bequeaths to his cousin Thomas Button, both cutlers of Chelmsford, his house in Margaret Street in Thaxted and his tools (1601).

John Knappyng, the solitary 'bladesmith', devises to his son Thomas his 'dwelling house, mill house, stables and shop', but mentions no implements (1597). Of several Colchester cutlers' wills, that of Robert Weeles of St. Mary's parish is quite exceptional in the list of debts owing to him (1583) :

> Keeping the armour of Stanway parish for 2 years, 5s. 7d.
> Due by the parishioners of Lexden for keeping and trimming of their parish corselet for 2 years, 2s. 4d.
> Owing by Mr Stanton of Wickham for keeping of his armour 2 years, 4s., for a rapier trimming, 18d., also for trimming of a sword, 14d.
> Owing by Robert Burges for dressing of his swords and dagger at sundry times and other things, 2s. 10d.
> Owing by William, Old Mr Stanton's man of Wickham, for trimming of one almain rivet and a sword and a dagger, 20d.
> For a headpiece to the same almain rivet, 3s. 4d.
> By Greene of Saint Toffes (St. Osyth) for a sword, 8d.

The Acts of 4 & 5 Ph. & Mary, cc.2,3 (1558) had followed the renowned Highways Act (1555) in adopting the parish as the unit for a communal liability, the constables of each parish becoming responsible for providing a stock of arms to supplement those which the more substantial parishioners had to furnish privately (see p. 132).

Akin to cutlers are 'edgetool-makers', who produce sharp-edged instruments such as knives, chisels and swords. Their craft is illustrated by a single will, that of Richard Cooper of North Weald Bassett : 'to my son John my anvil and bolt hammer, an upright hammer, two pair of tongs, a pair of forebits, and a pair of crotches' (1591). The stock of kettles possessed by the only tinker testator was mentioned under Kitchen Implements.

With its great abundance of brick-earth and suitable clay for earthenware, Essex among the English counties in times past had an above-average number of brick- and tile-makers and potters. (Over 40 Elizabethan testators thus term themselves.[15]) We learn from the account-books of Sir William Petre of Ingatestone Hall that he paid a local brickmaker for '4,600 bricks at 4s. the thousand, 18s. 4d.; 50,000 of earth to make brick at 20d. the thousand; 1,250 paving tile, 50s.' (1550). His most detailed book, under 'Building expenses', discloses that as many as 240,000 bricks were made on the estate (1555), the best brick-earth being at East Horndon.[16] Only six testators tell us anything about their manufacturing equipment : meagre as compared with the informative weavers and smiths.

Walter Dadrye *alias* Rawlyn of Buttsbury, brickmaker, devises to his son William 'my house with the tylekell (tile-kiln) and working house adjoining' (1566); Thomas Castell of Stock, brickmaker, bequeaths to his son James 'my dungcart and all my tools, planks, boards and implements about my workhouse' (1590); and Ralph Jenewaye, in addition to a loom to his son, leaves to his wife 'my shed and bricks at Potter Row' (1601).[17] The few tilemakers are silent about their trade except for Richard Duke of Layer-de-la-Haye (1575) and the two John Fynches of Ingatestone, (1573, 1603), each of whom refers to his tenement called the Tilehouse; and 'my tiling hammer and tiling trowel' are among the assets of a South Hanningfield man. Potters are equally reticent. Harlow and Stock, the two main Essex centres of the industry, are both of medieval origin (see p. 254); the high-sounding 'Metropolitan Slipware' is the product of the potters who gave their name to Potter Street in Harlow. Edward Hankin of Stock gives his son William 'all my boards with the pot kiln and outward things about the kiln or workhouse' (1599), he was later in trouble in the manor court. Robert Hylles leaves 2s. each to Edmund Reve, Emmanuel Emyng and John Wright, all four being potters of Latton, close to Harlow, but makes no mention of his equipment; the Emyngs are well-known potters (1592). The same remark applies to William Livermore of Wethersfield, potter, who, like Jenewaye, leaves 'a pair of looms to weave in '(1589). In fact, the sole appearance of potters' ware is included in the schedule of debts given by John Lambe of Easthorpe, turner : 'Of Humphrey Palmer of Stock either to have of him 17 dozen pots or else 15s.' (1559). It is interesting to note the probable existence a generation later of some form of organized group : in 1622 'the potters of Stock and Buttsbury' complained about an unapprenticed neighbour, 'taking away the living of married persons who have wife and children'.

Debtors oblige two testators to record what is still due. Bartholomew Rawlin of Buttsbury, labourer, declares : 'Debts owing to me—of John Bonner of Rayleigh, brickmaker, for making of brick and tile at Rayleigh, 59s.; of William Sheene alias Sheine of Pleshey, brickmaker, upon a reckoning of my wages after 20s. from May Day to Michaelmas about 20 years since or thereabout, 14s. 6d.'! (1589). In the next extract, taken from 'debts as appeared by tallies' owed to John Backhouse of Woodham Ferrers (1590), the reference is to making bricks in stacks in the open, not in kilns : 'To my son John all the money due from my master for the delivery of lime, brick and tile and the burning of a clamp of bricks and for the casting of brick earth'.

The house-builder does not appear until the 18th century. A carpenter, a tiler, a bricklayer (if bricks are used), and so on are all separately engaged for the work. Robert Barker of Thaxted is the only glazier (a comparatively recent craft) who refers to 'all his glass and tools', bestowing it on William Ellice 'his late servant' (1598).

John Bentall of Halstead, beerbrewer, leaves 'to Agnes my wife all my brewing, baking and tunning vessels during her life, keeping them in sufficient reparation' (1588). A few brewing implements were referred to in the section on House Fixtures. For large household brewing an extraordinarily interesting list of implements—perhaps the most detailed contemporary record that has survived—is found in the Petre archives.[18]

Not a single water- or wind-miller describes his equally elaborate equipment, because it is normally an integral part of the structure of his mill; but Thomas Howe of Netteswell, (water-)miller, refers to 'all the implements and tools, bushels, pecks, baskets, tubs, crows of iron and wimbles which appertains to the mill wherein I dwell' (1569). Baking the miller's product, on the other hand, demands only simple implements. A solitary baker, John Stucke of Moulsham in Chelmsford, mentions his 'rolling beetle (a heavy-headed instrument, usually of wood) and pin' (1595), but not his peel (the long-handled shovel for withdrawing his loaves).

Two butchers refer to their premises and heavy equipment. John Harte senior of Thaxted bequeaths 'one great scalding tub and one great cauldron, and all such trees (trestles?), gambles (bent pieces of wood or iron on which to hang carcases), iron pins, and all other trees and instruments that I have pertaining to my trade'; he also alludes to 'the chipyard' (1594); and John Pumfret junior of Walden devises 'my shops and slaughter housen' (1576).

A most illuminating list of utensils is recorded by John Hawkens of Coggeshall, cook (i.e. keeper of a cookshop) : 'a pewter basin, 2 platters, 3 dishes, a porringer and a saucer (i.e. a dish for salt or sauces) containing in weight 17 lb., a two-eared pan of brass weighing 22 lb., a brass pot weighing 31 lb., a brass pot and a posnet weighing 33 lb., a kettle weighing 13 lb., also in pewter, a charger, 2 platters, 3 dishes, 2 porringers and a saucer weighing $19\frac{1}{2}$ lb., a latten chafing dish the biggest of the twain, a goblet of silver, a quern, a boulting tun, an axe, a hammer, 2 wedges and a piercer, a spit with a foot, and a new kettle; and all the corn in my house' (1575). He appoints as the supervisor of his will Thomas Paycocke, a member of the rich clothier family whose name is perpetuated in Paycocke's house in Coggeshall.[19] Edward Reade the elder of Maldon, another cook, lists 'a quart pewter pot, in the buttery the greatest kettle, two little skillets, a chafing dish, a skimmer, a steel ladle, basting ladle, an old tinker's kettle of a pottle, a tinker's kettle of 6 quarts, a little graven (engraved) saucer, 2 fruit dishes', and a number of porringers (1588).

The trapping of the tidal water by the mudbanks in the Essex creeks produces high salinity. Salt-making on certain marshes can be traced back to Roman times, and the Essex Domesday has many references to salt-pans. First there is partial evaporation of sea-water in shallow pits, or pans, strengthened by planks to prevent the earth from falling in and apparently lined with lead. The salt is then extracted by slow boiling (much wood being used as fuel) in small buildings or sheds known as salt-cotes.[20] Until fairly recently our knowledge of the manufacture of 'bay salt' in Elizabethan Essex was almost nil,[21] though it was assumed that the remains of salt-works at Goldhanger, Paglesham, Heybridge and a few other places were of ancient origin;[22] and place-names, including field-names in the Tithe Awards of about 1840-50, provide further evidence.[23] The survey of the manor of Woodham Ferrers, 1582, refers to six salt-cotes (two being 'wasted') that 'do make white salt' (purified by dissolving in clean water, and re-evaporating) (p. 330), the memory of which survives in the farmhouse still called Saltcoats (close to the head of Clements Green Creek), meaning, like the village of Salcott, 'salt-cottages' near salt-pans. The earliest record of the Woodham salt-works is in 1332.[24] Just outside our period we note the wills of John Creke, 'weller' (salt-boiler) of Hockley (1547),[25] William Shetelwoode of Fambridge, 'saltman' (1605), and of Edward Bird of Stow Maries, 'salt weller' (1608).

Apart from an East Donyland salter (an ambiguous term), our wills yield those of two salt-makers, father and son, who died within a year of each other. Their salt-cotes lie in Woodham Ferrers, but their dwelling is in Rettendon, on the west side of Woodham. The chief items of interest are the terms used for their equipment and the hints about keeping the manufacturing expertise in the family. It will be observed that salt-making, probably inactive in winter, is combined with pastoral farming. Thomas Stammer, who calls himself a yeoman, provides (1571):

> To my son Thomas my saltcote called Marten Stammers saltcote in the parish of Woodham Ferrers. To Thomas five leads and all the wood at the saltcote, all the tubes, dung cart, harrows, and striking boards, and half the salt in the cote. To my son Edmund one saltcote called Mundes cote in the parish of Woodham Ferrers and all the leads, tubes, baskets and other implements. To Edmund half of my marsh called Little Struwed. I ordain that Richard Allard my servant have the occupying of the cote until my son come to the age of 19 years, upon condition that Richard do instruct him in the mystery (i.e. craft) of saltmaking and pay yearly farm (i.e. rent) 26s. 8d. to Edmund's use. To my wife Joan 5 of the best of my horses and 1 cart, 17 kine and bullocks and 40 of my best sheep.

Thomas Stamer, the son, has to make different arrangements for passing on the business (1572): 'To William my brother my cote called Marten Stamers cote, with 5 leads and all the wood and salt there, and the tubes, dungcart, harrows, and striking boards. I will that Thomas Radle, my father-in-law, have the occupation of my cote for 4 years, paying yearly unto my brother William 26s. 8d.' Perhaps dried dung, like peat, is used because of its slow combustion.

While Alderman Thomas Burlz of Maldon left his son Thomas a saltcote in Stow Maries, which adjoins Woodham Ferrers on the east, it is doubtful whether he actually worked it (1585).

A letter dated at Ipswich, 1567, from a certain Edward Gooddinge to Sir William Cecil, gives a brief account, the writer having been 'sent for by Mr Grymston' (Edward Grimston, an Essex J.P.?), about two 'salt-houses' in Essex and Suffolk. He cannot definitely state the quantity made, 'for that I made it in trials of the ovens and pans, yet I think there is about 200 bushels made in both houses'—apparently one in each county, but there is no indication where these are.[26]

Although rock salt was not to be found (in Cheshire) until 1670, English coastal bay salt (obtained by evaporation) did not supply all the demand for this vital commodity. A parish historian remarks that 'the bay salt exported from Brightlingsea to London' in our period 'is not necessarily of local manufacture, some at least having been first imported from Rochelle, a centre of the French industry'.[27]

The packsaddles and other equipment of itinerant dealers are referred to in the section on Horses. The wills of two other dealers each mention 'ped', an obsolete word for a wicker pannier. Valentine Wheler of Buttsbury, rippier (fishcarrier), leaves to 'Richard Swyfte my servant a grey gelding called Dycke, with pack-saddle, peds, halter, wanty (rope or band to fasten the pack), and girth', and his brown mare called Joan Twopence (1587); and Thomas Lentforde of South Weald, 'poulter', dictates that 'my three horses and all my stock of money with my peds, baskets and furniture for the horses shall be used by my son John' (1591). Robert Nevitt of Chigwell, collier (charcoal burner or supplier), has several horses, as well as some cattle (1563).

## Markets and Fairs

A valuable trade asset is a market-stall. Three wills mention them. 'All my market stalls in the market place of Rayleigh' are left to his son James by Nicholas Brodwater, a townsman who describes himself as a yeoman but refers also to 'my ware in my shop and my tallowhouse' (1592). William Cocke of Brentwood, linendraper, bequeaths 'my stall being freehold, wherein I sold my cloth in the town of Chelmsford in Potters Lane, abutting upon the house of old Free on the west and the stall late Edmund Saberys on the east' (1598). The same market is alluded to by John Rogers, shoemaker, of Moulsham, who passes on 'all the lasts and other working tools in the shop and my stall and tilt (booth) which I use in the market' (1601). Two other testators speak of their local markets: 'my house in (Great) Oakley market', of which little is known (Thomas Cambredg of Moze, 1567); and 'my house next the church gate towards the market house on one side, the other abutting next the lane towards Earls Colne' (Elizabeth Hodson of Halstead, 1598).

We have already mentioned complaints in 1593 about the fair at Thremhall Green on the boundary of Stansted and Hatfield Broad Oak.[28] Four years earlier Anne Bredg, a Harlow widow, had devised 'my lease of Thremnall Fair or Hatfield Fair to my son Edward'. The important livestock fair at Newport appears in several wills, e.g. 'My grey stone horse and my bay colt which I bought at Cold Fair' crops up in that of William Everard of Great Waltham, a substantial yeoman (1571); and two testators enjoin their executors to pay certain legacies 'next Cold Fair day', which, as Harrison tells us, is 6 November.[29] Henry Cooke 'the eldest' of Castle Hedingham leaves to Henry his son 'all the trestles, crotches, poles and boards belonging to the stall in Crowche Fair'. Lying by the ford over the Colne between Castle and Sible Hedingham, now bridged and known as Crouch Fair Green, it was the site of the ancient Hinckford hundred moot and was used for a cattle fair.[30] 'A brass pot that she bought at Stortford Fair' is among the kitchen implements left to his wife Joan by Thomas More, a yeoman of Little Canfield, seven miles from the Hertfordshire town (1566).

## Debts and Loans

To what extent do we find the lower-rank Elizabethans either giving credit or being given loans, with or without security? The heavy expenses and wild extravagance of many courtiers are well documented and the financial state of some of the nobility has been the subject of much recent research,[31] but there is a paucity of evidence about the ordinary people. A little information can be gleaned from wills, which are a source that does not seem to have been much used for the less exalted classes' debts, though Harrison tells us of the growing practice of lending money at interest.[32] About 200 Essex testators refer to debts owed to or by them. Thomas Hanes of East Mersea, for example, tells his executor: 'I owe goodman Pollard fire and lodging and my two keepers' board (during his last illness), and Nelson hath of mine a firkin of butter price 13s. 4d. and a roundlet of vinegar containing 8 gallons 2 quarts, price about 3s., and oweth me for a pair of new shoes 14d.' (1581). About 50 wills have a schedule of debts, chiefly of creditors. Attached to that of Thomas Meddowes, the East Tilbury blacksmith (1585), are two lists of 'the (56) names of those that are indebted to me', ranging from £3 to 6d., mostly by men living within a 4-mile radius including 'Mr Rytch (probably Edward Rich, esquire) in Horndon (-on-the-Hill)', and of 'those to which I am indebted' including 'Mr Jackson of London, ironmonger, £9'. Among similar but shorter lists of creditors are those of three other blacksmiths. Glode Friszille (or Fresell), a bricklayer of Prittlewell, names 11 local creditors, including 'Mr (John) Niccoulsone, parson of Southchurch'; they owe him in all £44 15s.

The ways in which testators deal, or try to deal, with debts owing to them afford some odd features. Debts, as we know from contemporary accounts, may be classed as 'sperate' (hopeful) and 'desperate'. Some people announce their waiving certain debts, but whether out of generosity or pessimism is usually not apparent. 'I forgive him all that he oweth me' is an occasional phrase. Or the testator may relinquish part of the debt, as William Cock junior, a Paglesham mariner: 'Whereas James Wett oweth me £5 10s., I forgive him all saving 47s. for the which I give him twelvemonth day payment' (1583); or, more simply, 'I forgive John Austeyn 4s. of the money he ought (owed) me'. William Gates, a Paglesham yeoman, goes one better: 'Whereas Thomas Howell our minister (the rector) oweth me two bushels of wheat, I forgive it him and give him two bushels more' (1584). Stating that William Annes, 'being beadle of Colchester, oweth me £4', Robert Beard of that town takes a stronger line: 'If he will quietly pay to my executors 50s. within a year and a half after my burial, I will forgive him the rest, and if he will not I will that he shall pay the whole due' (1566). We may observe Richard Poole of Rochford on his deathbed, suddenly remembering some unpaid debts and adding a postscript: 'Old Kinge of Strode Green (in Rochford) oweth me for 37 days work whereof 6 days in harvest, and I owe Stephen Hammond 4d. and Henry Prentice 4d.' (1581).

Not uncommonly testators adopt a shrewd method by combining a legacy with collection of a debt and leaving it to the executor or legatee to pursue the debtor. Thus, William Shawcroft of Aveley: 'I give my wife £6 which my brother oweth me, £3 which John Costell oweth, 3 bushels of rye and 2 of barley which Richard Humbers oweth, and Richard Cowdalle oweth 10s., (all) which I give to my wife' (1587). Stephen Cannon of Foulness deals with his overdue wages and livery: 'I will that my brother John shall receive of John Edwards my master 13s. 4d. and two yards of home made cloth which he oweth me for my quarter's service' (1573). That stern yeoman, Thomas Cottysforth of Tolleshunt D'Arcy (p. 116), assigns a debt to the officers of three parishes to recover: 'Whereas one John Baker of Tillingham oweth me 30s., he shall pay the same to John Caywood of Tillingham Hall presently after my decease', who in turn is then to pay the 'churchwardens and collectors (of the poor) of Bradwell-juxta-Mare, Tillingham and Dengie 10s. each' (1588).

A few wealthy persons appear as creditors. Robert Dickenson, a Romford carpenter, leaves his sons £31, which 'Master Cooke (Sir Anthony Cooke junior of Gidea Hall, Romford) oweth me' (1597); and William Walker of (Cold) Norton refers to £20 'owing to me by Mistress Osburne of North Fambridge (Hall)' (1602). In an unusual clause, Robert Spenser of St Osyth, 'servant to the right honourable Sir Thomas Darcy Lord Darcy of Chiche', dictates: 'To Henry Atkins, steward of my lord's house, 20s., which he now oweth me upon my accounts, together with all such money as is now due to me from my Lord as partly appeareth by my bills extant upon the files in the custody of Mr George Goldinge, my

Lord's auditor, and one dag (heavy pistol or handgun), which is now in my chamber' (1582).

We find three references to the ancient accounting method of scoring, or notching, a tally, or stick, which was then cleft lengthwise, each party to the transaction keeping one part as a record or receipt: an elementary but foolproof safeguard against cheating.[33] John Pearson of Great Easton, blacksmith, refers to 'all manner of debts and duties due unto me upon tally, score or otherwise', and William Cooke *alias* Barker of Layer Breton, tallowchandler, to debts 'upon my tallies and scores' (both 1584). The 'debts as appeareth by tallies' owed to John Backhouse of Woodham Ferrers (1590) are given in the section on Crafts (brickmaking).

Akin to debts are 'gages', or pawns, of which three examples have been noted. The legacy of Anne Browne of Ingatestone to her daughter Edy includes 'a silver spoon which is at gage, which I will that my son shall redeem and give unto her' (1589); the short inventory of her goods shows that she is poor. So also is Joan Finch of Chelmsford, 'maiden', who declares that her brother has refused to come to her deathbed and she has no friend; in a pathetic nuncupative will she refers to 'her cloak in pawn' (1597). A postscript to the will of Mary Harvy of Halstead, widow (1590), reads: 'I have in the hands of John Potter of Colne Engaine, yeoman, one salt silver and gilt and one stone pot lipped part with silver which lieth for payment of 40s., and in the hands of John Fuller of Halstead, yeoman, 8 silver spoons marked with S & H which lie for 40s., which I will my executors have, paying the said several sums towards the payment of my debts'.

---

[1] See A. Jewell, *Crafts, Trades and Industries: A Book List for Local Historians* (N.C.S.S., 1964).

[2] *V.C.H., Essex*, ii, 380-404, has a long section on Colchester. Recent research is embodied in J. E. Pilgrim's unpublished London M.A. thesis, 'The Cloth Industries of Essex and Suffolk' (1939) and his chap. 15 in J. G. Jenkins (ed.), *The Wool Textile Industry* (1972).

[3] Emmison (ed.), *Wills at Chelmsford, 1400-1620*, 319, 382, 465.

[4] *E.L.: Disorder*, 296-9, and Appendix B.

[5] A certificate of 1576 to the Privy Council of wool bought by 27 Coggeshall clothiers from staplers and 'broggers' (dealers) probably gives the names of all or nearly all of the resident clothiers (P.R.O., S.P. 12/114/47).

[6] Dorothy Hartley (ed.), *Thomas Tusser* (1931), 80, 82, quotes other contemporary accounts of linen production before bleaching.

[7] I am greatly indebted to Mr Pilgrim for several explanations.

[8] *E.L.: Morals*, 76, 193, 221.

[9] Bertha L. Stratton, *Sherman and Allied Families* (priv. printed, New York, 1951).

[10] *Trans. E.A.S.*, xxiv, 161.

[11] *Ibid.*, xxii, 334-40; xxiii, 1-17; xxiv, 132-48; see also xxiv, 162.

[12] For methods and equipment, see F. W. Waterer, *Leather Craftsmanship* (1968) and J. G. Jenkins, *The Craft Industries* (1972), 60-73. For indictments for leather goods stolen, see *E.L.: Disorder*, 299-300 and Appendix C.

[13] Listed in C. F. Innocent, *The Development of English Building Construction* (1916), 96-7, which also gives the medieval tools and those named in a Leicester carpenter's inventory of 1597.

[14] E.R.O., D/DP E2/23; Edwards (*see Note below*), 30-6.

[15] *Wills at Chelmsford, 1400-1620*, index.

[16] *Tudor Secretary*, 157, 299; *E.L.: Disorder*, 244.

[17] Potter Row in Inworth is not recorded in *Place-Names of Essex* (1935); the name could be derived from a man of that name (*cf. ibid.*, 255) or from one or more of that occupation.

[18] *Tudor Secretary*, 149.

[19] *Trans. E.A.S.*, 311-21.

[20] Harrison, *op. cit.*, 377-8; *Ess. Rev.*, lii, 186.   [21] *V.C.H., Essex*, ii, 445

[22] *Ess. Rev.*, ii, 184-88.   [23] *Trans. E.A.S.*, vols. v-ix.   [24] *Ibid.*, xxiv, 5-16.

[25] *Ibid.*, O.S., i, 154.

[26] P.R.O., S.P. 12/43/1; nothing else about the Essex salt industry occurs in the State Papers or Privy Council Acts.

[27] E. P. Dickin, *History of Brightlingsea* (1939), 165-8, 187. So little being known about the industry in Essex, we quote the following early entries in the E.R.O. Index of Subjects: bequest of a salt-cote in Hockley (1487); bequest of 50 ways of salt (1544); deeds of messuage and land in East Marsh in North Fambridge used for a salt-cote (1629).

[28] *E.L.: Disorder*, 67.   [29] Harrison, *op. cit.*, 396.

[30] *Place-Names of Essex*, 440; *Trans E.A.S.*, xviii, 185, 294.

[31] L. Stone, *The Crisis of the Aristocracy, 1558-1641* (1965) and the subsequent well-known controversy; Mary Finch, *The Wealth of Five Northamptonshire Families* (1956).

[32] Harrison, *op. cit.*, 202-3. The Act of 1571 gave semi-legal approval to interest not above 10 per cent. For charges of usury, see *E.L.: Morals and the Church Courts*, 72-4. For the useful facilities provided by the Maldon Court of Record regarding loans, credits and debts, see Dr. Petchey's thesis (p. 6).

[33] *Tudor Secretary*, 133-4.


NOTE.—Published just after my page-proofs were received, A. C. Edwards, *John Petre* (1975), 114-36, gives detailed bills (from the family archives in the E.R.O.) of a bricklayer, two blacksmiths, a carrier, a cooper, a London sword-cutler, 6 joiners, and a pewterer (1580-94).

# 6
# Family and Household
## Wives

In few records is the importance of the family emphasized more than in wills. Taking a last look at the beloved or greedy faces of the relations gathered around the bedside, the testator, perhaps suddenly taken ill, ponders anxiously. Who shall have my possessions? Who shall receive preference—eldest son or spouse? How many should I remember outside the family? Shall I prohibit as well as provide—veto the legacy to any child who marries without my wife's or executor's consent or that to my wife if she re-marry? Some go to infinite trouble in drafting or dictating their wills, with these and other problems on their minds.

Death, that comes like a thief in the night, may leave the rest of the family with problems where the head has made no will. But we are not concerned with intestacy. A large proportion of testators having a wife and children fall into three categories—they reveal more care for the widow than for the offspring, the reverse, or real consideration for both. Of the first, it is abundantly clear, although life for the great majority has been a hard struggle with little time for sentimentality, that many a man approaching death shows genuine affection by arranging for his widow's material comfort : all the more significant when we bear in mind that in certain respects the law regards her as little more than the husband's chattel. For these reasons, therefore, some wills afford a viewpoint of ordinary society that is of much interest, and it is relatively novel : a pleasant one, too, and a change from the pattern of disorder and immorality that filled so much of the two previous volumes. It warrants fairly full treatment.

Provision for the widow is given in a variety of ways—sometimes only one, but often a combination of several. We shall look at them in the following order : food; fuel; houseroom, sometimes with specific access to the only fire or other convenience; and manual help in the house or on the land.

Concern is commonly evinced by way of an injunction to the eldest or only son or daughter or to the executors to see that she has adequate victuals. At least a hundred of our wills include such a clause, often expressed only in general terms, as 'My son shall maintain my wife with meat and drink', but it may be strengthened by the executors or overseers being asked to ensure its being properly carried out. John Polley of Stebbing thinks ahead for his widow's happiness : 'To Edward my son, all my moveable goods unbequeathed, upon condition that he be a comfort to his mother and to see that she be honestly kept at bed and board for her diet' (1598). Such bare requirements are extended in many wills. Two, for instance, provide thus. William Byatte the elder of Stebbing directs : 'My daughter shall honestly keep at bed and board, washing and wringing my wife Alice' (1578); and William Sworder of Hatfield Broad Oak, yeoman, enjoins : 'Henry and William my sons shall well and honestly board, find and keep my wife with sufficient meat, drink and lodging, with washing and wringing' (1591). Specific legacies of food appear in another section.

Clothing, with extra care during illness, is frequently stipulated : 'To be kept with good and sufficient apparel, meat and drink in sickness and in health for the term of her life'. Or we find further forethought, as by John Tabor of Stock : 'My executors shall keep sufficiently with meat, drink and apparel my wife Amy, and if it pleases God to visit her with sickness to the impoverishment of her and my executors, then they shall sell any such things as I have given, to the succouring of my wife' (1586). In contrast, cash maintenance is rare : 'My son shall pay my wife 16d. every week so long as she shall live' has only two, and less definite, parallels.

Another humane consideration sometimes revealed is the provision of fuel for her cooking over the permanent fire in the hall or the outside kitchen as well as for warming a separate room assigned for her own use. 'During her life to have free liberty to come to the fire' is not an unusual clause. 'Meat, drink, fire and candle' is the briefest phrase. The quality and quantity may thus be left to the executors' discretion, but some wills are more precise. For convenience, we include here bequests to other kin; and for 'load', 'cubit' and 'billet' the reader is referred to the section on Timber above. One of the Stock millers, Charles Whiskerd, who has figured in both the preceding volumes, dictates that, 'if my wife keep house called Herdes and Picardye, she shall have 6 loads of firewood every year, otherwise none' (1587). The executors of John Ilger of Stansted Mountfitchet, yeoman, must deliver to his widow '4 usual cartloads of wood great and small between the Feasts of All Saints and Easter and allow her sufficient straw to heat her oven so oft as she shall bake and brew' (1600). John Smith of Great Birch, yeoman, bequeaths to his wife 'three loads of wood to be paid as long as she liveth yearly, or else 6s. 8d., and she to stand to the making and carriage' (1560). The wife of William Danyell of St Giles, Colchester, is left 'two hundreth of wood' (1567); that of John South of West Mersea, 'all my wood that I have provided for my winter burning, if she will tarry here to burn it' (1567); that of William Stede of Chrishall, 'two loads of wood, one of small, the other of great, at her removing hence' (1570); and that of Richard Man of Braintree, yeoman, 'sufficient firewood to be cut handsome (i.e. easy to handle) and laid in the great chamber' (1571). Thomas Bredge senior, a husbandman of Felsted, directs his eldest son Thomas 'to lay yearly in the yards five loads of wood for my wife's fuel and firebote' (1575). Similar provision for their wives is made by William Cooke of Stebbing for '3 loads of wood during her life, to be laid in the yard of the mansion house of Mertens for her use, to be burned in the house and not elsewhere' (1581); by Richard Gallowaye of Ramsey for 'four loads of cubit to be delivered at her house in Bridge Street' (1582); by Thomas Fuller the elder, a yeoman of Great Burstead, for 'three load of billet' (1585). Thomas Baw, an East Mersea seafaringman, arranges that his wife 'shall have one load of logs of the most doted (i.e. decayed) trees and half of one load of cubit every year' (1594); and Ralph Wenlock, a Langham weaver, likewise 'one load of wood yearly for her burning and one tree for logs' (1595). William Glascocke, a Fyfield yeoman, goes further (1579). His wife Thomasine is 'to have for her firebote every year 13 of the best lops and 1 old husband to make her logs, so that she shall fell no timber nor spoors what wood soever they be, and she to maintain the house and houses with sufficient reparations; and if my son William chance to fell any timber for his own use, my wife to have the lops and offal towards her firebote.' 'Husband', which does not occur in the *O.E.D.*, means a pollarded tree;[1] and 'spoor' apparently stands for 'spur', a short branch, especially one likely to produce fruit.

Two yeomen grant leave to fell timber also for farm implements and fences. John Elie of Little Bromley declares that there must be 'no waste in cutting, cropping or lopping any wood but only eight trees a year towards my wife's fence and fire' (1587); and John Sparrow senior of Sible Hedingham, in devising his capital messuage called Sparrowes to Joan his wife for life, makes it clear that 'she shall do no waste in the woods and timber trees but to take sufficient hedgebote, firebote, ploughbote, gatebote and cartbote to be expended on the premises only' (1590).

Although many men doubtless assume that the children will provide houseroom for their widowed mothers, others regard this age-old problem as too tricky to be left solely to their offspring or in-laws. They therefore give directions according to individual circumstances. It is in such clauses that a testator's kindliness manifests itself in an intimate way, though in others it may indicate a strong possibility of unkindliness on the children's part. Reservation of rooms is the most common criterion of a testator's forethought. For example, 'My wife to have the chamber I used to lie in and part of the sollar room above the chamber, without let, contradiction or molesting of my executor'. Other fairly typical clauses are : 'My wife to have and enjoy my loft over the hall or else the kitchen, for her life'; or, more fully, 'To my widow, dwelling in the house, these parcels, viz. the chamber over the hall, the kitchen, the yealding house (i.e. where the beer wort is left to ferment), and the buttery, with free ingress, egress and regress'. Robert Coote of Radwinter, husbandman, dictates: 'My wife Agnes shall quietly have as well the parlour belonging to my farm wherein I now dwell with the chamber at the end of the same parlour, as also free way, ingress and regress to and from them' (1585). In Thomas Bredge's will, already quoted, his eldest son Thomas is instructed to 'permit Margaret my wife to enjoy peaceably during her natural life where I now dwell the hallhouse, the parlour, the buttery and the soller over the parlour' (1575).

Likewise William Wyther assigns 'to my well beloved wife Sarah for life these rooms wherein I now dwell commonly called the Chequer in Chelmsford, viz. the parlour, the chamber or loft called the apple chamber, the chamber called the garret chamber, the chamber over the shop, and the little room under the stairs leading up to the same loft; also the little garden, and liberty to wash and bake within the kitchen and to have her water in the well' (1595). Other facilities are given by John Godfrey, a carpenter of Theydon Garnon: 'My wife shall have the garner and the one end of the sheepen and come to the fire in the hall and kitchen at all times to do her necessary business' (1587).

Even fuller provision for his wife is made by John Hart, a mariner of Harwich (1591):

> My parlour and the chamber over the parlour and the cellar under the parlour over the south side of my house, and the yard room that lieth from the cellar door to the backhouse ward (i.e. towards it), my backhouse and the soller over it, and the going of my cow, and half my tow house; also half my garden in the West Street and all my stall gear and the rooms in the street, with free passage through the entry to carry the stall gear every market day, and also to have free passage through the entry to the tow house and backhouse with her cow, and carriage of herrings to the tow house. To my son my hall and all other rooms and sollers and chambers unbequeathed.

Anxious for the future secure tenure of his wife, William Hewitt, a Braintree butcher, wills: 'To my son William my messuage called the Chequer in Braintree, he to permit my wife Dorothy and her maid to occupy all the hallhouse with a chamber on the south side of the hallhouse and all the houses, chambers and sollers on the north side as she hath before occupied as necessary houses for victualling' (1570).

Stephen Collyn of Beauchamp Roothing ordains: 'Ellen my wife shall have the two chambers where I now dwell to her own use for life, namely the old parlour and the nether chamber; and Robert my son shall keep her one cow winter and summer, and shall quietly suffer her to have free recourse to the fire at all times and the great salt trough in the nether chamber provided that she shall allow him to have free recourse to the trough' (1575). The advantage of a single cow also figures in the will of Nicholas Lacye of Widdington, yeoman: 'William my son shall suffer Grace my wife to have one chamber over the hall, and shall find her meat, drink and firewood with free use of the fire and table in the hall at her will, or else shall pay her yearly 40s. with the keeping of one cow to her use winter and summer' (1599). With rational brevity Thomas Dyddon of Orsett declares: 'I will that Isabel my wife, using herself tenderly as becometh an honest woman towards her children, have her abiding in the house and also commodities of my farm' (1567).

Various means of comfort are thought of by Nicholas Ruste of Debden, yeoman: 'To my wife Joyce during her life one chamber between the doors and the two sollers over them, and the hall to do her business and the kitchen to use the oven, half the apples, pears and other fruit, 1 bushel of pease and 2 bushels of barley before 17 November yearly, and sufficient fuel and firewood to be burned in the hallhouse and kitchen; my son Edward to use the fire jointly with my wife' (1597). To avoid distress temporary accommodation is arranged by two yeomen: 'She shall remain in my house one month after my decease at the charge of my executor, if she will; if not, God speed her well' (John Crimble of Hawkwell, 1578); and 'She shall have her dwelling in the kitchen adjoining to my house' for a year (John Underwoode senior of Greenstead-juxta-Colchester, 1593). John Haryson of Foulness island allows a choice: 'to have her dwelling either at the Temple (Farm in Sutton) or at Prestwood (in Foulness) at her best liking, with a chamber and place at her best liking' (1578).

Convenience and profit are carefully planned for Joan wife of William Law of Arkesden. She is 'to have the chamber where I lie and to use the quern, kneading trough, moulding board and boulting hutch when she need; 1 acre of barley and ½ acre of wheat and 1 acre of oats at her own choice at harvest yearly; also 4 hens to go in the yard and to bring forth a brood of chickens when it shall please her, and to bring up a pig till it be a hog, and to do so yearly as long as she liveth, and to have a sow going among my son Stephen's beasts, and to wean a calf amongst his to her profit, and to fare as they do winter and summer' (1574). Robert Bonde of Bradwell-juxta-Mare evidently knows that his wife Parnell would not wish the contents of a certain cabinet to be disturbed, so 'she shall have the occupation of the cupboard and table in the hall during life on condition that she enter into bond unto John Brooke of New Hall' (1573).

Access to the water supply is as important as use of the oven. The wife of Richard Abbot of Colchester, tanner, is to have 'free ingress to and from the pump in my great tenement called Redinges at all times from sunrising to sunsetting' (1571). William Stookes of Fyfield gives his wife 'his dwelling for 16 years after his decease', but insists that she 'maintain and cherish the spring, and at the end of the term to hand over to his son' (1581).

Even more illuminating are the ways by which the widow is to be afforded practical aid. It may be a brief, general phrase, such as 'My son shall be a guide with her'. The executors of Robert Nycoll of Colne Engaine are to provide 'a girl or wench to attend unto my wife at all times for her help and comfort' (1599). Farming assistance, especially at seed-time and harvest, is demanded for a number of widows. John Clerk of Takeley, husbandman, for instance, wills that his son Thomas 'shall are' (for 'ear', to plough) 'and till my ground every year during the time of his mother's life or so long as she shall occupy the same, also to carry her corn and hay, carry out the dung, and lay the wood for her spending at the house, and at all times a horse to the market or at any place at her desire' (1558). Few husbands could be more considerate. Walter Watter of Plaistow in West Ham, plasterer, offers his son a little bribe—'my best blue coat upon condition that he shall help my wife to get in her harvest' (1588); and Thomas Whyte of Great Hallingbury suggests to his wife Joan : 'She shall give to James my brother a ½ quarter wheat, a ½ quarter barley, a ¼ quarter oats and a ½ quarter of peasen for seeing her lands ploughed and sown in due season at her charges' (1558). Likewise Thomas Bucke of Littlebury, husbandman : 'My son Erasmus shall give to Joan my wife yearly during her natural life 1 acre of barley, 1 acre of wheat, 1 acre of oats, with 4 loads of firewood if she shall spend so much, and shall reap, mow and dress the said barley, wheat and oats and make them ready to the cart in such sort as he doth his own, the which he shall carry and lay in such place as my wife shall think meet at his own costs' (1581).

Thus, in diverse fashion, many a man provides for his widow's domestic comfort or makes her lot less desolate. It is an agreeable feature of family life in a period when people see nothing remarkable in language such as that of John Potter of White Colne, who refers to his spouse having 'been to me a good, honest, faithful and serviceable wife' (1573).

Sedulously attentive in his mortal sickness as his wife may be, there looms before many a testator the prospect of her finding a second husband. This eventuality, if not actually frowned upon, may not be kindly anticipated. Our extracts, entirely representative, make this abundantly clear; but the milder clauses of course merely ensure domestic peace for the son and heir. There is little doubt that the proportion of widows re-marrying is high by modern standards and is presumably due, in an age when love is not a paramount factor in marriage, to their usefulness in so many ways beyond ordinary household duties. John Till of Goldhanger leaves his wife all his copyhold lands for life, 'making neither strip nor waste, or else if she marry to take her third and to go her way'

(1570). John Gilbert *alias* Hale of Fryerning, yeoman, is exceptionally demonstrative. He assigns to his wife Anne for her life his house called Knapps and land called Helders (copyhold of the manor of Ingatestone); but 'if she happen at any time hereafter to marry—the contrary whereof she hath firmly promised and vowed—then she shall have but a third part and to avoid immediately the possession to John my son' (1574). William Buntinge of Halstead allows his wife Ellen to have 'her chamber furnished, but my gift to be utterly frustrate, void and of none effect if she at any time hereafter chance to be married' (1598). John Bullocke of Great Wigborough stipulates that his wife 'shall have the north soller of my house for six months after my decease, provided that if she happen to marry before that time then she shall avoid my house and soller' (1561). John Spiltimber of Stambourne, husbandman, states that 'if my wife Christian do marry after my decease, then she to depart from my farm' (1573). John Brockas of Havering Green, who describes himself as a painter (1582) and leaves some religious books,[2] bestows the residue of his property on his wife, 'but if she marry, then all those goods that are appraised in the inventory shall be equally divided into eight parts, whereof five shall be unto my five children, viz, Abisaye, Achior, John, Edmund and Elizabeth, and the three to my wife'.

Safeguarding the children's future welfare, should the wife marry again, is not infrequently dealt with by her having to enter into a bond for ensuring that their legacies are to be paid at the age stated in the will. Jeffrey Maydestone of Marks Tey, for example, insists that if 'Emma my wife marry, she shall be bound to the headmen of Marks Tey in a sufficient bond to bring up my children' (1583).

The law allows a widow, as her dower, one-third of the husband's real estate for her life. Some husbands are more generous or offer an alternative. In an unusual phrase, Thomas Pakeman of Wrabness gives Margaret his wife £8 'for the third foot of my house and my land' (1558). Legacies of greater value than her right are generally conditional on her making no claim to her dower, or 'if she challenge any third or dowry or freeboard the legacy is void'. George Malle senior, a Hornchurch yeoman, leaves his wife for life 'her dwelling in the upper chamber and her necessary meat, drink, apparel, firewood and attendance, in consideration whereof she not demand her dower' (1575). William Glascocke, a Fyfield yeoman, gives his wife Thomasine 'the choice whether she immediately after my death she will take the use of my house and land or else to take her jointure in Dagenham' (1579). A few men insert a proviso that, if the wife is dissatisfied with a specific bequest, she may instead have her dower; or they may provide, as William Lyncolne of Great Burstead, 'in the name of her jointure, because she shall not claim the third of none of my lands and house, every year 40s.' (1560).

The possessions that a bride had brought to the home, becoming by law her husband's, are left to her in many wills. 'I give unto Joan my wife all such household stuff as she did bring unto me when I married her', used by John Langley, a Colchester clothier (1572), is a normal clause. Lists of goods made at the time of their weddings are remembered by two testators, who 'give' their wives 'all that was hers before I married her and that appeareth by an inventory' and 'all such household stuff as appeareth by an inventory made at our marriage'. What these were is not vouchsafed, but full details are recorded by John Smith of Great Birch, yeoman (1560): 'I bequeath to my wife all such things as she brought to me, namely':

> 2 beds with all the appurtenances, 5 kettles and 2 pans, 2 brass pots, 2 skillets, 2 ladles and a posnet, a chafing dish, 1 posnet, 1 dripping pan, 2 frying pans, 1 skummer, 2 spits, 1 latten basin, 1 pewter basin, 2 pieces of pewter, 3 pewter pots, and a wine quart, 1 salt cellar, 3 candlesticks, 3 drinking cruses and a jug, a dozen of round trenchers and a pair of querns for malt, a pair of mustard querns, 2 aletubs, 2 tables and 2 forms, 2 round tables, the hangings over the table in the hall, and 2 or 3 pieces of stained cloths, a cobiron, an andiron, 2 spits, a fire shovel, a pair of tongs, a kneading trough, 2 old tubs, a tablecloth, 2 pillowbeers, 2 great hutches, 2 little hutches, 2 alecups, a cradle, a sieve, a tub, a ladder, 2 wimbles, a chisel, a pulling hook, and addis, a shave, 2 percers and a hammer.

The unique phrase of Thomas Bell of Thaxted, yeoman (1591), runs, 'To my wife all my handsel stuff', a rare word which seems to mean in this context the gifts she had already received from him, or more probably his wedding gift.

## Children and other Relations

Leaving aside the truism that the larger landowners (whose wills will be dealt with in the next volume) concentrate on the heir, we shall now examine some of the various ways in which the less affluent parents provide for their children, especially minors. That their young children will receive maternal care and love is of course taken for granted by most husbands. More explicit is John Mann of Harwich, mariner, 'being moved by Mr Hugh Branham, clerk' (vicar of Dovercourt-with-Harwich) 'and others to make his will': 'I have told my wife my mind, she hath been a good mother to my children and she hath promised me to be a good mother to them still, and I refer all to her conscience' (1602). In a curious little document entitled 'Instructions for the penning of his will', Thomas Boosey of Broomfield determines that if his wife 'refused the children', then two relations should step into her place.

Not uncommonly an ardent wish is expressed that religious guidance will be given by the widow; but, somewhat naively, John James, schoolmaster of Billericay, among other men, in leaving her the residue of his property declares that the bequest is conditional on her 'bringing up my children in the fear of God as my trust is as a faithful matron' (1599). Apart from spiritual considerations, a minority of men specifically enjoin their wives to bring up the offspring, and a few include the eldest son or daughter in the responsibility. Thomas Rutter of Hockley 'on-the-Hill', husbandman, for example, states: 'My wife Anne and my eldest son John shall carefully bring up my other three children, James, Mary and Martha, with meet and convenient meat, drink and cloth (*sic*) till such reasonable times as they severally shall be able to earn their livings' (1584). In another case, William Stock of Prittlewell uses the expression, 'My mind is that my wife Elizabeth and my daughter Elizabeth shall be helping and aiding to my daughter Joan' (1595). Fuller provision is made by Robert Keble of Great Oakley (1564), who incidentally uses 'educate' in its early sense of bringing up:

> I do pray and desire and nevertheless charge and require William my son, by the bond of filial duty that he oweth to me, to be aiding his mother to educate and bring up my said children with the occupying of my stock, shop and slaughter house, William having a chamber in my dwelling house and having meat and drink convenient and receiving 4 marks by the year at the hands of my wife for his wages, so long as he keepeth himself a bachelor, yielding up unto his mother an account weekly of all such money as he shall weekly receive and informing his mother weekly of all such meat as he shall deliver without ready money.

John Pecke the elder, of Burnham, husbandman, hopes to ensure both material and spiritual protection: 'My overseer to give my children sufficient meat, drink, apparel, lodging and all other necessaries, and also virtuously and honestly to bring them up in some good and godly arts or exercises during all the time of their nonage' (1584). In more general terms, an executor may be entreated 'to be be good to my children', 'hoping that he will be good to my daughters', or the like.

Many men make specific legacies of money, goods, livestock or land with which their wives are to maintain the children. The amount may be relatively small. For instance, John Battell of Leigh, probably an ancestor of Andrew Battell, the seaman whose adventurous voyages to distant lands were to give Samuel Purchas much of his material, leaves his four children, Robert, George and Richard at 20 and Margery at 20 or marriage, '40s. apiece, and my wife shall have the occupation of this money till the time be expired' (1558). But Edward Mighell of West Ham, giving his two sons Jeremy and William £10 each, insists that, 'if my wife doth marry before they be 21 years of age, then she shall deliver the £20 into the hands of my brother John Mighell the elder and my brother-in-law John Cokes and my gossip (i.e. godfather) Thomas Harte, by even portions, to have the custody of the money' (1560). The usual method is to allocate the 'residue' to the wife, for example, in the wills of Richard Pyke of Foulness, fisherman, 'towards the bringing up of my little children' (1602), or of John Martyne of Little Clacton, husbandman, 'all my household stuff, a cow and a yearling bullock, upon this condition that she shall bring up my son George until he comes to the age of 14 years' (1587). Or a temporary legacy may serve the purpose, e.g. Thomas Sterne of Great Fordham, yeoman, leaves his wife 'all the whitemeat (i.e. cheese and other dairy produce) in my house, 10 bushels of wheat, 10 bushels of maslin and 18 bushels of malt towards the maintenance of the house and bringing up of her children until Michaelmas next' (1599).

Of interest for early American history is the will of Elizabeth Bond, a widow of Hawkwell (1602). The testatrix desires that 'Mr Adam Wintrope after my decease to receive all my goods and chattels and use the profits for the maintenance of my children and bring them up until they come to the age of 20 years'. She adds, 'I entreat and make my well beloved friend Mr Adam Wintrope of Groton in the county of Suffolk gentleman executor and give him 20s. and make Jonathan Clemence overseer'. She signs by her mark. The trustee is not one of the witnesses, who are Jonathan Clemence, Robert Sansome and Nathaniel Newman.[3] The will is dated 26 February 1601/2 and proved 5 March following. Adam Winthrop is the father of John Winthrop, destined to become 'the Father of New England' and the first Governor of the Colony of Massachusetts. John was born at Groton Manor near Sudbury, but is later associated with Essex. At the early age of 17 he married Mary the only child of John Forth of Great Stambridge; three years later in 1608, they went to live at her former home there.[4] Have we here, in Mistress Bond's will, Adam's first link with Essex—Hawkwell is only six miles from Stambridge—and is it possible that young John, when accompanying his father to Hawkwell, first met Mary? John's third wife, whom he married in 1618, was Margaret daughter of Sir John Tyndal of Great Maplestead, and John's son, also John, who became Governor of Connecticut, married Elizabeth Read of Wickford.[5]

The future care of four orphans is specified by Margery the widow of Tristram Cooke of Romford, whose relationship to Sir Anthony and Lady Cooke of Gidea Hall, Romford, has not been traced. In her will, witnessed by Richard Atkins, curate of Romford, and made on her deathbed (1563), she makes the following provisions :

> I bequeath the keeping of Edward my son to Mr William Cooke, and I ordain that my brother John Bright, my sole executor, do handsomely clothe and deliver him to Mr William Cooke and the bay mare. I will that Mr William shall have the custody of him and his lands till he be of lawful

age. I will that my executor clothe George my son handsomely and take him into his own custody to bring up in the fear of God and to see him taught to write and read, and to have with him one cow. I will that Dorothy my daughter do remain with my lady and my executor do give her at the years of discretion my wedding ring of gold, my new silk hat, two pair of silver hooks, one silver pin and my best cassock caped with velvet, and two of my best capkerchers. I will that Elizabeth my daughter be in the keeping of Mrs Flouere and that my executor do array her handsomely and deliver a cow with her to her said mistress and two hives with bees.

But whether the children will be orphans or maintained by their widowed parent, there are other aspects of juvenile care that are more suitably committed to one or more guardians (often appearing as 'gardener' and once as 'guider', curious contemporary spellings unnoticed by the *O.E.D.*). Executors are commonly given this responsibility, especially by widowers. Thomas Damote of Coggeshall, for instance, asks them 'to have the oversight, government and keeping of Edward my son at their charges till he be set forth to the occupation of weaving to some honest man' (1567). Thus an executor, or occasionally an overseer, is asked to undertake an additional duty, without necessarily being termed a guardian.

Guardianship may also embrace the custody of the children's lands, goods or money legacies; or, without any personal obligation for the 'bringing up', may be limited only to their possessions. The guardian is often expected to give security by a bond or asked to render an account yearly or at the end of his stewardship.

A few representative wills illustrate such arrangements. Robert Marshall of Stock decides that 'Thomas Osborne my son-in-law shall have the custody of Margaret my daughter with her part of goods until she come to a lawful age or be married, putting in sufficient sureties unto my overseers' (1562). 'If God do call me at this time', thinks Margaret Over, a widow of Barking (the plague had recently visited London and this part of Essex), 'my brother William Sharles shall be guider and keeper of my daughter and to have her stock in keeping until she accomplish the full age of 18 years and put in sufficient sureties to the overseers for the performance thereof; and if William do die before, then my brother Thomas to have the tuition of her and her stock' (1574). John Coker of Woodham Mortimer, yeoman, appoints Richard Wilkes of Boreham, his brother-in-law, 'to be the gardener, governor and co-adjutor of Ralph my son, as also of my lands and goods, till he come to the age of 20 years' (1595).

Both guardianship and maintenance are dealt with by John Hewson of Rayleigh, who gives '£12 to Sarah my daughter, to be paid to my well-beloved friend and cousin John Ballard to take upon him the custody of my daughter until she come to her full age of 18 years, and to find sufficient meat, drink and apparel, and he to have for her keeping 40s.' (1575). 'My especial and well beloved friend Davy Sympson gentleman' is to be the governor of the unnamed son of Anthony Graunthame of Canewdon, yeoman (1565); he is to be 'delivered when he shall accomplish the age of 5 years, well apparelled both with linen and woollen, to bring up my son till he be the age of 21 years'. Richard Harwood of Harwich, yeoman, asks 'Mr James Harvye of Wengie in Dagenham (i.e. Wangey Hall in Ilford) and Thomas Cooper of the same, high constable, to be gardeners to my children' (1591). Bennet Welche of Little Thurrock, husbandman, arranges for a man and a widow 'to have the governance and bringing up of my two daughters during their nonage, willing my daughter Joan to be placed in London with a mistress', and leaves 20s. to each trustee (1587). John Hore of Fingringhoe, mariner, provides a succession of guardians : 'I ordain Joan my wife to be governor of Alice my daughter, but if Joan die before Alice come to the age of 18 Benet Westwood shall be governor and gardener of Alice, and if he die John Pollye to be governor and gardener; and I will then that John Pollye shall not meddle nor have to do with Alice during the life of Benet Westwood' (1567).

Servants occasionally ask their masters to take charge of one or more of their children in various ways. John Gladdin of Nevendon desires that 'Mr Roger Braunch of Corringham my master shall be gardener unto William my son till he come to the age of 21 years' (1600). The will of John Welles, 'servant to Roger Amyce esquire', who does not give his abode but wishes to be buried in Wakes Colne churchyard, relies on his employers' goodwill : 'I give my daughter Anne unto my very good Mistress Margaret Amyce, praying her for God's cause and for charity, either to receive her into her own service or else to place her elsewhere as shall be thought meet unto her; also I give my son William unto Mr Israel Amyce to be brought up as to his discretion shall be thought best' (1574). Roger Amyce had been an active justice of the peace until 1569, and Israel his son, of Tilbury-juxta-Clare, educated both at Cambridge and the Middle Temple, was to become a J.P. in 1586 [6] as well as a notable land-surveyor and map-maker.[7] Or a child's legacy may be entrusted to the master or mistress, e.g. John Hodge of Little Burstead, cook, begs that his son Richard's 'portion remain in the hands and custody of the right worshipful my very good lady and mistress the Lady Petre till he accomplish the age of 24 years' (1600). John Bennet of West Tilbury dictates : 'I give to Lady Champyon one seam of white wheat, desiring her good ladyship to stand good lady and mistress to my poor infants as she hath been always to me, good lady. I commit the keeping of my two sons to my nephew Robert Bretton and my son-in-law John Asheley, that is John the elder to goodman Bretton and John the younger to Ashlie, whom I make executor to the use and bringing up of my children' (1568).

An unusual double responsibility is handed over by William Basewicke of 'Steeple and Stansgate': 'Forsomuch as my wife hath not the use of speech, I do desire my cousin John Basewicke of Stansgate, whom I make my executor, to take my wife and child to and in his keeping and governance, with such lands and goods as I am now possessed with, to see them honestly kept and my debts to be paid out of the same' (1578).

By English custom, as well as by the legal and logical principle of primogeniture, houses and land normally pass to the eldest son, and many testators dispose accordingly, either by specific devise or by his being named as the residuary legatee. But some decide to apportion their house between their children. Margaret Browne, a widow of St. Nicholas, Colchester, has a large house in St. Helen's Street. It looks as though her five children, three of them married, live with her, and she attempts to divide it into what we should term independent apartments or flats, and even assigns shares of the garden (1585):

> To my son John the hallhouse with the entry coming and going in and from the same; to my son Richard and Joan his wife the chamber over the parlour in which he now dwelleth for term of their lives; to Anne my daughter now wife of John Glascock of St. Osyth the kitchen and to her heirs for ever; to my son Oliver and his heirs for ever the parlour in which he now dwelleth; to my daughter Katherine now wife of Robert Symon of Colchester weaver the shop with the little buttery in the entry and to his heirs for ever. Provided that if any of my children shall not be contented with the division of the said tenement he or she shall have 40s. in lieu of their portion.
> My garden and backside to be also equally divided between my said five children in form following, whereas I have already divided the same by stakes, John shall have one of the knots within, Oliver the other, Richard shall have the green place by the knots whereon the peartree standeth, and the other green yard shall be equally divided between my two daughters, and the stony yard shall be equally divided between John and Richard.

Vertical division of his house into three dwellings is decided upon by William Clark of St. Osyth, carpenter (1585):

> To John my son the hall and the soller above the hall and two little butteries at each end of the chimney and half the ground. To Joan my eldest daughter the parlour and the soller above the parlour and a little buttery at the end of the parlour chimney and a little garden plot by the parlour. To Mary my daughter the backhouse and the two shops and the other half of the ground. I give a way for every of them to go freely to the well to draw water, finding part and part alike for buckets and ropes.

No instance of a second or third son inheriting the whole family house or all the land, if any, has been found. The allocation of the property, except for the widow's right of dower or a third of any real estate, is of course a matter for the testator. Relatively few decide on a physical division of their dwelling: instead, as we have seen, there is often a clause enjoining the heir or executor to provide houseroom for the widow and occasionally for the younger unmarried children.

An alternative method and indeed sometimes the only effective way of providing children's legacies or maintenance or paying debts is to sell the family home and divide the proceeds. The transaction is generally placed in others' hands. William Rychardson of Black Notley directs: 'If my wife depart and my son William die without issue, then my house be sold by the churchwardens and the money equally divided among my children' (1560); and so, too, John Thorne, a glover of Thaxted: 'My house and shop in Mill End and my barns, stables, malthouses, kiln-houses and malt sollers to be sold by the churchwardens and the money divided among my sons, Thomas, John, Daniel and Samuel' (1592). Francis Sprigge, a shearman, also of Thaxted, asks that his house 'be sold by the mayor and bailiffs or in default by the vicar and church-wardens, and the money equally divided among all my children' (1591). Having left his house to Agnes his wife as life tenant, William Underwood of Walden, who calls himself a musician, makes a similar 'humble request' to the treasurer and churchwardens of the town (1596). Robert Longley of Boxted, husbandman, however, leaves the matter open: 'My house to be sold and the money equally divided into five portions among my wife and my four children at their age of 21' (1588). Thomas Webb of Radwinter gives all his sons slight preferential treatment at the sale: 'After the decease of Jane my wife, my house shall be sold unto the most advantage by the consent of Mr Monford and Thomas Smyth of Radwinter Hall, and the value be equally divided amongst my five sons, i.e. my eldest son John and my youngest son John, Thomas, Nicholas and Edward, and if any of my sons be able to buy my house and lands I will that he shall have it 20s. better cheap than any other man' (1583). John Connye of Coggeshall, weaver, leaving to his wife his tenement in West Street (evidently near Paycocke's mansion), enjoins that, after her death, the house 'be sold to the best profit that may be made by two such honest inhabitants as shall be nominated by all other the greater part of my children' (1597). John Osborne of Stock, fletcher, requests that 'my tene-ment be sold by the advice of the one of the churchwardens of Stock and another of Buttsbury, and the money I bequeath to my three youngest children, i.e. Ellen, Thomas and John' (1574); and William Stucke of Rochford wills his house at Prittlewell 'in the lordship of Earls Hall' to his wife Helen 'for the maintenance of my children', and 'after her death it be sold by the churchwardens of Prittlewell and the money equally divided between my children' (1575).

To pay for the expenses of keeping large families one, perhaps two, Braintree inns are to be sold. James Wylkinson, innkeeper, gives the following directions: 'My inn called the George in Braintree to my wife

Elizabeth for 14 years after my decease towards the bringing up of my children; at the end of the term to be sold by John Lawrence, Henry Shepherd, John Spooner and Gabriel Joslyn or by the survivors and the money to be distributed to every of my eight children £12 at the age of 21 years. I give to the same eight children £28, besides the £12, at 21'. After leaving the residue of his property to his wife, he concludes: 'I choose my friend Mr James Hille vicar of Braintree and John Sorrell of Old (Great) Saling the elder as supervisors; and I will that my executrix (his wife) shall bring up my children to their several ages of 21 years' (1599). Two years earlier his inn had been burgled and he lost silver worth £9.[8] William Skynner, whose occupation is not stated, likewise devises to his wife Emme 'my house called the Angel for ten years after my decease, (then) my brother Richard Skynner and my brother(-in-law) John Worden to make sale of the house and the money to be equally divided among all my children part and part like' (1565). The plan resolved by John Steward of Great Dunmow, husbandman, is that after his wife's death 'all my houses be sold to the uttermost penny to any of these my brethren, William, Thomas or Miles, if any of them will buy, or if not to any person that will give most for them, and the money to be immediately after divided equally between the children of my brethren' (1593).

Many testators decide on equal sharing of their goods—among the children or among the wife and children. Where there is a large family, such division, e.g. of 'all my sheep and lambs', certainly eases the problem of trying to apportion them: 'All my household goods to be equally shifted between my daughters', or 'they shall have all my linen shifted between them'. Some leave the matter to impartial nominees. Having divided his chattels among his seven children, Philip Meadow of Elsenham decides that 'the overplus be divided among my children that have most need' according to the discretion of four named men (1572); and Daniel Garington of Mundon husbandman requests certain assets 'to be parted by the customary tenants of (the manor of) Mundon' (1602). Other arbitrators are appointed by Thomas Taylor of East Mersea, in a nuncupative will: 'All the goods be equally divided between Agnes his wife and Thomas his son by the discretion of some honest men of the parish' (1589); by Richard Mott of Rickling: 'All my implements of household shall be equally parted amongst my eight children by the advice of six of the honest men of the parish' (1562); by Christopher Orsone of Hockley: 'All my goods to be by indifferent men shifted in six parts and praised (appraised, valued) and divided equally between my wife and five children' (1583); and by William Love of Thaxted, labourer: 'The residue of my goods shall be equally divided amongst all my children, part and part alike, by the good discretion of Mr Mayor, John Same and Peter Purcas' (1583).

Agnes widow of Thomas Pamphylyn of Elsenham essays to be just to as many as nine children by her two marriages (1597). She begins: 'I give unto my seven sons Richard Barnard, Nicholas Barnard, William Barnard, John Barnard, Avery Barnard, Edmund Pamphylyn and John Pamphylyn and to Thomasine Barnard and Margaret Barnard my two daughters one featherbed, a mattress, 2 bolsters, 2 pillows, 3 coverings, 2 blankets, and the chest standing in the parlour, to be equally divided amongst them'. How this is to be done she leaves to her executors. Then, undaunted herself, she proceeds to list all her furniture, kitchen implements and tableware, also 'to be equally divided'. She even thinks of the cost of providing her will, and this too must be borne by equal shares. But, in the end, she apparently has some qualms and decides to placate her executors 'for their pains' by giving them 'such implements and hostlements' (see p. 10) as is unbequeathed and forgotten or not named'! But of course the most common clause is of the kind dictated by Henry Almon of Burnham, mariner: 'All the rest I will that my seven children shall have it part and part like and to be equally divided amongst them' (1581).

Other circumstances, such as the absence of a willing successor to carry on the trade, craft or farm, may lead to a sale of goods or livestock, as enjoined by Richard Yonger, a smith of St. Mary (Magdalene), Colchester: 'My shop tools which I have not otherwise bequeathed shall be sold to the most advantage of money to be equally divided among my seven children part and part like' (1571); or by John Harvye, a Little Bardfield husbandman: 'The bull shall be sold and the money divided equally by my executors among my children' (1596). Sale because of the testator being childless or having apparently no relations is a rare feature. William Lowys, a labourer of Great Clacton, leaves his cottage to his wife for life, but 'if she fortune to have no issue then it shall be sold by the churchwardens and the money I will remain in a stock to the use of the poor people of the parish for ever or otherwise to bestow the money on some piece of land' (1588).

A few testators entrust livestock to their wives or executors. Thus, Rose wife of John Jose of Little Burstead is to have 'my 10 kine and bullocks now on the ground and a score of sheep towards the bringing up of our children, provided that she deliver to my five children, William, John, Bridget, Joan and Isaac, a cow' at 21 or at marriage (1567); and Anne Releson, a widow of Little Bentley, directs her executors 'to have the wool of 4 sheep and their 4 lambs and the commodity (profit) of the 3 kine towards the keeping of Anne my daughter until the Michaelmas after my decease' (1581). John Frinde of South Benfleet passes to Joan his eldest daughter '6 theaves (ewes of the first year) and Thomas Ranoles shall have the custody of the same sheep and sell them to the most profit and behoof of my daughter' when she is 21 or marries (1581). 'To my son one cow called Red Ear, which I will shall be put forth to the most advantage for him until he come of age' is typical of several similar bequests, though 'a cow and its vantage' is the commoner term for the looked-for natural increase; or it may be 'a farmable cow' (one that can be hired out), or '3 good farmable kine'.

Who can be trusted with legacies which children may not receive until they come of age or marry? These questions are uppermost in many testators' minds. Generally they are left to the widow's, executor's, overseer's or guardian's discretion, but some are required to give security, enter into a bond, or render an account. A typical safeguarding clause is inserted by Richard Fuller of Wydoms in the parish of Romford : 'To Anne my daughter £7 at the age of 20 years or marriage, and whoso hath her keeping shall have the stock with her in occupying until she doth come to the age or marriage, and he shall put in sureties to my overseers for the deliverance of the stock and for the well using of the child' (1560).

If we have dwelt somewhat fully on restrictions governing children's legacies rather than on their positive benefits, it is because this aspect has been neglected by most writers, who have concentrated more on the general desire of testators to provide suitable marriage portions for their offspring, especially girls, or for their sons' advancement. We must therefore conclude this section by stating briefly that the last word in the ubiquitous phrase 'at 18 (20, 21, or older) or marriage' usually indicates the improving of nubile maidens' expectations; and, indeed, many would-be bridegrooms cast their eyes on the girl's prospective dowry in preference to their physical charms : all the more so if the yoke-mate is likely to have some land. "Tis to be feared'—the shrewd comment of the worthy Dr Fuller, parson of Waltham Abbey in the next century—that 'they that marry where they do not love, will love where they do not marry', would prove to be a woefully prophetic reality with more than a few land-hungry swains.

Little is known about testators' care for incapacitated children, so that it is interesting to find three wills, each showing concern for a daughter. Henry Nevard of Ardleigh evinces paternal consideration for his unfortunate daughter (1563) :

> To my daughter Grace all my houses and lands in Ardleigh, keeping herself and unmarried because she is blind. My son Henry to have the occupation of them on condition that he keep Grace his sister as well with meat, drink and clothing as also with fire, lodging and all other things necessary and meet as well in sickness as in health. And if she complain for want of sufficient meat, drink and other necessities by honest indifferent men, then my son John shall occupy my house and lands.

Thomas Stone of Little Bentley, yeoman, is more open-hearted : 'To Christian my other daughter, who being a lame and impotent cripple, shall honestly be provided for with sufficient meat and drink and also needful linen, woollen, hosen, shoes, lodging, washing and other things necessary' (1588). Joan Risson of Wickford, a widow, tries to defeat any sinister scheme which may prejudice her apparently mentally deficient daughter by a previous marriage (1567):

> provided that the legacy given unto Eleanor Harris shall remain unto her towards her keeping during her life, but if any shall for covetousness of the same goods make any contract to the intent to get the legacy, she being an innocent and not able to govern herself, then I will it be clean taken away by my executors and given unto my daughters Eleanor and Sarah Harris.

Two facts of Elizabethan society—the low average age at death and the high frequency of pregnancy—often result in a legacy to the unborn. But there are three imponderables. Has the wife actually conceived? If so, will the offspring be male? Male or female, will it survive infancy? 'The child my wife now goeth withal' is the usual phrase; rarer, 'is pregnant'; or more sanctimoniously, 'if it shall please God to bless and preserve in life the fruit of my wife's body'. It may be qualified by 'if a man child' or 'if it so fortune that my wife have a man child', when the dying father's last hope of a male heir sometimes leads him to give the infant a better chance in life than if the wife produce a daughter. Various provisions are made for the awaited baby, especially by landed owners without a male heir. Yeoman lessees of farms also pass the unexpired years of their lease to the hoped-for infant if it proves to be a boy. Sample clauses are: 'All my messuages and lands to my well-beloved wife for her life, and after her decease to the child now in her womb', or, on a humbler level, 'to the child that my wife now goeth withal two sheep, to be put to the most increase until it come to the age of 18 years'. Two of the three 'ifs' may thus be expressed: 'If my wife be with child, I give unto the child if it fortune to live £10'. The older as well as the younger generation are considered by Valentine Byndley of Boreham, husbandman (1587):

> My executors shall put forth £10 in stock to some honest person that will enter into bond to pay yearly to my poor mother for her relief and comfort 20s. during her life; and after her decease the 20s. to be paid to my wife for the bringing up of my child which she now goeth withal, if God shall give it life, until it come to 21 years or may be put to some honest service, at which time the £10 shall be delivered to his master to have the use thereof until he come to 21 years to use it himself; and if my said child die before 21 years, 40s. to my wife and other £8 to my two sisters Anne and Bennett.

Where there is already one or more surviving children, the new infant will probably be treated like the others. Geoffrey Cuckok, a Colchester baker, for instance, determines: 'To John my eldest son, Geoffrey, Thomas, John the younger, Francis, Nicholas, Rose, Susan, Prudence and

Mary and the child my wife is now pregnant with, to either (i.e. each) £20, to my sons at 24 years and to my daughters at 20 years' (1584).

A humanitarian aspect of Elizabethan society is the recognition by a few testators of their illegitimate children. Robert Ewen of Great Bardfield gives 'Richard Ewen my base son 20 marks at 21' (1587). Sarah Seabroke of Black Notley singlewoman leaves £5, 'due to her by her late father's will, to Mary Lawson, her base daughter' (1594); administration is granted to John Lawson to Mary's use. Joan Elie, a widow of Rettendon, bequeaths to 'Richard Kitteridge and Bennet Kitteridge, my natural children, 19 nobles', i.e. £3 6s. 8d. (1597). In addition to bequests to his wife and children, Humphrey Garralde of Downham gives 'Elizabeth my bastard daughter 25s. a year during the term of nine years', some linen, a hutch, 'and the bed I now lie in, also my cloak withal' (1601). Exceptionally, one testator—George Virlee of Brook Walden in Walden, carpenter—parts with the substantial sum of £10 to 'John Whitnie the base son of Thomas Whitnie gentleman' (1577). Thomas Whitnie senior of Brook Walden gentleman, although giving his four children very big cash legacies (1603),[9] makes no mention of John, and appoints as executor his brother, also named Thomas, for whom no will exists. Three other cases may possibly relate to bastards but are more probably examples of kindness to orphans. Clement Cokoe of Great Clacton : 'I will that, if it shall please God to call me betwixt this and Allhallowtide, my executors shall provide and buy for little Gye the fatherless infant a grey frize coat, a cotton petticoat, two shirts, hose and shoes, which if I live shall be provided by myself' (1588); Alice Sorrell of Chelmsford : 'I will to Joan Watse, a poor girl that I have brought up and now dwelling with me, 40s., and my cow that I have going with Mr Longe', linen, a great kettle, a few clothes, and a ring (1587); and Edmund Beaumond of St. Osyth husbandman : 'I give to Mary Norman whom I have brought up from her childhood £10 at her age of 20 years' (1582).

Mothers' comfort and convenience, too, are attended to in a few wills. 'Even in the Middle Ages', writes a recent historian, 'provision for aged parents sometimes required additions or divisions of the house'.[10] Two men, perhaps both mortally sick and certainly anxious about their mothers who will probably outlive them, plan for their being looked after. James Riddlesdale of Little Clacton thus exhibits his love : 'As touching the maintenance of mine aged mother, I will that she shall remain and dwell here during her life, and I do allow her out of the yearly revenue of my lands as shall be thought needful in sickness and in health, and that no man shall here inhabit but such a one as will condescend (i.e. agree) to have some honest and careful regard to see to her daily in this her extreme age and necessity' (1600). One man voices his hope briefly : 'My son to be good to his mother and his sisters and brother'.

His mother-in-law is the concern of Reynold Willsum of Great Warley, husbandman: 'To William Reeve of Finchingfield, my brother-in-law, £30, on condition that he help Joan Reeve of Abbess Roothing my mother with meat, drink and apparel and all other necessaries which are fit for a woman of her degree and calling' (1597).

Sisters rarely get much consideration. Roger Smythe of Matching, bachelor, will enrich his sister with 'one table with the frame and one bench and form standing in the hall, if that she match herself with some one honest man whom my mother and my brother shall take liking of, (but) if she do contrary to their minds, then I bequeath them to Mary Smythe, my brother Michael's daughter' (1594); John Goodyeare of Mucking enjoins his wife 'to see Margery Goodyeare, my poor sister, honestly kept during her life with meat, drink, cloth and other necessaries' (1576); and John Pecke senior, a Burnham husbandman, provides his sister with 'four of the best lops yearly growing in the tenement for her firebote and as many furzen (i.e. gorse) as she shall need for her fuel, and yardroom to lay her wood and fuel' (1585). A brother is expected to look after himself as regards houseroom. Only once is he specifically offered 'lodging' in the testator's house, and that only 'if he behave himself'. Exceptionally, Bennet Welche of Little Thurrock, husbandman, leaves £8, 'to be distributed among my brethren and sistren (a late instance of its use) at Upminster' (1587).

Apart from normal legacies of household goods, cash and perhaps a few animals, little thought is bestowed on daughters after 18, 21 or marriage, when they usually become payable. Life for ageing spinsters in Elizabeth's time can hardly be regarded as other than dreary. Susan the daughter of Edmund Watkynson, a North Benfleet yeoman, is the sole recipient of fuel—'one old or reasonable tree to the use of logs yearly' (1591). Clearly, adult daughters are expected to leave home for domestic service elsewhere if not already employed. Unique direction is given to the wife of William Sledd, a Harwich shipwright (1603). Thinking on his deathbed of his step-daughter's needs, that he should 'not leave her fatherless and motherless, he caused Anne his wife to be called to him by Susan, which he had by his former wife', and by his nuncupative will gave Susan a posted bed and a trundle bed.

Grandchildren are remembered by quite a number of men and women. Amy Pease, a widow of Great Baddow, is surely a proud granddame. She leaves 6s. 8d. each 'to John, William, Robert, Ralph and Priscilla Pease, the children of my son John; to William, Grace, Thomasine, Amy, Margaret and Alice Bickner, sons and daughters of my daughter Bickner; and to Thomas, Anne and Amy Stamer, the children of my daughter Stamer' (1589). Unwittingly she may also earn gratitude from some of her descendants trying to trace their family history.

Bequests to godchildren frequently figure in Elizabethan wills—usually not more than a few shillings, or not uncommonly a lamb; one favoured godson gets six lambs. George Ridge of Walden, husbandman, gives 'all my goods to my goddaughter Grace daughter of Gregory Swallowe of the same, tailor' (1598); and John Blosson, late cook of Thomas Tirrell of Downham (p. 129), bestows as much as £3 on his godchild (1586); but these are unusually generous. William Cocke junior, a mariner of Paglesham, has four godchildren, viz. 'a girl of Dixon's, John Clerke's girl, a boy at Baker's, and John Crowche William Crowche's son', each of whom gets 10s. (1583). As many as ten godchildren benefit by a shilling each after the death of Hugh Maddocke, curate of Berners Roothing (1573). We often find small legacies 'to every godchild that bears my name'; once 'to every of my godchildren that be unmarried'; and once 'to every of my godchildren, if they can say the Lord's Prayer'.

## Disputes

In all ages some testators reveal anxiety about possible dissension arising from their wills. Others debar beneficiaries who will appear to their executors to be dissatisfied, e.g. 'If any of my children be not content with their gifts or go about to make strife or trouble, then my will and mind is that their legacies be clearly void'. Equally common is the sort of threat to children not likely to get on with their widowed mother. Jacob Ashlye of St. Leonard, Colchester, shipwright, for instance, ordains: 'If my sons Jacob and John do molest my wife wrongfully and contrary to this will for that land, then my gift to them shall be void' (1595).

A long will made by Thomas Wackefeilde of Radwinter husbandman, one of Harrison's flock, provides elaborate safeguards against matters going awry. 'If any of my children', he lays down, 'molest, trouble or vex my wife for any such bequests and will not be contented but seek strife and discord, to be utterly void of my bequest or gift, the one half to be divided amongst the rest of my children and the other half to the poor men's box in the parish of Radwinter'. He names as his executors John Coote his son-in-law and Thomas Wackefeilde his brother's son, to each of whom he gives 10s.; and if either should refuse, then Edward Mondeforthe should be an executor; and he names Thomas Mondeforthe gentleman as supervisor. Finally, 'if there fortune any controversy to fall out betwixt my wife and my children or between my executors and my children, then they shall be ruled by my supervisor. And I trust to God they will be without vexation, trouble or expenses in law' (1569). It is unlikely that Harrison drew up this will, as he is not one of the five witnesses, but it was proved a month later before him as the Archdeacon's surrogate at the Saffron Walden court.

Let us now see how the Elizabethan testator tried to forestall trouble caused by insubordinate children. Hugh Gryffen of Tolleshunt Major, husbandman, leaving his son Michael £20 to be paid at 21, adds (1559) : 'But if he will not be ruled and ordered by my executors and other his friends, then he shall not receive this my legacy until his age of 24 years'; and his two younger sons each get £10 'in like manner'. His attitude to his daughters, who will each get £30 at 20, is : 'If they marry before, having the consent of their mother and her friends, then they have it at the day of their marriage'. William Gates of Paglesham, yeoman, extends a gratuity for good conduct (1584). Assigning to his daughter Barbara 40 marks at 21 or marriage, he offers that, 'if she shall tarry till the same age of 21 or be ruled by the advice of my overseers, then I will her portion be amended to £30', i.e. an extra £13 6s. 8d. Stricter clauses are found in two men's wills. John Spiltimber, a Stambourne husbandman, dictates (1573) : 'I will my three daughters to continue to dwell with their mother so long as they be unmarried, and if any shall be stubborn, froward and wilful and will not be ruled, then that party so offending to depart and go away and to be allowed 12d. a quarter to help her in her service wheresoever she shall be placed, and yet to have her part (i.e. a quarter of all his goods) in the end nevertheless'. Anticipating trouble, the legacy that Edward Newman of Greenstead-juxta-Colchester, sailor, gives to his son is 'on condition that it be seen he is become reformable and obedient to his mother and a profitable member in the commonwealth' (1584).

Hoping to control the behaviour of his children after his death, Thomas Cottysforth of Tolleshunt D'Arcy, yeoman, inserts some severe disciplinary clauses in his will (1588). The £30 legacy to his daughter Mary is conditional on her dwelling with his son John in the testator's leased house called Langbrokes until she is 23 or married. Then mildly demanding that John shall provide sufficient food and drink for Mary, 'she behaving herself cheerfully and lovingly as a sister ought to live with a brother', he proceeds :

> Provided always that if my son shall neglect or refuse to live in the fear of God by haunting or using of any suspicious company or by wasting of his goods unlawfully by neglecting of his business in his vocation that God hath and shall appoint him unto, or procure his discredit any way (and being duly proved), and John will not, upon lawful admonition by four of his neighbours, namely Henry Eustace, William Belvis, John Tyll and John Bushe or the most part of them, be reformed, being by them lawfully warned two several times at the least, that then my will is that, upon trial by these men made or so many of them as shall be then living of any such abuse or offence, my son shall pay £40 equally to be divided among so many of three daughters' children as shall be then living, part and part alike. Item, my will is that, if any of my three daughters, being lawfully warned and forbidden by my supervisors, shall at any time attempt to steal, convey or embezzle any of my goods to my son before given, and the same being duly proved, they shall lose the benefit of the goods.

He appoints his son as his sole executor, Thomas Page of Peldon and John Fowle of Tolleshunt Major, his sons-in-law, as his overseers, giving them each 'a colt of two years old and the vantage' (i.e. profit), and the four neighbours, who are also the witnesses, as 'overseers to my son in his conversation (i.e. behaviour) only'.

With contrasting terseness, another man threatens 'whosoever of my two daughters breaketh concord shall lose two acres of land', thereby perhaps bequeathing his executors a ticklish problem.

Juvenile marriages are not common in Elizabethan times. 'Demographers have estimated that most brides wedded between 20 and 30 and most grooms between 25 and 30'.[11] By contemporary custom children are expected to accept their parents' arrangements for suitable matches, though this is applied more rigorously by the landed families, as we shall see when dealing with their wills in the next volume. While clauses such as 'To each of my daughters £5 at the age of 21 or at the day of their marriage, whichever be the sooner' are very common, a few parents leave nothing to their daughters unless they wed. Nothing, too, if they, or even sons in rare instances, commit themselves without the approval of their widowed mother, relations, executors or guardians. Witness what a stern Flemish father, Theodorus vanden Berghe, probably of Colchester, has to say (1598):

> If my beloved wife Elizabeth remains unmarried, she shall give to our four children which are yet unmarried, namely Samuel, Tobias, Mary and Elizabeth, £25 each at the day when with the good will and consent of their mother they shall give themselves to marriage or when they come to years of discretion. But if it should chance (which God forbid) that any marry without her consent, they shall lose the right of their portions.

Freedom in the choice of husband is also barred by Katherine George of Abberton, widow: 'I give to my daughter Martha £10 upon condition that in her marriage she be ruled by her uncle and her aunt' (1573). A legacy of £6 13s. 4d. (i.e. 10 marks) with various articles of furniture is to go to each of his eldest and two younger daughters, Mary, Agnes and Elizabeth, under the will of John Palmer of Tolleshunt Major, husbandman, 'at the day of her marriage, if she marry to my wife's mind, and if not then to have it at the age of 24' (1584): a measure without parallel in our wills.

Precautionary steps against the mother-in-law syndrome are taken by some men. Thomas Estwood of East Donyland, sailor, determines: 'If it please God to move my son to marry, and his wife and Margery my wife cannot agree together, then I give to my wife my house during her life and a new chimney to be set at both their charges for a better quietness of my wife, and to have the one half of the occupying of the fish houses and my son Edward the other' (1597). Robert Frend of Great Warley, husbandman, gives his mother 'a yearly pension of 4 marks to be paid quarterly by my wife, upon condition that she meddle not with the house which was her father's but suffer my wife quietly and peaceably to enjoy the same' (1587). Fears of similar domestic disturbance influence two more testators. One, after planning that his wife is to stay with his son, adds: 'And if she shall mislike and not be contented with her diet or any other thing', then the son is 'to pay her £5 a year on her departure'; and the other provides for 'what time she shall refuse any longer to dwell with my son'. Trying to smooth his wife's relations with her brother-in-law, John Bawden is apprised by Richard Bawden of Hornchurch: 'My will and pleasure is that he shall have his lodging in my house as before, so long as he behaving himself honestly and quietly it shall stand with my wife's good liking, otherwise to depart at her warning forthwith' (1588).

Expressed in more general terms are the doubts of a 'Dutchman', Nicholas de Hane the elder (probably of Colchester): 'Forsomuch as right and reason requireth that every one to whom the uncertainty of this life is known should endeavour to his power to leave no occasion of dissension among his heirs and successors' (1585); and of another man: 'Remembering the brittle and uncertain estate of this life and for the avoiding of discord and contention which among my children may happen to arise after my decease'. Gratitude as well as grief are recorded in the nuncupative will of Thomas Thomsone of Prittlewell, husbandman: 'I did lend to Thomas Harckewood of 'Wylde' (North or South Weald) £7; he hath been a very good friend to me, but my brother hath alway been my enemy and driven me to this hard state that I am now in. I will (if it please God to call me away to death) frankly and freely forgive Thomas the £7' (1590).

## Education and Books

While we may imagine the sort of teaching given by Shakespeare's 'pedant that keeps a school i' the church', it is not always easy to distinguish in wills between formal schooling and being taught to read and write by the village dame, the vicar or curate, or merely at home. The word 'education', in fact, has a double meaning in our period and the context may not indicate which is intended. Appearing in early Tudor times, it originally denoted a child's being reared or 'brought up' by food and clothing, by parental instruction in manners, or both. To provide means for maintenance is clearly the aim of Robert Keble of Great Oakley whose stock and shop are left 'to educate and bring up my children' (1564) and of Thomas Rawlins senior of Stock, brickmaker, who leaves 'two beasts, two bullocks and a mare only for the education and bringing up of my two sons' (1580). But there is ambiguity in that of Matthew Dale, a substantial yeoman of East Hanningfield, who entrusts 'the guardianship and education of my two sons to my brother John Hunte leatherseller and my cousin William Poynter mercer', both of London (1586).

Whether having first received some schooling or not, a relatively small percentage of boys get 'technical' education through a period of apprenticeship, but the majority remain bereft and go early into service in a craft, trade or husbandry, while most girls go into domestic service; nearly all, male and female, live in their employer's household. Virtually every mention of maintenance, schooling or academic education arises from the testator's expressed wishes or instructions to wife, relations, executors or supervisors; but, as we shall see, references to daughters' education are very rare. Richard Purcas of Thaxted, yeoman, leaves to his (eldest) son Ralph £10 at 21, or else to be laid out in the hands of some honest man under whom he shall be learned and brought up, putting in good assurance for the same, and my mind is that Ralph shall be kept at school one year after my decease' (1576). Provision is thus, as in other cases, in general terms: John Gooday of Coggeshall, for example, asks his wife 'to bring up both his sons in learning and to keep them at school' (1566); or executors may be required, for instance, to bring up a testator's two sons 'some year or two at school to increase their learning'.

Occasionally the leaving age or time is given. Richard Hart of Rickling, husbandman, appoints his brother(-in-law) Thomas Pamflyn as guardian to his son Thomas, to 'keep him with all necessaries and at school and learning till the age of 14 years' (1596); Robert Hubberd of Theydon Garnon, yeoman, leaves his wife £5 'towards bringing up my son at school to the full age of 16' (1599); and Henry Bonner of Chadwell writes, 'I charge my wife Joan that my two eldest sons Henry and Richard be kept to writing school for one year after my decease' (1589). Elizabeth Bylles of Thorpe gives 'to John my youngest son £6 to find him to school, and I will that my executor see him honestly arrayed both for holy day and working day. I will that he shall be put to board with my younger brother and to go to school at Bury' (St. Edmunds, Suffolk), apparently because her son-in-law, Robert Lunt, lives there (1561).

Two documents are of interest in giving, if we understand them correctly, the contemporary cost of feeding, clothing and generally 'bringing up' of a boy. Edmund Stamer of Little Warley, yeoman, provides: 'My wife shall have the bringing up of my son till he come to the age of 13 years, and my son's guardians shall allow her £3 yearly till he come to the age of 8 years and then till he come to 13 years £4 13s. 4d. yearly, so that she keep him to learning if he profit herewith; if not, my will is that he be a prentice to some good science, and he to have for his maintenance 20s.' (1594). The cost is broken up in the administration account (a rare survival for Essex) of John Barnes of Stansted Mountfitchet: 'Allowances demanded—for boarding and finding with meat and drink of Thomas my son for one whole year after my decease at 2s. the week £5; for his schooling for one year 10s.; for double apparel of him when he was bound apprentice 26s. 8d.' (1588).

The cost of education may be met out of a special fund. The wife of Thomas Merke of Langenhoe is to have certain lands, the income from which will keep his son Thomas 'to school to learn to write and read' (1559). 'My executors to sell all my goods, corn and cattle and make thereof a stock of money and to have the occupying thereof for 12 years for keeping my son John at school' is the intention of Thomas Martyn of Moze (1561). William Butler of Hawkwell husbandman bequeaths to John his brother 'all my goods and chattels upon this condition that he shall bring up my son William virtuously with good and godly education, and he to be taught to write, read and cast accounts, giving him £6 13s. 4d. at the age of 21 years' (1589). An interesting discovery shows that John Walker of West Hanningfield, the now renowned estate mapmaker, is left the house of Thomas Gilbert, a fellow parishioner, 'until such time as my son Thomas shall come to the age of 21, on condition that John Walker shall see Thomas virtuously and honestly kept and brought up in all things to him needful, as well to write and read as also to be taught and instructed in some honest trade or occupation whereby he may hereafter get his living'; and Walker is also appointed sole executor (1597).

Ability to cast up their own accounts and to ascertain the extent of their profits or losses is becoming an increasing need among farmers and tradesmen. Proficiency in the forerunner of the '3 Rs' (reading, 'riting and 'rithmetic) is therefore the basic requirement of such utilitarian education in many fathers' eyes. John Edwardes of Foulness island asks his son Edward 'to bear the charges of my son Michael's schooling until he can perfectly write and read and cast account' (1581); John Sawkyn junior of Goldhanger, husbandman, directs that his son Anthony be 'set to school to learn to write, read and cast accounts' (1594). But arithmetic is not demanded by Edward Man of Woodham Ferrers: 'I will that my son John be well educated and brought up with meat and convenient food and raiment and also in learning until he be able to read any English and written hand and to write well and legibly' (1600); a competence that William Stowe of Great Holland also desires for his youngest son William: 'to school till he can write and read written hand well' (1591). John Hayle the elder of Romford, who is to be the guardian of the children of John Marvyn of Ramsey yeoman, is to maintain them and 'to bring them up in the fear of God and with learning to set them to school till they can write and read English well' (1571). The religious aspect of education is thus frequently in evidence, especially in the wills of puritan-minded testators. Classical learning, however, finds favour only in that of Thomas Wood of Chelmsford, 'chirurgeon'. His wife Joan is to have his house and also one at Widford for life 'on condition that she bring up his son Tiberius at school until such time as he shall perfectly understand the English and Latin tongue and shall find him meat, drink and apparel fit and convenient for his calling', and he is to have £20 at 18 (1602).

Maintenance probably for a young relation is arranged by Joan Lacy of St. Osyth, a widow, who requires that 'John Cole shall keep Bartimeus Baxter and to set him to school to be learned to write and read and find him meat, drink and lodging until he be ready to go to service, John being paid for his learning or discharged from the teacher and paid 4s. a month for his meat and drink' (1598). Some testators are more specific. Richard Sandoll of Stanford-le-Hope yeoman wills that 'my wife shall bring up my children Richard and Thomas to school to learn to read, write and cast accounts and (then) place them with some honest men to learn some good art or science with which to get their living another day' (1580); and George Cuper, a millwright of East Mersea, wishes that 'my son George to be in the keeping of my brother(-in-law) Robert Halles, to keep him at school and to some good science to get his living, giving him (Halles) for his pains and charges therein £13 6s. 8d.' (1585).

'To place' or 'to get his living' of course normally refers to apprenticeship. William Gates of Paglesham yeoman directs that 'my brother-in-law shall have the bringing up of my son Richard to writing and reading school until he shall be meet to serve as an apprentice' (1584); and Thomas Andrew of Collier Row in the parish of Hornchurch asks his executor to 'set his son to school until such time that he be able to earn his living and put him prentice to some honest man' (1582). A cleric is entrusted with the private education of William Hills' son of Fobbing: 'My son William shall be with Mr (Philip) White parson of Fobbing, and his stock with him for the use thereof to bring him up withal in learning both to write and to read, and when he cometh to the age of 14 or thereabout then to bind him prentice in London with one Mr Young grocer or some other honest and godly man' (1586). Incidentally, we may quote here a clause in the will of Thomas Thorpe, 'minister dwelling in the parish of Great Burstead': 'I will that Mr Hawkyne minister shall pay unto his son Thomas Hawkyne the 6s. 8d. that he oweth me for schooling' (1570); 'Mr (Thomas) Bryce, parson of Little Burstead' is appointed supervisor of the will. Often neither schooling nor apprenticeship is specified, and the legacy is merely 'towards the bringing up of my two children until they shall be able to shift for themselves'.

A bequest of equipment to a child may be useless unless he can be instructed how to operate it, hence the provision by John Torner of Stansted Mountfitchet: 'To John my youngest son a pair of looms which are here in my house, and I will that my son Thomas should have the occupying of John's looms till he be 10 years of age and then if John will go to that occupation my will is that Thomas shall teach him' (1578).

The natural desire of many craftsmen, especially those who have built up a good business, to pass it on to one or more of their sons is evinced in other ways than leaving them their implements. Robert Allen of Ridgewell, who calls himself a husbandman, devises his house 'to remain to my son Edward upon condition that he be a chandler and follow his occupation' (1597).

University education for Elizabethan boys is of course not restricted to the upper classes; and here we may explain that university is a not uncommon contemporary meaning of 'school'. John Woode of Kelvedon *alias* Easterford leaves 'to William Wentford my kinsman, being a poor scholar of Cambridge, £4, to be paid to him towards his exhibition in two years, i.e. 40s. in one year and 40s. in another year' (1564). Thomas Salmon of Doddinghurst bequeaths 'to my son Thomas £5 at 21 and £20 to keep him at the school at Cambridge, and my executor shall keep him there at the school these four years and pay for his board these four years' (1581); and Alexander Wallforde of Shalford, yeoman, states that 'my wife shall yearly pay to my son Richard to keep and maintain himself at school in the University of Cambridge or elsewhere £10' (1580). Also referring to university education are the wills of Henry Cocke of Henham : 'to Henry my son £20 to the keeping of him to school' (1568); and of Robert Fenner of Halstead, clothier : 'to my son Peter £20 within five years after my decease by the yearly payment of £4 towards his exhibition and finding at school and learning' (1569). Richard Simson of Brightlingsea, yeoman, stipulates : 'To Esdrau my son £30 to be delivered to my supervisors, who shall bestow the £30 in training and bringing him up in learning at Cambridge or otherwise, according to their discretions'; but has second thoughts about leaving the decision entirely to them and indicates his own preference, 'but rather to learning' (1575). Thomas Woodd of Beaumont has clear ideas about his five sons' future. 'Thomas to be kept to husbandry. Robert to be brought up in learning so as if his capacity will serve him he may be a Master of Arts. Richard, John and George to read and write perfectly and cast accounts both with pen and counters. And if Robert happen to die before he be a Bachelor of Arts, then Richard shall be brought up in such sort' (1591).

Girls' education is of relatively little account. Few are taught to write. We quote the only four references in the entire series of the non-gentry wills. Jeremy Pavett of Great Dunmow, yeoman, provides for the 'bringing up in learning' of his daughter Anne till 16 (1590). John Smithe of Tillingham, husbandman, leaves £5 'to bring up and instruct my daughter in learning, both of the Book (i.e. the Bible) and also in sewing and some other profitable exercise whereby she may be able in time to earn her own living' (1583). On a slightly higher level Richard Hayward of Messing, yeoman, directs Grace his wife 'that she carefully bring up my daughter in setting her to school' (1585). In the much longer clause in the will of Ursula Kilby, a widow of Barking, it is doubtful whether 'education' has its modern sense : 'I devise the custody and education of my daughter Katherine to my dear and good friends Mr John Searle of Westbury gentleman and his wife, beseeching them that they will see her maintained and brought up as to their godly wisdom shall seem best, appointing my late good mistress Mrs Fanshawe to be made acquainted with their purpose from time to time how they shall appoint my daughter to be brought up, using her advice therein' (1591). In nominating John Searle as her sole executor, she 'beseeched him to bestow the said money to some profit towards the maintenance and education of my daughter, so as the remain shall be the greater to her at her marriage or at the age of 21'.

If, according to Aubrey the antiquary, Norfolk farmers carried a copy of Littleton's *Tenures* at their plough-tails, at least one Essex yeoman is found to own a copy, but he is exceptional, and our wills reveal little beyond spiritual instruction being sought in the printed word. While it is a truism that the only, if any, book possessed by the great majority of Elizabethans is the Bible, the oft-repeated bare mention of 'my Bible' may be slightly amplified by such bequests as 'my psalter book' bestowed by Richard Payne of Doddinghurst on Robert Browne the vicar (1571) or 'two books, viz. a testament and a psalter in English and two prayer books' (1603).[12] Apart from service books, there is the occasional mention of religious commentaries and books of sermons. Conditional gifts of two books are made by John Brockas of Havering Green, painter (1582) : 'To Samuel Brockas one Paraphrase of Erasmus on the Four Gospels and the Acts of the Apostles, in consideration that he shall be good to my wife and to the rest of his brethren and sister after my decease or else it shall be in my wife's power to give or retain the same if he be not good to them. To Richard my son one Bible translated by Miles Coverdale' (which had been first published in 1535,) with the same proviso. Arthur Newman, a Rayleigh tailor, leaves his son 'my bible and my book of Mr Calvin's Sermons upon Job' (1587); Alice Billing, a Leigh widow, gives another copy of the same work, 'my great new Testament' and 'my Great Bible' (usually denoting the translation of 1539) to her three children (1600); and Stephen Commynges, a Barking fisherman, bequeaths 'one English book of Mr Becon's work' (1588), Thomas Becon (1512-67) being a protestant divine. With religious spirit John Sommerson, husbandman of Great Birch, divides his books among his children, to be handed over by his executor as each reaches full age : 'To Tobias my bible; Robert one testament; George another testament; Peter my book with clasps; Elizabeth my book called The Governaunce of Vertue; Margaret my double psalter and my broad service book' (1573).

In the next extract (1591) 'Mr (George) Gyfford' is the well-known puritan preacher of Maldon : John Tayler of Asheldham, another husbandman, hands on 'to my son Ralph my bible and Bunnye (Edmund Bunny, 1540-1618) his Resolution and a Commentary written by Marten Luter upon the Galations, and a book of sermons written by Mr Gyfford upon Ecclesiastes, and a book called the Governance of Virtue', also at 21.

After the Bible, Foxe's *Book of Martyrs* is generally regarded as the most commonly read book in our period—only to give place in popularity to Bunyan's *Pilgrim's Progress* a century afterwards. Henry Wode of Prittlewell mentions 'my book of the Acts and Monuments of the Church' (the correct title of Foxe) and 'my little bible' (1582); and Thomas Hastler of Rettendon, yeoman, leaves his Book of Martyrs and his Geneva Bible, first printed there in 1560 (1582).

Four of the devout Flemish settlers in Colchester pass on the means of spiritual guidance. Nicholas de Hane gives his godson 'a new testament bound in board' (1584). Francis van Pradeles bequeaths to a young female cousin '7 great books, i.e. a bible, the Harmony of Calvin, the Commentaries of Calvin, the Decades of Bolingery, the Institution of Calvin, the Exposition of Bolingery of the Revelation, and the Book of Martyrs, to exercise herself therein' ! Not a case of

> Come and take choice of all my library
> And so beguile thy sorrows.
> (*Titus Andronicus,* IV, i, 34-5).

Nor is there any choice in the distribution by John de Roode of Messon (Meessen) in Flanders among his eight children (1593) :

> To John the Exposition of the five Books of Moses in the French tongue; to Samuel the Harmony upon the Four Evangelists and the Acts of the Apostles also in the French tongue; to Nathaniel the small bible and the book of Mr Calvin's Institutions; to Abigail the bible with the black cover; to Mary the bible with the red cover; to Sarah the Decades of Mr Bullinger with the Exposition upon the Psalms of David made by John Pomeranus; to Hester the Exposition upon the Apocalypse written by Mr Bullinger, the Book of Martyrs and the six books of Mr Bullinger against the Anabaptists, and the History of Josephus; and to Judith the Exposition of Mr Calvin upon the Epistles of St. Paul and the Disputation against the Anabaptists.

Finally, the inventory of John Soones of St. Giles, Colchester, reveals '2 Dutch bibles, Bullinger's Decades and 3 Testaments' (1602).

Apart from religious works, books prove to be only a minor feature of ordinary laymen's wills, but of course the illiteracy of most of the Elizabethan people is fairly well known. Thomas Pakeman of Wrabness, yeoman, leaves 'all my books which are in my study' to his son Christopher (1599), and another yeoman refers to 'a chest and all the books that be therein', and a smith leaves 'my books'. Thomas Andewe of Prittlewell, who does not give his occupation, bequeaths to his son Geoffrey 'my Latin bible and all my Latin books' (1578).

Coming to named books, the result is disappointing. John Truelove of Hornchurch, who calls himself a yeoman, leaves in addition to his bible 'these books : Littleton's Tenures, The Office of Justice and Balifes, The Doctor and the Student, The Pommander, and Alphabet of Prayers, and all the rest of my books' (1574). But, despite his being apparently a man of some standing (his other legacies include bow and arrows and even a lute), he does not seem to occur in any other records; he is certainly not a J.P.

The names of medical treatises are absent from the few relevant wills. Robert Searle (of Walden?) bequeaths to his son 'all my books appertaining to the science of surgery; also for other Latin books as a bible and such other I give to Robert my son' (1588); and John Evered, who gives neither abode nor vocation but whose stills and mortars suggest that of the apothecary, leaves his son John 'all my books, English and Latin' (1586). Although only a husbandman, the legacies of John Arsonne of Theydon Bois (1589) include 'my great chronicle called Fabian's Chronicle' —the famous *New Chronicles of England and Wales*, printed in 1516.

The seven clerical wills that mention books may be briefly quoted in order of date. John Lamkyn, vicar of Shalford : 'to the parish church of St. Leonard of Shalford all my books and ornaments that are meet for the said church' (1560); Alexander Gate, 'parson of Bosvile portion of Springfield' (one of the two moieties of the rectory) : 'books upon the Scriptures belonging to divinity' (1560); William Bettes, 'parson of Wivenhoe' : 'to my wife's two sons Paul Browne and John Kervyle, to be equally divided, my two books which are in French, Calvin upon Job and upon the Small Prophets, all other books to my wife' (1570); William Atkynson, rector of Nevendon : 'to John Cox, curate of Ramsden Bellhouse, my dictionary called Elliot's to Robert Freman, parson of Ashen not far from Stock (Stoke-by-Clare, Suffolk) College, 'my book called Concordantia Biblie' (1570); Robert Kneight of Great Ilford, clerk : 'to Master (William) Richardes my master, parson of Little Ilford, my book entitled Destructorium vitiorum and his own book Lyra upon the Four Evangelists, and Paul's Epistles' (1571); William Squire of Great Ilford, clerk : 'Cooper's Dictionary and Hewlett's Dictionary' (1588); and Thomas Hawlkins, curate of North Ockendon : 'to my son all my books' (1587).[13]

## Apprentices and Servants

As the Essex wills give virtually nothing about apprentices' instruction, we will link them with Servants rather than with Education. Thomas

Swetinge of Margaretting requires that 'my son John shall have the bringing up of my son Edward seven years to be his prentice in the fear of God' (1590). William Baylye, a Finchingfield blacksmith, leaves £10 to Henry his younger son, of which £5 'shall be to bind him apprentice to some good occupation at his age of 13' (1578). The legacy given to his son Richard by Richard Peacocke of Lambourne, glover, is conditional on the son's paying to 'Mr Butcher of Lombard Street in London, now his master, the £20 I promised him for taking my son his apprentice' (1593). Sensibly, a legacy may not be due until the term has been served : 'To my son', John Mede of Ugley dictates, 'a cow farmable' (i.e. that can be hired out), 'to be paid as soon as he come forth of his prenticehood' (1576); when similarly, by a mariner's bequest, there will accrue, 'my wearing apparel to my two sons' (1575). Morris Davison, a Chelmsford ostler, wills : 'To my brother(-in-law) Griffin Daved, apprentice to George Knight of Chelmsford, shoemaker' (whose own will was to be proved 20 years later), '£15 to be paid at the end of his apprenticeship and all the overplus that shall come and grow thereof during all that time', indicating that the money was to be put out to interest or other use. Alternatively, a legacy may be paid in two instalments, as arranged by Edward Finch of Fryerning, butcher : 'To my son £10 and another £10 when he shall come out of his prenticeship' (1595). Robert Peacoke of St. James, Colchester, carpenter, gives 'to Thomas my son all my working tools if he go to the science of a carpenter when he hath served his apprenticehood' (1577).

Other apprentices, not being related to the testator, are sometimes remembered. Robert Munson of St. Osyth, yeoman, leaves two of his apprentices 20s. and a third 40s. Faithful apprentices may become the owners of some or all of their masters' tools or goods. 'All the rest of my carpenter's tools to be divided equally betwixt my two prentices' is the reward given by Edward Nycholas of Chelmsford, carpenter (1589). Margaret Daniell of Great Wakering bequeaths 'to John the son of John Daniell of Sandon, my late husband's prentice, all my goods', and he is to be her sole executor (1592). William Skott of Maldon, barber-surgeon, helps to set up John Kemydd his apprentice with '20s., a case of knives, a comb, a pair of scissors, and a washing basin' (1583). Clothes, too, are sometimes left to them. 'To John Watson mine apprentice a pair of russet hose, which were my late husband's' (Margaret Willoughbye of Barking, 1583); 'To John Spryng my prentice 6s. 8d. and the breeches which be on my legs and the white stockings which I have on' (John Phyeff of Walden, cordwainer, 1603); 'The rest of my clothes which I brought to sea, to my father to give to his prentices' (Thomas Thorne of Manningtree, 1589). A former apprentice is remembered by Richard More of Braintree, tailor : 'To Anthony Todd, my late apprentice, my candlestick, my shop board and one stool, all in the shop' (1587). A little bribe (but the sum is left blank) is offered by Thomas Damote of Coggeshall : 'To John Evanse my prentice so that he tarry to comb the wool that is in my house' (1567). William Gyrten of Inworth, weaver, commands his wife 'to perform the covenants betwixt me and Thomas Shere my prentice, upon condition that he doth his service to my wife' (1559); and Stephen Mumford of Colchester, musician, directs that Nicholas Hunt his apprentice be provided for 'as I am bound to do by a certain indenture' (1594). Richard Ailet of Kelvedon, yeoman, by a codicil, asks that 40s. 'be delivered to one Edward Nevell, tailor, of Galleywood End (in Great Baddow) to take Richard Tabor his nephew apprentice to learn his occupation' (1585). Roger Fisher of Ingrave seems to be referring to an indenture, and the only mention of a maidservant's : 'I will that my wife see Joan Garroll my maid brought up until she be married or come to the age of 21 years and pay her at her marriage or at 21 4 marks according to the obligation which I stand bound in' (1573).

About three hundred testators, excluding the gentry and the richer yeomen and merchants, are found to have made bequests to their servants. The legacies may be as low as '12d. to every servant that dwelleth with me'—even so, perhaps equivalent to £10 or more in current (1975) money. The commonest figure is 3s. 4d. (quarter of a mark). A more generous provision is that of £3 made by John Buckley, a Barking tanner, to 'Ellen my servant' (1587) or by William Jennyngs of Matching, yeoman, to 'Joan Perse my servant £3 6s. 8d. at the age 20 or marriage' (1576). Among the biggest gifts of money noticed are £6 given by John Condall of Romford to 'Edward Rushe my servant' (1560), £6 13s. 4d. (ten marks) left by William Everard of Great Waltham to 'Richard Lyngeye *alias* Carter my servant' (1571), and a similar sum is promised to 'Margery Saward my servant at her marriage' (1573). William Leape of Wivenhoe, who terms himself a sailor, allocates £5 to be shared equally among his seven named servants, who may perhaps be his ship's crew (October 1588); had they possibly seen action against the Armada three months earlier?[14] Cash legacies often take the form of 'to every of my serving men 10s. apiece and my maidservants 5s. over and above their wages'. A bequest of £12 by Hugh Maddocke, curate of Berners Roothing, to 'Margaret Davye widow, my servant,' at the rate of 10s. a year, is in effect almost an annuity; she is also his residuary legatee.

More often servants get clothes, or clothes and a little cash. Robert Abbot, a Maldon baker, for example, asks his wife to deliver 20s. and a cassock price 20s. to one maid and a similar bequest to another, but not 'if they pre-decease her or depart out of her service' (1574). Likewise Alice Hurrell of Sible Hedingham, a widow, passes on 'my woollen apparel on this condition that she continue with me a dutiful servant during my life' (1603); and a similar proviso, 'if she stay with me all her life', occurs in another will. Joan Lytham, a Hornchurch widow, rewards her servant with 'my least kettle and my cassock which is unmade and the petticoat which she weareth on holy-days' (1571); 'Rebecca the girl of my house' gets a red petticoat and two lockram kerchers; a third employer dictates, 'I will that my servant be well apparelled and to have 10s.' John Ayers of Brightlingsea, yeoman, presents 'Ede my maid' with '10s. and her mistress' black morning gown which is of grograine and her grograine kirtle '(1585).

To the present-day reader the strangest legacies to servants are livestock : 'To Margery my servant my little black sow'; 'A lamb to every of my servants', five of them employed by alderman William Mott of Colchester (1562); 'I will to Bess my maid four sheep'; 'To my servant a lamb or 20d. the price of a lamb'. The nursery rhyme is to become a fact to one wench by the will of George Lentton of South Benfleet, who gives 'to Mary my master's maid, one lamb', which is followed by, 'To goodwife Charvell all the lambs' wool that I have' (1575). Henry Overeye of Dagenham gives 'to Dalle my maid and to Roger my boy to each of them a lamb with the keeping of them all the winter next following' (1562).

Unusual generosity is shown by William Stileman of Ulting yeoman : 'To Mary my servant a new chest and all things therein as it is locked, my best cloak, my feather bed with the best coverlet, the best brass pot, 2 new pewter platters and a chafing dish, 2 beasts, a bullock and a brown cow', not forgetting the beehives noticed under Food. One farmer's maidservant is remembered with 'one half quarter of barley'; another's manservant with 'my sword and buckler and 40s. of good money', and 'Robert my servant and apprentice' with 20s. A servant of Robert Newman of Great Clacton receives a good bounty. He enjoins his son 'to keep with convenient meat, drink and apparel Joan Hunte my servant during her life, and, if she shall overlive him, then to have 20s. and a cow, a bedstead, a flockbed, a coverlet, 2 blankets and a bolster' (1574). Benevolent maintenance is provided by William Lambe of St. Nicholas, Colchester (1574), whose trade or occupation is not given : 'To Humphrey Curryn my servant 40s., to be paid to any honest man whosoever will take him for 9 or 10 years as his apprentice or covenant servant and teach and instruct the same child in some good occupation or science whereby he may be able to live hereafter'; such a master is however to put in sureties for its proper fulfilment. Lambe also leaves him 'the posted bedsteadle standing in the chamber over the parlour, with a featherbed, bolster, pair of blankets, coverlet and things belonging'.

The plan of Michael Archer senior of Mistley, 'To Alice Saunder my girl that I kept for the town, 1 milch cow and 1 bullock of 2 years old and more and 2 sheep, to be kept for her use by my son until she come to the age of 24 years' (1575), is paralleled by that of Lancelot Ree of Chigwell, 'To Joan Mott my servant 1 sow pig and 1 ewe and a lamb, and the same to be kept and bred up for her best behalf during the time that she dwelleth with my wife' (1582) : a kindly looking ahead and a shrewd lien on their continued service—the Tudors were ever practical-minded. Likewise Thomas Binckes of Panfield : 'To Frances Alvin, my goddaughter and servant, £5 so that she be so faithful and diligent in her service to me and my wife as my wife and Roger Carr, parson of Rayne, approve of the same, and if they do not approve of her service to be faithful for the years she is bound to me I will that she shall only have 40s.' (1590).

Religious sanctions are imposed by William Gardiner, a Langham husbandman, on a girl about to go into service : 'To Beatrice Ford a calf to be weaned the next year and to run in the ground free until it be a cow and then she to let it out to her best advantage, conditionally that she learn the Ten Commandments and other principles of Christianity and behave herself honestly and obediently to her master and dame' (1578).

It is pleasant to find how many remember their companions in service. 'To my fellows in my master's house 10s. each' or thereabouts is a clause seen in at least twenty wills. 'To all my fellows and maids 5s. apiece' is left by John Tanner of Chigwell, himself a 'servant with Mistress Anne Stonarde' (1587). By her nuncupative will, Margaret Lichoras gives nearly all her goods (probably of little value) to Frances Elvey, 'her fellow servant unto Henry Appleton esquire' (J.P., of Jarvis Hall in South Benfleet) (1588).

Reynold Willsum, a Great Warley husbandman, gives the poor 40s. and a similar sum 'to Anna Drywood my dame, being my whole half year's wages'—not a cynical reminder of wages due, because he asks William Drywood of the same parish, gentleman, evidently his employer, to be overseer. He then names no less than eight 'fellow servants' (five male, three female), each of whom benefits by 3s. 4d. (1597). Thomas Wortham of East Hanningfield, husbandman, leaves 'to my fellow servants 5s. apiece (two names) and to the residue of my fellow servants which shall be in my master's service 12d. apiece' (1602). John Mellar, 'brewer, servant with George Bigges of Dedham', wants 'William Greive, his fellow servant, to have his best doublet and his venetians 5s. better cheap than any other man, they being (ap-)praised' (1586).

'I Thomas Docker have owing to me £20 for my half year's wages of my master Mr Thomas Tey esquire I lent my mistress at Layer Hall' is the unusual clause found in a superior household servant's will (1574). The nuncupative will of John Blossom, 'late cook to the worshipful Mr Thomas Tirell of Fremnels *alias* of Downham esquire', reveals how he disposes of his possessions (including £3 in gold to a godchild), 'reposing his trust in his friend and fellow Peter Snowe to take some pains for him' (1586).

A little sidelight into the Leighs Priory household reveals John Green of Little Leighs, cook and servant of the right honourable the Lord Riche, giving 'to David servant to my Lord and master in his kitchen 5s.' (1574); John Hodge of Little Burstead, cook, sets aside 5s. 'to my fellow servants in household at Ingatestone as shall take the pains to carry me to church', Lady Petre being his mistress (1600); and Richard Gaedge, 'servant to the right worshipful Sir Thomas Lucas, knight, of St. John's (Abbey) besides Colchester', leaves 3s. 4d. to 'the boy in my master's kitchen' (1603). In his brief nuncupative will, John Buckler, 'servant to the right honourable the Earl of Sussex', gives 'to John chirurgeon (surgeon) to the Earl of Sussex' 20s. and 'to Edward of the stable 5s.' (1601).

Five more wills, covering the whole of our period, illustrate upper servants' sincere or sycophantic regard for the gentry. Master or dame must not be omitted. Robert Robinson of Havering-atte-Bower, 'servant with the right worshipful Sir Edward Waldegrave, knight', leaves 'to my lady my mistress one old ryal; to my master Sir Edward my young bay gelding that is in Havering Park' (1559). John White *alias* Parker of Downham, 'servant to the right worshipful Sir Henry Tyrrell knight' (of Heron Hall in East Horndon) offers his compliments widely among the family: 'To my master 3 angels of gold, also to my master's son and heir Mr Thomas Tyrrell 20s. in gold or silver. To Mrs White of Hutton an angel and an half-angel. To Mrs Pascall of (Great) Baddow an angel and an half-angel. To Mrs Moone, my master's daughter, an angel and an half-angel and a sheep with 2 lambs. To my master's son John Tyrrell 6s. 8d. To Mrs Gertrude Tyrrell and Mrs Thomasine Tyrrell 6s. 8d. each. To Mr Thomas Tyrrell of Gyffordes (in Runwell?) an angel and an half-angel' (1572). William Smyth of White Notley bequeaths 'to my very good friend (and loving young master *struck through*) Mr John Rochester of Terling, my master's son, an angel of gold to help make him a jewel' (1588). John Alders of Danbury, 'servant to the right worshipful Mr Humphrey Myldmay' (of Danbury Park) dictates: 'I will special gloves be provided for my good master Mr Walter Myldmaye and my good mistress and my good friend Mr Pickeringe, if it please them to wear gloves for my sake' (1592). Finally, we quote from the same will of Richard Gaedge, Sir Thomas Lucas's retainer: 'to the worshipful Mr John Lucas esquire 40s., to Mrs Mary Lucas the daughter of my good master 20s. in gold; to Mrs Katherine Farmer who is now attendant upon my good lady and mistress 20s. in gold' (1603). All five, at any rate, have paid their respects.

More than once we see how a master or dame is the chief or sole beneficiary—'to my master all my goods and chattels', or is even the residuary legatee, as in the case of George Bigges just quoted. But the legacy may be conditional or qualified. Witness what Roger Norman *alias* Reynolde, servant to John Wyseman esquire, of Great Canfield, has to say: 'To all my fellows now servants with my said master 4d. apiece. To Mistress Margaret Wyseman my mistress, for divers good considerations me thereunto moving, all my house and grounds in Great Dunmow to her and her heirs for ever. The residue to Mr John Wyseman, my master, for to see my debts paid'; and he is named as sole executor (1579). Frequently, in fact, a superior, and occasionally a menial, servant nominates the master as an executor, doubtless with prior approval.

---

[1] Used in Kent (Halliwell, *Dict. of Archaic Words*). [2] See also *E.L.: Morals*, 185.
[3] Indexes to printed sources and the E.R.O. indexes yield nothing about the witnesses, apart from two facts: Jonathan Clements appears as sub-tenant of a messuage called Salmons at Hales in Hawkwell, 1607 (D/DHt T52/5) and as a freeholder, 1617 (Q/SR 217/95).
[4] *Ess. Rev.*, lviii, 58-63. [5] *Ibid.*, xvii, 1-11.
[6] *E.L.: Disorder*, 86, 110, 176, 289, 322.
[7] Emmison (ed.), *Catal. of Maps in E.R.O.*, esp. revd. reprint edn. (1969), xi.
[8] *E.L.: Disorder*, 269.
[9] P.C.C., Montague 29 (now P.R.O.).
[10] W. M. Barley, *The English Farmhouse and Cottage* (1961). [11] *E.L.: Morals*, 3.
[12] For books read, see J. B. Black, *The Reign of Elizabeth* (1936), 240-55.
[13] *Ralph Josselyn's Diary* (Camden Soc., 3rd. ser., xv).
[14] Wills of the clergy were mostly proved in the Consistory court of the Bishop of London, now in the Greater London County Council Record Office. It is remarkable that William Harrison, 'official' (i.e. deputy) of the Archdeacon of Colchester as well as historian, mentions neither legal nor literary works in his will.
[15] In 1582 Wivenhoe had nine ships, all under 80 tons (*V.C.H., Essex*, ii, 276).

# 7
# Weapons and Armour[1]

Although the ordinary weapons carried by Elizabethan civilians and soldiers are fairly well understood, the Essex wills illumine some of the lesser known details and even fill in a few small blanks in the broad picture.

Excluding esquires and gentlemen whose wills are not dealt, as always, with in this volume, the number of testators who mention weapons or armour amounts to 139. An analysis gives the following figures:

Swords, 34; rapiers 12; daggers 20.
Bills 2; pike 1; javelin 1; halberds 2.
Calivers 3; dags 2; handguns 2; fowling pieces 2.
Body armour 10.
Bows 48.

In some wills it is of course impossible to tell whether the weapons are for military or private use.

Dealing first with the former, the year before Elizabeth's accession saw the passing of two statutes for England's defence—for Arms and Armour and for Musters (4 & 5 Ph. & Mary, cc. 2, 3). Every adult male of substance was obliged to furnish horses and specified arms and armour in accordance with his status; those with goods worth between £10 and £20 had to provide 1 long bow, 1 sheaf of arrows, 1 steel cap or skull, and 1 black bill or halberd; and every parish became responsible for supplying armour and weapons for the other men and for storage in the church. In 1560 there were stolen from Feering church 4 calivers, 4 powder flasks and touch boxes, 5 swords, and a dagger, for which the thief was undoubtedly hanged.[2] A few later lists of armour kept in churches have survived in Essex parish archives.[3] The Maldon borough records include a list of 78 men assessed in 1569 for 'finding and maintaining 2 corselets furnished, with 2 pikes and 4 harquebuses furnished, with 4 morions' (vizorless helmets) assessed by Lords Rich and Darcy, commissioners for armour in Essex; also the names of the gentry and others, personally liable in 1573, e.g. 'W. Twedie gent. (rated at) £8, 1 coat of plate furnished, 1 black bill or halbert, 1 long bow, 1 sheaf of arrows and 1 steel cap or skull' and 'W. Vernon gent. (William Vernon, one of the bailiffs) £10, 1 almain rivet, coat of plate or brigandine furnished, 1 harquebus, 1 morion or sallet, 1 long bow, 1 sheaf of arrows, and 1 steel cap or skull.'[4] In the State Papers are preserved for various years certificates for each county of the number of able persons and horses and the number and kinds of armour and weapons chargeable under the Act, but without personal names, set out under each parish.[5]

Despite the emergence of fire-arms, Sunday practice at the archery butts with the longbow—the erstwhile pride of English victories over the French —was still obligatory. Although the longbow was already on the decline as a really effective weapon in military campaigns, another statute of 1571 enforced the importation of bowstaves, usually of yew (English yew not being good enough for the best bows).[6]

The Elizabethan fire-arms are the (h)arquebus or haquebutt, the caliver and the musket, the pistol and the dag, and the handgun. The harquebus is a gun supported on a stand and the caliver a light sort of musket; neither harquebus nor musket is found in the Essex wills, but the former, 'charged with hailshot', appears in a disseisin indictment of 1586.[7] The dag is a kind of heavy pistol. A caliver is mentioned in the inventory attached to the will of John Dyer of Great Maplestead (1570). John Pepper of St Mary-at-the-Walls, Colchester, yeoman, leaves his 'caliver with the furniture' (1593), and Richard Fytche of Steeple Bumpstead his 'caliver with flask and touchbox (i.e. primer) (1602). Robert Spenser of St Osyth, servant to Lord Darcy, bequeaths to Henry Atkins, the house-steward, 'one dag which is now in my chamber' and to his brother Richard his sword and dagger (1582).

Turning to weapons for private use, Parson Harrison says: 'Seldom shall you see any of my countrymen above 18 or 20 years old to go without a dagger at least at his back or by his side. Our nobility wear commonly swords or rapiers, as doth every common servingman that followeth his lord and master'.[8] Doubtless echoing his own fears in travelling about the north Essex roads, the perils of which the Quarter Sessions rolls illustrate by their unique details of highway robberies,[9] Harrison then describes the piked staves, up to fourteen feet long, carried by many, especially robbers and thieves: 'By reason of this, the honest traveller is now enforced to ride with a case of dags at his saddlebow or with some pretty short snapper (handgun)'. And in a later passage he says: 'No man travelleth by the way without his sword or some such weapon with us, except the minister, who commonly weareth nothing at all except it be a dagger or hanger (short sword) at his side'.[10]

Using a more recent composite work, the extracts that follow are from the pens of three different authorities. Writing on costume: 'A broadsword or dagger was the invariable equipment of every ordinary man. At the beginning of Elizabeth's reign even agricultural labourers, when at work, put down in a corner of the field their sword, buckler, and bow'.[11] On weapons: 'The Englishman's ordinary weapon in civil life was the back-sword or single-edged sword, which with the buckler' (the latter held in the left hand) 'was the national weapon until the thrusting rapier was introduced in Elizabeth's day, much to the disgust of the old-fashioned folk'.[12] On the Elizabethan Age generally : 'Young gallants practised much with the "dag", or pistol, and gave up the old-fashioned sword and buckler in favour of the newer, more stylish, and deadlier rapier. Young men of good position went armed in the streets, quarrels were frequent'.[13] Of these, there is ample evidence in our first two volumes. Many men sported both the right-handed rapier and the left-handed dagger, point upwards to ward off or to hold the opponent's weapon.

Among the many bequests of bladed weapons, sword or rapier is indeed often accompanied by buckler or dagger. Apart from such common items, we may cite 'my backsword and dagger' (1590), 'my Scottish dagger' (1592), and 'my dagger with black silk handle' (1566). Harrison's dictum that a few clerics carry a dagger is confirmed by Thomas Thorp, 'minister dwelling in Great Burstead' (apparently not the vicar), who refers to his dagger (1570), and by William Squire of Great Ilford, clerk (evidently the chaplain of Ilford Hospital or almshouses), who writes, 'To John Allen of the Crown (inn) my gilded dagger and knives as I now wear them, desiring him to wear them for my sake' (1589). Of composite references we find 'cloak, rapier and dagger, bows and arrows' (1600); 'all my longbows and quivers and all my arrows, also my buckler and my gauntlet', left by Charles Dabbs, notary public, to Francis Newman, tailor, both of Chelmsford (1588); and Thomas Coulson of Walden, 'servant to the right honourable the Lord William Howard' (of Audley End) directs that 'the rapier which my lord and master hath lent me shall be restored to his honour again' and also leaves to a fellow-servant his dagger and his 'crossbow and the rack and fowling piece' to others (1587).

A legacy of 'my bow and arrows' is very commonly met with, varied occasionally with 'bow and shafts', 'bow and quiver of arrows', 'long bow with sheaf of arrows and four shafts', or 'bow, bow-case, and quiver of 20 shafts'. Once we find 'an English bow and 16 arrows with a quiver' (1571); 'my best bow with the best sheaf of arrows' or 'my longest bow and my shortest bow'. Stephen Cannon of Foulness bestows on John Kirby, his father-in-law and sole executor, 'for his pains one bow and half my quiver of arrows' and on John Cannon, his brother, 'another bow and the other half quiver' (1573). John Barret of Little Thurrock, husbandman, leaves 'one ewen bow sinewed (i.e. of yew, strengthened) at the back, and 10 new shafts, or 6s. 8d. in money, and my other ewen bow and 10 shafts or else 6s. 8d.' (1600).

The longbow was being replaced in sport—and poaching—by the crossbow, 'handgun', fowling-piece and birding-piece.[14] Specific mention of crossbows is somewhat infrequent. John White *alias* Parker of Downham, servant to Sir Henry Tyrell of Downham, leaves 'my crossbow and all that belongeth to it and my long bow and arrows' to 'Mr Thomas Sandell' (1572). John Peacocke of High Ongar goes into more detail : 'To Mr

John Morris my crossbow with a windlass and a crossbow with a rack'.[15] Another man gives his son 'my tiller bow and all my arrows' (1585); the *Oxford Dictionary* defines tiller as the 'stock or shaft to a long bow to admit its being used as a cross bow, for greater convenience or precision of aim'. Richard Gemmynges of Romford, fletcher, passes to his son Nicholas 'my new bow and a dozen of arrows and a sheaf of strand heads' (1562). Both Francis Quick of Aveley, innholder (1590), and Humphrey Frith of North Ockendon, yeoman (1591) refer to their 'shooting bow and quiver'. One labourer, John Becke of Langdon Hills, mentions his bow, arrows, quiver and pikestaff (1590).

While some wills refer merely to 'my armour and harness', or 'all my armour', we quote most of those giving details. As to defensive equipment, that curiously archaic term, almain rivets—a kind of flexible light armour made of overlapping plates sliding on rivets, and, as the adjective denotes, first used in Germany—is commonplace in Elizabethan wills and muster rolls; corselet is the alternative word for body armour. We find : 'one pair of almain rivets' (John Byrde the elder of Ingatestone, yeoman, 1574); 'my almain corselet with the whole furniture that it hath, that is, sword and dagger, and all my arrows (Edward Crefeilde of Messing, yeoman, 1579); 'a caliver, two sheaf of arrows and bow, an almain rivet' (Andrew Brette of Great Burstead, wheelwright, 1582); 'to my son Edward an almain rivet with a bill thereunto belonging' (Joan Kinge, a Dunton widow, 1583); 'to my son William all my part of the corselet and armour which I have for service of the Queen's Majesty' (William Sturgen senior of Great Baddow, 1596); 'to my son John my coat of plate and my almain rivet with bill, sword and dagger thereunto belonging, and to my son Richard my war bow with sword and dagger furnished' (Richard Skott of Gosfield, yeoman, 1599). Robert Dunt of Romford, innholder, who leaves 'my shirt of mail', is the only testator to refer to it (1560), plate having virtually superseded mail (1560). As we do not deal with the wills of the gentry and the rich yeomen in this book, we find no other mention of plate-armour except in that of a yeoman of moderate means, viz., William Glascocke of Fyfield, who hands down to his son William 'two coats of plate, the best bow with the best sheaf of arrows, the best two gorgets (pieces of armour to protect the throat), the best sword and dagger, and the two steel caps' (1579). The gradual displacement of body armour owing to the improvement of hand firearms belongs to the end of our period.

Finally, a few miscellaneous extracts. Richard Bright of Great Warley, yeoman, refers to his 'sword, dagger, girdle and skull (i.e. skull-cap), a bow with a sheaf of arrows hanging in the hall, and one almain rivet hanging in the hall' (1572), and Richard Cotman of Plaistow in West Ham, bricklayer, to 'my new halberd that hangs in my hall and my little black Scots dagger' (1591). Thomas Harrison senior, a yeoman of Walden, possesses a 'harness girdle with three knops of silver and gilt' (1587), and Thomas

Walker of Chelmsford, baker, has 'one arming sword with a close halter' (1603). Here is the assortment distributed among his friends by Anthony Claxton, who fails to give his abode and rank (1600): 'To my son-in-law William Collard my sanguine [16] rapier and dagger; to Paul Smythe my russet arming sword and dagger, girdle and hangers; to my loving son(-in-law) Richard Scott my best armour, my best pick (pike?), my best musket with flask and touchbox; to his father Mr Scott of Barnston my grey hobby (i.e. horse, probably Irish-bred); to Mr Arthur Gregory my best crossbow and stonebow; to Samuel Ridley my russet [16] graven sword and dagger; to Thomas Collye of Ware (Herts.) my sword that he wore in Ireland': the only and very faint echo of arms used in warfare.

Pursuit of game is well illustrated in the will of John Andrewes of Creeksea, single man. He is careful to direct that 'my horse which my master, his worship, gave me, with my crossbow, arrows and other furniture and implements belonging to the use of the park, do return again to my master', who is not named but is clearly Arthur Harris, the active J.P. of Creeksea Place. Roger Martin of Walden refers 'the flourbow of 8s. price and the crossbow of 6s. price' (1598). Thomas Lok of Marsh House in Thorpe (1559) and Thomas Pakeman of Wrabness (1599) each has a 'handgun', and Thomas Viccars of Woodham Ferrers 'a gun, a javelin and best sword' (1592); all the guns perhaps being used for coastal or creekside wildfowling. John Gore of Great Bentley, husbandman (1596) and John Warden of Romford, yeoman, both own a 'fowling piece', and Thomas Standly of Widford, glazier, a 'birding piece' (1588). 'My gaming bow and shafts, my wardbrace[17] and my shooting glove' are given by Richard Justice of Mundon to his brother (1586). 'Pellet bow' (1581) is not represented in the *O.E.D.* until three centuries later, the pellet being described as a lump of hard clay. The caliver, too, is sometimes used for sporting purposes.

---

[1] I am grateful to Mr M. R. Holmes for kindly reading this section and for correcting and amplifying several passages; see notes below.

[2] *E.L.: Disorder,* 279.

[3] Emmison (ed.), *Catalogue of Essex Parish Records* (2nd. edn.), 17.

[4] For military weapons, see Harrison, *op. cit.,* 233-35; for details of 16th century body armour and armourers, see C. Blair, *European Armour* (1972), 112-40, 188-90. and M. R. Holmes, *Arms and Armour in Tudor and Stuart London* (London Museum, 1970), which includes a few items 'from an old farmhouse near Ongar'. On the Maldon borough extract Mr Holmes comments: 'Pikemen had to do hand-to-hand fighting, so they are equipped with corselets, while the four arquebusiers, operating from a distance, need only steel-caps in the way of defensive armour'.

[5] See *Calendar of State Papers, Domestic;* photostats of the Essex certificates are in E.R.O., T/A 407. For a sample full transcript, 1558, see J. C. Cox, *Three Centuries of Derbyshire Annals* (1890), i, 129-45.

6 On the decline of archery, see Harrison, *op. cit.*, 234-5.
7 *E.L.: Disorder,* 124.
8 Harrison, *op. cit.*, 237.   9 *E.L.: Disorder,* 180-3, 272-7, and appendix A.
10 Harrison. *ibid.*, 238.
11 *Shakespeare's England,* ii, 112.   12 *Ibid.,* i, 131-2.   13 *Ibid.,* i, 12-13.
14 *E.L.: Disorder,* 234-41, 254.
15 Mr Holmes explains: 'They wound up in different ways, one by a rack-and-pinion arrangement, the other by a hook and pulley'.
16 Mr Holmes kindly explains: 'The word *sanguine,* when applied to armour, denotes a certain amount of artificial oxydization induced partly for ornament and partly as a protection against rust; another popular colour was *russet,* a warmer red rather like a horse-chestnut—in your context it may refer to the blades or, quite possibly, to the hilts, of the sword or dagger in question'. In general, Mr Holmes adds: 'the various items found in the Essex wills might be required as (a) part of a gentleman's ordinary dress; (b) necessary, or at least advisable, when travelling; (c) useful things to keep in the house as a defence against robbers, if one had a large, rather isolated, farmhouse'.
17 Mr Holmes writes: 'Wardbrace (or garde-bras), generally known as a bracer, strapped to the left forearm to protect it from the friction of the bowstring on discharge'

# 8
# Deathbed and Probate
## *Sickness*

To most Elizabethans living outside the big cities neither doctor nor hospital is normally available. Instead the sick and dying who cannot call on relations are attended by a friend or a 'keeper', who may be rewarded or reimbursed. Here are a few representative extracts from deathbed testaments. William Godfri of Wrabness bequeaths to 'my hostess Deacon 20s. and my chest and clothes, in consideration of such kindness and friendship as she hath showed me in keeping me in her house' (1584). Michael Manners of Boxted, by his nuncupative will, declares: 'All other his worldly treasures he did give to John Creathorne the younger, his master's son, for the great pains that he did take about him during his sickness; to Margaret his keeper for her pains, 3s. 4d.' (1602). Thomas, 'servant unto the right honourable Lady Winifred Hastings', gives 'the poor women and men which have watched with me and taken pains in my sickness, for every day and night 6d.' (1583). William Ganslitt of Lawford, singleman, leaves to 'Elizabeth Wright being his keeper in recompense of her watching and painstaking all the time of his sickness 10s.' (1597). 'Besides their wages, mother Gaunt and mother Browne, my keepers', each get 2s. from Philalego Emson, a Wivenhoe labourer (1585). Other examples from nuncupative wills are those of Jane Pierson, 'maidservant with William Lambert of Ramsden Bellhouse', who, 'being demanded' (by three named women who witness her will) 'who attended her and kept her in her sickness, to whom she would dispose her goods, answered, "You shall have it among you"' (1589); and of Richard Byrde of Aveley, a tiler, who, 'in consideration that he had burdened and charged a long time Robert Harris of the said parish for his lodging, finding and keeping as well in health as in the time of his great infirmity and disease, declared that he should have all his goods and be his sole executor' (1584). Some can leave only a few miserable articles: 'To the woman which do keep me in my sickness now, a candlestick, a painted cloth, an old frock and a little kettle'.

Where nursing is given by a relation, the testator may feel it necessary to offer some payment; but the absence of other relations or friends from the sick-room may not be overlooked, and some bitter words are on record. Agnes Arbuster widow, 'dwelling upon St. John's Green by Colchester', wills that because 'I did board with my son in my great sickness the space of fifteen days, I do allow him for the boarding of me 7s.' (1560). Joan Bocher *alias* Adams of Ashdon, widow, decides that the residue of her small possessions shall go 'to my daughters Mary and Joan equally to be divided betwixt them in consideration for their great pains about me in this my time of sickness', but her son gets only 'one old covering, one old blanket, one old pillow and one towen sheet', and the two other daughters a few trifles including 'one platter each' (1596). In 1602 Thomas Emery of Danbury, yeoman, had designed his will especially 'to cause peace, concord and amity amongst friends, namely with my wife and children'. Apparently, however, a long illness ensued, and although he had intended to provide a dwelling for his eldest daughter he admits that he 'never could compass the same to my content.' So her solicitude leads him to draw up a codicil a year later. 'Forasmuch as I have found by a large and long experience', he records, 'that Anne Emery my eldest daughter hath been more painful and careful over me, and more helping and comfortable unto me, in the time of this my great distress and long visitation with extremity of sickness, than any of my other children have or could be'; she is therefore to be rewarded with his house called 'Peppers in Danbury Street' for the term of her life after his widow's decease. Pathetic but perspicacious is a clause in the will of Robert Whest of Hornchurch. After leaving John, Andrew, Anne and Elizabeth, his brothers and sisters, only 6s. 8d. each, he exclaims: 'All the rest of my goods I bequeath to my uncle Thomas Vere of Hornchurch towards the charges for all the whilst I was sick and not able to help myself and forsaken of all my friends' (1569).

We conclude with two nuncupative wills of Essex men taken sick when far from home and two wills of strangers being cared for in Essex. John Woodward, 'late of Harwich, mariner, being sick upon his deathbed in the house of Margaret his sister in the town of Gosper (Gosport) in the diocese of Winchester, gave Margaret his wife all his moveable goods and all his houses in Harwich freely on condition that she should bring up his children' (1584); and John Marteyne of Elsenham, 'being sick at the city of Bath, being demanded by Mr Richard Barlee esquire' (of Elsenham), then his master there present, answered that he had a note of his mind, will and meaning in his chest at Elsenham' (1589). Thomas Smyth, 'sailor of Blackwall near London' (a small group of houses on the bank of the Thames in the parish of Stepney, Middlesex), bestows on 'John Smyth my host of Harwich, in whose house I lie sick, all my moveable goods except two coarse pieces of calucot (calico) cloth' (1592); and Richard Page, 'late soldier at Newehaven (in Flanders) and now living at Billericay', gives 20s. 'to Mundayes' woman that doth keep me, while I am here' (1563).

Very occasionally a dying man may have to take into account his wife's imminent death. John Maryon senior of Inworth, for instance, states: 'If my wife Elizabeth, now living yet being very sick, do escape and outgrow this sickness, she shall have all my goods on condition she pay to my five daughters viz. Margaret, Elizabeth, Mary, Sarah and Martha, £10 each, and to my son John £10, to my daughters at 21 years and to my son at 26 years' (1594). Thomas Hawarde, parish clerk of Barking, in appointing his wife as sole executrix, adds: 'But if she die of this sickness that God hath laid upon us, then my brother William to be sole executor' (1582), referring apparently to one of several outbreaks of plague at Barking.[1] Apart from such epidemics, impending death is expressed in scores of ways, e.g., 'visited by the handiwork of God'; 'visited with the visitation of God'; 'visited with sickness and in peril of death'; 'grown old and troubled with diseases' (Thomas Honike (or Hunwycke) of Little Waltham miller, 1597). The large proportion of perilous childbirths may be occasionally exemplified by a deathbed will: 'in travail of child, sick and weak of body and urged by the wives present'.

To ensure against any doubts about the testator's sanity, it is common to find his declaring that he is 'whole of mind though somewhat diseased in body'; 'somewhat accrazed in body but of good and perfect remembrance, thanks unto God'; or 'sick in body and hale in spright' (spirit). In this context, it is far from unique to find that a scribe spells the testator's bodily condition as 'deceased'!

The twin subjects of longevity and fatal sickness, now being intensively studied by demographers and social historians mainly from parish registers, may also be indirectly illustrated from wills. Two recent statements, at first sight contradictory, are really complementary. The first runs: 'Very high infant mortality in spite of the enormous birthrate kept the population almost static during the period'.[2] The other writer, commenting on historians' emphasis on the heavy incidence of deaths through epidemics, childbirth and infantile sickness (the last was largely owing to gastro-enteritis), says: 'One reads with surprise in the documents of the extraordinary number of children who nevertheless had large broods of their own, and one begins to suspect that these easy generalisations about mortality rates in past centuries need some re-examination, especially for the three generations between c. 1560 and 1640, if no more'.[3] Male Elizabethan infants' expectation of life was still as low as forty, as medical care had not yet made much advance.

## Preambles, Witnesses, Executors and Overseers

The Essex wills thus provide many details, both colourful and sombre, for the wide canvas of social and economic conditions. We conclude this part with some further extracts of a more general nature showing briefly how wills were drawn up and put into effect.[4] Who writes (or drafts) the wills of the ordinary Elizabethan folk? In a small minority of cases, the testator, in pseudo-legal language or painful scrawl, attempts to deal himself with the disposition of his goods. Nearly all other wills are written by a clergyman, an attorney, notary public or professional scrivener, or a local man used to drawing up simple testaments. That of John Allen, a yeoman of Dovercourt (1599), is written and witnessed by John Forber, 'writer of the court letter of London', i.e. a member of the Scriveners' Company (the present writer is a liveryman of this ancient company).[5]

The preamble to a majority of Elizabethan wills is a declaration of orthodox Christian faith in fairly standard language, often inserted as a matter of course by the scribe, whether cleric or attorney. It is rarely an indication of the testator's religion. One of the commonest clauses, with minor variations, runs: 'I bequeath my soul to Almighty God, my Maker and Redeemer, fully trusting to be saved by the death and passion of his only Son Our Lord and Saviour Jesus Christ'. Some, however, clearly give a personal profession or confession, and the genuinely devout may thus perhaps be distinguished, as also the introvert. Even so, one cannot assume that it represents his own words, unless the preamble is long-winded and sanctimonious. Such phrases as 'when the last trump shall blow', 'answer at the dreadful day of judgement', or 'rise again at the latter day' are probably suggested by the scribe. Lawrence Newman, the puritan vicar of Coggeshall, writes and witnesses the wills of several of his flock in the 1590s; the preambles are identical.

The fell-sergeant Death will soon touch many on the shoulder. Thus, for example, William Birchett of Langham thinks, 'being well stricken in years and knowing nothing more frail and uncertain than life, which is a vapour and a bubble in the water' (1584); Robert Hilles of Great Chesterford, miller, opines, 'The life of man is like to the flower of the field which fadeth away' (1585); and John Mylborne of Wanstead exhibits his biblical knowledge, 'As Job sayeth, "Naked I came into the world and naked I shall depart" ' (1571). We could continue *ad infinitum*.

To the present-day reader, witnesses' names may be interesting from various points of view. As many as ten have been found, but the average number is three or four. They generally include the writer, clerical or lay. Not a single witness identifies himself as the parish clerk,[6] but John Walle, 'high constable' (of Freshwell hundred) occurs in a Hadstock will (1592).

It is a fairly common practice (which continues well into the eighteenth century) for the less humble testators to appoint one or more 'supervisors' (or 'overseers') in addition to one or more executors. Their function is advisory only: 'Overseers have no power to intermeddle, otherwise than by counsel or advice, or by complaining in the spiritual court';[7] in other words, they are not concerned with probate. John Pace of Barking fisherman, for example, names as his overseers two of his 'loving friends', also fishermen. Among the three overseers of the will of John Warde senior of

West Ham is Lewis Hilles, 'musician' (1585), but more than two are seldom found. John Harte senior of Thaxted, butcher, nominates Richard Taylor, physician there (1594). John Knight of Earls Colne, yeoman, confides the oversight of his will to 'my trusty and well-known friends Mr Thomas Harlakinden gentleman and Mr John Parkinson parson of the parish', and William Foxe of Barking, yeoman, to Humphrey Bowland of Wanstead, gentleman' (1562). Robert Rochel of 'Yng Peter' (Ingatestone) appoints Peter Preston (1565), who, twenty years later, in turn is to name 'the right worshipful my very good master Sir John Petre knight' as overseer, adding, 'If any question or controversy arise, to be settled by him', and he is the first witness (1585). Edmund Beaumond, a St Osyth husbandman, 'most humbly desires my master Mr Brian Darcey (of the Priory) to take upon him to be overseer' (1582). Thomas Graye, a Harwich mariner, uses 'umpires and overseers' instead of the usual term. Richard Albert of Maldon, woollen-draper, makes Thomas Reignald, a fellow townsman, his overseer, 'to whom for his pains I give my hat, and I forgive unto him all debts he oweth me, so that he do pay Robert Hardinge 20s. which I owe' (1559). Edward Cottrell of Rochford, yeoman, appoints John Walpole, 'clerk of my lord's kitchen', who gets a bullock, his patron being Lord Rich of Rochford Hall. John Rellison of Little Bentley is to receive 13s. 4d. and the bow and arrows of William Prior of St Botolph, Colchester, haberdasher, for acting as his supervisor (1568); John Gooday rewards his overseers by passing on his sword 'as a remembrance' to Thomas Paycock and his best doublet to his cousin Edward Gooday, all members of the Coggeshall clothier fraternity (1566); and Richard Yonge of Great Totham husbandman leaves £5 to Edmund Teale of Witham, grocer (haberdasher in his own will of 1608).

As a reward for their duties, a few executors 'have the use' of legacies until they are due for payment, but some trustees are requested or enjoined to 'increase' them or 'make profits' for the beneficiaries. Being without banking or other simple investment facilities, how are custodians to deal with the problem, so that the money will be available at the due time? The question is an intriguing one. It seems reasonable to assume that legacies thus made by ordinary folk are 'used' either by means of a loan to a local tradesman or farmer by oral or written agreement for a consideration (annual interest or a bonus on repayment) or in buying livestock in the hope that it will multiply. We quote nearly all the evidence.

Anne Newton of Marks Tey, by her nuncupative will, leaves '20s. to her mother to be put out to profit until Andrew shall come to age' (1602). Nicholas Ollie of Laindon, referring to his daughter Bridget, says: 'Her friends to have the governance of my child's goods until she come to 20 years of age and shall make her stock to increase' (1569). Likewise John Mylles of Lexden, yeoman, asks 'my loving friend Mr Matthew Stephens to be gardener (guardian) to my son John and to take the profit of all his lands till he come to the age of 23 years, and to make to my son an account' (1593). The carefully planned clause about a glover's stock has been noticed under Crafts; the same Solomon Whiskerd of Fryerning directs: 'I will that a book shall be made and kept of all manner of profits that shall come to my executors' hands until my children shall come to age, whereby they may be truly answered' (1561). The executors of Jeremy Pavett of Great Dunmow, yeoman, are 'to put forth the stock (of money) to my daughter's most advantage' until she is 16; and those of John Fenzham of Chigwell, carpenter, are to be 'countable for the interest of my children's stocks' (1595). Thomas Perrient, gentleman, is entrusted by Ralph Solme, both of Sandon, with 'the ordinary putting forth for the most advantage' of two children's legacies of £20 and £10 (1598). The curious story of the poaching gang involving Solme reveals how 'Mr Perryn, a gentleman', made a complaint against him in 1595;[8] if the gentlemen are identical this trusteeship shows an improved relationship! John Hammond of St Osyth leaves £30 to his son William, 'to be delivered into some honest man's hand by my executors and my supervisor, whereby some profit may grow to be employed towards my son's keeping' (1594). An optimistic labourer, John Northe of Thundersley, wishes even a trifling legacy to earn something: 'To every of my three children, Henry, Joan and William, 6s. 8d., which shall be put into goodman Wyatt's hands that he may put it forth so as it may be a benefit unto them to increase the same, as my trust is he will' (1581).

We discover a single concrete example of a rate of interest being charged for the use of a legacy. Joan Hickes, a widow of Tollesbury, dictates (1595): 'To my son Arthur Burles (by a previous marriage?) £50, which money is now in the custody of Mr Henworth of Danbury, to be given within 16 years; but if it appear to Mr Henworth or Mr Edward Lukis of Lawling Hall (in Latchingdon) that Arthur orderly and honestly behaveth himself, then the £50 be paid upon his sober behaviour when it may appear best to do him good; I will that Mr Henworth so long as the £50 remain in his keeping pay yearly to Arthur £5 for the use of the £50 or otherwise the principal, and Mr Henworth shall put in sufficient bond for it'. Under the Usury Act, 13 Eliz., c. 8 (1571), 10 p.c. was the maximum allowable rate, so the widow strikes a good bargain for her son's benefit. Perhaps her husband, John Hickes *alias* Stanley, yeoman, whose will is dated the previous 23 April, had advised her accordingly. Another specific 'increase', but with an unknown rate of interest, is found in the will of Richard Kennatt, the Goldhanger sexton (1568). He leaves £3 to be equally divided between his four grandchildren, the children of his daughter and John Garolde. The son-in-law is to have 'the money to the use of the children till they come to the age of 21 years or marriage, and then to be paid the whole stock and increase, on condition that he will make the stock by such time that every child (receive) 20s. apiece to be paid according to your (*sic*) conscience'. The earliest register of Goldhanger is lost, so that we cannot find their ages. More vaguely, Avery Lacye of Stansted Mountfitchet, fanwright, directs his executors 'to put to use the interest or loan money' (1600); likewise William Prior, haberdasher of St Botolph, Colchester, wills that 'the money I have bequeathed to my sons Edward, Henry and Valentine and to my daughter Ellen be put in the keeping of John Rellison of Little Bentley to be put to some use to their profit' (1568). Some Elizabethan writers expressed conflicting opinions about the ethics of lending money at interest, but it is clear that these testators expect their trustees not to allow the assets to lie idly, like the delinquent in the parable of the talents.

If no 'question or controversy arise', probate is remarkably expeditious, provided that the will, inventory and account are quickly produced before the spiritual court. Deathbed wills are thus seen to be proved within two weeks and even one: for example, that of John Brett of Latchingdon *alias* Purleigh Barns in Purleigh within six days (1566): a happy contrast to the delays and complications experienced in proving many present-day wills!

Following are two more examples of nuncupative wills and two ministers' certificates on behalf of aged legatees unable to attend the court.

> Katherine Garrold alias Bocher of Ridgewell, 1577.
> Speaking these words hereafter following in the presence of Rose Wade the wife of Thomas Wade of Tilbury next Clare and Katherine Motte the wife of Robert Motte of Nether Yeldham, viz.
> Goodwife Wade, I pray you bear witness whatsoever shall become of me, how I do give to this man John Levett all such goods of mine as he hath in his house and how all that is not a sufficient recompense for the great charges and pains he hath been at about me in my sickness, both now and at other times heretofore, and though it were a great deal more than it is he were well worthy to have it.
> She then said further, Levet standing by her bedside, 'John, thou hast my goods in thy house, I charge thee keep them, and if I wist thou wouldest not I would take some other order for them', Levet then answering, 'Mother, I would ye should not think but that I mind both to take your gift thankfully and also to keep them for your sake'. Furthermore she then said how she had before that set such things as she had, but she repented her of it wherein she had given Henry a hutch and a brass pan, but he should not have them, for he had his portion already and the other had no need of her gift nor none should have, for Levet had taken all the pains and been at all the charges, and therefore she did give him all, saving that immediately she required the said John Levett to give unto the aforesaid Katherine her daughter her black cassock, which is done accordingly.
>
> Agnes Beston of Earls Colne, widow, 1588
> 'Son William, I give unto thee all that I have, from the least to the most, within doors and without. All is thine, and I pray God bless thee with it, good son William.' And being moved to give her daughter somewhat for a remembrance, if it were but one of her gowns, she answered she would not, for that she had of her of late £20 and a great deal more.

These may be to certify you that Edy the wife of Richard Howell late of Margaret Roothing labouring man deceased is a very old and impotent woman, and therefore not able to travel to the Court neither on foot nor on horseback without peril. And so it is that the said Richard Howell made his will nuncupative, wherein he gave all that he had unto the said Edy his wife, and appointed her his sole executrix thereof in the presence and hearing of those persons whose names are hereunder subscribed. Wherefore, if it may please the Court that the parson there may take her oath and certify it into this Court, it shall be done, for the old woman cannot come herself as it hath been said.

JOHN PIGBONE parson (of Margaret Roothing, 1587).

Whereas Robert Martin of Coggeshall, a very aged man, is cited to the Court about the goods and chattels of Charles Amye late of Coggeshall deceased, these may be to testify that the said Robert Martin had not one pennyworth of the goods of the said Charles, but that money which he had, lying on his deathbed, he delivered to his father (blank) Amye of Abington in the county of Cambridge. And the rest (as far as the said Robert Martin understandeth) are in the hands of John Amye, servant to Nicholas Merill of the hamlet of Little Coggeshall and brother to the said Charles.

Being requested to certify my opinion of the truth of the premises, upon the testimony of these honest men, I have yielded willingly to write thus much, that in conscience Father Martin had none of those goods and that this certificate is wholly true. And further that the old man can hardly travel two miles, being very aged and weak.

LAWRENCE NEWMAN (vicar of Coggeshall, 1596).

---

[1] For that of 1564, see *E.L.: Morals and the Church Courts*, 107.
[2] W. S. C. Copeman, *Doctors and Disease in Tudor Times* (1960), 162.
[3] W. G. Hoskins, 'The Rebuilding of Rural Britain' (*Past and Present*, x, 56).
[4] The writer's terms of reference did not embrace examination of the act, cause, and deposition books of the Archdeacons' courts, which contain a great deal of information concerning the administrative machinery of probate, including contested cases and cases about failure to render account or inventory or to act as executor. See Emmison (ed.), *Guide to Essex Record Office* (revd. edn., 1969), 70-78. For form and probate, see R. Burn, *Ecclesiastical Law* (1763), ii, 503-774.
[5] F. W. Steer, *The Scriveners' Company Common Paper* (London Rec. Soc., 1968); he was apprenticed in 1563 and admitted in 1573.
[6] Little is known about rural parish clerks; see *E.L.: Morals and the Church Courts*, index, s.v. 'clerk, parish'.
[7] Burn, *op. cit.*, ii, 545.
[8] *E.L.: Disorder*, 238.

# PART 2—WORK
*(from Essex Petty and Quarter Sessions Records)*

## 9

# Employment

### The Statute of Artificers

The renowned 'Statute of Artificers, Labourers, Servants in Husbandry and Apprentices' (5 Eliz., c.4) was the work of her second Parliament (1563). It has been reprinted almost in full more than once,[1] and its main objects are sufficiently well known to require only a brief summary of its 40 sections. There was little novel in its actual provisions: it was in fact more in the nature of a codification of many earlier statutes, but the preamble expresses the specious hope that its execution would 'banish idleness, advance husbandry and yield unto the hired person both in the time of scarcity and in the time of plenty a convenient proportion of wages'. England's vital farming economy, it was hoped, would be assisted by maintaining sufficient labour on the land by restricting the rural exodus into the towns.

The three principal aims were rigorous control of contracts between employers and employees by means of public hirings, periodic assessments of wages by Quarter Sessions, and regulation of apprenticeship. Underlying the Act was the fear of discontent, if not rebellion, for the insurrection of 1549 was fresh in statesmen's memory. In Essex, as related in the first volume, there were to be, despite the Act, sinister threats of risings by Colchester weavers in 1566 and of poverty-stricken and hungry labourers in 1594-6.[2]

The basic provisions concerned mutual obligations and rights between masters and servants, both male and female, the former being divided broadly between those working in crafts and in husbandry. No artificers were to be hired for less than a year in the following crafts: 'clothiers, woollen cloth weavers, tuckers, fullers, cloth workers, shearmen, dyers, hosiers, tailors, shoemakers, tanners, pewterers, bakers, brewers, glovers, cutlers, smiths, farriers, curriers, saddlers, spurriers, turners, cappers, hatmakers or feltmakers, bowyers, fletchers, arrowhead-makers, butchers, cooks, or millers'.[3] Every unmarried male or female and every married man under thirty, 'having been brought up' or worked in one of these crafts for three years or more, unless he owned land worth at least 40s. a year or goods worth £10, could be compelled if unemployed, by any master working in that craft, to serve him. All other unemployed males between 12 and 60, except those having substantial lands or goods, were to be obliged to work in husbandry by anyone who required such labour. Two J.P.s could order any unmarried and unemployed female between 12 and 40 into menial service at reasonable wages.

While the Act was largely directed against the heinous sin of idleness, it recognized the labourer's right to work, in theory at any rate, as well as his duty. An unemployed adult who refused to work, an artificer who broke his contract, or a servant who left his or her master, was liable to imprisonment, and a master who unduly dismissed his servant could be fined 40s. Hours of work were set out: between mid-March and mid-September, 5 a.m. to 7 or 8 p.m. ($2\frac{1}{2}$ hours being allowed for meals), and dawn till dusk for the rest of the year. These were probably the normal hours before 1563, as indeed they were to be for long years to come, but the numerous festivals in the Church calendar, as well as Sundays, gave relief from toil.

Since the first Statute of Labourers (1349) there had been a spate of legislation attempting not only to restrict free movement of labour and demand for higher wages but also to punish those who refused to work. For Essex (and a few other counties for which medieval Sessions of the Peace records have been preserved), some details of their operation are known.[4] The duty of administering the Statute of Artificers in the counties rested squarely on the J.P.s and their subordinate officers in every hundred and township. To ensure that it was fully effective the county magistrates were to 'divide themselves into several limits', to meet twice yearly to make 'diligent enquiry' about its execution, and to impose severe punishment on offenders. Records of such divisional meetings in Essex are scanty and ambiguous, and even more so elsewhere.[5] The obligation seems to have been deputed to the high constables at their own sessions, though it is clear in Essex that one or two J.P.s were present on at least four occasions.

## *High Constables' Petty or Hiring Sessions*

In our attempt to describe relatively unknown aspects of Elizabethan social life, based on the rich Essex documentary sources, we shall now draw on a series of detailed records which, on account of their number and date range, may be justifiably termed unique.[6] We refer to the presentments to the county justices in Quarter Sessions from courts or meetings held before the high constables of the hundreds and called 'petty sessions', 'statute sessions', 'hiring sessions' (from their chief function), or 'inquisitions'.

There were two sorts of hundredal courts in Tudor times. What we shall term the *ordinary* hundredal sessions submitted regular presentments, or reports, of offences to county Quarter Sessions. Their returns concerned 'decayed', 'dangerous', or 'impassable' bridges, roads full of 'sloughs' or liable to flooding owing to unscoured roadside ditches, and unlicensed or disorderly alehouses, together with some other public nuisances or a few personal offences. A fair amount is known from the Quarter Sessions records of several counties, but these exist chiefly for the later years of the reign, whereas those for Essex cover the whole period—and there are over 600 of them. In our first volume we gave a fairly full account, relating mostly to bridges and roads, for 1562-68.[7] Owing to lack of space we were unable to continue beyond that date, but we explained that subsequent presentments were very similar in content and mainly of local or topographical interest.

Of the other hundredal courts—the *high constables'* sessions—Essex possesses returns from no less than 172 of their meetings for all its seventeen hundreds, ranging from 1562 to 1610. This noble run of archives bears mainly on the relations between masters and 'servants' (including employees in husbandry as well as in trade and crafts and also maidservants) and to a minor extent between masters and apprentices. A full transcript is embodied in the typescript calendar in the Essex Record Office.[7a] While the courts met shortly before each Quarter Sessions, it is possible that in some hundreds or periods they were limited to Easter and Michaelmas. To form the hundredal 'juries' every parish or township was obliged to send its constables (usually two, though only one for small parishes, a few had three, and populous parishes such as Barking and West Ham had constables for each 'ward'), together with a few 'inhabitants' (generally two, for some places one or three). Defaulters, including constables, were punished by a fine or the stocks.[8] The returns to Quarter Sessions are set out either parish by parish or under headings—jurors, defaulters, offences (almost all under the Statute of Artificers), 'covenants' (contracts or agreements by which an employer hired a servant), and occasionally apprenticeships. The documents were compiled from these parish presentments, and fortunately the county records preserve a few of the originals. Many places reported 'All well according to the Statute', or more often just 'All well'. Our limited space does not allow of citation of every single offence and of every covenant, but in general only very minor or purely repetitive cases have been omitted in the following pages.

Our account begins with the decade before the Statute of Artificers. The earliest Quarter Sessions rolls yield six documents about the operation of the pre-1563 legislation. In 1556 two Barking 'single men' ('single' is the usual term for a bachelor or spinster not in service) are presented as 'loiterers' (vagabonds), who 'refuse to serve with any honest man except at unreasonable wages'.

The first proceedings, dated January 1562, are headed: 'Hundred of Ongar. Presentments at a Petty Sessions before Robert Thurgood and

John Grene, chief constables'; as 'affirmed by the oath' of 14 men, being the jurors representing the parishes. Four 'bachelors, not in service', are reported from Bobbingworth, North Weald, Lambourne and Chigwell, and 'they are warned to find masters'. A Magdalen Laver 'garment-maker made stockings with worsted, contrary to divers warnings', for which he is fined 20d. A petty constable and six men from five parishes having defaulted in attending the petty sessions, the constable is fined 6s 8d., the rest 2s. each. And in an exceptional entry in our petty sessions records William Tynge of Stanford Rivers 'is ordered that he shall not further frequent the society of Joan Palmer, widow of Chipping Ongar, because they are suspected persons and of dishonest conversation, under a penalty of forfeit as often as they are found associating', the man 13s. 4d. and the woman 6s. 8d.

Harlow hundred presentment in the same year begins: 'Petty Sessions held before John Bevys and John Brydges, high constables, according to the form of the statutes of late made'. Roydon had reported that two men 'are bachelors and keepeth tailors' shops (i.e. workshops), as is found by the constables and others'; two parishes each that a man 'duly warned to appear before the high constables at the petty sessions has made default', one of whom used 'opprobrious words'; and the other places, 'All well'. Clavering hundred in 1562 and 1563 presents that all is orderly in almost every parish, except for a few unlicensed alehouses.

The other documents belong to 1562-63. In the roll for Epiphany Sessions 1562 there are two more original parish papers, evidently handed in at the Hinckford hundred petty sessions. The two constables and two other men of Great Maplestead report at some length on their having searched 'divers houses being suspect'. A constable and another man of Wickham St. Paul's present an offence against the laws concerning livery and maintenance, the signal abuse of which by the Earl of Oxford of Hedingham Castle in 1489 must still have been common talk because of the enormous fine imposed on him by Henry VII for parading his liveried retainers when he entertained his sovereign. Both these interesting documents and another parish presentment of 1567 have been printed in full.[9]

In 1566, for the first and only time, the grand jury presentment refers to two 'idle persons' who are masterless but will not 'obey the Queen's officers or dwell in the service of any person' and have defaulted in their summons to appear, one before the high constables and the other before the justices. Barstable hundred sessions in 1566 receives 'All well' presentments from most of its parishes, except for three single men out of service and two masters receiving men without a testimonial. But Mucking and Stanford-le-Hope each present a parishioner for buying butter, eggs, calves, lambs and chickens without licence (see next section).[10]

While high constables' juries very occasionally see fit to mention disorderly alehouses or unscoured roadside ditches—among the common features of the presentments by the ordinary hundredal juries[11]—the latter likewise include service offences among their normal presentments in a few rare instances. Two masterless single men and another who 'works as his own hand' are thus accused in 1565 and two more in 1567, but scarcely any subsequently by this means. The complementary nature of the functions of both kinds of sessions is evident from sporadic references in the ordinary hundredal reports to the high constables' sessions.[12] Only a few 'single men out of service' are in fact reported from the latter before 1568; also one who 'dwelleth with his father-in-law and is not able to set him a-work' and another who 'will not tarry with any man in service'.

It is for March 1568 that the first full record of statute sessions as a hiring court has come down to us, headed 'Petty Sessions held at Stanway in the hundred of Lexden before Edmund Bocking esquire, one of the justices, William Sammes and William Lynne, constables of the hundred'. This and nearly all of the eleven subsequent Lexden sessions form the most detailed series of hundredal returns for Essex and indeed for the whole country. All name the masterless males and females; all except that of 1572 give the terms of the hiring covenants—the masters and servants, their trades, and nearly always the wages; and most name the occupations of men and women who failed to attend the petty sessions. But the unemployed, in all the Lexden reports, are not presented as offenders; unlike every other hundred with the single exception of Witham in 1590, they are the names of those publicly 'proclaimed' as 'not being retained in anyone's service for a year but are free to give service to those who ask for it', or, in other years, 'if anyone wished to retain them in their service according to the Statute, let them come and be taken'; and their home parishes and occupations are also stated. Statistics from all the twelve Lexden petty sessions records are analyzed below (p. 152). Thus (1568) 20 men and 13 women are listed; in addition, a weaver 'retained in his service one man for a quarter of one year' at 13s. 4d. wages, 'contrary to the Statute'. Of the covenants (16 males and 3 females) we give five typical examples.

### LEXDEN HUNDRED SERVANTS' CONTRACTS, 1568

> John Sytheston of Wakes Colne husbandman agreed to serve John (torn) from 7th March, taking for his wages 46s. 8d.
> James Doddes agreed to serve John Sparke of (West) Bergholt, taking for his wages 40s. and 6s. 8d. clothing.
> Thomas Radley of Aldham, butcher, agreed to serve John Sperlinge of the same, butcher, taking therefor his wages 40s. and 6s. 8d. for his livery.
> John Chamberlen agreed to serve Thomas Byrde of Aldham bowmaker, taking for his wages 46s. 8d. yearly.

Joan Smyth agreed to serve Anthony Pulleyn from 8th March next, taking for her wages 16s. and one petticoat cloth yearly.

The entries are not wholly uniform, but each hiring is for 'one whole year' in accordance with the Act, in some cases starting from the day of the petty sessions. The only other masters whose occupations are given are a butcher and a glover (two of the 29 crafts enumerated in the Act) and 'Thomas Audley gentleman', probably of Gosbecks in Stanway. The wages range from 26s. 8d. to 46s. 8d. for men and from 16s. to 20s. for women, with or without 'a new tunic', or '6s. 8d. for a cloak'; three males, probably youths, receive 'sufficient victuals and clothing' but no wages. Five non-service offences are reported: four unlicensed 'common sellers of bread, beer and other victuals in his house', one of whom also allowed 'unlawful games, to wit, alleys (bowls), cards and slidethrift' (shovelboard, in much later years, shove-ha'penny [13]); and one man 'insulted the constables'. Continuing with the Lexden returns, that of September 1572 states that 'the constables, reeve and inhabitants' (unnamed) of eight parishes having defaulted in attendance, these parishes have each been fined between 10s. and 40s. The outstanding item is that no less than 48 males and 8 females 'are not retained in service but work by the day and month, contrary to the Statute; therefore they are warned to be lawfully retained in service by 1st October next or else they will be punished as vagabonds'. (Several Privy Council anti-vagrancy measures in 1569-71 had enforced compulsory service for masterless persons.) Exactly half this number are Coggeshall men, and nearly all of these, judging by the proclamation lists from 1582 onwards, are probably weavers or fullers, unemployed because of the cloth trade depression in the early 1570s.[14]

The Easter return in 1574 states that 13 constables of eight parishes failed to appear, all except one sick man being 'referred to the discretion of the justices', who fined them 12d. each. This is the only sessions in the reign in which a surety is named for each masterless person, e.g. 'to find a sufficient master before Easter next, by the surety of Thomas Byrde', four men being bound. For this year only we also have a return for the September petty sessions. Punishment in the stocks for four hours had been meted out, so the high constables report, to five servants who did not attend. Only one covenant is recorded. Next year a four-hour stocking was also awarded to three men, two being fathers who failed 'to bring his son'. In addition to five hirings, two apprentices to a fuller and a brickmaker are registered, each 'taking for his wages double apparel and 20s. (or 40s.)' at the end of his seven-year term.

At the Lexden hundred meeting around Easter 1576 21 men and women absentees are 'to be punished by the stocks at the discretion of the constables'. One, 'a slanderer of his neighbours and bears himself evilly towards the constable', is fined 3s. 4d.; another 'daily frequents tippling houses', fined 12d.; 22 men and 10 women 'are not retained in anyone's service, but are free to serve', only 6 Coggeshall men being named, without their occupation; and 4 men are ordered 'to provide themselves with masters before 28th April or to appear and be ready to serve anyone who may require them, on pain of imprisonment'. Of the four covenants, two are for a three-year term, one for husbandry, the other in blacksmith's work, each master providing 'sufficient food and clothing and other bodily necessities, and at the end of term double apparel' (Sunday and workday clothes), one also being given 16s. 8d. cash, the other 30s., a pair of shears, an iron mallet and a butt. Despite the end-of-term clothing and tools, these short apprenticeships seem to be illegal under the Act of 1563.

The presentment of March 1582, if our assumption is correct, reveals the return of serious unemployment at Coggeshall. This time the proclamation list includes 7 weavers, as many as 15 fullers, and 2 shoemakers, all males. But the Easter proclamations in the two following years apparently showed a marked improvement: Coggeshall reports only 4 weavers and 6 fullers in 1583 and 7 weavers and 4 fullers in 1584, only one weaver being in both lists. Those for 1586 and 1589 disclose 3 weavers and 4 fullers and 6 weavers and 3 fullers respectively. In all these years, however, the Coggeshall figures are by far the highest in the hundred. None of the other Lexden returns reveals anything out of the usual. Maximum wages at this last sessions remain much the same as before—46s. 8d. for service with a farmer and a blacksmith, 22s. for a single woman.

## LEXDEN HUNDRED PETTY SESSIONS, 1568-89

| Year | Absentees* male †fem. | Masterless male fem. | Orders§ male fem. | Hirings male fem. | Males' masters' occ'ns husb'y weav'g other | App's‡ |
|---|---|---|---|---|---|---|
| 1568 | — — | 20 13 | — — | 16 3 | — — — | — |
| 1572 | — — | — — | 48 8 | 0 0 | — — — | — |
| 1573 | — — | 4 4 | 4 — | 3 0 | 3 0 0 | — |
| 1574 | — — | 9 3 | — — | 1 0 | 1 0 0 | — |
| 1575 | 3 0 | 8 4 | 1 — | 4 1 | 1 0 4 | 2 |
| 1576 | 15 6 | 22 10 | 4 — | 2 2 | 1 0 1 | 4 |
| 1578 | 1 3 | 2 4 | — — | 4 1 | 4 0 1 | — |
| 1582 | 18 5 | 54 7 | — — | 9 5 | 8 2 1 | — |
| 1583 | 16 0 | 35 9 | — — | 16 3 | 6 4 6 | — |
| 1584 | 19 2 | 27 3 | — — | 9 2 | 7 1 0 | 1 |
| 1586 | 24 0 | 21 0 | — — | 13 3 | 5 8 0 | — |
| 1589 | 18 10 | 27 9 | — — | 6 2 | 5 0 1 | — |

*Petty constables who failed to attend are excluded.

†'Male and female' instead of 'men and women' because many, if not the majority, of the unemployed and of those hired were probably boys and girls, as the low wages—mostly far below the maximum rates allowed in the justices' wages assessments—seem to imply.

§To find or serve masters.    ‡Apprentices.

Leaving this abundant evidence for Lexden hundred sessions and reverting to our general chronological account, Ongar hundred is found in 1568 to present that 'certain (unnamed) young men were out of covenant and be appointed to service by the high constables'; and at Great Dunmow three single men, tailors by occupation, 'refuse to serve by the year and use great excess in their apparel for their hosen, contrary to the Statute': the latter referring to the sumptuary law against extravagant costume.[15]

Except for a recognizance given by John Lucas of Manningtree, gentleman, as surety for a tailor 'leaving off working at his own hand and to be retained in some honest service as a household servant', the Sessions rolls for 1569-71 lack records of the high constables' proceedings. But a 'declaration' in July 1572 before a justice and a petty constable by William Wryet shows that he had been servant to William Rede, both weavers of Harlow, for 'a year and more' at the rate of 12d., 11d. or 10d. 'for a dozen ells' (45 inches to the ell) 'according to the breadth and goodness of the cloth'. The master had agreed to retain him 'without a testimonial of his departure from where he before dwelt, and being warned that it is against the law' (Statute of Artificers, s.7) 'has notwithstanding very obstinately continued in the doing thereof'.[16]

The Michaelmas 1572 Sessions roll affords the fullest group of petty sessions records, no less than 12 of the 19 hundreds being represented. It looks as though some earlier slackness in forwarding the returns had occurred, for the normal memorandum for each Quarter Sessions written by the clerk of the peace states: 'The chief constables did orderly return and certify their Petty Sessions'. Furthermore, those of Chelmsford hundred sent in their records for the three preceding quarters, as well as that for the meeting held a week earlier, and Witham submitted a return for July. From the four Chelmsford reports, giving the particulars under each parish, we get the following totals of offences for the whole year 1571-72:

> 49 'single men' (or 'masterless men') out of covenant, including one bachelor 'working by his own hand'.
>
> 25 masters employing 34 men and 4 maidservants 'out of covenant', meaning probably, as stated in a number of cases, 'working by the day', or, in two instances, 'hiring by the week'; once specifically 'working in his house'. Of these a tailor takes in 'a journeyman of that occupation by the month, notwithstanding the constable's commandment', and one man 'keeps his two sons, single men, out of covenant, working about by the day'.
>
> 5 single men 'keep open shop and work at their own occupation, being under the age of 30 years'.
>
> 22 masters give their 31 covenant servants, including one female, 'excess wages'.

Unusual entries record that 'John Hasting, miller, is out of service and lieth loitering at one Howson's house in the hamlet of Moulsham'; a man has 'rescued' (in the sense of forcible removal) a maidservant from her master 'and keeps her out of covenant', for which he has been fined 12d. by two J.P.s; two Chelmsford shoemakers each keep a journeyman (i.e. one who has completed his apprenticeship but is not yet working on his own account), one out of covenant, the other at 'excess wages' of 53s. 4d.; and John Wood of Moulsham, shoemaker, 'uses the art of surgery', doubtless meaning that he also worked as a barber-surgeon. All except one of the illegal wages items are found in the returns for Midsummer; these 'excessive' rates range from £2 13s. 4d. and £6 13s. 4d. a year (mostly the lowest figure or £3); the solitary maidservant's wages are 33s. 4d. Christopher Wylson, a Chelmsford butcher, for giving his man £5 4s. 'at the rate of 2s. by the week', is fined 2s. by the justices. The highest sum appears against Walter Baker, also of Chelmsford, whose four servants are the largest number, the other three getting £4 or £3 6s. 8d. each. Unlike some of the masters, his occupation is not given, but he may be the man who kept a brothel in the town in 1567.[17]

Of the other hundreds, Waltham and Ongar report 'all well' in every respect; in Winstree the only offender is one who 'retained a pedlar in his service to carry fish (as a pedlar he should have been licensed); and Harlow names five labourers who 'have gone away to unknown parts' and another who 'will not work by the day at the time ordained but wishes to have 6d. a day'. Instead of supplying an itemized report, Hinckford puts in a 'certificate' from the high constables 'that they have held the petty sessions, as commanded by the justices' at the previous Midsummer Sessions, 1572. This is followed by a valuable comment on their other business in connection with apprenticeship, which is not so well illustrated as service: 'Whereas they found divers masterless men and women, they have placed the most part of them with masters and trust that they may place the rest of them, and have so charged the constables of the towns where any of them are, and they have taken the children of divers folk and put them to masters by indentures for reasonable years'. Uttlesford merely informs the Court that 'there were young men out of service, who were put in service by the high constables'. Tendring finds 23 men and 2 women 'not retained in service', 7 being weavers and one 'a knacker, for being a vagrant'. Dengie reports 4 unmarried men under 30, being vagrants and out of service, of whom one 'refuses to be retained and labours by the day, to the great depauperization of other labourers'. (Thus the high constable or his clerk pens or coins an impressive word in place of 'impoverishment', not to be recorded by the *O.E.D.* until nearly three centuries later and anticipating some Ph.D. thesis-writers' beloved jargon!) Thurstable adds a little more to the general picture, as in the entry for Great Totham :

Gideon Boreman, late servant to Thomas Martindale, is out of service, and Ralph Lidgard of Tolleshunt Major husbandman seek to retain him in his service for one whole year, and he is retained being paid for his wages 33s. 4d. and for clothing 10s., and he received 1d. as an earnest.

A dairymaid gets 20s. wages and a petticoat worth 5s.; a female 'hedge-breaker refused to be retained'; 5 men and women 'out of service, are found vagrants'; and another vagrant's father 'seeks to retain him', so he is 'committed to dwell there on pain of being punished for a rogue'.

The most informative document delivered in at Michaelmas 1572 relates to Dunmow hundred, the meeting being presided over by two J.P.s, Thomas Frank and Kenelm Throckmorton, as well as the high constables. No less than 34 masterless men and women are named. In addition, two of the town of Great Dunmow 'will quit their service' at Michaelmas, and being 'solemnly summoned, come with their masters, who will show themselves content for their departure', i.e. at the end of their year, thus making 38 to find employment; and three servants are 'freed from their service' and attended with the masters who were to engage them from Michaelmas. Dunmow hundred formerly included two hamlets, Berwick (or Barwick) Berners in the parish of Aythorpe Roothing and Birds Green in Beauchamp Roothing and Willingale Doe (the main parts of these parishes lay in adjacent hundreds). Being in a different hundred, these two hamlets were separate constablewicks, but this seems to be the only record of their individuality in the petty sessions returns. One of them reports 'a dweller there without service'. High Roothing goes a bit further in presenting a man 'taught in the art of a weaver, without service, who declared himself to be ready to serve in his art if required, whereof he has a day to obtain service, and in the meantime is not to frequent the common alehouses as he was wont'!

The Lexden return we have already noticed. Finally, and exceptionally, this roll has two recognizances, one given by John Cooke of Rochford, gentleman,[18] 'to keep in his service for a whole year' a Wakes Colne labourer 'who was found on inquisition to be a rogue within the compass of the Act of 14 Eliz.', the other by Thomas Mildmay of Springfield likewise to keep a Langley labourer, both having left their abodes many miles away; also a court order for a 13-year-old labourer of Wye (Kent) to remain as servant to Francis Harvye esquire and Mary his wife to the age of 24, 'according to the same statute.'

The presentment from the Becontree sessions, held at Barking in March 1574, gives the highest number of hirings and apprenticeships for any Essex hundred, mainly due to West Ham having already achieved a large population.

## BECONTREE HUNDRED PETTY SESSIONS, 1574

|  | Hirings | | Masterless | Apprentices | |
|---|---|---|---|---|---|
|  | male | female | male | male | female |
| West Ham | | | | | |
|   Church Street ward | 22 | 10 | — | 3 | 1 |
|   Stratford ward | 18 | 9 | — | 3 | — |
|   Plaistow ward | 3 | 1 | 1 | — | — |
| East Ham | 7 | 6 | 3 | 3 | 2 |
| Walthamstow | 6 | 3 | 5 | 1 | — |
| Leyton | 7 | 7 | 1 | 1 | — |
| Wanstead | 1 | 1 | — | — | — |
| Woodford | 4 | 3 | — | — | — |
| Dagenham | 11 | 17 | 3 | — | — |
| Barking | | | | | |
|   Town ward | \multicolumn{5}{c}{'All that inhabit there are fishermen'} | | | | |
|   Ripple ward | 8 | 1 | 1 | — | — |
|   Chadwell ward | 2 | 0 | 1 | — | — |
|   Ilford ward | 5 | 4 | 6 | 3 | — |
|  | 94 | 62 | 21 | 14 | 3 |

The masterless men (why no women or girls out of service?) are stated to be 'appointed' (or 'licensed') 'to get him a master' before a certain date. Of these, one, an Ilford bachelor, 'is commanded to depart within eight days'; another, likewise 'to depart from Leyton for that he is married and has children and dwells at Hatfield Broad Oak'. While the great majority are described as 'single men' or 'single women', 8 men are noted as 'married'. Several masters each take a few employees: in Church Street ward, William Rooke [19] hires 4 men and 1 woman, and Thomas Staples hires 3 men and also takes 4 apprentices, both tanners; and William Rooke, yeoman (the same person?) hires 4 men and 2 women. The terms are far from uniform. The majority finish at Michaelmas, others at Shrovetide, Lent, Palm Sunday, May Day, Whitsun, Midsummer, Lammas, Bartholomewtide, Hallowtide, Christmas, Twelfth Day, or Candlemas. This indicates that most hirings had been agreed before the sessions, which therefore serve chiefly as a registration court; only a few are 'to end at this day twelve months'. But 4 married men are hired only by the week, at between 14d. and 3s. 4d., 2 to smiths, 1 to a glover; and 1 bachelor 'is appointed to work by the day for that his mother is a widow and a poor woman and hath charge of children'. The yearly wages vary wildly, the highest at £3 6s. 8d. being given to William Rooke, a tanner's man, and for a woman, 26s. 8d. Some wages, even for a male, are as low as 13s. 4d. and presumably refer to boys. 'A high pair of shoes at 20d.' also goes to a husbandman's servant. The Plaistow constables report that Thomas Burton, yeoman, 'refused to come to the court or to certify any of his servants, therefore in example of others he is fined 40s.'; but perhaps, unknown to them, he was sick, as his will is dated three months later. Among the masters are four gentlemen: Anthony Bridges of Plaistow, Thomas Rampson of Walthamstow, Henry Parker of Woodford, and Thomas Smyth of Ilford. The other employers are mostly yeomen or husbandmen, with a sprinkling of brewers, tanners, smiths, shoemakers, tailors and wheelwrights, also a collier (charcoal-maker) at Woodford in Waltham Forest and a widow. The remark about the Town ward of Barking ('All that inhabit there are fishermen') is surely an exaggeration, for there must also be a few tradesmen and craftsmen in connection with the fishing and ancillary business who employ servants. This document is one of the three instances of the use of 'court' for the high constables' sessions. The apprenticeship terms vary between 4 and 9 years, but mostly 7; apart from 2 tanners, the other masters are several husbandmen (Thomas Sleape of East Ham takes as many as 3 apprentices), a shoemaker, a ropemaker, a wheelwright, and a brickmaker.

The Hinckford report in April 1574 is exceptional. Held on two successive days at Braintree and Castle Hedingham, the business is mainly with apprenticeships. But the Hedingham man is doubly in disgrace—for profiteering during the severe shortage after the preceding poor harvest and for illegal trading. Payment of wages by truck, i.e. goods instead of cash, of which his flagrant offence is the only case noted, was first forbidden by the Act of 4 Edw. IV, c.1 (1465), which declared that 'the clothier shall pay ready money to the weavers and spinners'. Bragge is ordered to appear at Quarter Sessions, but the result is unknown.

## HINCKFORD HUNDRED PETTY SESSIONS, 1574

John Freman of Bocking, having an apprentice by indenture for 4 years and at the end should have paid his apprentice, Roger Chamberleyn, 5 nobles, did devise to put him away, having served the most part of his time, to defraud him of his 26s. 8d.

Robert Wallys is a fugitive person and goeth like a vagabond from town to town and possesseth the name of a soothsayer.

George Hudswell of Bocking, a bachelor, occupies the trade of a shearman and never was apprenticed to the same.

John Edes of Bocking, weaver, has compounded with Thomas Reve, being bound for 7 years, and took 3s. for the release of one year's service, having served 6 years.

Richard Crouch, weaver, put away Philip Paule one year before his apprenticeship ended, and William Ballard of Bocking, weaver, put away Benjamin Rost, being bound 12 years and having served 11 years.

Reynold Grene of Halstead, single man, works by the day with John Harvy and Agnes Barnard single woman.

William Bragge of Sible Hedingham sells oatmeal and corn to poor people above the price of the market, and they are enforced to take it at his price, for that a certain clothier, whose name we know not, useth to bring wool to the house of Bragge to spin, and the poor can get no money for it but as they take it out in corn.

Thomas Pennell of Stebbing, carpenter, is a bachelor out of service, and liveth very disorderly and hath lived so for a long time.

George Byncks of Finchingfield, tailor, a singleman, keeps a shop and keeps as servants William Bynckes, John Brewster and George Bennett, to the hindrance of others.

Later details of apprentices are recorded only in 1575. In two returns from Waltham Abbey: a tailor takes a lad of 17 for 7 years agreeing to give him at the end 5s. and 'double apparel for workday and holyday'; a tanner has a boy for 8 years with 5s. only promised; and a man whose craft is not stated is in trouble for having retained a boy of 13 for 9 years, 'which retainer is void by Statute'. The final phrase is used also by Chelmsford hundred in the same year: a master 'retains single men in his service of other towns (i.e. from other villages) and retains them by the day and week to do his work and be not in covenant with him by the year, to the great hindrance of other poor men'. The return names Nicholas Shache of Great Waltham, single man, as 'out of covenant and works by the day in the harvest time and other times and yet refused to have any master': clearly a cantankerous fellow, and three years later he was to forbid the banns of matrimony of a local couple.[20]

The following entries, the first two from Lexden and the rest from Waltham hundred, all of 1575, are quoted as among the few examples of apprentices' terminal 'wages' or because they are unusual.

### APPRENTICES, 1575

At this sessions Thomas Almon, son of William Almon of Danbury, placed himself as apprentice to Thomas Burgeys of Bergholt Sackville (West Bergholt) in the work of fuller's craft from the Feast of the Annunciation next coming for 7 years, taking for his wages double apparel and 20s., as appears by indenture.

Edward Cock was apprenticed to John Neele of Inworth, brickmaker, from the same date, taking for his wages double apparel and 40s.

Aaron Yonge of Waltham Abbey, tailor, takes apprentice by indenture John Ethyn aged 17 years for 7 years, giving him at the end of his term 5s. and a double apparel convenient for workday and holyday.

Thomas Robinson of Waltham, tanner, takes Thomas Keyes for 8 years, giving at the end 5s.

Robert Hancock of Waltham has acknowledged that he has in his service Thomas Clarke aged 13, whom he retained for 9 years by 9d. giving him by the year, etc., which retainer is void by Statute, wherefore warning is given him to avoid the peril thereof, etc.

William Fynche and Robert Fynche of Waltham linendrapers, unmarried and masterless, keep shop, but for that the said William was prentice in the town he shall be permitted to remain 40 days, and Robert is enjoined to depart forth of the town presently.

At this stage in our study of the effect of the Statute we pause because space does not permit our continuing in such detail. Despite the remarkable number of the returns to Quarter Sessions, it will already be clear that they are far from being a complete series. Their existence in the rolls is apparently somewhat fortuitous, and it is impossible to say why some hundreds are poorly represented or why some years are a blank. The two high constables of every hundred are under an obligation to attend the County Bench. Even those of Chelmsford hundred, who handed in the largest number of returns, evidently failed to deliver some, if such delivery may be equated with their preservation on the rolls. We say 'some' instead of 'many', because there are hints that petty sessions are not necessarily held every quarter, as the great majority of the returns are in the Easter or Michaelmas Sessions rolls, suggesting that these are customary if not obligatory times, unlike the other quarters. To analyse or to total the number of the various offences under the Statute would therefore be a somewhat futile task. The information varies a good deal from hundred to hundred; and it is not always possible to differentiate between the male servants in husbandry and in other occupations : all the women, however, may be assumed, with few or no exceptions, to be in domestic service. An added reason for making a break in our account here is that after 1574 only a few of the returns give any large numbers of bachelors under 30 'working at their own occupation', persons 'out of covenant', or masters paying excessive wages. Even Becontree, with its high figures for 1574, subsequently puts in 'All well' returns or refers only to a few offences. We therefore now quote only exceptional items.

A minor point is that a small proportion of the males take service with their own fathers and one or two with brothers or uncles—at the usual wages. But, as an isolated instance, we find a Coggeshall weaver presented in 1599 for retaining his brother as a weaver or baymaker.

An Ingrave bachelor, out of service, is stated to be 'in summer a tile-maker and in winter a tailor', and 2 Brentwood bachelors 'occupy butcher's craft', being under 30 (1573). A Lindsell man is out of service 'and is a very good servant', and a Willingale Doe smith, 'a good workman, is fugitive and will not keep service nor be bound' (1574). A labourer 'of the age of 50 years and unmarried, being a decrepit and lame person, is in house' with a widow, 'endeavouring himself to labour about all her necessary labours, and is willing to be retained with anyone' (1574). Dengie hundred presents 7 men and women who 'refused to serve in husbandry when they were required by divers persons, and the constables are ordered to bring them to the justices residing nearest to their parishes' (1574).

The Waltham half-hundred return for 1575 has four unusual entries. The first extract illustrates the fact that some persons fail to get hired, to which we refer again later. 'John Lampley of Epping, a servant of a smith or farrier, came and showed he had been out of service' since last Christmas 'and desired to be retained, but upon proclamation made there was none that would retain him, wherefore upon report made by the constables of his good behaviour he was appointed to repair again to Epping and not to depart from thence'. Two Waltham Abbey tailors, 'being unmarried, keep open shop, not having any masters; therefore they forthwith be put in the stocks, and henceforth do no more so'. A husbandman 'came and sought to retain' a youth of 18 for another year, 'and does so, giving him 20s. and pasture for two sheep, and has given him for earnest 1d.' (1575). Thomas Stubberfyeld, a Waltham shoemaker, 'keeps 2 journeymen at least who are not hired by the year' (1575): section 26 of the Act of 1563 obliged clothmakers, fullers, shearmen, weavers, tailors and shoemakers to keep 1 journeyman for every 3 apprentices. A young Shenfield tailor 'hath been warned to provide him a master, but he will not but doth linger at home with his father who is not able to maintain him' (1577).

An original presentment by the petty constables of High Easter in 1574 discloses 3 men out of service, 1 because his master and he cannot agree about wages, but 2 bachelors each 'intend to marry shortly'. The same constables, according to the normal petty sessions return, have found that 'Lady Jates (*sic*) doth keep secretly one William, a stranger, in tailor's craft but not as a covenant servant'. (Dame Mary Gates, widow of Sir John, was sheriff in 1550, privy councillor, and owner of Pleshey Castle.) The next item, for Uttlesford hundred, comes from the ordinary (not the high constables') jury, also in 1574: 'There is at Arkesden one William Hilles, single man, being under 26, who has neither lands to the value of 40s. by the year and uses the craft of a tailor and sets other single men awork with him, to the great hindrance of many other of the same art, being poor men married and with children; and he has often been desired to serve with some of the same art, which he does refuse'. Two years later, this obstinate fellow and 4 other tailors of the same area, 'all unmarried and masterless', are indicted for the same offence, as also in 1571 4 Boreham bachelor tailors 'to the great prejudice of other poor households of the same occupation'. The principle, either ethical or economic, of safeguarding heads of families is voiced, in fact, in several other presentments: the man with a wife and children to support must not be injured by bachelors 'working by their own hand', setting up by themselves 'to the hindrance of the poor householders', or some similar phrase. In the interests of the community generally their earning capacity must be protected against unfair competition.

The two Bynkeses are reported again, not only for 'keeping a tailor's shop together, under the age of 30', but also as seditious papists (1577).[21] Richard Ingram and Osias Hearne, Chelmsford tailors and single men, are also presented (1577) for 'keeping a shop together'. (The will of the former, then termed a tailor of West Hanningfield, was to be proved in 1609.)

Illegal discharge before the end of the year is reported by petty sessions only in three instances. Among them, John Wynter of Stanford-le-Hope, having stolen a sheep, is also charged with turning away John Goose his servant (1587), perhaps the querulous unlicensed schoolteacher twice in trouble in the Archdeacon's court.[22] But it was doubtless thought unnecessary to present employers for dismissing unmarried servants found to be pregnant, this being regarded as a breach of their covenant.

A Marks Tey man who refuses to serve a White Colne husbandman for 48s. wages is to be arrested by the constable (1583); a Feering husbandman for similar refusal to work in husbandry for a Coggeshall man at 48s. wages is fined (1584); and 3 Coggeshall weavers refuse to serve masters (1586). For a 2-year term in husbandry a husbandman gets 'for his wages sufficient food and clothing' but no money; and a girl who agrees to serve for 7 years gets the same, plus double apparel and 20s. at the end (1584). Dunmow hundred presentment (1586), instead of merely listing the masterless, states that 8 males and 3 females, 'unmarried and without service, live idly'. Thurstable hundred reports John Sawkin of Tollesbury for 'not having a master, because no-one requires his service, therefore a day is given him until 10th October to find a master' (1589).

An interesting document, preserved in a Quarter Sessions roll for 1596, is the warrant signed by John Tyndall, J.P., at Bocking and directed to the Braintree constables. 'Whereas Richard Owtinge of the same', it recites, 'of the age of 30 years, brought up in the trade of a clothworker, being required to serve with Stephen Meres of the same, a man of the same trade, has alleged that he is yet bound as apprentice to Gideon Upsher until the Feast of the Annunciation next, whereof there is some doubt', Tyndall orders the constables, at Meres' suit, if Owtinge refused to serve, to bring him before 'the justices' (in Quarter Sessions) 'to show cause why he should not be bound to serve'.

After the fairly normal returns from seven hundreds to the Michaelmas and Epiphany Sessions of 1589-90, only a few brief presentments are found at the end of our period. Of these, two relate to Chelmsford hundred: 4 males without service, a female 'lives idly and is of evil fame', 3 fathers keep 5 children 'in idleness', all 10 'apt to serve' (1590); and 3 single men came into the town to dwell, 2 worked as tailors, the other as a weaver, none having been apprenticed (1591). It is very unfortunate that the high constables' activities in the four years 1594-97 of increasingly severe famine and unemployment through harvest failures (p. 177) are unknown. Following a long gap, there are reports for Barstable—3 masterless males 'having no living that they can prove', certified by 'John Preston, clerk to the constables for the said sessions' (1600); Uttlesford—18 males and 11 females 'masterless', and 5 males and 2 females 'placed' with named masters, for 2 of whom 'the parish to give' the masters small sums for keeping a girl 7 years and for clothing a boy (1602); Freshwell—15 males and 11 females 'not retained in service', and 3 boys apprenticed (1602); and Uttlesford—1 male and 4 females 'masterless' and 2 females 'placed', one man taking 3 of them (1602). The Freshwell sessions definitely terms their placing of the boys as 'apprenticeships', for 6, 5 and 3 years respectively, thus affording further instances of nonconformity to the statutory 7-year minimum. Finally, there is a solitary presentment (1601), with no reference to statute sessions, of an unmarried glover under 30 who had refused the St. Osyth's parishioners' demands to serve a master glover.

But, although we are somewhat bereft of normal petty sessions records at this date, the high constables are still busy. At the last Quarter Sessions of the reign, January 1603, the justices issue an order that 'all petty constables shall make monthly certificates to the high constables of the number of rogues and idle persons they have apprehended and punished', of licensed and unlicensed alehouse-keepers, and of 'all idle and masterless men working at their own hands or having no trade to live by, and that warrant shall be directed against any constables as shall be negligent'. And the high constables are enjoined 'to make a perfect book thereof' and present it regularly to the County Bench. No such 'book' has survived, but the justices' special order undoubtedly discloses their anxiety about the prevalent riotous rumblings of the poor.[23]

To complete the account we must go beyond our period—for a solitary and final record filed at the Epiphany Sessions 1611 : 'Waltham Half Hundred. The Petty Sessions there holden 20th December 1610', at which 14 'householders warned for this service' are apparently the jurors. Reported are '4 masterless men and others that work at their own hand', including a tailor 'not having served 7 years', and under 'servants to tradesmen' are 2 tailors and a smith who 'each keep 2 apprentices bound according to the law'; all of Waltham Holy Cross. There follow the names of 34 men of various parishes including 4 Epping innholders, all 'licensed as victuallers by the Lord Denny and Sir Robert Leigh', J.P.s, and 3 unlicensed victuallers including one in Waltham town who 'holds his house to be an inn'. The rest of the document is a statement of hirings and apprenticeships, arranged under the parishes. Thus ends the long sequence of returns of the hiring sessions. Of their post-Elizabethan counterparts in other counties, only scattered references survive. The Essex Quarter Sessions rolls are again silent about local sessions until 1632-33, when they are no longer concerned with masters and servants but with unlicensed alehouses and vagrants, three returns being sent in from the 'Petty Sessions held at Barking' by several J.P.s who received the petty constables' presentments.

We may now consider to what extent the high constables' sessions functioned for actual hirings as well as for retrospective registration. Although most contracts were made between the sessions, we noticed that some ran from the date of the sessions, denoting apparently that both masters and servants, were present and that the proclamations made at the Lexden sessions name those who were 'free for service', inviting them to come forward 'in open court'; but in 1582 and 1584 'no one came to seek their service'. Then there are the lists of those who defaulted in attending the sessions. Some of their names also appear in the proclamation list at the same sessions. Apart from a few absentee jurors they were apparently masterless men and women. We cannot be certain, but it looks as though a number of would-be employers were also present at each session. If these assumptions are correct, the high constables' meetings were fairly large public gatherings and therefore an important feature in Elizabethan society. Yet we emphasise our knowing only one reference by contemporary writers to these hiring fairs.[24] Regrettable as it is that the elder Breughel did not depict one and that printed literature and original archives elsewhere yield such meagre information, the Essex records thus prove to be all the more valuable to the economic historian.

The next point concerns the places where the high constables' sessions were held and the number of people who assembled there. At Dunmow, Witham, Chelmsford and Lexden sessions, for example, between 60 and 70 constables and others normally attended to represent their parishes. As many as 89 congregated at one Barstable sessions. For Becontree, however, each parish sent only one man, or two at the most, presumably the constables. The meeting-places were mostly in the market-towns, but a few hundreds had no towns or they were by no means centrally situated. So we find that Dengie sessions were held at Purleigh or Southminster; Thurstable at Goldhanger; Winstree at Peldon; Uttlesford at Wenden, Newport, Henham, or Stansted Mountfitchet; Freshwell at Hempstead, Radwinter or Great Sampford; Clavering at Manuden; Barstable at various places; and Lexden, generally at Colchester but twice at 'Fordham Ford'. The latter suggests a point near the bridge over the Colne at the boundary between Fordham and Aldham (the hamlet of Ford Street lies just over the river in the latter parish, and Fordham Bridge was presented as 'greatly decayed' in 1580). This, more than any other place, points to an open-air meeting (the medieval hundred courts are generally believed to have been held in the open), and with a large influx of people it seems entirely logical.[25]

What proportion of the total Elizabethan population were engaged as servants? Mr Peter Laslett's estimate is 'over one in seven'.[26] We have already pointed out that the term 'servant' had a wide connotation. Better expressed, 'This category contains not only domestic servants, but also servants in husbandry, or as we would call them, farm labourers, together with a certain number of industrial workers who were resident with their employers'.[27] Let us take the Lexden return of 1582 (see p. 152), showing about 100 servants and masterless persons. The population of the hundred, excluding Colchester, was approximately one-fifteenth of the whole county, which suggests a total of about 2,400 out of our tentative 'estimated *adult* population of (Elizabethan) Essex of 35,000-40,000,[28] or about 1 in

24. But it is probable that none of the returns really gives all the servants hired or available for service: the actual numbers were wholly dependent on the efforts of the petty constables in tracking them down. Our hypothetical figure need not therefore contradict that of Mr Laslett. Among several other subjects on which the high constables' sessions provide material for research is that of mobility. With very few exceptions, the contracts were for one year. The same writer states: 'It is apparent that, during the period of life spent as an in-servant, it was normal for a man to change jobs every year'; and he adds that instances of two-year hirings, though unusual, are also found and that 'the hiring year began in autumn at the hiring fairs and ended the following autumn when the farmer had the money, after selling his harvest, to pay the year's wages'.[29] What happened at the end of the short term? Did the servants normally renew their agreements with the same masters or find another employer? Research to try to answer this question is outside the present writer's terms of reference, but the index of persons to the typescript Calendar of Essex Quarter Sessions Records, which includes every name in the original rolls, would materially ease the task. Judging by the evidence collected elsewhere for the late 16th and the 17th centuries, the degree of movement of servants was remarkably high, but mostly only a short distance. It would seem that nearly two-thirds of their migrations lay under 10 miles and five-sixths under 20 miles; the lower figure in fact may perhaps be equated with 'a half-day's walking distance' to the hiring fair at the 'nearest market-town'.[30] Here again, the limitation to market-towns is in need of broadening, because a few of the Essex statute sessions were held, as we have just seen, at other places of easy access within certain hundreds.

## Wages

The making of wages assessments by the county justices at their Easter sessions was a practice that had prevailed long before the Statute of Artificers of 1563. The Ordinance of Labourers of 1349 had compelled all able-bodied men to work and established as the legal rate of wages the level of 1346, that is, just before the Black Death of 1348-49. The Statute of Labourers of 1351 fixed wages for certain occupations, 'though apparently limited to unskilled labour outside the craft gilds'.[31] An Act of 1390 gave the justices power to fix rates below the statutory limits. The Statute of 1563 and its predecessors stipulated *maximum*, not minimum, rates, the objects being to stop demands for 'excessive' wages, to encourage agriculture by preventing the drift from the country to the towns, and to restrict easy mobility of labour generally because it posed a threat to national peace. But the 1563 Act rejected the principle of a single *statutory* maximum and authorised the J.P.s to assess their own local maxima.[32]

Wages assessments in theory were made annually, but it was not uncommon for the county justices, despite fluctuating food prices, merely to renew existing rates over long periods. For Elizabethan Essex a solitary complete wages assessment has survived—for the borough of Colchester, made in 1583.[33] It sets out the rates in four sections. Under 'Servants of husbandry by the whole year' we find 'a bailiff of husbandry and able to discharge the same' assessed at 53s. 4d., with livery (allowance of cloth) 10s., 'a common servant of husbandry' of 20 or over at 33s. 4d., with livery 6s. 8d., and 'women servants of the best, being a cook and taking charge of an household or a dairy', of 18 or over at 20s., livery 10s. From 'labourers, harvest excepted, we extract 'Michaelmas to Easter by the day with meat and drink 3d., without meat and drink 7d.' Harvest rates are much higher, the best being 'mowers of corn by the day', with meat and drink 8d., without 16d. It ends with a long and detailed section headed 'Artificers, their servants and apprentices'. Masons, carpenters, wheelwrights and other craftsmen are put down for the winter half-year at 4d. with meat and drink and 10d. without. Alternative figures for certain piecework reveal wheelwrights being given 3s. 4d. for 'making a pair (of) wheels, finding themselves'. In addition, yearly wages of journeymen (apprentices who have served their term) employed by various craftsmen range from 40s. to 4s. 4d. with meat and drink, with livery 6s. 8d. to 10s. Artificers' 'servants and apprentices' receive from Michaelmas to Easter with victuals 2d., without 4d. The phraseology is typical of that found in most assessments. Of the very few others extant for our period, that for Buckinghamshire two decades earlier discloses much lower rates: bailiff 40s., livery 6s. 8d.; labourers in husbandry, Hallowtide to Easter with meat and drink 2d., without 5d.[34] The rates for Kent, 1563 and renewed annually without change until 1589, were: bailiff 56s. 8d., labourers 40s.; best woman 26s. 8d.; all without livery; labourers, winter by the day with meat and drink 3d., without 7d.[35]

No full Elizabethan wages assessment for the *county* of Essex has been preserved. We have, however, figures of recommended increases for some farm-workers and the more experienced women. These are recorded, quite exceptionally, in a presentment made in 1599 by the Grand Jury:

> We present ourselves to be offenders against the rate made at the Quarter Sessions held the 6th of April in the 40th year of her Majesty's reign (1598) for servants' wages, and desire the favour of the Court.
> 
> Item, we certify that the rates for servants for husbandry be too small, and think it be requisite to augment them as follows:
> 
> A bailiff of husbandry, taking charge and able to discharge the same, by the year 50s., and for a livery 10s.
> 
> The best ploughman and carter 50s., and for a livery 10s.

The best woman servant, being to cook or able to take charge of a household 26s. 8d., livery 6s. 8d.
For all the other rates for men servants in husbandry we allow of them, and likewise for women servants.
Item, we certify that the rates for labourers in husbandry be too small and think it requisite to augment them as follows:
From Hallowmas to Candlemas (i.e. 1 November to 2 February), with meat and drink by the day 3d., without meat and drink 8d.; all the rest of the year (haytime and harvest excepted), with meat and drink 4d., without meat and drink 10d.; and for the rest of the rates mentioned in the rule we do allow of them.

Regrettably, the decision of the County Bench is not recorded. The opening sentence implies that some, if not many, masters have been guilty of paying wages above those assessed (or, more likely, merely renewed) in 1598. The Statute of Artificers had imposed a penalty of ten days' imprisonment or a fine of £5 on masters giving wages higher than the rate and 21 days on servants receiving them; but there is ample evidence in Essex and some elsewhere that the maxima were frequently ignored.[36]

An appropriate comparison may be made with the Hertfordshire rates of 1592, shortly before the series of disastrous harvests. This lengthy assessment enumerates the wages for numerous kinds of artificers, but parallels with those suggested for Essex in 1599 are found only in the general classes: 'a man servant of husbandry of the best sort' (no distinctions about period or meat and drink), with livery 40s., without 46s. 8d.; the 'third sort' (apparently corresponding with ordinary labourers in husbandry), with livery 26s. 8d., without 33s. 4d.; 'the best sort of women servants', with livery 21s., without 26s. 8d.[37] Judging by the last figures, which afford the closest comparison, the Essex women's wages certainly needed to be raised owing to higher food prices. Indeed, by section 11 of the Act, Quarter Sessions had to take into consideration 'the plenty or scarcity of the time and other circumstances'.

The two earliest full assessments for Essex are those made in 1612 and 1651.[39] The lack of any complete Elizabethan Essex assessments is, however, partly compensated for by the figures given in the high constables' petty sessions returns to Quarter Sessions. These, unlike the formal maximum rates allowed by the County Bench, represent the actual wages received by those in service under their contracts. Thus, as already noticed, they range during 1568 and 1569 between 26s. 8d. and 46s. 8d. for men (the very lowest, 13s. 4d., apparently applying only to boys) and between 16s. and 22s. for maidservants. But we must not overlook the presentments for 'excessive' wages. Such illegal rates, in 1572 for instance, while mostly around £3, include wages as high as £6 13s. 4d. Nor are such breaches confined to a few masters, the Chelmsford hundred return alone disclosing as many as 22 employers of 31 covenant servants getting inflated sums. Yet, as we have seen, there are only slight hints in the county records of either masters or employees being punished. The law was being flouted, because market forces were more influential. Such figures of real wages as we are vouchsafed in Essex and elsewhere are a warning not to regard the published assessments as more than a rough guide to the sums received, a point emphasised again by a recent writer.[40]

We have further independent evidence in the account-books of Sir John Petre of Thorndon Hall. The servants are paid *quarterly,* like those of his father, Sir William Petre of Ingatestone Hall.[41] In the earliest year 1576-7 they run from 6s. 8d. for women to 15s. for the brewer and 16s. 8d. for the head gardener and the park-keeper. The male cook is rewarded with 25s. a quarter. The wages of the 'bailiff in husbandry' work out at 53s. 4d. a year, which may be compared with the 50s. recommended for such men by the grand jury in 1599. The last of the five years for which such accounts are preserved is 1593-4, which is one of the complete statements. The 7 maidservants still receive only 6s. 8d. a quarter, with one woman getting 10s. Of the male staff, the quarterly figures are: 22 at 13s. 4d., 1 at 15s., 5 at 16s. 8d., 8 at 20s., and two superior servants at 25s. and 33s. 4d., which broadly reveal more generous rates than those assessed for Hertfordshire in 1592. In addition, all servants are allowed summer and winter liveries of cloth.[42]

Perhaps the most complete account of covenanted wages is that for the whole of Waltham half-hundred, except Chingford, registered at the high constables' sessions in December 1610 and incorporated in their presentment to Epiphany Quarter Sessions 1611. No less than 104 servants' wages are given, males between 26s. 8d. and £3 6s. 8d. (mostly £2-£3) and females between 20s. and 50s. (mostly 26s. 8d.), the continuing general low level of maidservants' wages being noticeable.[43]

A few documents concerning wages, other than those in the petty sessions returns, are extant in the Quarter Sessions rolls. Six cases of refusal to pay wages, but with negligible detail, are found; in one instance the county justices ordered the master to do so. A dispute between two Hatfield Peverel men led Edward Meade, husbandman, to write in 1580 to the Bench complaining that he had 'faithfully served John Pilborough, gentleman, by covenant in husbandry' for a year, but his master had detained 19s. 8d., part of his wages, and 'utterly denies to pay the same'. Pilborough, enjoined to appear before Lord Rich, seems to be an upper servant of the Earl of Sussex living at New Hall, Boreham, and was often involved in other trouble.[44]

The records quoted are best considered against the economic background. During the second half of the century the condition of the labourer and artisan became gradually worse owing to prices rising more rapidly than wages, especially during the famine years of 1594-97. The Government was alarmed, and much paper was used by those concerned with trying to cope with the grave situation. From the various instructions issued, we will end by citing a circular letter addressed by the Privy Council to the justices of all the counties in 1595 :

> We are given to understand that sundry workfolks with their families .. are like to be very much distressed by reason the clothiers in this time of dearth do not anything increase their wages. We pray you heartily to deal earnestly with the clothiers in this behalf, procuring them to yield such reasonable increase of wages.[45]

## Apprentices

Apprenticeship was the normal means in medieval times by which the country was supplied with skilled labour. Seven years was the customary period—reckoned as fitting for master to instruct learner and learner to reciprocate with his labour. By the 1563 Statute the seven-year term became an obligatory minimum, and the apprentice had to serve to the age of 21; starting ages were to be over 10 and under 18. More important, it became illegal for anyone to exercise any craft unless he had served his full apprenticeship, offenders being liable for the severe penalty of 40s. a month. The conditions and phraseology in apprentices' indentures, although by no means uniform, are fairly well known. These include good behaviour and abstention from gambling and other unlawful games, fornicating, and haunting alehouses. At the end of his term he should receive from his master two suits of clothes, but no wages because he had benefited by tuition, board and lodging.

The whole subject of Master and Apprentice has been thoroughly studied for our period (and beyond) in a work that made use of both national and local records.[46] Of the latter, as we should expect, by far the richest source drawn on by the author is the Essex Quarter Sessions archives. The view of an earlier writer, that 'though apprenticeship was adopted primarily in the interests of trade and manufactures, it was regarded by the Government with additional favour as a partial solution of the problem of pauperism',[47] does not seem to be contradicted by more recent research nor by the Essex records, for example, in the unique omnibus indictment of many unapprenticed musicians, to be mentioned shortly.

In the last but one section, we noticed that some of the high constables' returns include new apprenticeships and the names of unapprenticed workers in trades or crafts as well as certain related offences. It would seem that, although most of the unemployed males and females were immediately or eventually hired for the yearly minimum period, a few at least were taken as apprentices. We shall now see what the normal Quarter Sessions records disclose about apprenticeship.

Presentments by the ordinary hundredal (i.e. not high constables') juries, or indictments, for non-apprenticeship number only six: a High Ongar single man working as a painter (1588); a basket-maker as a baker (1590) and a chandler as a basket-maker (1599), both of Barking; a Halstead weaver for baking and making starch (1592); a Coggeshall clothier as a baker (1600); and a Halstead tailor for working as such (1601). The only recorded fine, 3s. 4d., is that on the basket-maker, levied apparently in the lower sessions or by two J.P.s.[48]

In 1572 a petition was presented to the County Bench by William Cooke, Thomas Castelyn, Richard Grene, Thomas Waller and John Darbye, all mercers of Brentwood, stating that 5 tailors, a smith, a labourer and a widow of several rural neighbouring parishes, 'unlawfully use the occupations' (the usual phrase) 'of mercers, haberdashers and grocers' without having been apprenticed to the same, and desiring proceedings against them; 6 Chelmsford men, whose trades are not given, were also 'plaintiffs' against the same 8. The result is not on record, but the case recalls the major Essex town versus villages conflict which had been eased by the exemption in the Cloth Act (1 Eliz., c.15, 1558) of Bocking, West Bergholt and Dedham (Boxted and Langham were exempted by 27 Eliz., c.23, 1585) from prosecution by Colchester Corporation. This petition 'is of some interest as revealing one of the very few known cases in Elizabethan England of town retailers charging villagers with unapprenticed trading.'[49]

An intriguing document, dated 1573, exists in one of the few Assize files which have by chance been preserved among the Quarter Sessions rolls. Headed, 'A bill (i.e. indictment) to be made against those using the trade of musician, not being apprenticed thereto', it names no less than 56 men of parishes, nearly all rural, in all parts of the county. Their occupations are various, e.g. husbandman, tailor, etc., but no clue is afforded as to the form of the originating process—presentment, information or otherwise. We can surely discount their having been presented by professional musicians, fearing that their livelihood would be prejudiced by 'part-time' rivals. It seems possible that, under the vagrancy laws, always severe against wandering minstrels, they were arrested but not being vagabonds were prosecuted under the Statute of Labourers. The hypothesis, however, is a weak one, and the question still arises, What were the circumstances leading to this round-up? The anti-vagrancy measures of 1569-71 had involved some forcing of masterless men into service, but why this drive against 'musicians', apparently not unemployed, which was never repeated later? Their abodes are too scattered to suggest their having all congregated at one of the big fairs, and had they been spotted at fairs by a professional informer the document would have referred to his part in the charge. This indictment remains an enigma.

In 1594 Quarter Sessions received a petition from Robert Knowlden, a Bocking weaver, stating that he 'hath good liking' to take apprentice the son of a poor townsman, and as the justices had been informed by many Bocking men that the town 'is charged with poverty' the weaver's proposal was deemed a very charitable one. The lad having been brought for inspection before the county justices, they ordered his being apprenticed to the weaver. Failure to teach his apprentice resulted in a carpenter being bound over by a J.P. to appear at Quarter Sessions in 1589: the sole instance of this offence.

In the first volume we narrated the charge against an apprentice for assaulting his master.[50] The reverse occurred in two instances in which individual justices enquired into charges of battered apprentices. Roger Harlackenden had examined John Whitlock of Coggeshall concerning his apprentice's complaint, and the master refused to enter into covenants by indenture as agreed or to discharge the apprentice (1595). A high constable living in Coggeshall also testified to Whitlock's contemptuous behaviour to himself and the headboroughs. 'Wherefore', the J.P. concluded, 'I thought good to bind him over to abide the censure of the Court'. James Crowe was likewise bound over, with Richard Windell and Edward Benton as his sureties, all Bocking clothiers, because of ill-treating his apprentice. After returning to his father, Mr (Thomas) Bendysh and Mr (Henry) Maxey were 'to view the hurts' (1598). Crowe was ordered to 'bear all charges both for the case and diet, and the justices at the next Sessions to dispose of the apprentice at their discretions'. Standing *in loco parentis*, a master had a legal right to chastise his delinquent apprentice, and the two charges of abuse doubtless represent only a very small fraction of such incidents.

We must now introduce informers—those strange creatures through whose activities offenders against statutes providing a fine were brought to justice. Informers flourished from about the beginning of our period until late in the next century. In theory they could claim one-half of the appropriate penalty, the other half accruing to the Crown. Their mercenary efforts had been mainly pursued in the royal courts at Westminster until the Act of 31 Eliz., c.5 (1589), enjoined them to prosecute at Quarter Sessions, but generally without much effect. Its first results are found in the county records of Essex, Cheshire, and Staffordshire in 1591, the defendants being charged with not having been apprenticed.[51] In Essex, between that year and 1603, 8 informers produced 15 such delinquents. The periods of the alleged offences were nearly all for 12, 11 or 10 months, carrying the prescribed forfeitures of £24, £22 and £20, of which the informer claimed his half-share. The two first-named informers will appear again in the next section on Illegal Dealing. In 1591 Josias Portwaye, a Braintree tailor, prosecuted a Coggeshall draper, a Halstead victualler, and a Rivenhall wheelwright. Edward Hedd in 1597 sued Thomas Mussett of Barking, miller, for exercising that craft, Thomas Tyrrell of Woodford, gentleman, and John Hyndes of Epping for trading as bakers, Hyndes also as a brewer, and Richard Chapman of Stebbing and Elias Marredge of Little Easton as tailors. The remainder were brought by a carpenter against another carpenter, both of West Ham (1591); by a man whose occupation and abode are not given against a husbandman and a cordwainer, both of Maldon, for brewing (1594); by a yeoman against a husbandman, both of Great Chesterford, for trading as a petty chapman and haberdasher (1599); by a Horndon-on-the-Hill yeoman against a Mucking yeoman for brewing (1601); by an unidentified man against Edward Pasfeild for milling; and by Thomas Carder, hairclothmaker, against a shoemaker and a petty chapman for using the trade of a hairclothmaker, Pasfeild and the last three all of Wethersfield (1601-03). (Of this narrowly localised craft, more anon.) The Chesterford offender failed to answer the charge at four successive sessions and at the fifth was adjudged to have forfeited the £24 for 12 months' practice. This is in fact the only recorded instance in the surviving Elizabethan county records of Essex or elsewhere of the forfeiture having actually been sanctioned, perhaps because the man did not appear; and two years later he was arrested for refusal to pay.[52] 'Varlets', informers were sometimes dubbed, but the more active members of the tribe served in this indirect way to enforce some of the Tudor mercantilist measures.[53]

Our cumulative chronicle of breaches of the Statute of Artificers has revealed hundreds of offenders in the high constables' returns. But how effective was the Act? If the main criterion is the number and severity of the punishments, we are faced with the fact that the Quarter Sessions records do not contain a single indictment based on such returns, the explanation being apparently that the defendants were dealt with, if at all, by the local J.P.s. We learned incidentally, from the Chelmsford hundred returns of 1572, of their imposing fines of 12d. and 2s. Almost certainly delinquents were brought before justices acting in pairs 'out of Sessions' (i.e. Quarter Sessions), as was customary for various other offences. Further confirmation is found in the Dengie hundred report in 1574 that the constables were ordered to take masterless men and women to the nearest J.P.s. We also saw that failure to appear at petty sessions in 1574 earned one master the heavy fine of 40s. and five servants the stocks. On the positive side, there is abundant evidence that the high constables' sessions exercised important functions as labour exchanges and in enforcing as well as registering service contracts and to a lesser extent apprenticeship agreements.

Although the County Bench evidently delegated cases under the Statute to the divisional justices, it dealt directly with a few offences involving other relations between master and servant or apprentice. Enticement to leave service and so deprive the master is the subject of six charges at Quarter

Sessions. As early as 1562 we find two indictments resulting in a 12d. fine on each of the enticers. The Court's punishment is 10s. in the case against William Underell of Aveley, gentleman, for enticing a maid to quit her master and for 'still detaining her' (1564); and 3s. 4d. is the penalty levied by Thomas Mildmay and John Pynchon, J.P.s, on Edward Hales of Witham, the vicar, for 'instigating the servant to Edward Dawny to leave his service' (1570). Thomas Turner lured away the covenant servant of John Oxburowe, both of Great Henny (1582). Premature departure figures in two more indictments. In 1563 Roger Amyce of Wakes Colne, J.P., ordered the Coggeshall constables to arrest a weaver's servant for 'absconding before the end of his agreed term'; but adds, 'If the boy will be content to serve this bearer, his master, you shall not need to bring him the next sessions, otherwise you must needs have him there'; a sensible decision, but the presence of the document on the roll implies that the lad failed to return. Likewise in 1567 a maidservant absconded before the end of her year's contract with Nicholas Smythe of Rivenhall, gentleman, and this time her new employer, Thomas Burnett of Cressing, barber-surgeon, is also charged because he knew of her offence: 'fine assessed at 12d. by Thomas Smith (of Cressing Temple, J.P.) and others'. In the next four Quarter Sessions cases the emphasis is on the master losing his apprentice's labour. Thomas Myller, a Maldon collarmaker, went to the house of John Spigurnell there, and 'incited and procured' both his son and his apprentice to leave his service. Myller kept them for three nights, after which the son 'withdrew himself from the government' of his father for a further three weeks, so that he lost their service (1587). A youth left his master, Christopher Burrowes, a Purleigh tailor, only ten days after being apprenticed, and Thomas Thrussell, a Purleigh husbandman, retained him in service, knowing that he had departed without licence (1598). Thomas Robinson, a Waltham Abbey tanner, enticed away the female apprentice of Nathan Butler, a gentleman of the same town, and 'with others in his company led her up and down the country, not knowing now where she is become' (1599). George the son of George Chapman, an Epping innholder, apprenticed to a certain Bankes, a London cutler, had apparently run away (1601), so the father was bound by his own bail to ensure the son's return to his master and his appearance before the Masters of the Cutlers' Company.

---

[1] G. W. Prothero (ed.), *Select Statutes and Other Constitutional Documents* (1894 and later edns.); A. E. Bland, P. A. Brown, and R. H. Tawney, *English Economic History* (1914, many later reprints); R. H. Tawney and Eileen Power, *Tudor Economic Documents* (1924, later reprints).

[2] *E.L.: Disorder*, 62-5.

[3] The Act did not apply the one-year minimum generally; for this peculiar feature, see S. T. Bindoff, 'The Making of the Statute of Artificers' (in *Elizabethan Government and Society*, 1961).

[4] *Essex Sessions of the Peace, 1351, 1371-79* (ed. Elizabeth C. Furber, *Ess. Archl. Soc. Occl. Pubns.*, 1952).
[5] Margaret G. Davies, *The Enforcement of English Apprenticeship* (Harvard Univ. Press, 1956), 217-20.
[6] 'Piecemeal traces' of high constables' sessions are found in Norfolk Q.S. records Davies, *op. cit.*, 189). Three presentments (between 1564 and 1582) of offences under the Statute of Artificers are recorded for Middlesex (*Middlesex County Records*, i).
[7] *E.L.: Disorder*, 12-28.   [7a] Calendar of Q.S. rolls (15 vols., 1554-1603).
[8] Harrison, *op. cit.*, 92, has only a brief mention of high constables' sessions, 'called petty sessions', where servants, among others, 'are often reformed for their excesses'.
[9] *E.L.: Disorder*, 33-35.   [10] *Ibid.*, 31.   [11] *Ibid.*, 204-12.   [12] *Ibid.*, 35.
[13] *E.L.: Disorder*, index, *s.v.* shovegroat.
[14] In 1577 a report to the Privy Council of wool bought by Coggeshall clothiers lists 27 of them (see p. 196, n. 17).   [15] Cf. *E.L.: Disorder*, 30.
[16] For a forged passport for leaving a master's service, 1592, see *E.L.: Disorder*, 86.   [17] *E.L.: Disorder*, 26.
[18] In the same year, 1572, he was assaulted in the highway and his ward abducted (*E.L.: Disorder*, 194).
[19] William Rooke was involved in a church pew feud in 1576 (*E.L.: Morals*, 133); and the will of a gentleman of that name, of Upton in West Ham, was to be proved in 1597.
[20] *E.L.: Morals*, 150-1.   [21] *E.L.: Disorder*, 46-7.
[22] *E.L.: Morals*, 104, 186, 187.   [23] *E.L.: Disorder*, 64.
[24] At the statute (fair), folks do come of purpose to hire servants' (T. Deloney, *Thomas of Reading*, c.1600); Thomas Hardy (*Far from the Madding Crowd*) describes a hiring market in Victorian Wessex.
[25] Harrison's vague passages (*op. cit.*, 86, 89-90, 92) about high constables' petty sessions (no mention of hiring of servants) and the clerk of the market are curious and suggest that he never attended one, as indeed he had no cause to do.
[26] P. Laslett, 'Size and Structure of the Household in England over Three Centuries' (*Population Studies*, xxiii (1969), 219).
[27] P. Spufford, 'Population Mobility in Pre-Industrial England' (*Genealogists' Magazine*, vol. 17, no. 8 (1973), 422).
[28] *E.L.: Morals*, 1.   [29] Spufford, 423.   [30] *Ibid.*, 427-8.
[31] E. Lipson, *Economic History of England* (7th edn. 1937), iii, 251. For some early figures, see Furber (n. 4 above).
[32] For assessments, see R. K. Kelsall, *Wage Regulation under the Statute of Artificers* (1938); W. E. Minchington, *Wage Regulation in Pre-Industrial England* (1972); *The Local Historian*, viii (1968-9), 293.   [33] Copy in E.R.O., T/A 323.
[34] Printed in full in R. H. Tawney and Eileen Power, *Tudor Economic Documents* (1924, reprinted), i, 335-38.
[35] Printed in full in *Eng. Hist. Rev.*, xli (1926), 270-73.
[36] Lipson, *op. cit.*, iii, 275.
[37] Printed in full in W. Le Hardy, *Guide to the Hertfordshire Record Office*, Part I (1961), 15-19.
[39] See illustrations—for 1612, in Emmison, *Guide to the E.R.O.* (1st edn., 1946), 19 (a MS. list); for 1651 (a printed list), *ibid.*, 20; neither list is illustrated in 2nd edn. (1969).
[40] *The Local Historian*, viii, 293-9.   [41] Emmison, *Tudor Secretary*, 152-3.
[42] E.R.O., D/DP A18, 22.

[43] Printed in full in W. (now Sir William) Addison, *Essex Heyday* (1949), 94-5.
[44] *E.L.: Disorder,* 125, 195; *E.L.: Morals,* 103, 262.
[45] *A.P.C.,* xxv, 44. An Act of 1604 enjoined a *minimum* wage for textile workers.
[46] Margaret G. Davies, *The Enforcement of English Apprenticeship, 1563-1642* (Harvard Univ. Press, 1956), esp. the concluding chapter.
[47] J. Dunlop, *English Apprenticeship and Child Labour* (1912), 68.
[48] A trifle may be added to the extraordinary libel case in 1600 concerning the highly scurrilous Chelmsford ballads (*E.L.: Disorder,* 71-79). Filed under Midsummer Sessions 1597 is the apprenticeship indenture for 12 years of Micah son of (blank) Barker of Woodham Ferrers deceased, made with consent of his father-in-law John Arthure of Springfield, yeoman, to Clement Pope of Chelmsford, glover (*ibid.,* 72-3, 77). [49] Davies, *op. cit.,* 99, 154, 204, 259.
[50] *E.L.: Disorder,* 168-9. [51] Davies, *op. cit.,* 28.
[52] *Ibid.,* 51; also pp. 83 and 90 for statistics, undifferentiated by counties, and p. 203 for details of 12 Essex cases, all of informers' apprenticeship prosecutions in the Westminster courts.
[53] In her concluding chapters, Dr. Davies discusses in broad terms the rather imperfect evidence about the effectiveness of the Statute of Artificers in relation to apprenticeship.

# 10
# Dealers in Food Supplies
## Licensing

To understand the efforts of the Elizabethan Privy Council and Parliament to control the nation's economy, we must first look at the position in the Edwardian years. In 1550 the former attempted to restrain the rapidly rising prices of foodstuffs and other commodities caused by the debasement of the coinage and by bad harvests. It enjoined justices of the peace to make arrangements to discover cases of grain-hoarding in farm barns and houses and to release any surplus to the markets. In the councillors' eyes, the root of the evil lay, however, in black market and speculative dealings by that Tudor trio of traders known as forestallers, engrossers and regraters. Accordingly, a proclamation was issued forbidding them under heavy penalties to buy corn, livestock, butter and cheese for re-sale.[1] This proving insufficient, the Act of 5 & 6 Edw. VI, c.14 (1552), was aimed at controlling their iniquitous activities. To *forestall* was to purchase privately any such foodstuffs on their way to a market or fair : to *regrate,* to buy corn or other dead victual and sell it again in the same market or fair or another within four miles; and to *engross,* to buy up wholesale such corn or a standing crop, in order to retail it or to hoard it, awaiting higher prices; all three offences involving pernicious profit-taking on the transaction by raising the price and thus injuring the poor. Section 7 imposed severe restrictions on such dishonest middlemen, while necessarily giving safeguards against the prosecution of ordinary dealers, such as fish, meat and fowl wholesalers, innkeepers and victuallers. Similar protection was given to lawful 'buying of any corn, fish, butter or cheese, by any such badger, lader, kidder or carrier' selling in open market, but he had to be authorized by three local J.P.s; and it was extended, with the same proviso, to 'common drovers' buying cattle in accustomed localities for re-sale at reasonable prices at fairs or markets over 40 miles away. These privileges in all cases excluded any form of forestalling. If conviction was secured through the report of an informer, he could claim half the amount of the forfeiture or fine imposed on the defendant.

In order to tighten control and probably because of the poor harvest of 1562, a further statute, 5 Eliz., c.12 (1563), obliged every 'badger, lader, kidder or carrier of corn, fish, butter or cheese, or drover of cattle' to be bound by a pecuniary recognizance registered by the clerk of the peace after the issue of a licence by Quarter Sessions. Even so, such chapmen or itinerant dealers still remained subject to the existing market regulations.

Thus the Tudor government endeavoured to cope with some of the evils of inflation by attacking part of the problem, especially corn-hoarding, at the source. All victuals and food, with the recognized exceptions, were to be bought and sold in open market; to intercept it before reaching the stall or to create a neighbouring market for the same foodstuff was anti-social behaviour and a high crime against the State, because it increased the cost of the necessaries of life.

After the series of disastrous harvests of 1594-97, resulting in a severe dearth and greatly inflated food prices, the heavy hand of the Council came down on the counties and boroughs by means of drastic prohibitions. Ample information about these supervisory activities, drawn from their minute books and the State papers, is in print. Much of this concerns Essex, but lack of space precludes our quoting more than a few instances.[2] But of the actual effect of the statutes and Council orders—at any rate, outside the boroughs—virtually nothing has been known, except for the years of acute distress in the last decade of the century, because of the almost wholesale loss of Quarter Sessions records of earlier date, apart from those for Essex. The meagre evidence from the Sessions rolls of several other counties is noted later.

We shall therefore deal fairly fully with this aspect of economic life in Essex, first with the issue of licences and then with the closely-related offences of forestalling, engrossing and regrating and with corn-hoarding. It is an exceptional, if somewhat pedestrian, account.

In the 'Articles for the Petty Sessions' (the high constables' hundredal sessions), engrossing was among the offences for which the Essex Quarter Sessions about 1562 had especially demanded reports based on local enquiry.[3] Action was taken in June 1563 by a man (a J.P.?) writing from 'my house besides Charing Cross' to the clerk of the peace for the issue of a licence for 'a buyer, lader and carrier of victual, corn and grain' to a Dagenham dealer, 'a friend of mine', but the letter is unsigned. At the Easter Sessions, 1572, a combined licence was granted to Lynnet (*sic*) Crane and Richard Meres, both of Steeple Bumpstead, 'loaders', each to be 'a common buyer, seller, transporter and carrier of butter and cheese', the document being witnessed by Richard Twedy, Vincent Harris and Thomas Gent, J.P.s, and written by Gent's 'servant' (i.e. clerk). Three months later Roger Amyce, a Wakes Colne J.P., wrote to the clerk of the peace : 'At the special suit of a son of mine, a Fellow of King's College in Cambridge, I am to advise you to send me by this bearer a licence for one William Cockeley to be a pedlar and to buy and carry sea-fish and oysters from the sea to Cambridge. I know the man to be very honest and will undertake he shall and will observe all conditions contained in the Statute'. In 1580-85 the county clerk received further letters from several

J.P.s requesting or authorizing him to write licences: to William Rycard to buy and sell butter, eggs and other victuals (from Thomas Meade, written at Serjeants' Inn); to 'a neighbour and tenant of mine in (Great) Bardfield', to be a badger and kidder of corn (from Robert Wrothe, written at 'Durance' in Enfield, Middlesex); to John Goodwyn *alias* Gudgin, 'a miller and neighbour of mine', to buy and sell corn (from James Morice at Chipping Ongar); to Roke Johnson and Simon Wylmote of Walden for the same (from George Nycolls, apparently at Walden); and to Richard Steele of Barking, 'a man of good behaviour and very fit to be licensed as a common kidder and buyer of butter, cheese and other victuals' (from Thomas Pawle of Clay Hall (in Great Ilford) and Henry Archer).

There are preserved in 1574 six recognizances of licensed tanners, all of Witham and adjacent parishes, 'bound under the Act of 5 Eliz.' (c.8, 1563) 'touching tanners, curriers, shoemakers and other artificers occupying the cutting of leather'; also another tanner's bond, dated 1586, following the granting of his licence by Lord Darcy and Edmund Pirton.

## Illegal Dealing and Food Shortage

So much for the extant traders' licences: probably a tithe of those actually issued,[4] but sufficient to illustrate the positive aspect of the Elizabethan statute. There is far more information about prosecutions for illegal trading and hoarding of food supplies. Two important questions arise, to which the Essex records supply answers. Were there any determined campaigns against the nefarious activities of these dealers in times of economic crisis? What were the reactions of the County justices or the Assize judges to the Council's injunctions in such years? First we may note the years in which the harvests were 'deficient', 'bad', or resulted in a dearth,[5] scarcity of course continuing until the following harvest, which, more than once, was poor or disastrous partly because of shortage of seed-corn from the previous low yield. The critical years, which may be borne in mind for the rest of the chapter, were 1555 (bad harvest), 1556 (dearth), 1562, 1565 and 1573 (all bad), 1576 (deficient), 1586 and 1594-95 (bad), and 1596-97 (dearth). Wheat prices, according to the Assize of Bread taken by the borough of Colchester, show the following violent fluctuations:— 1581 (Feb., 26s.); 1586-87 (Sept.-June, 41s. 6d.); 1592 (June, 18s.); 1593 (March, 20s. 6d.; Oct., 24s.); 1594 (Feb., 28s.; Sept., 42s. 10d.); 1596 (Oct., 43s. 6d.; Nov., 48s.); 1597 (Aug., 48s.); 1598 (Jan., 52s.).[6]

Turning to the evidence, the last of the three surviving Marian Quarter Sessions rolls (January 1557) records a single engrossing offence, John Nuland of Orsett being presented because he 'doth buy certain wheat and rye on the ground and sold it again to divers persons unknown', but the verdict is not stated.

Whereas most charges arose out of the reports sent in by both the ordinary hundredal and the high constables' petty sessions, it is significant that the earliest Elizabethan record is a long presentment by the grand jury, undated but enrolled in July 1564. This deals solely with unlicensed buyers and sellers of butter. Of these, 8 belonged to West Ham, 2 to Steeple Bumpstead (the same pair who were to be licensed in 1572), and 1 each from Dagenham, Barking and Great Baddow; among them were 4 wives. This is the only occasion on which the grand jury concerned itself with the matter.

Failure of the harvest of 1565 caused much alarm about the food supply. The first case of corn-hoarding came from Great Bardfield in that year, when the ordinary hundredal jury presented Robert Corney (who had served as village constable a few years earlier), because he 'doth ingrate wheat to the number of 30 quarters and hath kept it so long that it is not meet or wholesome for man's sustenance, whereof 10 seam' (a seam contained 8 bushels) 'is not good, and hath sold of the same wheat 15 quarters as we think, contrary to the statute.' 'Let process be made' is noted. A similar incident was reported in 1566 by another hundredal jury in north Essex. William Scott of Pebmarsh 'did lay in at Halstead in the cellar of one Thomas Batman 8 or 9 seam of wheat and kept it there by the space of a year and was required by divers that would buy the same corn and would neither sell them of it nor bring any of it to the market, and thus we made certificate of it to the high constables and they to Sir Thomas Golding'. (The entry is marked 'void'.) The preceding paragraph, obviously based on articles of enquiry and confirmed by a further document in the same roll, reads : 'For engrossers, forestallers and regraters we have made certificate to Sir Thomas Golding, the Queen's Majesty's commissioner'. He was a J.P., but there is no record of his having been specially deputed to enquire into market offences.[7] A solitary hoarder in the south of the county 'hath in a loft wheat and rye to the value of 8 seams, and selleth none of it'. In 1565-66 further charges about dairy produce are found. A Barking labourer was bound over to give evidence against a servant of Andrew Hayz for forestalling 6 gallons of butter at Grays Thurrock and selling it at Sampford, 35 miles away. Indictments for trading in unspecified amounts of butter and cheese without licence were preferred against 6 men of West and East Ham and Wanstead, also against a Stansted Mountfitchet man who bought and sold at Great Thurlow, 5 miles from Haverhill, just over the Suffolk border. The constables of Mucking and Stanford-le-Hope each reported an unlicensed dealer in butter, eggs, calves, lambs and chickens, and an Epping labourer was indicted for carrying five quarters of corn there without licence.

In 1572 the Council intervened 'to force farmers to bring corn to market', condemning 'speculative dealers who were holding the stocks'.[8] Several documents filed at the Easter Quarter Sessions are of much interest. They show that the justices had issued an order to the hundredal sessions to send in parochial reports in answer to ten 'articles' of enquiry. The constables and jurors for Waltham (i.e. the market town of Waltham Abbey), Upshire and Sewardstone, hamlets in that extensive parish, gave their replies 'concerning the buying and engrossing of butter, cheese and corn and also for the prices of beer, ale and bread'. The last article was designed to ascertain whether there were any violations of the Assize of Bread and Ale. 'To the first article' they presented transactions at Waltham market, 9 on 15 November and 2 on 22 November 1571. Four were for buying butter: Richard Tomkines of Islington (Middlesex) 100 lb.; William Peele's daughter 100 lb., widow Franke 60 lb., and Robert Stanton's maid 50 lb., all of (West) Ham. The rest relate to buying grain: Robert Curtis 5 quarters of oats, Thomas Hinsdon 3 loads of wheat, and Richard Wibard 1 load of wheat, all of Enfield (Middlesex); and John Chapman 1 load of wheat, 'the miller' 11 bushels of wheat, and Thomas Bennet 2 load of wheat, all of Waltham. 'To the 2nd, 3rd, 4th, 9th and 10th, we can say nothing'. To the 5th and 6th, they presented Roger Boyer of Waltham, a beerbrewer, for selling strong beer at 8s. the barrel and small at 4s. 8d., and the same man, this time termed a baker, for selling 'both wheaten and household groat (i.e. 4d.), 2d. and ½d. bread'. Answers to the 7th and 8th name 'tipplers' (alehouse-keepers). It is not easy to tell whether any of these deals amounted to engrossing, though the miller's obviously was legal. No indictments resulting from their returns are preserved. Stanton we have met in both the previous volumes; he was a gentleman who lived at New Barns in West Ham and had confessed in 1566 to begetting another man's servant with child.[9]

Two other reports, both undated, come from two adjacent parishes in Ongar hundred, about a dozen miles from Waltham Abbey. Each is headed, 'A note of the quantity of corn within our parish.' The Fyfield return runs:

> At Master Barfote's [10] we find 10 seam wheat, 10 seam barley, and 6 oats and pease; at goodman Alyte's 4 seam wheat and 8 seam barley; in the same barn we find in our judgement 10 seam wheat that was bought off the ground by Clarcke of Willingale Doe; at Nele's barn 5 seam barley of the same man; at Fremane's 5 seam pease and oats; at Gilbert Ashewell 3 seam wheat and as much barley; at Overard 2 seam wheat and 5 seam barley; and at a barn in our parish 10 seam wheat of John Colens of Willingale Doe. This we find spare.
> And for the bread by weight 1½ lb. in a groat loaf of household bread and ¾ lb. in a white loaf of 2d.
> For the rest of the articles we have nothing to present.

The Norton (Mandeville) report, sent in by three men, 'signifies' that:

> William Stane hath 3 quarters of wheat to spare, and what he hath bought or sold we know not.
> Robert Adams hath 1 quarter of wheat and 10 quarters of oats, but the

oats though they remain yet in our parish they are already sold to one John Mayler of Little Laver.
Thomas Hogge hath 7 quarters of dredge barley to spare.
John Pechie hath 14 quarters of oats and 1 quarter of barley.
John Stane hath 2 quarters of malt to spare.
We have one Robert Sturdy, a keeper of a windmill in our parish, but what he or the other before named do buy or sell we know not.
We have by our mutual consent agreed that the poor shall have pease at 2s. the bushel and oats at 12d. to supply their want.
To the rest nothing.

The man who had some spare malt is one of the reporters. Although Norton had only a very small population, the penultimate entry is a noteworthy item for the early history of poor relief in rural parishes.

A fourth report, filed at the Sessions of January 1574 and also undated, almost certainly belongs to the same group and came from the same hundred. It reads, 'Bobbingworth's answer to the article given them in charge':

1. To the first they can say nothing.
2. They find that Robert Borne, gentleman, has 25 quarters of wheat and 100 quarters of oats, and John Poole has 16 quarters of wheat and barley and 100 quarters of oats.
3-7, 9, 10. They can say nothing.
8. They find that John Peper and Humphrey Sargiant are victuallers and that Peper is like to victual and that they sell without sealed measures.

In the county records are preserved two so-called 'Bridge Books' which were compiled by the clerk of peace about 1675, mainly as precedent books. While most of the entries relate to liability for repair of bridges, they contain a few items about other matters. Under 1572 he noted: 'It seemed there was a dearth of corn and victuals at this time, for all the presentments were what store or corn was in every man's possession'. 'All' strongly suggests that he saw many more of these returns, now lost, from the parishes.

In March 1574 22 cases under the food control laws came before the Assize judges (the previous harvest had been a bad one). They considered a composite indictment against 14 men for having engrossed in their own parishes 'great quantities of barley, wheat and other victuals'. Their abodes mostly range over central Essex; all are termed yeomen except John Welle of Moulsham in Chelmsford, bowyer, Thomas Durrant of Springfield, miller, and Henry Cocke of Kelvedon, glover. The document proceeds to itemize the commodities, beginning with John Harris of Mountnessing and Lawrence Smyth *alias* Salmon of Broomfield, 40 and 20 quarters of corn respectively. The others dealt with smaller quantities of corn or eggs and butter; 6 pleaded not guilty and the rest seem to have been fined. The fifteenth man, William Awgar of Shalford, yeoman, in an individual indictment for forestalling, was charged with having in the previous October 'at Maldon in the highway met an unknown man bringing a cart loaded with 6 quarters of wheat for sale at the market there and bought it from him there, away from the market, with the intention of selling it at a profit and did so'. He pleaded not guilty, but words of the verdict are torn away. This is followed by a less specific indictment against 7 yeomen for similar offences in various parishes—and annotated, 'Made fine'. Whether all these cases had been transferred by writ of *certiorari* from the County Bench is not clear, but 9 of their names also occur in the Sessions rolls. A pernicious case of grain profiteering at the expense of the poor was noticed under Wages.

A year later another omnibus indictment lay at the Assizes against 16 defendants from numerous places for having 'got into their possession oats, barley, butter, cheese and herrings, which John Love (Lone?) of Colchester' (one of them) 'carried beyond the sea contrary to the Statute'. The men include 4 millers, Lawrence (illegible) and Robert Northe, both of Colchester, and John Coole of Thorrington and Thomas Gladwyn [11] of Lexden. One was found guilty; 6 have no plea against their names; the rest pleaded not guilty. In 1573 and again in 1574 the Council, worried once more about the scarcity of corn, had sent letters to the justices of Essex, Suffolk and Norfolk, prohibiting 'the transportation of wheat and victuals beyond the seas'.[12] Further prosecutions for unlicensed export were made at the Midsummer Assizes in 1576. Stephen John, or Johns, of Colchester, merchant, had put two flitches of bacon worth 40s. and 1,400 'biscuit bread' (a contemporary term for biscuit) worth 8s. a 100 into his ship, intended for 'parts beyond the seas'; John Danbye of Colchester, sailor, had carried away there 1,500 of 'biscuit bread' of like worth and 3 'barrels of beef' worth £8 with the same intent; and Richard Frend of Sudbury, Suffolk, merchant, at Manningtree had carried away in a hoy (a small vessel) 170 quarters of pease worth £4. No other cases of illegal export occur, except for John Cooke, a Heybridge grocer, charged on the evidence of four parishioners in 1591 with buying butter and cheese and transporting it abroad; but the Council was much concerned with unlicensed export and with general restraint of corn and victuals in all the periods of scarcity.[13]

During 1574-76 charges of illegal dairy-produce dealing were prominent at Quarter Sessions. John Steward of Thundersley, husbandman or yeoman, engrossed 300 eggs, 2 leads of cheese (about 1 cwt.), and 20 dishes of butter (about 40 lb.) there and re-sold his wares at 'excessive prices in London';[14] and 18 men and women of West and East Ham and 4 of Walthamstow engrossed and regrated in the markets at Romford and Brentwood, each with 10 dishes of butter worth 5s., with intent to re-sell. Much bigger transactions involved William Townsend junior and John Wilson senior, each of whom likewise 'engrossed from divers persons within the hundred of Hinckford 3 horseloads of butter worth £6'; and in the following year (but a month or two before the harvest of 1576)

Wilson was again indicted for 'engrossing and forestalling in the open market' by buying 6 horseloads of butter, and Daniel Wilson of West Thurrock, husbandman, for 'engrossing 1 horseload of butter at Billericay', with the same intent. Finally, 6 unlicensed men, 5 being of Sheering, bought and sold butter, fowls and poultry and engrossed at Sheering and Epping butter worth 5s. in each case, and capons and hens worth 5s. There is a note, unassigned to any of these cases, that 'all those indicted for selling butter are assessed for their fines at 10s.' Thomas Cannon of Walthamstow, gentleman, and 5 husbandmen and a widow of Walthamstow, Waltham Abbey, West and East Ham were charged with similar unlicensed dealings in butter at Epping, Romford and Brentwood. In 1576 a Great Leighs husbandman bought 4 bushels of malt in open market at Braintree, but regrated it two days afterwards at Chelmsford market.

Pig-dealers and others were in trouble in 1578; 10 drovers, 5 butchers, a badger and a linendraper had bought and sold pigs without licence at Billericay, Romford, Cressing and Ingrave and had regrated 60 pigs each (presumably a round figure) worth 10s. each for re-sale. Verdict: no true bill against 6 (all drovers), true bill against the rest. Nicholas Cook, a miller, was up on four separate indictments with engrossing 25 quarters of corn worth £31, having bought it in four lots from John Glascock gentleman and 3 other men; all were of Hatfield Peverel. He confessed to all the offences and was fined as much as £10. A hundredal jury presented an Epping badger, who was accordingly indicted, for buying corn and 'converting it into meal that is not wholesome for man's body and hath sold it in Epping market'; he had also sold 3 bushels of maslin (mixed corn) there at 2s. 4d. a bushel without licence. Similarly next year a Great Dunmow yeoman engrossed 5 quarters of wheat worth £5, 'converting it into flour', and then selling it.

In April 1586 steps were taken by the Privy Council to regulate the corn supplies. Reports were sent in by many counties. Essex was first and within a few days the reply from Sir Henry Graye, Sir Thomas Mildmay, Sir John Petre, James Morice, George Nycolls and Jerome Weston, dated at London, stated that they had circulated the Council's order to each 'division'.[15] They enclosed, as enjoined, a list of the divisions, with the names of the market towns in each division and of the J.P.s 'to whose oversight the several market towns are committed'.[16] In September Lord Darcy (of St. Osyth's Priory) and Edmund Pirton, J.P.s, told the Council about the scarcity of grain at Colchester, adding that prices were likely to rise and desiring to receive a new commission to restrain its export.[17] The grain situation had worsened after the failure of the harvest, but the crisis left no special mark in the county records. In March the Cambridgeshire justices, because the town of Walden was desperately short of provisions normally supplied from that county, were ordered to remedy the deficiency.[18]

Minor prosecutions in 1586-88 reveal that several husbandmen had engrossed corn; a Castle Hedingham man had forestalled hogs and sold the bacon 'at excessive prices'; and the Ongar hundred jury presented '4 bachelors which take upon the trade of poultering, being unlicensed'. In 1590 greed brought Richard Aysone of Sheering to the notice of the hundredal jurors, who in turn reported him 'for buying 1 quarter of seed wheat, and he had well nigh 12 acres of wheat growing of his own, sufficient for his use'; and John Webster of Romford, yeoman, was fined 6s. for buying at Brentwood and Ingatestone 20 quarters of wheat worth £26 13s. 4d. and 20 quarters of malt worth £20, and then turning up early at Brentwood, Chelmsford and Romford 'to sell there before it should come to the markets'. A single indictment of the same year accused 9 men of 8 parishes, including John Pake of Broomfield, gentleman,[19] of engrossing grain for re-sale, precise particulars being given for each defendant: in all, 21 quarters of wheat (£28), 12 quarters on the ground (£16), 5 of barley (£5), 5 of barley (£5), and 30 of malt (£30); two being fined unstated sums. Growing crops appear again in 1591, when the Hinckford jury reported John Glascock, gentleman, this time described as of Stisted, for buying wheat, maslin, pease and barley 'in the ear' from several men, and selling it in Chelmsford market. The indictment is more definite, though the figures are again only approximate: 20 quarters of wheat (worth £5), 5 of maslin (£5), and 10 of barley (£10). In the next year Josias Portwaye, the informer we have already met, sued Richard Smythe, a Messing yeoman, for engrossing wheat worth £10 10s. growing on 5 acres belonging to Adrian Mott (of Braintree[20]), Portwaye claiming half the value.

The harvests of 1592 and 1593 yielded an abundance of corn with fairly cheap prices. But the economic pendulum then swung back sharply, a series of notoriously disastrous harvests causing widespread distress throughout the four years 1594-97. The menace of famine and the soaring cost of food (wheat prices nearly trebled) led to sporadic riots. Seditious speeches with threats of revolt in Essex, of which information came to light only recently and was related in the first volume, led to several prosecutions in 1594-96.[21] The Council's 'Book of Orders' for the control of the grain supply, issued in 1587, was re-issued in 1594. Exceptionally, the rolls for three sessions in 1594-95 are lost, but the others preserve several significant documents. (See *Addendum* on p. 189.)

Although it is impossible to ascertain precisely what the County Bench decided after the failure of the 1594 harvest, they had apparently ordered stringent action by the justices and high constables of each hundred. This may be assumed from a precept, surviving by chance in the Mildmay family archives.[22] Signed in December by George Harvy of Marks in Dagenham, J.P., it is addressed to the high constables of Becontree. They were enjoined to summon before him at Barking a few days later at 8 a.m. 51 named men and 'all bakers, brewers, taverners, victuallers, badgers, loaders, millers, corn hucksters (small retailers or hawkers), and maltsters'; victuallers and badgers were also ordered to produce their licences. This leaves no doubt about the pressure exercised by the justices meeting in their embryo petty sessions. The list of traders' and dealers' names runs : West Ham 19 (7 are termed corn hucksters), East Ham 14, Little Ilford 2, Walthamstow 2 including 'Mr Morgan of Mounes' (Moons), Woodford 3, Wanstead 1, and Dagenham 11 including 'Mr Timothy Lucye' (of Valence). More pertinent are the notes written in a different hand. To 8 of the names is added a measure—1 to 4 bushels of rye, 3 or 4 bushels of oats, 4 bushels of barley, or 2 bushels of pease, in all cases 'weekly'. Of these, 'Oats 4 bushels weekly till 6 quarters be out' and 'Pease 2 bushels weekly till 3 quarters be out' suggest that the men were willing, or were ordered, to sell their surplus grain in the emergency.

An interesting letter sent by George Nicolls of Walden, an active J.P., in January 1595, to the clerk of the peace, tells of the hardship suffered by two north Essex villages. He asked that 'a letter be granted to the bearer, John Bentley' (of Helions Bumpstead, whose will, 1608, terms him a yeoman), 'to bestow and lay out money for the provision of corn for the use of the poor within (Steeple and Helions) Bumpstead, which are pasture towns' (i.e. villages) 'and little or no tilling used by them, the occasion whereof at this present dearth of grain hath caused a great and lamentable cry of the poor there inhabiting'.

As already explained, the food shortage was now even graver. At Michaelmas 1596, the County Bench, spurred on by the Council's circular missive of August exhorting all courts to prosecute engrossers and to issue orders 'for the stay of dearth of grain',[23] sent out a stern injunction restricting the activities of corn dealers after the further terrible harvest :

> All badgers who now have licences to buy any manner of corn or grain, and all such other persons who use the trade of buying and selling corn, shall from henceforth presently forbear to buy any corn by virtue of any licence, either in market or elsewhere, until other order be taken for their liberty to use the same trade again; and likewise that no foreigners, either bakers or badgers, shall carry any manner of corn out of this shire.

The Court directed justices in their divisional meetings 'to have care to see this order duly executed, and also to take order that no carts with corn pass away by night'.

The Michaelmas roll yields three more documents. This is what Richard Thurgood of Roxwell, a husbandman, deposed when examined by a J.P. On 1 September he had taken to Romford market 12 bushels of wheat and 'might have sold it for 7s. a bushel'. But John Harmon, a Romford baker, came up, offering to take the corn for the poor and to price it at only 5s. a bushel, affirming that to be the figure laid down by the Council.

Thurgood asked him to take only half his supply, but Harmon bought it all at that price, 'to bake for the poor, as he said, but in fact to make a private gain, the poor getting none'. Sir Anthony Cooke (of Gidea Hall, Romford, J.P.) was asked to look into the matter and to see that Harmon brought to court a certificate showing how he had disposed of the corn. In the previous month Thomas Foxe of Bromley in Kent, loader, had been bound with Michael Foxe of Chelmsford, innholder, as his surety, to appear before the Bench and meanwhile to 'forbear to repair to the markets of the county to buy any kind of corn'; Thomas Hogge of Bethnal Green in Middlesex, another loader, was likewise bound; both in their own bail of £100, the bonds being taken before Sir Thomas Mildmay. Dunmow hundred jurors presented an Aythorpe Roothing man for buying 5 acres of wheat and 5 acres of barley from a Rayne farmer just before harvest. 'He seems to us', they added, not too sure of the confusing legal terms, 'to be an ingrater'. Next year we also find writs issued against 6 men for regrating, but without details, apparently as a result of activity on the part of Edward Hedd, of whom more very shortly.

Corn shortage led to inflated prices for poultry and dairy products. The Michaelmas Sessions 1595 held on 2 and 3 October (it rarely ran into a second day) was notified by the Council that 'the great numbers of buyers and sellers of poultry, butter and eggs do so swarm in every market, whereby the same are grown to extreme prices, for that they do buy the same at farmers' houses upon the highways and by way of forestalling'. The justices were to take urgent steps to remedy the abuse, as a result of which proclamation was made 'in open sessions that all higglers, buttermen and poulterers within this Shire shall presently forbear to buy any butter, eggs or any kind of poultry, until they shall be newly licensed'. The Court also ordered the production of their licences to the clerk of the peace within ten days. (But the justices' history was weak, for Essex was never a shire. Equally so two centuries later, when they named their new building the Shire Hall!)

Hedd, that sharp-eyed informer, had already been energetically descending on rapacious 'buttermen'. At the same Sessions the Court received his findings. The facts, as set out in his 'information', are that William Crane senior, husbandman, had engrossed 20,000 lb. butter worth £300 with intent to re-sell it, between 1 October 1594 and 28 September 1595; William Crane junior had done 'the like' (no figures); Richard Nerse and John Nerse had engrossed 10,000 lb. butter worth £150; and William Enever had engrossed 2,000 lb. butter worth £30; the last four between 1 May and 1 October 1595; Enever being of Great Easton, all the others of (Steeple) Bumpstead, the scene of the malpractices. The informer seems to be identified with Edward Heade of Elmdon, gentleman, who was to be involved in a poaching incident in 1601;[24] he is clearly the same man who was appointed a tile-searcher in 1596 (p. 194). Further butter-cornering charges were to come before the Midsummer Sessions 1599, at which Thomas Foster of London laid identical informations against Judith Townsend, widow, Daniel Wylson and Richard Barle, each for engrossing 20,000 lb. butter worth £300 at Brentwood; the first two being of West Ham and also probably the last. In all these cases the informers formally stated that the delinquents 'ought to forfeit' the stated values and sought half those sums for themselves. None of the informations bears any note of plea, verdict, sentence, or grant of the sum claimed. Dealing with the last point, there is little doubt, judging by the evidence of other sources, that the financial rewards of these men were in actual fact very much lower. Defendants were either allowed by the Court to compound for lesser sums or it decreed mitigated penalties: a statement based on extensive research by another writer,[25] who also shows that most informers were 'professional' prosecutors active in more than one county. Portwaie and Hedd have appeared under Apprenticeship, and Foster also informed in an offence against the Assize of Fuel (p. 193).[26] But it is doubtful whether any of them did more than supplement their normal livelihood, unlike those who often appeared at Westminster. There remains the problem of the quantities of butter alleged to have been involved in the various transactions. Apart from their being only approximate figures, it is impossible to say to what extent, if any, they are grossly exaggerated.[27]

When the county magistrates met at Epiphany 1596, they had before them a list of 22 'names of all the poulterers and higglers which have bought ware continually at markets and at home at farmers' houses', contrary to their order; 'and they notwithstanding do forestall at Chelmsford, Braintree, Dunmow and Billericay markets'. So 'Old Tomalyne of Widford, Young Tomalyne of Margaretting', and the others, including 2 women, were reported to their local justices. What is perhaps surprising is that these defendants were obviously not dealers in a big way. Poulterers do not figure again afterwards.

In October 1597 the clothworkers of Dedham were in a peculiar plight, so much so that they appealed to the Council to be 'licensed to make provision of some reasonable quantity of corn by reason of the small store of grain growing in that parish, in so much that the same consisting of 200 households none of them hath sufficient of their own for the provision of their families, and six score are utterly unfurnished of grain or other victuals, being poor people chiefly relying on the clothiers there'. In consequence the Council asked the Norfolk justices to send 100 quarters of barley and rye to Dedham, 'so as not to infringe the general order of restraint'. The Council, however, was not satisfied about local arrangements for dealing with the crisis and informed Sir Thomas Lucas and Francis Harvey, neighbouring J.P.s, that in their opinion 'there is some want of due care and government in the country' (i.e. district), urging them to watch the position. There was also distress at Colchester, and in January 1598 the Council made a similar order for 400 quarters of grain from Norfolk 'or so much as can be spared' to be dispatched for the relief of the townspeople.[28] But London of course was in very short supply, and Essex had to bear its share of help.[29]

The privy councillors, although relieved at the end of the four-year run of appalling harvests, were sternly moralizing in 1597. Their penetrating, if rhetorical, fulmination may serve as an epilogue to our own account of how the Essex justices tried to deal with the avaricious middlemen and the grim situations. The Council refer [30] to the

> late dearth of all kind of grain and of butter and cheese and other victuals in the most part of this realm (but God hath now yielded us a change in this latter end of summer to the great comfort of all sorts of people), yet there are seen and found a number of wicked people in conditions more like wolves or cormorants than to natural men that do most covetously seek to hold up the late great prices of corn and other victuals by ingrossing the same into their private hands, bargaining beforehand for corn, and in some parts for grain growing, and for barley before it be made malt, and for butter and cheese before it be brought to ordinary markets, for to be bought for the poorer sort.

Among such 'wicked people' we must not overlook 'Wm. Shackespere' who appears as one of the chief hoarders (10 quarters of malt) in a Stratford-on-Avon list dated February 1597. (Just before publication, the County Archivist found in a recent addition to the Barrington family archives, 17 N.W. Essex parish returns (1597), about corn stocks and dealers in and processors of grain, victuallers, bakers, etc., in response to 'articles' issued by J.P.s in their divisions, apparently made after the re-issue in 1594 of the 'Book of Orders'.[30a])

To this story of widespread scarcity and severe restriction, the county records add little for the rest of the reign, doubtless because the yields of the six harvests of 1598-1603 were all average or good. In January 1598 the Hinckford jurors complained that Arthur Bettes of Finchingfield had bought '4 bushels of wheat of goodman Stock's as an engrosser, some for 6s. a bushel, and has always wheat to sell'. The Sessions roll for Epiphany 1597 has an order by Sir Thomas Mildmay (as chairman of the Bench) to the high constables of Becontree hundred to search for Henry Browne, loader, dwelling in Stratford Langthorne and to bring his brother(-in-law) George Hixon, miller, being both resident in one house. In the meantime they were prohibited from lading, badgering, or carrying corn in any market. Browne was indicted for engrossing 1 quarter and 4 bushels of wheat worth £3 and was fined 40s. Thomas Grene of Earls Colne, another miller, was presented in 1601 because 'he bought 3 bushels of wheat of John Hunnicke for 4s. 6d. the bushel and sold it to a baker, notwithstanding the same bushels being before that time promised and sold to Henry Bridge for 4s. a bushel'. A year later Chelmsford hundred reported

Edward Keale of Great Baddow for engrossing and forestalling barley, pease, oats, butter, cheese, and bacon, 'with great store of hay, to the great hurt of the poor and commonwealth'; he was fined 20s.

The last document about the control of food supplies in Essex is preserved in the file for the summer Assizes, 1601. It is headed, 'A presentment of all such persons as have made starch within the County sithence the making and publishing of her Majesty's proclamation for the suppressing of such persons'. Here we have apparently the only known record of action taken locally in any county except for true bills against 8 persons, mostly of Clerkenwell, in 1600-01 for making between $\frac{1}{2}$ and 2 cwt. of starch.[31] The decree, dated August 1598, was for 'punishing forestallers, regrators, and engrossers of corn and for the prohibiting of making any manner of starch'.[32] Proclamations were a device used by Tudor and Stuart sovereigns in place of parliamentary legislation or to publicize it. The list names no less than 29 persons. They include John Thorowgood of West Ham, Zachary Jones and William Brooke of (Great) Ilford, and John Brystowe of Wanstead, gentlemen, and Richard Pett of West Ham, miller. The rest are mostly termed yeomen or labourers, apart from two women, and nearly all are of West Ham. The quantities of starch made range fairly evenly between $\frac{1}{4}$ cwt. and 20 cwt., all except one of the offences having been committed in September 1600. No further details are afforded. In addition a man and a woman, both of West Ham, are reported for selling starch. The presentment is witnessed by three men, none of whom is recognized as an informer for other offences. Of the 31 persons charged, 27 are found guilty, but the punishment inflicted is not recorded. A considerable supply of flour is known to have been produced in the West Ham watermills, but there is little other contemporary evidence that starchmaking was a principal industry in the parish, only two West Ham starchmakers' wills being extant (1603, 1618),[33] neither testators' names occurring in the list. At the same Assizes John Tapp and Benjamin Baynarde, both termed gentlemen of West Ham, were indicted for stealing in May 1600 2,000 lb. of starch made from wheat and selling it in September to unnamed persons. The witnesses are the same three, but the accused are stated to be 'at large'. All the so-called gentlemen prove to be elusive, no wills for instance being traced. There can be little doubt, however, that these prosecutions, although an isolated affair, reveal a determined campaign to divert wheat from being converted into the stiffening of 'ruffs of the largest size, quarter and half deep, gloried richly with blue starch',[34] as we see depicted, for example, in the famous painting of the Queen dancing La Volta with the Earl of Leicester, attributed to about 1580.

We may now see what the few Elizabethan records of other counties tell. For unlicensed or illegal corn-dealing 4 true bills were found (3 in 1573 and 1 in 1581) against Middlesex men.[35] Several unlicensed badgers and forestallers occur in the Staffordshire and Hertfordshire records in 1594 and 1599.[36] The first Wiltshire minute book contains over 200 badgers' recognizances, 1574-89: the sole extant Elizabethan register compiled under the Act of 1563.[37] That is virtually all about licensed and unlicensed trading, except for informers, already mentioned.

[1] W. K. Jordan, *Edward VI: The Threshold of Power* (1970), 471-6.
[2] See especially the *Acts of the Privy Council*, indexes, s.v. 'Essex', 'Colchester', 'Maldon', and other towns. [3] *E.L.: Disorder*, 29. [4] Judging by the unique Elizabethan register of the Wiltshire badgers' bonds (p. 189).
[5] W. G. Hoskins, 'Harvest Fluctuations and English Economic History, 1480-1619' (*Agric. Hist. Rev.*, xii (1964), 28-46). Professor Hoskins, in this important article including full tables for each year, uses 'deficient' to indicate average wheat prices of 10-25 p.c. above the norm, 'bad' for 25-50 p.c., and 'dearth' for over 50 p.c. [6] *Ess. Rev.*, lii, 117. [7] The Privy Council minutes are lost for most of 1566.
[8] W. Cunningham, *Growth of English Industry and Commerce* (3rd edn., 1903), 51. [9] *E.L.: Morals*, 287. [10] Apparently the rector (*E.L.: Disorder*, 237).
[11] Cf. *E.L.: Morals*, 15.
[12] *A.P.C.*, *1571-75*, 135, 139, 286; cf. M. B. Pulman, *The Elizabethan Privy Council in the 1570s* (1571), 147. Certain Maldon clothiers and others were alleged in 1582 to have conspired with London merchants for 'conveying great quantities of wool out of the realm' (P.R.O., S.P. 157/3).
[13] *A.P.C.*, viii, 139, 286; ix, 160, 183, 297.
[14] Lead and dish: for these measures, see Emmison, *Tudor Secretary*, 136-7; *Ess. Rev.*, lxiii, 131. [15] *Cal. S.P.Dom., 1581-90.*
[16] P.R.O., S.P. 12/189/5 (copy in E.R.O., T/A 407/51).
[17] *Cal. S.P.Dom., 1581-90*, 350. [18] *A.P.C.*, xiv, 382.
[19] Lessee of the lay rectory of Broomfield (*E.L.: Morals*, 245).
[20] Emmison, *Early Essex Town Meetings* (1970), index, 'Mott'.
[21] *E.L.: Disorder*, 64. For discontent in Kent, Norfolk and Sussex, see *A.P.C.*, xxvii, 55, 88, 92. [22] E.R.O., D/DMs O7; cf. *Ess. Rev.*, lviii, 77.
[23] *A.P.C.*, xxvi, 81. [24] *E.L.: Disorder*, 242. [25] Davies, *op. cit.*, 50-54.
[26] None of the informers except Hedd occurring in the Essex Q.S. records is identical with those named by Davies, *op. cit.*, 40-62.
[27] For the somewhat larger number of prosecutions by informers in the Exchequer and Queen's Bench Courts, *op. cit.*, 92 (table 4, charges against 'retailers' and 'food processors'); examination of the Public Records is outside the present writer's terms of reference. [28] *A.P.C.*, xxviii, 69, 89, 230.
[29] For precepts issued by the Council to the justices of the Home Counties for the supply of grain to London, see *A.P.C.*, xxv, 72 (1595); xxviii, 44 (1597); xxx, 791 (1600). For the abuses of grain-engrossing in Hertfordshire in 1595, see Mildred Campbell, *The English Yeoman* (reprint 1960), 192.
[30] *A.P.C.*, xxvii, 359. Harrison's own complaints (*op. cit.*, 133, 248-53), usually to the point, are somewhat rambling in this case.
[30a] E.R.O., D/DBa O3; cf. E. Lipson, *Econ. Hist.*, iii (1943), 440-5.
[31] J. C. Jeaffreson (ed.), *Middlesex County Records*, i, 261, 272.
[32] Society of Antiquaries, Royal Proclamations, vol. 2, no. 121: a collection of mostly rare documents.
[33] Emmison (ed.), *Wills at Chelmsford, 1400-1620*, 93, 110.
[34] Greene, *Conny Catch* (1592), 16. [35] *Middx. County Records*, i, 84, 165.
[36] *Staffordshire Quarter Sessions Rolls*, iii, 45-50.
[37] *Hertfordshire County Records*, i, 30-1.

# 11

# Control of Trade

## Weights and Measures and the Clerk of the Market

Weights and measures and the price of victuals and some other commodities were regulated by statutory ordinances known as 'assizes', the best known of which were the Assize of Bread and Ale and the Assize of Fuel. The enforcement of the former was a function of manor courts, as we shall find in Part 3. Deficient or illegal weights and measures and kindred offences under the same assize also came before Quarter Sessions mainly through the agency of the hundredal juries. The number of delinquents reported by them is relatively small, the majority being dishonest bakers or victuallers. In 1571 4 bakers and 2 brewers of Chelmsford were indicted in 1571 for selling their wares at excessive prices; each was fined 5s. From Danbury in 1577 were presented John Mumford, shoemaker and victualler, because 'he sold bread of his own baking and of others, lacking weight', and Francis Hixe, Thomas Stevens and Richard Newtone, victuallers, also sold their own bread by short weight. Two Kelvedon innkeepers, Thomas Leveriche at the sign of the 'Angel' and Robert Shoyle of the 'Bell', were reported in 1585, each for making 'his own horse-bread too light' by 13 or 11 oz. for every pennyworth. The Act of 32 Hen. VIII, c.41 (1540) had prohibited innholders from making any horse-bread (which was produced from beans, bran, etc.) In 1594 Joseph Pagge of Stratford-atte-Bow, Middlesex, baker, 'serveth bread to East Ham which wanteth weight 5 oz. the penny white loaf, and the wheaten loaf wanteth in weight 7 oz.' Three years later the County Bench twice received presentments from Becontree hundred of similar breaches committed by Thomas Score (or Scory) of Stratford-atte-Bow and Thomas Rolfe (or Relfe) of West Ham, both bakers, whose dishonesty has afforded us some precise facts about sizes and prices of loaves. The first was charged thus : 'Whereas his 1d. wheaten loaf should weigh 8 oz., wheat being at 7s. 6d. the bushel, it weighed but 6 oz.; and whereas his 2d. household loaf should weigh 22 oz., it weighed but 18 oz.; and whereas his ½d. loaf should weigh 2¼ oz., it weighed but 2 oz.; this bread was weighed and thus found on 13 October 1596 and sold in West Ham to the value of 9 dozen a day'. The weights of the other man's loaves were : 1d. loaf (6½ oz.), ½d. (2¼ oz.), 2d. (17½ oz.), weighed on 15

October, 20 dozen; and on 12 January following 'when the 1d. loaf should have weighed 10 oz., wheat being bought by him for 50s. a quarter', his was only 6½ oz., while the 2d. loaf, which should have been 26 oz., was a mere 19 oz., 25 dozen a day being sold. In June the same pair and Joseph Page of Stratford-atte-Bow were in trouble for selling a total of 100 dozen short-weight loaves, with similar particulars, and Relfe for making groat (i.e. 4d.) bread against the Statute, 'and he saith he will do so, whosoever saith to the contrary'. A pity that we do not know what his recalcitrance cost him.

An early presentment (1566) complains that 'Clarke the Orsett beer-brewer sells beer by the kinkerkin' (i.e. kilderkin, or 18 gallons), but the price is illegible. From West Ham also (1587), two alehousekeepers were reported because 'they sell but a pint of ale for a 1d. to travellers and inhabiters' (instead of at the usual rate of ½d.).

Millers' greed is revealed in three being accused of extortionate toll. William Brodbelt of Great Saling windmill took as much as 1 in every 4 measures for grinding the wheatmeal of John Pechye of Bardfield Saling, husbandman (1564); John Humfrey of Shenfield levied 39 lb. for 2 of his neighbours' 6 bushels of wheat, 'contrary to the ancient custom of the realm' (1573); and one Kitching of Hadleigh windmill took an excessive ½ bushel toll for 2 bushels of wheat (1589).

Various earlier statutes had enjoined every borough and market-town to have 'a common balance and a common bushel and weights sealed and according to the standards in their shire town'. Failure to provide standards crops up twice. In 1590 it was presented that 'there is no common measure belonging to the market of Brentwood'; and in the following year 'no market bushel nor other sealed measures, greatly to the hindrance of the poor' was reported. Two years later the Court was informed that the Countess of Rutland 'is to find weights to weigh bread and measures in Walthamstow as heretofore hath been used', as well as a cucking-stool and a pillory; she was the widow of Edward Earl of Rutland, lord of the manor of Walthamstow.[1]

Excessive verification fees led the jury for Hinckford and Freshwell hundreds to present the royal clerk of the market in 1582: 'He doth take of every bushel 2d., also of every peck 2d. which hath been sealed with the Queen's seal, and for every clothier's weight 4d., for every smith's weight 4d., and from victuallers 4d., from millers (although their dish be sealed) 4d., and thus continueth from year to year as well sealed as unsealed'. Five years earlier Harrison, whose vicarage lay in Freshwell hundred, had inveighed against 'the covetousness of many clerks of the market'.[2] Seven years later, impersonation of the Bishop of London's clerk of the market fooled many Kelvedon tradesmen.[3] Quarter Sessions issued a precept in

1581 to the officers of the borough of Thaxted for 24 jurors to appear before the clerk of the market there at 7 a.m. in connection with weights and measures. This is all that the county records disclose about clerks of the market. Originating as a member of the Royal Household, deputies attended markets and fairs at which their chief function was to control weights and measures and to punish market offences. Many royal liberties, certain manors with appurtenant market rights, as we shall see later, and various boroughs, appointed a clerk of the market.[4]

Very little is known, before the 17th century, of the actual work of the courts held by the Clerk of the Market and the deputies.[5] But a fairly recently discovered account-book of (Sir) John Petre of Thorndon Hall during his term of office as sheriff of Essex in 1574-75 reveals the local courts in action all over the county and adds to our knowledge of trade control.[6] Its chief interest perhaps is to confirm fully the official statements indicating the wide range of market offences that came within their jurisdiction. Such private shrievalty records are extremely rare. In this book Petre, or more likely his steward, kept a full chronological record of all fines and forfeitures collected, not only at Quarter Sessions and Assizes but also at the hundredal petty sessions and at the sessions held in Essex by the deputy to 'the Clerk of the Queen's Household', usually abbreviated to clerk of the market. For the last category, the document gives each individual's offence and his fine.[7] False weights were traced mostly to bakers, but we also find a few victuallers, an innholder and a vintner. The treasurer of the town of Walden was accused 'because he has not common weights and balances', and another man 'because he has a greater measure than the standard and buys by the same'. John Grene, a Halstead constable, 'deceitfully altered the market bushel', for which he was very heavily fined at 40s. A few millers 'accepted excessive toll'. Sale at excessive prices was the charge against several beer-brewers and tallow-chandlers. Some bakers were presented for 'breaking the assize of bread'; one did not bring along his weights for inspection. A few cordwainers made 'deceitful shoes'. There is also the occasional presentment for engrossing corn and of a solitary butcher for killing and selling calves during Lent. The bailiff of Waltham hundred was reported for not having 'a pillory within the town to punish offenders'. Finally, we note that a few hundredal chief constables and bailiffs and many petty constables failed to turn up at the sessions.[8]

The deputy clerk held his sessions in respect of each hundred, usually in a village rather than a market town. Exceptionally, he sat at Stortford, just over the border in Hertfordshire, for Clavering hundred. Comparison of the dates reveals that he apparently settled his itinerary to suit his own convenience; and, as the following table shows, on at least one occasion both the ordinary and the clerk's sessions for Uttlesford hundred were held on the same day, though in different villages.

## SESSIONS OF THE HUNDREDS AND OF THE CLERK OF THE MARKET

| 1575 | Hundred | 1575 | Clerk of the Market |
|---|---|---|---|
| 8 Mar. | Becontree, at Barking | 26 Jan. | Tendring, at Manningtree |
| 16 Mar. | Chafford, at Aveley | 27 Jan. | Lexden, at Fordham |
| 19 Mar. | Barstable, at Horndon-on-the-Hill | 13 Feb. | Chafford, at Brentwood |
|  |  | 15 Feb. | Becontree, at Barking |
| 29 Mar. | Lexden, at Stanway | 18 Feb. | Chelmsford, at Chelmsford |
| 29 Mar. | Clavering, at Manuden | 1 Apr. | Uttlesford, at Newport |
| 1 Apr. | Uttlesford, at Wenden | 2 Apr. | Clavering, at Stortford |
| 13 Apr. | Freshwell, at Hempstead | 31 May | Freshwell, at Hempstead |
| 15 Apr. | Chelmsford, at (blank) |  |  |

The Act of 7 Edw. VI, c.7 (1553), known as the Assize of Fuel, laid down the sizes and prices of 'talwood, billet, faggot and coals' (charcoal). Contravention of the Act in 1587 resulted in John Harre of Heybridge being indicted for 'false marking of wood' : 'He hath altered the mark of 1,000 billets marked and assayed, viz. 400 single billets for one cast, 500 for 1 cast to 2 casts, and 100 for 2 casts each to 3 casts'. Evidence had been given against him by Jason Woodwarde, miller, and a sailor and a glazier, all of Heybridge. Found guilty, the case was forwarded to the Assizes, but the records are silent. In 1599 Thomas Foster informed against Robert Taylor of Langdon Hills for selling 100 cartloads of logwood worth £20 'without lawful assize', claiming the statutory forfeiture of half that sum.

## Fairs and Miscellaneous

The principal yearly or half-yearly Essex fairs were at Epping, Harlow, Brentwood, Romford, and especially the Cold Fair at Newport, in all cases chiefly for cattle.[9] Various untoward incidents at these often disorderly gatherings were dealt with by Quarter Sessions.[10] The Church Courts were concerned with fairs held on Sundays or in churchyards.[11] William Shepherd, that devout but extrovert rector of Heydon (now in Cambridgeshire), preserved in his parish register copies of his letters about the abuses connected with fairs on holy days at Walden in 1578.[12] Curiously enough, five other fairs kept on Sundays came before the county justices via hundredal presentments—at Brentwood on 7 July; at Coggeshall on the first Sunday in August, 'which ought to be kept on St. Peter-ad-Vincula's Day'; at Little Dunmow on Sunday after Our Lady Day in harvest ('My Lord of Sussex' noted in the margin refers to its ownership by the Earl as lord of the manor); at Thaxted 'in like manner' on Sunday before Whitsuntide ('Thomas Saward, bailiff of the manor'); and at Chelmsford on 1 May.[13] (These annual dates may be compared with Harrison's.[14]) What action, if any, the County Bench took is unrecorded. It is not surprising that fairs, which were important events in the dull lives of most people, affording them unusual opportunities for trade and fun, should involve dishonesty, ebullience and even violence.

Several Cloth Acts had attempted to safeguard purchasers against dishonest clothiers, who stretched their cloth, by fixing standards of length, breadth and weight in each textile area in England.[15] By a further statute (43 Eliz., c.10, 1601), cheating was to be stopped by government inspectors. We know that such men were appointed in Essex because Sir Thomas Lucas and Edward Waldegrave, J.P.s, handed in at the Michaelmas Quarter Sessions 1602 bonds given by the 'overseers for the true making and working of woollen cloths' for Coggeshall, Boxted, West Bergholt, Earls Colne, Kirby, Manningtree, St. Osyth, Thorpe, and Great Oakley: 2 or 3 men for each parish, of whom Robert Cotton of West Bergholt and John Church of Earls Colne are gentlemen, the rest being termed yeomen. Bonds were also filed at the same Sessions by Lucas and Edward Grimstone for Dedham (as many as 4 overseers) and Langham. Going just beyond our period, we may note that Benjamin Clere, a Boxted clothier, who had informed against an Ipswich merchant in 1586 for exporting cloth illegally,[16] was himself indicted by the Essex magistrates in 1607 for 'resisting the overseers and searchers' of cloth for his own parish. Colchester of course was outside the county justices' jurisdiction. Within a few months after the passing of the Act of 1601, Quarter Sessions had expressed doubts about the wisdom of prosecuting a man 'for making of fustians' (a coarse cloth made of cotton and flax), following a complaint under the statute, 'for it appeared to the Court to be much profitable for setting the poor on work'.[17]

The work of similar inspectors of tiles is illustrated by two documents in the Sessions roll for Easter 1597. The first is the commission, dated 28 July 1595 and signed by John Wyseman and Edward Hubberd (Lord Morley was the third commissioner but did not sign), appointing Edward Heade and Richard Scott of Thaxted 'to make a survey and search of tiles, according to the Act of 17 Edward IV' (c.4). This statute of 1477 had empowered J.P.s 'to call before them such persons as have the best experience in the occupation of making of tile, to search and examine the digging, casting, turning, parting, making, whiting and annealing'. Accordingly these two 'searchers of tiles' made their report, on which, however, no action is recorded:

> We have surveyed all the tilekilns in Essex, being 46. At our first survey, made between July and Christmas 1595, finding all the 46 kilns to be defective and not lawful (some wanting length and breadth, some full of marline marble and chalk-lime, some not well whited and annealed, and some have not their earth cast up in time), so that there was no good order among them. Now forasmuch as every tilemaker had made his tile so that they could not remedy them, therefore we thought it good to give

them warning, otherwise it would have been to the undoing of a great many poor men. And afterwards we made a search again between 1 June and 28 July (1596), and we found 36 of the kilns amended and were willing to amend, and the other 10 would not amend by any warning but would still work them unlawfully, five of whom are not worthy to make tiles any more. Therefore we crave the Bench that they may be fined according to the Statute.

Here we see Heade, informer under the Statute of Artificers, acting in an official capacity.

In 1589 the Bench received a letter from the Privy Council referring to their having learned of 'sundry abuses committed by certain bad and lewd fellows concerning the levying of such penalties as might have grown by force of a statute made for sowing of hempseed and flax, for which abuses divers have been heretofore committed.' The document goes on to state that these men had been acting falsely under colour of letters patent granted to William Waad, one of the clerks of the Council, 'who never hath been privy nor consenting to their dealings', and had extortionately taken such penalties. The county justices were enjoined to forward the counterfeit commission to the Council and in the meantime to imprison the criminals and to await further directions. The Act of 5 Eliz., c.5 (1563), had increased the penalty in the original Act of 24 Hen. VIII, c.4 (1533), from 3s. 4d. to £5.

For centuries the adjacent parishes of Braintree and Bocking were at loggerheads : a rivalry that was not altogether eased by their enforced 'marriage' into a single Urban District in 1894. Quarter Sessions tried to solve their differences in 1599, ordering : 'The matter in variance between the clothiers and weavers of Braintree and Bocking shall be referred to my Lord Suffragan, Francis Harvye, John Tyndall, Ralph Wyseman, Henry Maxey and Thomas Walgrave esquires to determine all controversy between them, if they can'. (The first justice is John Sterne, suffragan bishop of Colchester and vicar of Witham, 1587-1607.[18]) A double criterion of the Court's realistic attitude to the problem is the large number of referees appointed and the most unusual *'if they can'* qualification in a formal order. That neither the result, nor indeed the cause of the dispute, is on record is tantalizing. But Puritan dissent and industrial depression were temporarily to unite Braintree and Bocking in 1629, when serious unemployment led them jointly to petition Quarter Sessions for relief.[19]

A few miles to the north lies the village of Wethersfield, where the highly specialized craft of haircloth weaving was plied. Their product was utilized in drying malt and hops, the hopgrowing district of Essex being centred in the neighbouring parishes. In 1590 6 men—2 tailors, 2 yeomen, a smith and a shoemaker—had intruded into Wethersfield and set up as haircloth weavers, so the local craftsmen promptly prosecuted them at Quarter Sessions.

We shall see in Part 3 how men using unsavoury trades often appeared as defendants in the manor courts. Several offenders were indicted at Quarter Sessions: Nicholas Want of Fairstead, a tanner, in 1592, for 'erecting floodgates at Fulsters Street there, obstructing the brook, and for putting skins and other foetid things into the waters so enclosed', to the great annoyance of John Drane dwelling there and other neighbours; and John Ingram, George Sewell and Anthony Bland, fullers (of Halstead), in 1593, for 'washing thicked bays in a river near Ingram's house, by reason of which the water in the river has become very noxious and insalubrious to those dwelling nearby', also Bland, 'for throwing filth into the river'.

---

[1] *V.C.H., Essex*, vi, 255.  [2] Harrison, *op. cit.*, 91, 251-2.  [3] *E.L.: Disorder*, i, 93.
[4] A copy of the 'inquest' of the clerk of the market at Norwich, 1564, is printed in Tawney and Power, *Tudor Economic Documents* (reprint 1951), 127-8.
[5] W. Cunningham, *History of English Industry and Commerce* (3rd edn., 1903), 94-8, gives a good summary of the royal proclamation of 1618 which sets out the functions of the office and the numerous abuses perpetrated by tradesmen.
[6] E.R.O., D/DP O58.
[7] Such details are not recorded in the Pipe Rolls (P.R.O.).
[8] An incomplete collation of the account book with the Quarter Sessions rolls shows that most of the offenders' names are common to both records.
[9] A large number of Essex fairs and their dates are among the list of the principal fairs in Harrison, *op. cit.*, 391-97
[10] *E.L.: Disorder*, index, s.v. 'fairs'.  [11] *E.L.: Morals*, index, s.v. 'fairs'.
[12] Emmison (ed.), *Catalogue of Essex Parish Records* (2nd edn., 1966), 135; *E.L.: Disorder;* 48-9.
[13] Cf. a presentment of 1592 that part of Stortford fair was kept in the churchyard (*Herts. County Records*, i (1905), 13).  [14] See n. 9 above.
[15] Esp. 4 & 5 Ph. & Mary, c.5 (1557), s.5. (Essex).
[16] Davies, *op. cit.*, 45. For Clere, see *E.L.: Morals*, 103, 140.
[17] Three contemporary documents in the State Papers relate to Essex clothiers: a reply from Lord Rich to the Council regarding the lack of wool among them (1566); a certificate to the Council of wool bought by 27 Coggeshall clothiers from staplers and 'broggers' (dealers), probably giving the names of all or nearly all of the resident clothiers (1576); and a memorandum to the Council as to the reasons for scarcity of wool (1577), in which the Essex clothiers agree with those of Wilts. who 'impute it to the greedy forestalling of wool before sheartime by the staplers at whose hands they are fain to buy', the former adding that they 'have of necessity bought wools of a number of staplers and broggers to occupy their clothing and to set poor men on work' (*Cal. State Papers, Domestic, 1547-80;* reproductions of originals in E.R.O., T/A 407/9, 34, 35). For the opinions of Essex clothiers on the dearth of wool in 1577, see another document in the State Papers (copy, T/A 407/34).
[18] *E.L.: Disorder*, 92-3, 97.  [19] Emmison, *Early Essex Town Meetings*, vii.

# PART 3—LAND
(*from Essex Manorial Records*)

## 12

# Manor Courts: The Social Background

The short title of Part 3 is not quite accurate. Although the Manor and Manor Courts were largely concerned with Land, the courts' functions were somewhat wider.

In the first volume we related how the State, through the county justices in Quarter Sessions and the royal judges in Assizes, dealt with secular crimes and offences.[1] In the second book we narrated how the Church, through the two Archdeacons' courts, tried to restrain moral lapses.[2] Part 2 of the present volume has described the means by which the justices and the hundredal high constables' meetings attempted to control trade and labour. But big gaps still remain in the wide canvas depicting the people's day-to-day business. We shall now strive to fill some of the blanks with scenes revealing how many of their ordinary affairs as well as other aspects of behaviour and trade were regulated by the Manor courts.

Service on the various juries and the common offences such as theft on the one hand, and the ubiquitous sexual misdemeanours and absence from church on the other, brought a significant proportion of the adult population to the civil or the ecclesiastical courts. But while some parishioners might infrequently or never receive a summons to them, 'suit of court', or compulsory attendance of the tenants, involved a much larger number of people at the manorial courts. The very general transgressions, including neglect to scour ditches or remove obstructions in the streets, breach of the assize of bread and ale and other trade offences, led to many others being charged to appear. All copyholders, and to a small extent freeholders, were also liable to attend as a result of changes through inheritance, sale or lease of their dwellings or lands. In the Elizabethan manor of average size, it is therefore not unusual to find a hundred persons, or even more, being present through one cause or another at a single session of the manor court.

Manor courts indeed exercised a far greater influence over the Elizabethans' lives than a mere count of the names in the rolls would suggest. Not only did they deal with all matters of tenure, but they also supervised the repairing of the tenants' dwellings, and their taking in lodgers; they managed in diverse fashion the commons, heaths and greens, and their timber felling rights, if any; they watched over the cleanliness of the streets; they kept a sharp lookout for dishonest dealings and bad workmanship of tradesmen and artificers; and they directed many of the inhabitants' other activities.

Military and other feudal services associated with the medieval manor were, however, seldom rendered by the Elizabethan period, and some insignificant manors had almost ceased to hold courts. But, in general, it is very necessary to emphasize that in most manors, especially urban manors, the court was still a vigorous organ of justice and government. So far from being in decline in these respects, there is abundant evidence that the 'New Men' of the middle of the 16th century were actively engaged in maintaining their courts and enforcing manorial customs—in their own favour—and such legislation as lay within the courts' powers.[3] As we shall see, there was a spate of new statutes during the reign, of which manor courts were obliged to take notice, and these among other factors had the effect of rejuvenating them. The Elizabethan age, in fact, is their high water-mark as units of local government. But the ebb began in her last decade, notably with the Poor Relief Acts of 1597 and 1601, which placed the responsibility on the overseers of the poor with the churchwardens, and the ancient parish vestry meeting was then transformed into a largely secular body. The late medieval period of decadence had seen the breakup of the *economic* structure of the manor. This, we must repeat, was followed by a remarkable resurgence of the *judicial and administrative* control of those who lived within the manor. From the 17th century onwards the courts gradually declined into sessions mainly concerned with registration of changes of tenancies.

Much of the regulation of the inhabitants' affairs depended on a major element that was largely peculiar to manors and their courts: a factor of ancient origins, though differing from manor to manor, which closely concerned the mutual claims of the lord over the tenants and of the tenants' rights against the lord; and which might even conflict with the common law of the country. This over-riding principle was known as the *customs of the manor*.

What these customs were will be fully illustrated in the last chapter by examining the custumals, or custom-rolls, of a number of selected manors in Essex; and in the following chapters, which deal with the various manorial offences, many of the customs will be exemplified from the court rolls of these and other manors.

The numerous fine series of manorial records in the Public Record Office, the British Museum and other national repositories are mainly medieval or pre-Dissolution in period. The Essex Record Office is equally rich in medieval court rolls and has infinitely more Essex manorial archives of later date. For the Elizabethan period it now holds records (mostly court rolls but also many account and estreat rolls, custumals, maps, surveys and rentals) for 210 Essex manors. Those which have been examined by the writer are distinguished as explained on p. 345.

Manor court rolls are the records of the proceedings of the Court Baron, the Court Customary, or the Court Leet. The differentiation between them was partly due to the writers of legal treatises on manors in the 16th and 17th centuries. The Court Customary (the bond-tenants' court) had at an early date become inextricably confused with the Court Baron (the freeholders' court). The existence of the Court Leet, on the other hand, pre-supposed a royal grant of special privileges and 'liberties', originally belonging to the royal courts represented locally by the sheriff's tourn. Despite the theorists' definitions, it is often impossible to distinguish rigidly between the business of the various types of manor court, though many stewards by our period headed the section dealing properly with the Court Baron, *'Nunc de Curia'* or 'Now of the Court (Baron).'

The *Court Baron,* which was the lord's own court, was held to determine questions concerning lands held of his manor. The chief business, briefly, was to register all transfers of tenancies, to deal with minor infringements of property rights, to collect his rents and other dues, to see that the tenants' buildings were kept in repair and to deal with dilapidations, to maintain continual watch against minor enclosures and illegal felling or stealing of timber or wood, to consider disputes affecting the boundaries of the manor and the tenants' holdings, and to impose fines on copyholders who had transgressed against the customs, especially those relating to the commons, open fields and meadows (in unenclosed manors), roads, ditches and the like. In certain manors the Court Baron also adjudicated in pleas, such as debt, detinue and breach of contract. Although the lord could legally insist on the tenants paying their suit of court every three weeks, meetings combined with those of the court leet were usually held only once or twice a year, and some inactive courts met even less frequently.

The *Court Leet with View of Frankpledge,* which was a court of record, elected the manorial officers and punished inhabitants who had committed 'nuisances' and 'misdemeanours'; felonies had to be certified to the Assizes. Its staple business was to deal with assaults and other quarrels, disorders in alehouses, trade offences, harbouring of undesirable inmates, and the multifarious annoyances such as obstructions in the streets and obnoxious privies. The offender was warned that repetition of the misdemeanour or failure to remedy the nuisance would result in his forfeiting a specified penalty, or he was summarily fined. The stocks or the pillory were reserved for the worst delinquents or more probably those known to be too poor to pay a fine. In theory it had to be held twice a year, within a month after Easter and Michaelmas, but generally in Elizabethan times there was only an annual court; in some manors it was held on Hock Monday (in Whitsun week).

As explained earlier in the general Introduction and because of limitations of space and our concern with society rather than with institutions, the legal basis of manorial courts will only be sketched briefly. There are many text-books of Elizabethan and later date, written by lawyers, which set out in full detail both the foundation and the procedure of such courts : procedure, however, in which, as already stated, their statements did not always wholly accord with practice.[4] There are also numerous publications giving full transcripts of manor court rolls, some with scholarly introductions, though the majority deal only with the medieval period. As is well known, the Webbs' standard book deals mainly with the period after 1689, but much applies equally to the Elizabethan manor.[5]

For Essex manors, there are several books and articles of outstanding interest. Of special importance for medieval manors are those of Writtle and Great Canfield; both deserve to be more widely known.[6] The first is concerned with the economy of one of the largest and most important manors in Essex and a royal demesne. That on Great Canfield deals with a rural manor and an 'average' one, in so far as any manor can be regarded as such; its arrangement is by subjects, the relevant entries being given in their original Latin in footnotes; and a remarkable feature is the identification of many of the medieval tenements with still surviving farmhouses and cottages. Among articles, with a few transcripts and translations, may be noticed those for the manors of West Mersea and Fingringhoe, 1547-58, and Salisbury Hall in Walthamstow, 1499-1507.[7] A good account of manorial organization is that on the rolls of Great Waltham (medieval) and Lyons Hall in Great Leighs (early 17th to early 19th centuries), with clear explanations of the origin of manorial tenures and incidents).[8] A more important and recent contribution, on which the present writer has freely drawn, covers various Essex manors.[9]

It is not part of our task to attempt to deal with the origin and the development of the manor, nor with its partial decline towards the end of the medieval period. The problem of giving a concise and accurate definition of the manor has always eluded historians, because of lack of uniformity, not only between manors in different parts of England and Wales, but even within a small area. A few remarks may be offered on more practical lines. In Essex, as in other counties, a manor was rarely co-terminous in area with that of the parish. A manor might include land in several parishes; a few scattered holdings might lie even in distant parishes. Thaxted, for example, had holdings at Haverhill on the Essex–Suffolk border. At Great Burstead court in 1574 the jurors presented that some land called 'Benerittes in the parish of Latchingdon (14 miles away) always pays 15s. annually to the lord of the manor of Great Burstead and has done for 40 years and as we believe from time whereof the memory of man is not to the contrary'. A survey of the manor of Eastwood, 1589, includes areas in the islands of Foulness and Wallasea. Such detached holdings in some cases originated in a former lord's ownership, and by what is known as 'manorial attraction' they were appropriated into his own manor. On the other hand, a parish might include the whole or parts of two or even ten manors. There were about 13,000 ancient parishes, but nobody has estimated the number of manors and sub-manors in the late medieval or Tudor periods. It would be highly inaccurate to base any such calculation on a county such as Essex, which was highly manorialized. At the time of Domesday, Essex had some 800 manors. More difficulty is experienced in trying to reckon their number in our period, but Morant and more recent sources suggest a total of between 1,200 and 1,500.[10] Of these, the Essex Record Office now holds some court records, medieval or modern, of nearly 1,000 manors and pseudo-manors.

Although feudal tenures were not to be abolished until 1661, freeholders' tenure by military service had survived only in a very few manors to the previous century. By our period, too, copyholders, who represented the medieval villeins, very seldom gave any 'bond' or predial services to the lord, and virtually all such boon works had been commuted into fixed money payments—the quit-rents paid by every copyholder.

Some Essex lords' income from freehold and copyhold rents has been briefly dealt with by Dr F. Hull,[11] who remarked that such 'rents of assize' (fixed rents) 'formed one of the least remunerative sources of revenue'. Emphasizing that leaseholds afforded lords a much higher income, as rents could be substantially raised on renewal of the leases, he supported his statement by figures of all three kinds of rent paid to seven manorial lords in his period. But by no means all took full advantage of this potential increase. The Petres, Sir William and his son Sir John, certainly took few steps to exploit or rack-rent their tenants and seemed satisfied to maintain a net income of little more than 5 p.c. on their investment; except for providing for payments in kind on renewal of some leases, the revised rents reveal no significant rises.[12]

Apart from such rents, an irregular income came from other kinds of tenants' 'services' and cash due on changes of tenancy. These comprised wardships, reliefs and fines (from freeholders and copyholders respectively), and, on rare occasions, forfeiture of the holding in consequence of treason, serious offences against the customs of the manor, or escheat (failure of heirs). They also had equally unstable receipts from amercements and penalties levied in the courts. Lords having certain 'liberties' were entitled in addition to deodands, waifs, wrecks, and estrays, all of which will be explained shortly. Income from these sources was known as 'casualties', because their rate of flow into the lord's purse was erratic. While the total in some years was considerable from active courts with many tenants, some of the smaller courts thus only just paid their way after deduction of the steward's fees and other expenses such as dinners given to the freehold tenants in a few manors when they paid their rents. John Townshend (who had recently succeeded his father, Sir Roger, the valiant

Armada captain), as lord of the important manor of Wivenhoe, could afford to pay the 15s. 2d. bill for the dinner.

A few quaint rents lingered on from medieval times. In the Epping rolls one occasionally spots an admission to a cottage, the tenant of which had to pay, in addition to the trifling quit-rent, *'unam gallinam vocatam* a smoke hen'; a list of 1631 names 33 'ancient tenements paying smoke hens'. Likewise at Berners Roothing one finds a presentment in 1583 that 'every customary tenant should pay at the Feast of the Nativity of St John the Baptist of old custom *unum pullum vocatum* a headborough chicken having a tail (*caudam*) three inches long'.

In Volume I (*Elizabethan Life: Disorder*) most chapters ended with a brief note of parallel evidence from the printed calendars of the relatively few surviving Elizabethan Quarter Sessions records of other counties. But many manorial records (court rolls, account rolls, custumals and surveys) have been published in full or in abstract,[13] mostly of medieval date. It is impracticable, therefore, to follow the same method in this volume. Instead, we refer only to a recent publication giving a full transcript (but no subject index) of the court rolls of a Yorkshire manor, 1544-1760, which readers who would like to compare the proceedings and customs of Essex manors with those in a distant county should consult.[14] The common misdemeanours, such as petty assault, scolding, woodstealing, failing to cleanse ditches, and so on, are found of course in manor court rolls everywhere. But it is hoped that a study showing the peculiar characteristics of manors in widely different localities may be undertaken, especially from unpublished original sources, by scholars. Such a task would be rewarding and a valuable contribution to social history.

We shall now give a short sketch of the groups of tenants whose duty it was to attend the court and of the various manorial 'incidents' which produced income for the lord. Readers whose interest lies with Elizabethan life, rather than with these prosaic subjects, may wish to skip the next chapter.

---

[1] *Elizabethan Life: Disorder* (1970).

[2] *E.L.: Morals and the Church Courts* (1973).

[3] E.g. pp. 215, 256, 271, 290. In a wider context, see J. Hurstfield, 'The Revival of Feudalism in Early Tudor England' (*History*, xxxvii, 1952, 131-45).

[4] Among such treatises may be mentioned J. Kitchin, *Le Court Leete et Court Baron* (1579) and Sir Edward Coke, *The Compleat Copyholder* (1650), in which is incorporated C. Calthrope, *The Relation between the Lord of a Manor and the Copyholder* (1635), *The Order of Keeping a Court Leet and Court Baron* (1650), and *Lex Customaria, or a Treatise of Copyhold Estates* (2nd edn., 1701). Calthrope and several other contemporary treatises have been reprinted in the Manorial Society's publications. A limited account of the medieval manor is N. Hone, *The Manor and Manorial Records* (2nd edn., 1912); more useful is H. S. Bennett, *Life on the English Manor, 1150-1400* (1938).

5 S. and B. Webb, *The Manor and the Borough* (2nd impression, 1924).
6 K. C. Newton, *The Manor of Writtle* (1970); G. Eland, *At the Courts of Great Canfield* (1949).
7 *Ess. Rev.*, 1, 189-200; *Walthamstow Antiq. Soc. Pubns*, no. 36.
8 A. Clark, *Ess. Rev.*, xii and xiii.
9 F. Hull, 'Agriculture and Rural Society in Essex, 1560-1640' (London Univ. unpublished Ph.D. thesis, 1950, a copy of which he presented to the E.R.O.).
10 These figures were kindly supplied by Mr W. R. Powell, Editor of the *Victoria History of Essex*.
11 Hull, *op. cit.*, 302.
12 Emmison, *Tudor Secretary*, 269-70.
13 For a useful list, arranged by counties, see J. West, *Village Records* (1962), 37-42.
14 *Court Rolls of the Manor of Acomb*, vol. I, ed. H. Richardson (Yorks. Archl. Soc., Record Series, cxxxi, 1969). Among the less common offences may be noted: bad workmanship (p. 58), eavesdropping (p. 60), keeping a mastiff (p. 63), disclosing the jury's secrets (p. 76), not wearing caps (p. 92), harbouring a pregnant woman (p. 94), dangerous chimney (p. 102), keeping an evil woman (p. 103). In many ways the offences and orders differ from those in court rolls of southern manors. For extracts from court rolls of five manors in Warws., Derbys. and Herefs., see Emmison, *Archives and Local History* (1966), 94-8.

# 13
# The Lord and the Tenants

At the beginning of each Elizabethan court roll are usually the names of the 'Chief Pledges with the Homage'. Because the court baron and court leet were usually merged, so, too, this short list combines the chief copyholders with the homage, or freeholders' jury. Each list may contain up to 30 or more names. Even a relatively unimportant manor like Yardleys in Thaxted sometimes mustered 14; but in some of the smallest manors, such as Cammas Hall in White Roothing, Abbess Hall in Great Wigborough, and Kensingtons in Doddinghurst, the tally of chief pledges with the homage was as low as 3 to 6. Attendances varied from year to year, as some tenants were 'essoined' (excused) or fined for default in attendance. Although gentlemanly status is sometimes recorded, the occupations of the others are only occasionally given, e.g. a tailor and a currier at the main Thaxted manor in 1571.

It was the duty of the chief pledges to bring with them their 'deceners' (the heads of tithings), but they are seldom named. In the records of the active court of Abells in Halstead, however, the deceners as well as their pledges are sometimes given; exceptionally, in 1581, the roll furnishes the names of 34 essoins, 22 defaulters, and as many as 87 attendances. In 1576, for the important manor of Felsted, the roll records, in addition to many essoins, the names of 27 men forming the 'homage with the chief pledges', and the appearance of 41 tenants and 70 deceners, with similar long lists in other years. The Purleigh roll for 1573 shows that 'the chief pledges were ordered to have here at the next court their deceners to swear and to perform their service'; this they failed to do, and they were accordingly fined 12d. or 2s. each. The proper procedure is evidenced at the court of Brook Walden in 1563, when 18 inhabitants, aged 12 or more, came and were sworn as deceners. At Thaxted, too, in 1574, all deceners above the age of 12 were commanded to be brought to the next court 'to be put in tithings', under pain of 12d. each. A final illustration may be drawn from Middlemead in Little Baddow, where in 1572 three youths 'of the age of 14 or more' were not in a tithing (*decenario*), so 'their masters are ordered to bring them to the next view', under a similar penalty. The evidence is abundantly clear: the tithing system was still being rigorously enforced in Essex manors.

A few stewards prepared a separate 'suit roll' giving the names of the suitors who were liable to attend. There are several suit rolls for the manor of Fingrith in Blackmore, marked with attendances and noting a few as 'dead' since the previous court. For most manors, however, the record of the names of defaulters, with the fines for absence, is in the ordinary court rolls. At Epping in 1578 39 'residents' who absented themselves were named and each was fined 1d. At Thaxted in 1571 19 tenants defaulted and were fined 3d. each, an average number for this manor. But as many as 59 names occur in 1599, when the homage presented that the cause was that the tenants did not have notice, and the lord, who was himself present in this meagre assembly, was obliged to pardon them. Most courts fined defaulters between 4d. and 1d., but occasionally a more affluent non-suitor, such as Sir John Mordaunt of West Horndon at Shenfield court or Robert Earl of Essex at Canewdon court, was amerced (but probably never paid) 6d. or 20d. respectively.

In general, suit of court was a duty imposed on all males above a certain age (usually 12, 14, 15 or 16, according to the custom of the manor), except freeholders exempt by charter or prescription, who possessed holdings within the manor, many of whom of course lived in neighbouring manors and some far away. The abodes of the latter are rarely stated, and it is important therefore to note that defaulters can rarely be equated with inhabitants: a slip which is made by some parish historians. In fact, the names of defaulters tend to be those of non-residents. At the North Benfleet court, for example, in 1603, the homage included Vincent Simpson, gentleman, but the twelve defaulters included Sir John Petre, Sid Edward Sulyard, Sir Edward Butler, Henry Appleton esquire, Rowland Trappes gentleman, Richard Jennings gentleman, the heir of Thomas Clopton esquire, and John Mustrum gentleman, most of whom are easily identifiable as lords of other manors. On the other hand, the local gentry did not automatically ignore suit of court. In the opposite corner of the county, at Brook Walden manor in 1565, the suitors included George Nycolls esquire, and Thomas Burgeant, William Smyth, Henry Whitney and Alexander Raye, gentlemen. It was not to be expected that such dignitaries as the archdeacon of Essex would pay suit at the Moulsham court, nor the Dean and Chapter of St. Paul's at that of Chingford Comitis; but it is doubtful whether St. Paul's bothered to pay the 2d. fine!

In addition to defaulters, who were fined, the steward usually received a number of 'essoins', which were excuses for not paying suit, almost corresponding to apologies for absence of modern times. Generally, but by no means always, an essoin was put in by another tenant. At the Great Burstead court in 1559 essoins were submitted in the names of 24 tenants by the same number of other tenants who were present. At some courts one tenant would tender an essoin for more than one absentee. Sickness, infirmity or other just cause of absence was occasionally advanced; in 1559 a Walden tenant was on war service in Scotland. A son might attend on behalf of his aged father or widowed mother; at Chelmsford in 1596 Thomas Mildmay of Barnes, esquire, was essoined by William Mildmay.

After the names of the chief pledges, homage, and those essoined for absence, the rolls of most manor courts record the payment of the 'common fine' to the lord. In medieval rolls sometimes termed 'cert money' or 'head silver', it originated as a contribution by the tenants towards the lord's cost of maintaining the court leet, thus relieving them from attendance at the Sheriff's tourn, with the privilege of having their disputes adjudged locally.

The common fine was 'certain' or 'uncertain', and this, like so many other incidents, depended on the ancient custom of each manor. 'We present that we give our common fine 13s. 4d.' is the regular, and typical, form of entry in the rolls of Fingrith in Blackmore. Other examples of common fines which were certain are: Bacons in Dengie 10d., Thaxted 20d., Brook Street in South Weald and Blunts Hall in Witham 2s., Berden 3s., Great Burstead 3s. 4d., Great Dunmow (the manor called the Borough) 4s., Great Bardfield, Eastwood Bury, and Great (South) Shoebury 6s. 8d., Purleigh 8s., and Debden 10s. At Epping court it was 10s. (6s. for the 'Town' and 4s. for the 'Upland'), and the amounts and named divisions at Chelmsford were the same.

'Uncertain' common fines were usually at the rate of 1d. or 2d. 'for each head' and 'of old custom'. At Rettendon in 1560 the 'chief pledges with the homage said they with the deceners give for each resident ½d.', which came to 23d.; it was 16d. in 1568, 22d. in 1588, thus varying considerably. The court of Alfreston *alias* Bigods in Great Dunmow, unlike the other Dunmow manor, had an uncertain fine of ½d. a head, which yielded between 6d. and 12d., while that of Middlemead in Little Baddow at ½d. each ranged between 2d. and 6½d. At Witham, where the courts for the manors of Newland and Chipping were held concurrently, the former paid between 4s. 9d. and 6s. 8d., the latter 17d. or 18d. The rate at Canewdon Hall 'for both chief pledges and deceners' was 1d. a head. The principle at Aveley was somewhat ambiguous. 'The common fine from the beginning I find to be 4s.', wrote the compiler of the survey of the manor of Aveley about 1625 after his extensive search of the old rolls, 'which at the first was computed to be 1d. of every decener as in 24 Henry 8 appeareth, but since I rather think the inhabitants have rated the common fine than stand upon the ancient order of 1d. for every decener, for 21 and 40 Elizabeth some were amerced 12d. apiece for refusing to pay 2d. towards the common fine, also the common fine as 4s. a year at 16 Eliz., note this.'

Some tenants of course refused to contribute to the common fine, or were remiss in doing so, as William Latham, esquire, of Upminster, a 'tenant who ought to pay for his common fine 4d., therefore fined 8d.' in

1561. At Walden in 1580 the court ordered a penalty for non-payment, and in the following year nine were fined 12d. for actual default; occasional fines were levied in later years. The Ingatestone court in 1573 and 1582 fined two men 4d. each for refusing to pay 'their decener's penny'. Because one tenant would not pay his penny, and was fined 12d., the Fryerning court steward in 1582 recorded that the common fine 'is 1d. for each tenant and resident, which amounts to 3s. 4d., which sum the jurors have assigned to their own use by the lords of the manor for their dinner.' Perhaps this concession originated in the pre-Dissolution period, when the Hospitallers owned the manor. Although 36 houses on the west side of Ingatestone High Street and 9 on the east side lay in the manor of Fryerning, the occupiers probably had no reason to crow over their neighbours on the east side, as they were well entertained as tenants of the manor of Ingatestone on Christmas Day and New Year's Day.[15] Those of West Mersea had the rare privilege of paying no common fine— an exemption which doubtless had its origin in the leet franchise having been acquired from Edward the Confessor by St. Ouen Abbey at Rouen, not by purchase but as a gift.[16] At the end of the century there was evidently some difficulty in securing attendance at the courts of Fingrith Hall in Blackmore. In 1599 not only were there many such defaulters, but also 9 tenants who refused to pay towards the common fine, each of whom was amerced 12d.

On the death of a manorial lord, his tenants were under an obligation, by ancient feudal law, to 'attorn' to the new lord, that is, to acknowledge the transferrence of their homage and services to him. The 'attornment of tenants' is accordingly entered on the roll of every lord's first court after acquiring, inheriting or succeeding to the manor.

The first Rettendon roll, 1560, is headed 'The view of frank pledge with the first court of Richard Bishop of Ely', and there follows the attornment of 25 named tenants; that of Brook Walden, 1561, begins 'The first court general of Thomas Duke of Norfolk with attornment of the free and customary tenants', and similarly that of a later lord, John Wentworth, 1588, both listing 70-80 names; while at that of the ancient (Domesday) but very small manor of Yardleys in Thaxted, 1588, 'The view of frankpledge and the first court baron of Jane Wiseman widow' received the attornment of only one tenant.

This initial acknowledgement of lordship in many manors was marked by the customary payment of 1d. by each person. At the first court of Thomas Lord Darcy of Chiche, son and heir of John deceased, 1581, 13 'free and customary tenants and lessees (*firmarii*)' of his manor of Beaumont came and attorned themselves and did fealty to him, paying 13d. between them. The same penny token was rendered to William Cooke for Mascallsbury in White Roothing, 1574, Thomas Tompson for

Shalford Hall, 1596, and Sir Thomas Lucas for Shenfield Hall, 1578 (53 tenants); and in 1559, at the Queen's manor of East Mersea, 'all the tenants who appeared at this court attorned themselves by payment to the Queen of 8d. and did fealty.'

After Arthur Breame had acquired the manor of Abells in Halstead, 1577, he received acknowledgement of fealty and 1d. each from 39 tenants including one of the churchwardens, in accordance with his deed of purchase from Sir William Waldegrave, the previous lord; and the bailiff was instructed to distrain for fealty at the next court 18 absent tenants, 8 being esquires or gentlemen. The roll for Rettendon, 1581, when the new lord was Richard Cannon, states: 'Whereas by ancient custom the customary and free tenants have given to the lord at the first court 40s. in the name of acknowledgement, but this was not forthcoming, therefore payment is postponed until the Feast of All Saints.'

The tenants of Moulsham, by ancient custom, rendered 'palfrey money' at their attornment. The estreat roll for 1567, when Thomas Mildmay succeeded as heir to his father, Thomas, records 6s. 8d. from 'divers customary tenants for their recognition or general fine called palfrey money due to the lord by custom at his first entry, as appeareth by many precedents.' Palfrey money was also paid for the manor of Chelmsford, which the Crown sold to Thomas senior in 1563. Chelmsford manor had belonged to the bishops of London until 1545, and Moulsham to Westminster Abbey until the Dissolution. There is a little scattered evidence that this custom, as in certain manors elsewhere such as Bulphan, a former possession of Barking Abbey, originated in the gift of a palfrey (which was a saddle-horse, not a war-horse) to ecclesiastical or monastic lords.[17]

From these ancient but financially trifling tokens of overlordship, we pass to the regular dues payable to the lord on changes of freeholds and copyholds on death or otherwise and to other dues in kind or money, which embrace further strange and archaic terms of customary law.

An heir or purchaser paid a sum of money to the lord of the manor on being 'admitted' to his copyhold. Such sums were either 'reliefs' or 'fines'. A relief was due from every freehold tenant if of full age at the death of his father or other 'ancestor' on his taking possession, and the sum was 'certain', that is, fixed. The actual amount depended on custom and might be half a year's, one year's, or two years' rent (quit-rent), usually one year. The Elizabethan customary of the manor of Horham Hall in Thaxted discloses that the tenants paid 'relief certain for every tenement 12d., for every acre of wood and meadow 12d., and for every acre of arable and pasture 6d.'

Even as late as our period echoes of feudal times were heard. In Elizabeth's last year, at Rettendon, the jurors found that 'John Cely gentleman, who held certain free land and tenement called Little Hayes', a farm still surviving, 'died since the last court, and because it is clear by the court rolls they were held of the lord by one half of a knight's fee the bailiff is ordered to levy 50s. for relief'. At Abells in Halstead in 1577 it was presented that 'William Hunwick gentleman, who held by charter and military service, viz. half a knight's fee, the manor of Boyes, died since the last court, whereon fell relief 50s., which the bailiff is ordered to levy, and Margaret and Petronella are his sisters and next heirs, and Margaret is 14 and Petronella under 14 and a ward of the Queen.' Bois Hall was a sub-manor to Abells, an extensive manor which included most of the parish of Halstead and lands in ten other parishes. William Hunwick of Great Dunmow had come to live at Bois Hall after purchasing it in 1554.[18] As an example of small freeholds may be cited that of Thomas Wood who had held by free charter a tenement called James in Beaumont, which he had devised to his son Thomas; the quit-rent was 8s. 4d., and the relief paid in 1592 was the same sum.

A 'fine' was payable by every copyholder on his being admitted through inheritance or purchase. It is not to be confused with an amercement, or fine, for an offence. Unlike the relief, the amount was at the discretion of the lord or his steward in nearly all manors. At Beaumont in 1580 one fine for admission to a small holding was as low as 6d., whereas Arthur Breame, lord of Abells, noted the receipt in 1588 of a £30 fine from John Ungeley for his admission on buying Towneford Mill. Other high fines were £26 at Dengie in 1591, and £24 at Shenfield in 1585 on the death of John Element, who held a tenement called Edwardes, for which he had paid £16 on its surrender seven years earlier by William Elyment. Many similar examples of these arbitrary fines being raised on each death or purchase could be given, but as such increases depended on the attitude of each lord statistics are of little interest to economic historians. Fines of between £5 and £10 were not at all uncommon in respect of the average yeoman's customary tenement. In law a tenant had the right to challenge the amount, if unreasonably high, but no such instance has been found.

The manor of Harlow Bury, owned by the Addington family since 1544, was one of the few in which, by ancient custom, the fine was certain. A legal authority, referring to 1577, wrote, '(John) Addington, lord of Harlow, would increase the fines of his copyhold tenants, which were proved to be certain; and it was holden that he could not increase them'; to which the author adds his own pithy comment, 'It shall be a good prescription to say, Always ready to pay such a sum and no more', a somewhat surprising remark, having regard to his hopes of selling the book to lords and stewards rather than to copyholders.[19] Other examples of certain fines are found at Little Bromley (1s. an acre) and Barking (two years' quit-rent).

In marked contrast to the often substantial sums received by the lord by way of fines and reliefs were the annual quit-rents payable by the customary, or copyhold, tenants. Originating in a money payment in commutation for the villein's works and other services, it remained a fixed one, and by Tudor times it had become a low, even nominal, amount owing to the depreciation in the value of money. Small copyholds paid only a few pence; even for larger holdings the quit-rent was seldom more than a few shillings. The actual sums are recorded in the rolls on the admission of a new tenant, and the total sums receivable in a given year are shown in rentals, which were usually prepared at regular intervals.

When a tenant no longer wished to live in his cottage, he could apply to the lord for a licence to 'demise', or let, the property. By the custom of the manor, the term was generally limited to 21 years, and the tenant usually paid a 'fine' to the lord for the licence. It might be for a shorter term, for instance, one for 17 years, the fine being 5s. 8d. Gratuitous licences are less common. After being admitted, Charles Cardinall, gentleman, was given authority by the lord of Beaumont in 1585 to let the holding without fine for 9 years; and the lord of Epping in 1580 allowed his servant to let his customary cottage for 21 years without fine. Licences were also granted by lords for permission to fell timber or to demolish dwellings or outhouses, sometimes on payment of a fee, as will be seen later.

Originally the return to a feudal lord of weapons on his tenant's death, the heriot had come to be the best beast. Heriots are very frequently met with in manorial records : a very large number appear in the Writtle rolls. A few cases from other manors will suffice. At an Epping court in 1578 a black bull, 'his best animal', was seized to the lord's use on a tenant's death, and two bulls in respect of two other holdings. Most heriots, unlike those at Epping, were valued by the jury, in which case the lord took either the animal or cash according to valuation; for example, at Beaumont, a cow valued at 23s. 4d., or at Shenfield, a black cow priced at 46s. 8d. The value lay within a wide range; from 'a little pig' worth 2s. to 'a bay horse' worth £5; or the entry might read, 'Nil, because she has no animal'. The heir of a tenant who himself had acquired by inheritance or purchase two or more separate holdings might be liable for more than one heriot, depending on custom. 'This land is now divided into three parts, therefore three heriots' is noted at Mascallsbury in White Roothing; three heriots valued at £6 were taken for one tenant's four holdings at Canewdon; and three cows price 21s. each at East Mersea. Occasionally the bailiff was ordered to distrain for the heriot; or, as at the Beaumont court in 1567, the heir named two men as pledges for the payment—a horse worth 53s. 4d. The typically detailed manorial surveys of Elizabethan date distinguish between holdings which were heriotable and those not heriotable, according to ancient custom.

When the inheriting tenant was a minor, the lord often claimed right of wardship, that is, the custody of his land and the income from it; but the natural guardian, mother, uncle or the like, was generally confirmed or appointed (subject to the lord's overriding right) on payment of a 'fine', or fee. Several grants of wardship to the age of 14 occur in the Beaumont rolls, where fees as low as 3s. 4d. and 2s. suggest that they were very small tenants; but one of 53s. 4d. was received by the lord of Debden in 1589. In the records of Fingrith Hall in Blackmore under 1571 is a separate bond for £40 given by Giles Collard, George Collard, both brickmakers, and John Dickison, carpenter, all of Walthamstow, to Edward Earl of Oxford, the lord, to render their accounts 'without covin' (fraud) of the lands of William Taylefor during his minority. When a tenant by knight service of the manor of Bulphan died in 1598, his son being aged 17, the roll indicates that the wardship had to be negotiated with the lord. The longest wardship record found in Essex was enrolled in the Fryerning court in 1572 at the request of Edward Ponde, 'guardian in socage' of John, Clemence and Anne, children of John Ponde, yeoman, deceased, then in the custody of Barnard Wharton, Nicholas Poole and Alexander Wylmot respectively, to whom Ponde paid in court the sums of 6s. 8d., 40s. and 40s. for their food, drink and raiment, as had been previously agreed. Ponde also handed over £4 13s. 4d. in court to John Bentley, gentleman, on behalf of Sir John Petre according to the agreement made under John Ponde's will. (Bentley was Petre's most trusted servant.)

To many manors, by grant or ancient prescription, belonged additional forms of income, which we shall now describe.

On conviction, a felon not only lost his life but also forfeited his lands, if any, and his goods, either to the sovereign or to the lord, if the right was attached to the manor. The hanging of a tenant was therefore reported at the court.

High treason rarely reverberated in the humble manor courts, but two cases have been found. At Kensingtons in Doddinghurst in 1593 it was presented that William Shelley, esquire, had been attainted of high treason, his lands therefore escheating to the lord. The copyhold property consisted of two fields and a wood called Bush Field *alias* Maleperdews, apparently in the adjacent parish of Stondon Massey and now represented by Mellow Purgess Farm. The bailiff was instructed to seize the lands into the lord's hands. Shelley had been found guilty of plotting for the cause of Mary Queen of Scots, but he must have obtained a reprieve, as he died in 1597 among his friends, though still under surveillance. His family seat was at Michelgrove in the parish of Clapham, Sussex.[20] The other case originated in the involvement of Thomas Abell, rector of Bradwell-juxta-Mare, in the seditious affair of the Holy Maid of Kent in 1534; he was executed in 1540. Soon after Elizabeth's accession, John Abell, gentleman, produced to the steward of East Mersea written authority from the Queen as owner of the manor to admit him to 19 acres of customary land, 'late of Thomas Abell clerk, attainted of high treason,' paying a 30s. fine and an 8s. 8d. annual rent.

In 1569 Richard Rogers, a brewer of Chelmsford, was found guilty at the coroner's court of the homicide of Stephen Bishop, the bailiff of the manor of Chelmsford being ordered to seize his goods. It was presented at Springfield in 1589 that John Smythe, who had been committed to the county gaol at Colchester (Castle) since the last court for stealing a gelding from Edward Bowser, possessed when arrested a double cloth of fustian, a woollen hose and a dagger, worth 12s., then in the custody of one of the constables, which were taken for the lord's use. The goods of Thomas Rampton of Purleigh, husbandman, 'lately attainted and hanged for felony', were seized by the bailiff in 1591, but their value is not recorded. John Wright, Thomas Melborne and Robert Barfford, all living in the manor of Harlow Bury, having been hanged for felony in 1583, their possessions were forfeited and were sold for 16s. 8d. At Epping in 1577 the jurors gave their 'verdict' that the bailiff should account for £6 5s. found on Robert Perle, arrested there for stealing 22 sheep, for which he had been sent to the county gaol and thence to the Marshalsea prison in London, and attainted. The lord of Epping also acquired two horses worth £5 in 1595 after the execution of two London men who had wounded the son of a Mr Cramphorne, robbing him of his money.

The jurors at Great Burstead in 1581 had a problem. John Potter of Tye Common on the west side of the parish, who had been convicted of manslaughter at Assizes, was freed by one of the Queen's general pardons. The chief pledges of the manor had duly prepared an inventory of his chattels because from time immemorial the lord had had the right to felons' goods, 'but whether they are forfeited because judgement was not granted against him they do not know, therefore it is referred to the judgement of the court.' This is not recorded.

Two cases of forfeiture of goods, one for felony and the other for outlawry, are found in the Moulsham rolls. In 1598 it was presented that Walter Fryer, an inhabitant, committed felony, and having been convicted and attainted had forfeited all his goods. The indictment had been preferred at the Assizes against Fryer, described as a cooper, and two others for poultry raids. His fellows were lucky : one read and was branded, the other was acquitted. In the following year Thomas Barnard, who had been declared an outlaw, was likewise adjudged to have lost his chattels, but 'afterwards the lord of his special grace and kindness and at the humble petition of Barnard pardoned the forfeiture on payment of £5 to him.'

Black Notley court learned in 1589 that Richard Bundock had murdered his father-in-law and his sister, and the jury listed for the lord's information his stock, clothes and other worldly goods. The Assize file has the gory details of the coroner's inquests on the victims, both of whom had been violently attacked one evening with an axe, receiving deep headwounds of which they died instantly. Robert Bundock had also been indicted for abetting Richard in helping to bury the bodies, but was found not guilty. This was one of the seventeen murders [21] of which no details were given in the first volume because it revealed no unusual details apart from being a double murder.

Other goods which were forfeited to the Crown, or to the lord if he could claim them by original grant or prescription, were deodands, waifs and estrays, wrecks, and treasure trove. No record of the last has been found in the Essex rolls that have been examined. A deodand was the personal chattel which had caused a person's violent or accidental death and was deemed to have been given to God (hence the term) as an expiatory offering. In 1595 the Stock jurors presented that Thomas Brock yeoman, an inhabitant, died after falling off a cart loaded with 40 wooden faggots because the binding of the faggots broke. They were valued at 2s., which the bailiff was instructed to levy in the name of a deodand.[22]

A fatal accident at Chelmsford in 1597 resulted in an unusual document, which was attached to the court roll. A 'caliver' (a light kind of musket), 'being charged with a bullet', apparently exploded, killing Christopher Tatem, a townsman (an innholder in 1590 [23]). Its owner was John Wortley, a Chelmsford grocer, who declared that he was unaware it was loaded. The coroner's jury returned a verdict of misadventure, but by law the defendant's goods were liable to confiscation to the lord, Sir Thomas Mildmay of Moulsham Hall. They were valued at £130, a very considerable sum. At the entreaty of the grocer's friends and kinsmen and out of 'commiseration and clemency' towards Wortley, his wife and children, Sir Thomas compounded with him for 20 marks (£13 6s. 8d.). A long deed of release, drawn up by a local lawyer, sets out these terms, including Wortley's declaration that he, his family, friends and kinsfolk were in duty bound to pray for Sir Thomas's 'long life and prosperous success in all good things.'

Suicides' goods were wholly forfeited. Those of James Stone of Moulsham, beerbrewer, valued at 32s. 2d., who hanged himself on an appletree in 1560, of Thomas Netherstrete of Epping, who likewise slew himself in 1584, and those of Isaac Tyball of Rettendon, husbandman, who drowned himself in 1581, were thus in each case taken to the lord's use. But when, in 1573, Alice Pepper of Ingatestone, committed suicide by drowning, her cow worth 30s. and her other chattels valued at £4, were not taken by Lady Petre, widow of Sir William, but graciously distributed by her to the poor and needy.

A waif was any property which was found ownerless; waifs included 'wreck of the sea'. An estray was an animal (not being wild) similarly found. By law, waifs and estrays had to be publicly proclaimed in the nearest markets and in the parish church. If not claimed by the owner within a year and a day, they were valued and fell to the lord. Such stray animals figure frequently, and only a few cases need be cited. At Purleigh in 1553, to quote a rather fuller than normal entry from a Marian roll, the homage stated that 'a black wether now remains at Fryarn within the precincts of this leet which was feeding there, a sheep called a theve remains at Segors, and a ram at Jenyns, that the owners are unknown, therefore proclamation to be made and order to seize them to the lord's use if nobody shall come to prove their ownership'. At the same court in 1592 a white and black spotted boar 'came as an estray into the leet, whereof proclamation had been made in Maldon market.' This action not fulfilling the law's demands, it was ordered that further proclamation be made in Chelmsford and Witham markets. At Epping in 1566 a gelding valued at 20s. and two sheep at 6s. 8d. had to be accounted for to the Queen, who owned the manor. It was reported at Yardleys in Thaxted in 1603 that two stray sheep had been taken by the bailiff, who was told to proclaim them 'according to custom.' Of three horses found at Debden in 1571, one had been kept in custody since Cold Fair day (the important horse fair at Newport). The Thaxted and Little Baddow courts ordered proclamations to be made at the nearest fairs as well as markets. On the other hand, publication in church has been noted only in the Ingatestone rolls. A unique estray case was reported at the court of Alfreston in Great Dunmow in 1581, a black ram worth 3s. 4d. and a brown mare worth 20s. being claimed 'to the use of the Sheriff of Essex because William Longe, tenant of Marhills, is a suitor at the Sheriff's tourn held at Dunmow for the hundred of Dunmow.' Whether this contention was proved is not stated. That lords did in fact enforce their claims is exemplified, among other cases, by the 'praising' (valuing) at 40s. of two old kine and a bullock which had remained in the manor of Fingrith in Blackmore for twelve months and a day since being taken up as estrays in 1571.

Waifs were less commonly recorded. The early sense of 'waive' implied abandoning goods, especially stolen goods, and most waifs had been cast aside by fugitive thieves when pursued in hue and cry. It was presented at Stock in 1570 that a vagabond had stolen two hens which he waived when fleeing.[24] The Shenfield roll for 1577 has this entry: 'Waif. The bailiff has seized 2 pair of shoes, a pair of hose, a piece of ravelling to make bolters, a pair of old boots, a new leather bottle, 100 nails, and a wallet as felon's goods'. ('Bolters' were cloths used for sifting meal or flour; 'ravelling', from ravel, to fray out a fabric, is a much earlier reference than that in the *O.E.D.*) At Purleigh in 1591 two ewes and a lamb worth 12s., 'lately taken by an unknown thief', had been waived.

Entries of 'wreck' occur occasionally in the rolls of maritime manors.

Four cases were presented at Great (South) Shoebury in 1592-99; a mast cast up on the demesne (valued at 10s.); pieces of masts, a rudder, boards and a sail cloth wrecked (25s.); 2 timber logs (5s.) and a 'cock boat or wherry' (16s. 8d.), wrecked on the foreshore; and a little anchor (4s.). Numerous papers, 1576-77, about the wreck of the *John Evangelist* off Foulness, are preserved among the manorial records in the Rich family archives.[25]

The heterogeneous sources of income which lords of manors received have been described, with one exception. At every court, except where the manor was a very petty one, an irregular sum accrued from the amercements (i.e. fines) and penalties for the various offences cognizable by customary law. The actual amounts were 'affeered', or assessed, by two tenants termed affeerers. They are recorded not only in the court roll, but also, if still extant, in the estreat roll, which the steward drew up after each court and submitted to the lord, deducting his own fee and other expenses. Whereas court rolls are almost wholly in Latin, the manor court being a court of record, the estreat roll (Norman-French for 'extract') was a private account and therefore written sometimes in English.

Although estreat rolls are in effect only a duplicate series of entries in the court rolls, they are obviously of much value to the historian where the main records are defective, partly illegible, or lost; and occasionally the language differs slightly from that in the formal rolls. If in English, the steward, instead of translating literally, might express the offence in somewhat different, and more illuminating, words. Some stewards totalled the fines and other fees at the end of each court roll, but many failed to do so, obliging the historian to do the work himself. Estreat rolls, however, necessarily give the totals.

Many of the 'New Men' who acquired manors at the Dissolution were government officials, used to keeping business archives and as intent as the religious houses were on receiving the maximum possible income. Such a man was Thomas Mildmay, one of the Auditors of the Court of Exchequer, who acquired from the Crown the manor of Moulsham. He had given instructions to William Sidey, his steward, to prepare a full statement of the income from his new local court. Sidey performed his task well, and few estreat rolls are more elaborately compiled and engrossed in Latin than the lengthy pair for two courts held in the autumns of 1545 and 1546. Whatever some historians may think about the petty amercements for unlicensed alehouse-keeping, breaking the assize of bread and ale, breaking heads, not cleansing ditches, and the like, Mildmay's court did not regard them lightly, as the peroration to each estreat roll reads:

*Manor of Moulsham*
A pain upon the Bailiff. Memorandum that the bailiff over and besides the substantial execution of all the seizures awarded in this estreat and levying

of all issues and other profits of this leet and court shall with all diligence and speed give special and particular warnings to all persons or else to their tenants or landholders upon whom any pains be laid in this court to endeavour to reform themselves and their defaults in every thing according to the precepts in this estreat comprised, under pain that in the bailiff's default thus to do he shall answer and pay of his own part all such sums of money as for lack of such sufficient warning shall happen to be forfeited at his peril. Examined by me, William Sidey steward there.

Equally unusual is Sidey's habit of including (though of course not as income) forfeitures that had been authorized, should an offence be repeated. Despite his sanctimonious hope that the tenants would reform themselves, had he inserted the penalties for future reference, expecting that inveterate transgressors would add more to his lord's receipts?

It is not generally realised that manorial lords had the privilege of settling the tenants' disputes in their courts baron : a privilege, too, and a valuable boon to the tenants, who thus had a domestic court of justice, saving them the trouble and expense of attending the royal courts and the Sheriff's tourn. Such disputes are easily recognizable in the rolls because each entry is nearly always annotated in the margin as *Querela* (plaint, or plea). The chief actions within the courts' jurisdiction were debt, bargain and contract, slander, trespass, assault, detinue, and waste; but the sum in dispute was normally limited to 40s.[26] But in royal (or 'ancient demesne') manors, such as Writtle, there was no such restriction : 'In relation to civil pleas, it was in effect an exempt jurisdiction, scarcely touched by the Hundred Court or indeed by the central courts. Meetings of its court involved the appearance of professional lawyers just as in the royal courts in London. This exclusiveness of jurisdiction in the matter of civil actions was paralleled in large degree in the execution of the criminal law'.[27]

At Lord Rich's manor of Felsted a very unusual action for fraud or breach of contract and 30s. damages was brought in 1561 against Thomas Parker by Roger Allyn on behalf of himself and the inhabitants, who were duly represented by William Parke, an attorney. The complaint originated in an agreement made two years earlier. For 2s. 6d. Parker had undertaken to fetch from Colchester, for the use of the parishioners, certain armour, viz. 'an almon revet fully furnished', which Roger Wood, one of the Felsted soldiers, had lately used and which Sir Thomas Golding, his captain, had recently sent to Colchester for delivering to the men of Felsted. But Parker, 'cunningly plotting to deceive and defraud' the inhabitants, had failed, after several demands, to deliver the armour.

Another curious action at the same court in 1578 describes how Thomas Ardon 'went into the house of Roger Allen on the first Sunday in Lent and opened the window, and seeing nobody in the house, opened the door and went in, and with his dagger drew back the iron bolt with which the other door was shut, and entered into a bedchamber, where, seeing the wife of Richard Drane, one of Allen's daughters(-in-law), said, *Itane es tu istic,* and then went away'. Taken by surprise, his own words were probably 'So you're here!'; doubtless preceded by a suitable expletive omitted by the steward. The result is not recorded, but at the same session, then termed 'Mr Piggott's servant', he was charged with 'shooting with a handgun at doves sitting on the tenants' houseroofs' and was warned that he would forfeit as much as £5 for a further offence. Cases of theft are also found in the Felsted rolls. In 1562, for instance, a tenant pleaded not guilty to the charge of stealing a pig.

Sir William Petre's manor of Stock also had the right of holding pleas in civil actions.[28] Among evidence from other courts may be cited a 'licence to agree' in a case of debt for a mere 2d. (Newport, 1572) and a plea of false imprisonment (Harlow, 1572).

As a corollary to exemption from the superior courts, the Felsted tenants were debarred by ancient custom from 'impleading for any plea in any other court or any royal court at Westminster nor elsewhere, under pain of forfeiting his goods to the lord's use.' Accordingly, in 1560, Edward Albert was summoned to answer to John Strayte of 'Valaunce' (Valence in Dagenham?) in a plea of defamation at Quarter Sessions [29] for having publicly declared 'John Strayte did take away a boar of mine and set his own mark upon it and kept it as his own'; on which he sought damages of ten marks (£6 13s. 4d.). Thomas Lyster also had to answer Strayte for saying, 'He did steal a sheep of mine and killed it and afterwards sold unto me a quarter of the same sheep'. Lyster pleaded not guilty, and the bailiff was ordered to summon a jury of 12 tenants to try the case. Three years later Albert was convicted for stealing three lambs of John Strayght and two sheep and a lamb of widow Moore. For this breach of custom the bailiff was ordered to seize Albert's lands.

Some latitude in enforcing the prohibition against suing elsewhere is seen in the case of Petre's manor of Ingatestone. In 1565 a general order was made forbidding any tenant or inhabitant from impleading another 'for any matter or cause, before he has warned the lord, so that the lord may determine the cause, if he is able or so wishes; if not, the plaintiff may commence his action and have his remedy elsewhere'. The very stiff penalty of £5 was set on anyone breaking this ordinance. The procedure in some of these actions was of a highly technical nature, following indeed that practised in the royal courts, and pleadings in some cases are found to be very lengthy.

The majority of the entries in Elizabethan and later manor court rolls are concerned with changes of tenancy of the copyholds, and, to a much smaller extent, of the freeholds. While it is obvious that these record important facts about the affairs and deaths of many people, most entries are of a somewhat routine nature and add few lively details.

Although customary (copyhold) dwellings and lands were nominally held 'at the will of the lord, according to the custom of the manor' (hence the term), the Elizabethan tenants, unlike their villein predecessors, had become free. In his examination of selected Essex manors, Dr. Hull found no evidence of eviction of copyholders or of their copyholds being replaced by leases, nor has the present writer. They were able to buy, sell, mortgage, bequeath, entail (and in some manors disentail by a fictitious suit called a 'recovery'). But all changes of ownership, including inheritance, had to be 'presented' at the next meeting of the court. A vendor or mortgagor had to 'surrender' his holding; a testator had to 'surrender to the use of his will'; and all new tenants had to be 'admitted', when they received their 'copy of court roll' as their title-deed.

How much land in each manor was 'registered' in the rolls? (The lord's demesne never appears in them.) Freeholds were recorded when the heir paid his relief and nominally 'acknowledged' the lord; copyholds, at every change of tenancy. The percentage of the total acreage affected varied a great deal from manor to manor. On some Essex manors freeholders were almost as numerous as copyholders.[30] The Elizabethan surveys of about fifty Essex manors mostly give the area in acres of every holding.[31] From these brief remarks it will be apparent that a vast number of owners, with particulars of their freeholds or copyholds, can be recovered from the manorial archives. It is not uncommon to find a court roll mentioning previous changes of tenancy, perhaps many years back. That for Wanstead, for instance, in 1563 refers incidentally to a surrender dated exactly a century before by Thomas Elvolde, the rector, of a tenement called Setweyes. These countless surrenders and admissions, with their vital facts, are a much neglected source for family historians, genealogists and biographers. If neither the parish register nor the contemporary annual copies ('bishop's transcripts') have survived, the approximate date of a person's death ('since the last court') may be deduced from that of his heir's admission. (The date may generally of course also be presumed to be soon after that of his will, if he made one, but it is guesswork.) The relationship of the heirs (e.g. brother, or several daughters with their husbands' names) to the deceased tenant is invaluable. An individual's removal from one parish to another and the date may occasionally be surmised from a surrender.[32] Little appreciated, too, by genealogists is the large number of names occurring in the other sections of the rolls: those who attended, essoined or defaulted, and the chief pledges and homagers; and the often long lists of those presented for the commonest offences. Although court rolls were mostly written in Latin until 1733, except during the Commonwealth, it requires relatively little effort to master the standardized forms of entry of surrenders and admissions; and the tenants' names can be quickly identified because they are often noted in the margin of the roll.

[15] Emmison, *Tudor Secretary*, 123. [16] *Ess. Rev.*, li, 99.
[17] Cf. *Ess. Rev.*, xxxviii, 156, 196-7; xlvi, 138.
[18] Morant, *History of Essex*, ii, 250-1.
[19] Calthrope, *op. cit.*, 65.
[20] *Ess. Rev.*, xxxiii, 109.
[21] *E.L.: Disorder*, 155.
[22] F. W. Austen, *Rectors of Two Parishes and their Times* (1943), 83.
[23] *E.L.: Disorder*, 175.
[24] Austen, *op. cit.*, 58.
[25] See 'The John Evangelist' (prize essay, E.R.O., T/Z 13/105); space does not permit quotation from the documents in this interesting case.
[26] Sir W. Scroggs, *The Practice of Courts Leet and Court Baron* (4th edn., 1728). Despite the holding of courts baron 'no oftener than courts leet, viz. twice in one year', the author thought fit, 'because many manors still retain their ancient power' to determine pleas, to include 'The method of holding a Court Baron for the Trial of Actions' (pp. 194-301); all the specimen pleas are in Latin.
[27] Newton, *The Manor of Writtle*, 87-89.
[28] For two cases of trespass, see Austen, *op. cit.*, 54, 58.
[29] The Sessions roll is not extant.
[30] Dr Hull calculated from the records of his selected manors, showing 640 freeholders, that they represented 43 p.c. of the whole tenantry and their average holding was about 15 acres.
[31] For the acreage of demesne, freeholds and copyholds, see Emmison (ed.), *Catalogue of Maps in the E.R.O.* and its three *Supplements* ('Manorial Surveys' sections).
[32] Examples of manorial admissions, surrenders, etc. are given in full, with notes, in A. A. Dibben, *Title Deeds, 13th-19th Centuries* (Histl. Assoc., revd. edn., 1971), 23-26.

# 14
# Original Presentments

To anyone who has read some thousands of verbose entries in Latin, engrossed on the long, rolled parchment membranes, the manor court assumes in his mind the full dignity of a superior lawcourt. The formal records of the surrender by a copyhold tenant to a purchaser or to the use of his own will, or of the admission of an heir, a new purchaser or a mortgagee, crystallized into set language by lawyers of past generations, follow each other in stately procession. The inhabitants' transgressions are chronicled in shorter entries, but, even so, formulæ such as the ubiquitous *insultum fecit et sanguinem traxit* take on the appearance of normal incidents of their lives, though we may usually discount the actual shedding of blood. At rare intervals, however, he will come across a few loose papers, perhaps crumpled up or torn, in a bundle of parchment court rolls. These are probably the draft minutes. He may be fortunate enough to find also the actual documents put in by the homage or jury, each headed with a statement that it is their 'presentment' or 'verdict'. Such papers are little treasures, for they give the manorial jurors' own language, often painfully penned in vernacular spelling. It was these presentments which initiated nearly all the business of the court. Written usually by the jury foreman, they expressed their neighbours' misdoings or neglects. But when the steward or his deputy prepared the Latin record, he adopted as nearly as he could the terminology of the printed formula books. By doing so, the inherent meaning of some of the jury's vivid phrases, with their homely or dialect words, was lost or suppressed as superfluous for his legal record.

To illustrate the interest of original presentments, a few entries have been selected from the 'verdicts' of the jury for the manor of Great Bardfield, forming part of a small group of papers which also include draft minutes for 1586-89. Evidently the steward noticed that a few entries did not give him enough information from which to draft the proceedings, and after questioning the jury he interlined certain words in his own writing; these have been copied within square brackets. Occasionally he was baffled by the jurors' meaning, or felt incapable of putting certain entries into Latin, so he resorted to the lawyers' device of copying the entry in English, preceded by a Latin phrase stating that the presentment was 'in these words'. Thus he complied in effect with the rule that the record should be in Latin. To one original entry, he added *bene*, apparently to indicate that all was well.

## Great Bardfield

We do paine Richard Michell to tourne the water course of the water which cometh from his stable that doth noye Edmonde Mylliente, uppon the paine if it be nott removed of xij d. to be forfeyted unto the lorde.

We do paine Thomas Ellice uppon the paine of ij s. for every bullocke which he shall have killed in his hall house after the Feaste of St. Andrewe the Appostell nexte cominge.

We do finde that [John] Pamphelon dide lately breake Thomas Sayers hedde.

We do fynnde John Badbroke the yunger aiere unto halffe a naker of lonnd in Monyfellde.

We fynnde John Numane have takenne in a passelle of grounde contayninge by estimacione iij parches of the lordes Commone not a greede for it a Cordinge to the Custome of the manner.

We fynde that Jhon Buttolf thelder made a defaulte in makinge a ditche upon his coppyholde against Mr. Kempes grounde, but since he hath digged the residue of ye greene there and made it playne with caryinge ye marle therof into his coppyholde lande [bene].

Richarde Bearnarde Surrendred into ye handes of Gefferye Poole and Jhon Warner customarye tenantes of this Mannor to ye use and behoof of Thomas Bearnarde and his heires all and singler his coppyholde landes holdinge of this Mannor.

We finde yt there hath bene felled and caryed out of Crowes beinge coppyholde of this Mannor in ye life time of William Bendolowes Seriante at ye lawe certayne oke spirkes like to prove tymber amountinge to a small iagge of woode felled by ye Tenante of ye same grounde and caryed awaye and spent by one Gyles Sirrha tenante to Mr. Bendlowes other grounde but not of that grounde.

We present John Ferras for setting a smythes shoppe uppon the lordes wast contrarye to the lordes will and that he remove yt betwene this and Mychellmas next commynge uppon payne to forfeete xl s.

We fynde on Alination from Robert Ewen to Doritie his wyfe a tenement called Thornes [by his last will *pro termino vite*].

We fynde Alination from William Robertsonne to Henry Redde otherwise Davie a tenement called Isoles [to him and his heyres].

Thomas Borley dide make defaute in his appearinge at this Courte we paine him at iij d.

There ys some controversie for that Jerome Bayliffe hath lopped ij asshes which doth stande in the pale betwene the Orteyarde of Jerome Baylyffe and a meadowe of Richarde Serles jun., uppon sighte thereof we do finde that the uppermoste ashe ys the saide Richarde Serles and the propertie of the lowermoste ashe ys in them both.

We finde that Roberte Cheekes man dide draue bloude on Mr. Smethes hedde the xij th daye of June.

We finde that Marye Brytaine shall voyde [remove] out [William] Townsend by Crystmas upon forfite x s.

We payne the dweller in a house called Stevens to scoure the ditche sufficientlye that is aboute that house against Mylfylde conteyninge xij pearches more or lesse, that ye water may so passe through the same ditch that it breake not over into ye highewaye at ye ende of ye shoppe there, which we payne to be done before Hallowmasse nexte, upon payne for everye pearch not so done to forfeyte iiij d.

We payne one Henrye Clarke to avoyde his tenante one Packman before Mychaelmasse nexte for that the sayde Packman his wife is berefte of ye use of her wittes, upon payne of twentye shillinges.

Thus we see the kind of language which lay behind the regular entries in the formal rolls. Except in the more populous manors, the steward must often have striven hard to maintain such little solemnity as the court had. It is virtually impossible to say how many sessions were opened with his reading a charge to the jury, after the style of the charges delivered to juries at Quarter Sessions or Assizes. But, whether they were told of their duties or not, the manor court witnessed groups of farmers, tradesmen, craftsmen and labourers declaring they were present or essoining those who were not, shuffling up to the steward's table to take their oaths, putting in their presentments, acknowledging or denying the charges against them, or paying their head-money, reliefs, fines, amercements and forfeitures to his clerk or the bailiff. The actual business varied between the minor farce of the very small rural court and the long day's proceedings of the substantial manor, at the end of which steward and clerk collected their records and the lord's cash, hoping that their scribbled notes would be intelligible when the time came to draft or engross the roll. The jurors, the old and new tenants, and probably some of the bakers, butchers and other offenders who made their appearance regularly, adjourned to the inn to eat and drink and talk about the affairs of the day, the mutual goodwill or illwill between the lord, the steward and them, the penalties imposed, the new bye-laws to which they had agreed, the good or bad qualities of the officers they had elected for the year. They were topics for some days, or even until the next court, which would be held on a given day—'according to the custom of the manor'.

# 15
# The Manorial Officers

'The steward', wrote Sir Edward Coke in 1650, 'sitteth as judge in court to punish offences, determine controversies, redress injuries, and the like; therefore sithence he hath this measure of authority and confidence committed unto him, the Lord shall do very well to be very careful in making choice.'[1] Only very rarely did the lord preside himself, for example, at Earls Colne in 1586.[2]

Large landowners possessing a number of manors in one county or adjoining counties usually had a chief steward, who sometimes presided in person; but on other occasions a deputy or an under-steward performed the office. Lord Darcy of St Osyth's Priory, for example, appointed Geoffrey Nightingale, who acted as chief steward of the manor of Beaumont (1581); he had been educated at Cambridge and Gray's Inn, was appointed a J.P., and lived at Newport.[3] The courts of Great Burstead, Felsted, and Chalkwell in Prittlewell in Elizabeth's first two decades are headed 'Before John Cooke, General Steward.' These were among the many Essex manors belonging either to Lord Darcy or to Lord Rich. In later years William Wyseman acted as steward for Rich's manors throughout Essex. William Waldegrave was steward of Felsted manor in 1603 and deputy steward both to Sir Robert Cecil, Principal Secretary, for the manor of Copford also in 1603, and to Thomas Powle, chief steward of East Mersea and of all the Queen's manors in Essex in 1583-98 (Copford, too, belonged to the Crown). William Ram, who was Clerk of the Peace for Essex as well as an attorney, termed himself vice-steward of the manor of Shenfield in 1578, John Cockerell being the steward then or a few years later. Other local attorneys held stewardships, such as Edward Markaunt, a Colchester lawyer, for Fingringhoe in 1553, and John Adye for Thaxted in 1599. A few stewards will be mentioned in later chapters, but by no means all Elizabethan rolls name them.

The lord also appointed a bailiff, or reeve, whose duties were to summon the tenants to court, to collect fines, heriots and quit-rents, to be on the spot to watch the lord's interests in such matters as the state of repair of the copyhold buildings and the proper care of the lord's woods and 'wastes' (commons), to report cases of trespass such as unlawful felling of timber, to keep accounts of the manorial court income and expenditure, and generally to carry out the court orders. The bailiff, acting on the lord's behalf, had power to levy distress for arrears of rent or to seize a tenement.

Among the numerous orders which the Ingatestone court gave the bailiff were those to warn defaulters to scour their ditches and lop their roadside trees, to summon the inhabitants to repair the stocks, to proclaim stray sheep in neighbouring market-towns, and to see that a hedgebreaker and his scold of a wife left the manor; once he was abused when executing his office, and once he was himself presented for allowing sale of goods in the church porch and graveyard.[4]

At Abells in Halstead in 1578 the bailiff was ordered to seize 'two parts in five of divers customary lands and pasturing called Everardes, Hawes and Longmead, now in the occupation of Francis Archer who has holden them for divers years without any lawful title, as by the inspection of the rolls appears, and to answer for the profits.' How he managed to apportion the two-fifths is not explained.

A penal instruction given at the Moulsham in Chelmsford court a little before our period further illustrates the bailiff's duties. The roll for 1529 notes (in English) that he 'shall with all diligence and speed give special and particular warning' to all to pay up their fines 'under pain that, in the bailiff's default thus to do, he shall answer and pay of his own price all such sums of money as for lack of such sufficient warning shall happen to be forfeited, at his peril'.

The constables' chief tasks were to maintain the peace, to appoint the watchmen, to pass on vagrants to the next manor or parish, to raise the hue and cry after malefactors and fugitives, to execute justices' warrants for arrest, and to take charge of and repair the archery butts, stocks, cage, whipping-post and cucking-stool. The activities of these town and village Dogberries, and the abuse and ridicule to which they were often subjected, are well documented in the Essex Quarter Sessions rolls.[5] But one must not generalize about their lowly status. In the larger towns it may have been higher. The Chipping Walden court, for instance, in 1583 chose Thomas Raye gentleman, Simon Wyllymotte gentleman and William Bowlinge as constables for the town.

Constables first appear to have been elected at manor courts about 1400;[6] a little after our period small, decaying manors were among the first to relinquish their appointment to the vestry, the organ of the parish. Nearly every manor elected each year usually two constables, though some small manors were satisfied with one, as Brook Street in South Weald and Mascalls Bury in White Roothing. At Blunts Hall in Witham, another petty manor, a constable was only elected every few years. The important manors of Great Burstead, which included the market town of Billericay, Great Coggeshall, and Bishop's Hall *alias* Chelmsford seem generally to have chosen 3 constables, and Moulsham had 4 in 1559 though usually 2 in later years. Abells in Halstead, which usually had 2, elected 3 (1 of them being a clothier) in 1586 and again in 1587. Quite exceptionally

Horham Hall in Thaxted appointed 7 in 1599 and 1600, and the other Thaxted manor known as Thaxted-with-the-Borough and Spencer's Fee elected 6, but they served jointly for both manors. In 1601, at the 'Borough' court, 3 appeared and put in their presentments. The 3 others did not, and 'because they are elsewhere in the Queen's service they are acquitted and discharged.' A joint appointment of 2 constables was regularly made at the combined court for the manors of Chipping and Newland in Witham. But in the town of Walden, separate pairs of constables were elected for the manor of Brook Walden.

In theory, the manorial constables were able to call on the chief pledges in charge of each tithing for help when needed. No specific reference to such aid has been discovered, but at rare intervals one finds chief pledges also termed 'assistant constables'. After appointment, most constables, like other manorial officers, took the oath of their office. At Purleigh in 1591 they apparently defaulted and were ordered under pain of 40s. to attend before Arthur Harris, J.P., to take it; and at Epping in 1595 the bailiff was instructed to have an absent constable before Richard Raynsford, J.P. In 1593 the court of Ruckholts in Leyton ordered John Leice to pay 10s. to Richard Fletcher, 'which was promised to him by Leice in open court to serve as constable for him as by the oath of divers tenants doth appear'. Although service by paid deputy is occasionally met with in much later years, it is extremely rare to find a case in Elizabethan times and this has no parallel in Essex records. Unlike aletasters, breadweighers and similar officers, constables in some manors, among them Epping, East Mersea and Springfield, were expected to serve for two years, the 'old' constable being kept in office for a second year, while a 'new' one was elected who in turn bcame the 'old' constable the next year.

There is little doubt that constables' chief responsibility was to the justices of the peace [7] rather than to the manor court. In periods of acute economic distress and unemployment they had a heavy burden involving much waste of their own time in conveying groups of vagabonds before the local justice and then out of the manor.

Very occasionally, as at Purleigh (1577 and 1591), two 'surveyors of bread and ale' or 'surveyors of victuals' were elected; or at Great Canfield (1556), when a single 'bread and ale taster' combined both functions; but in urban and many rural manors the control fell to separate pairs of breadtasters and aletasters. Alternatively there were 'bread weighers' or 'bread searchers', two of whom were elected, as at Thaxted; or an 'ale founder', as at Fingrith in Blackmore (1558) and Harlow Bury (1556), or 'ale conners', noted at Kelvedon Hatch (1593), Fingrith (1567), and Rettendon (1560). All these terms are commonly found elsewhere. Any catalogue of the names of the manorial officers, especially the longer lists of the more important manors, looks very strange to modern eyes, as so few of their offices remain in present-day language. The lineal descendants of some of them bear the grander names of public health, shops, and weights and measures inspectors. Boroughs not only appointed constables, ale-tasters, bread-weighers and leather-searchers, but of course additional officers.[8]

A majority of courts, except those of small rural manors, chose two aletasters each year. While it was the duty of the constables and watchmen to make 'privy search' for those guilty of disorderly acts in alehouses and elsewhere, the aletasters had to present all cases of bread (as well as ale) that was deficient in quality or excessive in price. 'You shall truly see', their oath ran, 'that all bread do contain such weight according to the assize, and take care that all brewers do brew good and wholesome beer, and ale, and that the same be essayed by you, and at such price as it shall be limited by the justices of the peace; and all offences committed by brewers, bakers and tipplers you shall present to this court.' At the Petres' important manor of Writtle 6 aletasters were appointed, who served their office in pairs for Writtle township, Highwood and Roxwell, into which this very extensive manor was territorially divided.[9] As will be seen later, the rolls of Sir William's Stock manor bear evidence how his steward treated the duties seriously, especially in the way in which he recorded the proceedings. Another illustration of the precise nature of his entries is found under 1565 :

> At this View, by the assent of the whole homage and steward, William Haywoode and Henry Stonerde are elected to serve and superintend all bakers and brewers within the precinct of this View and to weigh the bread and to taste the drink for sale of every kind, and to measure the vessels containing the drink for sale, etc.; and to present on their oath anyone whom they detect at fault or acting unfairly and further to do and execute that which appertains to the office of a weigher of bread and taster of ale or of drink for sale, etc.[10]

William Heywoode, one of the officers so elected, was a nephew of the jester in Mary's court. In one of his plays he mentions :

> Ynge Gyngiang Jayberd the parish of Butsbery

which tickled him as much as an even slightly longer name of the manor amuses us.[11]

Vigilance in seeing that supplies of meat and fish exposed for sale were reasonably fit for human consumption was carried out in the more populous manors, especially those with market rights, by 'flesh tasters' and 'fish tasters'. At Thaxted, for instance, 2 'flesh and fish searchers (*scrutatores carnis et piscium*)' were elected annually, and at Chelmsford 3 'tasters and searchers of flesh, bread and other victuals' in 1564.

The products of tanners and glovers were also subject to inspection in some manors. 'Searchers and sealers of leather' (*scrutatores et sigillatores corei*) were elected at Great Burstead (which included the market-town

## THE MANORIAL OFFICERS

of Billericay) in 1560, 'searchers of leather' at Harlow in 1566, 'searchers of tanned leather' at Chelmsford in 1564, 'leather sealers' at Halstead in 1577, and 'leather testers' at Dunmow in 1577; a pair for each manor. At Thaxted 3 leather searchers were elected in 1574, but only 2 subsequently.

Manorial offices, like the parochial offices of surveyor of highways and overseer of the poor, were unpaid and usually unwelcome. Not surprisingly, cases of refusal to take office are met with now and again, as well as charges of neglect, such as those against the aletasters and leather searchers at Harlow, who were each fined 12d. in 1597. The same court in 1581 fined an inhabitant 2s. for refusing to 'help the aleconners' after being ordered to do so.

Apart from the lord's own steward, the officers commonly elected in most manors of average importance were therefore a bailiff or reeve, 2 constables and 2 inspectors (under various guises) of victuals, or bread and ale separately; together with 2 to examine the tanners' and glovers' wares in fewer manors. In addition, appointments of other officers are found in the records of some manors, chiefly because of local circumstances, but these men were not necessarily chosen each year. At Newport an order of 1568 refers to 'the herdman', and a presentment of 1571 states that a widow had forcibly 'rescued' 100 sheep from John Cowper 'the heyward'. Great Bardfield, in 1589 at any rate if not in other years, had a 'driver of our commons', and a similar solitary mention occurs at West Horndon in 1584 of 'le ketcher *pro communis*', ketcher being an archaic form of catcher, who was evidently another common-driver. The Chipping Walden court each year elected a 'collector of the lord's rents'—an office held by a man of some substance; and a 'beadle or collector' is referred to in the customary of the important manor of Barking in 1609.[12] Coggeshall had 2 water-bailiffs to supervise the river. At Berners Roothing in 1567 a single surveyor of highways was elected by the manor court, perhaps because the constables and churchwardens of this tiny parish failed to do so under the Act of 1555.

Depending on their population, manor courts in market-towns tended to make extra appointments or to increase the number of the normal officers. John Walker's survey of the manor of Chelmsford in 1591 shows that a clerk of the market and as many as 7 'searchers' were elected—2 for bread and ale, 2 for leather, and 1 each for meat, fish and victuals. The Moulsham court in Chelmsford in 1564 elected 2 'surveyors of nuisances' : whether an *ad hoc* appointment to deal with special circumstances is not clear, but it is surprising that such a logical arrangement was not arrived at in other towns where insanitary conditions were very bad. They re-appeared in 1600, when 2 street-surveyors (*stratorum* must indicate the built-up street, not the ordinary surveyors of highways) as well as 2 water-bailiffs were appointed. In 1577 the manor roll of Thaxted not only records the election of 2 breadweighers, 2 aletasters, 2 leather-searchers, and 2 fish and flesh tasters, but also that of mayor and 'the warden of the mistery or corporation of the cutlers'. The manor of Romford in the royal liberty of Havering elected a head constable, 2 sub-constables, an aletaster and a clerk of the market.

While these officers were elected at the courts, other officers were occasionally appointed by the lord. At Ingatestone, for example, in 1579 a woodward was chosen, and at Ramsden Crays in 1593 'the lord nominated and appointed Edward Croxeton and Titus Coker to the office of woodward for the preservation of his woods within the manor.'[13]

The royal manor of Writtle not only included within its bounds the numerous sub-manors in Writtle but also the adjacent parish of Roxwell.[14] Purchased from the Crown by Sir William Petre in 1554, the large income which he derived from the manor and its important court demanded a precise knowledge of its customs. The rolls, which were examined from 1379 onwards by Mr Newton, yielded references to various officers, some of whom were peculiar to Writtle. The very bulky Elizabethan rolls have not been read by the present writer, so that it cannot be stated how many of these officers were still being appointed in this period. It is probable, however, that most, if not all, were still functioning. These officers were the woodward of Edney Wood and High Wood; the 2 palers, who were in charge of the fences of Petre's Writtle Park and Horsefrith Park and whose wages were paid in kind by an annual rent of one or more bushels of wheat by those holding certain tenements; the 'coaler', or collier, by whose skilled craft charcoal was prepared in the big woods;[15] and the 'cater', or acater (from which the modern caterer is derived), who presumably provided food for the lord's household.[16]

---

[1] Sir Edward Coke, *The Compleat Copy-holder* (1650),    [2] *Ess. Journal* ix, 89.
[3] *E.L.: Disorder*, 284-5, 324.
[4] For misuse of church porches and churchyards, see *E.L.: Morals* 270-2.
[5] *E.L.: Disorder*, index, s.v. 'constables'.
[6] Cf. the election of a single constable, 1409 (*Court Rolls of Tooting Bec Manor* (1909), 123.    [7] *E.L.: Disorder*, index, s.v. 'constables'.
[8] For a reproduction of a list of the Maldon borough officials, see N. Rowley, *Essex Towns, 1540-1640* (E.R.O. Pubn. no. 53).
[9] Newton, *The Manor of Writtle*, 90.    [10] Austen, *op. cit.*, 57.
[11] *E.L.: Disorder*, 70.    [12] *Ess. Rev.*, lix, 6.    [13] *Trans. E.A.S.*, lix, 6.
[14] Newton, *op cit.*
[15] Emmison, *Tudor Food and Pastimes*, 64-6.    [16] *Ibid.*, 28, etc.

# 16

# Punishments

Manor courts enforced the great majority of their orders by means of penalties and fines (the ubiquitous phrase is *A.B. est in misericordia,* is in mercy, i.e. is fined). The court baron might order an offending tenant's dwelling to be pulled down, his land to be forfeited, or his tenement, animals or his goods to be distrained. The court leet had a wider range of punishments at its disposal. In the main they were all in the nature of temporary imprisonment, during which the victim was exposed to public view and ridicule. The physical forms of confinement conjure up colourful scenes of the implements used: stocks, pillory, cucking-stool (for scolds), tumbril (scolds and others), cage or lock-up; also, for stray livestock, the pound.

In Essex the only genuine survival of any of these instruments of correction of Elizabeth's time is the remarkable combined stocks and whipping-post, as well as an incomplete pillory, preserved in the porch of Waltham Abbey church, removed there about 1910, a drawing of which forms the frontispiece of Volume I. Carved at the top '1598', this post has iron clasps for legs and arms. A sketch of the pillory outside Barking manor courthouse is seen in the drawing of that building, dated 1595.[1] In 1930 Mr John Salmon wrote a valuable article on the then remaining Essex stocks, pillories, whipping-posts and cages, with some photographs.[2] Among those which have been preserved, all of much later date than 1598, examples are the stocks at Havering (on the Green), Doddinghurst (on the roadside), and Colchester (Museum); a pillory (Saffron Walden Museum); and the cage at Bradwell-juxta-Mare. The village stocks at Canewdon, which were made to hold three people and not two as was usually the case and were unfortunately pulled down about 1920, stood inside the cage, 'close to the pond where probably the cucking or ducking stool did service in old times.'[3]

Who were responsible for providing and maintaining these instruments? There was no statutory provision—unlike the archery butts, for which the inhabitants were always liable—and the obligation depended on the custom of each manor. A later textbook notes, 'Everyone that hath view of free pledges ought to have pillory and tumbril to do justice: also in every town where there is a leet there shall be stocks, and for default thereof the town shall forfeit £5';[4] but no Essex manor roll seems to furnish evidence of this sum being levied.

The court of Chipping Hill in Witham ordered the inhabitants of Chipping Hill (so named from the market-place close to the church) to 'make' the stocks there (1583); and that of Middlemead in Little Baddow, on learning that the stocks 'for the punishment of illdoers' were in decay, enjoined the inhabitants to repair them under pain of 10s. (1601); in each case, before Pentecost. A similar penalty was imposed at Ruckholts in Leyton in 1574. At Rettendon in 1561 and 1563 the stocks were reported to be broken, 'but by whose default we know not, and we seek a tree from the lord for making new stocks'; the lord granted a tree from the Common on condition that the tenants made new stocks before the next court. Thirty years afterwards the homage presented themselves for decayed stocks, and the township was fined the paltry sum of 12d. A similar record is found at Debden in 1583 : 'All the inhabitants humbly ask the lord for an oak to make the stocks, and the lord grants a suitable oak', which the bailiff was told to provide. The lord was the Duke of Norfolk, but it may be assumed that he knew nothing of the gift and that his steward had acted on his behalf. At Blamsters in Great Easton, however, the farmer (lessee) of the manor was ordered to repair both pound and stocks. A dual liability was also declared in 1581 by the court jury of 'Ging Joyberd Laundry Harvard Stock' (i.e. Buttsbury) that 'the stocks and the cuckingstool are now in decay, and the Bishop of Ely ought to make and repair them at his own expense.'[5] This is somewhat surprising, as the manor was owned by the Petre family, whereas the bishops were lords of Imphey Hall in the same parish.

The men of Aveley had allowed the pillory and the cuckingstool to become ruinous in 1587. Both these implements of punishment were lacking at Rettendon in 1593, when the inhabitants were fined a further 12d. Three years later stocks, pillory and cuckingstool were all 'unrepaired', and the fine became 20s. An order at Great Burstead in 1584 for repairing the pillory is exceptional in being addressed only to the inhabitants of the town of Billericay, which lay within the manor.

A little before our period, in 1550, the stocks and pillory of Bendish Hall in Radwinter were in decay, the inhabitants being commanded to repair; and in 1546 those of Moulsham petitioned Thomas Mildmay, the lord, for a pillory and a tumbril 'for the proper correction or punishment of divers malefactors', at his own cost. In 1587 at Earls Colne 'all the honest inhabitants' complained that they 'do greatly want a pillory and cuckingstool'. Contrast 'honest' with the decree made two years later that, 'if any lewd fellow be found either drunken or railing on any man, he shall either be sent to the stocks or otherwise punished by the constables or headboroughs'.

The cucking-stool appears less frequently. That at Aveley was again the subject in 1603 of a humble request to the lord to make one. The tenants and inhabitants of South Ockendon were told in 1561 to 'repair or build the cucking-stool for punishing scolds and babblers (*obiurgatrices et garrulatrices*!)' and sufficient timber from the lord's wood was assigned. In 1585 the Great Burstead inhabitants (not confined this time to Billericay townsmen) asked leave to make both pillory and 'cookstool' before the next court. Cucking-stools are mentioned incidentally in the rolls of Epping in 1568 and of Alfriston in Great Dunmow in 1575, and the cucking-stool pond at Walden in 1583. The sole reference to tumbrils, except for use as punishment, occurs at Rettendon in 1560, when the jurors admitted that they had 'neither tumbril, pillory nor stocks, etc.'

The paucity of references to cages is perhaps understandable on account of their being slightly more expensive to build (they were presumably all brick structures, though only intended to confine a few unruly persons). At Harlow in 1579 '*prisona vocata le cage* was ruinous, rotten (*putrida*) and insufficient to detain malefactors', and the inhabitants were ordered to repair; and at Moulsham in 1602 'the landholders, from the well next to the cage towards the Friary', were presented for failing to cleanse the common gutter.

We saw in the previous volume how the archidiaconal courts sometimes ordered drunkards sentenced to public penance to exhibit an empty tankard in front of them. Such an extra humiliating device was adopted by some manorial courts in punishing those convicted of stealing hedgerow wood; several instances will be described in a later chapter. In the same context we shall find that the Ingatestone court in 1600 warned wood-stealers that they would be whipped half-naked until they 'bleed well': the sole instance of whipping found in manor rolls.

[1] Reproduced in E.R.O. Publn. no. 53.
[2] *Ess. Rev.*, xxxix, 195-202.   [3] *Ess. Rev.*, xxii, 88 (with drawing); xxxix, 196.
[4] Calthrope, *The Order of Keeping a Court Leet* (1650), 44.
[5] Austen, *op. cit.*, 80; the author remarks that 'it seems highly probable that the cucking stool was placed by what is now known as the weir pond'.

# 17
# Offences
## *Felonies*

'You must understand', wrote the compiler of a 17th-century steward's textbook, 'that high treasons, petty treasons and felonies are to be enquired of and presented in the Court Leet, but not punishable there, the which offences ought to be set down in writing and indented, the one part to remain with the steward, the other with the jury, and the same must be delivered to the justices of the Assizes'.[1] He then listed the crimes in question, such as counterfeiting coin, murder, manslaughter, rape, burglary, robbery, arson, and larceny.

But it is doubtful whether his theory accorded with practice; for no such indenture, at any rate, has been found in the Essex Assize files or manorial archives. One might have concluded that the compiler was so far off the mark that such an 'indented' or duplicated certificate was in fact never made, were it not for a solitary Assize document preserved in the Queen's Bench records. Even so, the offences presented were not grave ones, but rather a case of one individual having committed so many that the steward, or his lord, decided to inform the Assize justices. It is significant that the manor court amerced him in the high sum of £5.

> *View of frankpledge with the court of Roger Harlackenden esquire of his manor of Earls Colne, 1592.*
> Henry Abbott junior hath drawn blood upon William Clerke and utterly hath maimed and lamed his finger.
> In the night time he hath in his shirt come out of his house and in the street hath disquieted the watchmen.
> Being commanded by the constables to ward the next day he refused.
> He hath railed upon divers of his honest neighbours and them in most gross terms and speeches greatly abused.
> Divers and sundry times heretofore he hath played at cards, dice, tables and other unlawful games and that very often.
> He is very much given to contention and moveth great strife and variance between his neighbours and many suits and actions have by him been moved.[2]

What action, if any, the Assize justices took is not recorded: possibly they deemed his heavy fine an adequate punishment. His iniquities, however, did not cease. The reprobate was presented two years afterwards to the Archdeacon's court for drunkenness and highly obscene language.[3] But it seems a little unfair that the two constables of Earls Colne were indicted at the Michaelmas Quarter Sessions, 1592, 'for not keeping their watch, neither appointing any of the inhabitants to watch from sunset to sunrise, according to the statute'. And as 'watch and ward' is a meagrely documented subject, we may note that the Earls Colne court in 1585 had decreed : 'If any person be found out of his house after 9 o'clock, except he can show a reasonable cause, he shall forfeit 3s. 4d.' The nearest parallel to this curfew-type order, not found elsewhere in Essex, is that issued against nightwalkers at Halstead, quoted later. Certificates of felonies were probably not sent to the Assize for two reasons. Stewards, acting on their lords' behalf, had no pecuniary interest in such offences, as manor courts could not punish nor even fine felons; and in the intervals between courts the constables doubtless brought culprits before individual justices, who sent them to prison to await trial at the Assizes or Quarter Sessions or bound them over to appear.

An exceptional decision was made by the Rettendon court in 1560, when a tenant, presented as having been punished by the justices for stealing a sheep, was 'given a day to remove himself, his wife and children outside the jurisdiction of the court before Michaelmas on pain of 40s.'

At Harlow in 1564-5 a woman who had committed a petty felony in stealing a 'kersey' (cloth) was put in the stocks for 3 hours, and another woman who had stolen 2 plough-irons was apparently given similar punishment. The Stock rolls for 1557 and 1565 tell how John Tavernor had committed 'small robberies', viz. a shoe worth $1\frac{1}{4}$d. from a horse belonging to John Mylles of Billericay (fined 4d.) and a lamb worth 4d. of widow Russhe after his dog had accidentally killed it (fined 6d.), and how James Chamberleyne killed and cooked a cockerel that had wandered into his house (fined 4d.).[4] These trifling items are cited because theft figures infrequently in manor rolls. Such charges of petty larceny, which were misdemeanours, not felonies, and concerned goods worth 12d. or less, normally went to Quarter Sessions, the records of which have many hundreds of such indictments.[5] But presentments for wood-stealing and hedge-breaking, which were really other forms of larceny, are a very common feature of manor rolls, and will be described later.

## Assault, Barratry and Rescue

It goes without saying that the human tendency towards assault is well represented. So much so that there were relatively few court days on which the more important manors did not deal with one or more offenders. The usual punishment was a 3s. 4d. fine—a sum that was stable throughout the reign; so it was relatively cheaper to indulge in battery in the later decades, owing to the depreciation in the value of money! While 3s. 4d. was levied for many years at Witham, it was reduced to 20d. about 1590 and only 12d. in 1594. At Halstead it was rarely less than

3s. 4d., but it was 20d. at Shenfield in 1579 and only 6d. in 1570 for an assault 'without reasonable cause'. The Chelmsford court consistently levied 3s. 4d. (8 assaults at one session in 1579 and plenty in other years); but Christopher Wilson of Chelmsford was fined 6s. 8d. in 1602 at the court of Copford, 20 miles away, perhaps because he was 'foreigner'. At Felsted in 1594 assaults cost 4 men 3s. 4d. each, but another had to pay 6s. 8d.

Sometimes the nature of the attack is given—with cudgel, hedging bill, billhead, stone, or fists. At Brook Walden in 1564 assaults were made with sword, staff and even candlestick, the fine being 3s. 4d. in each case. Edward Justice of Purleigh, blacksmith, of course used his hammer. In such instances the 'weapon' was 'seized into the lord's hands'. Most charges include *'et sanguinem traxit'* (and he drew blood), a phrase so general that it had become common form. It made no difference to the fine. At Chelmsford in 1571 a townsman fell on another and 'drew blood with a pewter quart pot'; the same court in 1575 fined Thomas Griffine, miller, for sanguinary assault on Thomas Mantle. The names of two south-west Essex landowners appear incidentally in 1595, when 'the servant of Mr Grevell made an affray on the servant of Robert Wrothe esquire with a crotch' (a forked stick). Fairly common, too, were cases of mutual attack. At Halstead 5 men were presented for assault and 2 for counter-assault. At Thaxted an entry beginning *'Effusio sanguinis'* was to the same effect; and the bailiff was ordered to distrain all the 10 men's 3s. 4d. fines. Only very occasionally did an affray lead to a different sentence. 'By the favour' of the Brook Walden court in 1562, an assailant was amerced only 20d. because he had already been punished in the stocks; the same initial phrase was used at Chipping Walden in 1583 when another man was 'pardoned for good and reasonable cause'.

After reading thousands of routine assault entries it was refreshing to come across an unusual one at Stock in 1574: 'Margery wife of John James brawled and scolded with Roger Veale the lord's bailiff for executing his office and made an assault upon him in the constable's presence with firebrands. Judgement by the steward: 'the constable to punish her upon the cucking-stool, to be dipped in water in the pond'.[6] A remarkable picture of slander and dissension emerges in the same year, when Agnes Sawen was accused at Quarter Sessions of bewitching Roger Veale's son.[7] Next year James and his wife were commanded to 'avoid out of Stock before Michaelmas with his household upon pain of whipping'; but evidently they sneaked back again, as Jeffrey Petycrewe was to be stocked in 1579 if he allowed James to remain in his house. In 1585 an indictment was preferred at the County Bench against a neighbouring rector for obscenely libelling 12 Stock men, including James and Petycrewe, as cuckolds.[8] In 1584, too, William Palmer was accused of a bloody battery upon Thomas Hilles, one of the watchmen, which deprived the assailant of 3s. 4d.[9]

The charge to the court leet jury generally included an injunction to present the names of 'any common barrators as scolders or brawlers to the annoyance and disturbance of the neighbours'. Barratry was a term beloved by lawyers. It covered a multitude of disorderly acts, mostly by undisciplined female tongues. But court rolls, unlike Quarter Session records,[10] rarely refer to barrators and prefer more down-to-earth words, such as *communis rixatrix* (brawler), *garrulatrix* (babbler), or *fabulatrix* (tell-tale), usually followed by 'common disturber of the peace' or 'scold'. The punishment awarded was usually a short term in one of the instruments of correction—stocks, pillory, cucking-stool, or tumbril. It is not uncommon, in a populous manor, to find a few of these women, mostly married, hauled up at almost every session. At Moulsham in 1559 a wife was presented as 'a contumelious, scandalous and opprobrious woman with her tongue, and a common scold'. The constable was ordered to put her in the cucking-stool 'as often as she offends'; and to ensure his own obedience he was to lose the large sum of 6s. 8d. 'for each time he fails'. An Epping wife, a scold, was pilloried in 1571, Edward Benton, the constable of Upland (the rural part of the parish), being commanded to carry out the order. In the same year 'Jane the wife of the vicar of Epping' (Edward Aulefer) 'was garrulous against her neighbours', so 'it was adjudged that she be punished by the tumbril according to the custom'. Another contentious (*seditiosa*) Epping wife 6 years later was warned of punishment in stocks or tumbril at the discretion of the constables 'and the inhabitants dwelling nearby, if she behave ill in future'. The Ingatestone court in 1565 not only sent a scold to the cucking-stool but also sentenced her to quit the parish. The man who compiled the analysis of the Aveley rolls about 1620 found that in 1596 'and in other courts common scolds were presented'; he added regretfully, in his usual castigating style, that had they not 'wanted (i.e. lacked) a cucking stool, they had received their reward'.

As we saw in the archives of the two Archdeacons' courts, such offenders were not confined to one sex.[11] Thomas Botesworth was presented at Stock in 1558 as 'given to much scolding, and by his scolding a disturber of his neighbours; therefore fined 4d. and warned to do no further injury under penalty of being placed in the tumbril, in English called the dungcart, and being carried in it through the whole vill on some feast day, and then being placed in the stocks and banished the vill'.[12] To be 'banished', or 'to avoid the manor', was one of the most severe condemnations of a manor court. How he obtained entry into another parish was his own concern, but to the social historian it is something of a puzzle. Male tongues as often as not had been loosened over the alepots, like those of the two Harlow men brought before the court in 1582 as common brawlers and drunkards.

To the lawyers, 'rescue' was a serious offence. It did not imply a courageous act on behalf of another human being, but the forcible taking of an animal or a person from lawful custody. In 1576 that troublesome vicar of Epping, Aulefer, and Phoebe his servant, forcibly rescued from Thomas Tawney, the bailiff, a cow and a calf which he had taken for distraint of two years' arrears of the lord's rent (fined 8d.). Newport rolls under 1570 tell how the shepherd of Margery Fox, widow, rescued from John Cowper, 'the heyward', 100 sheep doing damage in the common of the lady of the manor called the Pond, for which the widow was fined 3s. 4d.; and two years later Robert Martyn rescued his pigs from the heyward and had to pay 8d. The heyward, or hayward (from 'hay', or hedge), was an officer having charge of the fences, especially to prevent beasts from breaking through them from the commons or open fields.

'Pound breach', or forcible rescue of impounded animals, was in fact a common occurrence. A Rettendon tenant was taking some sheep to the lord's pound when their owner assaulted him and rescued them, for which he was fined 20d. (1562); James Stainford's servants who broke the pound and took their cattle away had to pay a similar sum at Blunts Hall in Witham (1570); a man who drove from the pound his own cattle, put there because of trespass in the lord's wood, had to find 6s. 8d. at Great Burstead (1582); and William Sympson of Stock, who drove out of the pound of the lord of the manor of Fristling Hall in Margaretting his 3 sheep which had trespassed on the lord's waste, was amerced 12d. (1583). Presentments of such unlawful recovery by 17 owners of their cattle occur in the Elizabethan rolls of Chipping Walden. Christopher Baker's wife violently rescued from the servant of William Smyth, gentleman, bailiff of the manor of Brook Walden, 'a distress of cows' impounded for damage in the lord's meadow; 'therefore for her grave contempt' she was fined 12d. From these and entries in other rolls, pound breach seems to have been a favourite act of stalwart wives.

Violent recovery of a prisoner—usually one being taken to gaol by constables or sheriff's officers—was more serious, though it sometimes afforded good entertainment to the bystanders, as those who witnessed the Amazonian rabble at Newport in 1575.[13] Such cases went to the County Bench. Almost as grave in the eyes of the law was the passive allowance of a prisoner to escape. Unfortunate constables who lost their charges were usually indicted at Quarter Sessions,[14] but at least two manor courts dealt with their own officers. In 1589 a constable of Aveley who 'suffered persons to escape' was fined. The other case, from Felsted in 1577, is peculiar. It appears that John son of Robert Sponer had stolen an ewe from William Pratt and taken it home. There it was traced, and the lad was 'imprisoned in Hare's house' (John Hare kept an inn or an alehouse). But, by the constables' negligence, he escaped. Worse still, one-quarter of the sheep was eaten during Lent by his father, 'being very sick'. The court fined each constable the extremely heavy sum of £5.

## Poaching and Unlawful Games

Manorial juries were specifically charged to present inhabitants caught poaching or playing illegal games. The more flagrant cases went to Quarter Sessions.[15] In 1561 a man was before the Wanstead court for keeping pursenets (used over rabbit-holes), ferrets and greyhounds. Typical of numerous orders is one issued by the court of Abells in Halstead in 1578: 'No person in future keep any greyhounds or pursenets except such as be allowed by statute', under penalty of 3s. 4d. Ten years earlier East Mersea men were prohibited from using 'any gins or harepipes for taking coneys, nor any ferrets, except on their own lands'. The statutory property qualification is set out by the Great Burstead court in 1581: 'No inhabitants keep a greyhound unless taxed for lands at 40s. a year or £5 for goods by the subsidy, upon pain of forfeiting 20s'.[16] At Kelvedon Hatch in 1567 'John Harrison and his son keep beagles and hunt coneys on the lord's waste'; they were fined 4d. each, and henceforth no inhabitant might keep beagles. Having disobeyed, the Harrisons, who were general troublemakers, had to pay a further 2s. Tracing hares led to a forfeit of 6s. 8d. at Crondon near Stock in 1586; and killing a hare in Lent cost two Ingatestone men 12d. in 1601.

The same Halstead rolls reveal an inveterate poacher named Alexander Vyne. First charged in 1581 with killing hares 'with nets and dogs' and as a 'common hunter and fisherman within the demesne' he was fined 5s., to be doubled for the next offence. This led to an omnibus decree forbidding all from shooting birds or animals, taking fish in the river, or netting coneys or any other fowls or animals, under pain of 10s. Five years later Vyne forfeited 3s. 4d. for shooting. Summoned again in 1592 for the same, he was fined the crippling sum of £10, as authorized by an Act of 1541 but rarely exacted. At Newport in 1571 George Jeppes *alias* Jeepp and Thomas Raffe shot with 'handguns at geese called mallards', and Richard Bottrell netted 'house doves' in his neighbour's dovecote (all fined 12d.). Presented at Felsted in 1578 'for shooting with a gun at doves sitting on roofs', Thomas Arden, servant of Mr Piggott, was warned that a second offence would cost him £5.

Fishing rights, which were the sole privilege of many lords, were jealously guarded. Found everywhere are entries such as 'John Manger fished in the river within the manor' of Kelvedon Hatch in 1565 (fined 2d.). 'All servants and other inhabitants' at Ingatestone were prohibited from throwing nets or bait in the ponds in 1559; and in 1578 one was presented for trespassing thus with hoop-nets. At Wanstead in 1588 (blank) Lawrence, gentleman, fished in the lord's water with a 'scoop'. The

Epping court in 1599 banned fishing in 'the Pond' without licence. Seven years later many were reported at Chelmsford for 'keeping a casting net'. In 1578 13 men were fined 12d. for fishing in the river of the lord of Abells manor 'with nets and in many other ways against the ordinance hitherto made; and they have done much other damage in the meadows and have broken the river banks with their feet in many places'; another prosecution would cost them fourfold. Rights of fishing in Leigh Creek on the Thames estuary, which figure in a jury presentment at North Benfleet in 1560, provide an example of non-seigneurial ownership: 'William Hare of Leigh fished in a creek without the lord's leave, and he took and tore to shreds a net of Henry Gray and Humphrey Smart thrown and put in the creek between Oyster Fleet and Knights Wick, the fishing belonging to the tenants of the manor'.

Lords of manors who had been granted 'free warren', or the exclusive right of keeping and hunting 'beasts or fowls of warren' (game), were especially vigilant over their privilege. The best catalogue of offences against free warren is found in the custom-roll of the royal manor and lordship of Writtle, granted as a mark of favour by Mary to Sir William Petre in 1554. Compiled about 1600 from the ancient rolls, it notes the fines levied on poachers chiefly in the 15th century: hawking and fishing, taking partridges and pheasants, killing hares and coneys, killing of deer, all within the lord's warren; also fines for keeping greyhounds and even for setting a harepipe in a tenant's own garden and taking a coney.

Every parish, however, was obliged to provide a net for catching 'noyful fowles and vermin'. By the Act of 24 Henry VIII, c. 10 (1533), 2d. was to be paid for every dozen old crows, rooks or choughs by the owner or occupier of the manor. It was renewed in 1566 by 8 Eliz., c. 15 (1566), which authorized a parish rate for their destruction. Echoes occur in the Abells rolls in 1592: 'The townsmen have not a crownet for the taking of fowls or noisome animals called vermin; therefore the town is fined 10s.'

Apart from alehouse licensees, individuals were seldom presented for unlawful games.[17] A Rettendon man was fined 3s. 4d. in 1560 for playing at bowls. In 1571-2 12d. was levied at Newport on each of 5 gamesters—3 for bowls, 1 for 'tables' (backgammon) and 1 for 'scales' (nine-pins, called 'cales' in the Unlawful Games Act of 1541), a mild sport rarely mentioned. Ten years later the Epping court threatened 7 men who had allowed unlawful games in their houses with a 12d. fine; next year 2 of them, (blank) Graye the cutler and John Baker, were duly amerced for card-play. Except for occasional references, such as that to 6 men who 'came humbly to court and were pardoned' with only a 12d. fine, Chelmsford showed no special concern until 1598, when a bye-law was directed against 'servants, handicraftsmen, victuallers and such as shall be found at unlawful games at unlawful times' (repeated two years later).

Sir William Petre was a rare upholder of the laws which forbade the lower orders of society to indulge in such pastimes. Regular amercements of inhabitants for gaming are found in the Ingatestone rolls. Card-playing and 'slide groat' (the later shove-ha'penny) figure a few times. In 1564 and 1565 no less than 14 men were fined in each year 4d. or 8d. for bowling. In 1568 several men had to pay 20d. for the double offence of playing dice and bowls. After the old councillor's death in 1572, gaming was presented only once before 1600.[18] The bowling-alley at Ingatestone Hall was in the adjacent orchard.[19] Another private alley lay next to Mark Hall, Latton.[20] 'The bowling place' just to the south of the town and close to the sea, marked on a map of Harwich of about 1610, would seem, despite the general veto, to have been a public one : perhaps the Essex counterpart of the Plymouth Hoe bowling-place, where tradition credits Drake with finishing his game before tackling the Armada. At Stock, another of Sir William's manors, gaming was treated in 1558 (a month before Mary's death) as a spiritual rather than a secular offence : 'A common victualler permitted 12 persons to play at cards after midday about the time of vespers on a feast day, on his own confession. Therefore he is in mercy 3s. 4d. and warned not to do evil any more under penalty of being placed in the stocks for 6 hours on some feast day, openly in the market place, and exiled'.[21] No more is heard until 1580, in the time of Sir John Petre, when 'any person dwelling in the parishes of Stock and Buttsbury' who indulged in football on a Sunday would bear a 3s. 4d. fine.[22]

In 1571, as shown later, the Chelmsford court showed unusual activity against butchers for selling meat unfit for human consumption in the market. Among those prosecuted were also Edward Lowe and Peter Snowe, butchers of Witham, whose offence at first sight might seem to fall into the same category. They were charged with having killed '4 bulls not baited by dogs, and sold the flesh in the market, for which they have incurred the statutory penalty, viz. for each bull 3s. 4d.' Next year Henry Andrewes and Thomas Segges, Chelmsford butchers, were fined 10s. and 3s. 4d. respectively for slaughtering 3 and 1 unbaited bulls. A single presentment was also made in 1601. These transgressions, however, were not against public health but against public sport. Although occasionally found elsewhere, no other references to unbaited bull's flesh have been discovered in the Essex rolls. They are a vivid reminder of the contemporary attitude towards bull- and bear-baiting. A good supply of bulls must be available for the people to watch their being attacked by fierce mastiffs : no bull must be taken to a slaughter-house before it had afforded people's entertainment. A century earlier a Colchester Corporation ordinance had directed butchers 'to kill no bull unbaited'; and a century later Ipswich

Corporation was paying men for ropes and collars for the bulls and for 'discovery of unbaited bulls'.[23] But, in contrast to the Puritans' fulminations against this brutal sport, Harrison wrote from his Essex rectory in full-blooded praise of English mastiffs, which were made even more courageous 'by teaching them to bait the bear and the bull'.[24] Innkeepers were prohibited from permitting games in their houses but not from allowing bulls to be baited in their yards.

## Archery Practice

A series of medieval statutes had attempted to ensure strict attention to archery practice. Not proving effective, that of 3 Henry VIII, c. 3 (1512), was followed by the sterner Act of 33 Henry VIII, c. 6 (1542), aimed at upholding practice and prohibiting unlawful games. Its provisions were comprehensive. Every father had to furnish his sons and servants between 7 and 16 with a long-bow and 2 arrows and to teach them; and at 17 it was every man's duty to provide himself with a bow and 4 arrows until 60. The penalty for negligence was 6s. 8d. It was obligatory on every parish to maintain archery butts for shooting every Sunday and holy-day afternoons 'and other times convenient'. The butts were mounds of earth, set at a fixed distance from each other, against which the targets were planted.[25] A detailed account of the cost of erecting butts occurs in the parish accounts of Eltham, Kent.[26]

Although the superiority of fire-arms was not fully acknowledged until after Elizabeth's time, the Henrician statutes failed to restore the popularity of the long-bow. Englishmen were more inclined to use their crossbows to shoot at deer than to practise long-bows at the butts. Contemporary writers deplored the way in which the obligations were disobeyed, and in 1566 and 1571 the Acts of 8 Eliz., c. 10, and 13 Eliz., c. 14, re-iterated the earlier provisions.

Reports of negligence in archery practice were made at manor courts but are fairly rare in comparison with those for decayed butts. The rolls for five manors only have yielded references. At Rettendon in 1560 the homage admitted that 'the inhabitants have failed to exercise themselves with bows and in having bows and arrows', and again in 1598 they 'submitted themselves to the lord's mercy' for the same reason. Those of Chelmsford in 1596 likewise confessed; 'therefore they beg the lord to accept 20d. in satisfaction of the penalty; and he of his special grace and favour accepts it'. At Purleigh in 1591 the inhabitants had 'made default in not shooting with longbows for 10 months, for which default they have forfeited the penalty under the statute; therefore the bailiff was ordered to levy 12d. from each and in default to levy on each refusing to pay 6s. 8d.' The court of Middlemead in Little Baddow in 1595 fined some inhabitants 2s. 6d. for neglect. Somewhat exceptionally, those of **Ruckholts** in Leyton in the same year were presented for being 'well provided with artillery' but failing to carry out their practice. It is noticeable that all except one of the presentments occur in the last years of the century; this and the similar reports about the butts provide clear evidence of the belated concern about defence.

No previous attempt seems to have been made to ascertain whether the contemporary allegations of neglect of the archery butts are exaggerated or not, but the Essex rolls fully bear out the literary comments. Failure to keep up the butts was so general as to be damning. Of the manors for which rolls have been searched, virtually all record lack of maintenance. The common entry is that the 'metes or butts are in ruin' (or 'in great decay') and that 'the inhabitants ought to repair them' before a certain date or incur a penalty. This is found to range widely between 8d. and 20s. At Rettendon, for instance, it was 12d. in 1593, but further failure led to its being raised in 1596 to 3s. 4d. and in 1602 to 10s. At Berden and Debden, among other manors, the order was repeated many times, apparently with little success. In some manors the constables were responsible for repairs; in others, the bailiff. In 1560 the Stock court ordered that the butts should be made by the inhabitants of Stock and Buttsbury, which had always been closely-linked parishes.[27] Very small manors were not exempt from the obligation: the usual orders were made, for example, in 1583 at Berners Roothing where the butts were still 'not sufficiently repaired' in 1592, and again in 1603. The court of West Horndon, with few inhabitants apart from Sir John Petre's household, set a 6s. 8d. penalty in 1580: a deputy lieutenant could not overlook dilapidated butts.

Occasionally the rolls tell us where they were: 'To make up a pair of butts in Blackmore town's end against Michaelmas under pain of 6s. 8d.' (Fingrith Hall, 1563); or 'at Mulberry Green' (Harlow, 1591). Of more interest is the unique precept seen in the Great Burstead rolls under 1577 concerning the butts on the big green lying between the village and the town of Billericay: 'Those who dwell around South Green and others who used to put their cattle on it henceforth put no cattle on it on Sundays or feast days in the afternoon between Easter and Michaelmas, because it is a hindrance and nuisance to the bowmen who of old shoot on the green'. In 1583 the East Mersea court commanded the constables to remove the 'old butts' and re-site them near the church at the cost of the parish.

The question arises, How many manors are found to have ordered repair shortly before the threatened Spanish invasion? The strange answer is, None; though presentments and orders about butts occur in almost every other year of the reign. A marked increase, however, as pointed out, occurs after the defeat of the Armada and during the next decade when England was again imperilled.

The justices had a concurrent jurisdiction over the state of butts, and many parishes were reported by the hundredal juries to Quarter Sessions, at which similar penalties were imposed. The high constables' hundredal juries were in fact enjoined in their articles of enquiry to answer about their condition.[29]

## Highway Duty

The Act of 2 & 3 Ph. & Mary, c. 8 (1555) introduced compulsory labour. Every farmer had to send a cart with two of his men and every cottager to give his own work for 4 days each year, increased to 6 days by the Act of 1562. Neglect or refusal was to be presented by the parish surveyors of highways to the nearest J.P. for certification to Quarter Sessions. Although Parliament imposed this duty on the parish, not the manor, it chose the constables as well as the churchwardens to put the statute into operation, the former being manorial officers. Social historians' knowledge of the effect of this legislation before about 1600 is mainly confined to the few counties for which late Tudor Sessions rolls have been preserved, those for Essex being the most complete.

Apart from lists of fines on nearly 100 defaulters in the adjacent parishes of Coggeshall and Feering in 1566 and 1567, relatively few offenders for other places were presented.[30] But Harrison's scathing remarks about the indifferent manner in which road maintenance was carried out are undoubtedly based on his own experience. 'Scarcely two good days' work are well performed', he wrote. So the weak or mainly negative evidence in the County Bench records has to be set against his dogmatic strictures. A more favourable picture, however, can be drawn from a much-treasured source. Detailed surveyors' accounts are extant for one Essex parish—Great Easton, 1581—possibly a unique Elizabethan survival.[31] This record of a single year shows that 12 farmers sent their carts, 12 cottagers performed their labour, and, rather surprisingly, 27 'compounded for their work by money', paying apparently the equivalent of the fines authorized by the Act of 1555. There is not the slightest hint of refusal or slackness.

In the following centuries an increasing proportion of those liable for 'statute duty' compounded by money payments, but the Act of 1562, with later modifications, remained largely the basis for the upkeep of all English roads until the later creation of turnpike trusts for the more important highways. The Essex manor records add a few trifles to our scanty knowledge of the operation of the statutes.

The Marian Act fixed penalties for disobedience: 10s. for not sending a cart and 12d. a day for failing to work. It also gave strangely elaborate directions for distraint of such fines by the bailiff or chief constable of the hundred, who on receipt of the money was then to hand it back to the churchwardens, who in turn were to use it for repairs of their roads. That such a troublesome method was actually followed is borne out from a very long entry in a Stock roll of 1567. The surveyors had reported to the constables, who on oath had informed the jurors, and they presented defaults for 4 and 3 days respectively. Instructions were accordingly given to the bailiff and chief constable to levy the 7s., being the total fines due, on the two men, and to account for the money to the wardens.[32] Only three other manors provide any facts about neglect. In 1580 Robert Pare of Kelvedon Hatch, who had 'not worked in the highway with his cart this year', forfeited £3 (10s. for each day); the same sum was levied in 1593 on John Sedcole of Epping for not sending his 'cart and team'. Chelmsford fined one man 6s. for 6 days' absence from work in 1591. The most intriguing items, however, do not concern failure but refer to a special rate. In 1574 the Chelmsford and Moulsham courts passed identical orders: 'No inhabitant henceforth refuse to pay the tax imposed by the townsmen for the repair of the street (*de emendatione strati*) under pain to forfeit 12d. to the lord'. It looks as though Thomas Mildmay had persuaded his tenants to supplement statute labour, but we must not read too much into what is a unique pair of entries. Not until many more manorial records of the period have been examined would it be safe to generalize about the efficacy of the two Highways Acts.[33]

## The Commons

One of the most important functions of courts baron was their control of commons, heaths and village greens. The soil of commons, known to lawyers as 'manorial waste', was vested in the lord, but by ancient usage the tenants generally had certain rights of pasturage. They also had similar rights over the open arable fields and meadows after corn and hay harvests. All such facilities were the subject of countless offences in manor rolls and of much litigation in the superior courts. Common land on the boundaries of adjacent manors was also a fruitful source of disputes, such as the three riot cases tried at the Essex Quarter Sessions.[34] As is well known, many commons and heaths and virtually all the remaining open fields and meadows were enclosed during the parliamentary enclosure period, running, in Essex, from about 1800 to 1860. There were many large expanses of manorial waste. In the north-east lay the big heaths around Colchester and the vast Tiptree Heath containing about 5,000 acres and extending into six or seven manors. In the south-west were the immense areas of woodland, chiefly in Waltham Forest. Most of the villages in the north-west were surrounded by open fields, usually called 'common fields'. It must be emphasised, however, that rights of common, if any, belonged, not to the inhabitants in general, but only to the manorial tenants. These were, principally, the right to pasture their animals, to fell timber for repairing their buildings, to take wood and other fuel, and to dig clay and other materials. The extent of these privileges depended wholly on the customs of the individual manor. In one of his many sallies against the rich, the rector of Radwinter commented : 'Some owners, still desirous to enlarge those grounds as either for the breed and feeding of cattle, do not let (i.e. restrain or delay) daily to take in more, not sparing the very commons whereupon many townsmen now and then do live'.[35]

A composite picture of tenants' common rights must therefore be drawn from the custumals and bye-laws described later, as well as the orders issued from time to time by most courts, and of course the presentments. The information in the rolls about these rights is often of a somewhat negative character, e.g. 'No one dwelling outside the leet shall keep their cattle depasturing in the precincts, under pain of 12d.' (Foxearth, 1568), or 'No inhabitants of the (adjacent) parish of Doddinghurst shall place any lambs on the lord's common called Kelvedon Common, upon pain of forfeiting 20s. (Kelvedon, 1580). The most frequent trespass was 'overcharging' the commons with too many animals. It is not easy in some manors to ascertain what these animals were, or their number : they were known to the courts, but seldom vouchsafed in specific terms. A few presentments, however, all made in the Queen's first decade, will illustrate their activities. William Wortham 'overburdened the lord's common called Crays Common with his steers', also 'William Seymer of Billericay with his beasts, to the grave detriment of the tenants, where he had no common of right' (Ramsden Crays, 1559); two tenants 'unlawfully drove their beasts to pasture on such part of Galwode Common as belong to this manor, to the grave overcharging of the tenants and against the special bye-law of this manor', and they each forfeited 6s. 8d. (Moulsham, 1560); a tenant 'overcharged Fairing Common with 5 cows, 2 foals, 1 horse and sheep', fined 5s. (Felsted, 1568); and 'George Daye has put 4 horses, 4 cows and his sheep on the Common against the order', fined 3s. 4d. (Newport, 1569). Of these commons, Galleywood Common survived the enclosure period. Trespass in the open arable fields is exemplified by the presentment of John Ferrer of Littlebury, who 'unjustly commoned and depastured his sheep in the common ways and fields of this manor where he ought not to have done, to the injury of the tenants' (1564) : a normal sort of entry, but not what follows— 'He also beat the children and servants' of three tenants 'in resisting it' !

Rights of pasturage on the commons restricted to a certain number of animals were called 'stints', and in manors with a relatively small area of commons or a high population they were constantly protected against persons without rights. At Clavering, for instance, 'No bachelor shall keep more than one horse on the Common' (1600). In 1571 the Epping court defined pasture rights in terms apparently not found elsewhere in Essex :

> No bachelor or other dwelling within the town, not being a householder, shall in future put his cattle to depasture within the Forest within this demesne unless they are contributors to the inhabitants within the vill, *anglice* that they shall bear scot and lot according to the accustomed sum between themselves, under penalty for each offence 10s.

Even in places like Rettendon, with an extensive common, we find many offenders who had 'overcharged the Common with too many beasts' and others from the neighbouring manor of Runwell who had 'many times depastured there, where they have no common of pasture'. Great Bentley, which had several heaths and greens, is one of the very few Essex manors for which the stints are clearly recorded—in an undated order:

> *Custom as to the Commonage.* For every copyholder of 20 acres of land, 2 horses or 4 cows or 20 sheep, or 10 sheep in lieu of 1 horse or 5 sheep in lieu of a cow, and so in proportion for a greater quantity of land; and for every small copyholder, 1 horse or 2 cows or 10 sheep; and all cattle fed on the Commons shall leave a brand with their owner's name and also a distinguishing mark for the manor.

Fuller details about common rights in this manor will be given in the last chapter.

In Lord Rich's manor of Wanstead inhabitants of the neighbouring manors were fined between 2s. and 10s. in 1563 for 'commoning on the lord's common': Thomas Hall of Upton (in West Ham) with 80 sheep and 4 oxen, John Pemmerton of Little Ilford with 16 sheep, Francis Franke of Little Ilford with 8 cows and 2 colts, William Atkynson of Upton with 2 mares, Ralph Harrison of West Ham with 4 cows, Thomas Mosse of East Ham with 9 cows and 3 horses, and Matthew Wood of West Ham with 6 oxen. Occasionally, instead of reporting offenders, the tenants asserted their claims, and Rich's steward in 1574 had to enrol their presentment that 'All the tenants and inhabitants have or ought to have, from time whereof the memory of man is not to the contrary, common pasture on the green called Wanstead Heath for all their beasts, goats only excepted'. Here, it is to be noticed, the rights were not restricted solely to the tenants. Wanstead, of course, lay within the Forest of Waltham, but the subject of common rights in the Forest is too complicated to deal with in our own limited compass.[36] Cows are still pastured in number on Wanstead Flats, and occasionally get into nearby gardens!

As much as 10 miles upstream the tidal Mar Dyke, which runs into the Thames at Purleigh between the estuarian Wennington and West Thurrock Marshes, lies Bulphan Fen—the repetitive name of the parish is taken from the 'fanne' ('-phan'), a horseshoe-shaped fen or marsh, the head of which adjoins the Mar Dyke. This great fen, an important local asset, like the equally large Orsett Fen to the south, had from medieval times been strictly controlled by the manor court through its elected fan- or fen-reeves, whose chief duty was to supervise the fen-drivers in their ceaseless task of keeping out unauthorized cattle. In order to conserve this rich marsh, the tenants were under various communal obligations and prohibitions. They had to repair the several gates and bridges at the entrances to the Fen; to fine any who left the gates open; to suppress any attempting to make new ways across it or to fix annual rents for such rights-of-way; to stop hogs rooting; above all, to watch that none overcharged the Fen and to fine offenders; to fine tenants who 'took on' cattle from neighbouring parishes by way of agistment; to see that no tenant put in the Fen 'more than 2 geese to one gander' or any 'tups (rams) out of season'; to control the tenants' own marks for their beasts; to impose fines for cutting down willows; to ensure that all tenants having common rights scoured 'the great ditch called the West Fanne Merdich'; and to fine any non-tenant who fished in the Dyke. All this is derived from the proceedings of the Bulphan court in our period, extracted in a precedent book, compiled about 1700, which also cites much earlier orders and fines. While giving a superficial impression that the Fen was regulated by an oligarchy of substantial tenants, a more democratic note is struck in a bye-law of 1583 : 'No tenant who lets to farm (i.e. leases) shall reserve to himself the common of pasture belonging to his tenement, but he who holds the land shall have the common of pasture and herbage also'. The court was quite firm, too, in 1592, in disclaiming the parson's right, but, despite that, rector Edmund Williamson was warned four years later that he would be fined 10s. per head if he 'fed the Fen with any cattle'.

All the marshes around the Essex coast and along the Thames estuary were protected by sea-walls, the vital maintenance of which was directed by commissioners of sewers, the actual responsibility being that of the owners or occupiers of all lands 'which lay subject to peril' from sea-floods.[37] On that account, sea-walls do not figure prominently in the rolls of coastal manors with marshland. Those of the royal manor of Havering, however, afford an interesting example of the operation of the two marsh-reeves chosen annually by the tenants to supervise Hornchurch Marsh. It was presented in 1574 that John Bushe of Hornchurch, who held 5 acres, was by custom liable for 25 rods of the sea-wall, but had recently allowed his section to fall into grave disrepair. This had been brought to the notice of Sir Anthony Cooke, high steward of the liberty, who ordered Thomas Heard and John Quick, the marsh reeves, to investigate and to obtain materials for mending the wall. Attending the court, they reported having purchased timber and chalk at a cost of £7, which Bushe was enjoined to repay and to use the materials in completing repairs within four months on penalty of 12d. per rod.[38]

In the days before accurate estate maps were made, the boundaries of commons, especially along parish boundaries as at Rettendon, were sometimes in dispute.[39] The inhabitants of Theydon Bois, for example, who had 'encroached upon the Queen's waste within the Forest (of Waltham), by estimation 30 acres', were presented at Epping court in 1571. There was controversy in the manor of Middlemead *alias* Bassetts in Little Baddow in 1575, when 'the tenants were ordered diligently to enquire concerning the metes and bounds of the common of this manor called Hockam Hills, containing 4 acres'. The jurors accordingly reported after consulting 'the old tenants and residents', gave a detailed account of the boundaries of Wyckey Green, and stated that 'the commons contain in all by estimation 100 acres, and are known by the names of Wyckey Green, Leigh Hill, Crab Hill, Hockam Hills and Loves Green'. Trouble had also occurred about the big Galleywood Common at the extreme south end of the manor of Moulsham. In 1561 the rolls give 'the special verdict on the right, use and possession of part of Galwood Common after enquiry'. Too long to quote, it is of much interest for local topography and refers to intercommoning rights of the tenants of Moulsham and Great Baddow. A presentment was made in the same year at the court of Bacons in Dengie, that 'the landholder of a tenement called Bowngas unjustly ploughed up a dole which divides the parishes of Dengie and Tillingham and cut down a bramblebush (*rubum*) that likewise divides them in the same place where it stood of old'; he was commanded to replace the marks. Another open space known as Harlow (Bush) Common and Latton Common is referred to at Harlow Bury in 1578: 'Thomas Barrett dug and carried away a bank dividing' the parishes. At the next court he forfeited 10s. for not 'rebuilding' it; and two other men who dug the same boundary bank were fined 3s. 4d.

Boundary points between strips in the open fields and meadows, where ownership was intermixed, were in some places marked by posts for the avoidance of disputes. In 1581 Harlow court decided: 'All those having lands in Harlow Marsh before 10 October shall meet there to place stakes between their lands so that they know their own lands certainly'; and in 1599 John Shelley, who had ploughed up a dole in Bore Field, was told to replace it on pain of 10s. Two more cases concerning common-fields and common-meads will suffice: at Rettendon (1581), John Joyce dug up a 'mark bank' in Herd Marsh *alias* Rettendon 'Fanne' (Fen); and at Chingford (manor of St. Paul, 1595), Edward Harman ploughed up the boundary marks in Great Man Field between Rames Acre and lands belonging to a house called Pimpes (later Pimp Hall Farm).

Most manor courts tried to control the livestock and other animals on the commons and roads, and owners were liable to be presented on various grounds. Numerous regulations were made, designed to prevent damage caused by the beasts. Typical of such orders are those found at Fingrith in Blackmore (1564): 'The tenants are warned not to allow cattle on the highway without a follower'; at Brook Walden (1564): 'No inhabitant to pasture in the Queen's highway any of his great cattle beyond the number of two heads, and always to have a sufficient keeper at tending of beasts for indemnifying his neighbours from destruction of their corn, meadows or pastures, on pain of 12d.'; and at Rettendon (1567): 'Nobody thenceforth shall put any mares on the commons after Michaelmas or forfeit 3s. 4d.' A stiffer bye-law was issued at Purleigh (1577): 'Agreed by the whole homage and tenants that if any person allow beasts to wander in any common street without a keeper he shall forfeit 20d.; and any tenant or others having lands next to the streets may drive beasts into the common pound and impound them until the lord be satisfied with the penalty'.

The roll of Bendish Hall in Radwinter for 1564 is headed: 'Lord Cobham, Warden of the Cinque Ports—Thomas Mountford the lessee'; Cobham had presented Harrison to the rectory five years earlier. Because 'the inhabitants have frequently pastured their beasts in the Queen's highways and have broken their neighbours' hedges', the court banned them from the roadside verges; culprits would forfeit 4d. for each beast, one half to the impounder, the other to the lord. Geese, too, were an occasional source of trouble, as at Debden on the roads (1570) and at Tollesbury where they were to be kept off Salcott Green (1566).

Among the countless individual offenders were two rectors of Stock. Oliver Clayton was presented (1557) because, 'contrary to the custom, he places hogs, geese and other animals of his to feed and wander on the Common of the lord' (Sir William Petre). Fined 3s. 4d. for his cattle and geese (1560), he was later told not to 'keep his chickens on the lord's common' under pain of 40s. (1567); but William Pynder, his successor, broke the order and was actually fined that sum (1589).[40] A penalty of 3s. 4d. was incurred by 8 men (2 of South Hanningfield) for putting mares on Rettendon Common (1587). A street scene is recorded at Earls Colne (1584), when John Knight, 'who daily rideth his horses in the highway near his neighbours' doors and layeth his dung there', was ordered to remove it and 'to ride no more to their annoyance'. At Epping (1579) a tenant was amerced 4d. for his hogs 'taken in the common called le-dryfte' (possibly Epping Long Common, the narrow greenway on the Nazeing boundary); and the court of Chingford Comitis (1559) warned John Rampton, esquire, not to allow his hogs to destroy grass in 'Wymede and le Ney' on pain of 6s. 8d.

Hogs were undoubtedly the worst offenders. To restrain them they had to be ringed, or, as expressed by Tusser:

For rooting of pasture ring hog ye had neede.

To prevent their breaking through hedges or fences some were also yoked. But swine's unruliness and men's carelessness necessitated bye-laws in at least half the Essex manors. They were made, for example, at Epping (1566): 'Any resident who allows his hogs or porklets to dig *anglice* to wrotte in the Queen's waste shall forfeit 2d.'; at Walden (1561): 'No person shall put forth any hogs above the age of half a year unringed or unyoked under pain of 4d. for every hog'; and at Chelmsford (1564): 'No person shall suffer any of their swine, old or young, to wander at large openly in the streets or highways, except only to drive them to their grounds, under pain for every hog found 2d. and every pig 1d.' (and in 1569 the bailiff was 'ordered diligently to warn all'). A long order was issued in 1560 for the forest manor of Chingford Comitis. 'Because hogs and pigs for lack of yoking and ringing have done much hurt', swine so taken between 1 March and Bartholomewtide (28 August), not on the owner's own land, would cost the owner 4d. a hog and 2d. a pig; 'and this order to continue yearly until some better order be taken'. The Kelvedon Hatch court in 1568 outlawed the pigs and piglets of inhabitants living around the Common between Lady Day and St. Bartholomew's Day; but dwellers on Church Green in South Ockendon were restricted in 1561 to ringing their hogs only from Michaelmas to Easter. Ingatestone not only made a similar order in 1560 but also, doubtless at Sir William Petre's instigation, decreed that none were to be kept in the lord's park or the churchyard (the latter was declared out-of-bounds again in 1570). At Epping in 1586 townsmen who let them wander in the market-house on market days between 8 and 3 o'clock would pay a 6d. fine.

Occasionally, as at Ingatestone in 1561, a tenant was charged with allowing his dogs to worry cattle on the common. A man claimed damages at the Felsted-with-Grandcourts court in 1563 because '5 mastiff curs' had attacked his sow. Bitches on heat were also the subject of complaint. The Epping bye-laws were reported in 1569 to have been broken by 4 men who had let their 'salt bitches' run at large; and an Eastwood Bury survey dated 1589 re-affirmed a similar 'custom, as appeareth in anno 9 Henry VIII' (1518), concerning bitches. At Rettendon the owner of '2 noisome dogs' was told to get rid of them within 12 days or pay 10s.

Long before the numerous Diseases of Animals Acts of later centuries, some courts did their best to deal with infection. Clayton, the recalcitrant rector of Stock, was fined in 1560 for putting a diseased boar on the lord's common and ordered to keep it on his own glebe.[41] At Ingatestone in 1596 a general order forbade putting horses on the roads if they were suffering from 'mangery or versey'. The *O.E.D.*, which found no example of this spelling, defines 'farcy' as a disease, especially of horses, closely allied to glanders. The Act of 32 Henry VIII, c. 13 (1540), had in fact tried to provide against this danger.

The manorial pound, or pinfold, as already seen, was the place in which stray or distrained livestock was put—by the pinder, where appointed, or by the bailiff, constable or person who found the animals. Like the stocks and other places of temporary confinement for human beings, the appearance of pounds in court rolls is occasionally due to their being in a deficient state. Liability for their maintenance depended on the local custom. At Rettendon in 1560 it was presented that 'the pound of the lord and tenants is not lawful (*legale*), through the bailiff's default.' The court decided otherwise, giving the tenants a date by which to repair it under pain of 3s. 4d. Two years later those of Wanstead reported that 'the lord's pinfold is ruinous'. The jurors at the Brook Walden court in 1565 reported that the pound was in great decay and humbly begged the lord (the Duke of Norfolk), 'if his Grace pleases', to repair it within a short time because of their great necessity. Likewise at Felsted, where they begged that it be repaired before the next court. Six years after the Queen's death, the pound in the royal manor of Barking was presented to be 'His Majesty's charge.'

Even before our period the increasing scarcity of timber, and therefore its value, was serious. Unlawful felling or lopping of timber trees on the lord's common is found as frequently as pasturage offences. The court baron dealt with it as committing waste, rather than theft (which was triable at Quarter Sessions), though the lawyers were disinclined to differentiate between larceny and such forms of waste. The matter is further confused by the fact that waste may mean, according to the context, either this transgression or the lord's waste—a generic term for a manorial common, heath, green or wood, the soil of which was vested in the lord. What follows therefore relates mainly to waste committed on the waste!

An injunction to the bailiff of Fingrith Hall in Blackmore in 1559 exemplifies a ubiquitous kind of order : 14 men and women were warned that 'none hereafter cut down any wood or timber growing upon any of my lord's woods', though most courts refer to 'commons'. In communities which were largely self-supporting, the commons, heaths and woods were a valuable source of supply, and the bailiff and other officers (and probably also the lord's gamekeeper, if he had one) kept a sharp lookout for depredation by tenants and outsiders. It is sometimes difficult to distinguish between timber-stealing and hedge-breaking (see below), which through dishonesty or poverty brought so many of our Elizabethan forefathers into trouble. In some manors the tenants were permitted to take timber and other 'commodities' from the commons provided that the lord gave them a licence, for which a fee was paid. In others, a licence was demanded for felling trees on a tenant's own land. While this generally implies his intention to sell the timber, the right to use it even for repairing his dwelling was not always conceded.

The great Norsey Wood, still surviving to the north-east of the town of Billericay, appears in the Great Burstead rolls in 1573 : 'No person dwelling within the town or elsewhere shall cut any timber or trees in the lord's wood called Norsey or elsewhere within the demesne or on their own lands without licence, under pain of 10s. or being imprisoned for 24 hours, as may seem the better to the officers' : a discretionary power given presumably to the constables. An unusual case comes from Middlemead in Little Baddow in 1572 : 'Three have trespassed on the lord's common and cut down and lopped trees without his licence, riotously in unlawful assemblies (*conventiculos*) with divers other unknown persons; and because they are poor and have nothing to answer therefor, the constables are ordered to punish them in the stocks for 2 hours on Sunday next'. It has to be remembered, however, that in law a group of three or more persons involved in assault or trespass was deemed a riot, and 'divers unknown' is not always to be taken literally.[42] At Epping in 1571 a 5s. penalty was imposed on 'any who carry away wood *anglice* spray from the Forest without the licence of the woodward' (spray is defined as 'twigs for fuel'). This bye-law resulted from a charge against two tenants who were fined 3s. 4d. because they had 'made faggots (*fasciculas*), contrary to ancient custom, of wood called spray within the Forest of Waltham within the Liberty of Epping, to the damage of the poor and ill example'.

The rolls of Kelvedon Hatch yield some interesting information. A byelaw of 1561 insisted that 'nobody shall cut furzes on the Common but only tenants'. But the big heath, with its abundant supply of 'furze' (gorse, or whin), was a temptation to 'foreigners', despite the prickly nature of such inferior fuel. Dried furze was employed in making malt;[43] and it was apparently also used to patch up 'hovels' (open sheds or cattle shelters), for Tusser wrote :

With whinnes or with furzes thy hovell renew.[44]

Men caught carrying them away were fined between 6d. and 3s. 4d., probably according to the quantity; 'one cartload of furzes and bushes' led to a 6s. 8d. mulct. To cope with this thorny stuff, one offender used a 'sled'; and the fact that 'John Wright tailor, not being a tenant, takes fuel excessively from the Common', fined 3s. 4d., leaves no doubt about its other use. Still, however, gorse-collectors came, so, in 1581 : 'We ordain that if any do fell any furze for their own use or otherwise, not being a tenant, they shall forfeit for each load 5s., for every jag 3s. 4d., for every sled 12d.' (a jag was a small cartload). By 1603 the fine, paid by John Howe of Navestock for 'cutting down and carrying away lez furzons on the lands called the Lord's Common', reached as much as 8s. While the lord thus gained a little money from non-tenants, he drew a larger income from licences to tenants for felling or lopping trees on their own copyholds. The first is found in 1568, when John Grene paid £6 13s. 4d. 'to cut down all trees and bushes growing on his customary land containing 4 acres called Paynes Hill (except and reserved to the lord all oaks and timber trees)'. This sum was far exceeded in 1574, when for £25 he gave leave 'of his special grace and on the petition of Richard Stonley gentleman, a customary tenant, to fell in his coppice 100 of the best timber trees, except husbands and pollingers, and to leave untouched to the lord's use the standles and standers, as by the laws of the country should be left'. Both husbands and pollingers are rare words for pollards, the former in fact having previously been noted only in Kent;[45] standles are explained below. In 1584 and 1586 the steward also recorded : 'The lord certifies that he had sold' for £6 13s. 4d. to Richard Stanley esquire '40 bushes and little oaks', with similar sales of 'alderns' (alders) and lops of 100 trees to William Mawlter for £5, and further 'lops' to the latter and other tenants for £7; but one tenant gave him 2 fat capons instead! A few years before, Bartholomew Greene felled on his land '8 oaks being pollengers, whereof 4 were cleft for blocks to serve for fire, against the custom of the manor', meaning presumably without the lord's licence. The reference to standles originated in the Act of 35 Henry VIII, c. 17 (1544), which was designed to arrest the appalling destruction of woodland. Where any coppice wood of under 24 years' growth was felled, 12 standles (saplings) were to be left standing for further growth. At least one court, that of Chingford Comitis within the Forest of Waltham, re-iterated in 1559 this little-known legislation by decreeing that 'no inhabitant shall fell any coppice woods or standles, upon pain for every time 3s. 4d.', which was the statutory penalty. But that loyal Englishman, Harrison, bewailed the way in which the Act was evaded : 'Within these 40 years', he wrote, 'we shall have little great timber growing above 40 years old; for it is commonly seen that those young staddles (*sic*) which we leave standing at one-and-twenty years' fall are usually at the next sale cut down without any danger of the statute, and serve for firebote if it please the owner to burn them'.[46]

In 1565 William Reve, a Walden basket-maker, reported as a 'common trespasser in cutting down and stealing a great number of willows growing in the several wood of the lord', was fined 12d. with the threat of 2s. 6d. for any future theft. At Witham in 1583 a tenant felled 4 ashes, an oak, a little crabtree and branches of a willow, and also carried away 'a summer hedge', all growing in his meadow, against the custom. The bailiff was ordered to seize the meadow and to account for the profits. For 'lopping a willow' at Shenfield a man was amerced 6d. A fine of 10s. was levied on a Rettendon man in 1562 for custom-breach in cutting down crabtrees and lopping peartrees on the Common. A presentment is found at Beaumont in 1568 against Richard Borne, 'being guardian in socage of the lands of John Wright', because he had 'cut down *anglice* did girt an ash on his lands to the said John's damage', and he was warned that any repetition would cost him 20s. Felling speres, maples and sallows and girding timber-trees are among the charges against tenants at Wethersfield; and carrying away a cartload of thorntrees at Wanstead.

In some manors, as already seen, felling, even on tenants' own copyholds, necessitated their seeking authority. A widow sought a licence to carry away half a jag of timber on her customary land and had to give 16d. to the lord. If they took it clandestinely from the lord's waste, and were unlucky enough to be caught, they were fined. In 1600 no less than 14 men and women carried away wood and furzes from the Frith and Galleywood Common; each was fined 3s. 4d. or 5s. These are places well known : Moulsham Thrift, an ancient wood, is now surrounded by Chelmsford Golf Course, and Galleywood Common is still bearing its colourful cover of gorse.

Three Purleigh men who had cut down trees and furzes on the lord's waste called Purleigh Fee in 1591 were to be 'proceeded against at common law for trespass'; but there is no evidence that the court passed the charge to Quarter Sessions. A Harlow Bury bye-law in 1573 threatened anyone charged by proper witnesses with 4d. for each 'bundle' taken from the lord's wood. Among further cases, a word, the exact meaning of which has not been ascertained, is found at Epping in 1586 : Richard Raynesford 'cut down an oak called a brawler to the quantity of one load of timber to the lord's damage'. In 1576-77 Edward Aulefer, the Epping cleric, was fined 12d. for felling '3 oaken speres' on the demesne (a spere is a young oak after it has passed beyond the sapling stage);[47] and John Bridgeman was reported to have cut down '4 pollard elms containing 60 feet of timber on land next his customary tenement'. Adam Richardson, rector of Panfield, trespassed in the adjacent manor of Shalford in 1562, felling and taking away 8 cartloads of wood. Hornbeams, indigenous to Waltham (now Epping) Forest, are specifically mentioned only once, in 1603, when a woman was fined 12d. for cutting one down in 'Wintery Park', a large glade next to Wintry Wood near Epping.

The rolls of Great Canfield reveal how the right to take wood for fuel led to a bitter controversy. At the first court of John Wiseman, who had just acquired the manor in 1580, a tenant was amerced 12d. merely for taking 40 withies from the demesne wood to bind his faggots. At the next there was an inspired ordinance forbidding the use of underwood for fuel. Six months later, in 1581, no fewer than 30 tenants were prosecuted for infringing this order, everyone being fleeced as much as 30s., whether for 1 or 17 trees. As the local historian remarks, Wiseman 'was fighting the tenants, and chose timber-cutting as a means of extorting money'.[48] In 1585, presiding in person, he gave leave to a tenant to lop trees and cut firewood on his copyhold, for term of his life, but he had to pay as much as 26s. 8d. for the privilege. Had he waited seven years, he could have had the wood for nothing, as Wiseman's avarice in breach of the wood-cutting and other customs resulted in his losing a case in Chancery, as described later.

Although there were rarely any fruit trees on the commons, other commodities had to be restricted. Two lively little scenes can be visualized, in which boys were probably the culprits. In 1581 the Kelvedon Hatch court 'ordained that, if any do beat, shake or lebeat any trees bearing acorns growing within the waste of this manor, he shall forfeit for every tree so beaten, shaken or lebated to the lord, 2s.' The third verb seems to be otherwise unrecorded, though its meaning is obvious. The other entry is unique and intriguing. An order was issued at Harlow Bury court in 1562 that 'walnut pickers (*jugland' collectori*) called acrepickers, not having enough for his own use, must not shake the trees', under pain of 12d. 'Acrepickers' apparently refer to tenants having a customary right to take walnuts on some part of the lord's waste.

In conclusion, it seems clear that lords saw that their timber rights were rigidly protected. If a tenant wanted timber, even on his own land, he had to get a licence, unless the local custom gave him freedom to fell; if he wanted timber from the waste, he had to pay for leave to do so.

Other tenants illegally dug clay or marl on the commons. When puddled and mixed with withies or thin branches and cowdung, clay was used to fill in the 'mud' walls between the studs, or uprights, of timber-framed buildings, while marl, a rich clayey soil containing carbonate of lime, was a good manure. Many courts prohibited the taking away of such material. At Epping in 1570 a tenant was fined 5s. 'for carrying away soil from divers parcels of the Queen's waste'; and in 1578 'any person who digs clay on the lord's waste shall stop up the place within 2 days' or pay 12d. The Aldham Hall court in 1584 admonished the tenant of 'Bowsers Hall' (Bourchiers Hall *alias* Little Fordham, the other Aldham manor) because he 'had dug and carried away much clay from the common called Gallowtye'; and it decreed a penalty of 12d. on any future offender. Shenfield fined a Brentwood man 2s. in 1567 for digging 2 cartloads of clay on Aldeash Common without licence. A marl-digger on Great Bardfield Green was noted earlier under 'Original Presentments'. Inclined as we are to think of the safeguarding of village greens as a modern idea, other records testify to some degree of care, as at Earls Colne in 1590, when a man was charged because he did 'annoy the highway with laying the garbage of his cattle upon Hall Green and digging gravel there'.

Clay of course was also employed by potters. Making pottery was a thriving industry at Stock from as early as 1482 until at least the end of the 17th century,[49] but no offending potters were before the court in Elizabeth's time. The roll for the other Stock manor, which boasted the name of Ging Joyberd Laundry *alias* Blunts, shows that 7 potters obtained the lord's licence for 'digging out clay' in 1606-7, when the court directed that all potters digging 'loam and white clay on Stock Common for cups, tiles, bricks or other earthen vessels shall fill up their pits right up to the top immediately after the carting out of this white clay', under a penalty of 5s. for each pit.[50] Harlow, too, had suitable clay, and in 1578 the Bury court ordered that 'all potters who dig potter's earth (*argillam*) on Harlow Common fill up the pits made by them within 4 days', or forfeit 12d. Five years later they were forbidden to dig clay on the Common 'no nearer the highway than is assigned to them', with a 10s. penalty.

Everyone required fuel for warmth and cooking; everyone needed wood for making or repairing domestic implements. When the poor man's garden, orchard or 'backside' failed to furnish it, his eyes turned elsewhere, especially to hedges, which offered a more copious supply. No doubt he sometimes took hedgerow fuel furtively after dusk. Unfriendly watchmen might catch him, but, if he had real necessity, other officers probably cast a blind eye at the load. The fact remains, somewhat surprisingly, that 'hedgebreaking', as it was called, was regarded as theft, though there seems to have been no definition of a minimum load or weight. Most courts, especially after a minor wave of hedgebreaking, passed a bye-law stating the automatic fine and the penalty for a further offence. It was 12d. at Epping (1578) and Middlemead in Little Baddow (1592), and 12d. and a session in the stocks at Witham (1587). Repeated transgressions were to cost twice as much at Rettendon: 'for the first 12d. and for the second time 2s.' But in 1568 the Chelmsford court, increasingly active under its new lord, Sir Thomas Mildmay, set a highly minatory rate of 6s. 8d.

Although 'timber' normally implied larger girth than hedgerow wood, it is occasionally used in hedgebreaking cases, as at Bendish Hall in Radwinter in 1564: 'Anyone taken for hedgebreaking and taking away timber shall forfeit 12d., half to the aggrieved party, the other half to the lord.' At Halstead in 1587 it was defined as 'stealing poles, crotches and cockhedgestaves', to which 'spentes' was added in a similar prohibition two years afterwards. A most pertinent attack on such wood-stealers came from the pen of the compiler of the Aveley survey, quoted later in the concluding custumal. But, among the precedents cited, he omitted this order made in 1594: 'Warning be given in church that if any be taken with hedgewood, or breaking any hedges or stiles, they shall be set by the heels (i.e. put in the stocks), with the wood before them, upon a market day'.

The court of Canewdon Hall was equally vigorous in 1588 in its efforts to suppress hedge-stealing:

> Order by the tenants and residents with the assent of the lady. Whereas heretofore divers persons within the Leet have used to break hedges and carry away wood without licence of the owners, to the great hindrance of their neighbours and contrary to all good order, for reformation thereof to be had it is ordained that from henceforth no person shall do so without licence, upon pain to forfeit 6d. and to be set in the stocks by the constable, upon knowledge thereof to him given on the next Sunday, for 2 hours, on pain to the constable to forfeit for everyone by him not punished 5s.

The Chelmsford bye-laws, issued in 1564, were much sterner where the offence was repeated:

If at any time hereafter any inhabitant shall be taken, proved or found in breaking of any hedge and carrying away of any part to burn, either of the lord's demesne and lands or of any of the tenants, every offender shall be punished for the first offence openly in the stocks by the constables, with the wood so stolen set before them, and for the second offence like punishment and within one month after to be avoided the town.

But no record of such drastic action occurs. Newport produced its own version in 1567 : 'None shall break their hedges nor carry away wood on their shoulders, under pain of 6d. and another 6d. from those who shall carry'; while Felsted in 1581 preferred physical censure : 'Any persons breaking any hedge or stealing wood be put next Sunday or holyday in the stocks for 2 hours at the least, and the wood be placed before them, signifying the cause of the punishment'. Much earlier, in 1562, this court had heard a plea of trespass and claim for 20s. damage for 12 perches of broken 'quickset hedge'.

Despite these and similar general orders, hundreds of transgressors were caught. A tenant at Epping in 1583 not only broke his neighbours' hedges but also 'sold their timber'. The charge of selling, however, is not often met with, and it is clear that wood-pilfering was mostly for household use. The Halstead court fined as many as 21 'common carriers of timber and common breakers of hedges against the ordinance' 6d. each, and on another occasion mulcted 7 'common hedgebreakers' a groat (4d.); but elsewhere 1s. or 2s. was usual. A most illuminating entry is seen in the same rolls in 1595: 'Richard Darginson and his wife walk about at unlawful times in the night-time to milk their beasts, and under colour thereof take timber and break hedges'; both fined 2s. Hop-growing, which was already established in several places in North Essex, is referred to indirectly in the same records in 1577, when two townsmen had to pay 12d. for collecting hop-poles, and another was charged in 1595 as a 'hedgebreaker and stealer of hop-poles'. Doubtless owing to penury, the offence was far from being confined to adult males. At South Ockendon, for instance, in 1561, the 9 'common breakers of hedges and carriers of timber' were nearly all wives or widows. A Rettendon man was not only accused himself, but also for allowing his children to pilfer : 'They have carried away 2 bundles of stakes worth 4d.' At Berden in 1568 a child was twice found taking away a bundle of hedgewood, against the bye-law. The father's fine would have been 2s., but because he was adjudged a pauper it was halved.

No manor court dealt so regularly with hedge-breakers and wood-stealers as that of Ingatestone, which, as previously noticed, was strictly controlled by the Petres' stewards.

*Orders made at Ingatestone manor court*
1559 general order against hedgebreaking
1561 similar order especially against paupers
1565 bailiff to summon woodstealer to leave manor with wife and children
1565 order against stealing wood

1568 hedgebreaker and stilebreaker, never buying wood, fined 2d. but pardoned
1568 hedgebreakers to be put into stocks by constable
1569 occupiers of leased premises not to cut down neighbours' wood
1569 tenant's sons breakers of neighbours' hedges, stiles and other wood
1570 6 tenants fined 20d. each for hedgebreaking
1572 inhabitant ordered not to allow his sister to break neighbours' hedges
1572 widow ordered not to break hedge after warning by bailiff
1573 order to 2 inhabitants that neither they nor their boys and girls nor their servants break others' hedges nor carry away wood without licence
1574 father fined for allowing son to break hedges
1581 general order against carrying away wood and poles from groves and springs
1582 7 presented for breaking hedges and allowing their families to do so
1583 general order that those guilty of breaking hedges, stiles, bridges or pales or of cutting wood to be put into stocks for 8 hours without food or drink or other relief
1593 bye-law forbidding everyone from taking wood from lord's waste or grounds not his own between Feast of SS. Philip & James and Midsummer, on penalty of 12d. for every 'burthen' (load) or 3 hours in stocks
1595 hedgebreakers to forfeit 12d. on proof of offence and to sit in stocks for 4 fours
1600 hedgebreakers and woodstealers to be whipped naked from the 'girdlestead' (waist) until they 'bleed well'
1600 receivers of stolen wood to be fined 3s. 4d. or set in stocks next Sunday or holyday from 9 a.m. until 1 hour after evening prayer; overseers of the poor to pay 6s. 8d. for every neglect of this order, constables being charged jointly with them to execute it.

The severe double injunction in 1600 may have followed a wave of woodstealing by the poor. Manor courts had no power to issue orders to the 'new' officers, the overseers of the poor, let alone to threaten them with 6s. 8d. penalty for default. But Ingatestone court had always held supreme sway over the inhabitants, and evidently Sir John Petre had no intention of allowing the parish vestry only to control the overseers.

Man's insistent need for fuel is emphasized by an entry in the estreat roll of Wivenhoe in 1584 :

> If any person whatsoever be taken carrying away any of the lord's park pales or it can be proved by one sufficient witness that any hath conveyed away pales, he shall forfeit for every offence 20d. and be set in the stocks, to remain for 3 hours at least.

In general, few customs could have been valued more highly by copyhold tenants than those governing the rights to take timber or wood. That these privileges were open to dispute is seen in an award made at a slightly later time by Robert Willan, D.D., Robert Sandford esquire, and two other men, who had been appointed in 1623 as arbitrators in a controversy between Thomas Bowes, lord of Great Bromley, and the copyholders, who were able to prove their 'right of hedgebote and firebote in furze, shrubs and underwood on Bromley Heath'; but the award reserved to the lord the exclusive right to 'any pollinger or bowling of oak, elm, ash or aspen'. The apparent plight of the poorer inhabitants of Wivenhoe, despite its being a thriving little port, seems to show that the demands of London for the 'sea-coals' from Newcastle left little for other towns. In any case, we know that the cost of Mistress Quickly's 'sea-coal fire' went up steadily while Shakespeare lived in London, from 4s. to 9s. per chaldron,[51] which would be beyond the pockets of most inhabitants of Wivenhoe or indeed of other places. We know, too, that the price of timber trebled during the reign, because of the gradual exhaustion of the Wealden forests and other woodland. While too much must not be read into the very numerous timber-felling and hedge-breaking charges, of which the merest selection has been given, the evidence also points to a general awareness of the need to husband the declining supplies of timber.

Compulsory provision of a store of winter fuel is referred to in orders made in several manors. In 1561 the Brook Walden court enjoined: 'Every inhabitant shall have in his yard 2 loads of wood at Hallowmas next upon pain for every offender 6s. 8d., and every inhabitant or landlord having any tenant shall pay for the offence of his tenant'. Repeated in the following year, an additional clause explains why: 'He shall provide 2 cartloads for winter fuel without occasion to break his neighbours' hedges'. That tenant here means sub-tenant, the actual occupier, may be deduced from a Beaumont bye-law of 1581: 'All tenants having a sub-tenant to obtain and provide annually for each of them 2 cartloads of timber'. Breaches of a Walden precept were reported in 1582: one man forfeited 6s. 8d. for neglecting to get in his winter store; 3 others who had 'broken the bye-law' by hedgebreaking (2 of them 'through their children') were fined 16d. each. Somewhat similar injunctions for self-provision of fuel were issued at Wethersfield in 1573 and 1575. The same conception underlies an Ingatestone order in 1572: 'No owner of houses to let them except to those who bought sufficient wood'; and in 1589 the qualification for new arrivals at Earls Colne was placed at 4 loads of wood per person.[52]

A dual threat voiced at Walden in 1561 further typifies the generally stern attitude towards the indigent. It is the sole reference to the ancient custom of gleaning found in the rolls that have been searched:

*Orders for breakers of hedges and collectors of corn*
Every hedgebreaker taken in breaking of hedges and carrying of suchlike wood shall pay for every such offence 16d. and 3 hours punishment in the stocks; and the money thereof coming and forfeited to be delivered, 4d. to the lord, to the owners of such wood 4d., to the bailiff 4d., and to him that shall take an offender 4d.
Every gleaner found gleaning before the corn, both sheaf corn and raking, be clean carried shall have 3 hours punishment in the stocks and shall pay 6d., 4d. to the lord and 2d. to the bailiff.

An even more stringent decree was passed in 1587:

Each inhabitant who shall take or shall see any person stealing hedges or any other wood of his neighbours or gleaning against the bye-law shall make presentment so that he be punished without favour or concealment, upon pain for each offence 2s.

## The Tenants' Buildings

Every copyholder, or his lessee, was bound to keep his dwelling and outhouses in repair at his own charges and to the lord's satisfaction. So vital was this obligation that a tenant who allowed his house to fall into decay was liable to forfeit it to the lord, according to the custom of many manors. As the subject is of some importance to economic historians, a fairly full series of both representative and exceptional extracts will be given.[53]

A very clear picture may be drawn from the records of Old Hall with New Hall in Beaumont, where the tenants' duties were rigorously enforced at the courts of John Lord Darcy. In addition to injunctions to effect repairs under a money penalty, several offenders were peremptorily told to spend a specified number of days on the work. By the first order (1560), 4 men had to repair their barns, with '1 (or 2) days' work' (penalty for neglect 12d.). The direction in one case was to 'thatch and tile'; in another, to 'repair with straw' (thatch). Next year an inhabitant who had disobeyed an order to put in 3 days' repair forfeited 3s., with the prospect of losing a further 6s. if not dealt with by laying a 50-foot groundsel, a length which probably refers to a farmhouse. Three others had to lay groundsels 10, 30 and 20 feet in length, or pay 2d. for each foot. A groundsel, the essential groundplate in a timber-framed structure, is a term still occasionally heard in Essex.[54] In 1563 and later the scribe preferred to use the bastard Latin *daywarcatum* or *daywercatum* for a day's work, and as many as 12 tenants were told in 1564-66 to do repairs with thatch for 1 or 2 days, or lose 8d. But a few years afterwards Darcy, or more likely his steward, rode through the manor and was evidently still dissatisfied with the condition of the buildings. A long entry in 1568 shows that 11 tenants were ordered to thatch or tile their dwellings or barns under the threat of 12d. or 2s. Destruction by act of God did not exonerate a tenant. In 1564 Richard Darcy (whose relationship, if any, to the lord is not known) was enjoined to rebuild a tenement called Sewalles, 'lately burnt by fire', before the next court under penalty of 40s.

A single instance of arbitrary action by the lord is seen in 1597, among the ordinary copyhold admissions in the Beaumont rolls:

> It is found by the homage that John Felgate has newly built a cottage on his customary lands where there was no cottage before and has cut down certain timber trees for the building, against the custom. Therefore he puts himself in the lord's grace, and the fine is assessed by the lord at 5s., which the bailiff is ordered to levy. But the homage say that they can take timber

from their customary lands for the building and repair of their ancient houses.

The lawyers, certainly by the next century, were quite as definite as the Beaumont jurors that a tenant had the right to fell timber on his holding for repair of his own dwelling or outhouses.[55] Confirmatory evidence from other manors will be quoted later. This privilege, however, was in doubt at Epping in 1577, when Lawrence Stace was charged with having felled without the lord's leave 3 oaks on his land for repairing his house. 'The rolls to be examined concerning the custom' was the resultant order. Nor was Stace the only alleged offender, four others being similarly presented at the same court, despite one having cut down only an oak which was 'doted' (decayed inside). Stace, at any rate, managed to withstand the challenge, as he was granted leave retrospectively to cut down the trees; and having stoutly defended his right the licence was enrolled at his request. The dispute had probably arisen from the steward's action, because at the same court he ordered the bailiff 'diligently to enquire' if another tenant previously in trouble had in fact 'expended in repairing his customary tenement an oak which he cut down in his customary meadow', and search was also to be made regarding the remaining tenants. Flouted as the steward had been, curial dignity demanded close investigation, but apparently no custom-breach was proved.

Uncertainty, too, prevailed at Ramsden Crays. John Darbye had felled a timber tree on his land without leave, 'but said that he cut it down to repair his tenement; therefore he is to speak with the lord':[56] a slightly sinister phrase met with now and again elsewhere. The tenants of Fingrith in Blackmore also were unsure about their customary rights, though they knew that it was their duty to report felled trees. The jury's recorded presentment in 1575 is so illiterate that the steward made a fair copy for his own reference: 'We present Thomas Salmon hath felled 7 oaken trees in his land'. This is followed by 10 similar entries which refer to 4 oaks, 6 elms, 6 timber trees, and 'Posmer Grove wherein was timber growing'. Of other tenants' actions they claimed: 'He hath felled for his reparations and building at all time as he had need, and so did his father before him without any denial', and 'with the timber he built upon the copyhold and the wood he sold'. They concluded: 'All other tenants have felled and sold wood and timber from time to time as they had need, and so we may do (so far as we know)'.

The records of many other manors evince a good deal of attention to dilapidations. The original presentments of Fingrith in 1565, which are in the vernacular, show:

> We do pain Richard Gey and Margaret his wife in 20s. to reparation (*sic*) their house against next court day at Clatterford End.
> We do present father Brodye's house at Hookes End for fault of reparations against next court day under pain of 20s.

The Epping rolls have numerous repair orders. In 1576 five inhabitants had to renovate their 'decayed houses'. Penalties for failure range widely from 16d. to 53s. 4d. Control was so firm that in 1569 the court even ordered John Baker, a tenant, to 'remove his woodstack next his barn wall because it is detrimental to the wall'. This recalcitrant fellow's name often recurs on other pages. Alternatively, ruinous cottages had to be rebuilt. In 1571 a precept was given to Baker, who had 'wasted' a house against Cattes Lane without the Queen's licence (she granted the manor of Epping in the following year to Thomas Heneage and his wife), to rebuild it before the next court under pain of 20s. Another man was fined 3s. 4d. for a dilapidated barn on his tenement called Gaytons in Lindsey Street.

There were few manors, however, in which a tenant of a sound structure was allowed to convert or rebuild without licence. This is illustrated by the charge against Thomas Parker at Shenfield Hall in 1559 because he had 'decayed, altered, changed and taken away a messuage called Fusses alias Ropers of copyhold and builded a new house to the use of a milkhouse and garner, contrary to the custom'.

Presenting a tenant's death in the manor of Great Burstead in 1591, the jury added that his dwelling and garden fence were both 'in great decay'; the fearsome penalty of £5 was imposed on his son and heir if the defects were not quickly remedied. On the other hand, a forfeiture of 10s. for not complying with an injunction to repair an old house at Rettendon in 1567 was 'pardoned for 8s. because of poverty'. An East Mersea man's kitchen, burnt down in 1568, was to be rebuilt under penalty of 40s.; and in the following year Henry Greeneward had to restore 'his house, in which Cocke dwells, against wind and rain'. Tempest, like fire, was no excuse; and house insurance was still a long way ahead. In 1591 Richard Hodshone, clerk (the rector), and his brother John 'begged to be admitted to a tenement' at Debden, 'but because it is in great decay through lack of repair by reason of rotten timbers, and is wasted to the disinheritance of the lord, admission was respited' (deferred); at the next court they were pardoned, but had to bear a 'fine' (i.e. normal manorial fee) of 53s. 4d. on admission.

A few more typical restoration entries may be briefly quoted: presentments of 4 dwellings 'ruinous both in timber and plaster' at Bacons in Dengie (1559) and of 2 dwellings in Purleigh which had become ruinous through defective 'thatch, tile and daubing', with penalties of 26s. 8d. and 20s. if not promptly repaired (1592); John Bridges to repair the 'Crown' in Harlow 'in groundsels, daubing, tiles and thatching' or pay 40s. (1587); and repairs to 'groundselling and thatching' ordered at Great Burstead.

By the custom of many other manors, timber-felling for house repairs was vetoed unless specific permission was granted. At Debden (1571), for intance, the bailiff was authorized to assign an oak to 3 tenants to repair their dwellings; and at Mascalls Bury in White Roothing (1583) the bailiff informed the court that he had allotted 2 oaks on a tenant's land for repairing his barn.

Although offenders, as pointed out, were liable to have their buildings confiscated, actual forfeiture seems to have rarely ensued. Two revoked confiscations at Canewdon will be described shortly. A flagrant violation was dealt with at Old Hall in Boreham in 1560, when it was in the Queen's possession. Richard Twetty, gentleman, a customary tenant, had recently cut down without curial licence 300 'English oaken spires' in Groves Field containing 20 acres together with a grove, and he had rebuilt a house thereon with the timber; whereon the bailiff had a precept to seize the land into the sovereign's hands. Twetty (or Twytty), who lived at Stock, was the founder of the Stock almshouses, still surviving.[57]

Dilapidated outbuildings, such as barns, hayhouses, hogscotes and sheep-pens, figure as frequently as dwellings. There are many reminders that kitchens were often separate buildings; for instance, a decayed one in the manor of Mascalls Bury, for which timber was allotted in 1559. Occasionally leave was granted to demolish without having to rebuild. In 1580 a Great Canfield tenant paid 5s. to pull down his ruinous kitchen (an outbuilding) at Strattons in Thorpe End;[58] and another at Dengie in 1577 compounded for 20s. with the lord of Bacons to demolish his barn. A tenant of Stanstead in Halstead, who had repaired his shed without authority, was reported for having 'cut down on his customary lands timber called spurkes, viz. 4 asps, 6 oaken spurkes and 1 sallow'. (Spurk seems to be an otherwise unrecorded variant of spire.)

Entries about the building of new cottages or rebuilding are regrettably meagre, the Ingatestone evidence already cited being somewhat exceptional. In 1565 the lord of Harlow Bury licensed a tenant to build a cottage (apparently on a vacant site on his land), for which he gave 5s. Next year leave was granted to George Dyrrington 'to make a separate tenement of his old house, next to that of Joan Rede widow and the chimney of the tenement, by building anew the said part of the house, when it shall please him'. Does this relate to Moor Hall, of which George Derrington was the lessee?[59] Moor Hall was a sub-manor to Harlow Bury. At Alfreston *alias* Bigods in Dunmow Frances Carver, a widow, who had been ordered to build 'a new framed house' in place of her ruinous one but failed to do so, was threatened with a penalty as high as £6 for further non-compliance.

A significant affair is recorded in the rolls of Canewdon Hall in 1588. It arose from the jury's presentment and has been left to the last because the resultant trouble to which the steward went is an interesting illustration of the importance of manorial custom.

## THE TENANTS' BUILDINGS

Whereas at the last court the bailiff was ordered to seize a customary and heriotable tenement called Perfelde Hyll and 15 acres called Tenauntries and 2 tenements and 10 acres of land called Paternosters and Gayes *alias* Bowers, because Thomas Redman tenant thereof made waste by sale and destruction on the premises by cutting down 18 timber elms worth £3 growing on the lands without licence, and the issues being assessed at £10; and William Makin, the bailiff, was ordered to retain the lands in the lady's hands and to answer for the issues. And whereas this the homage (9 names), *not* being charged to enquire about any wastes, say on their oath that the custom is and was from the time whereof the memory of man runs not to the contrary that customary tenants of this manor used to have and cut down on their lands their timber growing on their customary lands for the repair of their customary tenements, and also to lop their trees growing there, *without* licence.

The spontaneous statement by the homage (the second sentence) having annoyed the steward, he had got out the old rolls, searched through them, and eventually found evidence as far back as 1405[60] that was contrary to the jury's uninvited opinion. He extracted no less than 18 later cases ranging from 1479 to 1578, all against the interests of the tenants, showing that they could not fell without first securing licence. A few of his extracts will be quoted.

In 1555 the lord had granted such a licence to Richard Broman to lop all the trees on his bondlands called Watsmythes and to cut down an elm to repair '*unum naviculum vocatum* a boat' on payment of 13s. 4d. No similar case has been noted elsewhere in Essex; in his will made in 1563 he described himself as a mariner of Great Stambridge, an adjacent parish. Coming to our period, the steward found that 4 tenants had obtained licences between 1567 and 1576 : John Castlyn, to lop 15 elms and cut down a rotten elm (for 3s.); Thomas Hull, to lop trees and cut down 8 'doted' elms, leaving sufficient 'hedgeboote and stackboote' (10s.); Thomas Stykerde, to lop trees and cut down 16 trees (20s.); and John Coker, to cut down 20 elms in his holding on the south side of 'Totham Cawsye *alias* the Churchweye' (5s.). Then, from 1563, actual seizures appear. Edward Bulman, having unlawfully felled 4 elms worth 20s. on his lands, redeemed his holding for 30s. In 1571 Thomas Pyke had cut down elms, intending to rebuild a dwelling on other bond tenements, whereon the bailiff seized the trees, with a warning that a further offence would result in forfeiture of his house. The court acted accordingly when, only three years later, Pyke again committed 'waste' by cutting down 30 elms worth 2s. 6d. each and felling 'by the middle' 30 elms and ashes. He humbly acknowledged his grave offence. On this occasion the lord himself (Thomas Armiger) presided, and he 'graciously' restored the holding, which was formally re-granted by John Barnardiston, gentleman, the steward. Pyke, however, had to pay the enormous fine of £10.

At the session in 1589 following their rash presentment the jurors were confronted by the steward's announcement of his search. Thomas Redman then confessed, acknowledged forfeiture as an accredited custom, and placed himself at the lady's mercy (Jane widow of Thomas). Having paid a similar penalty of £10 in court, confiscation was cancelled, and he was re-admitted. Were the jurors of 1588 unaware or forgetful of Pyke's £10 punishment only 15 years earlier? If not, they were an intrepid lot, feigning ignorance and taking the chance that the steward, who was apparently new to the job, would not challenge their false statement about the custom. But he called their bluff, and it is surprising that they also were not fined. Redman disposed of Paternosters before the end of the year, when John Locke was admitted. Eight years afterwards, Paternosters figured in an extraordinary incident. Locke, then 'of Ratcliff, Middlesex, sailor', perhaps learned that his lessee had sub-let the house without his (Locke's) leave. He and his son paid a surprise visit at dawn. Bolting themselves in, the family withstood a violent assault. Those besieged counter-attacked by throwing down 'leads of cheese' (a lead weighed 56 lb.)! The bizarre story, which is gathered from depositions in the Quarter Sessions records, has been fully narrated elsewhere.[61]

Throughout the centuries men have illegally appropriated small plots on which to put up their own dwellings. Now called squatting, the term originated in America about 1788; but the ordinary Elizabethans had no known word for such unauthorized acts, though the lawyers called land so filched 'purprestures'. Many cottages of the period may still be seen on the edge of commons and on wide roadside verges. The majority have no title apart from long user, because all such manorial waste was vested in the lords, who seldom made grants until the 17th century. The courts exercised constant vigilance against these unlawful encroachments. When hastily-built cottages were presented, the courts either ordered their removal or seizure, or less often allowed them to remain after the payment of licences, thus giving copyhold 'title'.

The Middlemead (Little Baddow) jury in 1576 found that 'James Wever without the lord's licence entered into Hockham Hills (see p. 247) 'by the instance and desire' of the lord of Tofts in the same parish, 'and there built a new cottage to the lord's grave damage and disinheritance and against the custom of this manor'; the bailiff was ordered to seize it. The sequel reveals a major dispute between the two lords; it also shows that a tenant's perjury could result in confiscation:

> Whereas contention has arisen between the lords of this manor (Richard Blake and Mabel his wife) and John Smythe knight, lord of the manor of Tofts, concerning the limits of this leet, the homage affirms that the said parcel of common since time immemorial belongs to this manor; and it is decreed by the whole homage, with the steward's assent, that John Draper has forfeited, because of his false evidence, all his customary lands and tenements, and that they be immediately seized by the bailiff into the lord's hands.

## THE TENANTS' BUILDINGS

Three of the few grants discovered may be quoted. At Epping in 1571 half an acre of waste in Epping Common was assigned at an annual quitrent of 2d.; the lord of Middlemead in 1572 gave a plot 30 perches long and 3 perches wide, being 'parcel of the waste lying under the park pales called le lane', at 2s. rent; and at Walden a man was admitted in the normal way to 'one purpresture lying in Danyelles Lane'. It is not clear whether these were intended for building plots.[62] (Exemption licences to poor tenants given by lords under the 'Four acres to each cottage' Act of 1589 are somewhat different as we shall shortly see.)

Orders to pull down illegal cottages are frequently recorded, but of those which survived by licence or escaped the courts' attention a contemporary author pithily remarked: 'Then build they up a cottage, though but of elder poles, in every lane end almost, where they live as beggars all their life after'.[63] The presentment at Blunts Hall in Witham in 1584 that 'the tenant of Old Barns hath erected a cottage or purpresture in a certain lane there without licence' leaves us in the dark, but a typical case may be taken from Purleigh in 1591. A tenant having built a cottage on the manorial waste called Purleigh Fee and dwelling there without licence, its removal was ordered under pain of 40s. Far more common were outbuildings put up surreptitiously. In 1588, for example, the homage stated that 3 tenants had built on Rettendon Common several carthouses; each was fined 12d. and their removal before the next court was ordered under penalty of 2s. 6d.; 3 others had erected dwellings there (fines 10s. and penalties 20s.). In the same year the Great Burstead court found that 2 tenants had built 3 cottages in Hobsters Lane and Norsey Corner, all of which were to be pulled down; and 'the inhabitants of Great Burstead have built for Thomas Jackson and his wife now deceased a new house, who beg the lord to allow it to remain for the use of the parish by the rent of 1d. a year'. Nothing further about this curious presentment is seen. Was it the desire of the parish to use it for housing pauper families?

Several Chelmsford men, including Thomas Wood, 'chirugeon', were charged in 1599 with having encroached with their 'penfolds'. A blacksmith at Kelvedon Hatch who impinged on the waste was fined 10s. and ordered to remove the encroachment. Some lords even frowned on minor breaches. In 1599 the court of Fingrith found that a tenant 'hath encroached and set his barn half a yard and better upon the lord's waste', which he was peremptorily told to remove; and a similar order with a 4d. fine was imposed on a Newport man who 'put a mud wall on the lady's waste', default to cost him 3s. 4d. An Epping tenant who 'behaved himself ill towards the lord in continuing his encroachment' saw the bailiff arrive to seize his cottage.

The alternative of monetary composition for unlawful erection is most fully exemplified from the Epping rolls. In 1577 the troublesome John

Baker was reported for having built 'divers years' ago on the lord's waste at the back of his house a shed 6 feet wide, also a carthouse 8 feet wide. Four tenants who had each put up a hogscote or a carthouse behind their dwellings had to compound for 'continuing' them; two more in 1579 at 2d. annual rent for unlawfully building cottages at Epping Heath and Wintree Common *alias* Wintree Wood; and drastic action was taken in 1583 because John Gladwyne, one of the offending pair, 'had not compounded for his continuancy; therefore he has forfeited £3, and on the verdict of the jury he is ordered to pull down the cottage under similar penalty.' Finally, in 1592 James Carr encroached on the waste with posts by his 'forge'; and three years later his widow was told to remove the forge.

The problem of traffic along narrow streets in main thoroughfares occasionally arose even in Tudor times. The little market town of Newport lay on the London–Cambridge road. The court could not allow any further straitening, so it fined John Aldyche 12d. because he had 'encroached on the Queen's highway one foot and more with a house newly built there in the High Street.'

In London and other cities the projecting overhangs or 'jetties' of some houses brought the uppermost storeys so close together that the occupants could shake hands across the street. Possibly Mildmay, who knew London's streets well, was determined that the narrowest parts of Chelmsford Back Street should not develop in this way. The exact implication in an extraordinary encroachment case in 1594 is not clear, but offenders against our present-day building bye-laws are only rarely punished so severely. At any rate, Thomas Watson was ordered 'to remove or otherwise destroy all the new building adjoining his free tenement in which he now dwells, which is to the ill and pernicious example of all the other inhabitants, under penalty of £20'. Next year he was again presented, because, although he had removed 'his new built eaves' on the front of his dwelling which apparently overhung the old eaves 2 feet 3 inches, the new eaves still 'overhung the old eaves at the back 15 inches', resulting in his forfeiting the £20. Doubtless dismayed by this crushing sum he confessed his fault at the next court, offering £12 'in satisfaction and humbly begged the lord to accept it'. Mildmay 'graciously' did so and even forgave him the balance. The streets of Walden were much straiter, and in 1571 John Gyver was ordered to demolish his cottage 'that overhangs the house of John Strachie', on pain of 6s. 8d.; the Strachies were influential townsmen.

Failure to maintain fences or hedges was an equally common offence. The penalty might be levied according to the length, e.g. 20d. for 20 perches (manor of Middlemead), or 3d. a perch (Thaxted); but in others

## THE TENANTS' BUILDINGS 267

it was fixed, irrespective of length, e.g. 'to amend her fence', 10s. (Epping), 'to make a pale or hedge at his watercourse at Park Bridge', 5s. (Thaxted), or 'to repair 60 rods of hedge at the Cock', 40s. (East Mersea). In 1565 Hugh Williams was ordered to repair his hedges at the end of the pale of Wanstead Park in Lord Rich's manor. By special custom, the upkeep of the lord's park pales was sometimes the tenants' burden, as at Great Bentley. Broken hedges or fences could lead to much damage and loss of crops through animals getting into the open fields; this in turn resulted in disputes and bad feeling, as evidenced from the frequent pleas of trespass.[64]

The value of these petty entries lies chiefly in the detail of local topography, especially names of streets and lanes. Many other spot-names occur; for example, orders 'to make his fences in his close called the Bull Yard', 'to repair his fence in the Town Garden' (Halstead, 1559, 1580); 'to repair his hedge next to the common well' (Kelvedon Hatch, 1568); to the tenants of the 'Dolphin' 'to put their hedge, as of right they should, against the glovers' pits' (Harlow, 1596).

It is not easy to learn what steps the Elizabethans took to prevent or to stop fires, although we know that long poles with hooks were kept at some churches for pulling down flaming thatch from dwellings and barns. But even in London there were only very crude fire-fighting arrangements, and elsewhere little was done to prevent fires from consuming whole towns and villages. The slightest references to fire prevention are therefore of interest. In 1577 a Chipping Walden tenant was ordered to destroy a 'hearth in a solar' (upper room) in his dwelling, after which he was not to allow any fire there. An instruction in 1583 to an Epping man to 'amend the chimney in his house' may have been concerned with fire prevention. Where there was no chimney, the smoke from the fire on a brick or rammed-earth hearth in the middle of the floor of the single-storey 'hall' escaped as best it could from a hole in the roof, with the constant risk of fire. As related in the first chapter, most of the medieval one-storey cottages in Ingatestone High Street were newly built or reconstructed with two storeys between the middle and the end of the 16th century, chimneys doubtless being incorporated at that time. In one instance, however, this apparently was not so, for in 1600 presentment was made that Thomas Hinds, inhabiting 'a room in which there is no suitable place for a fire, nevertheless keeps a fire in this room, to the great danger and alarm of the neighbourhood'; he was ordered to make a 'chimney or reredos' in the room under penalty of 10s. Hinds was copyhold tenant of a house called 'Stiles' backing on the churchyard, which about 1556 was a single-storey cottage but had recently been given a second floor. A reredos was generally a thick stone or new back to a firehearth; in this entry the meaning is a chimney : until the regrettable destruction of the house a few years ago, one could see the stack, probably inserted by Hinds through the roof where it came down over a low back-room. Certainly he never paid the penalty, and the map of 1600-01 shows the house with a chimney.

## Cottages and Inmates

Of the nine Tudor poor relief statutes, that of 31 Eliz., c. 7 (1589), concerned with building cottages and harbouring inmates, has perhaps received the least attention from social and economic historians. It included two important prohibitions:

> No person shall make or build any cottage for habitation, nor convert any building used as a cottage, unless he lay to it 4 acres of land, being his freehold, lying near it, upon pain to forfeit to the Queen £10. Every person that shall continue any such cottage to be erected shall forfeit 40s. for every month.
> There shall be no inmates or more families than one dwelling in any cottage, made or to be made, upon pain that the owner or occupier wilfully suffering it shall forfeit to the leet 10s. *per mensem*.

To the penal provisions about new cottages there were two exceptions. The statute was not to apply in any borough or market-town, and churchwardens and overseers of the poor, by the licence of the lord of the manor or of Quarter Sessions, might build cottages for 'poor people'. A few licences to build without the four acres were granted by the Essex Bench as a result of local petitions. The legislation of 1589 was new in regard to cottage-building, but the mandatory clause affecting inmates merely authorized action which most manor courts had been taking for many years.

An inmate, in the Tudor sense, was a lodger or 'subtenant'; more specifically, one who was unable to maintain himself. Inmates were deemed to be potential paupers; hence the watch for entry into the parish of intruders who might become chargeable to the poor rate, especially after the great Acts of 1597 and 1601; but it is observable after the semi-compulsory Act of 1572, and even earlier as a result of the voluntary Acts of 1550 and 1563. Inmates were also regarded as lazy persons who were harboured in cottages. Contemporary opinion tended to draw little distinction between inmates and vagabonds. We shall now see how manor courts dealt with the problem before 1597, when it became that of the parish vestries, though some manors continued to enforce the Act of 1589 until the Settlement Act of 1662 placed the matter squarely on the parish officers' shoulders.

Among the few instances of authority being given by lords for building cottages without the necessary land three entries will exemplify the procedure. The Springfield roll of 1585 records that 'the lord of his kindness, at the humble petition of Thomas Longe of Springfield labourer,

COTTAGES AND INMATES 269

has granted a parcel of Springfield Green containing 1 rood with the intention of his building a dwelling house, at the rent of 6d.' It was reported at the court of Blamsters in Great Easton in 1601 that 'a pauper had built a cottage on a piece of land with the consent of the lord, the tenants and other residents'. Two Woodham Ferrers copyholders who were granted 'a parcel of waste soil or vacant ground' on which each had built a cottage must have also received a licence; they are mentioned, without date, in the manorial survey of 1582.[65] Offences against the 4-acre clause are rarely found. Two shops converted into cottages were reported at Wethersfield in 1598, when owners of cottages not having one (sic) acre of land were forbidden to let them to 'strange persons likely to be charged to the inhabitants without the consent of four principal inhabitants'. Both sections of the Act were disobeyed by an Aveley inhabitant, who was accordingly charged with 'making a tenement out of an out-house, and so keeping an inmate contrary to the order', which cost him 6s. 8d.[66]

Examination of the post-1589 court rolls leaves no doubt that, whereas inmates were the bane of almost every manor and severe action was taken against them, the land clause was regarded as a utopian measure and not likely to solve one of the problems of poor relief. The paucity of offences and licences in the manor records leads to the conclusion, as far as Essex is concerned, that the statute was little more than a sanguine piece of legislation, despite some efforts at first made to enforce its provisions. Neither do the few published volumes of Quarter Sessions records of other counties, restricted mainly to Elizabeth's last two decades, show more than scanty activity elsewhere : building without laying four acres resulted in four pre-1603 indictments in Lancashire and none in Worcestershire, though they were fairly numerous in the latter county between 1603 and 1642.

The court rolls of Epping, like many other manors, indicate how frequently those who took in inmates were prosecuted. The following is a mere sampling :

*Action against tenants receiving inmates*

1561 Any tenant who receives a subtenant into his house 'to dwell together' to be fined 40s. unless permission is granted by the whole homage
1573 4 such offenders each forfeited 40s.
1577 William Gifford fined 4d. for harbouring Francis Gifford, a person suspected of having no lands or livelihood, and John Baker fined 5s. for harbouring another man, with another 1s. for harbouring beggars 'against the statute'
1577 Agnes Foster widow to remove (blank) Graye from her house because he is 'of evil conversation' (i.e. dealings) with his neighbour, under pain of 20s.
1582 Thomas Browne to remove a woman dwelling in his house
1583 Any person who harbours Thomas Browne and Thomas Payne more than two days to forfeit 3s. 4d.

1590 Thomas Redhedd ordered to remove his wife's sister from the town, under pain of 10s.
1591 Helen Sobie widow to remove her widow subtenant, under pain of 20s.
1593 5 named tenants to 'put in sufficient bonds to the chief inhabitant to discharge the township of their undertenants, being strangers lately taken in and like to prove a charge', under pain of 20s. each.

The court of Abells in Halstead waged incessant war against inmates. The risk of their becoming chargeable is illustrated by an injunction in 1576 to a townsman 'not to allow his tenant to use the trade of a baker' beyond Lady Day, under pain of 40s., unless the former gave 'a bond to discharge the town of the burden which may fall by reason of the baker dwelling there'. In the following year the inhabitants were prohibited from allowing any to dwell in their houses 'without the consent of the constables and 4 chief inhabitants', under the same penalty; but, in fact, a year later 2 offenders forfeited only 10s. and 5s. Then, in 1586, the campaign was intensified. One man was peremptorily told to remove an unmarried mother and her newly-born child, and 'none shall receive her into their houses'; another, to remove a tenant who dwelt suspiciously in his house; another, to clear out '2 women whom he keeps suspiciously'; and a man and his wife, to evict 4 persons, 3 'being of ill fame and likely to become a charge', and nobody to receive them without giving security by bond. All this led to a further veto, especially against pregnant women. The result was still unsatisfactory. Several of the offenders forfeited penalties in the next year, when yet another similar order was issued. In 1589 fines of between 40s. and 10s. were paid by 5 townsmen. Finally, in 1595, 4 householders were each warned to remove an inmate or pay 20s., and another to expel a pregnant woman, while any person who took her in would lose 40s.

The Ingatestone rolls tell much the same story. At least 7 inhabitants between 1564 and 1602 had to 'evict' a sub-tenant. At Wethersfield 8 men and women were presented for taking in 'strangers or inmates', one being described as 'not a good liver' and another having been given houseroom 'without the assent of the chief pledge'.

The Moulsham (Chelmsford) court in 1559 recorded that 'William Mildmay gentleman' (brother of Thomas, the lord) 'has forfeited his two several penalties of 20s. in all because he did not expel 2 tenants taken in by stealth and otherwise obnoxious to their neighbours'. At Fingrith the bailiff was instructed in 1560 to warn Thomas Saman 'to suffer but one tenant to dwell in his tenement upon pain of 3s. 4d.', implying that he had let his dwelling; and in 1575 : 'We pain William Brodye to avoid out of his tenement Ambrose Grove between this and Midsummer Day at night under pain of £10', an abnormally high sum.

It was reported at the Bishop's Hall (Chelmsford) court in 1571 that 4 inhabitants, who 'maintained more tenants than they ought to do', had incurred the penalties under the bye-laws of 6s. 8d. each, which would be raised to 20s. for each month if they were not removed. The court (Thomas Mildmay having also acquired this manor in 1563) took a serious view of intruders, for in 1574 William Weste, a barber, was directed to quit the town within a month or pay £3 6s. 8d. (i.e. 5 marks), 'to be levied on his goods'. His case led to a general precept on the same day: 'None receive any strange or unknown tenant without letters of testimonial from the place where he last lived for a whole year and the testimonial be allowed by the constables and lay ministers of the town, upon pain of forfeiting 40s.' This in turn was followed by an injunction to one Pechye 'the minstrel' to remove himself to Woodham Ferrers, his birthplace, before Christmas under a similar threat. He was clearly *persona non grata* in the town, as Moulsham court passed a similar order in the same year against 'Theophilus Pechie the minstrel and all his family'. Some musicians, as we noted earlier, were treated as vagrants. The court had evidently felt the need for a clearer definition of 'landlord' in one of its bye-laws: 'Landlord shall be meant of those that be as well owners of the freehold as others that take in under-tenants which are like to be noisome and burdensome to the township in any case'. This was succeeded by orders at intervals to a number of inhabitants 'to remove themselves from this town': in 1591 four received a command to quit. Exceptional action was taken in May 1600, when 8 tenants were presented for having inmates. Of these, 3 had each housed a man and his wife for a few months; another, 2 married couples for 6 months; the fifth, 5 couples; the sixth, in his dwelling called the Pipe, 2 couples and 3 widows; William Griffin had kept in his house called Spittle Barn 2 couples and a widow for 2 years; and Thomas Bowsey had allowed a couple, 2 men and 4 widows to stay in his house called Tye Hawe for 7 years. All offenders were ordered to remove their inmates before Michaelmas under pain of 20s. Were all these men lodginghouse-keepers, who had 'let' rooms to elderly, poor people, with or without the consent of the court under the Act of 1589? If so, it may be that the Act of 1597 had influenced the overseers of the poor to report this widespread infringement. The Spittle Barn was perhaps one of the surviving outbuildings of the dissolved Friary, the refectory of which had been converted into the 'Chelmsford Free Grammar School of King Edward VI'. The final anti-immigration decree reads, 'No man shall receive any person into his house hereafter without the consent of 6 of the chiefest headboroughs'.

Harlow had begun to get tough with inmates following the Act of 1563. Tenants were warned to evict them in 1565, and several forfeitures of 20s. were incurred; next year the injunction was repeated and was directed especially against those having houses in 'Harlowmarket and Churchgate'. The court of Felsted Bury in 1577 told 'Mr Ruste' (the vicar) to expel his tenant 'because he is like to be a charge to the parish' and another man to remove his mother-in-law, each under threat of 40s.; and 'the homage with the assent of the steward and bailiff' determined that 'if any tenant in future takes in any stranger into his house who was not born or has not dwelled in the parish for 3 years, such tenant remove such person within 3 months' or be liable for a £5 fine. Earls Colne ordained in 1589 that inhabitants having inmates remove them or pay 20s. for default, unless they had lived together for 3 years or gave indemnity against poor relief.[67]

The penalty varied a good deal from manor to manor. Before the lord was entitled to it, the offence had to be presented by the jury. All the manors in Witham, for instance, imposed 40s.; East Mersea and Great Dunmow 20s.; Little Baddow 12d. a week or 3s. 4d. a month; Beaumont 4s. a month; Harlow Bury between 10s. and 20s.; Shenfield Hall only 6d. in 1569 (7 offenders) but 6s. 8d. in 1593. Berden set a penalty for the removal of a man and 'all his children' at 20s. in 1579, increased on his disobedience to 50s.; and 20s. was to be levied if another refused to remove 'his nursechild'. The severest sentence is found at Canewdon in 1589 : 'Thomas Saffolde has received a certain Gregory Frauncys to dwell with him in one house for 8 months last, therefore he has forfeited for each month 10s., which totals £4'. The new Act was profitable to the lord.

A minority of manors permitted sub-tenants if their credentials were satisfactory. At Beaumont, it was 'with the assent of 3 or 4 inhabitants' (1586) or '4 chief pledges' (1594); at Halstead also, 'with consent of 4 of the best chief pledges' (1579); at East Mersea, 'unless the inhabitants consent' (1566); and at Harlow Bury, 'with the special consent of 6 of the best men' (1579). Great Burstead manor (including Billericay) forbade 'letting of tenements to any person who is a charge without the consent of 10 or 8 of the chief parishioners' (1581); putting strangers into their houses, 'by which the parishioners be charged, without the consent of 8 inhabitants' (1588); 'without the leave of 6 honest or chief inhabitants' (1591); or 'without the assent of the inhabitants' (1598).

The Springfield with Dukes court expressed the matter somewhat differently in a bye-law of 1576 : 'No owner of any messuage or cottage in future to allow 2 subtenants to dwell without the consent first had of the churchwardens and constables' ('2' implies that the owner had let the house). In 1599 Stock prohibited any parishioner of Stock and Buttsbury from taking an inmate without the leave of the wardens and overseers. At Kelvedon Hatch in 1578 it was ordained that 'no free or customary tenant in future receive any subtenant without the consent of 4 of the better pledges'; and this was re-iterated in 1588. Shenfield Hall in 1577 insisted on the assent of 'Master Gascoyne esquire and Master Pope gentleman' (not J.P.s), and in 1593, 'No paterfamilias shall receive any inmate' without the authority of 6 chief men.

The only difference in the proceedings before and after the Act is merely one of language. The post-1589 entries usually refer to it and adopt the statutory term 'inmate'. That is all. One example, from Purleigh, shows how the steward tried to cope with the new word in the middle of his Latin entry. The charge was for taking in *'unum le inmate* for one month and more; therefore he has forfeited the penalty in the statute, viz. 10s.' (1591). But the steward of Rettendon had already forgotten the correct penalty, and 3s. 4d. was levied on a man who had allowed an inmate to stay for a fortnight (1593).

The Thaxted steward was more long-winded in 1600 :

> It was presented that Rooke Westley, an inhabitant in this View of Frankpledge, took into a cottage at Bardfield Green John Stebbynge coming from a foreign hundred, being poor and unable to summon both to be at the next court to show why 40s. should not be paid for the nuisance according to the customs and bye-laws; and in the meantime Stebbynge is to find sufficient pledges for his good behaviour or Westley to remove him.

Perhaps this steward's fees depended on the number of membranes of parchment he filled. If so, he did well, as Westley's charge was followed by similar entries concerning 10 more offenders for harbouring inmates in their cottages in the Town Street, Newbiggen, Market Street, Mill End, and Sibley's Green, and an eleventh who took a stranger to work in his 'shop' at Mill End and to dwell in his home.

'Enquire if there be any vagabonds or those which walk by night and sleep in the day' was among the articles of enquiry with which courts leet were charged. But such undesirables were rarely reported, because vagrants were taken immediately by the constables to the nearest J.P. Only where tenants were found to be sheltering 'suspected and ill-disposed vagrants' was the offence presented, as on single occasions at Fryerning and Harlow. A Moulsham landlord was fined 3s. 4d. in 1560 because he was found to be harbouring a 'sturdy beggar', which led the court on the same day to order the constables *'totaliter* to remove and expel all strangers and beggars', under the threat that a defaulting constable would be fined 20s. : a clear indication of the court's attitude.

At Ruckholts in Leyton in 1567 the inhabitants were forbidden to take in vagrant women for more than 24 hours. Somewhat exceptionally in 1572 the Ingatestone constables were told to remove a man out of the town and to punish him in the stocks as a vagabond if he refused to work. No specific presentment of any 'Egyptians' (gipsies) has been discovered, except possibly that of a Rettendon man in 1603 who 'put cattle of wandering persons (*peregrinorum*) outside this leet on the Common'.

A nightwalker and his wife have already been mentioned, and another was accused at Wethersfield in 1586. Akin to nightwalkers were evesdroppers, 'which stand under walls or windows, by night or day, to hear tales and to carry them to others, to make strife and debate between their neighbours'.[68] An 'evesdropper and carrier of tales' was fined 6s. 8d. at Chelmsford in 1567.

We make no apology for the length of this section, which is designed to illustrate one of the most prevelant problems of the time; yet only a small fraction of the entries about inmates has been quoted. Perhaps the most scathing attack on these undesirables is that made by the man who made the survey of Aveley, about 1620. 'Many of these inmates', he declared, 'being of lewd sort as whores, scolds, lazy and idle people, have brought horrible and not to be named sins and wickedness into the town'. To those in authority, too, inmates were idlers, and idleness led to poverty and chargeability. Manor courts had no need to be spurred to activity by the Act of 1589. As explained, the only practical changes resulting from the late Tudor poor laws were that the parish boundary replaced the manor boundary as the crossing-point for intruders and the vestry meeting instead of the manor court dealt with them. The end of our period was transitional in this respect.

One problem remains unsolved. Why did people continue to take in these inmates, since the penalties were heavy? Were some takers-in the kind-hearted ones, the 'do-gooders', the socially conscious folk of the Elizabethan community? It seems doubtful. Rent is the probable answer.

## Clothes and Caps

In medieval times most European countries passed 'sumptuary laws' against private extravagance, especially in food and clothing. More than one Elizabethan writer censured both sexes for wearing costly dress. 'Except it were a dog in a doublet', wrote Harrison in a well-known passage, 'you shall not see any so disguised as are my countrymen of England'; and a great deal more in the same strain.[69] Even manor courts were expected to do what they could to suppress finery being worn by the lower classes: 'You shall enquire whether any have used in any of their garments, velvet, satin, damask, taffata, sarcenet, chamlet, or any fur . . . or gold or silver, otherwise than the statutes made in the 14 year H. 8 and 1 & 2 of Ph. and Mary do allow; you shall present the offenders'.[70] Writers and lawyers might condemn expensive costume, but manorial jurors very rarely did so; and the sumptuary laws largely remained a dead-letter. In our searches only a single case has been found. Three men were reported at Ingatestone in 1568 for wearing apparel beyond their social status, as well as for unlawful gaming, and each was fined 20d. Sir William Petre, at any rate, knew the law, and he may perhaps have persuaded one of his servants to present.

The Act of 13 Eliz., c. 19 (1571), attempted to benefit the wool trade, especially the cappers, by enjoining that all 'citizens, artificers and labourers' above the age of 7 should wear woollen caps on Sundays and holy-days, with a fine of 3s. 4d. for each day's transgression. Unlike the penalty for not exercising with bows and arrows, it was an absurdly low fine because it was generally construed as a levy of 3s. 4d. on the township, not on each individual, despite the fact that the owner of the court leet was to have one-half of the forfeit (the poor were to get the other half). It has been stated by more than one social historian that this statute also was a failure, but little precise evidence has been produced. The Essex manorial records certainly confirm their view, so much so that few other Tudor Acts appear to have been so universally disobeyed. The reason, however, is not clear. Was the 'statute cap', to be made of 'wool, thicked and dressed in England', an object of ridicule?

Although it is customary to find the fine being levied, there was a good deal of extra-statutory variation. Some courts interpreted the Act according to their own discretion. The parish of Epping was divided between the 'Town' and the 'Upland' (the latter, containing the parish church, having only a small population as compared with that in the town street with its market). Regularly each year the court imposed a fine of 3s. 4d. on the Town, but only 2s. on the Upland. In 1582 'the inhabitants again submitted themselves to the lord's fine of 3s. 4d. because they have not worn their caps on Sundays and holy days, and they have elected Robert Gore to be collector of this sum'. Yet, in a single instance immediately after the Act was passed, one Epping man was separately fined 12d. Perhaps to obviate the trouble of apportioning and collecting so small a sum as 3s. 4d. Great Canfield decided in 1577 to levy it only on the well-to-do (*ditiorbus*). In 1579 the fine was 2s.; in 1581 it was the full penalty but 'reduced by the lord to 20d.'[71] Shenfield fined the inhabitants 2s. in 1598; and Springfield set the same sum in 1585-89, but, perhaps realising that 2s. was not the legal amount, raised it to 3s. 4d. in 1591. At Walden, in the same year, 'many inhabitants have not worn their caps and humbly beg that the lord of his grace will pardon the offenders to the extent of 3s. 4d.', which was granted. Another deviation is recorded at Canewdon in 1588, when 'an agreement was made between the lady of the manor and the inhabitants', under which they were to pay '2s. for all forfeitures under the Act'. In the little manor of Berners Roothing in 1583 the fine on the tenants was as low as 6d.

The reluctance of the Elizabethans to pay up is also illustrated at Berden. 'All the inhabitants have offended', they confessed in 1583, but they 'humbly beg the penalty to be moderated, viz. that each be pardoned at 1d. and granted for this once (*pro hac unica vice*)'. Did they, in possible ignorance of the terms of the statute, fear that the fine of 3s. 4d., as in the normal case of common assault, was to be paid by each one? Two years later they were mulcted as a whole in 12d., and in 1589 they again sought a mitigated penalty of 2s., 'and the lord granted this favour'. Finally, in 1590, they had to pay 20d. The rolls of Debden, owned by the same lord, reveal a very similar story. At Kelvedon Hatch in 1578 every offender was fined 2d. But any doubts about its being a collective fine were removed at Thaxted in 1575, when three 'residents above the age of 21' each had to bear 3s. 4d., and the bailiff was ordered to 'answer to the lord for one half and the other half to the poor'. At the court of Alfriston *alias* Bigods in Great Dunmow, too, it was not a case of 'all the inhabitants', but 6 names; the amount is left blank. There was, however, a further risk of much heavier fines, because the 3s. 4d. applied to each Sunday or holy-day, and long-term disregard, in theory, could have produced a sizeable income for the lord and the poor. Only two instances of this effect had been found. At Purleigh in 1591 the homage reported all the inhabitants for neglect 'since the last court', and they had 'forfeited the penalty for each day, viz. 3s. 4d.', so the bailiff was told to levy 10s., one half to each party. The other example comes from Rettendon. In 1602 it was presented that 'the inhabitants have not worn their caps, therefore each of them (*quilibet*) has forfeited 20s., viz. for each day 3s. 4d., which sums the bailiff was ordered to levy to the use of the lord and the poor and to answer therefor'. But the obligation had been repealed by the Act of 39 Eliz., c. 18 (1598)! Parliamentary protection for the cappers had been, by and large, ineffectual.

---

[1] *The Order of Keeping a Court Leet and Court Baron* (1650), 10.

[2] P.R.O., Queen's Bench Indictments Ancient, 683, part 1, no. 33 (from typescript calendar in E.R.O.).

[3] *E.L.: Morals*, 47.   [4] Austen, *op. cit.*, 57   [5] *E.L.: Disorder*, 256-61, 316.

[6] Austen, *op. cit.* 59 (misread as 'Neale').

[7] A MS. map of *c*. 1575 shows their adjacent cottages at Crondon Park (Emmison, *Catalogue of Maps in E.R.O.*, plate viii).

[8] *E.L.: Disorder*, 68-9.   [9] Austen, *op. cit.*, 81.   [10] *E.L.: Disorder*, 139-47.

[11] *E.L.: Morals*, index, *s.v.* 'barratry', 'scolds'.   [12] Austen, *op. cit.*, 57.

[13] *E.L.: Disorder*, 172-3, also 106, 159, 178.   [14] *Ibid., passim.*

[15] *Ibid.*, 218-55.   [16] *Ibid.*, 242-3.

[17] For unlawful games offences at Quarter Sessions, see *E.L.: Disorder*, 218-27.

[18] Emmison, *Tudor Secretary*, 218n.   [19] *Ibid.*, 35.

[20] MS. map, 1616 (photograph in E.R.O.).

[21] Austen, *op. cit.*, 57.   [22] *Ibid.*, 60-1.

[23] *Trans. E.A.S.*, xiv, 206-7.   [24] Harrison, *op. cit.*, 343.

[25] *Ess. Rev.*, xii, 237.   [26] *Shakespeare's England,* ii, 384 (given in full).

[27] Austen, *op. cit.*, 57.   [28] *Ess. Rev.*, xii, 217-8.

[29] *E.L.: Disorder*, 6, 26, 29, 31, 227-8.   [30] *Ibid.*, 14-17.

[31] *Catalogue of Essex Parish Records* (1st. edn. only, 1950), frontispiece.

[32] Austen, *op. cit.*, 59-60.

[33] Some tentative conclusions were offered in my 'Was the Highways Act of 1555 a success?' (*Ess. Rev.*, lxiv, 221-34).

[34] *E.L.: Disorder*, 113-14.   [35] Harrison, *op. cit.*, 256.

36 Some scrappy details are in W. R. Fisher, *Forest of Essex* (1887), 265-311, but it is hoped that Mr W. H. Liddell's extensive researches on the subject may be published before long. Lengthy extracts from the court rolls of some of the Forest manors are in the voluminous printed proceedings of the Epping Forest Commission, 1871-74 (copy in E.R.O.).

37 Hilda Grieve, *The Great Tide* (Essex County Council, 1959), 1-14; also Emmison (ed.), *Guide to the E.R.O.*, 2nd edn. (1969), see index, s.v., 'Sewers', 'Sea-walls'.

38 Marjorie K. McIntosh, 'The Cooke Family of Gidea Hall' (unpubld. Harvard Univ. Ph.D. thesis, 1967), 281.

39 The remarkably early Essex estate maps of the Walkers, already mentioned, show boundaries of manors. Occasionally a manorial survey describes the boundary fully, e.g. that of the royal manor of Barking, 1609 (*Ess. Rev.*, lix, 1-3).

40 Austen, *op. cit.*, 53-5, 81.   41 *Ibid.*, 54 (author's translation, 'wild boar'!).

42 Cf. *E.L.: Disorder*, 132-3.   43 Harrison, *op. cit.*, 136.

44 Tusser, *Hundreth Good Pointes of Husbandrie* (1557).

45 J. O. Halliwell, *Dictionary of Archaic Words*.   46 Harrison, *op. cit.*, 283.

47 Cf. W. R. Fisher, *The Forest of Essex* (1887), 250n., and Austen, *op. cit.*, 83.

48 G. Eland, *At the Courts of Great Canfield* (1949), 15-16, 55.

49 Austen, *op. cit.*, 26; Emmison (ed.), *Wills at Chelmsford, 1620-1720*, 7; *V.C.H., Essex*, ii, 414.

50 Austen, *op. cit.*, 83; for the Stock potters, see Crafts *supra*.

51 *Shakespeare's England* (1916), i, 336.   52 *Essex Journal*, ix, 128.

53 Comparable entries of medieval date for the manor of Great Waltham are printed in *Ess. Rev.*, xiii, 146-48.   54 Eland, *op. cit.*, 58.

55 Cf. the long passage in *The Order of Keeping a Court Leet and Court Baron* (1650), 39-40.   56 *Trans. E.A.S.*, xxii, 223.   57 Austen, *op. cit.*, 68.

58 Eland, *op. cit.*, 59.   59 *Ess. Rev.*, xlvi, 43.

60 The Essex Record Office series dates from 1485.

61 *E.L.: Disorder*, 126, referring to J. Holmes' article in *Ess. Rev.*, lxiv, 259-66.

62 The same remark applies to 16 grants of 'waste' at Earls Colne (*Essex Journal*, ix, 89).

63. Philip Stubbes, *The Anatomy of Abuses* (1585).

64 For Quarter Sessions and Assize cases, see *E.L.: Disorder*, 135-6.

65 *Trans. E.A.S.*, xxiv, 12.   66 *Ess. Rev.*, xv, 121.   67 *Ess. Journal*, ix, 128.

68 *The Order of Keeping a Court Leet and Court Baron* (1650), 17.

69 Harrison, *op. cit.*, 146.   70 *The Order of Keeping a Court*, 21.

71 Eland, *op. cit.*, 75.

# 18
# Nuisances
## *Rivers, Bridges and Ditches*

The distinction between offences and nuisances dealt with by manor courts is by no means a rigid one; much of what has been said about animals in the section on Commons, for instance, could just as well go into this chapter.

In every generation owners or tenants of watermills have been accused of various nuisances connected with their necessarily erratic control of the flow. Ancient and other complex mill-rights led to endless litigation in the central courts, while minor disputes about watermills and mill-weirs were a common feature of manorial courts' business. Old records were therefore sometimes quoted. At the court of survey in 1576 of the manor of Blunts Hall in Witham, which belonged to Mary Lady Darrell widow of Henry Fortescue, all tenants had to produce their 'copies of court roll'. One of the millers duly brought along a lease dated 1494 by Henry, Fortescue's ancestor, to George Armond of Coggeshall, a clothmaker, of Machins Mill, with the milldam and millrace and fishery rights. Under this, the lessee had to repair the millhouse and the mill in 'tiling, daubing, groundselling and timber-work as well under the water as above the water' : evidently it was used as a fulling-mill. All Local Record Offices hold deeds and leases of hundreds of watermills, some with interesting details.

Notoriously dishonest, many a miller was charged with mercenary disregard of his neighbours' meadows by excessive 'pending' of his millrace, thus flooding their land. Disputes affecting Moulsham Mill on the Chelmsford–Springfield boundary illustrate the sort of complaints that so often arose. The Springfield court in 1572 received a presentment that Robert Gryffyn the miller had built *'purpresturam vocatam* a wharf' near Treen Bridge in the two parishes, next 'the Watering' of John Noke of Chelmsford, 'to the great nuisance of the lord's mill called Springfield Mill and of the adjoining meadows between the mill and the highway, and that the wharf was '3 inches higher than it used to be'. Nine years later the homage gave their 'verdict' that the miller of Moulsham Mill must in future *'exhaureat fluminem anglice* draw le flashe at le Waterynge' of John Noke, so that the water 'can have its course by the same, and not to continue to the nuisance of the Queen's highway and the inhabitants dwelling nearby'. A 'flash' was a contrivance for raising the head of water and may be the same as the 'wharf' in its obsolete sense of dam or sluice; and 'treen', which is an archaic form of 'wooden', distinguished this bridge from the Stone Bridge, referred to shortly.

At the court of Middlemead in Little Baddow in 1580, Thomas Hawes, miller of Grayes Mill in Hatfield Peverel, was accused of encroaching on the demesne lands by diverting the watercourse into a 'back ditch' and by planting osiers in the ditch, 'to the disinheritance of the lord and the enlargement of the lands belonging to the mill'. He was commanded to scour the ditch and eradicate the osiers, under penalty of 20s. Three years afterwards the roll records a perpetual grant to the same miller of the use of the lord's sluice-gates (*januarum fluminarum*) on the demesne land and a free footway from the miller's channel (*alveo*) through part of Normead next the river and through the Great Marsh belonging to the manor, as well as the right to take fish in the sluice; the grant was made for the 'preservation' of his water and stream.

There was trouble with the mills in the manor of Brook Walden. Thomas Mead, miller, was reported in 1559 because he 'annoys all the inhabitants by stopping up the water there, on account of which it is agreed and ordered that he shall make his flow to agree with the nether spur of the Angel gate', upon penalty of 10s. 'if he be presented by 2 or 3 tenants'. Four years later the court decreed that 'the miller do not keep his water stopped up beyond the old boundary mark (*dolam sive limitem*) viz. towards le Netherspore of Kyngs (*sic*) gate' and not beyond, under a similar pain. At the next session Hamon Carter was fined for disobeying the order. In 1565 the bailiff warned Thomas Witney, gentleman, the 'farmer' (lessee) of the lord's watermill, that 'he or his deputy (i.e. the miller) do not stop up the water before his mill to the damage of his neighbour to a greater height than previously used', again with the same penalty.

The Abells (Halstead) court was more than once involved in complaints about the big mill on the Colne below the town, on the site of which still stands the Courtauld family's silk-mill built about 1825. In 1577-79 'the miller of Townesforthe Mill' was directed not to allow his water to overflow, and 'John Buste the miller of Towneford Mill do not henceforth pend the river above the usual mark or pend, whereby the grounds of such as dwell by the riverside is flowed' (flooded), under penalty of 3s. 4d. 'for every time so wilfully offending'. The Town Mill then appears in the registration of changes of tenancies. First, a licence to Robert Rande in 1584 to lease 'Towneforde Mylne' for 21 years at a rent of 40s.; then, in 1587, a surrender of the mill, milldam and sluicegates by the same Robert (who had succeeded Thomas Rand in 1569) to John Ungeley. The lord would have refused to admit Ungeley, had he been able to do so legally. In the margin is written : 'Memorandum that I Arthur Breame had for a fine of John Ungeley £30. He should have bought the mill for me and he bought it for himself'. Breame had purchased both this manor and

Stanstead Hall, the other chief manor in Halstead, in 1576. It is interesting and very rare to find a lord's personal notes on a court roll.

Obstructing the flow through overhanging trees was another offence sometimes found. The court of the manors of Newland and Chipping in Witham in 1581 instructed 'the landholders between Dodfordes Mill and Newland Mill on both sides of the river to cut down overhanging trees' and to scour the river, or forfeit 3d. for each perch, increased to 2s. in 1587.

Obstructions to rivers and streams were not confined to mills, as many entries in the Abells records show. In 1578 the tenants of the lands from the Bridge towards an orchard on both sides of the river were enjoined to remove their encroachments made with 'stakes, piles or banks'. On the other hand, in the previous year the court reprimanded two tenants who had taken away 'lez hillockes', by reason of which a watercourse had been diverted; also several tenants who had 'allowed water to overflow to the nuisance of many near the stream'. In 1579 John Barnarde, gentleman, was admonished 'not to cast the weeds of his osier ground or any other earth or rubbish into the river at Parsonage Bridge against Jernygons Mead where he hath landed the river and stopped the watercourse'; and in 1586 Henry Scott likewise to remove hop-poles that obstructed the watercourse. A presentment was made in 1594 at the Stanstead court that John Kinge, tenant of Jerninghams 'osierground', had not rooted up the osiers, being an obstruction. In these ways some courts dealt with the choking up of rivers from specific causes, but it is doubtful whether they had wider powers to give general directions for cleansing rivers. The only order of this nature—to a tenant of Fingrith (Blackmore) in 1563 'to scour the river against his orchard'—relates merely to a stream running into the little river Wid.

To control the water, small wooden sluices, sometimes termed watergates, were sometimes constructed in meadows and marshes. Deficient sluices were occasionally reported; more often, orders were given to make a sluice, probably when an old one had rotted away. At Epping between 1571 and 1582 this aspect of drainage is referred to three times in orders 'to make a sluice at the end of his meadow called Tylers Mead and Cobbing Bridge'; 'to make a watersluice between Pond Lees and Sones'; and 'to amend his watergates.' Halstead court in 1577 told a tenant 'to make a sluice so that the water may be drawn off the highway into the lands called the Moor.'

Protection of the common meadows was another function of the courts. The tenants who had rights in Haslow Common Mead at Great Canfield were instructed in 1566 to make a 'dam at the breck there', probably referring to a breach in the bank of the stream.[1] The rich meadows along the Stort at Harlow figure in the rolls more than once. In 1563 a tenant was accused of not having made a sufficient bank (*defensionem*) against Symons Mead in Harlow Marsh and others against Chantry Mead and

Bridgeman Mead; and in 1597 William Taverner was directed to 'amend the breach against Chantry Mead, as the water has an unlawful course'.

In the first volume the involved question of liability for bridge repairs was studied in some detail from the Essex Quarter Sessions records for the first decade of the reign.[2] In most cases it was seen from the hundredal juries' presentments that the lord was held responsible, and where streams form boundaries between manors the lords on each side were usually named, whether known to be liable or not, unless the burden could be otherwise ascribed. In a few instances it was put on the town or the parish, or on the whole county, but occasionally the reporting jurors had no idea on whom to place it. Unfortunately the records of the Essex Bench give little evidence of direct action to remedy the deficient condition of bridges, because no Elizabethan order books are extant.

A somewhat similar picture emerges from manorial archives. Many manors were in the possession of the Crown. It is not surprising therefore to learn, as from the county records, that Elizabeth, one of the most parsimonious of monarchs, did nothing towards repairing bridges in her manors. At Epping (1571) 'Cobbing Bridge is in great decay and is to be repaired at the Queen's own costs' (repeated in 1572); at Witham (1587) 'the bridge at Chipping is in great decay and the Queen of old custom from time to time has repaired it' (repeated in 1588); and at Copford (1601) 'half Stanway Bridge ought to be amended by the Queen and is in great decay'.

At Thaxted in 1571 'two bridges against the great sloughs' were presented as ruinous, 'and the lord' (Sir John Cutte of Horham Hall) 'ought to repair one of them, viz. that beyond Milletts gate, and widow Key ought to repair the other'. At Ingatestone in 1567 Arnolds Bridge was reported to be in a bad state and the lord (Sir William Petre) and the lord of the adjoining manor (probably one of his manors in Mountnessing) ought to repair it (re-iterated in 1568, 1569 and 1572).

Near the north end of Newport on the right-hand side of the road to Walden lay St Leonard's Hospital, suppressed at the Dissolution. In 1567 the court ordered the lessee of the hospital (*firmarius domus hospitalis*) to repair his part of New Bridge, evidently that known later as Toll Bridge (repeated in 1571).[3]

To be able in 1587 to cite a record of the hundred court in 1417 would have been remarkable, as it is believed that such courts rarely kept written proceedings, were it not for the fact that an extract was presumably preserved in the diocesan muniments in connection with the ordination of the vicarage. Be this as it may, the Harlow Bury manorial jury quoted this to their own purpose: 'Pernell Bridge is ruinous, lying near Churchgate Street, and ought to be repaired by Richard Harrison, the vicar, at his own cost, as is shown in le terror made by the verdict of the homage at the hundred court of Harlow held in 4 Henry V, when the vicarage was ordained, on pain of 3s. 4d. to repair the bridge'. The actual date of ordination was 1398, and no mention of liability for the bridge occurs in the deed.[4] 'Le terror' refers to a terrier, or list of lands—perhaps a separate document. In the roll for 1591, however, a brief entry states that Pernell Bridge was to be repaired by the lord. Ten years earlier the jurors had declared that 'the bridge which lies between Mudbury Green and Stony Lane is very ruinous, but who ought to repair it they know not'. This clearly refers to the same bridge, between the green and Churchgate Street, over the stream running into the Stort. The present and more pleasant name of Mulberry Green is a corruption, through 'mud-' from 'mot', the moot or meeting-place of the hundred.[5]

Three cases are found in which the township was held to be liable for repair. 'A common horse bridge in the Queen's highway between Estwryghtes and the lands of the rectory is ruinous'; so the jury at Purleigh presented in 1592, adding that the township (*villata*) was responsible; 'therefore the inhabitants are ordered to repair it under pain of 40s.' In 1547 orders were made at the court of Blamsters Hall in Great Easton for the repair of Elsworth and Gybbes Bridges by the tenants and of Easewell Bridge at Duton Hill by the 'inhabitants and residents'.

Although the problem of repair of major bridges was one for the county justices to try to solve, it is perhaps strange that the matter seldom seems to have been initiated in the manor courts, which could have reported to Quarter Sessions. The sole reference to an important bridge has been noted in the Springfield roll for 1576:

> They present on the information of William Hore, one of the homage, that the Stone Bridge in Springfield was formerly built at the charge of the country (*patrie*); that Richard Brewer, late of Springfield, aged 80, William's father-in-law, said to him that the bridge was built at the charge of the country, and that Richard said to him that he had heard his father say that he knew when no bridge was in that place where the bridge now existed.

This bridge, close to Chelmsford High Street, lay over the Springfield—Chelmsford boundary on the Roman road to Colchester. The 'Springfield Bridge made of timber'[6] was perhaps that over the nearby branch of the Chelmer (now filled in); Springfield Stone Bridge is not to be confused with the Stone Bridge over the Can, dividing Chelmsford and Moulsham.

This history of bridge maintenance in Elizabethan England is not an easy one to write, partly because, apart from Essex, Quarter Sessions records survive only for a few counties and for the last decade or two of the century. But the great number of manorial records now available in public custody is an almost untapped source. Admittedly, as already stated, they seldom throw much light on bridges spanning the wider rivers, most references in manor rolls concerning small structures, some only built of wood, such as that still existing at Great Easton. Typical of scores of little bridges is that mentioned in the Brook Walden roll for 1565 : 'The jurors beg that the lessee of Castle Mill, for his own convenience and for the safe passage of all his customers (*custumariorium*) frequenting his mill, make a sufficient bridge extending beyond the water leading from Brook Walden towards Duke Street and amend the causeway'. His response to this tactful approach is not recorded. Even so, there are hundreds of minor bridges all over the country to which special interest attaches.

Court rolls seldom distinguish between cartbridges and footbridges, but persons with local knowledge can often do so. Those who use the busy A106 highway through Leyton to the City cross one of the branches of the Lea by Temple Mills bridge half a mile beyond the former manor house of Ruckholts. There was no river bridge at Temple Mills until the last century—only a small one over a stream between Ruckholts and its mill. This is what the Ruckholts manor roll reveals about the local topography when Sir Henry Compton was the lord : 'Mr Tompson to make a good and convenient causeway or footpath from Ruckholt to Temple Mill and to amend the bridge in the highway; and the farmer (lessee) of Temple Mill to amend the banks between the river and the highway and to amend the highway to the mill upon pain to forfeit £10' (1576). Tompson defaulted, so his own penalty was raised from 3s. 4d. to £6 13s. 4d. (1577). Further, 'The lord shall make a sufficient bridge and footpath betwixt Temple Mill and the manor house of Ruckholts upon pain to forfeit 40s.' : a nice instance, somewhat rare, of manorial juries using democratic powers against their lord, but whether he bowed to their 'verdict' is another matter.

Somewhat unexpectedly footpaths seem to figure less frequently in manor rolls than bridges. Nearly all references to the former in the Quarter Sessions rolls recently appeared in an article by the present writer.[7]

In an interesting chapter on 'Manorial Control', a recent and scholarly local historian rightly remarks, 'The offence of unscoured ditches receives scant attention in many books which have been examined for the purpose';[8] all the more surprising as this is perhaps the commonest of all the offences which came before the manor courts. In the surviving Elizabethan court rolls for Essex there are several thousands of presentments of uncleansed ditches and drains, mostly those by the roadside. Strangely enough, however, Mr Eland overlooked what William Harrison had to say, after enduring many years of journeying about north Essex : 'Such as have land upon the sides of the ways do utterly neglect to ditch and scour their drains and watercourses, for better avoidance of the winter waters, whereby the streets do grow to be much more gulled than before and thereby very noisome for such as travel'.[9]

For most manors the records merely give the offenders, over whose names is usually noted the fine for not scouring their part of a ditch before a certain date or the next court. At Thaxted, for instance, in 1577, 12 tenants, some living in adjacent parishes, were assigned penalties of between 4d. and 4s. In some manors the approximate length of the presented ditches of each individual is also given. At Rettendon, where 6 inhabitants had each neglected 40 or 30 perches, the penalty for further neglect was set at 13s. 4d., and at Great Canfield 13 tenants were told that they would lose 4d. for each perch still uncleaned by the next court;[10] both examples belong to 1559.

Less commonly, those liable for a specific roadside watercourse or ditch were dealt with impersonally, as at Abells in Halstead in 1578, when a general order was made on 'all tenants of lands from the Chapel to the Bridge'. In 1576 'all the inhabitants of the Street of Epping' were directed 'to cleanse the ditches against their houses before the Feast of St Peter-ad-Vincula and thence from time to time, under pain of 4d. for each yard'. The Chelmsford court took an unusual decision in 1589 : 'All inhabitants who ought to contribute to the scouring of the ditch from behind the Falcon each to pay to the labourers (*operariis*) by his particular before 1st October under pain of forfeiting 10s.', which suggests that they were individually assessed towards paying a special rate. The ditch in question, which drained into the Chelmer just above Springfield Bridge, was an important one. It ran at the end of the 'backsides' of the houses on the east side of the High Street [11] and is clearly marked on Walker's map of 1591.

The countless presentments of short lengths of foul ditches or small watercourses gives a routine impression, but a few specific complaints confirm that some roads were almost impassable after heavy rain. Witness this presentment made at the court of Brook Street in South Weald in 1562, when each stretch of ditch was 'stopped up with muck, branches and other filth (*fimis, frondibus et aliis sordibus*)' : the tenants of lands in Goobards Lane, 6 perches; the tenant of the Spital (Hospital) and another, 16 in Spital Lane; the same Spital tenant, 40 next Wood Lane; another, 6 against the highway from Brentwood towards London; all of whom were enjoined to remedy the defect or forfeit 3d. a perch. Similarly, definite charges against a tenant whose ditches in 1592 were 'stopped up, by default of scouring, behind the house called the Freres in Moulsham' (a reference to the former Dominican friary), and against Thomas Parker, gentleman, owner of the advowson of Shenfield, who in 1573 had 'stopped up a watercourse in Sawers (now Sawyer's Hall) Lane in Shenfield, which is very muddy'.

The jurors of Ruckholts in Leyton were explicit in 1595 : 'The want of scouring of the ditch at Hollowell Down is the cause of the badness of the Queen's highway, wherefore it is ordered that the Right Honourable the

Countess of Derby at her charge shall scour it all alongst her grounds upon pain of 20s.'; but the countess probably took no notice. Similarly at Fingrith Hall in 1563 : 'Mr Hall hath not scoured 40 perches of ditch against Hulcroftes, wherefore he hath lost 6s. 8d.; we command him to scour' or to forfeit 4d. a perch, i.e. double the sum for further inaction.

Entries expressive of the boulder-clay mud in north Essex often appear, such as orders 'to scour on both sides of the highway in Thaxted from Cutlers Green towards Debden Vicarage against the great sloughs' (1571) or 'the ditch towards Hamling Slough' in Debden (1568). The little court of Berners Roothing in 1587 enjoined the tenant of 'Rowse' (probably Rowe's Farm just over the Willingale Doe boundary) to clean 40 perches against a very minor lane from Willingale to Good Easter, 'two spits deep'. The same depth (*in altitudine ij spittorum*) is mentioned at Purleigh in Mary's last year. A spit was a full spade-depth, about a foot.

Not quite so numerous as road ditches are orders about agricultural drains, as at Beaumont in 1559 : 'The tenants of lands in Beaumont Field to sufficiently scour 50 perches of ditch against North Field, under penalty of 2d. a perch'. Such evidence of open-field cultivation is rare in north-east Essex, whereas in the many unenclosed parishes in the north-west the courts often exercised useful control, as at Newport in 1572, when two tenants were told 'to turn the water in Holford Field into its right course as of old'. Fleam, or fleme, ditches occur occasionally and refer either to a stream or to an artificial channel or drain somewhat wider or deeper than the ordinary ditches. The word is found at Purleigh in 1578, also at Rettendon in 1563 when 'the tenants of Fowles' had to scour 15 perches of the 'fleme ditch'.

Cases of overflowing ditches yield many topographical details, e.g. '10 perches of ditch between Berden Green and Dewes Green' in 1568 (the earliest record of the latter in the standard work on place-names being 1777), or incidental references like 'the tanhouse' at Shenfield in 1582. Could an injunction to the vicar of Epping (our old delinquent, Edward Aulefer) in 1571, under pain of 3s. 4d. (which he forfeited and incurred a distress warrant), to scour his ditch against Court Maple Croft refer to the tree near which the court was originally held? By Tudor times, at any rate, manor courts are thought to have been no longer kept in the open. A rare word is found in an order of 1570 to scour a ditch from '*puteo anglice* his wayer to Lockehatch corner at Epping'. The 'town wayer', or wayour, meaning a horse-pond, lay at the west end of Maldon.[12]

We shall see in the next but one section how courts were dealing concurrently with insanitary town kennels or street drains as well as with road ditches and field drains. The aim with the first was to reduce pollution; with the others, to remove surface water. The emphasis depends largely on whether the manor was fairly populous or mainly agricultural. The pollution aspect has been cursorily considered by some writers interested in the history of Public Health administration, who have noticed what was being done several centuries before the terrible cholera and other epidemics of Victorian times. But nobody, as Mr Eland states, seems to have studied field-drainage in Tudor or medieval times. Before writing the model history of Great Canfield, he tramped over the whole parish; and his chapter on field ditches is probably the only published account by a writer who, as Professor W. G. Hoskins always urges, made himself as familiar with his terrain as with his documents. Great Canfield lies in a heavy, wet area, in which hollow-draining was imperative, and it was necessary to dig very wide and deep ditches for carrying off the water. Mr Eland gives an intriguing reference to the discovery of some 'very ancient drains' at Roxwell, not far away. 'The difficulty', he writes, 'of getting rid of surface water where the subsoil is a boulder clay must always be very great; and to-day, with pipe-drains and mole-drains, it is common to see some of the ditches mentioned in our rolls which are six feet deep or more. The very large number of cases in the rolls directly concerned with ditches, affecting the lord, the largest tenants and the smallest, certainly seems to indicate an important policy, with a common interest in its effective performance'.[13]

Drainage is a prosaic subject, but all three kinds of drains affected the lives of the people in one way or another, and there is abundant evidence of the incessant efforts made by manor courts to deal with the defects.

## Highway Obstructions

There were of course other public 'nuisances'. Of these, the commonest group concerned the highways, especially the town and village streets. Through human perverseness or carelessness, every kind of obstruction was perpetrated. Some of the obstacles were highly dangerous to road users, and while manor courts gave little thought to long-distance or even local travellers, they were mindful of their own inhabitants who might be involved in fatal accidents. The vast majority of streets were unpaved, the width of the carriageway was undefined, and after dusk there was the constant risk of falling over unseen impediments or even into open pits of one sort or another. The street or road was all too convenient for dumping discarded materials. It was a useful place, too, for storing woodstacks and other heavy or bulky goods when there was no room in house, shop or yard. So, in Essex as elsewhere, thousands of presentments are found in the manor rolls against those who had transgressed, wilfully or otherwise.

Laying timber in front of the house was a very common offence. The Chipping Walden court in 1574 modified a general order for the removal of wood and timber from the streets by adding 'unless within the eaves-drops', which refers to the narrow strip under jettied houses, so many examples of which still remain in this unspoiled town; the injunction had to be repeated more than once in later years. A Chelmsford bye-law of 1564 directed every inhabitant 'having any blocks or logs by or under the eaves of his house or before his door' to remove them or suffer a 12d. fine, and any future infringement would mean a 20d. fine. Nine years later, 'all who put tree trunks, firewood (*phocalia*) or timber in the streets in front of their houses' were to clear them away. Epping in 1561 ordered tenants who had 'woodstacks in the Street' to take them away or forfeit 3s. 4d., and a somewhat similar order was made five years later for removal of dungheaps and timber from 'Epping Street' (the High Street). A Halstead tenant was told not to 'put tree trunks in front of his door'. Narrow roadside greens have always been tempting as free storage places, and Henry Clarke, who was enjoined by the Mascalls Bury (White Roothing) court in 1575 to remove his timber 'lying on the green in the Queen's highway', was only doing what others did everywhere.

If there were piles of wood above ground, below were probably dangerous pits from which useful materials had been dug in the roadside verges. 'We find a great annoyance', the Fingrith Hall jury declared in 1563, 'at a place nigh Horse Fair Lane; therefore we require that he may be enjoined in a great pain to fill up the pit'. Two years previously he had been warned to fill in the spot 'where he digged sand in the highway', under penalty of 3s. 4d.; and he was now given a second chance or pay 20s. In 1559 Ingatestone fined a man for not railing in a gravel-pit, and others later were told to fill in sand- or clay-pits. Orders to cover in such wayside holes were in fact fairly common. Clay was dug in order to daub the wattles between the studs of timber-framed cottages, and claypits were presented, for example, on three occasions at Wethersfield. When the nuisance became too frequent a general prohibition 'not to carry away any clay or sand in any street' was issued, as at Thaxted in 1600.

At Harlow in 1582 'the potters were ordered not to dig clay in Harlow Common no nearer the highway than is assigned to them, upon pain for each pit 10s.'; and in 1596 the Chipping in Witham court told two millers named Porter and Bright to fill in pits that they had dug in the highway from Chipping Hill towards Cressing Temple or to lose 20s. in default. Each roll uses the term *argilla* (potter's clay).

Deep sawpits were also perilous. A Stebbing man, for instance, was fined 4d. for digging one in the highroad and instructed to remove it under pain of 6s. 8d.[14] Unprotected roadside wells were another hazard. At Kelvedon Hatch a tenant was commanded in 1568 to 'make his hedge next the common well'; and in 1588 John Cole was warned to repair at his own cost the common well in Wantes Lane at Newport, 'as he ought to do'. The jurors at Southchurch Hall in 1555 presented a pit in the highway against the demesne lands, 'to the peril of the Queen's people', and the inhabitants were held responsible. The 'peril' attending such pits or wells was a real one, and the Rettendon court took a grave view in 1573. The homage had presented that a servant-girl of John Joyse of Little Hayes in the parish 'by ill fortune fell into a well and was drowned'. At the next court, after a survey had been taken by 12 named tenants and the bailiff, Joyse was ordered to cover up the well, which was probably by the street rather than in his own grounds.

Yet another obstruction to free transit was overhanging trees, presentments being fairly common. At Rettendon such a tree led to the adjacent landowner being directed to cut off the branches under penalty of 5s. 'Two oaks growing in the lands called Nether House overhanging the highway, so that the inhabitants are denied convenient passage' resulted in an order at Purleigh in 1577 to cut down both trees. A tree 'overhanging the highway towards the tilekiln' at Halstead had to be felled in 1577. The Thaxted court in 1588 instructed an owner to cut down branches overhanging Cursall Lane; likewise the tenants of lands 'against the street between the Hermitage and Water Lane' and 'against lands between Horham Park gate and Cutlers Green'. Richard Sparke, gentleman, and Richard Charitye were told in 1567 to cut down their hedges overhanging Mill Lane at Newport.

It was of course a far cry from 1285, when the Statute of Westminster decreed that the verges by the sides of principal roads were to be cleared of trees that afforded lurking places for robbers. Although this Act was probably a dead letter long before Elizabethan times, very wide verges may be seen, for example, in a map of about 1600 showing the Chelmsford to Billericay highway between Temple Wood and Crondon Park pale to the south of Stock.[15] There is, however, a solitary echo of the ancient Statute at Bicknacre in Woodham Ferrers in 1553, when the lord received a 'supplication' from his tenants concerning the trees growing on each side of the highway, in which they emphasized their 'grave fear of murderers and robbers'.

A generation before Harrison became parson of Radwinter the jury of the manor of Bendysh Hall in that parish anticipated his later strictures on the deplorable condition of the roads : 'In the clay or cledgy soil', he was to write, 'they are often very deep and troublesome in the winter half'.[16] Of course they were full of sloughs and the dual cause was expressed by the Bendysh Hall tenants in 1551 : 'The Queen's highways are a nuisance because of default in scouring ditches and cutting down branches of trees at Brookes 40 perches through the default of Thomas Mountford gentleman and another tenant'. Perhaps the jurors got some satisfaction in naming Mountford, who was in fact the lord's bailiff. Other courts sought to remedy the wet state of the roads. The tenants of Roughaye (now Roffey) Hall in Harlow were ordered in 1580 to lop the trees and clean out 30 perches of ditch. In 1586 the Kelvedon Hatch court recorded : 'The occupiers of Stondon Park land shall clean ditches and cut trees, which are a nuisance to the Queen's highway'. Two years later

John Petit, gentleman, had disobeyed an order concerning his ditch at Kelvedon Hatch gate and trees overhanging the highway, so he paid up at 4d. a perch, which came to 3s.

Deep pools of stagnant water or thick mud in the roads were indeed common impediments to traffic, except where the streets were paved or cobbled. 'A very miry slough' into which Christian and Pliable 'did suddenly fall; here they wallowed for a time, being grievously bedaubed with dirt' : Bunyan's description of the Slough of Despond applied with equal force in the preceding century. 'Foul and miry sloughs' are among many vivid epithets found in the Essex Quarter Sessions rolls.[17] Roadside hazards called 'the slough', which occur in most manors, as already noticed at Debden and at Blunts Hall Green in Witham in 1575, indicate their permanent nature in the winter, and the counterparts of Bunyan's Bedfordshire sloughs have been perpetuated in Foulslough Farm and other places in north Essex.

Diverting surface water from one's land into the road was a ubiquitous temptation which had to be suppressed. An order to a Wethersfield tenant 'to stop water flowing into the highway' and a counter-diversion order in 1568 to that stubborn man John Baker at Epping to 'turn his gutter in the lands called Trowles now running in Grove Croft Lane to the nuisance of the inhabitants' (he forfeited his penalty) have parallels in other courts. A massive dunghill 'which stoppeth the water running towards Dame Bridge' at Blackmore tells of another kind of obstacle.

At Moulsham in 1599 a tenant forfeited 6s. 8d. because he had 'not made a better and longer wholve (*hulvam*) for passing the water course towards his barn near Moulsham Cross'. Although 'wholve' is accorded, in the form of 'hulve', only a single quotation (as late as 1764) in the *O.E.D.*, it is found in scores of Essex rolls, from at least as early as 1421 (at Great Waltham).[18] As a cheap contrivance, a tree-trunk, hollowed out, served many a farmer as a simple drainpipe under a field-track or road, especially under a gateway; but nobody knew how to spell it, so stewards did their best with hulve, wholve, and occasionally wolf ! Let two stewards supply their own definitions : 'The tenants of Little Mill Field are ordered to put a wholve there, by which the water can be conveyed from the ditch there' (Mascallsbury in White Roothing, 1572); and two tenants were warned 'to lay a sufficient wholve in the lane from Bumpstead to Aveley' (the road from Upminster), 'so as the water may have free passage there, as of right it ought to have' (Belhus in Aveley, 1594). Typical orders are those 'to put a wholffe in the north part of Ardeleys Lane' (East Mersea, 1561); 'to make a sufficient wholve in the Common Field' (Harlow, 1577); 'to put a wholve in the Queen's highway from Canewdon Street towards Crixsey Ferry against Wood's Corner' (Canewdon, 1589); to the inhabitants to make '*gurgitem anglice* the hulve in Graves Lane' (Berners Roothing, 1583).

Two tenants at Chipping Walden in 1583-84 were enjoined 'to stop up the gutter of a whelm, a nuisance to the highway', and a third, to 'make a water whelm or trunk so that the Queen's lieges may cross with carts and horses'. A whelm, for which the *O.E.D.* has quotations from 1576, was a synonym for wholve. A direction at the Ruckholt in Leyton court in 1587 to 'make a through for conveyance of water out of the highway into his ditch' exemplifies a further dialect, and self-explanatory, term.

## *Public Health*

The squeamish reader may be wise to pass over this section! But, if he does so, he will not be able to appreciate a remarkable aspect of Elizabethan life mirrored in manor court rolls. Should he read it, however, and is then avid for even stronger word-pictures, he could find ample further material by examining borough records.

In the first volume we pointed out that 'Merrie England' originally referred to its being a pleasant, not mirthful, land to live in. The splendid achievements of Englishmen in the realms of exploration, music and drama earned for their country the retrospective epithet of the Golden Age. We have already seen in Volumes I and II other concepts. Few facets will be less merry or golden than those which we now observe from the unbiased language of the Essex manor courts. With the aid of these archives, but without having to bear the awful stench, we may inspect the town dung-heaps and the common kennels, even the unauthorized urinals; we may look closely at people's mixens, or cesspits; and we may peer into their privies, 'houses of easement', or 'jakes' (the one honest non-euphemism for such necessary places). It is a disagreeable picture, but this part of the Elizabethan canvas is faithfully painted.

We first visit Ingatestone. Its High Street formed part of the old Roman road through which passed droves of cattle and livestock destined for the London food markets as well as horse and cart traffic. In a few seconds we may make a 40-year survey of typical scenes in its insanitary streets.

### *Orders made at Ingatestone Manor Court*
- 1559 non-repair of common gutter between houses
- 1562 general order to scour the common gutter
- 1562 tenant to re-site his jakes
- 1562 general order forbidding the placing of dead pigs, dogs or other carcase on any public way, lane or other place
- 1564 inhabitant to remove a dunghill and not to put dung or gore of slaughtered animals on highway, not to block up the common gutter, nor to cause evil and stinking odours
- 1564 general order forbidding tenants to erect jakes above the common gutter which runs under their houses and to remove jakes so that it is not stopped up and harmful stenches not emitted

PUBLIC HEALTH                                                              291

   1565  general order to clean the common gutter and the sinks (drains) and to
         remove privies erected over it (for details, see below)
   1565  tenant to remove a dunghill from a lane
   1566  similar order to another tenant
   1567  tenant to remove a dead pig lying in a ditch
   1569  6 tenants not to permit the filth of jakes to run into the gutter under
         their houses but to attend to the gutter
   1573  general order not to throw dung in the Square or in the lane to Stock
   1574  2 inhabitants to remove dung from highway
   1584  inhabitant to remove his privy
   1591  inhabitant to remove dung in the highway
   1596  similar order to another inhabitant
   1596  16 tenants to scour their gutters in the Square in front of their houses
         (repeated, 1597)
   1598  8 inhabitants to scour, mend and keep their gutters so as not to be a
         nuisance to others
   1598  inhabitant to remove dung and dirt in front of his tenement
   1601  3 tenants to scour their gutters (repeated, 1602)

From this brief chronological summary it is clear that the outstanding problem lay with the main street drain, the 'common gutter', and the drain in the Square. The former gutter got blocked up. When such a drain or stream ran in the open street, as also in some other towns and villages, the garbage and filth could easily be removed and the blockage cleared. But the course of that at Ingatestone ran underneath some of the buildings, and more than one inhabitant had been tempted to turn his privy into it, creating trouble. The summary omits the most interesting part of the general order of 1565, which had been necessitated 'as it has proved impossible to establish where or by whose fault the gutter is stopped up'. In consequence, several inhabitants were nominated as clerks to superintend what was to be done and to inform the steward at the next court of any defaulters. But, by 1569, at least 6 householders were in disgrace for the same offence. Similar presentments recurred near the end of the reign; and in 1598 3 tenants were also ordered to make 'grates' over their drains.

The nuisance in the Square refers to the gutter in front of each building. The repetition of the precept to 16 culprits in successive years suggests that every occupier facing it was at fault and that this was the number of houses and shops on the two sides at right angles to the High Street. The north-west side of the latter lay in the parish and manor of Fryerning, whose steward collected a 6s. 8d. forfeiture from a tenant for disobeying an order about his privy. It is ironical that, about the time when the Ingatestone court was confronted with the menace of jakes sited over the common gutter, Thomas Larke was writing his laudatory account of how Dr William Petre, 20 years earlier, had tackled the problem at his new house, Ingatestone Hall, and had produced one of the most modern systems in the country. It embraced, not only underground drainage and sanitary arrangements for the 'houses of office', but also surface-water drains and drinking-water taps; there was apparently even a combined inspection and flushing vent-hole.[19]

The rolls of Chipping Walden afford another good account of sanitary provisions. The chief efforts were concentrated on the Slade, the southern brook coming down from Sewards End and running through the town. Into the Slade some inhabitants flung their garbage. In 1574 a general order was passed that none should 'throw filth in the river at time of flood, so that it is carried into the Slade'; next year 4 tenants were presented for 'annoying others with their excrement and privies by allowing the river to carry away the filth into the Slade'; in 1576 a further order, against 'annoying the watercourse called the Slade with filth'; and in 1590 a townsman had to remove a pile of ordure and others were enjoined to cover up the privies of their houses there. From time to time the inhabitants were enjoined to scour their sewers, privies or 'sinks', to open, remove, or stop up their gutters or sinks; to 'make a sink to receive dirt and filth arising in a tenement'; or to 'remedy foul water and corrupt matter' issuing from a house. Another precept in 1583 forbade them to allow water from 'cisterns' to flow into a pond. A few more directions to individual tenants having offensive drains show slight variations in language, and the lack of uniformity in the entries confirms the impression that persistent vigilance was exercised in the efforts to suppress insanitary conditions, though it is impossible to gauge the actual effect. In 1577, for instance, a man was ordered to 'stop up his gutter along which foul water runs to the annoyance of his neighbours', and another to 'make his gutter wider so that the filth can better escape'.

The state of the Walden streets is illustrated by the many presentments for allowing dung to lie about and the equally numerous orders to remove it. Matters evidently reached a head in 1575, when a bye-law was issued against 'excrement and filth in the streets', to which the homage added a rider in language rarely found in manor rolls: 'a very great nuisance daily growing'. Despite this, similar orders to householders to remove dung from the street were given in 1576, 1580 and 1590. An intriguing order in 1573 obliged 6 tenants to 'clean up the Northeast gate and not to annoy it again'; but, as Walden had no town walls, it must refer to a wooden gate, doubtless to prevent animals from straying from the common fields into the streets at this point. In adjacent rural manor of Brook Walden 'certain women have annoyed the watercourse with filth' (1559), so the bailiff was ordered to warn them that any repetition would cost them a groat.

The product which gave Walden its distinctive prefix had its nuisance element. A decree in 1574, re-iterated in 1583, prohibited growers from 'throwing saffron flowers within 20 perches of the town except on their own enclosed land'; and another in 1575 against 'throwing of saffron flowers and other rubbish into the river in time of flood so that it is carried into the Slade'. The penalty on conviction was to be two days and nights in the stocks, the severity of which is a criterion of the extent of the pollution.

Through the main street of Chelmsford ran another small watercourse or 'common gutter'. The first of the bye-laws made at the Chelmsford (Bishop's Hall) court in 1564 ordained that 'every inhabitant from Roger Webbe's house to Colchester Lane, should clean the part in front of his house once a month' or be fined 12d. The rolls are then silent until 1591, when it was required that 'all the inhabitants on both sides of the street from the fence (or pale) of widow Clarke to the end of Colchester Lane' should scour the gutter 'from time to time hereafter as is necessary as they were wont to do'; defaulters would pay 3s. 4d. In the following year a repeat of this order refers to *'contributores* according to a rate made', and defaulters were to forfeit 12d. for each offence, the money to be levied on their goods. The Latin word and 'rate' seem to indicate an actual payment based on an assessment; if so, one may guess that Mildmay, one of the leading Essex justices, was behind this *ad hoc* innovation.

The unhygienic state of the market cross was brought to the attention of the court in 1571. The inhabitants were ordered to desist from treating it as an open latrine; any servant or apprentice caught in the act would be whipped. In 1574 an injunction was made that 'no inhabitants near the cross throw any filth near the cross' on pain of 12d. Somewhere in the town, probably behind the main street, lay the common dungheap or dungpit (*commune sterquilinium*), and in 1598 several tenants were forbidden to throw their 'stable dung' on to it.

Across the river, and also in the parish of Chelmsford, lay Mildmay's other manor of Moulsham. This court recorded in 1559 that 7 named tenants 'and their servants have divers times annoyed the occupiers of the house, late the Friary, both in making within the gate of the house their common mixens (*fimarios*), in consequence of which the air there is infectious and corrupt'. Any future error would cost them 12d. The estreat roll for Moulsham, under 1594, anticipating Hogarth, adds the contents of 'chamber pots' to the filthy street scene!

The records of Halstead (manor of Abells) yield similar evidence, which leaves little to the imagination. In addition to the usual reports about the watercourse in the town street being contaminated by privies standing over it and so forth, the court decreed in 1578 a fine on any inhabitants 'between John Buntynge's tenement and the bridge who henceforth threw filth or any strange thing (*rem absurdum,* a novel Latin euphemism) into their gutters or made ordure in them'. Next year John Harrye, shearman, who lived near Townford Mill cast 'filth, slud and puddle before his door in the street or into the water there'. 'Dead dogs or carcases and other filth' thrown into the river were the subject of a presentment which led, as so often elsewhere, to a general prohibition, in this case bearing a 3s. 4d. penalty. Orders forbidding owners of pigs to let them wander in the streets are often found, but the Halstead court went farther in 1581 in warning them 'not to suffer their hogs to go at large in the streets, whereby they do defile the brook and watercourse'.

The townsmen of Thaxted in 1577 were told to remove 'le myre' in Newbiggin Street (the road to Walden) against the vicar's house, also those in 'Newbiggin' who had any gates 'beyond le Lane towards Pigs Fields no more shall put any filth on the backsides'. In 1601 it was again ordered that 'all inhabitants carry away their ordure' from the backsides of their houses. In the previous year several tenants who had not removed their nuisances pleaded inability owing to floods and heavy rain and were enjoined to do so before Pentecost.

Privies and cesspits gave trouble in every town. At Witham between 1587 and 1593 Edward Hales, gentleman, was ordered to cleanse his 'sink' running from his house into the market place (*plateam*) and other privies were to be 'enclosed' or one 'lately built over the ditch' of neighbouring tenants to be removed. The last nuisance was likewise to be suppressed at Aveley in 1591. At Dunmow in 1577 a householder who had not made '*puteum suam anglice* his close sink in his backside' was fined 2s. 6d. A privy, at any rate, was better sited in the backyard than a 'wardrobe hanging' from the upper storey of another Dunmow house two centuries earlier:[20] a rare reference to an ordinary dwelling having a garde-robe, which is usually associated with castles. The Great Burstead court in 1590 censured those who 'cast their pits into the spring'. It had passed a very unusual decree in 1573 : 'All who dwell on South Green shall put *stolas suas anglice* their washing stools in an appropriate place there viz. so that their filthy water does not run into *magnum rivum anglice* the flood ditch'. At Harlow Bury a bye-law was issued in 1580 that none 'henceforth shall wash their bucks and clothes in Harlow Market by the well there'. 'Bucks', a rare word, were 'washing tubs in which to steep clothes in lye'.[21]

The Epping inhabitants in 1584 and 1593 were warned not to cast filth in the Back Street nor to put any ordure on the path from the town to the parish church—the ancient church at Epping Upland—under penalties of 3s. 4d. and 6d. respectively. The refractory John Baker was amerced 8d. in 1568 for throwing a dead pig into the highway; and another tenant had to 'make a ditch to cleanse *fedum anglice* his sink'. The common town gutter, or 'kennel', also gave rise to complaints. In 1577 11 inhabitants were commanded to 'gravel from the front of their houses to the kennel', under the harsh threat of a 20s. fine; in 1581 another had to clean his kennel or pay 2d. and yet another to cover his kennel by the highway or lose 3s. 4d. Six years afterwards three men were to cleanse the kennel 'running from the pump against their tenement' or risk forfeiting 4d. for each yard 'unmade', also to cleanse it every month under a similar penalty. In 1589 this was trebled and the order extended to 'all the inhabitants from the upper end of the market house on both sides of the highway'. Dunghills, too, must have been lying everywhere in the High Street, despite the frequent removal orders accompanied by a 5s. threat.

In 1588 the Great Burstead court also tried to deal with the dung heaps: 'If any inhabitant of Billericay or Burstead shall make any dung hill in the market-place or in Church Street, and allow it to remain for more than one month, he shall forfeit for each dung hill 3s. 4d.'; and in 1590 two tenants were told to clear away their dunghills 'behind the chapel' (the ancient chapel-of-ease in Billericay High Street). Sanitary regulations in two other towns may be quoted. Great Dunmow was created a borough in 1555, though it remained a Duchy of Lancaster manor. The corporation's bye-laws, drawn up in 1571, contain the provision: 'Every householder shall cause the street before his door to be made clean quarterly on pain to lose 3s. 4d.'[22] While unsavoury conditions were naturally most prevalent in the larger market towns, some of the villages were by no means free. At Wethersfield and Tollesbury, for instance, presentments about dung and other filth put on the streets are found. The rector of Debden, one 'Hoddunsdon' (instituted as Richard Hodson) was accused in 1587 of having a privy that polluted the 'common stream' and annoyed the lessee of the manor. He was instructed to remove it within 10 days or forfeit 10s. The interesting bye-laws of Dedham include two anti-pollution clauses against beavers and washerwomen endangering the drinking water, as described later in the chapter on Custumals. A tenant of the manor of Mascallsbury in White Roothing in 1559 had to remove 'his house of easement or house of office to the great nuisance of all others' on pain of 12d; having neglected to do so, his penalty was doubled. But Stock seems to have been little bothered with unhygienic conditions. The rolls of this active court show only one complaint, 5 men being admonished in 1585 to take away 'heaps of mud and compost' from one of the roads in the village.[23] At Great Canfield, too, the few nuisances were restricted to manure heaps on the roads.[24]

Thus, without salaried sanitary inspectors, inspectors of nuisances and similar officials rarely appointed before Victorian times, some Elizabethan manor courts grappled in a ceaseless struggle with the problems of foul drainage and filthy dumps.

Another kind of nuisance over which manor courts exercised some control concerned offensive trades, for instance, as seen earlier, in the general prohibition at Ingatestone against discarding carcases. Butchers, again, were the chief culprits, and their habit of throwing offal into the street, or clandestinely at night into a stream, is referred to in the rolls of most urban manors. At Walden in 1575 a tenant was warned not to allow anyone to slaughter in his own house or curtilage except for his own use.

One of the Chelmsford ordinances of 1564 forbade townsmen to slaughter in their own houses 'to the annoyance of their neighbours', with the stiff penalty of 20s. A parallel is found in the Dunmow borough bye-laws of 1571, which commanded butchers 'to carry their gore and entrails of their slaughter houses into some place convenient out of the town where it may less annoy', under a 3s. 4d. penalty. The same Chelmsford bye-laws proclaimed that 'neither the butchers nor any other person at any time hereafter shall cast any horns, bones or any other filth in the street or the river'; and in 1575 they were again cautioned against throwing entrails into the street. In 1574 the court came down sharply on Thomas Taylor, who was threatened with a weekly fine of 6s. 8d. unless he 'no more annoy the inhabitants dwelling about his tenement with butchers killing in his yards, neither with his excessive number of swine or by the preserving of paunches and entrails of beasts for the feeding of them'.

At Epping in 1591 a tenant, doubtless a butcher, was ordered not to 'hang any carrion in Lyme Street'. A South Ockendon butcher was reported in 1561 for casting rotten meat and *alia excrementa* into the streets. In 1577 Thaxted court ordered that neither a certain butcher nor any of his neighbours in future should 'put their guts nor dead flesh under the church wall'; and a butcher who 'threw gore or garbage' on the roads at Wethersfield was presented more than once.

There were also those engaged in the malodorous manufacture of leather. At Wethersfield tanners were reported almost every year, and tawers, who prepared white leather, now and again. At Epping (1583) a tenant had to cease depositing his skins in the pond; and an almost identical order at Canewdon (1591) refers to skins put in a roadside pond. A glover was among 8 Thaxted men (1571) who had dumped rubbish in Mill Lane (all fined 12d.); and a Chelmsford glover (1594) had to fill in his limepits and to remove his 'drench tub belonging to his craft, being a nuisance to his neighbours' (40s.).

Two Epping men (1582) were ordered, 'on the suitors' verdict', to 'stop up the sawpits behind their tenements which were a nuisance to their neighbours', presumably on account of the dust. It was evidently a fishmonger there who was enjoined (1591) 'henceforth to keep the Queen's highway clean from fish water'. To ensure a clean street after the Friday market, rather than to care for the inhabitants' health, was probably the aim of an order at Chelmsford (1596): 'Each owner of the fishstalls to wash them out each week before noon on Saturday'; and an estreat roll of the same manor (1574) refers to a forfeiture of 8d. to be levied on fishmongers who, between the Feasts of the Annunciation and St Michael in any year, 'cast out their fish water at their stalls in the fish market'. The Halstead court (1581) commanded 'everyone that shall set up any stalls in the street for any chapman shall immediately after the market or fairs cleanse the place of straw or suchlike'.

Though slightly beyond our period, references to the important pottery industry at Stock are too valuable to be left out. In 1607 an 'offensive' act obliged the court to direct William Hankyn to 'remove outside the streets all refuse, dung, clay and other things of that kind, which he by reason of his art of pottery-making cast out, raised up all around and heaped up in the same'.[25] We have already seen (under Crafts) how the kiln was bequeathed to him by his father.

The question arises, in connection with nuisances generally—on whose initiative were these attempted reforms made? Some offences were clearly presented by neighbours annoyed by stench or other unpleasant conditions. But the fact that general orders for prohibiting or removing certain nuisances were often issued immediately after a specific charge suggests that in some manors the lord or his steward, personally angered or inconvenienced, arranged for a reliable tenant to report the worst offender. A more interesting enquiry concerns the degree of success resulting from suppression decrees. While penalties imposed on individuals were usually effective, some offenders who disobeyed forfeited the penalty, while others were threatened at the next court with double or much higher fines. In a few manors it is possible to recognize one or two tenants whose intransigence led to frequent presentments for the same or similar offences of this nature: a not uncommon feature of the much later sanitary inspectors' reports. Examination of the selected Essex rolls gives the impression that the courts brought about a fair amount of improvement. It would seem that manors in which recorded nuisances were numerous were not necessarily those in which unhealthy conditions were the worst, but rather that the number is a criterion of the efforts to reform them. There appears to be a link between the stern attitude or control evidenced in certain manors and their being owned by lords actively engaged in central or local administration. The lord who was also a government official, a member of parliament or a leading J.P. was more inclined to redress nuisances in his own domain than one with little experience. The unusual steps taken in Mildmay's manor of Chelmsford for cleansing watercourses is a case in point. It is evident, at any rate, that such courts in Elizabethan times were exercising functions, much later to be known as Public Health, three centuries before the creation of Urban and Rural Sanitary Authorities and Local Boards of Health. But, owing to historians' infrequent use of Tudor manorial archives until quite recently, little specific information on this vital aspect of social life has appeared in print. Credit may be given to many courts for coping, in diverse and elementary fashion, with the multifarious problems of public health, of which another aspect will be seen in the next chapter.

[1] Eland, *op. cit.*, 45.
[2] *E.L.: Disorder*, 6-7, 19-26, 37; see also p. 148 *supra*.

[3] Map of Essex by Chapman and André (1777).
[4] Newcourt, *op. cit.*, ii, 310.   [5] *Essex Place-Names*, 37.
[6] *E.L.: Disorder*, 20, 25, 36.
[7] 'Elizabethan Footpaths and Footbridges' (*Essex Journal*, viii, 119-24).
[8] Eland, *op. cit.*, 39.   [9] Harrison, *op. cit.*, 443.
[10] Eland, *op. cit.*, 42.
[11] Miss Hilda Grieve kindly confirmed the course.
[12] See Mr W. J. Petchey's reconstruction map of late medieval Maldon in *Towns of Essex* (E.R.O. Publn. no. 57).
[13] Eland, *op. cit.*, 43.
[14] *Ess. Rev.*, xliv, 61.
[15] Reproduced in K. C. Newton, *A History of the Highways and Byways of Essex* (E.R.O. Publn. no. 48).
[16] Harrison, *op. cit.*, 443; also 424, where he states that the 'lordship of Bendysh Hall (is) now worn out of knowledge and united partly to Radwinter and partly to Ashdon'; but the E.R.O. has a rental of the manor in 1605.
[17] *E.L.: Disorder*, 18-19.   [18] *Ess. Rev.*, xv, 211.
[19] Emmison, *Tudor Secretary*, 36-38.
[20] *Ess. Rev.*, xlix, 157.
[21] *O.E.D.*, in which this definition, now confirmed, is queried in connection with a single quotation of 1530.
[22] E.R.O., D/B 1/1; *Ess. Rev.*, xxviii, 169.
[23] Austen, *op. cit.*, 81.   [24] Eland, *op. cit.*, 41.   [25] Austen, *op. cit.*, 83.

# 19
# Control of Trade
*Prices, Markets, and the Assizes of Commodities*

In Part 2 we saw how Quarter Sessions dealt with various offences coming under the heading of 'breaking the assize'. They also figured very frequently in the manor courts. From its first enactment in 1266 the 'Assize of Bread and Ale' had attempted to regulate the cost of staple victuals according to the prevailing price of wheat and malt; and such 'assize' control was extended to other commodities such as fuel. Enforcement of the assize by manorial courts was generally in the hands of the aletasters and other 'searchers of victuals', though in some manors possessing markets it was in the hands of the clerk of the market, acting as deputy for the lord. Assize jurisdiction also included vigilance over the quality of provisions. Prices were adjusted by altering the weight or measure of bread, ale and the like upwards or downwards (generally the latter, because of the depreciation in money values during Elizabeth's time), rather than raising the price; in other words, a variable amount of loaf-bread or ale would be bought for a penny.

The Abells (Halstead) court in 1589 fined four men for selling ale 'above the price of 2d. for the jug (*lagena*)', which was probably a two-quart jug or tankard; in 1600 an Aveley man was amerced 2s. for 'not selling a quart of beer for 1d.'; and a Purleigh man in 1591 was fined 12d. for selling ale 'excessively' at 1d. a quart, with 10s. for a second offence. A few months after Elizabeth's death the Act of 1 James, c. 9, obliged alehousekeepers to sell not less than a full ale quart of best ale or beer for 1d., and small beer at 2 quarts for 1d. At the beginning of her reign strong ale had been half the price, as witness an interesting entry from the estreat roll of Colne Priory manor in 1559 : 'Inhabitants who sell ale shall sell out of their houses one thyrkyndell for ½d. and in their houses one quart for ½d.', under pain of 3s. 4d.' A thirdendeal was reckoned as three pints : so 'off-licence' ale at Earls Colne was cheaper ! The order evidently followed on the presentment of three tenants for 'refusing to sell beer out of their houses for 1½d. the gallon and 2d. the gallon in their houses', each being fined 6d. At Wanstead in 1561 victuallers were enjoined to sell their ale at ½d. a quart under penalty. A Billericay baker, selling his bread at Aveley market, was presented in 1583 because he 'doth make bread not according to the assize, and also unwholesome to be eaten; therefore he is ordered to make according to the rate of 20s. a quarter and to amend his size (assize) before the last day of the present month, upon pain of £3'. But the Aveley court summoned him on later occasions, as in 1594, when his fine was 10s. with a double penalty for a further offence.[1] The anonymous compiler of the Aveley survey culled the following entries from the rolls : 'Bakers amerced 3s. 4d. apiece for making 3d. loaves'; 'one amerced 2s. for not selling of a quart of beer for 1d.' (1600); also an order that 'the alehousekeepers should sell no beer but by the pewter quart pot'. The Chelmsford court decreed in 1600 : 'No brewers of ale shall brew any ale to sell it either within their doors or without (except) such as shall be willing to afford all buyers a full quart for 1d.'.[2]

So routine a matter, in fact, were these offences that the stock phrase is merely 'broke the assize', from which it is not always known whether excessive price or insufficient measure is implied, though the former is the more probable, as at Ingatestone, and some other manors, where victuallers, innholders, butchers and bakers regularly broke the assize by overcharging. As in other ways, butchers earned a good deal of discredit. At Wethersfield, in fact, the majority of the sessions saw one or more butchers presented for overcharging, for selling unwholesome meat, or for both.

Many millers, like some in later generations, were equally dishonest or rapacious, and reports of their 'taking excessive toll' for grinding corn abound in court rolls, furnishing incidentally a partial millers' directory. At Chelmsford, which boasted of several watermills, four avaricious millers, Robert Ronde, Thomas Durrant, Thomas Griffin and Richard Wells, were fined 12d. in 1581; at Wethersfield Christopher Grove and Robert Goodfellow, the millers, were fined 6d. or 8d., court after court; and in a few other places the miller paid 12d. for extortionate toll of his neighbours' flour nearly every year. In these manors it was in effect an informal annual licence fee. But Bulphan court in 1577 threatened a 10s. forfeiture 'if any miller take excessive toll'. An unusually specific charge was laid at Rettendon in 1594 against Alexander Watson, windmiller, for 'taking excessive unlawful toll, viz. John Hull for 1 bushel of wheat, 8 lb., and from Josuah Thornton for 1 bushel, 10 lb. and for 2 bushels, 1 peck', for which the homage amerced him 20s. The proportion of flour or grain taken by millers as toll varied from manor to manor. Fishmongers, too, though less often, were cited for overcharging.

In 1573 the Chelmsford court accused 5 innholders of making improper gain in the sale of horse-bread and hay. In 1577 no less than 12 unlicensed leather-tanners had sold in the market at excessive profit. Several tallow-chandlers had retailed their tallow or wax candles too dearly, John Munke being presented in 1574, 1579, 1582, 1583 and 1599. The operations at Newport against poor craftsmanship, of which more anon, were combined with an attack against Thomas Cole, brewer and baker,

William Bordells, draper, and 4 butchers for profiteering. Action was apparently taken more than once at Halstead. In 1577 a double charge of excessive profit and breach of the assize was levied against 2 innholders, 4 bakers, 5 tipplers (victuallers), 3 white-tawyers, 4 tanners, 4 butchers, and 3 brewers; but they were all fined a mere 2d., the steward entering in the margin, 'Divers delinquents in their trades'. At Chipping Walden court in 1592 15 bakers, brewers and butchers were mulcted between 2d. and 6d. for the same dual offence.

Some manors had the oversight, by prescription or charter, of weights and measures: an important function, but usually restricted to those having markets. Courts leet with this right were charged to enquire 'if any have and use any measures of bushels, gallons, yards or ells, or false balances or pounds'.[3] The general impression gained from manor court rolls is that regulations against false measures were enforced. It was presented at Chelmsford in 1564 that the manor lacked a market bushel. At Thaxted in 1575, search in the ancient rolls produced an order of 1520 that 'nobody within the manor shall buy or sell with a bushel unless it be sealed with the king's seal'. The most frequent charge was in fact that of using unsealed measures or deficient weights or measures, and the commonest delinquents were sellers of liquor, including occasional alewives. Alehouse-keepers were under a statutory obligation to sell only by sealed quart pots. No less than 18 sold ale at Chelmsford in unsealed measures in 1578 and had to pay between 4d. and 12d. At Great Burstead 6 'tipplers of ale' were fined 2d. each in 1560 for selling by short weight, and 10 paid 3d. in 1585 for selling ale in bowls and cups (*discos et sciphos*) and not in sealed measures; 10 at Harlow who sold in unsealed measures forfeited 12d. in 1563; and 10 Dunmow innholders were fined in 1579 for unlawful weights and measures.

Occasionally wholesalers also were guilty of dealing in illegal containers. Chelmsford brewers in 1598 were threatened with a 20s. fine: 'Those which keep tuns and brew beer in their houses and sell it out by the vessel shall sell no more by the vessel'. Bakers, too, did not abstain from dishonesty, as at Witham in 1592, when a tenant was caught for selling lightweight bread. Three dealers from Tilbury, Upminster and Stifford selling butter 'wanting weight' at Aveley were fined 6s. 8d. each in 1598. In 1567 at Fingrith in Blackmore the entry was in general terms, 'to see good order for weights and measures'.

Excessive prices and light weight are both exemplified in the following extracts from one of several estreat rolls of fines levied at the court of the clerk of the market[4] for Sir Thomas Mildmay, 'lord of the manor of Chelmsford with the hamlet of Moulsham', in 1583.

*Fines at Chelmsford manor (market) court, 1583*
William Rogers is a common baker and hath broken the assize in his penny white loaf 3 oz., and kept a common inn or hostelry and taketh therein

excessive gain as well in his bread, beer and other victuals for man as in hay and bread for the horses, amerced at 13s. 4d.

John Muncke is a common baker and his penny white loaf wanteth weight 3 oz., and besides he useth the mistery of common chandler and selleth his lights at excessive prices, and further useth tippling in his house in form of a common inn for man and horse and taketh excessive gain, amerced at 5s.

William Perry butcher for using one weight called a pound weight unsealed or unallowed, amerced at 3s. 4d.

Ellis Backouse for that his pound weight is too light by the standard above the weight of 16d. of silver, amerced at 3s. 4d.

Walter Baker is a common beerbrewer and uttereth the same at great excessive prices to the great impoverishing of the Queen's Majesty's subjects, viz. his barrel [5] of double beer at 6s. 8d. and his barrel of small beer 4s., and greatly breaketh the assize, and concealeth in his house one measure called a bushel and not brought to the trial and correction of the officer, neither presented himself at this court as he ought, amerced at £5.

Robert Platt is a common vintner and selleth French wines, Rochelle wines and other hedge wines after the rate of 2s. the gallon and other sweet wines after the rate of 3s. 4d. the gallon and useth of the said wines to the great hurt of her Majesty's subjects, and also selleth cakes wherein he gaineth above 10s. in a bushel of wheat baking, amerced at £5.

Thomas Griffin miller for using one false measure called a toll dish far exceeding the standard, amerced at 6s. 8d.

It is commanded to all common bakers that every of them from henceforth do usually bake halfpenny white bread and penny wheaten bread and no bread of odd sizes, on pain to forfeit to our sovereign Lady the Queen for every offence 40s.

This estreat roll names in all 25 offenders (18 for the manor of Chelmsford, 7 for Moulsham), several of whom were fined for more than one weights or measures offence.

It is not easy to assess the actual effect of the innumerable presentments for breaking the Assize. One gets an overall impression that it was being enforced—severely so at Chelmsford. But Harrison's strictures give a different picture. 'In most of these markets', he wrote, 'neither assizes of bread nor orders for goodness and sweetness of grain and other commodities that are brought thither to be sold are any whit looked unto, but each one suffered to sell or set up what and how himself listeth, and this is one evident cause of dearth and scarcity in time of great abundance.'[6] In some manors the fines were apparently little more than a permanent, if minor, source of court income. Although more than 30 brewers and regrators of ale and up to 10 bakers might be presented for breach at any one of the three courts held each year for taking the assize, the monotonous regularity with which the same names occur compels the conclusion that the amercements varying from 1d. to 1s. were regarded by the offenders as payment for licence to continue as before. Much the same applies to tanners who sold badly tanned leather at excessive prices and to the two millers who used unsealed measures, as we shall see shortly, at Chelmsford manor (market) court in 1583. Perhaps the best criterion of the courts' attitude is the amount of the fine or penalty : an offender fined or pained 2s. or more would probably realize that it might be wise to amend his ways. Thus, the courts served a useful, if limited, means of protecting the consumer in Elizabethan times, shortly before the more serious trade offences came under the control of the justices of the peace and long before the appointment of paid weights and measures and shops inspectors. We may be near the truth if we suggest that the degree of enforcement depended largely on whether the manor court was actively controlled by the lord or his steward, as was the case of the twin manors of Chelmsford and Moulsham, which functioned so vigorously.

Among the important privileges possessed by some lords of manors was the right to hold a weekly market and one or more annual fairs. Over thirty Essex manors had markets of ancient origin, mostly created by Crown grants. New market charters superseding those of medieval date were secured by the lords of Waltham Abbey (1553 and 1560), Halstead (1562), and Epping (1575). Active markets provided them with a regular and substantial income, but decadence had already set in or the markets had ceased to function at Horndon-on-the-Hill, Woodham Ferrers and Aveley by about the end of the century. Horndon wool market was not operating by 1594, but the court roll records the purchase of 'three butchers' stalls' in 1601.

Bye-laws, orders and other regulations concerning markets are found in the rolls of most urban manors. Examples have already been quoted. In 1573 the Great Burstead court, which controlled Billericay market, ordained that all corn and flour dealers must 'sell publicly in the market and not elsewhere', under pain of 12d. for each bushel; and in 1582 a miller was warned under pain of 6s. 8d. to sell his flour at the market cross (*in cruce mercati*) of Burstead manor, perhaps an otherwise unrecorded mention of that of Billericay. Halstead in 1585 forbade any artificer to set up stalls in the market-house 'to the nuisance of sellers of victuals'. At Epping in 1582 a shoemaker was told to remove into his house on market days his stalls in front of it or in the market. Next year all having 'removable stalls in Epping (High) Street' were instructed to carry them away at the finish of the market or on the following Sunday, to stop their being a nuisance to the inhabitants. Movable stalls in Chelmsford market-place are referred to several times, as well as temporary and fixed stalls (*mobile sive immobile*) in the fish-market, the leather-stalls and the salt-bin, also the Potters Row and the Shop Row. These stalls, as in many other English market-places, later became 'islands' of permanent shops. The roof of the 'great cross called the Market Cross' at Chelmsford was reported to be ruinous in 1564. This open market-house, in which Quarter Sessions and sometimes Assizes were held, is now well known from the drawing on John Walker's map of 1591.[7] The only surviving Elizabethan

Essex market-house is that of Horndon-on-the-Hill. The ancient 'court house' of Barking manor was destroyed in 1926.[8] The Great Burstead court in 1573 also decided that 'all persons who henceforth buy and sell butter in the market before the ringing of the bell' should forfeit 5s. Aveley market, too, was opened by bell, but dealers from Kent had to wait for the second bell. Elsewhere there are occasional names of outside traders, but court rolls provide only meagre evidence of a market town's zone of influence in this way.[9] A recent writer doubted 'the oft-quoted assertion that a market town (in Tudor and Stuart times) could draw trade only from the countryside within a day's return journey on foot, a distance variously estimated at from five to eight miles'.[10] The Essex rolls indicate a somewhat larger hinterland. Even the decayed market of Aveley attracted a baker from Billericay, involving a 25-mile return journey.

It is interesting to find that Mildmay's courts of Chelmsford and Moulsham were occasionally reinforcing the authority of the Church courts in regard to Sunday trading. At several sessions around 1591-92 butchers and other tradesmen were presented for opening their shops 'on divers Sundays against divers ordinances'.

Although fairs figure occasionally in manor rolls, those read for the present book are bereft of mention. Harrison's list of fairs in England and Wales, arranged under months, is a somewhat enlarged version of that borrowed from Stow.[11]

## Unwholesome Food

Another aspect of public health functions was the elementary control of what is now termed food hygiene. In the words of a somewhat later treatise 'If any butchers, fishmongers or other victuallers sell any corrupt victual, not wholesome for man's body, it is enquirable'.[12] Inspection of meat and fish was especially necessary to ensure that it was 'wholesome'. Centuries before refrigeration became generally practicable, one of the few available preservatives was salt. Most of the beasts were killed around Martinmas (11 November) because of the shortage of winter feed and the beef was salted down. It is, however, no longer believed that there was very little fresh meat by the end of winter, and the kitchen account-books of Sir William Petre confirm that the more substantial farmers were able to eat (and no doubt to sell) limited supplies of fresh meat in these months.[13] Enormous quantities of salted and dried fish were of course consumed in Lent and on the two weekly fishdays observed under the ecclesiastical and secular laws.[14] But it is obvious that, at most times of the year, butchers and fishmongers were tempted to sell supplies that were unfit or nearly unfit for human consumption.

Presentments were fairly numerous and significant of the courts' attitude. Butchers were the commonest offenders, usually for selling 'bad', 'unwholesome', 'corrupt', or 'putrid' flesh. Yet fines were generally only 6d. or 12d., and 4 Great Dunmow butchers who sold such meat in 1578 were mulcted at a mere 3d. each. Not unnaturally, other butchers kept a sharp lookout for 'foreigners' who brought their own meat to sell in the market. In 1586 a Hatfield Broad Oak butcher was summoned to Epping court because he had brought unwholesome meat to the market, and was fined 2s. In 1571 there was a round-up of erring butchers at Chelmsford market. Several were reported for putting on sale 'flesh of pregnant ewes, against the laws and ordinances of this manor', paying 12d. each. At the same time 7, including one from Witham, were fined between 12d. and 20d. for selling 'measled flesh' (pork affected with the swine disease known as measles); one of them also for selling a heavily pregnant cow, for which he paid an extra 12d. In 1574 at Thaxted a man, finding a dead pig, 'unlawfully prepared it for sale as fit for human consumption'. At Earls Colne in 1559-60 two butchers were prosecuted, one for selling 'unwholesome flesh to the infection of the Queen's people', the other, in order to make it swell and look bigger, because he 'useth to blow his meat with his mouth, to the infection of the lord's tenants and others'.[15]

The Epping court in 1587 received a presentment against a baker who had used unwholesome flour, and a few similar cases are found elsewhere. The petty delinquency of a female baker provides an illuminating entry in the East Mersea roll for 1577 :

> Ordered by the suitors and jurors at this leet that the widow Flower hereafter, being admonished by the alefounders, do make good and wholesome bread, both white and brown; and that she do not boult out (sift) the first for cakes and make whitebread of the next, under pain of forfeit for every batch 12d.

In this manor the ale-tasters also had the job of bread-searchers.

Rotting fruit was found for sale in one market in 1570 :

> Thomas More of Ramsden Bellhouse grocer put bad prunes for sale in Chelmsford market, and because by the scrutiny of the officers of the town and others of that trade they were found to be corrupt, therefore they were adjudged to be burned in the market, and he is fined 2s.; and More sold unlawful shoes in the same market, against the statutes and ordinances of this kingdom, and he is fined 3s.

Two men each forfeited 3s. at Chelmsford court in 1578 for selling bad oranges on Sunday before Morning Prayer, against the bye-law. Exceptionally, the Newport rolls have a single reference to unwholesome cattle food.

To what extent did the watchfulness of the searchers or tasters of flesh, fish, bread and other victuals, elected annually at the more active courts, have any effect on the quality of food? The actual number of presentments for selling bad meat or fish seems to vary within a wide range from manor to manor—in Essex and elsewhere—so that it is difficult to generalize. Stiff fines probably had a salutary result, but in many rolls the same butchers and fishmongers crop up year after year. It is clear that in such cases the almost derisory fines were more in the nature of payment for leave to continue as before.

## Bad Workmanship

With the decline of the trade and craft guilds, the manor courts to some extent stepped into the breach in so far as watching the quality of goods was concerned. 'It is to be enquired' (by the court leet jury) 'if all the artificers do make good work as they ought, and if any make deceit in the same, you ought to present their names'. It is fairly common to find juries presenting cases of bad workmanship. A minor campaign was waged at Newport in 1567. The key phrase is that the craftsman *'non fecit officium suum in ministerio suo debito modo'*, which may be loosely translated as 'he has failed to discharge his obligatory duty in his craft'. William Nytingale, George Nytingale, Stephen Nytingale, William Barnarde and John Brande glovers, Richard Bucke and William Harrys tanners, and Richard Bettrell and William Bagley shoemakers were thus fined between 2d. and 6d. The charge against Brande was more explicit: 'He does not make good leather'. So was that against Thomas Hawkes tallowchandler, who 'does not make good and sufficient candles' and had to pay 4d. Next year all of them, together with Robert Harvye tanner, were again fined. Such poor products, like unwholesome food, but in contrast to deficient weights and measures, seem to have resulted in fairly low fines, again almost akin to routine licences. At Great Burstead similar action was taken in successive courts in 1559 and 1560 against three tanners and three butchers 'who use their artifices ill'. Wethersfield tanners and curriers were often presented for deficient workmanship.

## The Flemings at Halstead

The vital part which the Flemish refugees (called 'Dutch' by Essex folk) played in the growth of the cloth trade, especially in Colchester and Norwich, is well documented.[16] Early in the 1570s they had established the trade in 'bays and says' and other textiles known as the 'New Draperies'. Of these, some strange names are given in the list compiled for our first volume.[17] Not so well known, however, is the settlement of a small 'Dutch congregation' as Halstead in 1576. Despite the prosperity which they brought to Halstead, it is not surprising that the local clothiers resented their presence, and restrictions which threatened their trading eventually led to the Flemings going back to Colchester in 1589, with disastrous results for Halstead people. The town quickly became 'full of poor people' and there was general distress.[18] Too late, the leading men regretted their xenophobia. Petitions for the compulsory return of some of the baymakers were sent to the Privy Council from Halstead (the 50 signatories were headed by Arthur Breame, lord of the manor),[19] supported by similar petitions from eight neighbouring parishes. Despite this massive testimony to the Flemish clothmakers, none of them took up their craft again in Halstead. While living there, one of them, Adrian Loy, 'alien', made his will, but it is uninteresting apart from being witnessed by as many as seven countrymen (1587); and Henry Ozell of Colchester, 'alien', bestowed 10s. on 'the poor people' of both the Colchester and the Halstead 'Dutch congregations' (1582).

A little fresh evidence of the animosity shown to them may be gathered from the Abells rolls. The first charge against the Flemish immigrants was made in 1577. It falls under the heading of pollution or offensive trades, and a general prohibition was issued :

> The Dutchmen nor any of them shall wash out their bays, after the thicking or dyeing of them, in the river before the mill, whereby the water shall be defiled or annoyed with the filth of the same bays (so as they may have liberty to wash them behind the mill), on pain to forfeit for every time so offending after warning given, 6d.

The order was coupled with another against working on Sundays or festival days, the penalty in this case being 20d. The parenthetical phrase makes it clear that they were authorized to wash their bays only 'behind the mill', and to placate the miller the court passed another order in the following year :

> Forasmuch as the Dutchmen have their liberty to wash their bays in the mill stream and mill dam, whereby they do annoy the water and the miller of Townford Mill doth sustain some discommodity thereby, as well by standing by the bank of his mill dam as also by defiling of his water which he should occupy for his meat and drink; all such Dutchmen as do make any bays or do work of the said bays shall from time to time grind their corn and grist which they shall spend in their houses at Townford Mill, on pain of every one doing the contrary for every time grinding elsewhere, so as the miller lawfully use them in grinding, 6d. for every bushel.

The villeins in medieval times were generally under compulsion to have their corn ground at the lord's mill, but it is very rare to find this obligation still being enforced in our period. Here, however, at Halstead there was a special reason for reviving an ancient burden in order to compensate the miller, so that he got a monopoly for grinding the flour needed in the Flemings' homes. Next year (1579) there is a sinister hint of their being obstructed. John Harvy, shearman, was directed to 'take up a post which he hath set against his house leading towards Townford Mill, wherewith he doth stop the passage to the mill'; which seems to imply that he had wilfully blocked the Flemings' only access to their washing-place. Then, in 1581, the roll for the first and only time gives the names of 'certain residents within this leet, commonly called in English Dutchmen', who had defaulted in attending the court. Intent on their business, they probably had no knowledge of the obligation on all male inhabitants to appear at the court leet. 'Godescalf, Dole, Grendela, Boonefale', with their christian names latinized as far as possible, look strange : there are 28 of them, but their fine was merely the normal one of 2d. There after the rolls are silent apart from a general and usual order against inmates, in which 'except aliens' was inserted to obviate their being accused as inmates. They stayed in the town for another nine years.

1 *Ess. Rev.*, xv, 123.
2 For the 1d., 2d. and 3d. household loaves and prices of beer at Colchester, together with average wheat prices and the assizes of bread recorded there, 1581-98, see *Ess. Rev.*, lii, 116-19.
3 *The Order of Keeping a Court Leet and Court Baron* (1650), 17.
4 The clerk of the market of royal liberties and certain manors having a market or other franchise appears occasionally in Elizabethan records. For Writtle, see K. C. Newton, *The Manor of Writtle* (1970), 90; for the liberty of Havering and Romford market, see Marjorie McIntosh, 'The Cooke Family of Gidea Hall' (unpubd. Ph.D. thesis, Harvard Univ., 1967, copy in E.R.O., p. 280); for the solitary appointment in 1567 of a tenant as clerk of the market of Stock, see Austen, *op. cit.*, 56.
5 Apparently 64 gallons (Harrison, *op. cit.*, 458).
6 Harrison, *op. cit.*, 247.
7 *E.L.: Disorder*, plate 2.
8 The open bays on the ground floor were used for the corn-market; in one of the bays stood the manorial standard bushel, chained to a post. It was a timber-framed two-storeyed building surrounded by wooden 'shops' or stalls. The detailed drawing dated 1595 is reproduced in E.R.O. Publn. no. 53.
9 For Malden market's zone, see Dr Petchey's thesis (see p. 6), map opp. p. 80.
10 H. B. Rodgers, 'The Market Area of Preston in the Sixteenth and Seventeenth Centuries', quoted in *Geographical Interpretations of Historical Sources* (1970), 112.
11 Harrison, *op. cit.*, 391-97.
12 *The Order of Keeping a Court* (1650), 18.
13 Emmison, *Tudor Food and Pastimes*, 40.   14 *Ibid.*, 45.
15 *Essex Journal*, ix, 89; cf. 'Custumals' under Dedham *infra*.
16 *V.C.H. Essex*, ii, 386-91.   17 *E.L.: Disorder*, app. B.
18 *V.C.H.*, ii, 389-90.
19 For a full list of their names, see P.R.O., S.P.Dom., Eliz., 146, no. 63 (copy in E.R.O., T/P 121/1); the petition is printed in *Tudor Economic Documents*, ed. Tawney and Power (reprint, 1951) i, 319. See also *Acts of the Privy Council*, xix, 127

# 20
# Contempt of Court

'The courts were kept always with great solemnity and gravity' appears in the Aveley manor survey introduction: 'In 21 Henry 8 one was soundly amerced for misbehaving himself in the face of the Court; and the homage of the leet also were wont with care and great secrecy to proceed in their presentments; in 29 Eliz. one of the homage of the leet was amerced at 6s. 8d. for discovering (i.e. revealing) his fellows' counsel before verdict'. Stewards were empowered summarily to punish by fine any contempt committed in court. The solemnity of Shenfield Hall court was disturbed in 1559, when Thomas Parker (who owned the farm called Ropers) 'railed contrary to all good order against the lord in reviling him and calling him knave and fool at this leet day in the presence of the lord's steward and the homage; therefore he is amerced 10s.' Parker's oral abuse had followed on his being presented for pulling down and altering his buildings. Another refractory tenant was presented at Newport in 1571 as a barrator in 'refusing to allow the homage to see his lands, being a great nuisance to the lady's miller and to others, and publicly using opprobrious words in the court to the steward, homage and suitors', for which he was fined 3s. 4d.; and 5s. was set on John Foster, an inhabitant of Epping, for similar words against the jurors there in 1593. The Felsted roll, recording a steep fine of 20s. on Thomas Belchamp, a tenant, in 1594, quotes the 'opprobrious words': 'None would find fault with his dunghill but some prowling thievish knave that cometh over in the night time'! But contemptuous comments at manorial courts were rarely as vociferous as the epithets shouted at the officers of the archidiaconal courts.[1] A superlative example, however, was found in the court rolls of the royal manor of Hitchin (Herts.). 'Only once was any discourtesy shown to the steward, but that was discourtesy indeed: "It is presented that Humphrey Woolcot did exclaim and rail against Bostock Toller, gentleman steward of this manor, as a mountebank attorney and the lord's hireling creature, and that he would have the court books out of his hands and cast them on the common laystall (dunghill) and, often as the bailiff cried the court, he did sing out lustily, Come, come away to the tavern, I say, so that none that stood by was able to hear" '.[2] Premature disclosure of a presentment, which affronted curial dignity, is also revealed in the proceedings at Bulphan in 1567: 'John Pepercorne, a juryman, before the verdict given in, had unlawfully and against his oath discovered to one John Payne the secret communication between him and his fellows touching things in charge with them and the verdict to be given, in contempt of the Queen and her court and to the pernicious example of others'. Likewise at Ingatestone in 1578, when a juror was fined 20d. for revealing part of the jury's verdict. Of inactive contempt, all who defaulted in their suit of court were nominally guilty, but only once is the term specially used. In 1603 the Rettendon bailiff was told to levy 40s. on Humphrey Hasler because he absented himself after being sworn as one of the jury of enquiry; 'which fine was imposed by the steward in full court for the contempt'. In 1568 a headborough at Chipping Walden was fined 5s. for 'withdrawing without the consent of the jury, having been elected'.

[1] *E.L.: Morals*, 307-12.
[2] R. L. Hine, *History of Hitchin* (1927), i, 56-7.

# 21
# Custumals, Bye-laws and Surveys

Manorial custom, as we have seen in the foregoing chapters, is a subject of considerable interest. Each individual manor had its own customs, and although some were fairly general except for minor local differences, others varied widely from county to county, and a few are believed to be unique. They are most fully described in documents, if surviving, known as customaries, or, more usually, custumals; they may be incorporated in surveys; they may be entered, occasionally, in ordinary court rolls as a complete statement or as particular customs to be reinforced; or they may appear as new bye-laws, to acquire in due course the validity of customs. In the more important urban manors, upwards of a hundred separate customs may be found.

It is not surprising, therefore, that no social or economic historian has so far attempted to give a comprehensive description of manorial customs over the whole country. The mind boggles at the immensity of the task, but there is no doubt about the importance attaching to such a study, even allowing for the fact that the content or effect of some kinds of customs, especially those dealing with inheritance, timber-felling rights and repairs to copyhold buildings, was broadly common to a large number of manors. Wide research would also afford a much clearer idea of the manors in Sussex, Middlesex, Suffolk and Surrey, and, to a lesser extent, Essex, in which the custom of Borough English prevailed, and it would determine the extent to which the custom of gavelkind obtained outside Kent. Under Borough English, in general terms, lands descended to the youngest son (excluding all other children) of a tenant who died intestate, and in a few manors to the youngest sister, uncle or aunt. It has been stated that Borough English customs, wholly or partially, obtained in 25 Essex manors.[1] Under gavelkind, among other matters, the property was inherited equally by all the sons, the widow getting one-half instead of one-third as her dower, and a tenant could alienate his lands at the age of 15. Thus primogeniture was not restricted to males, and certain other peculiarities were contrary to common law. Examination of manorial documents in all counties would reveal manifold strange customs associated with forests, marshes, moors, mining districts, areas with special fishery, wharf and similar maritime rights, open-field regions, and other parts of the country having characteristics inherent in local conditions. Manors in boroughs and market-towns are known to have had an extraordinarily wide diversity in their customs: in fact, urban manors and their relationship with the municipal bodies would alone form an important piece of research.

The Tudor and later writers of text-books for the guidance of lords and stewards differentiated somewhat theoretically between the court baron (the lord's court) and the court leet (the court for petty offences against the common law or the customs and bye-laws of the manor). They elaborated over what constituted 'reasonable and unreasonable' customs, explaining why the latter might be held to be void, but no example of a custom challenged on this ground has been found in Essex. The legal writers declared that 'four things are required to make a good custom—Antiquity, Continuance, Certainty, and Reason', and they attempted to distinguish between custom, presumption and usage.[2] In practice, however, the vital element was that the custom had been used 'time out of mind'.

Some custumals begin with the customs concerning attendance at the courts (the chief pledges with the deceners and the homage or jury and the customary or copyhold tenants, the earliest age at which suit of court was demanded, and excuses for absence), attornment of tenants to a new lord, their 'acknowledgement' at his first court by way of an offering in money or kind, such as 'palfrey money', and the common fine or annual money payment to him. On the custom also depended the officers elected every year: some were common to most manors, as constables and aletasters; some were peculiar to forestal, riverine, or coastal manors, as woodwards, marsh-reeves, and others with strange names like ketchers and common-drivers. There is sometimes a series of customs about changes of tenure through inheritance or purchase, the fines, reliefs and heriots payable to the lord on such transfers or for leases to under-tenants, widows' rights of dower, the amount of rents, and the lord's right of seizure of holdings for various tenancy offences. Other customs set out the liability for maintenance of the tenants' buildings, including the oft-disputed rights of cutting down timber for repairing or making their carts and ploughs. Less frequently are found customs concerning maintenance of bridges, gates, fences, ditches, rights of way, and so forth— factors in ordinary life which produced innumerable disputes that could be obviated and expense avoided if exact knowledge were established in a written custumal. Pasturage and mineral rights over the commons, heaths, greens and woods—the manorial 'waste'—also varied very widely, depending partly on their extent and quality. Control of the highways and streets included the removal of every sort of obstruction and filth and the banning of various animals; in manors with markets and fairs there were additional customs governing rights or nuisances.

Somewhat akin to customs were certain ancient privileges exercised by some lords, which were generally associated with special 'franchises' or 'liberties' granted by royal charter, such as the claim to exclude the sheriff's officers or to debar the tenants from lawsuits in Quarter Sessions and other superior courts or the right to fugitives' or convicted felons' goods. Most lords claimed deodands, waifs, estrays, and, in the case of coastal manors, wrecks. While nearly all these liberties were in theory derived from the Crown, some originated in a charter, and others were based on prescription, usage, or immemorial custom.

It was therefore imperative that the lord should ascertain as precisely as possible what the customs were. It was equally important for the tenants to know the extent of their own rights, in order to defend them, if needed, against abuse by an aggressive or mercenary lord or steward, either of whom might decide to search the rolls for earlier entries about customs, bye-laws, orders, fines or other punishments, or for similar precedents which might have acquired the force of custom. This desire for knowledge was occasionally so paramount that the search extended far back, even to the 14th century, if ancient court rolls had survived. If a lord decided to over-ride any established customs his tenants could sue him in the central courts. Such action would be a costly business for them, but the Chancery records reveal examples for most counties. In Essex they include a determined suit brought by the tenants of Great Canfield against their grasping lord. John Wiseman's activity in extracting money for wood-cutting has been mentioned. By 1592 he had gone too far, and the tenants' claim was four-fold. They contended that they had the right to cut timber and underwood on their holdings and for repairing or 'new making of any houses and buildings, without any licence of the lord'; to make leases of not more than three years; to dig marl, etc. on their copyholds without licence; and to pay on admittance a fine certain, not an arbitrary one, at the rate of 5s. an acre. These rights they had always enjoyed until Wiseman, with his 'covetous mind, conceiving some displeasure against some of the copyholders, did threaten to impeach and avoid all the customs'. They had first complained, though paying him the big sum of £40 as 'a gratuity for his favour and goodwill', on which he ratified the customs in writing, only to repudiate the agreement soon afterwards. He was completely defeated, and the Court of Chancery accepted his full acknowledgement of the disputed customs.[3]

In some manors the steward or the jury of tenants, perhaps convened as a 'court of survey', set out all or a number of the more important customs as a special statement, which was either enrolled in the proceedings of the court or compiled as a separate custumal. Although the initiative usually came from the lord or steward, it sometimes arose from the tenants, who were entitled to put forward the customs as part of their 'presentment'. The abnormal example found in the Canewdon rolls has already been noticed. In some instances it was obviously intended as a check on the lord's arbitrary will. While a lord belonging to a new family, or a new steward, might wish to ensure his position by a search, the tenants had the advantage of oral tradition passed on by many generations. Even so, the lord had the right to fine them heavily if they produced an inaccurate statement or suppressed any customs that were in his favour.

The highly interesting surveys of the manors of Felsted, Chelmsford, Boxted, Woodham Ferrers, and Aveley, all of which fortunately include sections or notes on the customs, have been chosen, with certain custumals, for our final chapter.[4]

In most manors we also find some quasi-customs. Every court could make new bye-laws, which in time had the same effect as the ancient customs and were binding. Sometimes they were termed 'general orders', or merely 'orders', instead of bye-laws. Urban manors required such bye-laws to deal with the common problems of town life. In order to reinforce their validity, many courts re-issued the bye-laws periodically, with or without amendments or additions. In Elizabeth's last decade the Witham court decreed every year, 'The bye-laws to stand', a phrase also observed elsewhere.

The fact that land tenure was the basis of manorial economy inevitably led to the careful recording in many manors, at intervals, of the tenancies, rents and services, together with definition of the bounds and abuttals of each holding. The resulting documents were extents, surveys and rentals, the first being mostly a medieval term. A manorial survey may concern itself primarily with the lord's demesne, with perhaps a brief description of manor-house, park, windmills, dovecote, parsonage, woods, commons, greens, heaths or wastes, fisheries, and boundaries of the manor. Or, more generally, it may comprise an account of the copyholds and freeholds, without any description of the demesne. It may also reveal interesting facts about market and fairs, school and free chapel, church and advowson, glebe and tithes, newly 'inned' marshes, timber, enclosure of commons or open fields, depopulation, disparking, and so on. The kind of information which one hopes to find in a fairly detailed survey is of course partly related to geographical and other physical factors. It will emphasize the numerous topographical (as well as economic) differences inherent in manors with open-field or enclosed, urban or rural, nucleated or discrete, low-lying or moorland, forestal, pastoral, coastal, or other characteristics. Surveys of Elizabethan date may give the acreages and names of every field and even the names of the adjacent owners or occupiers or fields, as well as the tenants' names. For some manors a map may also accompany the survey. Essex is particularly rich in late Elizabethan manorial maps. Even without a map, some surveys are so detailed that many, if not most of the holdings and the fields can be identified (though it is a laborious job), with the aid of later maps such as the parish tithe or enclosure award maps or the first edition of the ordnance survey 6-inch maps; the field-names in the tithe maps, however, often differ a good deal from the earlier names. Three remarkable maps of Saffron Walden showing the town about 1600 were thus reconstructed from the 16th and 17th century manorial surveys.[5] Much less detailed are the rentals, which generally give only tenants and rents, sometimes acreages, but few other facts.

The selection that follows cannot afford a full account of the customs and supplementary bye-laws which affected the tenants' lives. It would have been tempting, too, to say a little about the medieval customs and strange services by which a large number of the Essex manors were originally held from the Crown, or lands held from the lord. There were, for instance, the serjeanty of serving with a towel at the coronation—the duty by which one-half of the manor of Heydon was held of the Crown; the serjeanty of keeping 5 wolf-dogs for the King, by which a tenant held his land at Boyton in Finchingfield; and the vigil and guard at the high altar of Barking Abbey church one night each year, by which the lord of Clay Hall in Barking held the manor from the abbess and convent.[6] But all these and similar customary 'burdens' in other manors had probably fallen into desuetude by Elizabeth's time. The last two occasions (apart from the modern revivals) of the grant of the flitch of bacon to faithful couples, so adjudged by a jury of men and matrons at the court of Little Dunmow Priory, were in 1701 and 1751, but unfortunately there are no Elizabethan rolls of the manor, so we are not entitled to say more of this famous jocular custom.[7]

## Ingatestone

The manor of Gynge Abbess, or Gynge *ad petram* (at the stone), formerly belonging to Barking Abbey, was purchased from the Crown at the Dissolution by Dr William Petre, who promptly pulled down Abbess Hall, the ancient manor house, and built the present Ingatestone Hall. When not engaged at Court or in other official duties, this was always his country home. He aptly re-named the manor Ging Petre *alias* Ingatestone![8] An undated document, comprising 'Customs' and 'Liberties', was drawn up about 1575 as a result of search in the abbey's rolls from 1 Richard II (1377); they are in fact extant from as early as 1279. The section on customs has 19 articles, several of which such as overcharging the Common, are of course represented in most manors. 'Full age' was reckoned when the heir reached 12 (in some manors, 15). Two items refer to a fine given by a tenant for licence to put two of his sons to school and to a distraint for 'custom works' not carried out, but these are from rolls of Edward III and Edward IV, and it is very doubtful whether they were extracted to enforce similar action; evidence of the survival of boon works in Elizabethan Essex is extremely meagre. Under the heading of 'Suits at the Common Law' there is cited: 'A tenant is amerced for suing one other tenant in an action of trespass and commanded to forbear his suit, upon pain of forfeiture of his customary lands' (1489). The 'palfrey money' paid on the accession of each abbess was still being rendered at Ingatestone in Elizabeth's time when the tenants attorned to a new lord (as also in several other pre-Dissolution Barking Abbey manors). It is made clear that tenants who committed waste by cutting down trees on their holding without the lord's licence or by failing to repair their dwellings were liable to forfeit their copyholds.

The usefulness of precedents is exemplified several times by quotation of cases of bad workmanship and unauthorized disclosure of court business, and the action taken against two women, probably harlots, was also worth noting for future reference:

> Shoemakers amerced for ill sewing of shoes (29 Hen. VI). Amercements for uttering the counsel of the court (35 Hen. VI). A suspected woman commanded to avoid the town by a day or else to be set in the pillory (8 Edw. IV). One amerced for not putting out of his house a light woman (35 Hen. VI).

The fairly common doubts about the responsibility for bridge repairs ('Who should repair it we know not'), which caused infinite delay when the 'ruinous' bridges were presented to Quarter Sessions,[9] was doubtless known to the steward. The three entries about bridges reveal examples of liability both on the 'village' and on the lords of Ingatestone and adjacent manors: Rey Bridge evidently stood at the point where the boundaries of four manors met.[10]

> Rey Bridge is to be repaired by the lords of Ging Petre, now Sir William Petre, the parsonage of Buttsbury now Sir William Petre, the lord of Ging Hospital now Leonard Berners, and the lord of Ramsey Tyrell now Sir Henry Tyrell (1, 8, 9 & 10 Edw. IV and 1 Mary).
> Hey Bridge, being a foot bridge and lying by Hey Field and Magges Mead, is to be repaired by the village of Ingatestone and the lord of Thoby now Leonard Berners (8, 9 & 10 Edw. IV and 1 Mary).
> Street Bridge, a foot bridge lying by Hey Field, is to be repaired by the village of Ingatestone (8 & 9 Edw. IV).

Ging Hospital was another name for Fryerning; Ramsey Tyrell and Thoby were manors in Buttsbury and Mountnessing.

The second section begins: 'Liberties of this manor be very great, which be contained in my letters patent dated 1539, but more amply in the letters patent granted to the late Abbey of Barking'. These comprised the right to deodands, waived felons' and outlaws' goods, 'the order of victuals and victuallers and punishment of them', the right to free warren over the whole manor, and the prohibition to tenants from taking partridges, pheasants, conies and hawks. Also attached to the manor were the lord's special privileges, under the royal grant, of barring the sheriff and the bailiff of the hundred from arresting tenants and the royal household purveyors from commandeering provisions. Citations from the rolls of

Richard II and Henry VII are precedents showing that the tenants, not the lord, were liable for the stocks and archery butts. Finally, another roll of Richard II was evidence that 'if any question be whether a customary tenant be an idiot, the same shall be examined and adjudged by the steward in the presence of the homage'.

More than one major dispute between lord and tenants led to thorough searches by the steward, who also compiled 'An abstract of the rolls touching felling, lopping and disposing of timber and wood by the customary tenants'. His first extract is dated 1310-11 : 'It is found by the inquest that Robert le Locksmith made waste in his customary tenement in cutting down oaks and ashes, to the great prejudice of the abbess—fined 3d.' The 20 cases ending in 1553 are either charges of 'estrepement' (waste) or lord's licences to fell or lop trees. Another document, prepared about 1635, consists of extracts from the account-books of all sums paid for such licences between 1581 and 1633. The 30 Elizabethan items include the following :

> Robert Clarke of Fryerning, glover, for licence to lop certain pollenger trees growing upon his customary lands, late parcel of the tenement called Campers, and to expend the same at his house in Fryerning, 8s. (1582).
> Anthony Brasier, clerk, for licence to lop 8 pollengers on his customary land called Broade Lands and to burn the same in his rectory, 3s. 4d. (1582).
> Robert Clarke, for licence to dispose of 40 faggots made of the offal (waste wood) left of his hedging, 12d. (1590).
> Thomas Tabor, for licence to fell 40 trees and lop 60 trees in Collyers Croft, customary, as the same were marked out, £8 (1597).
> John Bonde, re-admitted to a tenement customary called Hyckes-at-Hyde by reason of waste done upon his tenement against the custom of the manor, 100s. (1601).
> Isaac Bett, for licence to cut down a coppice and 12 dottered (i.e. decayed) pollenger oaks upon the customary lands called Packmans and Morkyns, 50s. (1602).
> John Humfrey, gentleman, for licence to fell and to lop certain trees upon his customary lands called Helders, 60s. (1603).

## *Dedham*

In 1558 this manor had become Crown property, annexed to the Duchy of Lancaster. The document, undated but *c.* 1575, is in two parts—customs and bye-laws. It has been published in full,[11] but several remarkable points deserve repetition. Inheritance was to the youngest son, i.e. Borough English. Tenants had the fullest freedom to pull down or sell their houses and to fell or sell timber on their lands without the lord's leave. The other tenurial customs were not unusual, except that 'No man shall plough any ley land in any our commons until Candlemas Day following, and any man shall take but one crop of his common meadow in the year, but all the roughen and feeding of the edish (i.e.

aftermath) is free for the township and parishioners until Candlemas following, and they that feed their ground shall mow now by old ancient custom holden here time out of mind'. The loyal tenants finish with 'God save the Queen'.

Then follow 'The bye-laws made by the tenants made in the Court Leet for to have good order, by the old assent of the homage'. Dealing with 18 different offences, each carrying a fine, they form one of the longest sets of Essex manor bye-laws known to the writer. Owing to the paucity of husbandry or agricultural bye-laws in this county, their initial emphasis on control of the common meadow is of interest. The first three articles were aimed against tenants damaging the hay in Broad Meadow. The 6th custom was reinforced as a bye-law : 'If any doth ear (i.e. plough) upon ley lands or edish in common time', the fine would be 20s. Several bye-laws concern Dedham Heath, one of the largest in Essex. To suppress overstocking, tenants were forbidden not only to exceed their stint (not specified but in proportion to the size of their holdings), but also to 'take in any agistments' (rate at so much a head for pasturing livestock). Cutting down any 'lind' (linden, or lime) trees on the Heath was prohibited, possibly because the lime was one of the trees from which charcoal was made. Animals, live and dead, were controlled in the streets as well as on the Common; no tenant to allow rooting hogs; none 'to let any beast stand in the heat of the day and beat down men's banks and walls with their heads'; none 'to cast carrion of swine or dogs undelved in the ground'; no butcher in Church-gate Street 'to cast any horns or bones in the street so that men's horse doth stumble, ready to hurt both horse and man'. Butchers were also singled out for a dishonest trick occasionally mentioned in borough records and previously noticed only in one other Essex manor : 'If any butchers within Dedham do blow their flesh with their mouths or prick it to the intent to let in the wind or to lift up the neers of mutton, veal or lamb with pricks', the forfeit would be 20s. ('Neer' is a dialect word used in Eastern England for the kidney.) The fraud is referred to by a contemporary writer : 'They do blow the flesh, and cause it to seem fat and fair'.[12] Two articles deal with poaching, by means of ferrets, hayes, or fishing-nets. The bye-laws yield an anti-pollution order which is unique in its mention of beavers :

> If any manner of persons have any beaver pits at their woodhouses against the common brook, they shall always be kept cast so that the thick paste be kept out of the said brook for noyage of the common water. Also no person lay fish in the same water for to water it nor wash their linen therein because there be many that have none other water to dress their meat and drink with, but that who doth the contrary shall forfeit to the lord 40s.

'Woodhouses' probably means beavers' 'lodges', and 'kept cast' implies that they should be cast down. If both these interpretations are right, the bye-law directed that all beavers' dens be regularly broken down to prevent the drinking water being defiled or thickened with their mud.[13]

## West Mersea, Fingringhoe and Pete Hall

An elaborate custumal of these manors, the last being in Peldon and all in the same ownership, was compiled in 1497. It was 'entered and renewed' in 1572 by Thomas Cammock,[14] 'general surveyor' to Lord Darcy. In 1719 it was again 'read over and passed' by the tenants, who added, 'We find the same to be part of our verdict', i.e. presentment, which demonstrates the importance attached to ancient custumals. The original document, of 1497, known from copies made about 1650 and in 1719, begins: 'The usage, custom and customary used time out of mind of man for the customary tenants'. The custumal consists of no less than 34 articles, also printed in full,[15] so only a few of the outstanding customs will be noted.

The heriot payable to the lord on a tenant's death was 'his best beast whatsoever it be, horse, ox, cow, sheep, swine, pig, goose, cock or hen, and if he have not a beast then the lord to have no heriot'. It is rare to find such trifling heriots as domestic fowls. Even rarer in an enclosed manor was the custom allowing every resident tenant 'to stray upon the lord's demesne grounds with as much of his own cattle as his land may keep, winter and summer, except ploughed lands, from St Giles' Day until Christmas Day, paying for a horse or cow 1d., and for a bullock ½d., and from Christmas to Candlemas to pasture their sheep upon the demense and to pay nothing therefor'. The next article reads: 'If any tenant stray his plough team or any draft beasts, then he shall come to the lord's barns or manor place and ear a journey (day's ploughing) of land in wheat season and another in oat season, and to have his meat and drink of the lord or his farmer' (i.e. lessee); such a custom has not been found elsewhere in Elizabethan Essex.

The customs affecting females were also peculiar: 'No inheritance be shifted (i.e. partitioned) between females, but the eldest daughter or kinswoman only to be heir of the copyhold lands'; such heir, by the lord's licence, to be admitted at 15, but not to surrender, give or devise by will until she be 21. If under 15, the lord was to commit the custody 'according to the common law in socage tenure' and to have one-half of the lands until then, the guardian to have the other moiety for keeping the child, 'without waste or estripment'.

The widow's position was also contrary to common law: 'If any tenant die sole of any copyhold lands in fee simple or fee tail, without any surrender making thereof, then his wife to have all his lands during her widowhood for her free bench'. The free bench, or dower of a widow, was the income of one-third of her late husband's land; the normal provision and that of inheritance by the eldest son (Borough French) was over-ridden in manors having the custom of Borough English, in which not only did the widow have the whole of his land for life but the youngest son succeeded. Tenants were prohibited from suing each other outside Pete Hall court for debt, trespass or any other action determinable in the court ('general courts' for all three manors were held at Pete Hall).

The lord or his lessee was bound to keep 'a common bull and a boar for the easement of the tenants', both at West Mersea and at Fingringhoe. In these three maritime manors the lord had the 'advantage of the admiralty of the sea, and the finder of any wreck to have the one half or like advantage, after the use (usage) of the Admiralty Court'. The effect of some of these customs is seen in the rolls for 1547-58. In 1549 the lessee (appropriately named John Bullock) had failed to provide the obligatory bull and boar and was threatened by the homage with a penalty of 6s. 8d., which he forfeited two years later; for further negligence it would be 10s.[16]

The inheritance customs of the three manors were thus a curious mixture: while free bench was one of the normal criteria of Borough English, succession, where no surrender had been made, went to the eldest son; but, in case of no male heir, to the eldest daughter—all against the common law. The abnormal but restricted recognition of a female at 15 was another hybrid custom, savouring of one aspect of Kentish gavelkind, under which a tenant could alienate his lands at 15, but this right was specifically denied in West Mersea and Fingringhoe.

## Great Bentley

The customs were set down from oral evidence given in 1583-84 at the request of the lord, Roger Townshend, by 10 men who had held their tenements for between 7 and over 40 years and by 14 other tenants, all named, in consequence of the withholding of 'the book of written customs' by a certain John Goodwin. This lengthy compilation, which has survived only as a copy, *c.* 1750, consists of a statement of the customs and the answers to 38 articles, the actual questions not being given.

The tenants declared: 'Long ago the leet was usually holden on St. Gregory's Day in Lent, and about 40 years ago it was altered unto the Friday next after Twelfth Day and so continued 20 years upwards, and since it hath been holden upon several days uncertain'. They added: 'The manor extendeth into Frating and we think into Weeley. We cannot certainly set down the bounds, but on procession have been used, beginning at Cross House to go thence to Frating Heath and so to Wyland in Tendring, thence to Dry Brook and through Custrick Hall ground, thence down to Froodwick to Willy Hill and so to Borefleet Bridge'. Guttridge Hall and Frowick Hall are in Weeley and St Osyth parishes.

Somewhat unusual was the composition of the jury of 'headboroughs', or chief tenants, but if insufficient in number cottagers filled their places.

Apparently the headboroughs averaged 32 in Great Bentley and 8 in Frating Street. A headborough by custom was obliged to repair his dwelling but might allow his outbuildings to fall down, whereas a cottager, quite exceptionally, suffered no penalty for letting even his dwelling collapse. A cottager, too, contributed nothing to the common fine nor was he liable for a heriot; and only a single heriot was paid by a headborough tenant, although he might have two or more holdings.

One of the most illuminating replies concerns the former park:

> We say that before Bentley Park was disparked, there were certain tenants that did bestow every year one day's work in paling, that was to set up one rod of pale, the posts and rails and pales being laid at or near the place where they should be set up, by the Lord or park-keeper, and the tenants were found meat and drink for their work by the Lord or keeper, but since the park hath been disparked it hath not been done, neither can it well be done. Likewise before the disparking there were some tenants did bestow every year one day's work in the park in mowing or brakes, having meat and drink found them, but since the disparking the most part thereof (is) hedged. And divers which did those works have since paid money for not doing the same, viz. for every day's work 4d., being at their own choice whether they would do their work or compound.

The nearest parallel of park-pale maintenance is seen in a survey of the royal park at Havering in 1586, where 'the workmanship of paling for the most part is done at the charges of freeholders thereto adjacent'.[17] At the Crown manor of Havering, 1560, two persons were amerced at 12d. for each perch of decayed park-pale in their own sections.

The lord having been granted no liberties, the tenants could sue each other at common law in the hundred or the county courts in matters which could also be determined in the manor court, and they also had the alternative of presenting offences in the hundred court. Nor had the lord the right of 'free warren, sheep course, swan mark, nor fishery, except in the ponds in his park'. The mill was 'decayed', but the tenants did not know the owner.

Great Bentley was another manor in which the youngest son inherited, but, most unusually, the custom did not apply to the whole manor, the eldest son inheriting if the copyhold lay at Frating Street. Another peculiar custom, 'although it be contrary to law', so the tenants testified, governed widows' right to her thirds, or dower. While she could have it if she came to be admitted, she could not if her husband had previously sold his copyhold.

The fences and hedges of the demesne were maintained by the adjacent copyholders, 'who shall have all the wood and trees whatsoever that groweth, with the crumfall upon the lord's demesne in so far as the bank is higher than the other ground'. The word 'crumfall' seems to have eluded lexicographers, though the meaning of this minor customary right is fairly clear; it may be connected with 'crome, cromb', a stick with a hook at the end, to pull down the bough of a tree.

No other Essex manor court has preserved such detailed timber-felling customs:

> Now to shew you how we may use our timber upon our copyhold lands. We may sell it without the assignment of the Lord or his bailiff, and we may build or repair any new house or any piece of a new house or any barn or stable.
> We may rail or pale in any orchard or garden with pales and make it as big or as little as we will, or rail in any field or wood that we have with rails of timber, or make stakes of timber to set or stand in any hedge we have about our copyhold lands to hedge withal, or to make any bridges over slippers, waterways or brooks where any pathway or through way lieth with (within?) our copyhold lands.
> We may take it and use it for plough timber, timber or cart timber, i.e. we may repair or make any new carts, ploughs, tumbrils, drags or sleads to carry our own carriage, and to plough our own land, or to carry any other men's carriages, or to plough any other men's lands with the same ploughs, carts, tumbrils, drags or sleads.
> Thus may we use the timber that groweth upon the copyhold lands or for any other necessary reparations that we shall think good of about our copyhold lands.
> If we fell timber to build or repair withal and if we fell more than shall serve our turns at that time, whether it be a tree, 2 or 3 or how many or few soever it be, the same timber or trees may lie by us so felled down until such time as we have cause to use them about any such things as is before mentioned.
> Now to shew you what we have done or may do with the refuse of our timber or timber tops, i.e. the refuse of our timber we have riven out to blocks or logs and with the tops we have made billet, talwood and cubit, those blocks or logs, billet, talwood or cubit we may either burn them or sell them, which of them we will by our custom.
> For all our woods or underwoods upon our copyhold lands, we may take them, fell them down and sell them, and any of our husband trees we may stub them down and rive them out and make them out to blocks and logs, and we may burn them or sell them, which of them we will.
> We may stub up any row of trees we have within our copyhold lands and lay 2 or 3 fields, pightles or closes or more to one.
> By our customs we may girt, crop or lop any tree that we have about our copyhold lands, whether oak, elm, ash, asp, beech, or any other 3 whatsoever.

This is followed by two customs concerning digging rights: 'We may dig or take clay upon our copyhold lands to make brick and tile'; and 'We may take sand upon any of the commons in Bentley Magna or upon our copyhold lands to make brick and tile withal, and that brick and tile so made we may sell it to any man'.

The tenants then declared that the Commons were 'Bentley Green, Anger Green, South Heath, Puttock Tye, with 2 or 3 other parcels which have no certain names; but what quantity of acres they contain we cannot well esteem; and we say that the tenants of the tenements lying in Great Bentley may common in them and none else, and they may common there all manner of cattle except it be a byelaw against horses made by a few which bindeth none but those which made it'.

> Customs for our Commons
>
> The commons in Bentley Magna are not commons general to all men, neither are they commons special to 1, 2 or 3, but they are commons appendant to as many copyholders as belong to the court baron of Bentley Magna, and also they are commons appendant to as many freeholders in Great Bentley as can shew by their deeds that they common and to none other.
>
> And we do suit and service to the Lord as well for our commons as for our copyhold lands, and we pay fines for our commons as well as for our copyhold lands.
>
> We let our lands and tenements the dearer in that the commons are dependent upon our copyhold lands, and so by that means the lord hath a bigger fine.
>
> By our customs a copyholder may take any tree upon the Common that standeth or groweth within 7 feet of the outward brow of the ditch against our copyhold lands.
>
> By our customs we may take any furze, broom, bushes, bramble or thorns that grow upon the commons, that is to say, whitethorn, blackthorn, crabthorn and bramblethorn, and these furze, broom and bushes we may cut down and carry away off the commons.
>
> The Lord's bailiff and some of the tenants have used to drive the commons, and if the bailiff would refuse the tenants only have driven the same.

The last clause refers to driving cattle together for the purpose of identifying the owners. The custom regarding copyholders' stints over the commons was set out in the chapter on Common Rights.

## Hatfield Broad Oak

'The customs of this manor as they be warranted either by precedents in the rolls or by the presentments of the homage'. With these words one of the most comprehensive Essex custumals, prepared about the time of Elizabeth's death, begins and extends to four closely-written pages :

> There is belonging to this manor, by custom time out of mind used, a view of frankpledge commonly called a leet or law day, which by like custom hath been held at a day certain, viz. on Tuesday in Whitsun week, at which day both the leeters, freepledges with their deceners and also the tenants do usually appear without any summons or warning given. For the service of this leet there are two several juries, the one all of leeters, the other of the lord's tenants. Of the leeters there are commonly twelve sworn or more, as the steward thinketh good; of the lord's tenants Four and Twenty; if so many do appear. The office of the leeters is to enquire of all matters concerning the leet, and to put their presentment in writing and deliver it up to the steward, who is to engross the same and to amend it

in form, not altering the substance, and then to deliver it unto the Four and Twenty, whose office is to enquire of such offences as are omitted, forgotten or concealed by the leeters.

The firm hand of custom is evident in this long preamble, and throughout the keynote is a double one : service and discipline. Of particular significance is the Four and Twenty, a privileged oligarchy, paralleled in Essex by the Four and Twenty who had emerged about a generation earlier as the self-electing and self-perpetuating Vestry of Braintree, which by the first or second decade of the next century had largely superseded the manor court as the governing body of the town.[18]

As it appeared upon search of the ancient rolls that the common fine was uncertain, 'some rolls giving 1d. a poll (i.e. head), some ½d. a poll, some ½d. for a decener and 1d. for a headborough or chief pledge, it is therefore agreed by the consent of the leeters and tenants and of the steward that henceforth it shall be ½d. for every decener and 1d. for every headborough'.

The most curious article is an explanation, for the benefit of the ignorant, of the term 'common fine'. 'The jury present that the common fine is not in respect of the Common which is within this leet, for not any have common except he be a tenant or a sharrier, for if he be only a leeter he is to have no benefit of the Common, and therefore they present that the common fine is due in respect of the liberty of the leet'. 'Sharrier' seems to be an undefined term. The manorial wastes are then set out : 'All the highways and waste grounds are the lord's freehold, also all trees growing on them except in Hatfield Forest, which was lately sold by his Lordship'; after which the numerous 'ends' within the manor boundaries are named.

Any concealment of offences in the jury's presentment 'found by the Four and Twenty' would be punished by a crushing fine of 21s. on each juror. The same hierarchy by ancient custom appointed the constables, ale-founders, fish-tasters and leather-searchers. For appointing the chief pledges, the leet was 'divided into certain divisions', and they had 'the oversight of ten which are called decenarii, and they ought to see that they were of good behaviour, and to make their appearance at the lord's leet and lawday'. It was the constables' duty, 'at some convenient time before the court, to go from house to house and to take the names in writing of all the headboroughs, chief pledges and deceners who are couchant within the precinct of the leet'. By old custom, too, the Four and Twenty were entitled to have a dinner at each court day, but not the leeters. The jury admitted that the responsibility for the stocks, cucking-stool and pillory lay on the inhabitants, the lord providing the timber. They were also liable to 'find weights, scales and measures for the keeping of the assizes of bread and beer'. In this connection the jury added a further duty, not recorded elsewhere : 'Also a book of the acts of parliament which set down the assizes for bread and beer, which book, scales, weights and measures ought to be delivered to the ale-founders and constables to the end they may see that the assizes be kept according to the law, and if any default be herein, all the inhabitants ought to be amerced'.

Thus, in 15 long and separate bye-laws, only the most outstanding of which have been quoted, the inhabitants of the small market town of Hatfield Broad Oak were controlled and governed, perhaps as effectively as in any Essex manor.

## Fingrith Hall in Blackmore

The diversity of manorial customs and the uncertainty regarding some occasionally led a lord or a tenant to seek counsel's opinion. In the records of this manor is a file of papers endorsed, 'Certain questions upon acts done touching copyhold lands and the answers'. They belong to the 1580s and include the following questions put to a Mr Branthwaite,[18a] with his opinion on each:

> Remembrances for Mr Branthayte
> Whether copyhold lands sold for free lands by indenture be a cause of forfeiture?—If livery and seisin was made or any other thing used such is proper unto freehold land I do take it to be a forfeiture.
> Whether a customary tenant to him and his heirs according to the custom of the manor may lawfully without licence erect upon his lands divers dwellings building them with the lord's timber, yea or no? And whether it is a trespass or a forfeiture, yea or no?—It is a forfeiture as I take it unless there be a custom to maintain it.
> Whether a customary tenant having granted him by the Earl of Oxenford late owner of the manor all the wood, underwood, timber and trees growing upon the same to have, hold, fell, cut down and carry away, to the said tenant, his executors, administrators or assigns for ever, and after the said Earl selleth the manor unto Sir Walter Mildmay before there is any of the wood felled, the question is whether nevertheless the tenant may fell or dispose of the said woods and if he may so do whether his executors or any other may do the like by force of the same grant after his death?—The buyer, his executors or any other interested in the trees by the copyholder may fell them etc.

Attached is a copy of the Earl's deed of sale for 40s., paid by Richard Stonley of Doddinghurst, esquire, of 'all the wood, underwood, timber and trees standing on one piece of copyhold ground called Colemartyns'.

## Chelmsford

In 1591 a detailed survey and a map of the manor of Chelmsford *alias* Bishop's Hall were prepared for Sir Thomas Mildmay by John Walker senior. The 'book of the survey', made by 'exact view and upon the search of the court rolls, rentals, and other material escripts', was presented at the court held before 'Edward Moryson esquire, surveyor, John Lathum gentleman, steward, John Walker, measurer, and the tenants and suitors'. The map, which had long been lost, was discovered by the present writer in 1939. After a brief description of the town,[19] the survey sets out the 110 freehold and 99 copyhold tenements. It ends with two full statements of 'the liberties and franchises' and 'the customs and services'. Of these, the first is unusual in putting a valuation on each 'liberty'. The court baron and court leet, with their fines, heriots, waifs and estrays, were worth £20; the right of free warren and fishing in all the streams of the manor, £20; the privilege of holding pleas and of excluding the sheriff's officers, only 6s. 8d.; the fines and forfeitures of the inhabitants, whether the lord's tenants or not, levied on them in the royal courts at Westminster and at Assizes and Quarter Sessions, £11 13s. 4d.; the right of appointing the clerk of the market, the coroner and the escheator within his manor, with income from these officers, £6 13s. 4d.; and the right to the goods of felons and fugitives, £3 6s. 8d. But the weekly market and the annual fair are not valued, as the bailiff 'accounteth for the profits'. It is surprising that the townsmen did not seek borough status, as those of Thaxted and Dunmow had done in the previous reign; perhaps they concluded that Mildmay would have opposed an application which might have reduced his own powers.

The 'customs' section, compiled as a result of search of the rolls from as early as 1382, is fairly brief and on the whole unremarkable. The manor belonged to the bishops of London until 1545, when it became Crown property, and it had been acquired by Mildmay in 1563. The ancient render of 'palfrey money' to each bishop continued to be paid to the new lords at their initial courts. Every tenant, as in most manors, was liable to have his copyhold seized in case of waste or failure to maintain his dwelling house in good condition, but on grant of the lord's licence he could apparently demolish his outbuildings; and a special licence was required if a tenant wished to lease or sub-let his tenement.

It is perhaps surprising that Walker omitted to mention the 'schedule' of the bye-laws appended to the court roll for 1564. Admittedly, there are only six, relating chiefly to the common gutter, pollution and the like, some of which we have quoted in earlier chapters. But the preamble is formal and pompous, and the peroration equally so. A full copy had been given to the bailiff, 'to be always in readiness in his hands', and the bye-laws were also to be delivered at every leet to the jury, 'whereby the more effectually to enquire, find and truly to present upon their oath all the offences done or permitted in any thing contrary to the ordinances, so as by means thereof the offenders therein may be worthily punished, the lord justly answered of the forfeitures, and the abuses to be so much the sooner redressed'. William Sidey, the steward, had evidently enjoyed writing this prologue.

## Felsted

A very long survey embodying a custumal of this important manor was compiled for Lord Rich of Leighs Priory in 1577 as a result of the tenants' statements 'affirming' that they had been 'used and approved from time to time'. In many respects, indeed, they bear the stamp of ancient usage.[20] A brief note dated 1567 reveals that they were remarkably free in two respects: 'For our wood and timber, by our customs, we may do what we will, and for our houses of our copyholds we may take them down and do with them what we will'. The memorandum also includes a rare tithing composition: 'Our custom is for river mead 4d. an acre, for land mead 2d. an acre for tithe of hay', which probably refers to tenants' strips or doles in the common meadows.

The liberties attaching to Rich's manor were extensive. In addition to the usual deodands and kindred rights, he had jurisdiction over weights and measures, although he did not possess a market, and he took the fines and other income from the sheriff's tourn as well as exemption from the sheriff's and royal purveyors' activities. Not only were the tenants protected from arrest by the sheriff, but they also claimed through the lord the unusual 'privilege or liberty' of freedom from arrest in the neighbouring market-town of Braintree for debt or trespass, though not for felony, murder or treason. There are faint echoes, even from Saxon times and rarely heard elsewhere in Elizabethan Essex, for not only was ordinary justice restricted to his court but his manor had the ancient privileges of 'infangenthef' and 'outfangenthef'—the lord's right to arrest and punish a thief caught in the act within his boundaries as well as to pursue him outside.

The tenancy customs were especially detailed and were based largely on yardlands, half-yardlands and quarter-yardlands, all of which are fully described.[21] The customs are too lengthy to quote, but a few of the less normal ones may be mentioned. The fine payable on alienation, exchange or death by every customary tenant of one yardland was fixed at 10s., with 5s. or 2s. 6d. for each half- or quarter-yardland. Each 'unsettling tenant', or lessee, of a yardland, half or quarter, rendered a corresponding fine at the rate of 2d. an acre, but in his case no heriot could be claimed. Primogeniture at Felsted applied also to females, the copyhold descending to the eldest daughter in default of a male heir.

Remarkable testimony to the importance of the customs is seen from the fact that the Essex Record Office has acquired from different sources no less than four contemporary and later copies, two in Latin and two in translation.

## Great Dunmow

The two Essex parliamentary boroughs—Colchester and Maldon—are outside the scope of this book, but not the two manorial boroughs—

Dunmow and Thaxted. A most informative example of the bye-laws of such a borough is that of Great Dunmow, created by royal charter in 1555, for which a series of 25 'Orders and Bye-laws', written in English, was made in 1570. They have been published in full.[22] In addition to the usual officers—2 constables, 2 leather-searchers and 2 ale-tasters—the corporation was empowered to appoint a bailiff, a town clerk, a serjeant, and 12 head burgesses, the last being the counterparts of the chief pledges of ordinary manors. The bye-laws corresponding closely with those of many urban manors are five aimed at providing for clean streets and slaughter-houses, maintaining order in alehouses and inns, and controlling strangers. No inmates were to be taken in without the prior consent of the 'bailiff and his company or the most part of them'. Stern bye-laws subjected victuallers to monthly night search by the constables; the former must not lodge a stranger or wayfarer infected by the plague and were prohibited from allowing resort on Sundays or holy-days by 'men's sons or servants'. Apprentices and servants were subjected to equally strict supervision. Every artificer or householder was to bring his servants, journeymen and apprentices with him to quarterly meetings of the 'common assembly'. They and all sons were to be in their masters' or parents' homes by 9 p.m., and for default to be 'imprisoned for 2 hours' (presumably in the stocks or perhaps the cage), with a longer session if found in an alehouse or at unlawful games. If 'stubborn or disobedient to their masters', they were to be arrested and a second offence would result in 'open punishment'. Unmarried persons out of service were to be examined by the bailiff and two 'discreet burgesses', and if suspect were to be taken to a justice of the peace. Three bye-laws insisted on the burgesses' 'reverence' to the bailiff, and any burgess guilty of 'unseemly words' to another or to the officers was to be fined.

## Thaxted

This manorial borough had only very limited status and privileges. The medieval cutlery industry, as explained earlier, was no longer thriving. Hoping to revive the town's affluence, the inhabitants sought and obtained a Crown charter of incorporation in 1554. The new municipal borough's mayor, however, 'did never sit to keep court, but was commonly of courtesy called thereunto by the lord's steward', and he paid 2s. for his cushion! There ensued a long and bitter controversy between the two factions—the lord and the manorial officers on the one hand and the new borough officials on the other—for control of the town, no proper account of which has yet been written. We can refer only to two documents, drawn up in 1574-75 and entitled 'Liberties and Customs of the Manor and Borough' and 'Ordinances and Constitutions previously made'; the latter, like some of those already described, was based on search of the rolls, from Henry

VII onwards. In general, the customs do not differ materially from those of some other urban manors. Precedents quoted from earlier Elizabethan rolls include orders against the throwing of ordure or wood into the streets and dead pigs or dogs 'into Hall Garden or in the backsides or corners of the town'. Occupants of shops or stalls in the market were to keep them clean. Inmates were disallowed unless they bought and delivered to the householder 4 cartloads of firewood : another instance of compulsory self-provision of winter fuel. Anyone felling timber without the owner's leave would be fined 12d. and put in the stocks at the constables' discretion. Finally, 'There is an old custom that any having free land pay at each alienation or death 6d. for each acre of pasture and 12d. for each acre of meadow, on his admission'.

## Rivers Hall in Boxted

The survey of this manor is Walker's earliest but one known work, dated 1586, and was commissioned by John Ive, the lord. Unlike Walker's later maps drawn on vellum sheets, this is in the form of a paper book containing a series of small maps of farms, opposite each of which he wrote a statement of their names and acreage. After some introductory remarks, he recorded the customs, which he had gathered from nine named customary tenants.

> They hold their lands at the will of the lord according to the custom of the manor. Their fines are at the lord's will. They may not cut down any trees of oak, ash or elm without the lord's licence, neither may they girt or crop any timber tree. Any trees that have before been cropped, or cobed as they call it, they may crop for the use of their houses either for firebote, hedgebote or such like, not to carry or convey away any manner of woods from one copyhold to use upon another. Timber they must have upon their lands for the maintenance of their houses and other things needful to be taken, by licence and assignment of the lord or his appointed deputy, bailiff or other officer. Their rents to be paid half yearly and at their accustomed times. Heriots they pay generally at every decease. Suit and service they do owe as well unto the lord in the prince's service as also unto the courts or otherwise. Their use and custom of surrendering their lands is to be made and taken by 2 tenants and the bailiff or 2 tenants and any one man for the bailiff in his absence. Their usual fellable springs they may sell or fell by their custom at their wills.

'Cobe' is an otherwise unrecorded Essex dialect word, though evidently akin to 'cope', from the later sense of French *couper,* to cut.

## Woodham Ferrers

In 1582 'John Cooke gentleman, steward and surveyor', prepared on the instructions of the lord's lessee, Walter Fysshe, a London merchant tailor, a 200-page survey and custumal, which was beautifully bound in embossed leather. It presents a vivid picture of a rural manor. The owner was Robert Audley, and it formerly belonged to Thomas Lord Audley of Walden, Lord Chancellor. It was by no means uncommon for substantial land owners to farm out some of their manors, nor for Londoners to take leases for their country seats. Cooke had first met Humphrey Kenwelmarshe, Peter Jerome, William Boode, gentlemen, and 13 other named tenants, and then proceeded with his task. He prefaced his record with an informative introduction, setting out the potential advantages of the manor, and appended an illuminating account of the customs. A fairly full description of the survey and custumal has been published.[23]

> The manor of Woodham Ferrars alias Ferys . . . having very near thereunto two wharves or creeks of the sea called Clements Green and Woodham Fen in the parish, very fit and daily used for transporting and conveyance of billet, hostry, faggot, talwood, butter, cheese and corn to and from the city of London and elsewhere, for bringing thither of chalk, fish, bay, salt and other merchandise; and near also unto the same wharf be certain saltcotes which do make white salt . . . and certain oyster-layings. The most part of the grounds standeth by pasturage of milch kine and ewes, for the making of butter and cheese.

While the making of salt and ewes'-milk cheese in these parts adjoining the Crouch, as already seen, is true enough, Cooke's comments on likely profits were too optimistic. His remarks about the transport of timber from the wharves to London afford a useful comparison with that of his more distinguished fellow surveyor, John Norden, writing in the next decade, to 'creeks, which lead to certain ladings, where they take in wood, which carry it to London, which places are called upon the Thames woodwharves'.[24] The Woodham creeks are almost the farthest inland penetrations of the sea in Essex. The manorial fair, evidently for sheep, was now a very third-rate gathering, although still held for three days. The Saturday market, too, was nearly dead, for there were only 1 butcher and 2 victualling houses. There used to be, Cooke stated, as many as 6 butchers and 6 victuallers attending to the people's needs, from which it might be argued that the fair had once been of some importance in this area of sheep-producing marshes.

The long custumal, containing most detailed provisions regarding the copyholders, lists no fewer than a dozen different causes of forfeiture. They were strictly charged with maintaining their buildings in repair, but if there was no timber on their holdings the bailiff had to assign some from the demesne. Tenants were forbidden to common their swine and to dig gravel or tile- and brick-earth on the waste called the Hoe, and offenders were to be punished. By ancient custom, the tenants of Woodham and of the manor of Bicknacre in the north of the parish 'intercommoned together' on what was later called Bicknacre Common.

The manor of Woodham Ferrers, held of the Duchy of Lancaster, possessed full liberties. The lord and the court leet controlled the assize of bread, ale, beer and wine, weights and measures, waifs, strays, free warren, pillory, 'cuckingstool alias tumbrel', stocks, pound, treasure trove, and felons' goods, as well as hearing pleas under 40s. The sheriff, together with the Duchy officers, had to hold his tourn at Woodham, when the reeve and 4 men presented 'such offences as were concealed in the leet and none other'. Cooke may have prided himself as steward of these liberties, but they were now somewhat meaningless and profitless, owing partly to the low state of the market and fairs.

## Aveley

The undated survey of this manor near the Thames estuary can be assigned to a decade or two after Elizabeth's death, but life in the manor can hardly have changed since her time. It draws a fascinating picture of a small, declining market-town, though not so decayed as Woodham Ferrers. The survey proper is preceded by some exceptional remarks filling several pages.[25] 'The manor of Alvethlie', the compiler wrote, contains 'a poor (if not rude) town, where the market is kept'. The inhabitants and the steward in the court leet had in times past 'not only made certain orders and bye-laws, but by corporal and pecuniary punishment' endeavoured 'to redress and reform the misdemeanours and malefactors'; and he praised their efforts. He then gave his opinion on what he considered were the most serious offences: 'I cannot but observe that three things there be which, most of all, did and doth trouble the inhabitants, viz. the market, inmates, and hedge breakers and wood stealers'. The document re-creates lively scenes of market dealings before the authorized hour of 9 a.m. when the first bell was rung. Evasion of this regulation was all too rife, especially by strangers, who, 'thinking that the townsmen's hands by the order were bound, would before the bell did ring buy up all the cheese and butter, and so would either prevent the townsmen of their provision, or else they should buy butter and cheese at the second hand of them'. Strangers found guilty of such forestalling were to forfeit their purchases.

He cited six separate orders between 1564 and 1598 in the continual attempts to rid the manor of the potential burden of relieving unauthorized inmates. In 1568 householders were forbidden to take in any such 'undertenants' unless they had 'shown the constable a testimonial from 6 of the best men of the parish where such tenant last dwelt, of his good a-bearing'. Conversion of a barn, kitchen or outhouse into a dwelling as a means of eluding the anti-inmate order was to cease. The last order, perhaps unique in Essex, went so far as to threaten a 20s. fine on any owner whose inmate brought with him infants or others 'that should not carry themselves well', with a similar penalty on failure to turn out the subtenant within two months. From inmates the writer passed to the idlers and the unemployed. Retrospectively and fulsomely, he patronized those who 'hath so pursued their good service to their township that if any suspected person or able person to work did but linger or loiter within the township they did presently present them'. In 1538 'Robert Longnose and his wife and Great Meg'—expressive nicknames—had been commanded 'to avoid the town before Christmas', and he also found two Elizabethan cases of householders fined for harbouring young men and maids who refused to serve. Returning to the attack, he fulminated : 'Notwithstanding all the aforesaid orders and care of the inhabitants, yet hath the town from time to time so swarmed with inmates that not one court is passed without some presentment against inmates, and many of them, being of lewd sort as whores, scolds, lazy and idle people, have brought horrible and not to be named sins and wickedness into the town, insomuch as besides perpetual drunkenness, frays and bloodshed and such like as by name are many times presented, some of the inhabitants are amerced for suffering in their houses things not be spoken of nor tolerated'. All this from the pen of a secular surveyor, not a puritan preacher. Inmates, too, received his final censure. 'The third sort be hedgebreakers and woodstealers—people engendered of the inmates—for wheresoever you find a presentment against inmates the next presentment is inseparable from them who be hedgebreakers and woodstealers'. In 1563 the 'landlord' of any such offender was to bear a fine of 10s., but, 'because this order gave no scare to the tenants because there was no punishment appointed unto them', the loophole was closed in 1581 by an injunction to fine them 12d. and put them in the stocks for a night and a day. The court also decided in 1598 that the master of any boy or girl woodstealer should pay a 2s. fine. Perhaps the spasmodic campaign was against undesirables who came downstream from London or ferrywise from Kent.

At any rate, in the Aveley survey and in court rolls elsewhere, we have seen how numerous were the attempts to raise the curtain walls against intruders before the Poor Law Acts of 1597 and 1601 heightened the walls still further. Demographers so far have not studied manor court rolls in depth to find out what they tell on the problem of mobility, though it seems that collation of evicted inmates' names with those in parish registers might yield some fruitful results.

Nor, the present writer confesses, with many manorial records not unrolled by him, has he studied the Essex rolls as fully as he had intended. And so, like the anonymous surveyor of Aveley manor three and a half centuries ago, he concludes :

> And these things breifflie be as much as upon the cursorie reading of the court rolls I thinck fyt to observe, omitting no doubt of many other matters more worthy of observacion.

No doubt, too, the verdict against the author, as in the time-honoured phrase, will be:

*Ideo est in misericordia.*


[1] *Ess. Rev.*, li, 100n.
[2] Sir Edward Coke, *The Compleat Copy-holder* (1650); *Lex Custumaria, or a Treatise of Copyhold Estates*, by 'S.C.' (1701).
[3] Eland, *op. cit.*, 18-20.
[4] All manorial surveys and maps are analysed in Emmison (ed.). *Catalogue of Maps in the E.R.O.* and its three *Supplements* (1947-68).
[5] Reproduced by Mrs D. Monteith, 'Elizabethan Manorial Surveys' (*Geography*, xliii, 1958). Also one of Maldon, by Mr W. Petchey, in *Essex Towns, 1540-1640* (E.R.O. Publn. no. 53).
[6] R. S. Charnock, *Ancient Manorial Customs, Tenures, etc., in the County of Essex* (1870): antiquarian, not scholarly; although drawn partly from Beckwith's later edition of Thomas Blount's *Ancient Tenures of Land* (1679), it contains much from other sources.
[7] See F. W. Steer, *History of the Dunmow Flitch Ceremony* (E.R.O. Publn. no. 13).
[8] Emmison, *Tudor Secretary*, 22-27.
[9] *E.L.: Disorder*, 23.   [10] *Ibid.*, 20-23, for similar cases.
[11] In the printed version the headings of the two sections have been interchanged in error: for 'Bye-laws' read 'Customs', and *vice versa* (G. H. Rendall, *Dedham in History*, 1937, 33-36).
[12] Balfour, *Praticks* (*c.* 1550), cited in *O.E.D.*
[13] I am grateful to my friend James Wentworth Day for this note.
[14] Apparently the Thomas, the story of whose elopement with Frances daughter of Lord Rich was told in *E.L.: Disorder*, 186-7.
[15] *Trans. E.A.S.*, xiii, 82-85. There are several transcription errors, e.g. in article no. 15, read 'coverte' for 'court', and in no. 19, read 'shiffted' for 'shifsted'
[16] *Ess. Rev.*, l, 189-200; li, 32-42, 88-100.
[17] Brit. Mus., Lansdowne MS. 47, no. 19, quoted by Mrs M. K. McIntosh in her unpublished Harvard Univ. Ph.D. thesis, 'The Cooke Family of Gidea Hall, 1460-1661' (1967).
[18] Emmison, *Early Essex Town Meetings: Braintree and Finchingfield, 1619-34* (1970).
[18a] Probably Richard Branthwayte, serjeant-at-law, London, whose will was proved 1594 (P.C.C.).
[19] This initial paragraph was printed by Morant, *History of Essex*, ii, 2 n
[20] See *Ess. Rev.*, xxviii, 62-76; *Trans. E.A.S.*, xiv, 209-19.
[21] The yardland represented the medieval virgate, or average-size villein's holding, and was generally reckoned at about 30 acres, though with local variations depending on several factors; 30 a. is also the figure given by John Norden in his *Surveyor's Dialogue* (1607), 59.
[22] *Ess. Rev.*, xxviii, 165-72.
[23] *Trans. E.A.S.*, xxiv, 6-16.
[24] Norden, *Description of Essex, 1594* (Camden Soc., 1849), 10.
[25] Full transcription in Dr. F. Hull's thesis (copy in E.R.O.), appendix 10. For the medieval and Tudor manor court rolls of Aveley, see *Ess. Rev.*, xv, 113-32.

# Index of Subjects

NOTES. (1) *Occupations*.—The normal cross-references have *not* been made between the numerous crafts and craftsmen, or trades and traders, e.g. between brickmaking and brickmakers, cloth industry and the various artificers engaged in it; brickmakers, etc., are all brought together under 'crafts and occupations'.

(2) *Unusual words* are all brought together under 'words, rare, archaic, or local'.

access for relations to rooms, fire, well, etc., 7, 95-100
accounts, learning to cast, 120-1
acorns, 253
acts of parliament, 29, 44, 52, 55, 86, 132-3, 143, 146, 157, 169, 170, 175, 177, 190, 193-5, 199, 238, 242, 249, 265, 268, 271, 274, 288, 299; book of, 324
Admiralty Court, 320
admissions and surrenders, manorial, 208-10, 217-8, 221, 259, 261, 313-4, 317, 329; at age of 15, 319
advowson, 284
affeering of fines, 215
agistment, 318
agriculture, 33-58
alehouses, unlicensed or disorderly, 148-9, 151, 162; 328; *see also* inns; victuallers
aletasters, 225-8, 307, 324, 328
aliens, 307; *see also* 'Dutch'
alleys, *see* bowls
America, North, 3, 25, 61, 78, 103-4
animals, dead, 290-1, 293-6, 305, 318, 329; *see also* estrays; heriots; livestock
apprentices and apprenticeship, 119-21, 125-7, 146, 151-8, 328; *see also* journeymen
arable, 37-8; *see also* fields, open

archery practice, 240-2
Armada, 62-3, 127, 241
armour, *see* weapons
Artificers, Statute of, 146-64
assault, 170, 220, 233-4
Assize of Bread and Ale, 177, 179, 189, 192, 226, 299-303, 324, 331; of Fuel, 190, 193
Assizes, indictments at, 169, 180-1, 187-8, 212-3, 232-3, 326; account of fines, 192; case transferred to, 193
attornment, 207-8, 312; *see also* palfrey money.
aumbry, 21
'avoid' (eviction from manor), 221, 234-5, 256, 270-3

bachelors, out of service, 146, 149, 152-4, 156, 159-60
backgammon, *see* tables
bacon, 10, 29-31, 53, 181, 183
badgers, 175-89
bailiffs of manors, 208-333, esp. 223-4
baking, 96, 98
barges, barks, 60-3, 66
barns, repair of, 6, 259-62, 331
barrators, 235, 309
basket-making, 44
bastards, provision for, 113
bays and says, 196, 306-7
beadle, 227
beagles, 237
bearing sheet, 15
beavers polluting brook, 318

beds and bedding, 3, 12-16, 31-2, 110
beer, 1, 5, 29-30, 299-302; *see also* brewing; hops
bees, 30, 105; *see also* honey
beggars, 269; *see also* vagabonds
benches and benchboards, 9-10, 18-19
bitches, salt, 249
blind children, 111
boar, common, 320
boat, licence to cut timber to repair, 263; *see also* ships
bonds, 101, 105, 111-2, 119, 143, 270
bond (boon) services, 201, 210, 315, 321
books, 4, 123-5
Borough English, 311, 317-21
boroughs, manorial, 225, 228, 311, 326-9; Gt. Dunmow, 295; Thaxted, 225, 228
boulting-trough, 28
boundaries, manorial, viii, 243-7, 264, 314, 324; marks, 279
bowls, 151, 238
brass utensils, 25-7
bread, 28, 36; weighers, 225-8
brewing, 87-8, 98; implements, 9-10, 27-8
bricks and brickmaking, 3, 86-7, 322, 330
bridals, 41
bridges out of repair, 148, 281-3; *see also under* individual parishes
buildings, repair of, 7-8,

# INDEX OF SUBJECTS

259-64, 309, 311-3, 316-7, 321, 324-7, 330; conversion, 331; unlawful, 259-66, 317; right to demolish or sell, 254, 317, 321; *see also* houses
bulls and bullocks, 50-2; common, 320; unbaited, 239
butter, 5, 10, 28-33, 45-8, 104; dealers in, 175-86
butts, archery, 133, 317, 240-2
bye-laws, 248-331

cage, *see* punishment
calico, 139
calves, statute about rearing, 52-3
candles, bad or excessive prices, 81, 300, 306
caps, not wearing woollen, 274-6
caravel, 60
carding, 75
cards (game), 151, 232
carpets (table), 15, 17; (floor), 17
carriers, 90, 175-6, 187
carts, 54-5, 82
casting sheet, 15
catch, *see* ketch
cattle, *see* drovers; livestock
causeways, 283
ceilings, 9, 13
chairs, 18-9
chamber pot, 16
Chancery cases, 253, 313
charcoal, 55-6, 83, 318; *see also* coals
charities, 6; almshouses, Lt. Ilford, 134; Stock, 262
chapels, free, 314
chapmen, 175; *see also* dealers
cheese, 4, 5, 10, 28-33, 45-8, 104; dealers in, engrossing, 175-86, 330-1
children, employed at young age, 76; provision for, 102-12; incapacitated, 111-2; illegitimate, 113; insubordinate, 116-7; pilfering, 256-8; cost of bringing up, 119
chimneys, 3, 6, 7, 25, 107, 117; *see also* hearths
church, arms stored in, 132
churchwardens, sale of goods by, 108, 110
churchyards, hogs pasturing in, 249
'clampole', 82
clay, digging, 254-5, 287, 322
clergy, wills of, 125; as writers of wills, 115; *see also under individual parishes* in Index of Persons and Places
clerks of the peace, 175-6, 223; parish, 140-1; town, 328; of the market, *see* market, clerks of; of the kitchen, 142; to J.P., 176
close-stool, 16
cloth, industry, 75, 169; depression, 151; inspectors, 194; materials, 13-15, 24; painted, *see* hangings, wall
clothes, apprentices, 126, 129; servants, 92, 150-2, 158, 161, 165-7; holyday and workday, 31, 119, 127-8; *see also* sumptuary laws
coals (sea), 16, 55-6, 83, 258 *see also* charcoal
coastal trade, 59-66, 258, 330
cock-boats, 60-70, 215
coffers, 19-21, 24
commissioners for forestalling, 178
common-driver, 227
common fields, *see* fields, open
commons, 34, 49, 314; encroachment on, 221; overcharging, 244-6, 318; damaging, 236, 247-9-54; felling timber, 250-4; Aldham, 254; Gt. Baddow, 244, 247, 253; Lt. Baddow, 251, 255; Gt. Bardfield, 254; Gt. Bentley, 245, 247, 320-1; Clavering, 244; Epping, 248, 265-6; Felsted, 244; Harlow, 254, 287; Hockley, 51; Kelvedon, 251; Navestock, 251; Newport, 236, 244; Purleigh, 254; Ramsden Crays, 244; Rettendon, 245, 252, 265, 273; Stanway, 37; Shenfield, 254; Stock, 254; Wanstead, 255; Woodham Ferrers, 330; *see also* enclosure; greens; heaths; marshes
conies, 237, 316
constables, high, 106, 141, 149-63; manorial, 224-5, 233; petty, 148-9, 151, 178-9, 228, 234, 236, 241, 251, 255-7, 270-3, 312, 324, 328-31; high, *see* Sessions, High Constables'
contempt of court, 309-10
cooking, 1, 24-6, 41
copyholds, *see* manors
corn, dealers in, 179-89; sale at excessive prices, 157; *see* export, illegal
coroners, 212-3, 326
cottages, four acres to, Act, 265, 268; out of repair, *see* buildings
counsel's opinion, 325
courts baron and leet, 199, 216, 229, 233, 301, 306, 312, 317-8, 320, 323, 331; hundredal,

148-62; county, 321; *see also* sessions, high constables'
covenants for hiring servants, 148, 150-2, 165-6-7, 171; in leases, 37
cows, 44-53
cradle, 13
crafts, *see* trades; craftsmanship, poor, 300
crayers, 60, 66
crops, 33-44; acorns, 36; barley, 27, 35-9, 180-4; bullimong, 35-6, 39; corn, 4, 5, 10, 29, 30, 33, 35; dredge, 36; flax, 44, 76; hemp, 44; hops, 33, 39-40, 195, 256, 280; maslin, 29, 35-6, 104, 181, 183; mixed, 35-6; oats, 30, 35-6, 179-81, 184, 188; osiers, 44; peas, 36, 179-84, 188; rye, 4, 35-6, 184; saffron, 34-5, 40-4, 292; wheat, 30-1, 35-6, 181-4, 187; rotation, 37
crosses, Moulsham, 289; Chelmsford, 293, 303; Billericay, 303
cuckingstools, *see* punishments
cuckolds, 234
cupboards, 21, 99
cushions, 17
Customs, Board of, 59
customs, *see* manors
custumals, 238, 311-6
cutlery industry, 83-6

dairy, 28; *see also* butter; cheese; wicks
daubing, 5-6, 8, 261
dealers in food supplies, 90, 175-89; illegal, 149, 157, 177-90, 303
debts, 62, 67, 87, 91-3, 108, 217; pleas of, 320, 327
deceners, 204-7, 312, 323-4
deeds, title (evidences), 20

demesne, 314, 319, 321, 330
deodands, 213, 316, 327
depositions, 41
dice, 232, 239
diseases of animals, 249; *see also* food, unhygienic
disputes under wills, 115-8
Dissolution, 315
ditches, unscoured, 148-9, 221, 283-6
dogs, 249
Domesday Book, Essex, 201
dovecotes, 314
dower, 101-2, 311, 319, 321
dowries, 111
drainage, land, 285-6; street, 290-2; *see also* ditches
'Draperies, New', 75, 77
drink, *see* beer; milk; verjuice
drovers, cattle, 175, 290
drunkards, 230-5, 332
'Dutch' (Flemings), 306-7
dyeing, 75

eavesdroppers, 273
eavesdrops, 286
'educate' (meaning), 103, 118, 123
education, 105, 118-23; cost of, 120, 122; religious, 103, 120, 122; at universities, 106, 121-2; at inns of court, 106; of girls, 119, 122
eggs, dealers in, 177, 180-1, 185
embroidery, 15, 18
employment, 146-74
enclosure, for sheep-farming, 37; for parks, 37; of open fields, 37, 314; of commons, 49; parliamentary, 243-4
encroachments, *see* purprestures
engrossing, 175-89, 192, 331

escape, 236-7
escheats, 211-2
essoins, 204-5, 218
estrays, 214
estreat rolls, 215, 257, 299-302
estripment, 317, 319
ewes, milking, 34, 45-9
executors, *see* wills
export, 68; illegal, of grain, etc., 181-2
extents, 314

fairs, 175, 192-4, 303-4, 314; list of, 193; servants' hiring, *see* sessions, high constables; Blackmore, 287; Chelmsford, 326; Hatfield Broad Oak, 91; Hedingham, 91; Newport, 9, 214; Woodham Ferrers, 330
fallow, 35, 37, 39
family and household, 95-131
farming, *see* agriculture
fealty, 208
felonies, 212, 231-3; felons' goods, 211-2, 316, 326, 331
fens, 245-7; *see also* marshes
fences and hedges, failure to maintain, 266-7
ferries, Creeksea, 289; Fambridge, 72
fertilizers, 35
feudal incidents, 208-10
fields, open, 37-8, 243-7, 267, 285, 289, 292, 311, 314, 317; *see also* enclosure; meadows, open
fines (amercements), Part 3, *passim;* at high constables' sessions, 149, 151, 171; at ordinary hundredal sessions, 148, 169; at Quarter Sessions, 166, 192; for engrossing, etc., 182, etc.
fines (fees) for admission,

## INDEX OF SUBJECTS

etc., 206, 208-10; for licences, 210, 317; common, 206-7, 312, 321, 324
firebote, 252, 257, 329
fire prevention, 10, 267; destruction by, 259, 261
fish, 53, 63, 65, 69-72; named, 70; salted, 304; value of, 326; tasters, 226-8, 324; carrier, 53; *see also* mussels; sprats; oysters
fisheries, 59-72, 311, 314; illegal fishing, 237-8, 318
fixtures, 8-10, 17
flax, 44, 76
flax, Act relating to, 195
flesh, blowed, 305, 318
food, 28-31, 33; London market, 35, 48, 290; provision of, for widows, 95-6, 101; unwholesome, 239, 304-5; inspectors, 226-8; servants' liveries, 21; utensils, 26-31; *see also* bacon; bread; butter; cheese; fish; dealers; harvests; milk
football, 239
footpaths, repair of, 283
forestalling, 175-89
forfeitures, monetary, Part 3, *passim;* of copyholds, 252, 265, 316, 326, 330; *see also* informers
forges, 85, 266
forests, 311; Hatfield, 324; Waltham, 243-6, 251
forfeiture of goods, 217; of felons' goods, 211-2, 316, 326, 331; of holdings, 224, 259-64; (fines), *see* fines
'Four and Twenty', 323-4
fowling, wild, 70-1, 134, 136

frame of house, 5-6; *see also* houses, timber-framed
frankpledge, view of, 199, 207, 233, 323
free bench, 319-20
freeholds and freeholders, 201, 204-5, 208-9, 217-8, 314, 321, 323, 328-9
friary, Moulsham, 284
fruit, 31, 99; rotten, 305; trees, 10, 107
fuel, provision of, for relations, 95-101, 114; compulsory provision of, 258, 329; broom, furze, hedgewood, 44, 56, 251-8, 323; *see also* coals
fulling, 75; *see also* mills
funerals, 65
furnace, 27
furze, *see* fuel
furniture and furnishings, 9, 12-24; *see individual articles*

games, unlawful, 238-40; *see also* bowls; bull-baiting; cards; dice; football; scales; slide-groat; tables; *also* poaching
gaol, county, 45, 212
gardens, 10, 107
gavelkind, 311, 320
geese, 248
genealogy, 218
gittern, 23
glass, 8-9, 22; *see also* mirror
gleaning, 258-9
gloves, searchers of, 227
godparents and godchildren, 104, 114-5, 129
grain, dealers in, 179-89; dearth of, 176-86; hoarding, 175-9, 187; wheat prices, 177; rye, 177; parish returns (1571-4), 179-80;

illegal export, 181; *see also* crops
gravel, digging, 330; pits, 287
graveyard, sale in, 224
greens, 221, 314; Berden, 285; Gt. Burstead, 241, 294; Epping, 248; Harlow, 241, 282; Rayleigh, 51; Rochford, 92; Salcott, 248; Springfield, 269; Witham, 289; *see also* commons
greyhounds, 237-8
guardians, 105-6, 119, 143, 319
guns, 237
gutters, common, 231, 326; *see also* kennels

haircloth-weaving, 195
hangings, wall, and painted cloths, 7, 9, 13, 22, 78
harbouring, *see* inmates
hares, 237-8
harvests, deficient, 175-7, 183, 187; hay, 243; wages at, 165-6; help for widow at, 100
hawks, 316
haymaking, 36-7, 243
hayward, 236
headboroughs, 271, 310, 320-1, 324
hearths, 1-3, 7-10, 267; implements, 25; *see also* chimneys
heaths, 34, 39, 314; Bromley, 258; Dedham, 318; Frating, 320; Tiptree, 243; Wanstead, 245
hebbing-boat, 63
hedge-breaking, 250, 255-64, 331-2; failure to maintain, 266-7; hedgebote, 97
heirlooms, 8
hemp, 44; Act relating to, 195
herdman, 227

## INDEX OF SUBJECTS

heriots, 54, 210, 319, 326-9
highways, animals on, 248-9; impassable, 148; obstructions on, 40, 286-9; encroachment on, 266; uncleansed ditches, 284-5; repair of, 242-3; surveyors of, 227
hoggerels, 46-7
hogs, 10; wandering, 248, 294, 318
homage, 204-8, 218, 259, 263-4, 309; *see also* juries, manorial
homicide, 212
honey, 30; *see also* bees
hops, *see* crops
horses, 53-4; on commons, 248; horse-fair, 91; horse-mill, 9
hospitals, Chelmsford, 271; Ilford, 134; Newport, 281; South Weald, 284
household utensils, 10, 24-30, 88, 102
houses, rooms names of: backhouse, 5, 107; bedroom, 1-4; buttery, 1-2, 5, 27-8, 107; cellar, 4; chamber, 1-4; guest's chamber, 4; hall, 1-4, 18; hallhouse, 98, 221; kitchen, 2, 5, 10, 261-2; longhouse, 7; outhouses, 5, 24, 97-8, 261-2, 265-6; pantry, 1; parlour, 1-3, 98; service rooms, 1-2, 5; sollar, 3-4, 97-8, 101, 107, 267; stairs, 4; study, 4; *see also* fixtures; glass
houses, surviving medieval, 1-3, 200; new, 5-7, 261-8, 322, 325; enlarged, 5-7; jettied, 266; timber-framed, 254-62; petitions to build cottages, 268-9; *see also* buildings
hoys, 60-2, 70, 181
hue and cry, 214
hundredal courts, 321; record of 1417, 281-2
husbandmen, *passim*
husbandry covenants, 37
hutches, 19-21

idiot, 317; *see also* lunacy
immoral offences, 149, 316
implements, farm, 54-5; craft, 74-90; kitchen, 25-8, 88, 102
industries, *see* trades, *also under individual industries*
infangenthef, 327
informers, 170-1, 175, 183-8, 193, 195
inmates (sub-tenants), 258, 268-74, 328-32
innkeepers, 45, 135, 162, 172, 175, 190, 192, 213, 300-1; *see also* alehouse-keepers
inns, 190, 328; named, 39, 77, 108-9, 261, 284; *see also* signs
intercommoning, 330
insanitary conditions, 221, 227, 290-8
interest, legacies and loans at, or profit, 51, 91-3, 103, 111, 126, 142-4; *see also* vantage
intestacy, 95
inventories, 2, 26, 27, 31, 35, 44 n. 33, 54, 66, 81, 93, 102 (*in full*), 124, 133, 144
islands, *see* Canvey; Foulness; Wallasea

jakes, 290
jetties, 286
jewellery, 20, 105, 130; *see also* plate
journeymen, 154, 165, 326, 328; *see also* apprentices
juries, grand, 149; manorial, 204, 217, 220, 309-12, 315, 323; *see also* sessions
justices of the peace, 44, 106, 129, 136, 147, 151-5, 162, 165, 170-8, 182, 225, 273, 297, 328; divisions, 182; clerk to J.P., 176; *see also* Quarter Sessions

keddles, 70-1
keepers (sickroom), 91, 138-9, 144
kennels, 290-5
ketches, 60, 66-9
kettles, 26-7; tinker's, 26, 86
kidders, 175, 177
kilns, 108, 195
kitchen implements, 25-8, 88, 102
kitchens, separate, 2, 5, 99

labourers, 1, 110, 138, 178, 268, 284; hungry, 146; Statute of, 146-64
lace, bone, 15
lading-places, 65
larceny, petty, 233
lattices, 9
law day, 323
laynes, *see* oysters
lead (cauldron), 9
leases, 37, 46-8, 72, 90, 112, 201, 246, 248, 278-9, 330; stock, 46-51
leather crafts, 79-81, 177; searchers, 226-8, 324, 328
Lent, 237; killing calves in, 192
libel, 234
liberties, manorial, 199, 201, 207, 216, 228, 238, 312, 315-6, 326-8, 331; royal, 192
licences, to dealers in food supplies, 175-89; tanners, 177; to fell timber, 136, 210, 250-62, 265, 268-9, 317, 329; to demolish buildings, 210; to put son to

## INDEX OF SUBJECTS 339

school, 315; *see also* alehouses; victuallers
lighter, 63
linen, 76; bed, 13-16, 20; wearing, 20
livery and maintenance, 149
liveries, servants', *see* clothes
livestock, 35-6, 39, 44-5; common or pasture rights, 243-6, 318; killed at Martinmas, 304; bequests of, 110, 113; dealers in, 178, 182-3, 249; *see also* animals; bulls and bullocks; calves; cows; ewes; hoggerels; hogs; horses; oxen; pigs; runts; sheep; theaves
l(o)aders, 175-6, 185, 187
loans, 91-3; *see also* interest; pawns
longevity, 140
looms, 75, 77, 121
lunacy, 221; *see also* idiot
lutes, 23

malt, 4, 5, 27, 30, 104, 180, 182, 188; furze used in making, 251
manor courts, social background, 197-203; lords and tenants, 204-19; original presentments, 220-22; officers, 223-8; punishments, 229-31; offences and nuisances, 232-98; control of trade, 299-308; contempt of court, 309-10; custumals, byelaws and surveys, 311-33; held in open?, 285; lord's income, 201, 215-6, 228, 251-2, 272, 276, 326; pleas at, 216-7, 320-1, 327; *see also* admissions; forfeitures; freeholds; *for* deodands, etc., *see under* those titles; *for* individual

*manors, see under names of parishes in index of Persons and Places*
manor-houses, 314-5
manorial documents in E.R.O., 198, 201; searches in ancient rolls, 263, 278, 301, 313-9, 324-8
maps, estate, 284, 288, 325, 329; tithe, 314
market, clerks of the, 191-3, 227-8, 299-302, 326
market houses or places, Barking, 304; Billericay, 296; Chelmsford, 303; Epping, 249, 296, 304; Halstead, 296; Horndon, 304; Witham, 294
markets, 41, 44, 90-8, 299-304, 314; list of, 182; charters, 303; zone of influence, 304; officers, 227-8; bushel, 301; lacking weights, 191; fish, 63, 296, 303; horse, 53; leather, 303; meat, 48; wool, 303; illegal dealing at, 175, 178; London food, 35, 48
markets in Essex: list of, 182; Aveley, 299-300, 303-4, 331; Billericay, 182, 186, 303-4; Braintree, 182, 186; Brentwood, 181-3, 191; Chelmsford, 182-3, 296, 186, 303-4, 326; Dunmow, 186; Epping, 182, 303, 305; Halstead, 303; Horndon-on-the-Hill, 303-4; Newport, 53; Romford, 181, 183-4; Thaxted, 329; Waltham Abbey, 179, 303; Woodham Ferrers, 303, 330
marl, 35, 254-5

marriage, legacies conditional on, 114, 116-7; juvenile, 117; portions, *see* dowries
marshes, coastal, 34-6, 45-50, 71, 314; riverine, 39, 48; Mar Dyke; 245; Harlow, 247; Orsett Fen, 245; Lt. Baddow, 279
masters and mistresses, 123, 129-31, 139; *see also* apprentices; servants; Sessions, Hiring
masterless persons, *see* Sessions, High Constables'
mayor of Thaxted, 328
meadows, 36-7, open (common), 37-9, 44, 280, 243, 247, 317-8, 327
measures, coomb, 36; cheese, 264; dish, 29; lead, 30, 264; seam, 36; timber, 82; wey, 29-30; wood, 55; *see also* weights
meat, 10, 47; unhygienic, 300
medicine, books relating to, 125
mentally deficient, 112; *see also* idiot
milk from ewes, 34, 45-9
millers, 20, 28-9, 43, 96, 140-1, 146, 153, 170-1, 177-82, 187-8, 191-3, 278-80, 287, 300, 302, 307, 309
mills, water-, obstructions to rivers, 278-80; Gt. Bentley, 300; Chelmsford, 300; Coggeshall, 37; Halstead, 209, 279, 307; Hatfield Peverel, 279; Leyton, 283; Springfield, 278; Walden, 279; West Ham, 188; Wethersfield, 300; White Roothing, 289; Witham, 278, 280; fulling, Gt. Baddow, 39

# INDEX OF SUBJECTS

mills, wind-, 314; Norton Mandeville, 180; Rettendon, 300; Gt. Saling, 191
millhouse (domestic), 5; horsemill, 9, 28; handmill, 28
mirror, 21
mobility of population, 163
mothers, provision for, 112-3; unmarried, 270; in-law, 117
mongers, 60, 62, 68-70
murder, 212
musical instruments, 23-4
mussels, 68-9
musters, 132, 135

names, children of same Christian, 108, 112
New England, *see* America, North
nightwalkers, 256
nine-pins, *see* scales
'North Seas', 66
notaries, public, 134, 141
nuisances, public, 148, 278-98; surveyors of, 227
nuncupative wills, *see* wills

occupations, *see* trades
offensive trades, 307
open fields and meadows, *see* fields; meadows
orphans, 104, 113-4
orders made at manor courts, 233-308
osiers, 279-80
outlawry, 212, 316
overcharging by tradesmen, 299-301
overseers, *see* poor; wills
oxen, plough, 51
oysters, 60, 68-72, 176, 330

painted clothes, *see* hangings, wall
'palfrey money', 208, 316, 326
pardons by lords of manors, 261, 266, 275

parks, 34, 37, 267, 321; in Gt. Bentley, 321; Epping, 253; Havering, 321; Ingatestone, 249; Southminster, 71; Stock, 288; Stondon Massey, 288; Thaxted, 288; Wanstead, 267; Wivenhoe, 257
parsonages, 314; Gt. Dunmow, 56
partridges, 316
pastoral farming, 33, 35-6, 45-53; pasture rights, 243-8; 'pasture towns', 184; *see also* agistment; livestock
pawns, 93; *see also* loans
pedlars, 176
peterboats, 60, 63
petitions, 169; to build cottages, 268-9
petty sessions, *see* Sessions, High Constables'
pewter, 16, 27, 32, 88
pheasants, 316
pigs, 49, 53
Pilgrim Fathers, 62
pillory, *see* punishments
pinder, 249
pinfolds, 249-50
pits in roadside verges, 287
plague, 105, 140, 328
plate, 24, 93, 102; *see also* jewellery; silver
pleas at manor courts, *see* manor
pledges, chief, 204-6, 212, 218, 225, 272, 312, 324, 328; *see also* headboroughs
ploughs, 54-5
poaching, 237-8, 316, 318
pollution of watercourses, 290-8, 307, 318, 326
poor, 36, 160, 194, 265, 275-6, 307; testators, 138; bequests to, 110, 115; of Dedham, 186; supply of grain to, 180, 184-5; collectors, 92; overseers, 257, 272;

fuel for, 256-8; *see also* charities; dealers, unlawful; inmates; prices; truck; vagabonds
population, of Dedham, 186; mobility, 163
ports, 59-60, 63, 258; Colchester, 56
pottery industry, 86-7, 297
poultry, 54, 99, 248; dealers in, 178, 182-6
pounds, 248-50, 331; breach, 236
preachers, 78, 124
presentments at High Constables' Sessions, 148, 178; at Quarter Sessions, 148; to ordinary hundredal sessions, 177; articles, 176; at manor courts, Part 3, *passim;* premature disclosure of, 309, 316
prices, excessive, 175, 179, 181, 190-2, 299; wheat statistics, 177; of beer, 179; butter, 91; chairs, 18; lodging, 139; sea-coal, 258; shoes, 91; timber, 258; vinegar, 91; *see also* wages
primogeniture, 107, 311, 319; eldest daughter, 319, 327
privies, 16, 290-5
Privy Council, orders by and reports to, 44, 151, 168, 173, 175-90, 195, 307; 'Book of Orders', 183, 187
privy search, 149, 226
proclamations against dealers in food supplies, 185; against starchmakers, 188; at high constables' sessions, 150-1, 159, 162; by Privy Council, 175
public health, offences against, 290-98

# INDEX OF SUBJECTS

pump, access to, 99
punishment, implements of, Parts 2 and 3, *passim*; at manor courts, 229-31; cage, 328; cucking-stool, 191, 230, 234, 324, 331; pillory, 191-2, 234, 324, 331; stocks, 148, 151, 160, 233-4, 239, 251, 255-8, 317, 324, 328-32; *see also* fines
purprestures, 264-5
purveyors, vii, 316, 327

Quarter Sessions, 41, 53, 147-9, 161-6, 169, 171, 176-90, 233, 236, 242-3, 264, 268-9, 281, 303, 316, 326; *see also* justices
quay, Barking, 63

rate, to scour common gutter, 293
rebellion in Essex, abortive, 146, 183
rectories, Ingatestone, 317; Purleigh, 282; Springfield, 125
reeves, 151, 227, 331
registration of holdings, 217-9
regrating, 175-89, 302
reliefs, manorial, 208
religious education, 103
removals, *see* inmates
rents, manorial, 201, 315; rentals, 314-5
rescue, 154, 227, 236
rivers, Cam, 56; Crouch, 68-9, 330; Roach, 68; Thames, 48, 62, 330; filth thrown into, 292-5; obstructions to, 196, 278-80
roads, *see* highways
robberies, highway, 133, 288
rogues, *see* vagabonds
rooms, provision for separate rooms for widow, 96-9

runts, Welsh, 47

saffron, 34-5, 40-44, 292
salmon, 63
salt(-cellar), 24
salt and salting, 10, 28-32; salt industry and saltcotes, 88-90, 330
sanitation, 290-8
sawpits, 287, 296
scales (nine-pins), 238
schools, 314-5; education at, 119; cost of, 120; meaning university, 122; Chelmsford grammar, 271
scolds, 231, 234-5
'screens', 1
sea-coals, *see* coals
searchers, 227; *see also* leather
searches, privy, 149, 226
seawalls, 8, 246
'second best', 31-2
seisure of copyholds, *see* forfeitures
serjeanties, 315
servants, 13-14, 17, 21, 64, 100, 328; superior, 92, 129-34, 138, 142, 167, 176, 211, 217, 234-8, 257; bequests by and to, 127-31; testimonials, 149, 153, 271, 331; liveries, *see* clothes, servants'
service, put to or hiring for, 106, 112, 114, 119, 146-64, 178; working by the day, 151, 153, 157-8; enticing from, 172
Sessions, High Constables' Petty, or Statute, 146-64, 183, 187; clerk to, 161; places at which held, 163; ordinary Hundredal, 147-50, 160, 169, 178-9; embryo petty, 184; *see also* juries
settles, 9, 19
sheep, 35; flocks, 45-50,

52; pasture, 244-5; milking of ewes, 30, 33-5, 45-8; walks, 39; stealing, 212, 233
sheriff, tourn, freedom from attendance at, 206, 214, 216, 326-7; held at Woodham Ferrers, 331; barred from arrest within manor, 316, 327
ships, 59-72; 'Mayflower', 62 (*rest not indexed*)
shooting, 237-8
shops (workshops), 10, 107-8, 126-9, 221; bachelors keeping, 149, 160
shotts (furlongs), 38
shove-ha'penny, *see* slide-groat
sickness, deathbed, 138-40
signs (alehouse or inn), 9, 63, 79, 98, 267
silver articles, 24; *see also* plate
'single man', meaning of, 148
skeys, 60, 69
skiff, 70
slander, 151, 232, 234, 309
slaughter-houses, 328
slays, 76
slide-groat (shove-ha'penny), 151, 239
sloughs, 148, 281, 285, 288-9, 294
smuggling, 64
socage tenure, 319
soldiers, 216
soothsayer, 157
spinning, 75
sprats, 70
squatting, 264
stall-boats (staw-boats), 60, 63
stocks, parish, *see* punishment
stools, 18
storm, 261

# INDEX OF SUBJECTS

stints, 244-5, 318
stover, 44, 51-2
strangers, *see* inmates
streets, insanitary, 290-8, 328; narrow, 266
suicides, 213
suit of court, 199, 204-5, 310, 323, 329
sumptuary laws, 153, 274
Sunday, work on, viii, 304, 307
surveys of manors, 200, 227, 255, 309-15, 325-33; courts of, 278, 313, 320, 325
surveyor, estate, 106, 325, 329, 332 (*see also* maps); general, 319; of highways, 242-3

tables, 9, 10, 16-17, 99
tables (backgammon), 232, 238
tableware, 24
tainters, 75, 78
tallies, 51, 80, 84, 87, 93
tanhouses, 79, 285
tanners, inspectors of, 226
tapestry, 15, 22
teasles, teasling, 75
thatching, 5-6, 8, 10, 259, 261
theaves, 49, 110
theft, 40, 212, 214, 217; *see also* hedge-stealing
tideboat, 63
tiles, kilns, 86-7, 288; inspectors of, 194
timber, 5-9, 40, 193, 252-3, 258, 330; ploughbote, 322; *see also* wood
timber-framed, *see* houses
tithes, viii, 314, 327; of hops 40
tithings, 204, 225
toll, excessive, 300, 302
tools, *see* implements
towels, 24
tow house, 98
town clerk, 328
trade, control of, by Quarter Sessions, 175-96; by manor courts, 299-308
trades, offensive, 196, 295-7
traders, unlawful, *see* dealers
trades and occupations [*see Note on* p. 334]; *for* alehousekeeper, clerk, clergy, dealer, husbandman, innkeeper, labourer, miller, servant, steward, surveyor, victualler, yeoman, *see* these names; anchor-smith, 83; apothecary, 125; arrowhead-maker, 146; attorney, 141, 216; bailiff in husbandry, 165-7, 192; bailiff, manorial, Part 3, *passim*; bakers, 88, 112, 136, 146, 169, 171, 179, 184, 187, 190, 226, 270, 299-307; barber-surgeon, 126, 154, 172, 271; bargeman, 62; basketmaker, 169, 252; baymaker, 159; beadle, 92; blacksmith, 56, 83-5, 91, 126, 152, 234, 265; bladesmith, 86; bowyer, 146, 150; brewer, 87, 146, 157, 167, 171, 179, 184, 190-2, 213, 226, 300-2; bricklayer, 14, 91, 94, 135; brickmaker, 86-7, 118, 151, 157-8, 211; builder, 87; butcher, 45, 80-1, 88, 98, 126, 146, 150-1, 154, 192, 239, 295-6, 300-7, 318, 330; capper, 146, 274-6; carpenter, 12, 49, 54, 81-2, 92, 98, 107, 113, 126, 143, 157, 165, 170, 211, 271; carrier, 53, 90, 94, 175 (*see* fish-carrier); chandler, 169, 302; charcoal-maker, (*see* collier); chirurgeon, 120, 130, 265 (*see also* surgeon); clothier, 49, 74-7, 102, 122, 142, 146, 157, 168, 171, 191, 197-205, 224, 306-7; clothworker, 74, 146, 161, 186; clothmaker, 75, 80, 307; collarmaker, 81, 172; collier, 56, 157, 228; cook, 88, 106, 130, 146, 165, 167; cooper, 82, 94, 212, cordwainer, (*see* shoemaker); croker, 41 (*see also* saffron-man); currier, 79, 146, 177; cutler, 8, 85-6, 94, 146, 172, 228, 238; draper, 170, 301 (*see also* linendraper, woollendraper); drover, 175, 290; dyer, 75, 77, 146; edgetool-maker, 86; fanwright, 83, 144; farmer, 74-5, 185, 242; farrier, 85, 146, 159; fenreeve, 245-6; fish-carrier, 154, 176 (*see also* rippier); fisherman, 63-72, 104, 123, 141, 156-7; fishmonger, 296, 300, 306; fletcher, 82, 108, 135, 146; fuller, 75, 151-2, 158, 196; garment-maker, 149; glazier, 87, 136, 193; glover, 5, 79, 80, 108, 126, 143, 146, 151, 162, 174, 180, 227, 267, 296, 317; grazier, 45; grocer, 142-3, 169, 181, 213; haberdasher, 142-3, 169, 171; haircloth-maker, 171, 195; hat-maker, 146; herdman, 227; hosier, 146; hoyman, 61; joiner, 12, 81, 82, 94; knacker, 154; leathermaker, 79, 306; linendraper, 90, 158, 182; maltster,

## INDEX OF SUBJECTS

184; mapmaker and measurer, 106, 120, 326; mariner, 20, 59-73, 92, 102, 106, 110, 139 (*see also* sailor); marshreeve, 246; mason, 165; mercer, 70, 169; merchant, 23, 181, 194; millwright, 83; minstrel, musician, 108, 127, 142, 165 169, 271; mower, 165; notary public, 134, 141; ostler, 126; painter, 101, 123, 169; painter-stainer, 7, 78; pall-maker, 7, 82, 228; park-keeper, 321; pedlar, 154; pewterer, 94, 146; pinder, 249; plough-man, 165; plough-wright, 83; pointmaker, 81; potter, 86-7, 254-5, 287, 297, 303; poulterer, 90, 178, 182-6; rippier, 53, 90 (*see also* fish-carrier); ropemaker, 83, 157; saddler, 146; saffron-man, 41 (*see also* croker); sailor, sea-faringman, 59-73, 103, 116, 193, 264; salt-maker, 88-90; sawyer, 82; schoolmaster, 103, 118, 121, 161; scrivener, 141 (*see also* notary public); sexton, 143; shearman, 75, 78, 127, 146, 157, 294; sheep-walker, 47; shepherd, 236; shipmaster, 63; shipwright, 63, 65, 83, 114-5; shoemaker, 9, 53-4, 79-81, 90, 126, 146, 152, 154, 157, 177, 190, 195, 306, 316; smith, 10, 54, 83-5, 110, 124, 146, 157, 162, 195, 221; spinner, 75-6, 157; spurrier, 146; starchmaker, 188; steward, household, 92; steward, manorial, Part 3, *passim;* surgeon, 22 (*see also* barber-surgeon); tailor, 78, 115, 123, 126-7, 146, 149, 153, 157-62, 169-72, 195; tallowchandler, 81, 93, 192, 300, 306; tanner, 4, 15, 79, 127, 146, 156-8, 172, 177, 196, 227, 296, 300-2, 306; tawer, 80, 301; tilemaker, 86, 194; tiler, 138; tinker, 26, 86, 88; tucker, 146; turner, 82, 146; vintner, 192, 302; waxchandler, 60; weaver, 8, 74-7, 105-8, 127, 146, 150-9, 169-72, 195; weller, salt, 89; wheelwright, 83, 135, 157, 165, 170; woollendraper, 50, 142; woolman, 74, 75; wright, 83

travel, dangers of, 133
treasure trove, 213, 331
treen (wooden) utensils, 24, 28
trees, overhanging, 288
trespass on commons, 247-52-4, 267
truck, *see* wages
trustees, *see* wills
tumbrels, 54-5

universities, *see* education
usury, 143

vagabonds, 148, 151, 154-7, 162, 169, 225, 268, 271, 273
'vantage' (profit), 117
verjuice, 31
vermin, 238
vestries, parish, 224, 257, 268, 273, 324
vicarage, Harlow, 282; Thaxted, 294
victuallers, 162, 170, 179, 184, 190, 192, 238, 299, 306, 316, 328, 330; un-lawful measures, 180; *see also* alehouse-keepers; innkeepers
viol, virginals, 23
Virginia Company, 61
voyages, 46, 66-68

wafer-irons, 28
wages, 103; under Statute of Artificers, 146-8, 150-8; assessments, 164-8; payment by truck, 157
waggons, 53
waifs, 213-4, 326, 331
wainscot, 9
walnut trees, 10; pickers, 254
wards of parishes, 148
wardships, 209, 211
warming pan, 16
warren, free, 238, 321, 326, 331
washing clothes, 18, 294; provision for, 98
'waste', meanings of, 250; 97, 100; grants of, 265, 269; *see also* buildings, repair of; commons; estripment; wood
watch and ward, 226, 232-4
water-bailiffs, 227
watercourses, *see* ditches; rivers
watermills, *see* mills
water supply, 99-100, 107; *see also* pump; wells
weapons and armour, 82, 86, 132-7, 216, 234, 240
weights and measures, illegal, 180, 190-4, 226, 299-304, 324-7, 331; *see also* measures
weirs, 70, 72; fishing, 63
wells, common, 107, 267, 287
wey, 29
wharves, 330
whipping, 234
whitemeat, 29
wholves, 289
wicks, 33, 45-8, 71

widows, provision for, 36, 44, 95-101
wills, Part 1, *passim,* 263; executors, 103-20, 123, 131, 142-5; overseers, 103, 109-18, 122, 129, 141-2; trustees, 111, 143; nuncupative, 23, 138-45; preambles, 140-1; witnesses, 141; writers, 68, 141; quick probate, 144
windmills, *see* mills
wines, 30, 302
witchcraft, 234
wives, 95-102; second marriage, 98-9; pregnant, provision for, 112-3; *see also* fuel
wood (trees), kinds of, 12, 16-20, 24, 55-6, 81-2, 193, 252-3, 258, 260, 317-8, 323; felling, lawful and unlawful, 33, 221, 250-6, 259-62, 311-3, 316-8, 322-30; *see also* buildings, repairs of; fuel; hedge-stealing; timber
wood-stealers, *see* hedge-breakers
woodwards, 228
wool, 4, 15, 35, 46, 48-9, 74-6, 110, 127; Horndon market, 303
words, rare, archaic, or local (*for implements used by clothmakers, woodworkers and smiths, see* 78, 81-4): acrepickers, 254; battleden, 28; bedsteadle, bedstock, 12-13; butt, 42; carr, 39; clampole, 56; cobe, 329; crumfall, 321; curb, 27; daywork, 259; dicker, 79; engelments, 72; flash, 278, flemeditch, 285; flotts, 28; goff, 36; halling, 22; hapharlot, 14; handsel, 102; hoke, 71; hostlements, 10, 110; husbands, 97, 252-3, 322; jag, 251-2; keep, 21; ketcher, 227; lebeat, 254; neer, 318; outmark, 8; paste, 318; pellet, 136; pitcher, 64; pollinger, 252-3, 317; ravelling, 214; rowen, 36; roughen, 318; sharrier, 324; shifted, 109, 319; smoke hen, 202; spents, 255; spoor, 97; spurk, 262; stackbote, 263; standle, 253; starling, 55; storven, 56; strake, 64; suckle, 50; through, 290; trussband, 36; versey, 249; wardbrace, 136; wash, 69; wayer, 285; whitage, 29; whelm, wholve, 289-90; yealding house, 5; yotting vat, 27
workmanship, bad, 306, 316
'worst', meaning of, 31
wreck, 213-5, 320
writers, *see* wills

yardlands, 327
yeomen, *passim*

---

For *maps* of Essex, showing hundreds and parishes, see *Elizabethan Life: Disorder* (Norden's map, 1594) and *Elizabethan Life: Morals and the Church Courts* (modern map)

# Index of Persons and Places

NOTE. *Names of manors*, the Elizabethan records of which (in the Essex Record Office) were read by the writer for Part 3 (pp. 197-333) are in *italics*. (The rolls of a few manors, e.g. Chigwell, yielded no items of interest not already exemplified from those of other manors.) For periods covered and catalogue-marks, see Emmison (ed.), *Guide to the Essex Record Office* (2nd edn., 1969).

Abberton, 117
Abbot(t), Hen., 232; Rich., 99; Rob., 127
Abell, Jn., 211; Tho., rector of Bradwell-juxta-Mare, 211-2
Adams, Rob., 179
Adams, Bocher *alias*, Joan, 139; Mary, 139
Addington, Jn., 209
Adsley (Adeslie), Joan, 28; Tho., 77
Adye, Jn., 223
Ailet, Rich., 127
Albert, Edw., 217; Rich., 142
Alden, Wm., 50
Alders, Jn., 130
Aldham, 150; Bourchiers Hall, 254; Ford Street, 163
Aldyche, Jn., 266
Alexander, Tho., 48
Allard, Rich., 89
Allen (Allyn, Alline), Christr, 48; Edw., 122; Jn., 134, 141; Joan, 4; Rob., 122; Roger, 216, 217; Tho., 78
Almon, Hen., 64, 110; Tho., 158; Wm., 49, 158
Alresford, 34
Althorne, 47, 69
Alvin, Frances, 129
Alyte, goodman, 179
America, North, 78, 103; *see also* New England; Virginia
Amyce, Israel, 106; Margt., 106; Roger, J.P., 106, 172
Amye, Charles, 145; Jn., 145
Anderkyn, James, 69; Margt., 69

Andewe, Geoff., 125; Tho., 124
Andrew(es), Agnes, 60; Jn., 136; Hen., 239; Lancelot, 60; Tho., 55, 60, 121
Annes, Wm., 92
Appleton, Hen., J.P., 129, 205
Arbuster, Agnes, 138
Archer, Frs., 224; Harry, 4; Hen., 177; Mich., 128; Wm., 3; Mr., 16
Arden, Tho., 216, 237
Ardleigh, 34, 80, 111; 'Cock', 78
Arkesden, 99, 160
Armiger, Jane, 264; Tho., 263, 264
Armond, Geo., 278
Arsonne, Jn., 125
Arthure, Jn., 174
Ashdon, 56, 139
Asheldham, 124
Asheley (Ashlye), Jacob and Joan, 65, 115; Jn., 106, 115
Ashen, parson of, 125
Ashewell, Gilbert, 179
Aspland, Rob., 39, 43
Atkins, Hen., 92, 133; Rich., 133; Rich., curate of Romford, 104
Atkynson, Wm., 245; Wm,. rector of Nevendon, 125
Aubrey, Jn., antiquary, 123
Audley, Tho., Lord, 330; Tho., 151; Rob., 330
Aulcefer, Edw., vicar of Epping, 235-6, 253, 285; Jane, 235
Aunsell, Joan, 76

Auste(y)n, Jn., 92; Rich., 37
*Aveley*, 92, 135, 138, 172, 193, 206, 230, 236, 255, 269, 274, 289, 294, 299-304, 309, 311, 331-2; Belhus, 289; Marsh, 37; market, 331-2
Awgar, Wm., 180
Awsop, Frs., 67
Ayers, Jn., 23, 128
Ayme, Jn., 55
Aysone, Rich., 183

Backouse, Ellis, 302; Jn., 87, 93
Badbroke, Jn., 221
Badcock(e), Geo., 6; Jn., 77
Baddow, Gt., 20, 80, 114, 130, 135, 178, 187, 247; Mead, 39; Galleywood End, Common, 127, 244, 247, 253; fulling-mill, 39
Baddow, Lt., 29, 204, 206, 214, 230, 240, 247, 251, 255, 264, 272, 279; *Middlemead alias Bassetts*, 204, 206, 230, 240, 247, 251, 255, 264, 265, 266, 279; Tofts, 264; Hockam Hill, 247, 264; Wickey Green, 247
Bagley, Wm., 306
Baker, Christr., 236; Jn., 92, 238, 261, 266, 269, 289, 294; Mich., 174; Walter, 154, 302; Wm., 43; —, 115
Ballard, Jn., 105; Wm., 157
Bank(e)s, Joan, 66; Tho., 66; —, 172
Barber, Rich., 49

# INDEX OF PERSONS AND PLACES

Barfford, Rob., 212
*Bardfield, Gt.*, 28, 77, 82, 84, 113, 177-8, 206, 221, 227; Green, 254, 273
Bardfield, Lt., 83, 110
Bardfield Saling, 81
Barfote, Mr., 179
Barker, Rob., 87
Barker, Cooke alias, Jn., and Wm., 81, 93
Barking, 39, 49, 53, 59, 79, 81, 105, 123, 126, 127, 141, 142, 148, 155, 157, 162, 169, 170, 177, 178, 183, 193, 209, 227, 229, 250, 304, 315, 316; abbey and church, 208, 315-6; Fish Row, quay, 63; Clay Hall, 315; Westbury, 123; parish clerk, 140; *see also* Ilford, Gt.
Barle(e) (Barley), Rich., 139, 186; Mr., 43
Barling, 59, 69
Barnard(e), Agnes, 157; Avery, 110; Hen., 37; Jn., 110, 280; Margt., 110; Nich., 110; Rich., 110, 221; Tho., 212, 221; Thomasine 110; Wm., 110, 306
Barnardiston, Jn., 263
Barnes, Jn., 119; Tho., 120
Barnston, 14, 136
Baron, Rich., 23; Thomasine, 23
Barret(t), Jn., 134; Tho., 247
Barrington, Anne, 56; Rich., 56
Barstable, hundred, 34, 149, 161, 163, 193
Barthlett, Rob., curate of Lt. Thurrock, 37
Bartholomew, Christr., 65; Tho., 65
Bastwicke, Jn., 72, 107; Wm., 107
Bat(e)man, Rob., 82; Tho., 178

Battell, And., 103; Ellen, 31; Jn., 31, 70, 103
Baw, Tho., 97
Bawden, Jn., 118; Rich., 118
Baxter, Bartimeus, 121
Bayliffe, Jerome, 221
Baylye, Hen., 126; Jn., 84; Wm., 84, 126
Baylye, Smyth alias, Rich. and Tho., 6
Baynarde, Benj., 188
Beane, Tho., 7
Beane, Danwood *alias*, Tho., 84
Beard, Rob., 92
Beaumond, Edmd., 113, 142
Beaumont, 122, 207-11, 223, 252, 258-60, 272, 285; *Old and New Hall*, 259; (North) Field, 285; *see also* Moze
Becke, Jn., 135
Becon, Tho., writer, 123
Becontree hundred, 34, 155-6, 159, 163, 183, 187, 190, 193
Bedfordshire, 289
Bedle (Bedill), Erasmus, 83; Jn., 62
Belchamp, Tho., 309
Bell, Tho., 102
Belvis, Wm., 116
Bendlowe(s), Clement, 84; Jn., 84; Wm., 221
Bendysh, Tho., 170
*Benfleet, North*, 114, 205, 238
Benfleet, South, 46, 59, 110, 128; Jarvis Hall, 129
Bennet(t), Geo., 158; Hen., 82; Jn., 106; Tho., 179
Benoll, Wm., 6
Bentall, Agnes, 87; Jn., 87
*Bentley, Gt.*, 136, 245, 267, 320-3; mill, 300; Park, common and greens, 321-3

Bentley, Lt., 110-11, 142, 144
Bentley, Jn., 23, 184, 211
Benton, Edw., 170, 235
Beston, Agnes, 144; Wm., 144
*Berden,* 4, 38, 241, 256, 272, 275; B. Green and Dewes Green, 285
Bergholt, West, 150, 169, 194; Bergholt Sackville, 158
Bettes, Arthur, 187; Wm., parson of Wivenhoe, 125
Bettrell, Rich., 306
Bevys, Jn., 149
Beylde, Wm., 60
Bickner, Alice, Amy, Grace, Margt., Thomasine and Wm., 114
Bigges, Geo., 129, 130
Billericay, 36, 50, 103, 139, 182, 186, 195, 224, 227, 230-3, 241, 244, 250, 272, 288, 295, 299, 303-4; South Green, 241; Norsey Wood, 250; schoolmaster, 103; *see also* Burstead, Gt.
Billing, Alice, 123
Binckes (Byncke), Geo and Wm., 158, 160; Tho., 129
Birch, Gt., 51, 96, 101, 123
Birchett, Wm., 141
Bird(e) (Burde, Byrd(e)), Edw., 89; Jn., 30, 81, 135; Rich., 138; Rob., 65; Ste., 63; Tho., 150, 151; Wm., 23, 63
Bishop, Rich., 207; Ste., 212
Blackmore (*Fingrith Hall*), 205-7, 211, 214, 225, 241, 247, 250, 260, 265, 270, 280, 301, 325; Dame Bridge, 289; Horse Fair Lane, 287
Blackmore, Wm., 50

# INDEX OF PERSONS AND PLACES

Blackwater river, 47, 64, 68
Blake, Mabel, 264; Rich., 264
Bland, Anth., 196
Blossom, Jn., 115, 129
Blyth, Wm., 83
Bobbingworth, 149, 180
Bocher *alias* Adams, Joan, 139; Mary, 139
Bocher, Garrold *alias*, Kath., 144
Bocking, 75, 157, 161, 169, 170, 195
Bocking, Edmd., 150
Bond(e), Clement, 64; Eliz., 104; Jn., 51, 317; Margt., 64; Parnell, 99; Rich., parson of S. Fambridge, 51; Rob., 99
Bonner, Abr., 66; Hen., 119; Jn., 87; Margt., 54; Rich., 119; Wm., 66
Boode, Wm., 330
Bonefale, —, alien, 308
Boosey, Tho., 102
Bordells, Wm., 301
Boreham, 105, 112, 160, 167, 262; New Hall, 99, 167; Old Hall, 262
Boreman, Gideon, 155
Borley, Tho., 221
Borne, Rich., 252; Rob., 180
Botesworth, Tho., 235
Bottrell, Rich., 237
Bowen, Margt., 48
Bower, Blanche, 62; Wm., 62
Bowes, Tho., 257
Bowland, Hum., 142
Bowlinge, Wm., 224
Bown(d)e, Marion, 69; Nich., 69; Tho., 68
Bowser, Edw., 212
Bowsey, Tho., 271
Bowtell, Ralph, 50
Bowyar, Joan, 79
Boxted, 82, 108, 138, 169, 194, 311, 329; *Rivers Hall*, 329

Boyer, Roger, 179
Bradey, Tho., 76
Bradwell-juxta-Mare, 48, 54, 59, 64, 92, 99, 211, 229; rector, 211
Bragge, Wm., 157
Braintree, 75, 79, 97-8, 108, 126, 157, 161, 170, 182-4, 195, 324, 327; 'Chequer', 98; 'George', 108; vicar, 109; market, 182
Brande, Jn., 306
Branham, Hugh, vicar of Dovercourt, 102
Branthwaite, Mr. (Rich.?), 325, 333
Brasier, Anth., rector of Ingatestone, 317
Braunch, Roger, 106
Breadcake, Ste., 62
Breame, Arthur, 208-9, 279, 307
Bredge, Anne, 90; Edw., 91; Margt., 98; Tho., 97
Brentwood, 83-4, 90, 159, 169, 181, 183, 186, 193, 254, 284; market, 182, 191; fair, 193
Brest, Nich., 51
Bret(te), Andrew, 135; Anthony, 7, 23, 24, 30; Edw., 135; Jn., 144
Bretten, Rich., 40; Rob., 106; Susan, 40
Brew(st)er, Jn., 31, 48, 158; Margt., 31; Rich., 282
Bridgeman, Jn., 253
Bridges, Anthony, 157; Jn., 149, 261; Jn., rector of Paglesham, 30
Bright, Jn., 104; Rich., 135
Brightlingsea, 8, 23, 59, 66, 72, 90, 122, 128
Brock, Tho., 213
Brockas, Abisaye, Achior, Edmd., and Eliz., 101; Jn., 101, 123; Rich., 123; Sam., 123
Brodbelt, Wm., 191

Brodwater, James, 90; Nich., 90
Brodye, Wm., 270; father 260
Bromley, Gt., 44, 49, 81, 257; Heath, 258
*Bromley, Lt.*, 97, 209
Brooke, Jn., 99; Wm., 188
Bro(o)man, And., 81; Jn., 10; Rich., 81, 263
Broomfield, 102, 180, 183
Browne, Anne, 93; Edy., 93; Hen., 187; Joan, 107; Jn., 47, 77, 80, 107; Margt., 107; Paul, 125; Rich., 107; Rob., 47, 77, vicar of Doddinghurst, 123; Tho., 85, 269; Wm., 80
Bruce (Bryce), Tho., rector of Lt. Burstead, 10
Brystowe, Jn., 188
Brytaine, Mary, 221
Bucke, Erasmus, 100; Joan, 100; Rich., 306; Tho., 100
Buckinghamshire, 165
Buckler, Jn., 130
Buckley, Jn., 127
Bullock(e), Jn., 101, 320
Bulman, Edw., 263
*Bulphan*, 51, 208, 211, 300, 309; Fen, 48, 245-6; Mardyke, 245
Bumpstead, Helion, 184
Bumpstead, Steeple, 18, 84, 133, 176, 178, 184-5
Bundock, Rob., 213; Rich., 212, 213
Bunny, Edmd., writer, 124
Buntinge, Ellen, 101; Jn., 293; Wm., 101
Bunyan, Jn., writer, 124, 289
Burchett, Joan, Mary, Rich., Susan and Wm., 51
Burgeant, Tho., 205
Burge(y)s, Rob., 86; Tho., 158
Burles (Burlz), Arthur, 143; alderman Tho., 89

Burnett, Tho., 172
Burnham, 61, 64-5, 69, 72, 103, 110, 114,
Burrowes, Christr., 172
*Burstead, Gt.*, 36, 97, 101, 121, 134-5, 200, 205, 212, 223-6, 230-1, 236-7, 241, 250, 261, 265, 272, 294-5, 301-6; South Green, 241, 294; Tye Common, 212; minister, 134
Burstead, Lt., 4, 44, 106, 110, 130; rector, 10, 121
Burton, Tho., 156
Bury, Day *alias*, Rob., *see* Day
Bushe, Jn., 116, 246
Buste, Jn., 279
Butcher, Mr., 126
Butler, Sir Edw., 205; Jn., 120; Nathan, 172; Wm., 120
Buttolf, Jn., 221
Button, Jn., 85; Tho., 85
Buttsbury, 50, 53, 81-2, 86-7, 90, 108, 230, 239, 241, 272, 316; *Ging Joyberd Laundry alias Blunts*, 226, 230, 254; Ramsey Tyrells, 316
Bryckett, Wm., 36
Byatte, Alice, 96; Wm., 96
Bylles, Eliz., 119; Jn., 119
Byndley, Anne, Bennett, and Valentine, 112

Calvin, Jn., writer, 123-5
Cam, river, 56
Camber, Rich., 64
Cambredg, Tho., 90
Cambridgeshire, J.P.s of, 182; Abington, 145; Cambridge, 106, 176; Ely, bishop of, 207, 230; University, 122, 176; *see also* Chishall; Chrishall; Heydon
Camden, Wm., topographer, 35, 42, 45-6
Cammock, Tho., 319

Campe, James, 84
*Canewdon*, 47-8, 54, 59, 64, 69, 70, 75, 106, 205-6, 210, 229, 255, 262, 272, 275, 289, 296, 305, 311; Paternosters, 263-4
*Canfield, Gt.*, 130, 200, 225, 253, 262, 275, 280, 284, 286, 295, 313; Haslow Common Mead, 280
Canfield, Lt., 91
Cannon, Jn., 134; Rich., 208; Ste., 92, 134; Tho., 182
Canvey Island, 45-7
Carder, Tho., 171
Cardinall, Charles, 210
Carr, James, 266; Roger, parson of Rayne, 129
Carter, Hamon, 279
Carter, Lyngeye *alias*, Rich., 127
Carver, Frances, 262
Casse, Hen., 35
Castell, Jn., 86; Tho., 86
Cast(e)lyn, Jn., 263; Tho., 169
Caster, Frs., 76
Catonne, Jn., 84; Nich., 84; Tho., 56, 84
Cawderon, Roger, 53
Caywood, Jn., 92
Cecil, Sir Rob., 223; Sir Wm., 89
Cely, Jn., 208
Chadwell, 36, 119
Chafford hundred, 193
Chamberlayne (-len), Jas., 233; Jn., 80, 150; Roger, 157
Champyon, Lady, 106
Chapman, Dr. Edmd., 78; Geo., 172; Jn., 179; Rich., 65, 171
Charitye, Rich., 288
Charvell, —, 128
Cheeke, Rob., 221
Chelmer, river, 39, 282, 284
Chelmsford (*Bishop's Hall, alias Chelmsford*), 28, 34, 53, 81-2, 85, 88, 90, 93, 98, 113, 120, 126, 134, 136, 153-4, 160, 163, 169, 171, 174, 180-6, 190, 206, 208, 212-3, 224, 234, 238-40, 243, 249, 255, 265-6, 270, 273, 278, 284, 287-9, 292-3, 296-7, 300-5, 311, 325; High St., 282; Potter Lane (Row), 90, 303; 'Chequer', 98; Grammar School, 271; market (cross), 182-3, 193, 214, 303; fair, 193; mills, 300
*Moulsham*, 88, 90, 154, 180, 205, 208, 212, 214, 224, 227, 230, 231, 235, 243, 244, 247, 270, 271, 273, 282, 284, 293, 301, 302, 303, 304; Hall, 278; Friars, 284; Mill, 278; Thrift, 253
Chelmsford hundred 153, 158-61, 166, 187
Cheshire, 90, 170
Chesterford, Gt., 33, 42-3, 141, 171
Chesterford, Lt., 43
*Chigwell*, 49, 81, 90, 129, 143, 149
Chingford (*Comitis and St. Paul*), 167, 205, 247-9, 252; Pimp Hall, 247
Chishall, Gt. (now in Cambs.), 42-3
Chishall, Lt. (now in Cambs.), 42
Chrishall (now in Cambs.), 84, 96; Bildon Mead, 44
Church, Jn., 194
Clacton, Gt., 34, 47, 50, 110, 113, 128; Jay Wick Marsh, 47
Clacton, Lt., 104, 113
*Clavering*, 37, 193; Common, 244
Clavering hundred, 34, 149, 163, 192, 193

## INDEX OF PERSONS AND PLACES

Claxton, Anthony, 136
Clay, Wm., 61
Clayton, Oliver, 248, 249
Cleiveland, —, 76
Clar(c)k(e) (Clerk), Alice, 75; Edmd., 75; Ellen, 65, 66; Hen., 221; Israel, 76; Joan, 107; Jn., 56, 76, 79, 80, 100, 107; Margt., 75; Mary, 107; Rich., 65; Rob., 80, 317; Stephen, 50; Tho., 63, 66, 100, 158; Wm., 107, 232; wid., 293; —, 179, 191
Clemence, Jonathan, 104
Clere, Benj., 194
Clopton, Tho., 205
Cobham, Lord, 248
Cock(e), Edw., 158; Hen., 122, 180; Ralph, 78; Rich., 66; Rob., 69; Sam., 78; Tho., 69; Wm., 69, 90, 92, 115
Cockeley, Wm., 176
Cockerell, Jn., 223
Cocket, Jn., 38
Coggeshall, Gt., 22, 36, 75-8, 82, 88, 93, 105, 108, 119, 127, 142, 145, 151-2, 159, 161, 169-72, 193-6, 227, 242, 278; West St., 108; Machins Mill, 278; Paycockes, 75, 88, 108; church, 75; vicar, 141; combs, 14; fair, 193
Coggeshall, Lt., 145
Coke, Sir Edw., 223; Joan, 66; Wm., 66, 67
Coker, Jn., 105, 263; Tho., 105; Titus, 228
Cokes, Jn., 104
Cokoe, *see* Cuckok
Colchester, 8, 9, 17, 49, 59, 62-3, 67-8, 75-7, 82, 86, 92, 99, 101, 107, 112, 117-8, 124, 127-8, 163-4, 169, 181-2, 187, 194, 216, 223, 239, 243, 282, 306-7, 327; Castle Gaol, 45, 68, 212;

Kingswood Heath, 34; New Hythe, 56, 61, 65; St. John's Abbey and Green, 130, 138; Westness, 72; Museum, 229; 'Dutch' congregation, 76, 307; borough, 165, 177, 194; scarcity of grain, 182, 187; wages assessment, 165; weavers, 145
St. Botolph, 82, 142, 144
St. Giles, 9, 56, 96, 124
St. James, 126
St. Leonard, 56, 61, 63, 65, 115
St. Mary, 8, 84, 86
St. Mary-at-the-Walls, 133
St. Mary Magdalen, 110
St. Nicholas, 17, 81, 107, 128
St. Peter, 80
St. Runwald, 9
Colchester, Bishop of, J.P., *see* Sterne
Cole, Jn., 121, 287; Tho., 30, 47, 300
Collard, Geo., 211; Giles, 211; Wm., 136
Collin (Colens), Ellen, 98; Jn., 179; Rob., 98; Ste., 56, 98; —, 79
Collye, Tho., 136
Colne, river, 39, 91, 163, 279; oyster-fishery, 68
Colne, Earls, 20, 22, 44, 75, 90, 142, 144, 187, 194, 223, 230, 232-3, 248, 254, 258, 272, 299, 305; Priory, 299; parson, 142
Colne Engaine, 82, 93, 100
Colne, Wakes, 106, 155, 172, 176
Colne, White, 100, 150, 161
Commyn(ge)s, Rob., 79; Ste., 63, 123; Wm., 63

Compton, Sir Hen., 283
Condall, Jn., 127
Connye, Jn., 76, 108
Cook(e), Sir Anthony, 92, 104, 181, 185, 223, 246, 329, 330; Dorothy, 105; Edw., 104; Eliz., 105; Geo., 105; Hen., 91; Jn., 80, 151, 181, 329-30; Lawr., 80; Margery; 104; Nich., 182; Rich., 80; Tristram, 104; Wm., 30, 40, 97, 104, 169, 207; Lady, 104; —, 39, 83
Cooke *alias* Barker, Jn., and Wm., 81, 93
Cooper, Jn., 86; Rich., 86; Tho., 106
Coote, Agnes, 98; Anne, 75; Jn., 115; Rob., 31, 82, 98
*Copford,* 35, 223, 234, 281
Coppin, Mark, 80
Corney, Rob., 178
Corringham, 106
Costell, Jn., 92
Cotman, Rich., 135
Cotton, Rob., 194
Cottrell, Edw., 142
Cottysforth, Jn., Mary, and Tho., 92, 116
Coulson, Tho., 134
Coverdale, Miles, translator, 123
Cowdalle, Rich., 92
Cowling, Frs., Harry, and Toby, 82
Cowper, Jn., 227, 236
Cox, Jn., curate of Ramsden Bellhouse, 125
Crammer, Nich., 35
Cramphorne, Mr., 212
Crane, Lynnet, 176; Wm., 185
Cranham, 36
Creathorne, Jn., 138
Creeksea, 69, 136; Ferry, 289; Place, 136
Crefeilde, Edw., 135
Creke, Jn., 89

Cressing, 172, 182; Temple, 172
Crimble, Jn., 99
Crip(pes) (Crypes), Eleazar, 62; James, 71; Joan, 62; Jn., 24, 62, 70, 71; Mary, 71; Rich., 70; Rob., 70; Wm., 31, 70, 71
Crompe, Agnes, Jn., Hen., and Sarah, 69
Crouch, river, 62, 68-9, 330; ferries, 72
Crouch (Crowche), Jn., 115; Rich., 157; Wm., 115
Crowe, James, 170; —, 221
Croxeton, Edw., 228
Cuckok (Cokoe), Clement, Frs., Geoff., Gye, Jn., Mary., Nich., Prudence, Rose, Susan, and Tho., 112, 113
Cuper, Geo., 121
Curryn, Hum., 128
Curtis, Rob., 179
Cutler, And., 64
Cutte, Sir Jn., 281
Cuttle, Ellen, 62; Rob., 62

Dabbs, Charles, 134
Dadrye *alias* Rawlyn, Walter, 86; Wm., 86
Dagenham, 39, 83, 101, 128, 176, 178, 183-4, 217; Wangey, 106; Marks in, 183; Valence, 217
Dale, Joan, 21; Mat., 18, 118; Rich., 82
Damote, Agnes, 36; Edw., 105; Tho., 36, 105, 127
Damyon, Wm., 64
Danbury, 6, 47, 130, 139, 143, 189, 190; Park, 130; Horne Row, 49; St. Clere's, 49
Danbye, Jn., 181
Daniell, Jn., 126; Margt., 126; Wm., 9, 96
'Danske', 68

Danwood *alias* Beane, Tho., 84
Darbye, Jn., 83, 169, 260
Darcy, Brian, 142; Jn., Lord, of Chiche, J.P., 92, 132-3, 177, 182, 207, 223, 259, 319; Rich., 259; Sir Tho., 92; Tho., Lord, 207
Darginson, Rich., 256
Darrell, Lady Mary, 278
Daved, Griffin, 126
Davison, Morris, 126
Davy(e), Margt., 127; Peter, 56; —, 221
Dawny, Edw., 172
Day *alias* Bury, Rob., rector of Stapleford Abbots, 23
Daye, Geo., 244
Daynse, Harry, 50
Deacon, 138
Debbet, Jn., Margt., and Peter, 63
*Debden*, 53, 99, 206, 211, 214, 230, 241, 248, 261, 275, 285, 289, 295; Hamling Slough, 285; Cold Fair, 214; vicarage, 285
Debenham, Jeremy, 3
Dedham, 39, 75-8, 129, 169, 186, 194, 295, 317-8; Heath, 318; 'Classis', 78
Dengie (*Bacons*), 92, 206, 247, 261-2
Dengie hundred, 33-4, 46, 154, 159, 161, 163, 171, 209
Dennis, Rose, 32
Denny, Lord, J.P., 162
Derby, Countess of, 285
Derbyshire, 203
Derrington, *see* Dyrrington
Devereux, Rob., Earl of, 205
Dickenson (Dickison), Jn., 211; Rob., 92
Dixon, —, 115
Docker, Tho., 129

Doddes, James, 150
Doddinghurst, 122-3, 204, 229, 244, 325; *Kensingtons*, 204, 211; vicar?, 123
Dole, —, alien, 308
Donyland, East, 66, 89, 117; Rowhedge, 59
Dorrell (Durrells), Prudence, Rich., and Tobias, 65
Dovercourt, 48, 64-6, 141; vicar, 102
Downes, Jn., 75
Downham, 10, 113, 115, 134; Fremnels *alias*, 129
Dowsett, Wm., 85
Drake, Sir Frs., 239
Drane, Jn., 196; Rich., 217
Draper, Jn., 204
Drywood, Anna, 129; Hum., 46; Wm., 129
Dudley, Rob., Earl of Leicester, 188
Duke, Edw., 8; Rich., 87
*Dunmow, Gt. (Alfreston alias Bigods)*, 4, 15, 56, 76, 79, 82, 109, 122, 132, 143, 153, 155, 163, 182, 186, 206, 209, 214, 227, 231, 262, 276, 294-6, 301, 305, 326-8
Dunmow, Lt., 193; Priory, 315; fair, 193
Dunmow hundred, 33, 155, 185, 214
Dunt, Rob., 135
Dunton, 135
Durrant, Tho., 180, 300
Durrisse, Edw., 51
'Dutch', 75-6, 124, 307-8, *see also* Flanders
Dyddon, Isabel, 99; Tho., 99
Dyer, Jn., 30, 133
Dyrrington (Derrington), Geo., 261

Easter, Good, 285
Easter, High, 160
Easton, Gt., 84, 93, 185,

INDEX OF PERSONS AND PLACES 351

230, 242, 269, 282-3;
*Blamsters,* 230, 269,
282; Elsworth and
Gybbes Bridges, 282
Easton, Lt., 171
Eastwood (*Bury*), 31, 48,
75, 200, 206, 249
Edwards, Edw., 120; Jn.,
92, 120, 157; Mich.,
120; Tho., 63
Element (Ely-), Jn., 209;
Wm., 209
Elie, Joan, 113; Jn., 97
Ellice, Tho., 221; Wm., 87
Ellyot(t), Joan, 72; Jn.,
72, 83; Wm., 48
Elmdon, 185
Elmstead, 4, 34, 49
Elsenham, 109-10, 139
Elvey, Frances, 129
Elvolde, Tho., rector of
Wanstead, 218
Emery, Anne, 139; Tho.,
47, 139
Empsall, —, 30
Emson, Philalego, 138
Emyng, Emmanuel, 87
Enever, Wm., 185
*Epping,* 159, 162, 171-2,
182, 193, 202, 205-6,
210-4, 225, 231, 235-6,
238, 243-4, 247-56, 260-
1, 265, 266-9, 275, 280-
1, 284-9, 296, 305, 309;
Forest, 35; High St.,
287, 303; Lyme St., 296;
Upland, 206, 235, 275,
294; Cobbing Bridge,
281; (Long) Common,
248, 265; Lockehatch
Corner, 285; Wintry
Common (Wood), 266;
vicar, 235-6, 253, 285
Estwood, Edw., 66, 117;
Jn., 66; Margery, 66,
117; Tho., 66, 117
Essex, Earl of, *see*
Devereux
Ethyn, Jn., 158
Eustace, Hen., 116
Evanse, Jn., 127

Eve, Alice, 4, 15; Geo.,
54; Wm., 56
Everard (-ed), Jn., 125;
Wm., 91, 127
Eversson, Cornelius, 81
Ewen, Dorothy, 221;
Rich., 113; Rob., 113,
221
Fabian, —, 125
Fairstead, 56, 196; Fulsters St., 196
Fambridge, North, 72,
92, 94; Hall, 92
Fambridge, South, 89;
parson, 51
Fanne, Jn., 56
Fanshawe, Mrs., 123
Farrant, Alice, 39; Geo.,
39; Rob., 39
Faukoner *alias* Stockmer,
Rich., 14
Fawbott, Wm., 83
Feering, 161, 242; church,
132
Felgate, Jn., 259
Fellexe, Rob., 85
Felsted (*Bury-with-Grandcourts*), 77, 84,
97, 204, 216-7, 223,
234, 236-7, 244, 249,
250, 256, 271, 309, 311,
327; Fairing Common,
244; vicar, 271
Fenner, Peter, 122; Rob.,
122
Fenzham, Jn., 49, 143
Ferras, Jn., 221
Ferrer, Jn., 244; Wm., 85
Filbye, Grace, 61; Nich.,
61
Finch(es) (Fynch), Dennice, Grace, Margt.,
James, and Joan, 67;
Edw., 126; Jn., 87;
Joan, 93; Rich., 133;
Rob., 158; Wm., 158
Finchingfield, 83-4, 114,
126, 158, 187, 315;
Boyton, 315
*Fingringhoe,* 55, 65, 81,
106, 200, 223, 319, 320
Firlye, Jn., 67

Fisher, Roger, 127; Tho.,
79
Flanders, Flemings, 15,
20, 25, 40, 75, 124, 307-8;
Meesen, 124; Newehaven, 139; *see also*
'Dutch'
Fletcher, Agnes, 79; Rich.,
225; Tho., 79
Flower, wid., 305; Mrs.,
105
Fobbing, 62; parson, 121
Foockes, Wm., 7
Forber, Jn., 141
Ford, Beatrice, 129
Fordham, 29, 37, 40, 104,
163, 193; Bridge and
Ford St., 163
Forest, Geo., 83
Fortescue, Hen., 278
Forth, Jn., 104
Foster, Agnes, 269; Jn.,
309; Tho., 186, 193;
Wm., 10
Foulness island, 24, 29,
31, 47, 63, 71, 92, 99,
104, 120, 134, 200;
Hall, 71; New and
East Wick, 71; East
End, 71; Prestwood,
99; rector, 31; wreck of
*John Evangelist,* 215
Fowle, Jn., 117; Peter,
64; Tho., 64
Fox(e), John, martyrologist, 124; Margery, 236;
Mich., 185; Tho., 185;
Wm., 142
*Foxearth,* 244
France, 125; Rochelle, 90;
Rouen, St. Ouen Abbey,
207
Frank(e), Frs., 245; Tho.,
J.P., 155; widow, 179
Frating, 34; Heath, 320
Frauncys, Gregory, 272
Freman, Jn., 157; Rob.,
parson of Ashen, 125;
—, 179
Frenche, Jn., 68; Rich., 68
Freshwell hundred, 33,
141, 161, 163, 191, 193

Fr(i)ende, Joan, 110; Jn., 71, 110; Rob., 117
Friszille (Fresell), Glode, 91
Frith, Hum., 135; Jn., 36
Froste, Jn., 3
Fryer, Walter, 212
*Fryerning*, 5, 10, 53, 79, 101, 126, 143, 207, 211, 273, 291, 316-7
Fuller, Anne, 111; Eliz., 61; Hugh, 61; James, 63; Jn., 93; Rich., 111; Tho., 36; Dr. Tho., parson of Waltham Abbey, 111; Wm., 49, 53, 61; —, 103
Fyllupp, Wm., 43
Fysshe, Walter, 329

Gaedge, Rich., 130
Gale, Jn., 65
Gallowaye, Rich., 97
Gammedge, Alice, 78; Tho., 78
Ganslitt, Wm., 138
Gardiner, Lucy, 61; Wm., 129
Garington, Dan., 109
Garrat, Agnes, 56
Garol(d)e (Garralde), Eliz., 113; Ellen, 10; Hum., 10, 113; Jn., 143; Joan, 127
Garrold *alias* Bocher, Kath., 144
Gascoyne, Mr. (Geo.?), 272
Gaunt, mother, 138
Gate(s), Alex., rector of Springfield, 125; Barbara, 116; Sir Jn., 160; Dame Mary (Jakes), 160; Rich., 121; Wm., 92, 116, 121
Gawderne, Nich., 47
Gelbard, Tho., 49
Gemmynges, Nich., 135; Rich., 135
Gent, Tho., J.P., 176
Genye, And, 65
George, Agnes, Eliz.,
Kath., Martha, Mary, 117
Gestingthorpe, vicar, 22
Gey, Margt. and Rich., 260
Gifford, Frs., 269; Geo., preacher of Maldon, 124; Wm., 269
Gilbert *alias* Hale, Anne, 101; Jn., 101; Tho., 120
Gilden, Jn., vicar of Ridgewell, 13; Tho., 13
Gladwyn(e)(Gladdin), Jn., 106, 266; Tho., 181; Wm., 106
Glasco(c)k(e), Anne, 107; Jn., 49, 107, 182-3; Matth., 67; Oliver, 107; Rich., 49; Thomasine, 97, 101; Wm., 10, 83, 97, 101, 135
Godescalf, —, alien, 308
Godfrey (Godfri), Jn., 98; Wm., 138
Golding(e), Geo., 92; Sir Tho., 178, 216
Goldhanger, 48, 64, 89, 100, 120, 143, 144; East and Vaughty Wick Marsh, 47
Golston, Jn., Mary, Naomi, Rose, and Tho., 62
Good(d)ay(e), Edw., 142; Jn., 119, 142; Tho., 79
Goodfellow, Rob., 300
Goodwin (Gooddinge), Edw., 89; Jn., 320; Wm., 60
Goodwyn *alias* Gudgin, Jn., 177
Goodyeare, Jn., 114; Margery, 114
Goose, Jn., 160
Gooson, Tho., 63
Gore, Jn., 136; Rob., 275
Gosfield, 135
Gouldthayte, Tho., and Wm., 82
Graunt, Ant., 49
Grauntham(m)e, Ant., 29, 48, 75, 106; Edmd., 48
Gray, *see* Grey
Grendela, —, alien, 308
Gre(e)n(e), Alice, 61; Barth., 252; Jn., 10, 61, 130, 149, 192, 251; Kath., 10; Reynold, 157; Rich., 84, 167; Tho., 187; —, 86
Greeneward, Hen., 261
Greenstead-juxta-Colchester, 99, 116
Gregory, Arthur, 136
Greive, Wm., 129
Grenelefe, Tho., 35
Grevell, Mr., 234
Grey (Gray), Charles, 60; Sir Hen., 182; Hen., 238; Margery, 22; Sam., 60, 61; Winifred, 61; Tho., 61, 142; —, 238, 269
Griffin (Gryffyn), Hugh, 116; Mich., 116; Rob., 278; Tho., 234, 300, 302; Wm., 271
Grimston, Edw., J.P., 89, 194
Grove, Ambrose, 270; Christr., 300; Emmanuel, Jn., Rich., Rob., and Tho., 61
Gudgin, Goodwyn *alias*, Jn., 177
Gunby, Kath., 55
Gyles, Wm., 66
Gyllett, Wm., 63
Gynis, Rich., 68
Gyrten, Wm., 127
Gyver, Jn., 266

Hache, Rich., 65
Hadleigh, 47, 63, 191
Hadstock, 39, 141
Hager, Agnes, Geo., Hen., and Rich., 42; Jn., 38
Hainault Forest, 35
Haiver (Hay-), Tho., 38; Wm., 38
Hale(s), Edw., 172, 294; Jn., 120

# INDEX OF PERSONS AND PLACES 353

Hale, Gilbert *alias*, Anne, 101; Jn., 101
Hall, Anne, 56; Jn., 80; Tho., 245; Mr., 285
Halles, Agnes, 77; Rob., 121
Hallingbury, Gt., 84, 100
Hallingbury, Lt., 10
Halstead (*Abells*), 75-6, 79, 87, 90, 93, 101, 122, 157, 169-70, 178, 192, 196, 204, 208-9, 224, 226, 233-4, 237-8, 255-6, 262, 267, 270, 272, 279, 280, 284, 287-8, 293-4, 296, 299, 301, 303, 306-7; *Stanstead*, 262, 280; Bois Hall, 209; Townsford Mill, 279, 307; 'Bull', 79, 267
Ham, East, 157, 178, 181-2, 184, 190, 245
Ham, West, 45, 64-5, 82, 100, 103, 142, 148, 155, 171, 178-91, 245; Church St. ward, 156; Plaistow, 100, 135, 156, 157; Stratford Langthorne, 82, 187; Upton, 245; starchmakers, 188
Hammon(d), Eliz., 6; Jn., 143; Ste., 92; Wm., 143
Hampshire, Gosport, 139
Hancock(e), Jn., 71; Rob., 158
Hane, Nich. de, 118, 124
Hanes, Tho., 91
Hankin (Hankyn), Edw., 87; Wm., 87, 297; —, 56
Hanningfield, East, 118, 129
Hanningfield, South, 87, 248
Hanningfield, West, 49, 56, 120, 160
Har(c)kewood, Hen., 10; Tho., 118
Hardinge, Martha, 50; Rob., 142
Hare, Jn., 236; Wm., 238

Harlackenden, Roger, 170, 232; Tho., parson of Earls Colne, 142
*Harlow* (*Bury*), 20, 78, 90, 153, 193, 209, 212, 217, 225, 227, 231, 233, 235, 247, 253-4, 261-2, 271-3, 287-9, 294, 301; Common, 283; Common Field, 289; Marshes, 39, 247, 280-1; Churchgate St., 282; Potter St., 87; Mulberry Green, 241, 282; Moor Hall, 262; Roughay Hall, 288; Pernell Bridge, 281-2; 'Crown', 261; 'Dolphin', 267; market, 294
Harlow hundred, 34, 149, 154
Harmon, Jn., 184, 185; —, 83
Harre, Jn., 193
Harris (Harrys), Agnes, 7; Arthur, J.P., 136, 225; Eleanor, 112; James, 29; Jn., 7, 180; Margery, 7; Rob., 138; Sarah, 112; Tho., 5, 7; Vincent, J.P., 176; Wm., 306
Harrison (Haryson), Jn., 29, 47, 99, 237; Ralph, 245; Tho., 135; Wm., author, rector of Radwinter, 3, 13, 14, 24, 36-7, 40-6, 91, 115, 131-4, 191, 193, 240, 242, 248, 252, 274, 288, 302, 304
Harrye, Jn., 293
Hart(e), Jn., 46, 80, 88, 98, 142; Rob., 119; Tho., 104, 119
Har(e)vy(e), Frs., J.P., 155, 186, 195; Geo., J.P., 183; James, 106; Jn., 110, 157, 307; Mary, 93, 155; Rob., 306
Harwich, 59-72, 80, 83,

98, 101, 106, 114, 139, 142, 239
Harwoode, Eliz., 17
Hasting, Jn., 154
Hastings, Lady Winifred, 138
Has(t)ler, Hum., 310; Tho., 124
Hatfield Broad Oak, 38, 83, 90, 96, 156, 305, 323-5; Common, 324; Fair, 91
Hatfield Chase (Forest), 34, 324
Hatfield Peverel, 167, 182, 279; Grayes Mill, 279
Haughton, Cecily, 43
Haukin, Tho., 70
Haverhill, 178, 200
Havering, 130, 228, 246, 321; Green, 101, 123, 229; Park, 130; Pyrgo Street, 22
Hawes, Jn., 65-6; Tho., 65-6, 279
Hawkens, Jn., 88
Hawkes, Tho., 306
Hawkyne, Mr., 121; Tho., 121
Hawkwell, 99, 104, 120, 131
Hawlkins, Tho., curate of North Ockendon, 125
Ha(y)ward(e) (Haywoode), Grace, 122; Jn., 62; Rich., 122; Tho., 5, 140; Wm., 140, 266
Haywards, Saunder *alias*, Edw., Jn., and Peter, 76
Hayz, Andrew, 178
Heade (Hedd), Edw., 170, 185-6, 194-5
Heard, Tho., 246; —, 64
Hearne, Osias, 160
Hedingham, Castle, 40, 91, 149, 157, 183
Hedingham, Sible, 40, 91, 97, 127, 157; Nunnery Meadow, 39
Hempstead, 82, 163, 193

## INDEX OF PERSONS AND PLACES

Heneage, Tho., 261
Henham, 122, 163
Henny, Gt., 172
Henworth, Mr., 143
Herefordshire, 203
Hertfordshire, 43, 91, 166-7, 189; Hitchin, 309; Sawbridgeworth, 39; Stortford, 192-3, 196; Ware, 136
Heschell, Justice, 70
Hewitt, Dorothy, 98; Wm., 98
Hewson, Jn., 105; Sarah, 105
Heybridge, 89, 181, 193
Heydon (now in Cambs.), 193, 315
Hickes, Joan, 143
Hickes *alias* Stanley, Jn., 143
Hill(e)s (Hylles), James, vicar of Braintree, 109; Lewis, 142; Rob., 43, 87, 141; Tho., 234; Wm., 121, 160
Hinckford hundred 33, 91, 149, 154, 157, 181, 183, 187, 191; Crouch Fair Green, 91
Hinde(s), Jn., 171; Tho., 3, 267
Hinsdon, Tho., 179
Hixe, Francis, 190
Hixon, Geo., 187
Hockley, 6, 89, 94, 103, 109; Beeches Common, 51; Hullbridge, 59
Hodge, Jn., 106, 130; Rich., 106; Wm., 48
Hods(h)on (Hoddunsdon), Eliz., 90; Jn., 261; Rich., rector of Debden, 261, 295
Hogge, Tho., 180
Holderness, Anth., 63; Nich., 63
Holland, Gt., 120
Holman, Nich., 15
Honike, *see* Hunnicke
Honor, Rob., 66
Hood, Robin, 22

Hore, Alice, Joan, and Jn., 106; Wm., 282
Hornchurch, 15, 23, 31, 79, 80, 101, 118, 121, 125, 128-9, 246; Collier Row, 121; Hare Street, 79
Horndon, East, 86; Heron Hall, 130
*Horndon, West*, 205, 227, 241; Thorndon Hall, 167, 192
Horndon-on-the-Hill, 60, 91, 171, 193; market, 303-4
Howard, Tho., Duke of Norfolk, 207, 230, 250; Lord Wm., 134
Howe, Jn., 251; Tho., 88; Wm., 36
Howell, Edy, 145; Nich., 46; Rich., 145; Tho., rector of Paglesham, 92
Howson, —, 154
Hubberd (-t), Edw., 194; Jn., 38; Rob., 119; Roger 38
Hudswell, Geo., 157
Hull, Jn., 300; Roger, 30; Tho., 263
Humbers, Rich., 92
Humfrey, Jn., 191, 317; Rob., 48
Hunt(e), Jn., 119; Joan, 128; Nich., 127; Rob., 38
Hunwick(e) (Honike, Hunwycke), Margt., Petronella and Wm., 209; Jn., 187; Tho., 20, 140
Hurrell, Alice, 127
Hurt, Wm., 48
Hutton, 55, 130
Hyde, Jn., 64

Ilford, Gt., 84, 156-7, 188; Clay Hall, 177; Hospital, 125, 134; Wangey Hall, 106; 'Crown', 134

Ilford, Lt., 184, 245; parson, 125
Ilger, Jn., 96
Ince, Edw., 61; Jn., 61
Ingram, Jn., 196; Rich., 160
*Ingatestone*, 23, 30, 53, 58, 87, 93, 101, 135, 142, 183, 213-4, 217, 224, 228, 231, 235, 237, 239, 249, 256-8, 262, 270, 273-4, 281, 287, 295, 300, 310, 316; Hall, 27, 39, 130, 239, 291, 315; High St. and Square, 3, 207, 267, 290, 291; Arnolds Bridge, 281; Rey Bridge, 316; map, 3; *see also* Petre, Sir Wm.
Ingrave, 127, 159, 182
Inworth, 127, 139, 158
Isaac, Gilbert, 3, 9
Ive, Jn., 329

Jackson, Tho., 265; Mr., 91
Jacob, Gregory, 64
Jakes, *see* Gates
James, Jn., 103; Margery, 234
Jeppes *alias* Jeepp, Geo., 237
Jenewaye, Ralph., 86, 87
Jenkyn, Jn., 9; Kath., 9
Jennynge(s), Rich., 205; Tho., 20; Wm., 127
Jerome, Peter, 330; Mr., 23, 24
John (or Johns), Stephen, 181
Johnson, Jn., 63; Peter, 68; Rich., 61; Roke, 177; Wm., vicar of Southminster, 54
Jones, Christr., 62; Zachary, 188
Jose, Bridget, Joan, Jn., Isaac, Rose, and Wm., 110
Joslyn, Gabriel, 109
Joyce, Jn., 15, 247, 288

# INDEX OF PERSONS AND PLACES 355

Justice, Edw., 234; Rich., 47, 136

Keale, Edw., 187
Keble, Rob., 10, 103, 118; Wm., 103
Keche, —, 84
Kelvedon, 84, 122, 127, 180, 190-1, 244; 'Angel', 'Bell', 90
*Kelvedon Hatch,* 225, 237, 243, 249, 251, 253, 265, 267, 272, 275; 287, 288-9; Common, 251
Kempe, Mr., 221
Kemydd, Jn., 126
Kennatt, Rich., 143
Kent, 62, 165, 167, 185, 189, 211, 252, 304, 309, 320, 332; Bromley, 185; Erith, 63; Eltham, 239; Gravesend, 72; Margate, 67; Wye, 155; Cinque Ports, 248
Kenwelmarshe, Hum., 330
Kervyle, Jn., 125
Key(es), Tho., 158; wid., 281
Kilby, Kath., 123; Ursula, 123
Kinge, Joan, 135; Jn., 280; Wm., 135
Kirby, 194
Kirby, Jn., 134
Kitching, —, 191
Kitteridge, Bennet, 113; Rich., 113
Knappyng, Jn., 86; Tho., 86
Kn(e)ight, Geo., 126; Jn., 142, 248; Rob., clerk of Gt. Ilford 125
Knowlden, Rob., 167

Lacye, Avery, 83, 144; Grace, 99; Joan, 121; Nich., 99; Wm. 99
Ladd, Jn., 69
Laindon, 142
Lake, Wm., 52
Lambe, Beatrice, 61; Jn.,
61, 87; Jos., 61; Rich., 61; Wm., 128
Lambert, Nathl., 65; Mr., 84
Lambert, Oliffe *alias,* Joan, 70; Wm., 70, 138
Lambourne, 79, 126, 149
Lamkyn, John, vicar of Shalford, 125
Lampley, Jn., 159
Lancashire, 269; Preston, 308
Lancaster, Duchy of, 295, 317, 331
Langdon Hills, 53, 135, 193
Langenhoe, 120
Langford, 7, 23, 30
Langham, 4, 36, 51, 77, 97, 129, 169, **194**
*Langley,* 39, 155
Langley, Joan, 102; Jn., 102
Larke, Tho., 291
Latchingdon, 144, 200; Lawling Hall, 143
Latham, Jn., 326; Wm., 206
Latton, 87, 239, 247; Common, 247; Mark Hall, 239
Laver, High, 67
Laver, Lt., 180
Laver, Magdalen, 149
Law, Joan, 99; Ste., 99; Wm., 99
Lawford, 138
Lawrence, Jn., 109; —, 181, 237
Lawson, Jn., 113; Mary, 113
Laye, goodman, 7, 78
Layer Breton, 23, 81, 93
Layer-de-la-Haye, 87; Hall, 129
Lea, river, 39
Lea (Lee), Edw., 72; Ralph, vicar of Gestingthorpe, 22; Rob., 72
Leape, Wm., 127
Learke, Jn., 85
Lees, Tho., 69

Leice, Jn., 225
Leicester, 94
Leicester, Rob., Earl of, 188
Leigh, 59-62, 66, 70, 103, 123; Creek, 238; Oyster Fleet, 238
Leigh, Sir Rob., J.P., 162
Leighs, Gt., 182, 200; Lyons Hall, 200
Leighs, Lt., Priory, 130, 327
Lentford, Jn., 90; Tho., 90
Le(n)tton, Geo., 46, 128; Tho., 46
Leonard, Rob., 28
Leveriche, Tho., 190
Levett, Jn., 144
Lewger, Jn., 51
Lexden, 81, 86, 142, 150-2, 155, 158, 162-4, 181, 195; Heath, 34
Lexden hundred, 33, 150, 151, 152, 153, 163, 193
Leyton, 156; *Ruckholts,* 225, 230, 241, 273, 283-4, 290
Lichfild (Lychefeild), Hen., 23
Lichoras, Margt., 129
Lidgard, Ralph., 155
Lincolnshire, Boston, 66
Lindsell, 159
Littlebury, 43, 100, 244
Littleton, Sir Tho., 123, 125
Livermore, Wm., 87
Livesgate, Nich., 80
Lo(c)ke, Jn., 264; Tho., 136
Locksmith, Rob. le, 317
London, 6, 60, 89-91, 106, 119, 121, 126, 176, 182, 187, 212, 216, 258, 266-7, 284, 326, 329-32; Gray's Inn, 223; Middle Temple, 106; Serjeants' Inn, 177; Cutlers' Company, 172; Marshalsea prison, 212; food market, 35, 44, 48, 63, 290;

plague, 105; writer of court letter, 141
London, bishop of, 191, 207; St. Martin-le-Grand, dean of 38; St. Paul's, dean and chapter of, 205; Westminster Abbey, 208
Longe, Tho., 268; Wm., 214; Mr., 113
Longley, Rob., 108
'Longnose', Rob., 332
Lorde, Baron, 51
Love, Jn., 66; Wm., 109
Love (Lone?), Jn., 181
Lowe, Edw., 239
Lowys, Wm., 110
Loy, Adrian, alien, 307
Lucas, Jn., 153; Kath. and Mary, 130; Sir Tho., J.P., 130, 186, 194, 208
Lucye, Timothy, 184
Lukis, Edw., 143
Lun, Grace, Hugh, and Rich., 72
Lunt, Rob., 119
Luter, Robinson *alias*, Edw., Ralph, and Miles, 77
Lyddye, Jn., 40
Lyncolne, Wm., 101
Lyngeye *alias* Carter, Rich., 127
Lynne, Wm., 150
Lyse, Wm., 65
Lyster, Tho., 217
Lytham, Joan, 128

Maddock(e), Hugh, curate of Berners Roothing, 115, 127; Tho., 72
Maior, Jn., 66
Maiston, Emme, 28
Makin, Wm., 263
Maldon, 7, 9, 59, 76, 88-9, 94, 124, 126-7, 142, 171-2, 180, 189, 285, 327, 333; 'Spread Eagle', 9; St. Peter, 7; borough, 69, 132; market, 214

Malle, Geo., 101
Manger, Jn., 237
Man(n), Edw., 120, Jn., 102, 120, Rich., 97
Manners, Mich., 82, 138
Manninge, Eliz., 9; Jn., 9
Manningtree, 59, 60, 65, 80, 126, 153, 181, 193-4
Mantle, Tho., 234
Manton, Jn., 77; Wm., 77
Manuden, 163, 193
Maplestead, Gt., 30, 40, 104, 133, 149
Mar Dyke, 48, 51, 245-6
Margaretting, 126, 236; Fristling Hall, 236
Markaunt, Edw., 223; *see* Merchaunt
Marshall, Margot, 105; Rob., 105
Marredge, Elias, 171
Martin (Marteyne), Christr., of the *Mayflower*, 46; Ellen 66; Geo., 104; Jn., 104, 120; Rich., 83; Rob., 145, 236; Roger, 136; Tho., 120
Martindale, Tho., 155
Marvyn(e), Jn., 48, 120
Maryffe, Rich., priest of Stapleford Abbots, 23
Maryon, Eliz., Jn., 139; Margt., Martha, Mary, and Sarah, 139-40
Mason, Wm., 81
Master, Edw., 56; Jn., 56
Matching, 114, 127
Mawlter, Wm., 252
Maxey, Hen., 170, 195
Maydestone, Emma, 101; Jeffrey, 101
Maye, Rob., 53
Mayler, Jn., 180
Me(a)d(e), Agnes, 4; Edw., 167; Jn., 126; Tho., 177, 279
Med(d)ow(es), Philip, 109; Tho., 91;
Meatham, Nich., 65·
Melborne, *see* Mylborne
Mellar, Jn., 129

Merchaunt, Wm., 56; *see* Markaunt
Meres, Rich., 176; Stephen, 161
Merke, Tho., 120
Merill, Nich., 145
*Mersea, East*, 59, 62, 65-6, 91, 97, 109, 121, 208, 210, 212, 223, 225, 237, 241, 261, 272, 305; Blockhouse Marsh, 48; Ardeleys Lane, 289; 'Cock', 267
*Mersea, West*, 7, 59, 66, 96, 200, 207, 319, 320
Messing, 122, 135, 183
Michell, Rich., 221
Middlesex, 173, 188, 309, 311; Bethnal Green, 185; Clerkenwell, 188; Enfield, 177, 179; Islington, 179; Ratcliff, 264; Stepney, 139; Stratford-atte-Bow, 190-1
Mighell, Edw., 64; Jeremy, Jn., and Wm., 103
Mildmay, Humphrey, 130; (Sir) Tho., 155, 172, 182-7, 208, 230, 213, 215, 243, 255, 266, 270-1, 293, 297, 301, 325-6; Tho., of Springfield Barnes, 206; Walter, 130; Wm., 206
Miller, Tho., 172; Wm., 63, 64
Mills, Jn., 67-8, 142, 233; Tho., 84
Mistley, 61, 128; Heath, 34
Mon(de)forthe, *see* Mountford
Moone, Mrs., 130
Moore (More), Joan, 91; Rich., 126; Tho., 91, 305; wid., 217
Moptayd, Jn., 65
Mordaunt, Sir Jn., 205
Moreton, 85
Morgan, Mr., 184
Morice (Morris), Edw.,

## INDEX OF PERSONS AND PLACES 357

65; James, 177, 182; Jn., 83, 135; Tho., 77-8
Morley, Lord, 194
Moryson, Edw., 326
Mosse, Tho., 245
Mott(e), Adrian, 183; Hen., 64; Joan, 129; Kath., 144; Rich., 109; Rob., 144; alderman Wm., 128
*Moulsham, see* Chelmsford
Mountford (Mondeforthe, Mumford), Edw., 115; Jn., 190; Ste., 127; Tho., 115, 248, 288; Mr., 108
*Mountnessing*, 180, 281, 316; Thoby, 316
Moyse, Jn., 10; Margt., 10
Moze, 64, 90, 120; *see also* Beaumont
Mucking, 36, 114, 149, 171, 178
Mun(c)ke, Jn., 300, 302
Mundon, 30, 47, 64, 109, 136
Munson, Rob., 126
Mussett, Tho., 170
Mustrum, Jn., 205
Mylborne (Melborne), Jn., 141, 212
Mylliente, Edmd., 221

Navestock, 251
Nazeing, 248; Mead, 39
Nele, —, 179
Nelson, —, 91
Nerse, Jn., 185; Rich., 185
Netherstrete, Tho., 213
Netteswell, 88
Nevard, Grace, Hen., and Jn., 111
Nevell, Edw., 127; Tho., 56
Nevendon, 106; rector, 125
Nevitt, Rob., 90
New England, houses, 3, 25; Governors of Connecticut and Massachusetts, 104

Newman (Numane), Arthur, 123; Edw., 116; Frs., 134; Jn., 221; Lawr., vicar of Coggeshall, 141, 143; Nathl., 104; Rob., 128; Tho., 56
*Newport*, 43, 56, 163, 193, 217, 223, 227, 236-8, 285-8, 300, 305-6, 309; Cold Fair, 53, 91, 193, 244, 256, 265-6, 281; Hospital, 38, 281; New Bridge, 281; Mill Lane, 288; Holford Field, 285; Wantes Lane, 287
Newton, And., 142; Anne, 142; Rich., 190
Nichol(e)s (Nycolls), Edmd., 81; Geo., J.P., 177, 182, 184, 205; Jn., 81; Rob., 100; Wm., 65
Nicholson (Nickel-), Ant., 81; Jn., parson of Southchurch, 91; Tho., 63
Nightingale (Ny-), Geoffrey, 223; Geo., 306; Ste., 38, 306; Wm., 306
Noak Hill, *see* Romford
Noble, Jn., 56
Noke, Jn., 278
Norden, Jn., topographer, 34-5, 42, 45
Norfolk, 39, 123; J.P.s of, 181, 186-7; Norwich, 306
Norfolk, Duke of, *see* Howard
Norman, Mary, 113
Norman *alias* Reynolde, Roger, 130
Norrys, Jn., 36
Northe, Joan, Jn., Hen., and Wm., 143; Rob., 181
Northen, Wm., 77
'North Seas', 60, 66-7
Northumberland, Newcastle, 56, 68, 258

Norton, Cold, 92; Hall, 49
Norton Mandeville, 84, 179-80
*Notley, Black*, 108, 113, 212
Notley, White, 83, 130
Nuland, Jn., 177
Nycholas, Edw., 81, 126

Oakley, Gt., 10, 85, 90, 103, 118, 194
Ockendon, North, 135; curate, 125
*Ockendon, South*, 230, 249, 256, 296; Church Green, 249
Oliffe *alias* Lambert, Joan and Wm., 70
Ollie, Bridget, 142; Nich., 142
Ongar, Chipping, 67, 149, 177
Ongar, High, 134, 169
Ongar hundred, 148, 153, 154, 183
Orsett, 99, 177, 191; Fen, 48, 245; Crondon Park (in detached part of O.), 10, 237, 288
Orsone, Christr., 109
Osbonde, Geo., 64
Osborne, Edmd., 66; Ellen, 108; Jn., 108; Rob., 77; Tho., 105, 108; Mistress, 92
Over, Margt., 105
Overeye, Hen., 128
Owtinge, Rich., 161
Oxburowe, Jn., 172
Oxford, Earl of, *see* de Vere
Oxfordshire, 19
Ozell, Hen., alien, 307

Pace, Jn., 141
Page, Jn., 85; Jos., 191; Rich., 139; Tho., 117
Pagett, Lady, 43
Pagge, Joseph, 190
Paglesham, 64, 68-9, 89, 92, 115-6, 121, rector, 30

## 358 INDEX OF PERSONS AND PLACES

Pake, Jn., 183
Pakeman (Packman), Christr., 124; Margt., 101; Tho., 101, 124, 136; —, 221
Palmer, Hum., 87; Joan, 149; Jn., 117; Wm., 234
Pamflyn (Pamphelon), Agnes, 110; Edm., 110; Jn., 110, 221; Tho., 119
Panfield, 129; rector, 253
Pare, Rob., 243
Parke, Wm., 216
Parker, Hen., 157; Jn., 81; Tho., 81, 216, 261, 284, 309
Parker, White *alias*, Jn., 130, 134
Parkinson, Jn., parson of Earls Colne, 142
Pascall, Mrs., 130
Pasfeild, Edw., 171
Passeslye, Wm., 64
Pattiswick, 82
Paule (Pawle), Phil., 157; Tho., 177
Pavett (Pavyet), Anne, 122; Jeremy, 122, 143; Jn., 56; Tho., 56
Paycock(e), Tho., 88, 142; *see* Peacocke
Payne, Jn., 310; Rich., 123; Tho., 269; Wm., 4, 49
Peaco(c)ke, Jn., 134; Rich., 126; Rob., 126; Tho., 126; *see* Paycocke
Pe(a)rson (Pierson), Jane, 138; Jn., 84, 93; Rob., 84
Pease, Amy, Jn., Priscilla, Ralph, and Rob., 114
Pebmarsh, 178
Pecke, Jn., 8, 103, 114
Peeke, Rich., 71
Peele, Wm., 179
Peldon, 65, 117, 163; *Pete Hall*, 319-20
Pemmerton, Jn., 245
Pennell, Tho., 157

Pep(p)er, Alice, 213; Jn., 133, 180
Pepercorne, Jn., 309
Perle, *see* Purle
Perrient, Tho., 143
Perry, Wm., 302
Perryn, Mr., 143
Perse, Joan, 127
Pe(t)chey (Pe(a)tch(i)e), Eliz., 61; Jn., 61, 84, 180, 191; Joan, 84; Rich., 84; Rob., 84; Theophilus, 271
Petit, Jn., 289
Petre, Sir John, 10, 23, 142, 167, 182, 192, 201, 205, 211, 239, 257, 281; Sir Wm., 23, 47, 70, 86, 167, 201, 213, 217, 226, 228, 238-9, 248-9, 274, 291, 304, 315-6; Lady, wid. of Sir Wm., 106, 130, 213
Pett, Rich., 188
Pettican, Eliz., 24
Petycrewe, Jeff., 234
Phyeff, Jn., 126
Pickeringe, Mr., 130
Pierson, *see* Pearson
Pigbone, parson of Margaret Roothing, 144
Piggott (Pygot), Rob., 67; Mr., 217, 237
Pilborough, Jn., 167
Pirton, Edmd., J.P., 177, 182
Platt, Rob., 302
Pleshey, 87; Castle, 160
Pollard, goodman, 91
Polley (Pollye), Adam, 61; Agnes, 61; Edw., 96; Giles, 48; Jn., 96, 106
Polter, Hen., 61; Jane, 61; Joan, 61; Rob., 61
Ponde, Clemence, 211; Edw., 211; Jn., 10, 53, 211
Poole, Geoffrey, 221; Jn., 53, 180; Nich., 211; Rich., 92

Pope, Clement, 174; Mr., 272
Portugal, 67
Portwaye, Josias, 170, 183, 186
Potter, Jn., 100, 212
Powle, Jn., 93; Tho., 223
Poynter, Wm., 119
Pratt, Wm., 236
Preble, Wm., 79
Prentice, Hen., 92; Ste., 23; Tho., 75
Preston, Jn., 161; Peter, 142
Prior, Edw., Ellen, Hen., and Valentine, 144; Wm., 142, 144
Prittlewell, 59, 62, 80, 91, 103, 108, 118, 124, 223; *Chalkwell*, 48; Earls Hall, 108; Milton, 48, 59
Pulleyn, Ant., 151
Pumfret, Jn., 88
Purc(h)as, Geo., 103; Margery, 103; Peter, 109; Ralph, 119; Rich., 103, 109; Rob., 103; Sam., 63, 103
Purle (Perle), Rob., 212; Wm., 79
*Purleigh*, 51, 163, 172, 204, 206, 212, 214, 225, 234, 240, 245, 248, 261, 265, 273, 276, 285, 288, 299; Barns, 144; P. Fee, 253
Pygot, *see* Piggott
Pyke, Rich., 104; Tho., 263-4
Pynder, Wm., 248
Pynchon, Jn., 172

Quick, Frs., 135; Jn., 246
Quilter, Tho., 82

Rabbett, Agnes, 14
Radcliffe, Hen., 3rd Earl of Sussex, 167; Tho., 5th Earl, 130
Radle(y), Tho., 89, 150; Wm., 89
Radmoll, Edw., 31

## INDEX OF PERSONS AND PLACES 359

Radwinter, 14, 31, 41, 75, 98, 115, 163; Hall, 108; *Bendish Hall*, 230, 248, 255, 288; rector, *see* Harrison, Wm.
Raffe, Tho., 237
Rainham, 49, 65
Ram, Wm., clerk of the peace, 223
Rampson, Tho., 157
Rampton, Jn., 248, Tho., 212
Ramsden Bellhouse, 138, 305; curate, 125
*Ramsden Crays*, 228, 260; Common, 244
Ramsey, 48, 97, 120; Bridge St., 97
Ramsey, Lady, 38
Rande (Ronde), Rob., 279, 300
Ranoles, *see* Reynoldes
Ravens, Wm., 81
Rawlin(s), Barthw., 87; Hen., Mary, and Tho., 118; Wm., 62
Rawlyn, Dadrye *alias*, Walter, 86; Wm., 86
Raye, Alex., 205; Tho., 224
Rayleigh, 3, 6, 9, 26, 50, 87, 90, 105, 123; Sprats Green, 50; New Marsh Ho., 71; church, 71
Rayne, 185; parson, 129
Rayner, Hen., 83
Raynsford, Rich., J.P., 225, 253
Read(e) (Rede), Edw., 88; Eliz., 104; Joan, 261; Roger, 23; Wm., 253
Redde, Hen., 221
Redhedd, Tho., 270
Redman, Tho., 263, 254
Ree, Lancelot, 128
Re(e)ve, Edmd., 87; Jn., 78; Jean, 114; Tho., 157; Wm., 114, 252
Releson (Rellison), Anne, 110; Jn., 142, 144
Relfe, *see* Rolfe
*Rettendon*, 15, 48, 61, 75, 89, 113, 124, 206-8, 213, 225, 230-3, 236-41, 245-52, 255-6, 261, 273, 276, 284-8, 300, 310; Common, 245, 248, 265; Fen, 247
Reynolde(s) (Ranoles, Reignald), Roger, 46; Tho., 46, 110, 142
Reynolde, Norman *alias*, Roger, 130
Rich(e) (Rytch), Edw., 91; Frances d. of Lord, 333; Rich., 1st Lord, 216, 267; Rob., 2nd Lord, 71, 130, 132, 142, 167, 223, 245, 327; Lady, 69
Richardson, Adam, rector of Panfield, 253; Rich., 80; Wm., 80, 108
Richard(es), Wm., 177; Wm., parson of Lt. Ilford, 125; —, 83
Rickling, 109, 119
Riddlesdale, James, 113
Ridge, Geo., 115
Ridgewell, 122, 144; vicar, 13
Ridley, Samuel, 136
Risson, Joan, 112
Rivenhall, 170, 172
Roberts, Parnell, 46
Robertsonne, Wm., 221
Robinson, Rob., 130; Tho., 158, 172
Robinson *alias* Luter, Edw., Ralph, and Miles, 77
Rochel, Rob., 142
Rochester, Jn., 130
Rochford, 48, 92, 108, 142, 155; Hall, 142; Strode Green, 92
Rochford hundred, 33, 34
Roe, James, 37
Rogers, Jn., 84, 90; Rich., 212; Wm., 62, 301
Rolfe (Relfe), Tho., 190
Romaine, Wm., 43
Romford, 10, 49, 92, 104, 111, 120, 127, 135-6, 181-5; market, 193, 228; Noak Hill, 30, 55; Gidea Hall, 92, 104, 185, 308; curate, 104
Ronde, *see* Rande
Roode, de, Jn., 124
Rooke(s), Agnes, 42; Wm., 156
Roothing, Abbess, 114
Roothing, Aythorpe, 35, 54, 155, 185; Berwick Berners, 155
Roothing, Beauchamp, 56, 98, 155; Birds Green, 155
*Roothing, Berners*, 202, 227, 241, 275, 285, 289; Graves Lane, 289; curate, 115, 127
Roothing, High, 155
Roothing, Margaret; parson, 145
Roothing, White; *Mascallsbury*, 207, 210, 224, 262, 287, 289; *Cammas Hall* [formerly in Morrell R.], 204
Roper, Jn., 81
Rose, Eliz., 78; Nich., 78
Rost, Benjamin, 157
Roulles, Jn., 42
Roxwell, 2, 26, 184, 226, 228, 286
Roydon, 83, 149
Runham, Anne, Jane and Wm., 43
Runwell, 245; Gyffordes, 130
Rushe, Edw., 127; wid., 233
Russell, goodman, 67, 68; Wm., 68
Ruste, Edw., 99; Joyce, 53, 99; Nich., 53, 99; Wm., vicar of Felsted, 271
Rutter, Anne, James, Jn., Martha and Mary, 103
Rutland, Countess of, 191; Edw., Earl of, 191

Saberys, Edmd., 90

Saffolde, Hen., 54; Martha, 54; Tho., 272
Saffron Walden, *see* Walden
St. Lawrence, 76
St. Osyth, 59-61, 72, 80, 83, 86, 92, 107, 113, 121, 126, 133, 142-3, 162, 182, 194, 207, 320; Priory, 29, 223; Stone and Westmarsh Points, 72
Salcott, 64, 65, 70, 89; S. Green, 248
Saling, Bardfield, 191
Saling, Gt., 109, 191
Sallisbury, Jn., 78
Salmon (Saman), Tho., 122, 260, 270
Salmon, Smyth *alias*, Lawr., 180
Same, Jn., 109
Sammes, Wm., 150
Sampford, Gt., 6, 69, 81, 163, 178; Hampton Barn (Farm), 50
Sampford, Lt., 48
Sanden, Mary, 23
Sandford, Rob., 257
Sandoll, Jn., 44; Rich., 121; Tho., 121, 134
Sandon, 126, 143
Sansome, Rob., 104
Sapster, Tho., 69
Sargiant, Hum., 180
Saunder, Alice, 128
Saunder *alias* Haywards, Edw., Jn., and Peter, 76
Saward(e), Margery, 127; Tho., 39, 193
Sawen, Agnes, 234
Sawkyn, Ant., 120; Jn., 120, 161
Sayer(s), Susan, 48; Tho., 221; Wm., 48
Score (Scory), Tho., 190
Scotland, 205
Scott (Skott), Hen., 280; Rich., 135-6, 194; Wm., 126, 178
Sea, Francis, vicar of Ulting, 30

Seaborowe, Jn., 69
Seabroke, Sarah, 113
Se(a)rle(s), Jn., 123; Kath, 123; Rich., 221; Rob., 125
Sedcole, Jn., 243
Segges, Tho., 239
Sell, Jn., 43; Judith, 43; Marcy, 43
Sewell, Geo., 196
Seymer, Wm., 244
Shache, Nich., 158
Shakespeare, Wm., 31
*Shalford,* 40, 122, 180, 253; Hall, 208; church and vicar, 125
Sharles, Tho., 105; Wm., 105
Sharpe, Wm., 56
Sharpenton, Tho., 63
Shaw, Wm., 56
Shawcroft, Wm., 92
Shearman, Jn., 78; Hen., 78; Wm. (American General), 78
Sheene *alias* Sheine, Wm., 87
Sheering, 182-3
Shelford, Jn., 43
Shelley, 10, 211
Shelley, Jn., 247; Wm., 211
*Shenfield,* 160, 191, 205, 209-10, 214, 234, 252, 254, 261, 272, 275, 285; Aldeash Common, 254; Sawyer's Hall Lane, 284
Shepherd, Hen., 109; Wm., 193
Shere, Tho., 127
Shipman, Wm., 83
Shoebury, North, 59
*Shoebury, South,* 59, 206, 215
Shouncke, Tho., 22
Shoyle, Rob., 190
Sidey, Wm., 215, 216, 324
Sim(p)son, Davy, 106; Esdrau, 122; Nich., 49; Rich., 122; Vincent, 205; Wm., 236

Sirrha, Giles, 221
Skelton, Jn., 45
Skoot, Jn., 85; Nathan, 85
Skynner, Emme, 109; Rich., 67, 109; Wm., 109
Sleape, Tho., 157
Sledd, Anne, Susan, and Wm., 114
Slye, Jn., 66
Smart, Hum., 238
Smethe, Mr., 221
Smith (Smyth(e)), Joan, 151; Jn., 96, 102, 122, 139, 212, 264; Mary, 114; Mich., 114; Nich., 172; Paul, 136; Rich., 183; Roger, 114; Tho., 108, 139, 157, 172; Wm., 38, 82, 130, 205, 236
Smyth *alias Baylye,* Rich., 6; Tho., 6
Smyth *alias* Salmon, Lawr., 180
Snowe, Peter, 129, 239
Sobie, Helen, 270
Solme, Ralph, 143
Sommers, Wm., 26
Sommerson (and children), 123
Soones, Jn., 124
Sorby, Giles, 82
Sorrell, Alice, 113; Jn., 109
South, Jn., 96
*Southchurch,* 287; parson, 91
Southminster, 51, 85, 163; Park, 71; vicar, 54
Sparke, Jn., 150; Rich., 288
Sparrow, Joan, 97; Jn., 97; Wm., 79
Spenser, Rob., 92, 133
Sperlinge, Jn., 150
Spigurnell, Jn., 172
Spiltimber, Christian, 101; Jn., 101, 116
Spo(o)ner, Jn., 109, 236
Sprigge, Frs., 108

## INDEX OF PERSONS AND PLACES

Springfield (-with-Dukes), 155, 174, 180, 212, 225, 268, 272, 275, 278, 282, 284; Bridge, 282-4; Green, 269; Mill, 278; Cuton Mead, 39; parson, 125
Spryng, Jn., 126
Squire, Wm., clerk, of Gt. Ilford, 125, 134
Stace, Lawr., 260
Staffordshire, 170, 188
Stainford, James, 236
Stamage, Wm., 77
Stambourne, 101, 116
Stambridge, Gt., 65, 104, 263
Stam(m)er, Amy, 114; Anne, 114; Edmd., 89; Edw., 119; Joan, 89; Tho., 48, 89, 114
Stane, Jn., 180; Wm., 179
Stanford-le-Hope, 65, 121, 149, 160, 178
Stanford Rivers, 67, 149
Stan(d)ley, Rich., 252; Tho., 136
Stanley, Hickes alias, Jn., 143
Stansted Mountfitchet, 83, 90, 96, 119, 121, 144, 163, 178; Thremhall Fair and Green, 90-1
Stanton, Rob., 179; Mr., 86
Stanway, 37, 86, 150, 151, 193; Gosbecks, 151
Stapleford Abbots, 56; priest, 23
Staples (Stepell), Emme, 72; Jn., 71; Joan, 71; Mary, 72; Rachel, 72; Tho., 71, 156
Stayworthe, Jn., clerk, of Paglesham, rector of Foulness, 30
Stebbing, 30, 40, 84, 96-7, 157, 171, 287
Stebbynge, Jn., 273
Stede, Wm., 96
Steele, Rich., 177

Steeple; Stansgate, 30, 47, 107
Stephen(s) (Steven(s)), Jane, 63; Jn., 7, 77, 142; Matthew, 37, 142; Tho., 190
Sterne, Dorothy, 29; Jn., Bishop of Colchester, J.P., 195; Tho., 29, 104
Steward, Jn., 109, 181; Miles, 109; Tho., 109; Wm., 109
Stifford, 301
Stileman, Wm., 49, 128
Stisted, 183
Stock, 21, 86-7, 96, 105, 108, 118, 213-4, 217, 226, 230, 233-43, 254, 262, 272, 288, 291, 295, 297; Crondon Hall (Park), 10, 237, 288; Potter Row, 87; Gt. Greenwoods, 237
Stock, Eliz., 103; Joan, 103; Wm., 103; —, 187
Stockmer, Faukoner alias, Rich., 14
Stonarde, Anne, 129; Hen., 226
Stondon Massey, 211; Park, 288
Stone, Christian, 111; James, 213; Tho., 111
Stonley, Rich., 251, 325
Stookes, Wm., 99
Stort, river, 280
Storye, Ste., 61
Stour river, 39, 48, 59, 70
Stow Maries, 89
Stow(e), Jn., chronicler, 4; Wm., 120
Strachie, Jn., 266
Strayte, Jn., 217
Stubberfyeld, Tho., 160
Stucke, Helen, 108; Jn., 88; Wm., 108
Sturdy, Rob., 180
Sturgen, Jn., 135; Rich., 135; Wm., 135
Stykerde, Tho., 263
Styleman, Wm., 30
Suffolk, 29, 90, 189, 311;

J.P.s of, 181; Bury, 119; Groton, 104; Ipswich, 89, 194, 239; Stoke-by-Clare, 125; Sudbury, 181; Gt. Thurlow, 178
Sulyard, Sir Edw., 205
Sumner, Jn., 54
Surrey, 311
Sussex, 189, 311; Clapham, 211
Sussex, Earls of, see Radcliffe
Sutton, 99
Swallowe, Grace, 115; Gregory, 115; Margery, 79; Tho., 79
Swetinge, Edw., 126; Jn., 126; Tho., 126
Sworder, Hen., 96; Wm., 96
Swyfte, Rich., 90
Symon(d), Jn., 82; Kath., 107; Rob., 107
Sytheston, Jn., 150

Tabor, Amy, 96; Jn., 96; Rich., 127; Tho., 317
Takeley, 100
Tanner, Jn., 129
Tapp, Jn., 188
Tatem, Christr., 213
Taverner, Jn., 233; Wm., 281
Tawney, Tho., 236
Taylefor, Wm., 211
Taylor, Agnes, 109; Jn., 84, 124; Ralph, 124; Rich., 142; Rob., 142, 193; Tho., 109, 296
Teale, Edmd., 142
Tedemer, Ste., 47, 64
Tendring, 193, 320
Tendring hundred, 33-4, 47, 154
Terling, 56, 130
Tey, Gt., 83
Tey, Marks, 28, 101, 142, 161
Tey, Tho., 51, 129
Thackerwree, Gilbert, 76
Thames, river, 39, 45, 63,

70, 72, 238, 245, 246, 331; *see also* Mar Dyke
Thaxted, 56, 77, 83-8, 102, 108-9, 119, 142, 192-4, 200, 204-8, 214, 223, 225-8, 234, 266-7, 273, 276, 281, 284-8, 294, 296, 301, 305, 326, 328; Spencer's Fee, 225; Cutlers Green, 285, 288; Margaret (Market) St., 85, 273; Mill End, 108, 273; Newbiggin St., 273, 294; Cursall Lane, 288; 'Bell', 39; Hermitage, 288; Sibley's Green, 273; *Horham Hall*, 208, 225, 281, 288; *Yardleys*, 204, 207, 214; fair, 193
Theward, Rich., 62
Theydon Bois, 125, 246
Theydon Garnon, 3, 52, 98, 119
T(h)om(p)son, Tho., 118, 207; Mr., 283; —, 72
Thornton, Alice, 69; Joshua, 300; Tho., 69; Wm., 68
Thorne, Dan., 108; Jn., 108; Sam., 108; Tho., 108, 126
Thorpe, 10, 119, 194; Marsh House, 136
Thorp(e), Tho., 134; Tho., minister at Gt. Burstead, 121
Thorrington, 34, 83, 181
Throckmorton, Kenelm, J.P., 155
Thrussell, Tho., 172
Thundersley, 143, 181
Thurgood (Thorowgood), Jn., 16, 188; Rich., 184-5; Rob., 148
Thurrock, Grays, 62, 178
Thurrock, Lt., 106, 114, 134; curate, 37
Thurrock, West, 182, 245; Marshes, 245
Thurstable hundred, 154, 161, 163

Tilbury, East, 48, 91, 301
Tilbury-juxta-Clare, 106, 144
Tilbury, West, 48, 106
Till (Tyll), Jn., 100, 116; Tho., 76; Wm., 76
Tillingham, 92, 122, 247; Hall, 92
Todd, Ant., 126
Toller, Bostock, 309
Tollesbury, 47, 143, 248, 295
Tolleshunt D'Arcy, 92, 116; Tiptree Heath, 34, 243
Tolleshunt Major, 8, 48, 116-7, 155
Tomalyne, —, 186
Tomkines, Rich., 179
Tomlynson, Rich., 77
Tompson, *see* Thompson
Totham, Gt., 142, 154; Causeway, 263
Towns(h)end, Jn., 201; Judith, 186; (Sir) Roger, 29, 320; Wm., 181, 221
Trappes, Rowland, 205
Trewe, Jn., 77; Rich., 77
Trott, Jn., 10; Wm., 64
Truelove, Jn., 23, 125
Tubbes, Jn., 54, 80
Tucket, Christr., 61; Jn., 61; Wm., 61
Turner, Jn., 5, 37, 121; Tho., 121, 172
Tusser, Tho., author, 4, 36, 38, 42, 44, 54, 58, 76, 248, 251
Twedy (Twytty), Rich., J.P., 176, 262; W., 132
Twopence, Joan, 53
Tyball, Isaac, 213
Tyll, *see* Till
Tylnye, Jn., 64
Tyndall, Jn., J.P., 161, 195
Tynge (?Tinge), Wm., 67, 149
Tyr(r)ell (Tir(r)ell), Gertrude, 130; Sir Hen., 130, 134; Jn., 130; Tho.,

115, 129, 130, 171; Thomasine, 130

Ugley, 126
Ulting, 30, 49, 128
Underwood, Agnes, 108; Jn., 99; Roger, 51; Wm., 108
Ungeley, Jn., 209, 279
Uphaverringe, Jn., 79; Rich., 79
Upminster, 114, 206, 289, 301
Upsher, Gideon, 161
Uttlesford hundred, 34, 154, 160-3, 192-3

Vanden Berghe, Eliz., Mary, Samuel, Theodorus, and Tobias, 117
Vange, 47
Vassall, Jn., 61
Veale, Roger, 234
Vere, de, Edw., Earl of Oxford, 149, 211, 325; Edw., 75; Tho., 139
Vernon, Wm., 132
Viccars, Tho., 136
Vincent, Jean, 69; Tho., 83
Virgin, Agnes, 14; Clemence, 14; Ste., 14
Virginia, 61
Virlee, Geo., 113
Vygerous, Joan, 4
Vyne, Alex., 237
Vyvens, Rich., 80

Waad, Wm., 195
Wackefeilde, Joan, 75; Tho., 75, 115
Wade, Joan, 51; Rose, 144; Tho., 144; Wm., 51
Wailett, Eliz., 79; Mary, 79; Tho., 79; Wm., 79
Wakering, Gt., 8, 56, 69-71; Hall, 64, 70; Potton Creek and Island, 69
Wakering, Lt., 69, 126
Wal(de)grave, (Sir) Edw., J.P., 130, 194; Lady, 130; Tho., 195; Sir (Wm.), 208, 223

## INDEX OF PERSONS AND PLACES 363

Walden, Saffron (*Chipping Walden, Brook Walden*), 33-5, 38, 42, 43, 54, 56, 78, 80, 81, 82, 83, 88, 108, 113, 115, 125, 126, 134, 135, 136, 177, 182, 184, 192, 204, 207, 224-5, 231, 234, 236, 247-52, 258, 275, 279, 281, 283, 286, 289, 292, 295, 301, 310; Lt. Walden, 38; Audley End, 134; North End, 43; Pouncys, 38; Springwell, 30; Slade, 292-3; Castle St., 14; Castle Mill, 283; New Bridge, 281; Hospital, 281; Museum, 229; Guild, 43; vicar, 41-2; fair, 193
Walden, Tho., 65
Wales, 304
Walker, John, mapmaker, 120, 227, 284, 303, 325-6, 329; Tho., 136; Wm., 49, 92
Walle, Jn., 141
Wallasea island, 47, 64, 69, 200
Waller, Tho., 169; Wm., 49
Wallfleet oysters, 68
Wallforde, Alex., 122; Rich., 122
Wallys, Rich., 82; Rob., 82, 157
Walpole, Jn., 142
Walter, Wm., 83
Waltham Abbey (Holy Cross), 158-62, 172, 179, 182, 229, 303; Sewardstone, 179; Upshire, 179; parson, 111
Waltham Forest, 34-5, 56, 157, 243, 245, 251-3
Waltham hundred, 154, 158-9, 162, 167, 192
Waltham, Gt., 5, 7, 37, 77, 92, 127, 158, 200, 289; North End, 22, 43
Waltham, Lt., 20, 140

Walthamstow, 157, 181-2, 184, 191, 200, 211; Salisbury Hall, 200
Walton, 59
*Wanstead*, 141, 142, 178, 184, 188, 218, 237, 250, 252, 299; Heath, 245; Park, 267
Want, Nich., 196
Warde, Jn., 141
Warden (Wor-), Jn., 109, 136
Warley, Gt., 114, 117, 129, 135
Warley, Lt., 119
Warner, Jn., 221
Warren, Nich., 29
Warwickshire, 203; Stratford-on-Avon, 187
Wast, Tho., 8
Watkynson, Edmd., 114; Susan, 114
Watse, Joan, 113
Watson, Alex., 300; Edmd., 77; Jn., 126; Tho., 266
Watter, Walter, 100
Weald, North, Bassett, 81, 86, 118, 149
Weald, South, 10, 49, 81, 90, 118, *Brook Street*, 206, 224, 284
Webb(e), Edw., 108; Jane, 108; Jn., 108; Nich., 108; Tho., 108; Roger, 293; —, 200
Webster, Jn., 183
Weeles, Rob., 8, 86
Weeley, 32, 320; Borefleet Bridge, Guttridge Hall, Frowick Hall, 320
Welche, Bennet, 106, 114; Joan, 106
Welle, Jn., 186
Well(es), Anne, 106; Jn., 106; Rich., 300; Wm., 106
Wenden, 163, 193; Gt., 43
Wenlock, Ralph, 97
Wennington, 48, 245
Wentford, Wm., 122

Wentworth, Jn., 207
Weste, Wm., 271; *see* Wheste
Westley, Rooke, 273
Weston, Jerome, 182
Westwood, Benet, 106
Wethersfield, 85, 87, 171, 195, 252, 258, 269-70, 273, 287, 289, 295-6, 300, 306; mill, 300
Wett, James, 92
Wever, James, 264
Wharton, Barnard, 211
Wheatlye, Tho., 82
Wheler, Jn., 47; Valentine, 90
Whest, And., Anne, Eliz., Jn. and Rob., 139; *see* Weste
Whiskerd, Chas., 96; Solomon, 5, 79, 143
White (Whyte), Joan, 100; James, 100; Lawr., 80; Phil., parson of Fobbing, 121; Sybil, 20; Tho., 100; Mrs., 130
White *alias* Parker, Jn., 130, 134
Whitlock, Jn., 170
W(h)itney, Hen., 205; Jn., 113; Tho., 113, 279
Wibard, Rich., 179
Wicken Bonhunt, 43
Wickford, 29, 104, 112
Wickham, 22, 86
Wickham St. Paul, 149
Widdington, 99
Wid, river, 280
Widford, 120, 136
Wigborough, Gt., 48, 101; *Abbess Hall*, 204
Wilham, Tho., 44
Wilkes, Rich., 105
Wilkinson, Eliz., 109; James, 108; Wm., 82
Willan, Rob., D.D., 257
Williams, Hugh, 267
Williamson, Edmd., 246
Willingale Doe, 56, 155, 159, 179, 285; Rowe's Farm, 285
Willoughbye, Margt., 126

## INDEX OF PERSONS AND PLACES

Wilson, Christr., 154, 234; Daniel, 182, 186; Jn., 49, 181, 182
Willsum, Reynold, 114, 129
Wiltshire, 189, 196
Windell, Rich., 170
Winstree hundred, 154, 163
Winthrop (Wintrope), Adam, 104; Jn., 104
Wiseman, Jane, 207; Jn., 130-1, 194, 253, 311; Margt., 131; Ralph, 195; Wm., 223
Witham (*Chipping and Newland*), 16, 78, 82, 142, 150, 153, 172, 177, 204, 224-5, 230, 233, 236, 239, 252, 265, 278-81, 289, 294, 301, 305, 311; *Blunts Hall,* 224, 236, 265, 278, 289; Chipping Hill, 230, 280-1, 287; Dodfordes and Newland Mills, 280; market, 214; vicar, 195
*Wivenhoe,* 59, 66, 127, 138, 202, 257-8; parson, 125
Wix, 39

Wood(d) (Wode), Geo., 122; Hen., 124; Iverie, 56; Jn., 22, 122, 154; Joan, 120; Mat., 245; Rich., 122; Rob., 122; Roger, 216; Tho., 63, 120, 122, 209, 265; Tiberius, 121
Woodford, 157, 171, 184
Woodham Ferrers, 87, 89, 93, 120, 136, 174, 269, 271, 288, 303, 311, 329-31; fair and market, 330; marshes, 48; salt works 89; wharves, 330; *Bicknacre,* 288; B. Common, 330
Woodham Mortimer, 105
Woodland, Tho., 63
Woodward, Jason, 193; Jn., 139; Margt., 139
Woolcot, Hum., 309
Worcestershire, 57
Worden, *see* Warden
Wormingford, 24
Wortham, Tho., 129; Wm., 244
Wortley, Jn., 213
Wrabness, 4, 5, 101, 124, 136, 138
Wright (Wraight, Wryet), Eliz., 138; Jn., 65, 87, 212, 251-2; Mat., 65; Peter, 80; Tho., 65; Wm., 29, 153
*Writtle,* 56, 200, 216, 226, 228, 238; Park, 228; Edney Wood, 228; Highwood, 226, 228; Horsefrith Park, 228; inventories, 2, 21, 26
Wrothe, Rob., 177, 234
Wuddall, Hen., 84
Wyatt, goodman, 143
Wylde, Wyles *alias,* Hen., and Jn., 77
Wyles *alias* Wylde, Hen., 77; Jn., 77
Wyl(ly)mot(te), Alex., 211; Simon, 177, 224
Wynter, Jn., 160
Wyther, Sarah, 98; Wm., 82, 98

Yeldham, Lt., 144
Yngold, Jn., 83
Yonger, Rich., 84; Rob., 84
Yorkshire, Acomb, 202
Yo(u)ng(e), Aaron, 158; Rich., 110, 140; Mr., 121